1981

BUSINESS STATISTICS

BUSINESS STATISTICS

Concepts and Applications

William J. Stevenson

Rochester Institute of Technology

Harper & Row, Publishers

New York   Hagerstown   San Francisco   London

Sponsoring Editor: Charlie Dresser
Project Editor: Eleanor Castellano
Designer: T. R. Funderburk
Production Supervisor: Marion Palen
Compositor: Syntax International Pte. Ltd.
Printer and Binder: Halliday Lithograph Corporation
Art Studio: Vantage Art, Inc.

BUSINESS STATISTICS: Concepts and Applications

Library of Congress Cataloging in Publication Data

Stevenson, William J
  Business statistics.

  Includes index.
  1. Statistics. I. Title.
HA29.S798   519.5   77-16120
ISBN 0-06-046445-3

This Book Is Dedicated to You

contents

3. PROBABILITY

4. DISCONTINUOUS PROBABILITY DISTRIBUTIONS

5. CONTINUOUS PROBABILITY DISTRIBUTIONS

6. SAMPLING

14. REGRESSION AND CORRELATION

15. INDEX NUMBERS

16. ANALYSIS OF TIME SERIES

17. SUMMARY AND CONCLUSIONS

note to the student

WELCOME TO STATISTICS. You are beginning what should be an interesting and meaningful adventure as you explore one of the most basic tools of scientific decision making.

Unfortunately, texts on statistics are notoriously dry and uninteresting. In fact, many are downright boring. Furthermore, most students approach statistics with a certain amount of fear, simply because of the mathematics involved. Let me reassure you that I am well aware of these shortcomings.

I have long felt that there is a need for a clear, understandable textbook in statistics. The material should be easy to read and digest. Moreover, it should be interesting, not dull, and have plenty of examples for readers to follow. This book has been written with these ideas in mind. I have deliberately tried to present topics at a leisurely pace, and have refrained from including theorems and proofs. As for mathematical prerequisites, you will discover that a basic knowledge of algebra and a willingness to learn are all that are needed.

The intent here is to develop an intuitive understanding of statistics and statistical reasoning, while helping you to acquire skills in problem solving.

The text material is sufficient for either a one- or a two-semester course at the undergraduate level. For a one-semester course, optional material and selected chapters may be omitted without loss of continuity.

There are certain things you can do to get the most from this book:

1. Read the book carefully. Do not try to read it in the same way that you would read a novel. Work through examples, checking numbers taken from tables.
2. Use the chapter outlines and objectives provided at the beginning of each chapter to obtain an overall idea of what is contained in the chapter. Solve as many problems as you have time for. Answers to exercises are given at the end of the text. Also, use the review questions provided at the end of each chapter to gauge how effective your reading has been.

3. Use a calculator for working out problems.
4. Consider purchasing the Workbook and Study Guide that accompanies this book. If your bookstore does not stock it, ask that it be ordered. The Study Guide identifies important concepts and provides guided note-taking as well as a way to study notes prepared by you. In addition, worked-out examples (often starred exercises taken from each chapter) are given.

William J. Stevenson

preface

MY MAIN GOAL in writing this textbook has been to produce a clear, understandable textbook in introductory statistics. I have attempted to write a book that is interesting and informative, and one that illustrates the relevance of statistics to decision making. *Business Statistics: Concepts and Applications* is intended for beginning statistics courses in business and economics, specifically for students who need to understand how statistical decisions are made, but who may have little mathematical preparation. The text material presumes a course in high school algebra.

The key features of this book are:

1. Mathematical notation is used only where necessary, and proofs and derivations are avoided entirely. Explanations are informal and intuitive, and verbal explanations are often supplemented by visual displays.
2. The book is suited to a self-paced ("Keller Plan") approach as well as a lecture approach. A study guide is available that enhances learning with either approach, but is vital to a self-paced approach.
3. Answers to all exercises (except supplemental exercises) are provided at the end of the book.
4. Extensive tables for the binomial and Poisson distributions are provided.
5. Each chapter begins with a chapter outline and a list of chapter objectives that are to be mastered. A list of review questions follows each chapter.

In addition, a fairly unique and useful study guide, written by the author, is available. The chapters of the study guide correspond to the text chapters. Each chapter begins with a brief summary of the chapter. There is a study outline which guides student reading and note taking; moreover, there is an abundance of worked out examples illustrating the various techniques. These are taken from the exercises in the text (note the starred * exercises). Hence, students are able to see how the author would solve typical text exercises. The solutions are quite detailed—in many instances, even more so than in the Solutions Manual. Furthermore, each chapter contains tips on solving problems and/or identifies common pitfalls to be avoided.

The text contains sufficient material for a two-quarter or two-semester sequence. However, the text can easily be adapted to a one-quarter or one-semester course by deleting certain optional material. Chapters 1 through 10, part of Chapter 12, and Chapter 14 form the basic core; consequently, I recommend that all courses at least try to cover that material.

Finally, I would like to acknowledge the assistance of others in preparing this book. I am very grateful to George Telecki, Charlie Dresser, and Eleanor Castellano for their help and guidance in preparing the manuscript and various revisions. Thanks too must go to the reviewers for their many constructive comments and suggestions. Professor Paul Van Ness at the Rochester Institute of Technology and Professor James Vedder of Syracuse University were especially helpful in that regard. Mary Ellen McCrossen deserves praise for tireless efforts in typing and for editorial comments. Janice Van Knapp deserves thanks for checking the answers to the exercises. Thanks must also go to the many students who offered criticisms and corrections.

I want to acknowledge the patience and understanding of my wife and children for the many times I spent working on the manuscript that might have been spent otherwise.

W. J. S.

BUSINESS STATISTICS

1

introduction

Chapter Objectives

After completing this chapter, you should be able to:
1. Define the term "statistics"
2. Explain what sampling is and some of the main reasons for sampling
3. Answer the question, "Why study statistics?"
4. Give examples which show how a manager can benefit from a knowledge of statistics
5. Explain what models are and how they can be used as aids in decision making, and identify general advantages and limitations of models

Chapter Outline

SHORTLY AFTER the polls close on election day, a television announcer informs the viewing audience that a certain candidate has been projected by network analysis to be a landslide winner. What is more, the projection has been made after only 2% of the votes have been tabulated.

A manufacturer of flashcubes for cameras must determine what percentage of the flashcubes will not flash. If there is a large percentage that will not work, the manufacturer's reputation might be seriously affected. However, testing the cubes destroys them, so only a small fraction of the flashcubes will be tested, and a decision on whether to ship the cubes will be made on the basis of that small fraction.

The weatherman informs us that the probability of rain for today is 30%.

The government reports that the median income for a family of four is up 5% from a year ago.

An instructor announces to the class that the average grade on the midterm was 70.

These are some of the ways that statistics is used.

WHAT IS STATISTICS?

When some people hear the word "statistics," they think of such things as batting averages, accident rates, mortality tables, yards per carry, and so on. This branch of statistics, which uses numbers to describe facts, is called, appropriately enough, *descriptive statistics*. It involves organizing, summarizing, and generally simplifying information that is often rather complex. The purpose is to make things easier to understand, easier to report and discuss, and easier to keep track of. The Dow-Jones industrial average, the unemployment rate, the cost of living, amount of rainfall, average miles per gallon, and grade point averages all fall into this category.

Another branch of statistics deals with *probability*, which is useful in analyzing situations that involve chance. Games that involve dice or cards or coin flipping come under the heading of chance. Most games of sport, such as boxing, football, basketball, horse racing, and the like, are influenced to a certain extent by chance: the bounce of a ball one way or another often has a bearing on the outcome of a game; a horse or rider can slip; a boxer can be on the verge of clinching the fight one moment and be seeing stars the next. The decision by a cola manufacturer to undertake an extensive advertising campaign in order to increase the company's share of the market, the decision not to go ahead with an effort to immunize persons under twenty against a certain disease, and the decision of whether to risk crossing a street in the middle of the block all utilize probability, consciously or subconsciously.

A third branch of statistics is called *inference*. It deals with the analysis and interpretation of sample data. Sampling is a living example of the adage, "You don't have to consume an entire cake to know if you like it." Hence the basic idea in sampling is to measure a small, but *typical*, portion of some "population" and then use that information to infer (intelligently guess) what the entire population is like. Familiar examples abound. Dipping your toe into the water to judge the temperature of the pool. Trying on a new coat in front of a mirror to see how it looks. Watching a TV program for a few minutes to see if it will be worthwhile to continue watching. Browsing through a new book. Stealing a kiss. Taking a new car for a test drive. In addition, there are widespread applications of this concept in business and industry. Consider these examples.

A motion picture studio runs screen tests on prospective actors and actresses before deciding who to cast for each part.

Manufacturing firms often make a small number of pieces (pilot run) before going to full-scale production.

Many business firms stock thousands of items in inventory. Using sampling techniques, the dollar value of inventory can be estimated without resorting to a complete count of the items.

New products are sometimes test-marketed in key cities to determine the degree of consumer acceptance.

Business firms and government agencies sample for a variety of reasons. Cost is usually a major consideration. Like anything else, collecting data and analyzing the results costs money, and ordinarily the more data collected, the greater the cost. Sampling reduces the amount of data that must be collected and analyzed, and thus sampling reduces costs. Another reason for sampling involves the fact that the value of information is often short-lived. To be useful the information must be obtained and acted upon rather quickly. Sampling is often the only possible way to accomplish this. Sometimes examining items destroys them. Testing seat belts to determine their breaking point obviously destroys the product. If all seat belts were tested in that manner, there would be none to sell. These and other reasons for sampling are considered in more detail in a later chapter.

As you will soon discover, the three areas of statistics are not separate and distinct. Rather, they tend to overlap considerably. For instance, describing and summarizing sample data is a necessary first step in the analysis of the data. Furthermore, the theory and rationale of sampling is based on probability theory.

In a nutshell, then, there are three overlapping areas of concern in statistics: describing and summarizing data, probability theory, and analyzing and interpreting sample data.

Statistics involves descriptive statistics, probability theory, and sampling.

All three branches of statistics utilize the *scientific approach*, which consists of these five basic steps:

1. Carefully define the problem. Make sure the purpose of a study or analysis is clear.
2. Formulate a plan for collecting the appropriate data.
3. Collect the data.
4. Analyze and interpret the data.
5. Report conclusions and other findings in a way that will be readily understood by those who will use the results in decision making.

WHY STUDY STATISTICS?

It would not be unreasonable for you to ask the question, "Why should I bother to learn statistics?" Certainly it will require an effort on your part, and you probably are wondering what the benefit will be.

Now it is not unusual for students to feel that courses ought to be "relevant." You will be the final judge of that. But for now, consider the following:

1. Statistical reasoning is widely used in government and business, so it is possible that in the future some employer may hire or promote you in part for your abilities in the area of statistics.
2. Managers in many instances need a knowledge of statistics to make good decisions and to avoid being "snowed" by statistical presentations.
3. Subsequent courses will utilize statistical analyses.
4. The majority of professional journals and other literature contain frequent references to statistical studies.
5. The news media supply ample opportunities for statistical interpretation, as do many everyday experiences.

At this point, it is important for you to have a goal in your mind concerning what you should expect from your study of statistics. There are two very worthwhile and reasonable goals you might consider. The first goal is to develop skills in problem solving. This would include being able to recognize which technique applies in a given situation as well as being able to actually utilize that technique to obtain a solution to the problem. The second goal is more general: to develop an understanding of what kinds of problems statistics can be used for and what kinds it cannot.

THE USE OF MODELS IN STATISTICS

One of the major tools used extensively in statistics is the *model*. Models are simplified versions of some real life problem or situation. They are used to highlight certain aspects of the situation while avoiding a large number of details that may be irrelevant to the problem. Hence models can help to reduce the degree of complexity that must be dealt with.

There are many examples of the use of models in everyday life. A globe, for instance, is a model of the earth. It focuses attention on such things as the shape of the earth as well as the relative size, shape, and position of oceans and continents, while ignoring countless other details such as population densities, language differences, weather, manufacturing, record shops, and so on. Maps are models. Some show transoceanic routes of passenger planes, others relate to the weather, and still others to automobile travel. Mannequins are used to model clothing. Travel bureaus use fancy brochures to interest travelers, and magazines, newspapers, and billboards are loaded with pictures, sketches, and words designed to create an image and to sell a product in the process. Some other examples of models are rug samples, photographs, toys, diagrams, homework problems, definitions, form letters, recorded telephone messages, repair manuals, insurance forms, menus, stories, slide rules, and calculators, to name but a few. All are simplified versions of some more complex thing.

An interesting model, which can be used to illustrate sampling, is a large bowl containing many beads of various colors. The beads represent members of some population. It can be shown that if the beads are well mixed, a relatively small sample (say 50 beads) can be taken that will reflect the population quite well. That is, the breakdown of beads by color in the sample will closely match the actual breakdown in the population (bowl).

You will be introduced to a wide variety of *statistical models* as you progress through this book. There are frequent *definitions*, similar to the definitions of sampling, statistics, and models, already presented. Great emphasis is placed on intuitive models, such as the bead bowl example, to convey important concepts. Other models, such as *graphs* and *charts*, are used to create a mental image of an important idea. *Tables* and *equations* are used as aids to problem solving.

Descriptive statistics requires the use of numerical and graphical models in summarizing and presenting data. The main emphasis in this book will be on learning how to use existing models rather than on learning how to construct new models, thereby taking advantage of the knowledge and experience of experts in the field.

As an intuitive illustration of how models can be used in decision making, consider this situation. An architect has been asked to submit a proposal for a new town library. Obviously, there are many details the architect might concern himself with. However, some details, such as how much the town is willing to spend, the function and size of the building, and the style, are extremely important considerations. Other details, such as the color to paint the walls, the type of doorknobs to use, the number of shelves needed, and a whole host of other matters, can safely be ignored at the start. By reducing the mass of details to be considered, the architect makes the problem more manageable and thereby increases the likelihood of successfully handling the job.

As the project progresses, the architect will undoubtedly render rough sketches, and eventually blueprints, of the proposed structure. He might also make a scale model, especially if the proposal is to go before the voters. The architect might rely on these models as well as verbal descriptions to sell his ideas. Similarly, he might provide samples of the brick, stone, or wood he proposes to use to give town council members the opportunity to see and feel various textures. The architect would use numbers on the blueprints to represent dimensions, and he might use mathematical equations to determine the weight the supporting beams and columns would have to hold.

Needless to say, each type of model is incomplete in some way in the sense that it deals only with a portion of the problem. And yet this is precisely the purpose of using models—to focus on a small portion of the problem.

> A *model* is a simplified version of some real life problem or situation designed to highlight certain aspects of the problem without having to deal with every detail.

Models are useful in still other ways. Models can *communicate an idea or concept.* For instance, the architect's scale model and rough sketches can be used to convey his ideas in a nontechnical way to the town council members and other voters. Models are frequently used as ideals, which are *standards of comparison* against which something can be judged or measured. Thus the architect will undoubtedly make frequent reference to his blueprints as the work progresses to decide if things are proceeding according to plan. Models may involve *standard solution procedures.* For instance, building codes dictate certain standard procedures. Similarly, the architect will probably use standard techniques he found successful in previous work. Finally, models offer a *relatively inexpensive and safe way to test ideas before implementing them.* For instance, if the council members want to change the design of the building after viewing the scale model, the architect can readily accommodate them. However, once the foundation and framing are complete, such changes may be impossible to make, or they may require considerable additions in cost and time.

Still another important feature of models is that they force a manager or other user to quantify and formalize what is known about a problem. Problem definition in itself can be one of the most fruitful aspects of using models. In the process a manager is forced to recognize areas where knowledge or information are weak and where additional efforts, and perhaps expertise, are needed. One common mistake often made by someone who is anxious to "get on with it" is that insufficient attention is devoted to the crucial problem definition stage, and this generally results in a shoddy job or in retracing steps to correct errors. Another difficulty that frequently crops up is that necessary information is left out because it could not be readily obtained. In addition, human factors, many of which are either difficult or impossible to quantify, are sometimes ignored. Naturally, this detracts from the overall results obtained from using models. Similarly, important variables can be overlooked in efforts to simplify a problem. Nevertheless, when a model is used in the manner intended, by one who knows how to use it, it can be a powerful aid to decision making. Used incorrectly, it can lead to serious errors in judgment, which may have far-reaching consequences.

LOOKING AHEAD

The key issues in statistical analysis are (a) how to acquire useful data and (b) what to do with it after you get it. The first issue concerns methods of data collection, particularly sampling. The second issue is fairly broad; it involves the initial organization and summarization of the data in order to extract useful information and then the analysis and interpretation of that information.

Using this text, you will begin your study of statistics with a brief look at *descriptive statistics*, which involves techniques for organizing and summarizing data. These operations are necessary before any analysis of data can take place. Next you will learn about *probability*, which is used to quantify chance. Simple analogies like coin tossing, rolling dice, and drawing cards from a well-shuffled deck are useful for explaining many important probability concepts. *Probability distributions* incorporate both descriptive statistics and probability theory. They form the basis for all inferential statistics. In the chapter on *sampling*, you will learn how to obtain a representative sample, one that can be used to draw inferences about the population from which it was taken, and you will learn more about the importance of sampling. The chapter on *sampling distributions* will show you why inferences can be made if sampling is done correctly, as well as how probability distributions enter into, and are the basis for, statistical inference. The importance of sample size is one of the key issues. Another is determining how accurate sample estimates are. Finally, you will learn how to use sample data to make estimates about populations and evaluate claims about populations.

At this point you may wonder about the extent to which mathematics is used in statistical techniques, and perhaps you feel a pang of anxiety when you stop to think about it. While it is true that there is a certain amount of mathematics involved, nothing more than a basic understanding of elementary algebra plus the standard arithmetic operations (addition, subtraction, multiplication, and division) will be necessary. Furthermore, remember that statistics is not the sole property of statisticians. It is a collection of techniques, and ways of looking at certain kinds of problems, used by many people who cannot, by any stretch of the imagination, be considered statisticians or mathematicians. Managers, economists, market analysts, and others are all important users of statistical theory.

SUMMARY

There are three main branches of statistics: descriptive statistics, which involves organizing and summarizing data; probability theory, which provides a rational basis for dealing with situations influenced by chance-related factors; and inference theory, which involves analyzing and interpreting samples. Many examples are included throughout the chapter of the uses of statistics.

A knowledge of statistics is helpful in understanding statistical presentations, it can minimize chances of your being taken in by statistics, and, in general, it can serve as a valuable tool for decision making.

An important feature of statistics is the use of models. These are simplified versions (abstractions) of some real life problem or situation. The key feature of models is their reduction of complex situations to simpler and more understandable forms. They do this by focusing attention on only a few features of a situation while (perhaps temporarily) ignoring or de-emphasizing other aspects of the situation. Models come in many different forms. There are verbal (words and sentences) models, graphical models, numerical (numbers and equations) models, and physical (three-dimensional) models.

REVIEW QUESTIONS

1. What are the three major areas of statistics?
2. Define the term "statistics."

3. Define the terms "sample" and "population."
4. What are the primary reasons for sampling?
5. To be useful, what characteristic should a sample possess?
6. Give five examples of situations where statistics is useful.
7. Define the term "model."
8. What single feature do all models have in common?
9. State three ways that models are used.
10. Explain why each of the following would be considered a model, and state what each is a model of.

bicycle with training wheels	toy blocks
cadaver	phonograph record
wallpaper book	slide ruler
paint chip	8
$17.50	$y = 3x$
Sears catalog	author-title card catalog in a library
cash register receipt	

2

organizing, summarizing and presenting statistical data

Chapter Objectives

After completing this chapter, you should be able to:
1. Describe and give an example of continuous data, discrete data, nominal data, and ranked data.
2. Explain the distinction between data and information.
3. Discuss the need for organizing and summarizing data.
4. Use and interpret sigma notation.
5. Compute the various measures of center of sample data: the mean, the median, and the mode.
6. Compute the various measures of dispersion of sample data: the range, the standard deviation, the variance, and the mean absolute deviation.
7. Identify, compare, and contrast numerical methods for summarizing data.
8. Give examples and explain advantages and limitations of tabular and graphical methods for organizing and summarizing data.
9. Construct a frequency distribution for each type of data.
10. Compute summary measures for center and dispersion for grouped data.

Chapter Outline

Introduction
    Data versus information
Statistical Data
    Types of data
Sigma Notation
Analysis of Small Data Sets
Measures of Center
    The mean
    The weighted mean
    The median
    Comparison of the mean and the median
    The mode
Measures of Dispersion
    The range
    Measures of dispersion that use the mean as a reference point
    Mean absolute deviation
    The variance
    The standard deviation
    Other measures
Analysis of Large Data Sets
Frequency Distributions

INTRODUCTION

STATISTICAL METHODS involve the analysis and interpretation of *numbers*, such as annual earnings, monthly sales, test scores, number of defective parts, percentage of favorable responses to a questionnaire, service life, completion times, and so on. These numbers are referred to as *data*. To successfully interpret data, it is usually necessary to first organize and summarize the numbers. The purpose of this chapter is to introduce you to the most widely used methods of organizing and summarizing statistical data. Hence we now begin to address the question, "What do you do with the numbers after you get them?" Often an end in itself, the process of describing data also paves the way for additional analysis in terms of drawing inferences about a population.

Data Versus Information

In its raw or unprocessed form, data can be almost meaningless. Enormous quantities of numbers tend to confuse rather than illuminate, because our minds are unable to cope with the variety and detail that accompany large sets of numbers. We simply get bogged down with minor details.

Processing data helps us because it *decreases the amount of detail*. Moreover, it facilitates showing relationships. Processing transforms data into information by organizing and condensing it into graphs or into a few numbers, which then convey the essence of the data. The effect is to weed out minor details and highlight the important features of the data.

Graphs and charts are particularly attractive for processing data because they provide a visual portrayal of important data characteristics. Graphs not only serve as communicating devices but also help in conceptualizing problems. Numerical measures, on the other hand, are absolutely essential for computational purposes.

Both visual and numerical summaries play an important role in statistical analysis. Tables are often utilized in the process of organizing, summarizing, and presenting statistical data. Although they lack the visual appeal of charts and graphs, they offer certain advantages in terms of mathematical analysis. The variety of tables in use underscores their importance. Some commonly employed business uses of tables are the balance sheet (statement of assets) and income statement (earnings) most firms issue annually. Each essentially condenses the net results of a firm's activities into a few simple measures of performance, effectively bypassing the overwhelming detail that went into generating that performance.

STATISTICAL DATA

Statistical data are obtained through a process that involves observing or otherwise measuring such items as annual incomes in a community, test scores, amount of coffee per cup dispensed from a vending machine, breaking strength of nylon fibers, percentage of sugar in cereals, and the like. These items are called *variables*, because they yield values that tend to exhibit some degree of variability when successive measurements are taken.

Types of Data

For the most part, the choice of which procedure to use for analyzing or describing statistical data depends on the type of data involved. You must learn to identify and deal with four types of data: continuous, discrete, nominal, and ranked.

Variables that can take on virtually *any* value over an interval of values are referred to as *continuous*. Such characteristics as height, weight, length, thickness, velocity, viscosity, and temperature fall into this category. Data taken on these and similar characteristics are called continuous, even though, as a practical matter, measuring instruments have physical limitations that restrict the degree of precision.

> Continuous variables can assume any value over a continuous interval. Data taken on such variables are called *continuous data.*

Amount of coffee sold per day, gasoline sold per hour, air speed, reaction time, and elasticity of a rubber band all yield continuous data.

A *discrete* variable is one that can assume only certain values, usually *integers*. Discrete data arise by *counting* the number of items with a certain characteristic. Examples of discrete data are the number of customers in a day, children in a classroom, defects in a new car, injuries at a factory, truckstops, touchdowns, and so on.

> Discrete variables assume integer values. *Discrete data* are usually the result of counting the number of items.

Both discrete and continuous data are referred to as *quantitative* data because they are inherently numerical. That is, certain numerical values are naturally associated with the variables being measured. On the other hand, the remaining two types of data, nominal and ranked, involve variables that are not inherently numerical. These are called *qualitative* variables and must be converted to numerical values before they can be dealt with.

Nominal variables involve *categories*, such as sex (male or female), eye color (blue, brown, honey, hazel), field of study (medicine, law, business, biology, engineering) record of repair (excellent, good, fair, poor), and the like. None of these characteristics is naturally numerical. However, when applied to either a population or a sample, it is possible to assign each item to one class (e.g., field of study is business) and then *count* the number in each category (e.g., 15 are engineering majors).

Nominal data result when categories are defined and the number of observations falling into each category is counted.

Another kind of qualitative variable is that which typically concerns subjective evaluations when items are ranked according to preference or accomplishment. For instance, in baking, beauty, flower, and dog contests, entries are *ranked* first, second, third, and so on. Likewise, team standings are assigned integers 1, 2, 3, ... Alternatively, +'s and −'s might be used to designate improvement or worsening (e.g., writing performance after attending a course on creative writing). Now it might be possible to think of the underlying variable in each of these cases as being continuous, and yet we assign artificially the integers 1, 2, 3, . . . (i.e., ranks) either for convenience or for lack of a more scientific method.

Ranked data consist of *relative* values assigned to denote *order:* first, second, third, fourth, and so on.

It is interesting to note that many populations can give rise to all four types of data. For example, a load of beef might be classified into one of two (dichotomous) categories: acceptable or unacceptable. Or the beef might be graded according to some plan, such as USDA Good, Choice, or Prime (three or more categories). Both of these produce discrete data. If the concern is amount of fat per pound, or average weight per side of beef, or ratio of fat to lean, then the data will be continuous. Another example of how data can take on different characteristics is illustrated in Table 2.1. Similarly, grades can be recorded as measurements, categories, or ranks, as can velocity, appraised value, or just about anything else you care to study.

TABLE 2.1   The Same Population Can Give Rise to Different Types of Data

Population	Type of data			
	Continuous	Discrete	Nominal	Ranks
Third-Grade Class	ages, weights	no. in class	boys/girls	3rd grade
Automobiles	mph, mpg	no. of defects/car	colors	dirtiest
Real Estate Sale	$ value	no. of offers	overpriced	most expensive

EXERCISES

1. Identify the following in terms of the type of data:
   a. 17 grams   b. 25 seconds   c. 3 baskets
   d. 3 wrong, 7 right   e. shirt sizes   f. miles/gallon
   g. slowest   h. 2 vanilla cones   i. loveliest

SIGMA NOTATION

Many of the statistical procedures that you will learn, in fact, most, require computing the *sum* of a set of numbers. The Greek capital letter $\sum$ is used to denote a sum. Hence if some variable x has the values 1, 5, 6, and 9, then $\sum x = 21$. Likewise, if grocery expenditures y for the week are $8.82, $12.01, and $2.10, then $\sum y = \$22.93$.

Example 1   If values of x are 2, 4, 5, and 9, find $\sum x$, $\sum x^2$, and $(\sum x)^2$.

Solution:

$$\sum x = 2 + 4 + 5 + 9 = 20 \qquad \sum x^2 = 2^2 + 4^2 + 5^2 + 9^2$$
$$(\sum x)^2 = 20^2 = 400 \qquad\qquad = 4 + 16 + 25 + 81 = 126$$

If only a portion of the values are to be summed, subscripts are included to indicate those values to be summed. Thus

$$\sum_{i=1}^{5} x_i$$

means to sum the values of the variable x beginning with the first ($i = 1$) and ending with the fifth ($i = 5$):

$$\sum_{i=1}^{5} x_i = x_1 + x_2 + x_3 + x_4 + x_5$$

$\sum_{i=1}^{n} x_i$ means that n observations (all) are to be summed, and it is often shortened to simply $\sum x_i$ or $\sum x$.

Example 2   Using the given data, compute a) $\sum_{i=1}^{2} x_i$, b) $\sum_{i=2}^{4} x_i$, c) $\sum_{i=7}^{11} x_i$ and d) $\sum x_i$.

Data

i	x_i
1	8
2	2
3	3
4	6
5	7
6	8
7	9
8	4
9	5
10	4
11	1
	$\overline{57}$

a. $\sum_{i=1}^{2} x_i = 8 + 2 = 10$

b. $\sum_{i=2}^{4} x_i = 2 + 3 + 6 = 11$

c. $\sum_{i=7}^{11} x_i = 9 + 4 + 5 + 4 + 1 = 23$

d. $\sum x_i = 8 + 2 + 3 + 6 + 7 + 8 + 9 + 4 + 5 + 4 + 1 = 57$

Working the process in reverse, we can use this method to abbreviate a set of data we intend to add:

1. $x_1 + x_2 + x_3$ becomes $\sum_{i=1}^{3} x_i$.
2. $x_8 + x_9 + x_{10} + x_{11}$ becomes $\sum_{i=8}^{11} x_i$.

It is sometimes possible to simplify a summation operation by taking into account one or more of these three properties:

1. When each value of a variable is to be multiplied or divided by a constant, that constant can be applied *after* the values have been summed.

$$\sum cx = c \sum x$$

Thus

$$\sum_{i=1}^{4} 2x_i = 2x_1 + 2x_2 + 2x_3 + 2x_4$$

$$= 2(x_1 + x_2 + x_3 + x_4) = 2 \sum_{i=1}^{4} x_i$$

For example,

$$3(2) + 3(8) + 3(4) = 3(2 + 8 + 4) = 42$$

2. The summation of a constant is equal to the product of the constant and the number of times it occurs.

$$\sum_{i=1}^{n} c_i = nc$$

For example,

$$\sum_{i=1}^{6} 5_i = 5 + 5 + 5 + 5 + 5 + 5 = 30$$

or

$$6(5) = 30$$

3. The sum of a sum (or difference) of two variables equals the sum (or difference) of the individual summations of the two variables.

$$\sum_{i=1}^{n} (x_i^2 + y_i) = \sum_{i=1}^{n} x_i^2 + \sum_{i=1}^{n} y_i$$

$$\sum_{i=1}^{n} (x_i - y_i) = \sum_{i=1}^{n} x_i - \sum_{i=1}^{n} y_i$$

For example,

i	x	y	$(x - y)$
1	8	5	3
2	3	2	1
3	4	0	4
4	5	4	1
	20	11	9

$\sum(x - y) = 9$

$\sum x - \sum y = 20 - 11 = 9$

Now we may have two sets of numbers, such as hourly wages for various employees and the number of hours each worked.

i Individual	f_i Hours worked	x_i Hourly wage
1	1	$2
2	5	3
3	7	2
4	3	4
5	3	3

Suppose we want these sums: $\sum f_i$, $\sum x_i$, $\sum x_i^2$, $\sum f_i x_i$, and $\sum f_i x_i^2$ and $(\sum f_i x_i)^2$. The table below illustrates the necessary computations.

i	f_i	x_i	x_i^2	$f_i x_i$	$f_i x_i^2$
1	1	$2	4	2	4
2	5	3	9	15	45
3	7	2	4	14	28
4	3	4	16	12	48
5	3	3	9	9	27
	$\sum f_i = 19$	$\sum x_i = 14$	$\sum x_i^2 = 42$	$\sum f_i x_i = 52$	$\sum f_i x_i^2 = 152$

$$(\sum f_i x_i)^2 = 52^2 = 2704$$

Again, when the summation will be applied to *all* values in a set, the subscripts (i's) are usually dropped.

Finally, there are several instances where data are presented in a table. The subscripts i and j are used to indicate the row (i) and column (j), and the letter r is used for the number of rows and k for the number of columns. For example, we might want to examine data on gasoline mileage performance for different combinations of cars and drivers.

Car	Driver 1	2	3	4	Sums
1	22.3	23.5	20.5	19.8	86.1
2	20.4	20.1	19.0	20.8	80.3
3	23.4	25.6	19.6	21.7	90.3
Sums	66.1	69.2	59.1	62.3	256.7

The general notation for this table is shown below.

Car ($r = 3$ rows) $i/j \rightarrow$	1	2	Driver ($k = 4$ columns) 3	4	Sums
1	$x_{1,1}$	$x_{1,2}$	$x_{1,3}$	$x_{1,4}$	$\sum_{j=1}^{4} x_{1,j}$
2	$x_{2,1}$	$x_{2,2}$	$x_{2,3}$	$x_{2,4}$	$\sum_{j=1}^{4} x_{2,j}$
3	$x_{3,1}$	$x_{3,2}$	$x_{3,3}$	$x_{3,4}$	$\sum_{j=1}^{4} x_{3,j}$
Sums	$\sum_{i=1}^{3} x_{i,1}$	$\sum_{i=1}^{3} x_{i,2}$	$\sum_{i=1}^{3} x_{i,3}$	$\sum_{i=1}^{3} x_{i,4}$	$\sum_{i=1}^{3}\sum_{j=1}^{4} x_{i,j}$

EXERCISES

1. Expand each of the following:

   a. $\sum_{i=1}^{5} x_i$

   b. $\sum_{i=1}^{5} f_i x_i^{2}$

   c. $\sum_{i=1}^{5} x_i y_i$

   d. $\sum_{i=1}^{n} x_i/n$ for $n = 8$

   e. $\sum_{i=1}^{4} |x_i - \bar{x}|$

   f. $\sum_{i=4}^{8} 3i$

   g. $\sum_{i=1}^{6} (x_i - \bar{x})^2$

2. Write these sums in sigma notation:
   a. $x_1 + x_2 + \cdots + x_n$
   b. $(x_1 + x_2 + \cdots + x_n)^2$
   c. $x_1 + x_2 + x_3 + x_4 + x_5 + x_6 + x_7$
   d. $[(o_1 - e_1)^2/e_1] + [(o_2 - e_2)^2/e_2] + [(o_3 - e_3)^2/e_3] + [(o_4 - e_4)^2/e_4$

3. Compute each of the following quantities given the data below. (Note: n is the number of observations.)
   a. $\sum y$
   b. $\sum y^2$
   c. $(\sum y)^2$
   d. $(\sum y^2 - [(\sum y)^2/n])/(n - 1)$

e. $\sum(y - 12)$ $\qquad\qquad\qquad$ f. $\sum(y - 12)^2$

g. $\sum(y - 12)^2/(n - 1)$

y
15
10
5
9
14
20
6
17

4. Compute the following quantities given the data below.

   a. $\sum x_i$ $\qquad$ b. $\sum f_i$ $\qquad$ c. $\sum f_i x_i$ $\qquad$ d. $\sum f_i x_i^2$

i	f_i	x_i
1	3	10
2	5	11
3	9	15
4	10	19
5	2	21
6	1	26

5. Compute the following quantities, using the information in the table below.

   a. $\sum_{i=1}^{2} x_{i,1}$ $\qquad$ b. $\sum_{j=1}^{4} x_{1,j}$ $\qquad$ c. $\sum_{i=1}^{2}\sum_{j=1}^{4} x_{i,j}$ $\quad$ d. $\sum_{j=2}^{3} x_{2,j}$

	j			
	1	2	3	4
1	8	7	5	9
i				
2	4	0	10	2

ANALYSIS OF SMALL DATA SETS

The analysis of data often proceeds along different lines depending upon whether there is a large or small amount of data to be analyzed. When there are, say, 30 or less data points, the methods outlined in the pages that immediately follow are used; for larger amounts of data, computers, or techniques that first require *grouping* the data prior to analysis are most practical. These techniques are considered later in the chapter.

Very often a set of numbers can be reduced to one or a few simple numerical measures that summarize the entire set. Such measures are usually easier to comprehend than the original, or raw, data. Moreover, they are essential for computational techniques. Two important characteristics of data that numerical measures can bring out are (1) the center or most typical value of the set and (2) the dispersion, or spread, of the numbers.

The objective of this section is to introduce you to the most useful methods for summarizing data. While there is no one best measure for this purpose, different situations often lend themselves more to one technique than to another. The following discussion presents a variety of techniques and suggests some general considerations that can be used to choose among the various measures.

MEASURES OF CENTER

Measures of center are used to indicate a value that tends to typify or be most representative of a set of numbers. The three most commonly used measures are the mean, the median, and the mode.

The Mean

The arithmetic mean is what most persons think of when the word "average" is mentioned. And because it has certain desirable mathematical properties, it is the most important of the three measures we will discuss. The arithmetic mean is computed by finding the sum of the values in a set and dividing this sum by the number of values in the set. Thus the mean of the values 70, 80, and 120 is

$$\frac{70 + 80 + 120}{3} = \frac{270}{3} = 90$$

If a student has taken four exams and received grades of 83, 94, 95, and 86, that student's average grade is 89.5:

$$\frac{83 + 94 + 95 + 86}{4} = 89.5$$

The mean of a sample* is represented by the symbol $\bar{x}$ (read "x bar"), and its computation can be expressed in sigma notation as given in the box.

$$\bar{x} = \frac{\sum_{i=1}^{n} x_i}{n}$$

or, more simply, as

$$\bar{x} = \frac{\sum x}{n}$$

The *procedure* for computing the arithmetic mean is the same, regardless of whether a set of values represents sample observations or all the values in a

* The primary emphasis in this and the following chapters is on the analysis of sample data.

population. However, the symbol μ is used for the mean of a population and N for the number of items in the population:

$$\mu = \frac{\sum x}{N}$$

The mean has certain interesting and useful properties that explain why it is the most widely used measure of center:

1. The mean can always be computed for a set of numbers.
2. There is a unique mean for a given set of numbers.
3. The mean is sensitive to (affected by) every value in the set. Thus if any one value changes, the mean will change.
4. If a constant is added to each value in a set, the mean will increase by the same amount. Thus adding 4.5 to each value will cause the mean to increase by 4.5. Similarly, subtracting, multiplying, or dividing each value by a constant will decrease, multiply, or divide the mean by that constant.
5. The *sum of deviations* of the numbers in a set from the mean is zero:

$$\sum (x_i - \bar{x}) = 0$$

For instance, the mean of the numbers 2, 4, and 6 is 4:

$$\bar{x} = \frac{2 + 4 + 6}{3} = 4$$

Subtracting 4 from each number yields

$$
\begin{aligned}
2 - 4 &= -2 \\
4 - 4 &= 0 \\
6 - 4 &= +2 \\
\hline
&0
\end{aligned}
$$

A physical representation of the mean is to imagine a beam with equal weights at locations corresponding to the values in a set. The mean of the numbers 2, 4, and 6 could be illustrated as shown in Figure 2.1.

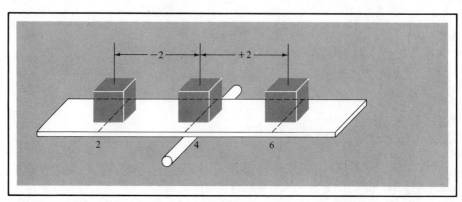

Figure 2.1   The mean is the balance point for the beam; positive and negative differences cancel each other out.

The Weighted Mean

The previous formula for computing the arithmetic mean assumes that each observation is of equal importance. While that is usually the case, there are exceptions. Take, for example, the situation in which an instructor informs a class that there will be two hourly exams, each counting for 30% of the course grade, and a final that will count for 40%. The computation of the mean must take the unequal weights of the exams into account. The following formula applies:

$$\text{weighted mean} = \frac{\sum_{i=1}^{n} w_i x_i}{\sum_{i=1}^{n} w_i}$$

where w_i is the weight of the ith observation. Thus a student who gets an 80 on the first exam, a 90 on the second, and a 96 on the final would have an average of 89.4:

Exam	Grade	Weight
no. 1	80	.30
no. 2	90	.30
final	96	.40
		1.00

$$\text{weighted mean} = \frac{.30(80) + .30(90) + .40(96)}{.30 + .30 + .40}$$
$$= 89.4$$

Suppose in another course that there is a midterm exam and a final and that the final is given twice the weight of the midterm. A student with a 95 on the midterm and an 89 on the final would have an average of 91.0.

Exam	Grade	Weight
midterm	95	1
final	89	2
		3

$$\text{weighted mean} = \frac{1(95) + 2(89)}{1 + 2} = 91.0$$

The Median

A second measure of the middle of a set of numbers is the median. Its key feature is that it divides an *ordered* set into two equal groups; half of the numbers will have values that are *less than* the median and half will have values *greater than* the median. To determine the median, it is necessary to first array, or order, the values (usually) from low to high. Then count off one-half of the values to find the median.

For instance, the median of the array 5, 6, 8 is 6; 6 is in the middle. In general, the median occupies the position $(n + 1)/2$. Hence for three numbers, the position is $(3 + 1)/2 = 2$, or the second position. Consider a second example. Find the median of these values: 7, 8, 9, 10. According to our formula the median's position is $(4 + 1)/2 = 2.5$, which is halfway between the two middle values, or 8.5 in this case. This leaves two values below and two above.

The procedure for finding the median is as follows:

1. Array or rank the values.
2. Count to determine if there is an odd or even number of values.
3. For an odd number of values, the median is the middle value. For an even number of values, the median is the average of the two middle values.

Here are some examples.

Even	Median	Odd	Median
a. 2, 3, 3, 4	3	a. 1, 2, 3, 3, 3, 4, 7	3
b. 1, 18, 19, 20	18.5	b. 9, 40, 80, 81, 100	80
c. 5.1, 6.5, 8.1, 9.1, 10.1, 15.5	8.6	c. 3.7, 9.2, 10.1, 11.8, 12.8	10.1

The median of a set of numbers is greater than or equal to one-half of the values and less than or equal to one-half of the values.

A measure closely related to the median is the *quartile*. Quartiles divide ordered data into four equal parts: 25% of the values will be less than the first quartile (Q_1), 50% will be less than the second quartile (Q_2 = median), 75% will be less than the third quartile (Q_3), and 25% will be greater than the third quartile.

Example 3 Determine by inspection the quartiles for these data sets:

$$1 \quad 2 \quad 3 \quad 4 \qquad 2 \quad 3 \quad 5 \quad 8 \quad 9 \quad 12 \quad 13 \quad 15$$
$$\uparrow \quad \uparrow \quad \uparrow \qquad\qquad\quad \uparrow \qquad\quad \uparrow \qquad\quad \uparrow$$
$$Q_1 \; Q_2 \; Q_3 \qquad\qquad\quad Q_1 \qquad\quad Q_2 \qquad\quad Q_3$$

It is customary to round up when a quartile does not equal either an integer or a value such as 2.5, 7.5, and so on.

Percentiles divide data into 100 equal subgroups. For instance, 76% of the values in a (large) set will be less than the value of the 76th percentile.

Percentiles and quartiles are mainly used in conjunction with frequency distributions, a matter we will take up shortly.

Comparison of the Mean and the Median

The choice of using the mean or the median as the measure of center of a set of numbers depends on several factors. The mean is sensitive to, or influenced by, *every* value in the set, including extremes. The median, on the other hand, is relatively insensitive to extreme values.

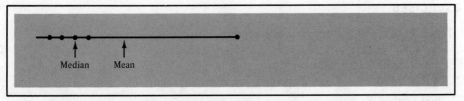

FIGURE 2.2   The mean is affected by extreme values.

Consider the data set shown in Figure 2.2. Notice how the mean is pulled toward an extreme value, while the median is not. Hence data on personal income or home values are usually more adequately described by the median, because a few very large values tend to inflate the arithmetic mean.

Generally speaking, the mean possesses certain mathematical properties that make it attractive. Furthermore, ordering the data in finding the median can be tedious, and computation of the median does not lend itself to use of a calculator, as does calculation of the mean.

The Mode

The mode is the value that occurs most often in a set. For instance, given the numbers 10, 10, 8, 6, 10, there are three 10s and one each of the other numbers. The most frequent value, the mode, is 10. The mode is descriptive when working with *count* data and will be considered in more detail at a later point in this chapter.

As compared to the mean and median, the mode is the least useful for most statistical problems because it does not lend itself to mathematical analysis in the same sense that the other two do (see Table 2.2). However, from a purely descriptive standpoint, the mode is indicative of the "typical" value in terms of the most frequently occurring value. The mode is most useful when one or two values, or a group of values, occur much more frequently than other values. Conversely, when most or all values occur with about the same frequency, the mode adds nothing in terms of describing the data.

> The mode is the value that occurs with the greatest frequency.

TABLE 2.2   A Comparison of the Mean, Median, and Mode

	Definition	Advantages	Limitations
Mean	$\bar{x} = \dfrac{\sum x_i}{n}$	1. reflects every value 2. mathematical properties attractive	1. can be unduly influenced by extremes
Median	half of the values are greater, half less	1. less sensitive to extremes than mean	1. difficult to determine if large amount of data
Mode	value with highest frequency	1. "typical" value: more values clustered at this point than at any other	1. does not lend itself to mathematical analysis 2. may not be a mode for some data sets

EXERCISES

1. Find the mean and median of each set.
   a. 4, 8, 7, 3, 5, 6   b. 2, 1, 7, 6
   c. .010, .020, .030, .020, .015   d. 309, 81, 452, 530, 70, 55, 198, 266
   *2. Fifteen CB radios are inspected prior to shipment. The number of defects per radio are

$$1, 0, 3, 4, 2, 1, 0, 3, 1, 2, 0, 1, 1, 0, 1$$

   Determine the mean, median, and mode for the number of defects.
3. Four friends work part time for a supermarket at these hourly wage rates:

   Bill: $2.20   Tom: $2.50
   Ed: $2.40   Don: $2.10

   a. Find the average hourly rate for the four friends.
   b. If Bill works 20 hours, Ed works 10 hours, Tom works 20 hours, and Don works 15 hours during the week, find their total wages and their average hourly wage.
   c. If each works 40 hours during a week, find the average hourly wage, and their total wages.
4. Can the mean ever be zero? Can it ever be negative? Explain.
5. Can the median ever be zero? Negative? Explain.

MEASURES OF DISPERSION

Two kinds of summary measures are necessary to adequately describe a set of data. In addition to having information concerning the middle of a set of numbers, it is also desirable to have some method for expressing the amount of dispersion or spread among the numbers. For instance, measures of dispersion indicate if the values are relatively close to each other or if they are fairly spread out. Schematically, this issue is illustrated in Figures 2.3(a) and 2.3(b). The observations in Figure 2.3(a) have values that are relatively close to each other, as compared to those in Figure 2.3(b).

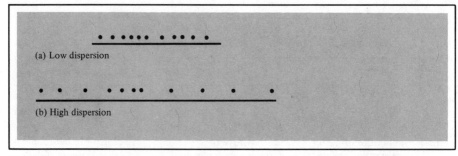

FIGURE 2.3   Dispersion measures how close values in a group are to each other.

There are four measures of dispersion that will be considered: the range, the average deviation, the variance, and the standard deviation. All these measures except the range incorporate the mean as a reference point. In each case a value of zero indicates no dispersion, while the amount of dispersion increases as the value of the measure (range, variance, etc.) increases.

The Range

The range of a group of numbers is generally the simplest measure to compute and to understand. It focuses on the largest number and the smallest number in the group (i.e., the endpoints). The range can be expressed in two ways:

1. The *difference* between the largest and smallest value.
2. The largest and smallest values in the group.

Consider these three values: 1, 10, and 25. The difference between the largest and smallest number is $25 - 1 = 24$. Alternatively, one might say the range of values is from 1 to 25. This latter method tends to be more informative. For instance, merely knowing that the range of a set of numbers is 44 does not convey anything else about the numbers; whereas stating that the range is from 300 to 344 provides additional information about the magnitude of the numbers.

The *range* can be expressed by stating the difference between the largest number and the smallest number in a group or by identifying those two numbers.

Some examples are given below.

Numbers	Range	
	Difference	Lowest to highest
1, 5, 7, 13	$13 - 1 = 12$	1 to 13
14, 3, 17, 4, 8, 73, 36, 48	$73 - 3 = 70$	3 to 73
3.2, 4.7, 5.6, 2.1, 1.9, 10.3	$10.3 - 1.9 = 8.4$	1.9 to 10.3

The advantage of using the range as a measure of dispersion lies in the fact that it is a relatively simple matter to determine the range, even for a fairly large set of numbers. Also, the meaning of the range is easy to understand. Unfortunately, some of the other measures of dispersion are not so easy to understand, at least intuitively.

The major limitation of the range is that it takes into consideration only the two extreme values in a set, and it does not tell us anything at all about the other values in the set. For example, Figure 2.4 illustrates three quite different sets of numbers, all with the same range. In the first set of numbers, the values are uniformly distributed and the range serves well. In the second set, the numbers

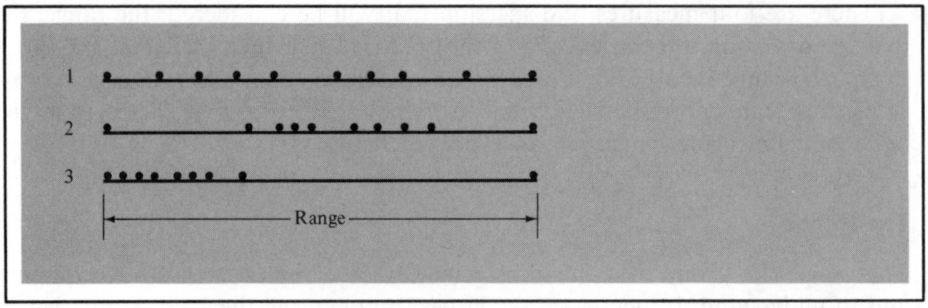

FIGURE 2.4   Three different groups of numbers, all with the same range.

are more tightly bunched, although the range still provides a crude measure of dispersion. However, the third set demonstrates how the range can be easily influenced by a few extreme values and might end up being quite misleading about the dispersion of a set of numbers.

Because of these problems, the range has a limited usefulness for the kinds of statistical analyses presented in this book.

Measures of Dispersion that Use the Mean as a Reference Point

Because of its mathematical properties, the mean of a set of data is almost always calculated. Consequently, a number of measures of dispersion have been developed that use the mean as a reference point. They all involve finding the deviation, or difference, between each individual value and the mean, $(x_i - \bar{x})$. We will consider three such measures. The first focuses on the absolute deviation from the mean, while the other two focus on squared deviations from the mean. The discussion will be primarily concerned with computations involving *sample* data as opposed to data from entire populations, with the idea being that sample statistics will be used to approximate the values of population parameters.

Mean Absolute Deviation

The mean absolute deviation (MAD) measures the average deviation of values around the group mean, ignoring the sign of the deviation. It is computed by subtracting the mean from each value in the group, eliminating the sign ($+$ or $-$) of the deviation, and then finding the average. In calculating the average deviation, it is necessary to take into account the fact that the sum of the positive and negative deviations from the mean will always (by definition) equal zero. Converting the differences to absolute values (all values are treated as positive deviations) before summing overcomes that problem. The mean absolute deviation is computed using the formula in the box.

$$\text{MAD} = \frac{\sum |x_i - \bar{x}|}{n}$$

where n is the number of observations in the set.

Example 4   Find the average deviation for this set of numbers:

$$2, 4, 6, 8, 10$$

Solution:

Find the mean:

$$\bar{x} = \frac{2 + 4 + 6 + 8 + 10}{5} = 6$$

Find the differences between the mean and each value:

$x_i - \bar{x}$

$$2 - 6 = -4$$
$$4 - 6 = -2$$
$$6 - 6 = 0$$
$$8 - 6 = +2$$
$$10 - 6 = +4$$
$$\overline{0} \quad \text{(check)}$$

Convert these differences to absolute value and sum:

$$4 + 2 + 0 + 2 + 4 = 12 = \sum|x_i - \bar{x}|$$

Find the average deviation:

$$\frac{\sum|x_i - \bar{x}|}{n} = \frac{12}{5} = 2.4$$

Example 5   Find the average deviation for this set of values:

$$1, 2, 3, 4, 5$$

Solution:

$$\text{mean} = \frac{1 + 2 + 3 + 4 + 5}{5} = \frac{15}{5} = 3$$

x_i	$\bar{x}$	$x_i - \bar{x}$	$|x_i - \bar{x}|$
1	3	-2	2
2	3	-1	1
3	3	0	0
4	3	1	1
5	3	2	2
Sums		0	6

Average:

$$\tfrac{6}{5} = 1.2$$

The *mean absolute deviation* for a set of numbers is the average deviation of the values from the mean, ignoring the sign of difference.

Although the mean absolute deviation is relatively simple to understand, it is not widely used as a measure of dispersion because other measures have more attractive mathematical properties. There are some uses for MAD in inventory control.

The Variance

The variance of a sample is computed in very much the same way that the average deviation is, with two minor exceptions: (1) the deviations are *squared* before summing, and (2) the average is found using $n - 1$ rather than n, because this purportedly provides a better estimate of the population variance than would the use of n.

The sample variance can be computed using the formula given in the box.

$$s_x{}^2 = \frac{\sum (x_i - \bar{x})^2}{n - 1}$$

If a set of numbers constitutes a population, or if the purpose of summarizing the data is merely to *describe* a data set rather than to draw inferences about a population, the $(n - 1)$ in the denominator should be replaced with n.

Example 6 Compute the variance of this sample: 2, 4, 6, 8, 10.

Solution:
We have already determined that the mean of this set is 6. The computations necessary are these:

x_i	$\bar{x}$	$(x_i - \bar{x})$	$(x_i - \bar{x})^2$
2	6	-4	16
4	6	-2	4
6	6	0	0
8	6	$+2$	4
10	6	$+4$	16
Sums		0	40

$$s^2 = \frac{\sum (x_i - \bar{x})^2}{n - 1} = \frac{40}{5 - 1} = 10.0$$

If these values had been *all* the values of a population, its variance would have been $40/5 = 8.0$.

The *variance* of a sample is the average squared deviation of values from the mean, computed using $n - 1$ instead of n.

In sum, the necessary steps in computing a variance are as follows:

1. Compute the mean.
2. Subtract the mean from each value in the set.
3. Square each of those deviations.
4. Sum the squared deviations.
5. Divide by $(n - 1)$ if sample data; divide by n simply to summarize the set or if the data are all the values of a population.

An alternative formula that is often used for computing the sample variance is

$$s_x{}^2 = \frac{\sum x_i{}^2 - (\sum x_i)^2/n}{n - 1}$$

(Again, substitute n for $n - 1$ in the *denominator* for the population variance.) This formula is sometimes easier to use than the previous one because it does not require calculating the mean and because there is no need to determine each of the deviations. For a mean such as 3.33333333, the former approach results in errors due to rounding.

Using the previous data, you can observe that the variance computed with this formula is identical to that previously computed.

x_i	$x_i{}^2$
2	4
4	16
6	36
8	64
10	100
$\sum x_i = 30$	$\sum x_i{}^2 = 220$

$$s_x{}^2 = \frac{220 - (30^2/5)}{5 - 1} = \frac{220 - 180}{4} = 10.0$$

The Standard Deviation

The standard deviation is simply the positive square root of the variance. Thus if the variance is 81, the standard deviation is 9; if the variance is 10, the standard deviation is $\sqrt{10} = 3.16$. To determine the standard deviation, compute the variance and find its square root.* The formulas for the standard deviation are

$$s = \sqrt{\frac{\sum (x_i - \bar{x})^2}{n - 1}} = \sqrt{\frac{\sum x_i{}^2 - [(\sum x_i)^2/n]}{n - 1}}$$

[As before, substituting n for $(n - 1)$ converts these to formulas for the population standard deviation.]

Example 7   Compute the standard deviation of this sample:

$$20, 5, 10, 15, 25$$

---

* There is a table of squares and square roots in the Appendix that is useful in this regard.

Solution:

Using the shortcut formula, compute $\sum x_i$:

$$20 + 5 + 10 + 15 + 25 = 75$$

Compute $\sum x_i^2$:

$$20^2 + 5^2 + 10^2 + 15^2 + 25^2 = 400 + 25 + 100 + 225 + 625$$
$$= 1375$$

Determine s:

$$\sqrt{\frac{1375 - (75^2/5)}{5 - 1}} = \sqrt{62.5} = 7.91$$

The standard deviation is one of the most commonly used summary measures for distributions, and it occupies an important role throughout statistics. It is worthwhile to note that the units of the standard deviation are the same as those of the mean. For instance, if the mean is in dollars, the standard deviation is too. If the mean is in meters, so is the standard deviation. The variance, on the other hand, is in square units (e.g., dollars^2, meters^2).

The *standard deviation* of a set of numbers is defined to be the positive square root of the variance

---

Other Measures

The previously discussed measures apply mainly to quantitative data, with the exception of the mode, which is also useful for working with nominal data, as we will soon learn. Another measure used with nominal data is the proportion, which is the fraction or percentage of items in a particular group or class. The proportion is computed using the formula

$$\text{proportion} = \frac{x}{n}$$

where x is the number of items having a certain characteristic and n is the total number of observations.

For instance, if we find that 10 persons in a sample of 40 own their own homes, we can say the proportion who own their homes is $10/40 = .25$, or 25%.

EXERCISES

1. a. Can the standard deviation ever be zero? Explain. Can it ever be negative? Explain.
   b. Can the mean absolute deviation be negative? Zero? Explain.

2. Compute the mean and standard deviation of daily sales:

$8,100, $9,000, $4,580, $5,600, $7,680, $4,800, $10,640

3. Determine the mean and median for each of these data sets:
   a. 7, 9, 2, 1, 5, 4.5, 7.5, 6, 2   b. 1, 2, 10, 7, 7, 9, 8, 5, 2, 11
   c. 30, 2, 79, 50, 38, 17, 9   d. .011, .032, .027, .035, .042
   e. 90, 87, 92, 81, 78, 85, 95, 80   f. 42, 30, 27, 40, 25, 32, 33
4. What effect would there be on the mean of a set of numbers if 10 is added to:
   a. One of the numbers?   b. Each of the numbers?
5. Compute the mean and variance for the following scores assuming the scores are a:
   a. sample   b. population

83, 92, 100, 57, 85, 88, 84, 82, 94, 93, 91, 95

6. Determine the standard deviation for the values in Exercise 5 assuming first a sample and then a population.
7. Compute the mean, median, and mode for the number of customers waiting in the lines of 12 tellers at the main office of a large bank:

1, 3, 4, 3, 4, 2, 4, 1, 2, 2, 1, 0 (behind a pole)

8. Determine the sample variance and standard deviation for the data given in the previous exercise using the shortcut formula.
9. Indicate the quartiles for the data in Exercise 7.
10. Compute the mean and standard deviation of reaction times for these sample data:

2.1, 2.5, 2.7, 2.3, 2.4, 2.0, 2.7, 3.0, 1.4, 2.4, 2.8

11. Find the median reaction time for the data in Exercise 10.
12. Determine the range for each of these data sets:
    a. Exercise 2   b. Exercise 5   c. Exercise 7
13. Find the quartiles for the reaction times in Exercise 10.
14. What effect would there be on (a) the mean and (b) the standard deviation if each value in a set is doubled? (Hint: Use these data: 1, 2, 3.)
15. Consider these sample data on price bids:

26.5, 27.5, 25.5, 26.0, 27.0, 23.4, 25.1, 26.2, 26.8

   a. Find the range.   b. Find MAD.
   c. Find the standard deviation.   d. Find the variance.
*16. Convert each of the following to a proportion:
    a. 5 children out of 25
    b. 7 of 9 patients
    c. 3 red, 4 blue, 5 green out of 12
17. Compute each of these proportions using the table shown in Figure 2.5:
    a. sunny days in June
    b. partly cloudy days in June
    c. sunny Sundays
    d. rainy weekdays
    e. snowy days

FIGURE 2.5   June weather.

ANALYSIS OF LARGE DATA SETS

Human beings require a fairly high degree of structure or *organization* in their lives to function properly. Consider, if you will, that your ability to locate a book in the library depends on the organization provided by a card catalog which lists library possessions *alphabetically*, by subject and by author and title, and by call numbers which indicate shelf location. Imagine how utterly impossible it would be to find a book if the system involved stacking books wherever there was space, with no call numbers and no card catalog. Similarly, consider the confusion that would exist if no traffic laws or signals were in use, and the only rule was "every man for himself."* Telephone numbers are organized into telephone books alphabetically by town; course schedules indicate when and where courses meet; there are bus, train, and airline schedules, and zip codes—all help us by *organizing* information.

The chief methods for *organizing* statistical data involve arranging items into subsets that contain similar qualities (e.g., same age, same purpose, same school, same city, and so on). Grouped data can be summarized graphically or in tables,

---

* It is generally accepted that most women would have too much common sense to venture out onto the highway under such circumstances.

and through the use of numerical measures such as the mean, range, standard deviation, and so on. The name for data arranged into groups or categories is a *frequency distribution*.

FREQUENCY DISTRIBUTIONS

Consider the data in the table that follows, which represent yields in bushels per tree for 40 peach trees. Even though the amount of data has been purposely kept small to simplify the discussion, it is still difficult to grasp an overall picture of yields from the data in its current form. Constructing a frequency distribution can enhance the data considerably.

Annual Yield (in bushels/tree) for 40 Peach Trees

11.1	12.5	32.4	7.8	21.0	16.4	11.2	22.3
4.4	6.1	27.5	32.8	18.5	16.4	15.1	6.0
10.7	15.8	25.0	18.2	12.2	12.6	4.7	23.5
14.8	22.6	16.0	19.1	7.4	9.2	10.0	26.2
3.5	16.2	14.5	3.2	8.1	12.9	19.1	13.7

A frequency distribution is a method of classifying data into classes or intervals in such a way that the number or percentage (i.e., the frequency) of each class can be determined. This offers a way of viewing a set of numbers without having to consider individual numbers, and it can be extremely useful in dealing with large amounts of data. The number or percentage in a class is called the *class frequency*.

A *frequency distribution* is a grouping of data into classes, showing the number or percentage of observations in each class. A frequency distribution can be presented in tabular and graphical forms.

The procedure for actually developing a frequency distribution for a given set of data depends on the type of data involved (i.e., continuous, discrete, nominal, or ranked data). Presumably, fruit yields (in bushels per tree) are measured on a continuous scale, so let us first consider that case.

Constructing a Frequency Distribution for Continuous Data

The main steps in developing a frequency distribution for sample data are as follows:

1. Establish the classes or intervals into which the data will be grouped.
2. Arrange the data into the classes by *tallying*.
3. Count the number in each class.
4. Present the results in a table or a graph.

Let us construct a frequency distribution for peach tree yields using the data given above. To establish the classes of the distribution, these steps are necessary:

1. Determine the *range* of the data. The largest yield is 32.8, the smallest is 3.2, so the range is 29.6.
2. Decide on the number of classes to use. It is best to use between 5 and 15 classes; less than 5 will hide important features of the data, while more than 15 will provide too much detail. One rule of thumb is to compute the square root of *n*, and adjust it to conform (if necessary) with the 5-to-15 limits. For instance, for 400 observations, $\sqrt{400} = 20$, and this would be adjusted to 15. For the 40 trees, we would have $\sqrt{40} = 6.32$, which would be rounded to either 6 or 7.
3. Divide the range by k, the number of classes, to obtain a class width: $29.6/6 = 4.93 \approx 5$.
4. Set up preliminary intervals, beginning with an integer just below the smallest value. For example, the first class is

$$\text{lower limit: } 3 \qquad \text{upper limit: } 3 + \text{width} = 3 + 5 = 8$$

The second class is

$$\text{upper limit of previous class} = 8 \quad \text{to} \quad 8 + 5 = 13$$

The third class is

$$13 \quad \text{to} \quad 13 + 5 = 18$$

The fourth class is from 18 to 23; the fifth class is from 23 to 28; and the sixth class is from 28 to 33.

It is important that the classes touch so that no *gaps* occur (i.e., there should be a class for every value), but the classes should not overlap (i.e., a value should belong to only one class). If the value 8.0 occurred, you might wonder whether to include it in the first class or the second, since both have 8 as an endpoint. There are various methods to use. Perhaps the simplest is to treat the intervals as

$$3 \text{ to } <8 \qquad 13 \text{ to } <18 \qquad 23 \text{ to } <28$$
$$8 \text{ to } <13 \qquad 18 \text{ to } <23 \qquad 28 \text{ to } <33$$

Once the classes have been set up, each data point can be placed in or assigned to the appropriate class by tallying. For example, the first value is 11.1, which falls into the second class. A frequency distribution can be formed by listing the intervals and putting a slash (/) in the correct class for each value and a diagonal line through each set for the *fifth* tally.

Class	Tallies	Count
3 to 8	////// ///	8
8 to 13	////// //////	10
13 to 18	////// ////	9
18 to 23	////// //	7
23 to 28	////	4
28 to 33	//	2
		40

Next the tallies are counted (see the table) by class. The frequencies can be shown in either a table or a graph, and they can be actual frequencies or relative frequencies. Thus a frequency table would appear as shown in this table:

Frequency Distribution of Peach Tree Yields

Number of bushels	Number of trees	Percentage of trees
3 to <8	8	$\frac{8}{40}$ = .200
8 to <13	10	$\frac{10}{40}$ = .250
13 to <18	9	$\frac{9}{40}$ = .225
18 to <23	7	$\frac{7}{40}$ = .175
23 to <28	4	$\frac{4}{40}$ = .100
28 to <33	2	$\frac{2}{40}$ = .050
	40	1.000

The same information can also be presented by a frequency *histogram*, which shows classes along the horizontal axis and frequencies (either actual or relative) on the vertical axis. The boundaries of the "bars" coincide with the endpoints of the class intervals. See Figure 2.6.

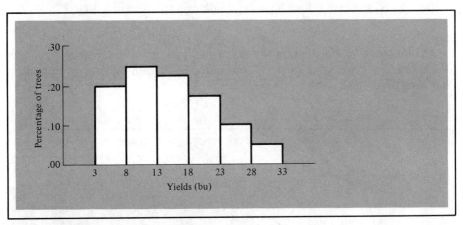

FIGURE 2.6   Relative frequency distribution for tree yields.

The sequence of steps for constructing a frequency distribution for continuous data is outlined below:

1. Determine the *range* of the data.
2. Determine the *number of classes*, $k \approx \sqrt{\text{number of observations}}$. (As a general rule, use 5 to 15 classes.)
3. Compute the *class width*, range/k, rounding to a convenient number. (Make certain that k times the width is greater than the range or else extreme values will not fit the classes.)
4. Establish preliminary *class limits*. Revise limits so they touch but do not overlap.
5. List the intervals and make a *tally* of data points by class. (Check to see that total tallies = n.)
6. Make a *frequency table* or a *frequency histogram*. See Figure 2.7.

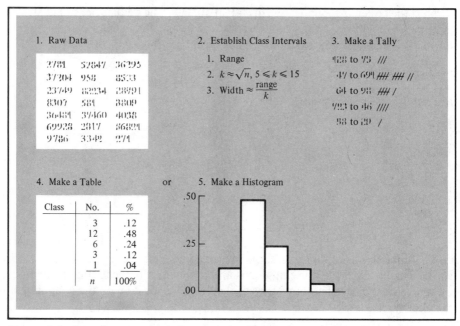

Figure 2.7   Steps for preparing a frequency distribution for continuous data.

An alternative to a histogram which is sometimes useful is a *frequency polygon*, constructed by connecting the *midpoints* of the histogram intervals with straight lines. See Figure 2.8.

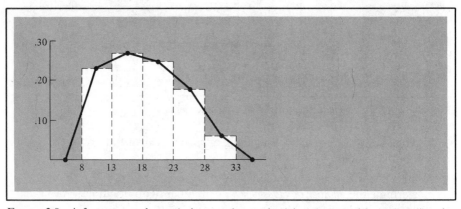

Figure 2.8   A frequency polygon (using peach tree data) is constructed by connecting the midpoints of histogram classes by straight lines.

Constructing a Frequency Distribution for Discrete Data

In constructing a frequency distribution using continuous data, a certain amount of information is lost because the individual values lose their identity when they are lumped into classes. This may or may not happen with discrete data, depending on the nature of the data and the wishes of the analyst. Consider the data below on the number of accidents reported per day for 50 days in a large parking lot.

6	9	2	7	0	8	2	5	4	2
5	4	4	4	4	2	5	6	3	7
3	8	8	4	4	4	7	7	6	5
4	7	5	3	7	1	3	8	0	6
5	1	2	3	6	0	5	6	6	3

Notice that the data consist of integers 0 through 9.

We can construct a frequency distribution with *no* loss of original values by using as our classes the integers 0 to 9.

Class	Number of days	Percentage of days
0	3	.06
1	2	.04
2	5	.10
3	6	.12
4	9	.18
5	7	.14
6	7	.14
7	6	.12
8	4	.08
9	1	.02
	50	1.00

We say there is no loss of information because it is evident from the table that the original data contained three 0s, two 1s, and so on. In other words, it would be possible to re-create the raw data from the frequency distribution. On the other hand, we could use as classes 0–1, 2–3, 4–5, 6–7, 8–9. The result is a distribution not unlike that for continuous data.

Class	Number of days	Percentage of days
0–1	5	.10
2–3	11	.22
4–5	16	.32
6–7	13	.26
8–9	5	.10
	50	1.00

Graphs of these two frequency distributions are compared in Figure 2.9. With no loss of information, the frequencies (either actual or relative) are shown as bars, whereas the distribution with loss of information is a histogram.

Generally speaking, a frequency distribution with no loss of information is preferred when:

1. Integer values make up the data.
2. Fewer than, say, 16 integers are involved.
3. There are enough observations to develop a meaningful distribution.

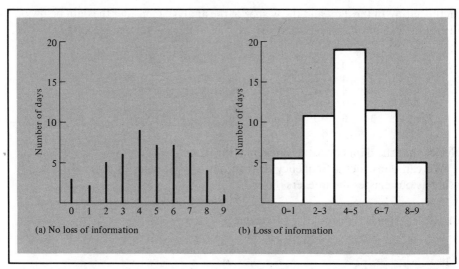

FIGURE 2.9 Comparison of a frequency distribution with and without information loss.

On the other hand, a frequency distribution in which grouping causes information loss is useful when:

1. Both integers and nonintegers (or nonintegers only) are involved.
2. Only integers are involved, but there are too many to develop a useful distribution.
3. The loss of information is of minor importance (for example, *rounding* the weight of a truck to the nearest pound, or annual income to the nearest dollar).

Constructing a Cumulative Frequency Distribution

A cumulative frequency distribution is designed to indicate the number or percentage of items that are *less than or equal to* some specified value. We can construct cumulative distributions for the accident data, for the distribution without loss of information, and for the distribution with loss. The previous distributions can easily be converted to cumulative distributions by successive summing of individual class frequencies (the data in the tables that follow are from previous discussions).

With No Loss

Class	Percentage of accidents	Cumulative frequencies
0	.06	.06
1	.04	.04 + .06 = .10
2	.10	.10 + .10 = .20
3	.12	.12 + .20 = .32
4	.18	.18 + .32 = .50
5	.14	.14 + .50 = .64
6	.14	.14 + .64 = .78
7	.12	.12 + .78 = .90
8	.08	.08 + .90 = .98
9	.02	.02 + .98 = 1.00
	1.00	

With Loss of Information

Class	Percentage of accidents	Cumulative frequencies
0–1	.10	.10
2–3	.22	.22 + .10 = .32
4–5	.32	.32 + .32 = .64
6–7	.26	.26 + .64 = .90
8–9	.10	.10 + .90 = 1.00
	1.00	

Thus we can see in the first table that 78% of the data points were 6 or less, and that 98% were 8 or less. Similarly, with information loss, we can see that 64% of the values did not exceed 5, and that 90% did not exceed 7.

The graphs for both cumulative distributions are shown in Figure 2.10.

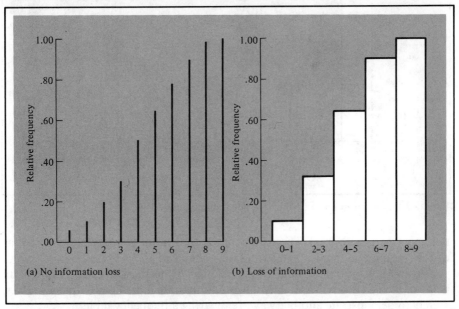

FIGURE 2.10   Cumulative frequency distributions for loss of information and for no loss of information.

Frequency Distributions for Nominal and Ranked Data

Perhaps the simplest frequency distributions to construct are those for nominal and ranked data. This simplicity stems from the fact that classes are more readily apparent, so computations are minimal. For instance, consider the nominal data in Table 2.3 on soft drink sales, which are arranged into a frequency table.

The categories are the various flavors of soft drinks. Notice the last category, Other. There may have been a number of flavors that had fairly low sales, such as cream soda, birch beer, and chocolate, and these were lumped together into a single category to make the data more comprehensible. As previously, we may want to present this information in a graph. This time it is more appropriate to use rods or bars instead of a histogram, signifying that the categories are nontouching, or

TABLE 2.3   One-Day Sale of Soft Drinks

	Frequency	
Flavor	Actual sales	Relative sales
Cola	600	60%
Lemon-lime	200	20%
Orange	100	10%
Grape	50	5%
Cherry	40	4%
Other	10	1%
	1000	100%

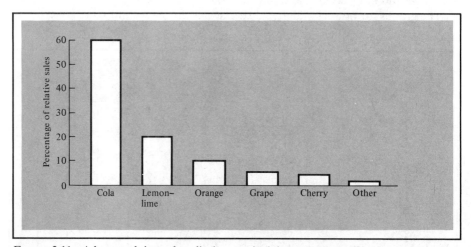

FIGURE 2.11   A bar graph is used to display nominal data.

nominal (see Figure 2.11). The graph can be shown horizontally or vertically, as can *any* graph of a frequency distribution.

Presentation of ranked data is quite similar. Consider the course rating data below, which is shown in a slightly different format than previous frequency tables, merely to demonstrate another way of preparing a frequency table.

	Course ratings					
	Poor	Fair	Average	Good	Excellent	Totals
Number	2	4	20	10	4	40
Percentage	5%	10%	50%	25%	10%	100%

Ranked data can be portrayed graphically as a bar graph similar to Figure 2.11.

Other Methods for Displaying Data

Figure 2.12 gives an indication of some of the many different ways of presenting data graphically.

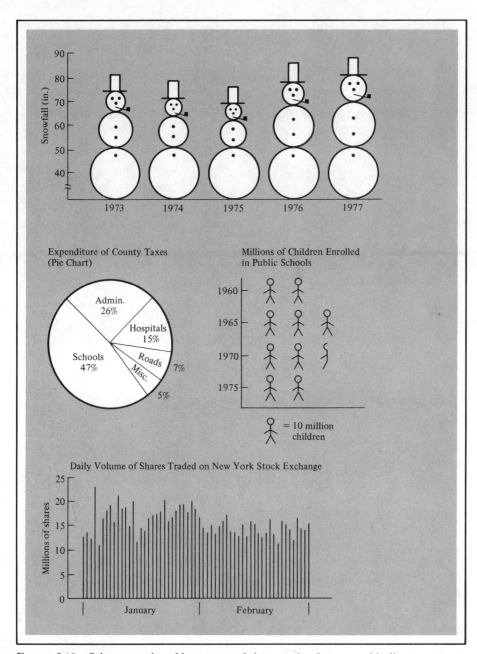

FIGURE 2.12   Other examples of how grouped data can be shown graphically.

EXERCISES

1. Construct two frequency distributions for these data: one without loss of information and the other with loss. Show the distributions in tabular and graphical forms.

Errors per page

9	7	4	3	6	5	8	2	3	6	2	3	0	3	0	2	1	3	1	5
11	7	4	2	3	2	4	7	3	2	1	3	2	1	0	1	2	2	2	3
3	2	5	4	3	6	2	8	2	3	4	1	2	1	6	1	3	2	1	1

2. The following data are for annual rainfall for the last 50 years recorded in a middle Ohio community. Construct a frequency distribution table and histogram for relative frequencies.

15.2	14.6	27.9	24.9	20.0	43.5	30.7	30.0	35.7	40.9
23.4	17.8	26.9	30.8	19.9	36.8	33.4	19.8	29.6	38.2
25.1	42.0	35.2	15.6	25.5	29.7	27.8	14.6	22.1	24.3
30.1	30.1	22.1	24.4	28.7	35.0	26.1	28.2	19.4	28.7
28.0	25.3	31.8	31.0	28.3	13.5	32.1	25.4	26.7	36.8

3. Arrange these 45 sample means into a frequency distribution table and chart. Use actual frequencies.

25.2	45.5	53.2	54.4	60.5	58.9	40.3	38.9	95.2
30.0	55.0	63.5	65.2	57.6	64.0	69.3	71.2	28.4
51.9	34.9	81.0	89.6	77.6	68.5	52.1	54.0	86.1
44.4	48.9	72.4	59.7	45.0	55.5	62.0	55.9	57.8
61.2	47.9	48.6	55.6	53.2	50.6	47.8	45.3	56.6

4. Criticize this suggested frequency distribution:

Classes	Data (mpg)				
10 to 19	8.6	22.8	30.5	28.9	23.7
20 to 30	12.0	20.1	26.8	9.5	18.6
29 to 40	42.3	34.9	20.3	13.5	11.8
	34.2	37.4	23.0	19.3	14.5
	25.8	17.5	12.3	25.7	28.4

5. Construct cumulative tables and graphs for the data in:
   a. Exercise 1 (without loss)   b. Exercise 1 (with loss)
   c. Exercise 2   d. Exercise 3

SUMMARY MEASURES FOR GROUPED DATA*

The key summary measures for grouped data are the same as those for small data sets, namely, the mean, median, and mode for measures of center and the standard deviation, variance, and range for measures of dispersion (MAD is not discussed because it is not widely used).

---

* Most of the computational methods discussed in this section were developed long before the advent of computers. For the most part they offer shortcut approximations for hand calculations. They are useful, though, when the original data are not given, as might be the case in working with published data.

Finding the Mean of a Frequency Distribution

A variation of the formula for computing the weighted mean can be used to find the mean of a frequency distribution. The class frequencies are substituted for the weights, and the formula becomes

$$\bar{x} = \frac{\sum f_i x_i}{n}$$

where f_i is the frequency of the ith class and n is the number of observations (equal to $\sum f_i$).

If there is no loss of information in the frequency distribution, the formula will yield the same answer as working with the original data; if grouping causes information loss, the x_i's are replaced with the midpoints of the respective classes, and the resulting mean is an approximation. The use of class midpoints treats the midpoints as class averages, which is not always the case. However, if the original data are not available, there is no other reasonable alternative.

Example 8   No loss. Find the mean of these data:

i	x_i	f_i	$f_i x_i$
1	0	2	0
2	5	4	20
3	10	5	50
4	15	10	150
5	20	2	40
6	25	1	25
7	30	1	30
		$n = 25$	315

Solution:

$$\bar{x} = \frac{\sum f_i x_i}{n} = \frac{315}{25} = 12.6$$

Example 9   With loss. Find the mean of these data:

Class	x_i Class midpoint	f_i Frequency	$f_i x_i$
0 to <10	5	2	10
10 to <20	15	1	15
20 to <30	25	5	125
30 to <40	35	8	280
40 to <50	45	4	180
		$n = 20$	610

Solution:

$$\bar{x} = \frac{\sum f_i x_i}{n} = \frac{610}{20} = 30.5$$

Note that the class midpoints are found by taking the average of the lower boundary of each class and the lower boundary of the next largest class.

Finding the Median of a Frequency Distribution

Here, too, the procedure and the results differ somewhat depending on whether the original data are available or not. If the original data are available, the procedure is as follows:

1. Identify the interval that contains the median.
2. Determine the rank of the median in that interval.
3. Rank the values *in that class*.
4. Identify the median.

Example 10   Suppose the distribution represents 73 values. We know that the median will be at the 37th position when the data are ranked (i.e., $\frac{73}{2} + \frac{1}{2} = 37$). Consider these values:

Class	Frequency	Cumulative Frequency
10–<12	5	5
12–<14	10	15
14–<16	17	32
16–<18	19	51—median is the 5th value in this class
18–<20	11	62
20–<22	4	66
22–<24	6	72
24–<26	1	73
	73	

The 37th value is in the class 16 to <18, and since 32 scores are less than 16, the median is the 5th value in this class: $32 + 5 = 37$. Hence array only the smallest values in this class and count off 5. Suppose the values are

	16.0	16.2	16.3	16.3	16.5	16.6	16.9
rank	1	2	3	4	5	6	7

Then 16.5 is the median.

Without the original data we are reduced to the assumption that the values in the class containing the median are *evenly spaced*. Continuing with the preceding example, in which the median is the 37th value, we can see from the frequency distribution that the median is in the class 16 to <18, which has a *class width** of 2. There are 19 values in that class, and we wish to find a value that represents the 5th value. In other words, with this assumption of evenly spaced values, we must go five-nineteenths into the class, or to the point $16 + \frac{5}{19}(2) = 16.53$. The concept is illustrated in Figure 2.13.

---

* It is important to keep in mind that class width is the difference between the lower boundary of one class and the lower boundary of the *next* class.

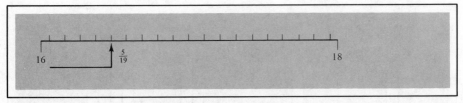

FIGURE 2.13   The median is the fifth value in a class of 19 values. Its location assumes the values are evenly spaced in the interval.

Finding the Mode of a Frequency Distribution

The mode of a frequency distribution indicates which portion of the distribution has the highest frequency of occurrences. It is often quite simple to identify the mode once data have been arranged into a frequency distribution. When there is loss of information, the mode refers to a "modal class" rather than a unique value. The mode can be easily seen in the two graphs shown in Figure 2.14.

Of course, the mode can also be determined from a frequency table:

Class	Relative Frequency
1	5%
2	3%
3	17%
4	35%—mode is 4
5	18%
6	15%
7	7%

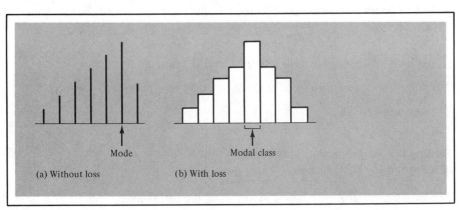

(a) Without loss   (b) With loss

FIGURE 2.14   Finding the mode on a graph.

Sometimes there will be two or more distinctive peaks of frequency in the data, and it is then meaningful to talk in terms of bimodal (two modes) or multiple modes. Furthermore, it is not strictly necessary to have two modes with equal frequencies. A bimodal distribution (see Figure 2.15) often signifies that there has been a shift in the population mean (i.e., that data have come from two or more populations).

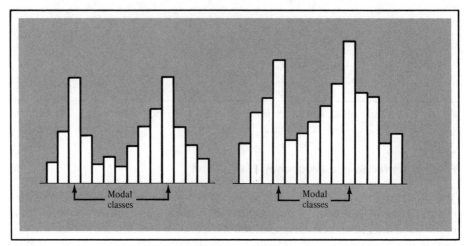

FIGURE 2.15   Bimodal frequency distributions.

The mode does not lend itself well to mathematical manipulations. Furthermore, if frequencies are fairly uniform, the importance of the mode as a decriptive measure is considerably diminished.

Finding the Range of a Frequency Distribution

If you have access to the original data, the range is simply the difference between the lowest and the highest values, or those values themselves. Without the original data the range must be considered as the difference between the lower boundary of the first interval and the upper boundary of the last interval, or the endpoints of the distribution.

Example 11   Given these class intervals, find the range:

$$0 \text{ to } <10, \ 10 \text{ to } <20, \ 20 \text{ to } <30, \ 30 \text{ to } <40, \ 40 \text{ to } <50$$

The range is 0 to 50.

Finding the Variance and Standard Deviation of a Frequency Distribution

The variance for grouped data is found using the formulas

$$s^2 = \frac{\sum f_i(x_i - \bar{x})^2}{n - 1} \quad \text{or} \quad s^2 = \frac{\sum f_i x_i{}^2 - [(\sum f_i x_i)^2/n]}{n - 1}$$

As previously, $(n - 1)$ is used if the variance is viewed as an estimate of the population variance, and n is used if the data constitute a population. Also, the standard deviation is the positive square root of the variance. For a distribution with no loss of information, the values will be exact; for loss of information, the midpoints are used for the x_i's, and the results are only approximations.

Example 12   Find the variance of this frequency distribution using the formula

$$s^2 = \frac{\sum f_i x_i^2 - [(\sum f_i x_i)^2 / n]}{n - 1}$$

Class	x_i Midpoint	f_i Frequency	$f_i x_i$	$f_i x_i^2$
0 to <10	5	2	10	50
10 to <20	15	1	15	225
20 to <30	25	5	125	3,125
30 to <40	35	8	280	9,800
40 to <50	45	4	180	8,100
		$n = 20$	610	21,300

Solution:

$$s^2 = \frac{21,300 - (610^2 / 20)}{19} = 141.84$$

Alternatively, find the variance using the formula

$$s^2 = \frac{\sum f_i (x_i - \bar{x})^2}{n - 1}$$

Note: $\bar{x} = 30.5$ (see page 45).

Class	x_i Midpoint	$\bar{x}$	f_i Frequency	$(x_i - \bar{x})$	$(x_i - \bar{x})^2$	$f_i (x_i - \bar{x})^2$
0 to 10	5	30.5	2	25.5	650.25	1300.50
10 to 20	15	30.5	1	15.5	240.25	240.25
20 to 30	25	30.5	5	5.5	30.25	151.25
30 to 40	35	30.5	8	4.5	20.25	162.00
40 to 50	45	30.5	4	14.5	210.25	841.00
			20			2695.00

$$s^2 = \frac{2695.00}{20 - 1} = 141.84$$

The standard deviation is 11.91.

Graphs of Frequency Distributions

There are continuous and discrete distributions. Continuous distributions are smooth curves [see Figure 2.16(a)]. Discrete distributions are formed using bars or rectangles [see Figure 2.16(b)]. One useful bit of information is whether the distribution is symmetrical (the left half is the mirror image of the right half) or whether the distribution is "skewed" (pulled) in one direction.

The shape of a frequency distribution has an influence on the values of the mean, median, and mode. For symmetrical distributions the mean and median are equal.

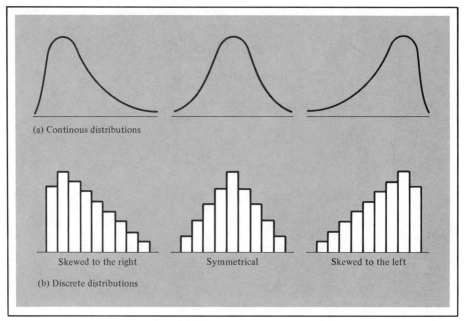

FIGURE 2.16   Examples of skewed and symmetrical distributions.

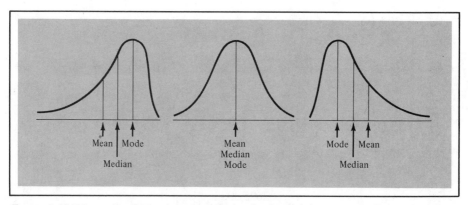

FIGURE 2.17 When a distribution is symmetrical and unimodal, its mean, median, and mode are equal. Otherwise, the mean and median are pulled toward the extreme values, the mean more so than the median.

For nonsymmetrical distributions (i.e., skewed distributions), the mean tends more toward the extreme values. See Figure 2.17.

EXERCISES

1. The age group of each of 50 visitors at a science exhibit was recorded. Find the mean age and find the class the median age is in.

Age	Number
0 to <10	6
10 to <20	18
20 to <30	11
30 to <40	3
40 to <50	0
50 to <60	8
60 to <70	4
	50

2. Find the average age of delinquent accounts and determine which class the median is in.

Months overdue	Tally
2–3	///// ///// ////
4–5	///// ///// //
6–7	///// ///
8–9	///// /
10–11	///// ////
12–13	///// ///// /
14–15	///// ///// /////
16–17	///// /////
18–19	/////
20–21	///
22–23	/////
24–25	
26–27	/
	99

3. Determine the mean and standard deviation of customer waiting times.

Minutes	
0 to <5	220
5 to <10	82
10 to <15	27
15 to <20	15
20 to <25	5
25 to <30	1
	350

4. Determine the modal class for the following:
   a. 1   b. 2   c. 3
5. Compute the variance for the following:
   a. 1   b. 2   c. 3
6. What is the apparent range in each of these exercises?
   a. 1   b. 2   c. 3
7. Determine the median for these exercises.
   a. 1   b. 2   c. 3
*8. Determine the mean and standard deviation for the data in Exercise 1, page 43.
   a. With no loss of information.

  b. With loss of information.
  c. Why are the two values different?
  d. Is one "better" than the other?

SUMMARY

Descriptive statistics involves organizing, summarizing, and presenting statistical data. Using graphs, tables, and numbers enhances data and makes data easier to work with because these techniques simplify and ignore many unimportant details.

Techniques for describing as well as analyzing data often relate to the type of data involved. Quantitative data are inherently numerical and can be discrete or continuous. Qualitative data involve nominal categories or relative values to which numbers must be assigned by counting or ranking.

Quantitative data are summarized by two principal measures, one for center and one for dispersion. Measures of center are the mean, the median, and the mode. Measures of dispersion are the range, the average deviation, the standard deviation, and the variance. The various measures all have advantages and limitations that must be taken into account in determining which to use for a particular situation. Nominal data can be summarized using proportions and the mode.

Frequency distributions are usually used for describing and analyzing large data sets. These can be graphical or tabular. Each type of data involves a different procedure for constructing a frequency distribution. Summary measures of center and dispersion are helpful in describing a frequency distribution.

REVIEW QUESTIONS

 1. Differentiate between data and information.
 2. Contrast quantitative data and qualitative data.
 3. Define continuous, discrete, nominal, and ranked data.
 4. Can the same population give rise to all four types of data? Explain and give an example of this.
 5. What advantages and limitations do graphical methods of summarizing data have?
 6. What advantages and limitations do numerical methods of summarizing data have?
 7. Why can it be advantageous to group data? Is there a penalty?
 8. Name three measures that can be used for the center.
 9. Name four measures that can be used to summarize the spread or dispersion of a set of numbers.
10. Under what conditions will the mean and median of a distribution be equal?
11. What is the importance of sigma notation?
12. What does the term "count data" mean?
13. What adjustment must be made if the formulas for variance or standard deviation are going to be used to summarize a data set or a population rather than to make inferences about population parameters?
14. Why are frequency distributions useful?
15. Are there different approaches to constructing frequency distributions for different types of data? Explain.

16. List the steps necessary to construct a frequency distribution for continuous data.
17. What does "skewed to the right" mean?

SUPPLEMENTAL EXERCISES

*1. Thirty students have taken a biology exam, with these grades:

84	88	90	78	80	89	94	95	77	81
83	87	91	83	92	90	92	77	86	86
99	93	83	94	76	98	70	81	76	87

   a. Find the mean and median of these scores.
   b. Construct a frequency distribution for the scores.
   c. Convert the frequency distribution to a cumulative distribution.

2. Given the following data on the number of defective items per lot for 40 lots, arrange the data into a frequency distribution without loss of information and determine the mean, median, and mode of the distribution. Plot a histogram.

5	12	9	1	10	11	8	7
7	3	8	0	9	8	2	3
8	4	4	3	3	4	5	4
0	7	5	6	5	3	0	1
10	8	3	7	2	6	2	5

3. Find the range, MAD, and variance for the data in Exercise 2.
4. Find the range and standard deviation of scores in Exercise 1.
5. For the frequency distribution below, find the mean, the modal class, and the median.

i	p_i Price	q_i Number of items
1	$0 to <$1	25
2	$1 to <$2	20
3	$2 to <$3	10
4	$3 to <$4	6
5	$4 to <$5	3
6	$5 to <$6	1
		$\overline{65}$

6. Find the total value of inventory, $\sum p_i q_i$, for Exercise 5.
7. Each person in a sample of 49 participants was assigned a series of tasks and the times recorded (minutes):

17.82	14.51	15.66	17.00	20.14	15.18	21.20
18.26	13.24	13.90	18.96	19.40	14.20	22.42
23.19	17.38	16.78	20.34	17.30	17.50	25.30
20.01	15.64	18.90	21.52	13.98	15.75	24.38
20.90	18.76	14.59	17.84	18.92	14.50	18.93
21.30	20.14	16.70	14.55	16.73	17.83	16.68
18.49	16.79	15.69	17.66	16.88	15.40	20.00

   a. Arrange the data into a frequency distribution (graph).
   b. Develop a cumulative frequency distribution.
   c. Using the original data, determine the median.

8. Consider the following data:

$$\$3.20, \$1.99, \$2.50, \$1.99, \$1.00, \$1.98, \$.79, \$.89$$

Find each of these quantities:

a. arithmetic mean	b. median
c. mean absolute deviation	d. range
e. variance (sample)	f. standard deviation (sample)

*9. Using the data below, compute b and a.

i	x_i	y_i
1	5	100
2	8	80
3	11	50
4	7	80
5	12	40
6	4	105
7	8	85
8	15	30
9	16	25
10	20	15

$$b = \frac{n\sum xy - \sum x \sum y}{n\sum x^2 - (\sum x)^2}$$

$$a = \frac{\sum y - b\sum x}{n}$$

3

probability

Chapter Objectives

After completing this chapter, you should be able to:
1. Define probability
2. Give examples of situations in which probability can be used
3. Explain what the term "experiment" refers to
4. Define the terms "sample space" and "event"
5. Describe the three possible approaches to probability: classical, relative frequency, and subjective
6. Identify situations in which each approach is used
7. Compute probabilities or odds for simple situations
8. Define the terms "set," "mutually exclusive," "collectively exhaustive," "complement," and "Venn diagram"
9. Explain what is meant by "conditional probability"
10. Contrast independent and dependent events
11. Compute probabilities for combinations of events
12. Relate counting rules to classical probability
13. Utilize permutation and combination formulas to solve problems
14. Tell what Bayes's Rule is and how it is useful

Chapter Outline

Introduction
The Probability of an Event
Sample Space and Events
Three Sources of Probabilities
    The classical approach
    Odds
    Long-run relative frequency
    Odds and relative frequencies
    Subjective approach to probabilities
The Mathematics of Probability
    Computing the probability that two events will both occur: $P(A \text{ and } B)$
    Computing the probability that at least one of two events will occur: $P(A \text{ or } B)$
Counting Techniques
    Multiplication principle
    Permutations and combinations
    Comparison of permutations and combinations
Bayes's Rule
Summary

INTRODUCTION

THE ORIGINS of the mathematics of probability date back to the sixteenth century. The initial applications dealt mainly with games of chance. Wealthy gamblers employed a knowledge of the theory of probability to devise betting strategies. Even today there are many applications involving games of chance, such as various state lotteries, gambling casinos, race tracks, and organized sports. The use of probability has gone beyond games of chance, however. Nowadays governments, business firms, and professional and nonprofit organizations are incorporating probability theory into their everyday decision processes.

Regardless of the particular application, the use of probabilities indicates that there exists some element of chance or uncertainty regarding the occurrence or nonoccurrence of some future event. Thus in many instances it may be virtually impossible to state in advance what *will* happen, but it may be possible to say what *might* happen. For example, if we flip a coin, we generally cannot say for sure whether heads or tails will appear. Moreover, through some combination of judgment, experience, and historical data, it is often possible to say *how likely* some future event is.

There are numerous examples of such situations in business and government. Predicting demand for a new product, estimating production costs, forecasting crop failures, buying insurance, hiring a new employee, preparing a budget, predicting the reaction of foreign governments to a change in defense policy, judging the impact of a tax rebate on inflation—all contain some element of chance.

Probabilities are useful because they can help in developing strategies. Hence some motorists seem to demonstrate an increased tendency to speed if they believe there is little risk of being apprehended; investors are more apt to lend their dollars if the chances for gain are good; and you are probably more willing to carry a raincoat if the probability of rain is high. Similarly, a firm may be more willing to negotiate seriously with a union if there is a strong threat of a strike; more willing to invest in new equipment if it thinks there is a good chance of recouping that money; more willing to hire a person who shows promise; and so on.

The central issue in all these situations is the ability to quantify *how likely* some event is. This chapter deals with definitions and rules that can be used to obtain probabilities.

Probabilities are used to express how likely some event is.

THE PROBABILITY OF AN EVENT

Probabilities are stated with reference to some event. The "event" in question might be rain, win, heads, a return of at least 6%, finish the course, score, and so on. The probability of some event A, denoted $P(A)$, is a number from 0 to 1 that indicates how likely the occurrence of event A is. The closer the number is to 1.00, the more likely it is that event A will occur; the closer the number is to zero, the less likely it is that event A will occur. An impossible event is assigned a probability of 0, while an event that is certain to occur is assigned a probability of 1.00. When the weatherman announces that the "probability of precipitation is near zero," he is saying, in effect, that it is highly unlikely that there will be any measurable precipitation during the forecast period (weathermen know from experience that nothing is impossible as far as the weather is concerned, so they usually refrain from assigning 0 probabilities).

Probabilities can be expressed in a variety of ways, including decimals, fractions, and percentages. For instance, the chance of rain can be stated as 20%, 2 out of 10, .20, or $\frac{1}{5}$.

The *probability* that an event will occur is given by a number that can range from 0 to 1.00.

SAMPLE SPACE AND EVENTS

One of the fundamental mathematical concepts used in the study of probability is that of a *set*. A set is a collection of objects or items that possess some common characteristic(s). For instance, the residents of Detroit, station wagons in Cincinnati, rivers in Georgia, retail drug outlets in Wisconsin, a shipment of calculators, and a classroom of students can all be thought of as sets. It is important to carefully define what constitutes the set of interest in order to be able to decide if a given object is, or is not, a member of the set.

A *set* is a well-defined collection of objects or items.

There are two ways to describe the elements of a set. One is to *list* all, or enough, of the items so that it becomes apparent what the members of the set are. The list is enclosed by braces. A second method of indicating a set is to state a rule or otherwise define the common characteristic(s) of the members of a set. Consider these examples:

$$\text{set } A = \{\text{Jones, Smith, Gungledorf}\}$$
$$\text{set } B = \{\text{all positive integers less than 9}\}$$
$$\text{set } C = \{\text{the winners of the first round}\}$$

Now probability has meaning only in the context of a *sample space*, which is the set of all of the possible outcomes of a sample or "experiment."* The term "experiment" suggests that the outcome is uncertain prior to taking observations. The outcomes of an experiment are called *events*.

A *sample space* is the set of all possible outcomes of an experiment or sample.

The outcomes of an experiment are referred to as *events*.

For example, the experiment could be flipping a coin 10 times and recording the number of times heads occurred. The sample space for the experiment would then be the possible number of heads that might result: 0, 1, 2, . . . , 10. Alternatively, the experiment could focus on number of tails in 10 flips.

Another experiment might consist of inspecting a manufacturing plant for safety hazards. The sample space is composed of the possible number of hazards that might be discovered: 0, 1, 2, 3, . . . , ∞.

Now consider the experiment "draw a single card from a deck of 52 cards." The possible outcomes are listed in Figure 3.1. There are 52 *elementary* events in the sample space. Other events can be thought of as *combinations* of these elementary events. For instance, the event "a heart is drawn" can be satisfied by any one of 13 elementary events. Likewise, the event "a five is drawn" consists of 4 elementary events, and the event "the card is red" consists of 26 elementary events, or $\frac{1}{2}$ of the elements in the sample space.

Probability calculations take into account how the various events of interest relate to each other. The terms "complement," "mutually exclusive," and "collectively exhaustive" are used to describe some of these relationships.

The *complement* of an event consists of all outcomes in the sample space that are not a part of the event. Hence the complement of "card is a heart" is the set of all cards that are not hearts (i.e., clubs, diamonds, and spades). The complement of "card is a king of diamonds" consists of the other 51 cards. The complement of an event can be denoted by a prime. The complement of event A is A'.

Events are *mutually exclusive* if they have no elements in common. Thus in drawing a single card, the events "card is a heart" and "card is a diamond" are mutually exclusive because a card cannot be both a heart and a diamond. Conversely, the events "card is a heart" and "card is a face card" are not mutually exclusive, because some hearts are face cards.

Events are said to be *collectively exhaustive* if at least one of the events must occur during an experiment. Thus the events "card is a heart," "card is a diamond," "card is a club," and "card is a spade" are collectively exhaustive; they exhaust all the possibilities. Similarly, the events "card is red" and "card is black" are collectively exhaustive.

---

* The terms "experiment" and "sample" are often used interchangeably in statistics to refer to the process of taking observations.

	Suit		
Clubs (black)	Diamonds (reds)	Hearts (red)	Spades (black)
♣ K	♦ K	♥ K	♠ K
♣ Q	♦ Q	♥ Q	♠ Q
♣ J	♦ J	♥ J	♠ J
♣ 10	♦ 10	♥ 10	♠ 10
♣ 9	♦ 9	♥ 9	♠ 9
♣ 8	♦ 8	♥ 8	♠ 8
♣ 7	♦ 7	♥ 7	♠ 7
♣ 6	♦ 6	♥ 6	♠ 6
♣ 5	♦ 5	♥ 5	♠ 5
♣ 4	♦ 4	♥ 4	♠ 4
♣ 3	♦ 3	♥ 3	♠ 3
♣ 2	♦ 2	♥ 2	♠ 2
♣ A	♦ A	♥ A	♠ A

FIGURE 3.1   A standard deck of 52 playing cards.

Finally, it is sometimes useful to note that an event and its complement are both mutually exclusive and collectively exhaustive.

> The *complement* of an event consists of all other outcomes in the sample space.
>
> Events are *mutually exclusive* if they have no elements in common or if they cannot occur at the same time.
>
> Events are *collectively exhaustive* if no other outcome is possible for a given experiment.

Here are some additional examples. These events would be considered complements:

1. Heads or tails on a single toss of a coin.
2. Injured or not injured in an accident.
3. Caught or did not catch the ball.
4. Answered or did not answer the telephone.

These events would be considered mutually exclusive:

1. The person has one brother, the person has two brothers, the person has three brothers.
2. The faces of a die.
3. Stan received an A in math, he received a B in math, he received a C in math, he received less than a C in math.

These events would be considered collectively exhaustive:

1. Any of the complements listed above.
2. The faces of a die.
3. Stan's math grade (above).

It is often useful to portray a sample space in graphical form, because this makes it easier to visualize the elements of the sample space. This can be accomplished by using a *Venn diagram*, which depicts sample spaces and events as circles, squares, or some other convenient geometrical shape. Some examples of Venn diagrams are illustrated in Figure 3.2.

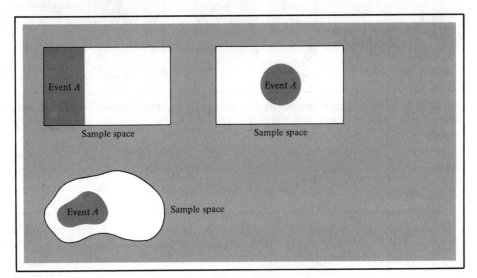

FIGURE 3.2   Some examples of Venn diagrams.

Figure 3.3 illustrates the use of Venn diagrams to portray complement, mutually exclusive and nonmutually exclusive events, and events that are both mutually exclusive and collectively exhaustive.

Now since a sample space consists of *all* the possible outcomes of an experiment, it follows that at least one of the outcomes in the sample space must occur. In other words, the probability of the sample space is 100%, or 1.00. Furthermore, because any event and its complement account for all the possibilities in the sample space, it also follows that $P(A) + P(A') = 1.00$. For example, when a coin is flipped, if we are willing to assume that it will not land on its edge, then we can say that the probability of heads or tails is 1.00. And if we somehow know that $P(\text{heads}) = .40$, then we can automatically say that $P(\text{tails}) = .60$ (i.e., $1.00 - .40$).

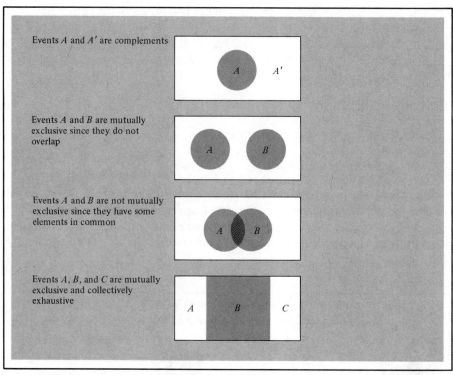

Events A and A' are complements

Events A and B are mutually exclusive since they do not overlap

Events A and B are not mutually exclusive since they have some elements in common

Events A, B, and C are mutually exclusive and collectively exhaustive

FIGURE 3.3 Venn diagrams can be used to portray complement, mutually exclusive and nonmutually exclusive events, and events that are both mutually exclusive and collectively exhaustive.

At this point, then, we can say the following:

1. The probability of any event A is represented by a value that can range from 0 to 1.00:

$$0.00 \leq P(A) \leq 1.00$$

2. The probability represented by the sample space is 100%:

$$P(\text{an event in the sample space}) = 1.00$$

3. The probability that an event will not occur is 1.00 minus the probability that it will occur:

$$1.00 - P(A) = P(A') \quad \text{or} \quad P(A) + P(A') = 1.00$$

EXERCISES

1. Identify the experiment and the sample space for each of the following:
   a. Giving an exam in math and recording the grades, which might range from 0 to 100.

   b. Giving a medical exam to prospective football players and passing or failing each one.
   c. Weighing turkeys and recording their weights. In the past these have not been less than 6 lb or more than 30 lb.
2. Briefly explain each of the following terms:
   a. set   b. experiment
   c. sample space   d. event
   e. Venn diagram   f. complement of an event
   g. mutually exclusive events   h. events that are collectively exhaustive
3. Which of the following pairs of events are mutually exclusive?

Event *A*	Event *B*
a. rain	not rain
b. B in chemistry test	C in same test
c. drive a car	walk
d. drive a car	talk
e. swim	feel cold
f. win a game	lose a game
g. win a game	tie a game
h. draw a queen from a deck of cards	draw a red card

4. State which of the following sets are collectively exhaustive:
   a. receiving either an A or a C on a test
   b. win, lose, or tie a football game
   c. a bottle being either empty or full
   d. happy or sad
   e. happy or not happy
   f. promoted or not promoted
   g. a tree is small, medium, or large
5. Determine the complement for each event:
   a. win a baseball game
   b. win a football game
   c. draw a heart from a deck of 52 cards
   d. draw a red card from a deck of 52 cards
   e. roll a two or three in one roll of a die
   f. less than 10 defectives
   g. 10 or less defectives
   h. pine paneling
6. Give three examples of statistical experiments other than those already mentioned.
7. Select one of the experiments listed for Exercise 6.
   a. Identify the sample space.
   b. Give an example of an impossible event.
   c. Give an example of a certain event.
   d. Give an example of a probable event.

THREE SOURCES OF PROBABILITIES

Before we delve into how probabilities are *used*, it will be helpful for you to have some idea of *where* they come from. There are three different ways of computing or estimating probabilities. The *classical* approach is used when sample spaces have equally likely outcomes; the *empirical* approach is based on the relative frequency of occurrence of an event over a large number of repeated trials; and the *subjective* approach uses personal estimates of probability based on degree of belief. The first two approaches are considered objective, the last subjective, as its name implies.

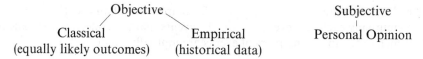

The choice of approach depends on the nature of the situation. It will be obvious as you go through the following pages that certain situations are more amenable to one approach than the others.

The Classical Approach

The classical approach pertains to situations that have *equally likely outcomes*. Games of chance, which often involve coin tossing, rolling dice, or drawing cards, usually have this characteristic of equally likely outcomes.

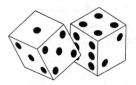

When outcomes are equally likely, the probability of each *outcome* is simply a function of the number of outcomes possible:

$$P(\text{each outcome}) = \frac{1}{\text{Number of outcomes possible}}$$

If each card in a deck of 52 playing cards has the same chance of being selected, the probability of drawing any one card will be 1/52: $P(A) = 1$ card/52 cards. The sample space for flipping a coin has *two* outcomes: heads and tails. Hence if the two outcomes are equally likely (i.e., the coin is "balanced"), the probability of heads is

$$P(\text{Heads}) = \tfrac{1}{2}$$

and the probability of tails is

$$P(\text{Tails}) = \tfrac{1}{2}$$

And in similar fashion we can compute the probability of getting one particular face in a single roll of a "balanced" die. Since there are six faces in the sample space, the probability of each must be

$$P(\text{any one face}) = \tfrac{1}{6}$$

And if we draw a single bead from a bowl with 321 beads, the probability of getting any one bead is

$$P(\text{any one bead}) = \tfrac{1}{321}$$

if we can assume the beads have been well mixed prior to selection.

The classical approach can also be applied to events that involve two or more outcomes. For example, we might want to determine the probability of drawing one of the four queens from a deck of 52 cards, or the probability of getting a number that is less than four in one roll of a die. In these and similar situations, it is necessary to first identify the number of "favorable" outcomes, and then divide that number by the total number of outcomes in the sample space. In other words, the probability of some event A is as given in the box.

$$P(A) = \frac{\text{number of outcomes associated with event } A}{\text{total number of outcomes possible}}$$

For example, the probability of drawing a queen, according to this definition, is

$$P(\text{queen}) = \frac{4 \text{ queens}}{52 \text{ cards}} = \frac{4}{52}$$

Similarly, the probability of rolling a die and getting a value of three or less (i.e., a one, two, or three) is

$$P(\text{three or less}) = \frac{3 \text{ faces}}{6 \text{ faces possible}} = \frac{3}{6}$$

If an event is impossible, it has a probability of 0. For instance, the probability of getting a nine with a single roll of a die is 0 because there are no faces marked nine on an ordinary die: $P(\text{nine}) = \tfrac{0}{6} = 0$.

Conversely, if an event is certain, it must have a probability of 1.00, or 100%. The probability of getting one of the six faces on a single roll of a die is $P(\text{one, two, three, four, five, or six}) = \tfrac{6}{6} = 1.00$, if we make the reasonable assumption that the die will not come to rest on an edge.

The interpretation of a classical probability, such as .25, is that if the experiment were repeated a large number of times, an event that has a probability of .25 will occur about 25% of the time.

Odds

Odds and probabilities are very closely related. In fact, odds are merely an alternate method of expressing probabilities. The only difference between odds and probabilities is that odds compare the number of favorable outcomes to the number of nonfavorable outcomes, whereas probabilities compare the number of favorable outcomes of the *total* number possible. That is, for probabilities we have

$$\frac{\text{number of outcomes in category } A}{\text{total number of outcomes possible}} = \frac{\text{number of outcomes in } A}{\text{number in } A + \text{number not in } A}$$

and for odds we have

$$\frac{\text{number of outcomes in category } A}{\text{number of outcomes not in } A}$$

Odds may be expressed in fractional form, as above, or they may be expressed in the equivalent form of a ratio:

odds in favor of A = number of outcomes in A : number of other outcomes

Let us consider some examples. Suppose we have a bowl with 10 marbles: 8 are red and 2 are green. The *probability* of selecting a green marble in a single draw is

$$P(\text{green}) = \frac{2}{2+8}$$

which can be reduced to $\frac{1}{5}$. The *odds* in favor of green are 2 : 8, which can be reduced to 1 : 4. Also,

$$P(\text{red}) = \frac{8}{8+2} = \frac{8}{10}$$

or $\frac{4}{5}$, while the odds of red are 8 : 2, or 4 : 1.

> The *odds in favor* of an event equal the ratio of the number of favorable outcomes to the number of unfavorable outcomes.

The odds in favor of heads in one toss of a fair coin are 1 : 1 (which is read "one-to-one"). An equivalent expression is that the chances are 50 : 50 in favor of a head occurring.

The odds *against* an event are

odds against = number of outcomes not in A : number of outcomes in A

Thus the odds against rolling a die and getting a two would be 5 : 1, and the odds against drawing a king from a deck of 52 cards would be 48 : 4. Refer to Table 3.1.

An important feature of classical probabilities is that they provide an intuitive, easy-to-visualize explanation of probability, especially when they are explained in terms of simple devices like coin tossing and rolling dice. In addition, there are numerous real life counterparts to these devices. The most significant feature of the classical approach, though, is that it is the basis for random sampling, a concept that underlies most of modern statistical inference theory. Hence the term "random sample" generally implies that all elements of a population have an equal chance of being included in the sample.

TABLE 3.1 Odds and Probabilities Compared

			Odds	
Experiment	Event	P(event)	For	Against
flip a coin once	head	$\frac{1}{2}$	1 : 1	1 : 1
roll a die once	roll a 3	$\frac{1}{6}$	1 : 5	5 : 1
draw 1 card from a deck of 52 cards	get a red 6	$\frac{2}{52}$	2 : 50	50 : 2
draw 1 card from a deck of 52 cards	get a jack of diamonds	$\frac{1}{52}$	1 : 51	51 : 1

Long-run Relative Frequency

The classical approach to assignment of probabilities is limited to those situations in which outcomes are equally likely. As you might suspect, there are many instances in which outcomes are not equally likely. For example, suppose you have a bent coin, and this causes you to question whether heads and tails are equally likely. One way to answer your question is to gather some *empirical data* in an attempt to *estimate* the probabilities. Thus it might seem reasonable to consider flipping the coin a number of times and observing the results as a simple experiment to test the assumption of equally likely outcomes. If you flipped the coin, say, 100 times and got heads 60 times, it might seem reasonable to estimate the probability of heads on any future flips as $\frac{60}{100} = .60$. Likewise, if laboratory records indicate that when 25 mice were administered equal doses of a test drug, the tongues of 20 turned bright green, then this percentage ($\frac{20}{25} = .80$) could be used as an estimate of the actual probability of this event occurring under *identical conditions*.

Hence according to the relative frequency approach to probability, we have the following definition:

$$P(A) = \frac{\text{number of times } A \text{ occurred}}{\text{total number of trials or observations}}$$

Now it is not absolutely essential to conduct an "experiment" to obtain sample data. In many cases historical information will be available, and it can be used in precisely the same way. This historical data might be in the form of published data, results of previous tests, or merely information accumulated in company files. For example, the records of a real estate firm might reveal that over a period of 16 days, the frequency of houses sold per day was

Number sold	Number of days
0	3
1	2
2	5
3	6
	16

If we can assume that the past is representative of the future (which is *not* always the case), we can determine the following probabilities: $P(0) = \frac{3}{16}$, $P(1) = \frac{2}{16}$, $P(2) = \frac{5}{16}$, and $P(3) = \frac{6}{16}$.

Thus according to the long-run frequency concept of probability, we imagine a recurrence of this same set of conditions many times, and then try to answer the question, "What percentage of the time did the event in question occur?" For instance, 2 houses were sold on 5 of the 16 days, so our estimate of the probability of that happening would be $\frac{5}{16}$. Similarly, we could estimate the probability of selling 3 houses in a day at $\frac{6}{16}$. Thus with the empirical approach, probability is treated as the *proportion*, or *relative frequency*, with which an event occurs.

When the empirical approach is used, it is important to recognize the following points:

1. The probability so determined is only an *estimate* of the actual value.

Just because we flip a coin 10 times and come up with 4 heads does not guarantee that we will get 4 heads every time we take 10 flips. Hence our empirical evidence will not usually provide us with an *exact* probability.

2. The larger the sample size, the better the estimate of the probability.

The number of observations is important, and generally speaking, the larger the number of observations (i.e., the sample size), the better the estimate of the relative frequency. A later chapter will take up this question in more detail. For now you will have to accept an intuitive explanation: consider flipping a coin one time and trying to decide if it is fair. The sample will always result in either 100% heads or 0%. Even a sample of two observations ought to leave some doubt in your mind as to the true probability of heads. On the other hand, after a hundred or so flips, you would undoubtedly feel more comfortable in assessing the probability of heads. Theoretically, the relative frequency definition of the probability of A is the ratio or fraction of times that event A occurs as the number of observations increases without limit.

3. The probability pertains only to a set of conditions that are identical to those under which the data have been acquired.

The validity of using the relative frequency approach depends on matching the two sets of conditions. Of course, outside the physical sciences it is often difficult or impossible to match conditions *exactly*. Unfortunately, in most business situations we are unable to control all the major factors involved. The implication is that the resulting proportions must be treated as less accurate approximations than those that might be obtained through more controlled experimentation. Consequently, the degree of belief you attach to such probabilities must take into account the degree of discrepancy between conditions under which data are gathered and conditions under which the resulting probabilities are to be applied.

Odds and Relative Frequencies

When relative frequencies are used, the corresponding definition of odds becomes

odds favoring A = number of times A occurred : number of times A did not occur

odds against A = number of times A did not occur : number of times A occurred

For instance, in the bent coin example, heads occurred 60 times and tails 40 times. Therefore, our estimate of the odds of getting a head on a single flip would be 60 : 40, while the estimate of the odds of our not getting a head would be 40 : 60. Similarly, if the weatherman tells you that the probability of rain is 20% (which can also be expressed as $\frac{1}{5}$), he is essentially saying that the odds in favor of rain are 20% : 80%, or 1 : 4.

Subjective Approach to Probabilities

Probabilities that are determined using either the classical approach or the empirical approach are called objective probabilities, because the probabilities are derived from facts. However, there are numerous situations that do not lend themselves to an objective approach—that is, situations in which the outcomes are not equally likely and historical data is not readily available. In these cases a "subjective" assessment of probability must be made. For example, will you fall in love next week? What grade will you receive on your next test? When will a labor strike be settled? Will a small tree grow straight and tall? Will a critically ill person recover? In such instances someone must decide what the "probability" of the event is under the given conditions.

It often helps to imagine a large number of identical situations, and then to try and answer this question: "What percentage of these situations will produce the event in question?" This can be done even when it is not practical to actually carry out such an experiment. And, except for the fact that data usually cannot be collected, the subjective approach is quite similar to the relative frequency approach. Thus we define subjective probability in this way:

> *Subjective probability* is a personal assessment of the likelihood of an event.

Subjective probabilities, then, are the result of an effort to quantify our feelings or beliefs about something. Lawyers, doctors, and most businessmen utilize this approach with reasonable success, although there are certain disadvantages of this approach. Among the disadvantages are the following:

1. Subjective estimates are usually difficult to support if questioned.
2. Biases can be a factor. Preconceived notions about what should happen can distort objectivity, as can feelings about what one wants to happen. It is sometimes difficult to eliminate these biases, because they are often subconscious. Training, experience, and professional attitude can help to overcome these difficulties.

EXERCISES

1. A single card is drawn from a deck of 52 well-shuffled cards. Find the probability of getting the following:

   a. a jack

   b. a face card

    c. a red card   d. a diamond
    e. a ten of clubs   f. a red nine or a black eight

2. List the possible outcomes for rolling a single die. Find the probability of each outcome and add the results.

3. A balanced die is rolled once; find the probability of getting the following:
    a. a six   b. a five, six, or seven
    c. an even-numbered face   d. a number less than four

4. There are 50 beads in a bowl:

Color	Number
blue	20
red	15
orange	10
green	5
	50

The beads are mixed and one is selected. Find the probability that the one selected is as follows:
    a. green   b. blue   c. blue or green   d. not red
    e. red or green   f. yellow   g. not yellow

5. Ten chips are numbered 0 through 9 and placed in a bowl. If one chip is drawn after the chips are mixed, find the probability that it is the following:
    a. the number 3   b. an odd number
    c. less than 4   d. the number 10

6. A motorist has a stone or nail in his tire and 20% of the tire is visible. The motorist coasts to a stop. What is the probability that the stone or nail will be in the visible portion?

7. There are 100 marbles in a bowl. Fifty are red, 30 are white, and the rest are blue.
    a. What percentage of the marbles are red?
    b. If the marbles are mixed and one is drawn, find $P(\text{red})$.
    c. Determine the probability that the marble selected will not be red.
    d. Find the probability that the marble will be blue.
    e. Find the probability that the marble will be red or blue.

*8. What is the probability of guessing the day of the week (e.g., Tuesday) that Abe Lincoln was born? George Washington? What assumption did you make? Does that assumption seem reasonable?

9. A single fuse is to be tested from a lot of 10 fuses. Determine $P(\text{defective})$ if
    a. 1 fuse is bad.
    b. 2 fuses are bad.
    c. 3 are bad.

10. One spark plug in an engine with six spark plugs is defective and must be replaced. Two of the spark plugs are located in positions that make changing difficult.
    a. What is the probability that the defective is in a "difficult" position?
    b. What is the probability that the defective plug is not in a "difficult" position?
    c. What is the probability that the motorist gets charged for a complete set of plugs?

11. Determine the odds in favor of drawing a queen from a deck of 52 cards. What are the odds against this?

12. Find the odds in favor of drawing a face card from a deck of 52 cards.

13. What are the odds in favor of tossing a fair coin twice and getting a head each time? (Hint: All possible outcomes, such as HT, TT, etc., must be considered.)

14. The probability of rain is 30%. What are the odds in favor of rain? Against rain? (Remember that probability is defined as the ratio of favorable ways to total ways and that total = favorable + unfavorable.)

15. A sports prognosticator states that the odds that the Cubs make it to the World Series are 38 : 52.
    a. What is the probability that the Cubs make it to the World Series, according to this prediction?
    b. What are the odds against them making it?

16. Nine times out of ten when John calls his wife at four o'clock, she is talking with her mother and he gets a busy signal. What is the probability that he gets a busy signal if he calls her at four o'clock today? What are the odds of a busy signal?

17. A random sample of 40 prison inmates showed 10 with high blood pressure. Estimate the probability that if another inmate is tested, he, too, will have high blood pressure. What are the odds he will not have high blood pressure?

18. Data compiled by the manager of a supermarket indicate that 915 out of 1500 Sunday shoppers' grocery orders exceed $10.00. Estimate the probability that any given Sunday shopper will spend more than $10.00.

*19. A truckload of 10,000 tissue boxes arrives at a warehouse. The boxes are marked "400 count," but a check of 300 boxes turns up 45 that contain less than 400 tissues. Estimate the probability that any one box in the shipment has less than 400 tissues in it.

20. A traffic survey conducted during the hours from 5 A.M. to 6 A.M. on a section of a state highway revealed that of 200 cars stopped randomly for a safety check, 25 had unsafe tires. Estimate the probability that a car stopped during that time period on the same stretch of road would *not* have unsafe tires.

21. Local weather data for the last 100 years indicate that the daily high temperature for the first day of summer exceeded 75°F in 79 of the years.
    a. Estimate the probability that this year on the first day of summer the temperature will exceed 75°F.
    b. What assumption did you make about the comparability of the years? Is this a reasonable assumption?

22. Hospital records for emergency room service indicate the following over a two-year period:

heart attack	12%
respiratory illness	20%
accident victim	32%
poisoning	16%
other	20%
	100%

   a. What assumption must be made before using the long-run relative frequency approach to generate probabilities using this data?

b. Assuming this is reasonable, find P(accident or heart attack).

c. What is the probability that the patient is not suffering from a respiratory illness?

23. A coin is flipped 10 times, resulting in 6 heads. The same coin is flipped 10 more times, resulting in 4 heads.

   a. Estimate P(heads) on the basis of the first sample of 10 observations.

   b. Estimate P(heads) on the basis of the second sample of 10 observations.

   c. Estimate P(heads) on the basis of the combined sample of 20 observations.

24. Repeat Exercise 23 for P(tails).

25. Jim and Tim find an old coin. Upon close inspection it appears that the coin has been altered so that one face will be more likely than the other. Jim decides to find out, so he flips the coin 40 times and discovers that heads occur 24 times. Tim then flips the coin 50 times and gets 28 heads.

   a. Can you say that either Jim or Tim have definitely obtained a true long-run relative frequency? Why?

   b. If you had to choose one of the two results, which one would you choose, and why?

26. An insurance salesperson estimates that the probability of selling a $10,000 whole life policy to a young married couple is $\frac{2}{5}$. What are the odds of this happening, assuming the assessment is correct?

27. A student believes that the odds that his application for medical school will be approved are 2 : 13. What is the student's subjective estimate of the probability of approval?

28. A high school football coach estimates that the probability of his team's winning this week's game is $\frac{4}{7}$. What odds of losing would be consistent with the coach's estimate?

29. Estimate the probability of rain next Sunday. What factors did you base your estimate on?

30. A bank president estimates that there is a 90% probability that a tax rebate will result in inflationary spending if it is approved by Congress. Interpret 90%.

THE MATHEMATICS OF PROBABILITY

Up to this point the discussion has focused on the various definitions of probability and on how these definitions can be utilized to determine certain event probabilities. These ideas are important, but they do not give you sufficient information so that you really understand how probabilities can be used in decision making.

Many applications of statistics require determining probabilities for *combinations* of events. There are two categories of combinations. Suppose we have identified two events of interest in the sample space, A and B. In some situations it will be necessary to find the probability $P(A$ and $B)$, which is the probability that *both* events will occur. At other times we will want to find the probability that *either A or B* occurs, $P(A$ or $B)$. For example, suppose there are two elevators in a building. From historical data it may be possible to determine the probability of an elevator being in use. Someone might ask, "What is the probability that *both* are in use?" This implies $P(A$ and $B)$. Or someone might want to know,

"What is the probability that *either* one *or* the other is in use?" This implies $P(A \text{ or } B)$.

It is important for you to be able to recognize which of the two combinations is called for. The real key is this:

> "both" implies $P(A \text{ and } B)$
> "either ... or" implies $P(A \text{ or } B)$

Computing the Probability that Two Events will both Occur: *P*(*A* and *B*)

The probability that two events will both occur is called their *joint* probability, and its computation differs depending on whether the events in question are independent or not.

Two events are considered to be *independent* of each other if the occurrence of one event is unrelated to the occurrence of the other. If two dice are rolled, knowing the outcome on one die will not aid you in predicting the outcome on the other. Likewise, placing a mathematics text beneath your bed and getting a high grade on a math test are presumably unrelated. So are sex (i.e., male or female) and IQ.

On the other hand, if events are *dependent*, then knowing that one has occurred can be useful in predicting the occurrence of another event. A flower must have water to grow. A child will usually cry when hurt. A glass will usually break if dropped. Knowing that a flower has not been watered can tell us something about the probability that it will grow. When we see that a child has been hurt, we expect the child to cry. And even before the glass hits the floor, we anticipate having to use the broom.

> Two or more events are said to be *independent* if the occurrence or nonoccurrence of one has no effect on whether the other(s) occurs.

If two events are independent, then the probability that both occur is equal to the *product* of their individual, or "marginal," probabilities:

$$P(A \text{ and } B) = P(A)P(B)$$

Example 1   Two fair coins are tossed. What is the probability that both land heads up?

Solution:
It is reasonable to assume that the outcomes of the two coins are independent of each other. Moreover, we know fair coins have $P(\text{heads}) = \frac{1}{2}$. Hence $P(\text{both heads})$

is

$$\begin{array}{ccc} \text{toss 1} & \text{toss 2} & \text{both} \\ (\tfrac{1}{2}) & \times \quad (\tfrac{1}{2}) & = \quad \tfrac{1}{4} \end{array}$$

Now suppose we want to extend this to three coins. What is the probability that all three land heads up?

$$\begin{array}{cccc} \text{toss 1} & \text{toss 2} & \text{toss 3} & \text{all 3} \\ (\tfrac{1}{2}) & \times \quad (\tfrac{1}{2}) & \times \quad (\tfrac{1}{2}) & = \quad \tfrac{1}{8} \end{array}$$

Example 2   One-third of the registered voters in a rural community are women, and 40% of the voters voted in the last presidential election. Assuming these two events are independent, find the probability of randomly selecting a voter from a list of all voters who is a woman that voted in the last presidential election.

Solution:

$$P(\text{women who voted in last election}) = \tfrac{1}{3}(.40) = .133$$

Example 3   John arrives home late for dinner 25% of the time. Dinner is late 10% of the time. If John's late days and the late dinners are unrelated, what is the probability that both will occur?

Solution:

$$P(\text{both late}) = P(\text{John late})P(\text{dinner late})$$
$$= (.25)(.10) = .025 \quad \text{or} \quad 2.5\%$$

Example 4   A large shipment of boxes of chocolate-covered peanuts is to be inspected. Historical records indicate that 2% of the boxes are underfilled. If two boxes are selected, what is the probability that both are underfilled, assuming this shipment is like the previous ones (i.e., 2% defective)?

Solution:
The probability that the first box chosen will be defective is 2%. However, if we can assume that the first box is not returned to the shipment before the second is drawn, the probability of the second box being defective will have changed slightly, depending on the results of the first box. Nevertheless, if the shipment is large, the impact will be extremely minor, and, for all practical purposes, P(underfilled) will remain about the same. Hence

$$P(\text{both underfilled}) = (.02)(.02) = .0004$$

If two events are *not independent*, the computation of $P(A$ and $B)$ must take this into account. Suppose we have two bowls of marbles. The first contains 8 red and 2 white. The second contains 5 red and 5 white. Thus

	Red	White	Totals
Bowl Y	8	2	10
Bowl Z	5	5	10

A single marble is to be drawn from one of the bowls. If the first bowl is selected, the probability that the marble will be red is $\frac{8}{10}$. If the second bowl is chosen, the probability of red is $\frac{5}{10}$. Hence $P(\text{red})$ *depends* on which bowl is selected. Thus the *conditional* probability of selecting a red marble, assuming bowl Y, is $\frac{8}{10}$. Using symbols this is written as $P(\text{red}|\text{Bowl } Y)$. The vertical line | means "assuming Bowl Y" or "given Bowl Y" or "if Bowl Y is selected." Likewise, it is apparent that

$$P(\text{red}|\text{Bowl } Z) = \tfrac{5}{10}$$
$$P(\text{white}|\text{Bowl } Y) = \tfrac{2}{10}$$
$$P(\text{white}|\text{Bowl } Z) = \tfrac{5}{10}$$

Now suppose that the bowls are unmarked and that the probability of selecting either one is $\frac{1}{2}$: $P(Y) = \frac{1}{2} = P(Z)$. What is the probability of drawing a red marble from Bowl Z? Our computation must take two things into consideration: the probability of selecting Bowl Z to begin with, and then the probability of getting a red marble *assuming* Bowl Z has been selected:

$$P(\text{Bowl } Z) = \tfrac{1}{2} \qquad P(\text{red}|\text{Bowl } Z) = \tfrac{5}{10}$$
$$P(\text{Bowl } Z \text{ and red}) = P(\text{Bowl } Z)P(\text{red}|\text{Bowl } Z)$$
$$= (\tfrac{1}{2})(\tfrac{5}{10}) = \tfrac{5}{20} = \tfrac{1}{4}$$

In a similar fashion we can compute $P(\text{Bowl } Y \text{ and red})$:

$$P(\text{Bowl } Y)P(\text{red}|\text{Bowl } Y) = \tfrac{1}{2}(\tfrac{8}{10}) = \tfrac{8}{20} = .40$$

As a general rule, then, we can say that the joint probability of two dependent events is the probability of one event times the conditional probability of the other:

$$P(A \text{ and } B) = P(A)P(B|A)$$

Since it does not matter which event is A and which is B, it follows that an alternative expression is

$$P(A \text{ and } B) = P(B)P(A|B)$$

Note that if two events are mutually exclusive, such as "marble is red" and "marble is white," then their conditional probabilities are 0, since, by definition, both cannot occur. That is,

$$P(\text{red}|\text{white}) = 0 \quad \text{and} \quad P(\text{white}|\text{red}) = 0$$

Finally, when two events are independent, knowing that one event has occurred will not tell us anything about the other. Therefore,

$$P(A|B) = P(A) \quad \text{and} \quad P(B|A) = P(B)$$

One rather important application of conditional probabilities is Bayes's Theorem, which is treated in a later section of this chapter.

Computing the Probability that at Least One of Two Events will Occur: $P(A \text{ or } B)$

The *addition rule* is used to determine the probability that either or both of two events will occur. The computation differs depending on whether the events are mutually exclusive or not.

When events are mutually exclusive, the probability that one event will occur (by definition, more than one cannot occur) is the *sum* of their individual probabilities. For two events A and B we have

$$P(A \text{ or } B) = P(A) + P(B)$$

For example, the probability that a single roll of a balanced die will produce either a five or six is

$$P(\text{five}) + P(\text{six}) = \tfrac{1}{6} + \tfrac{1}{6} = \tfrac{2}{6}$$

Likewise, the probability of drawing either a card in the heart suit or one in the club suit in a single draw from a deck of 52 cards is

$$P(\text{hearts}) + P(\text{clubs}) = \tfrac{13}{52} + \tfrac{13}{52} = \tfrac{26}{52} = \tfrac{1}{2}$$

When two events are not mutually exclusive, both can occur. In this situation the probability computation must take into account the fact that *either or both* can occur. As an example, suppose we want to determine the probability of drawing either a club or a ten from a deck of 52 cards. Because a card can be both, the events "ten" and "club" are not mutually exclusive. Simply adding their individual probabilities will overstate the true probability, because the ten of clubs will be counted twice, once as a ten and once as a club, as illustrated in Figure 3.4. Consequently, we must subtract the probability of the overlap if we are to avoid this trap. In a deck of 52 playing cards, there are 13 clubs, 4 tens, and one ten of clubs. Then $P(\text{clubs}) = \tfrac{13}{52}$, $P(\text{tens}) = \tfrac{4}{52}$, and $P(\text{ten of clubs}) = \tfrac{1}{52}$. Hence

$$P(\text{clubs or ten or both}) = P(\text{clubs}) + P(\text{tens}) - P(\text{ten of clubs})$$
$$= \tfrac{13}{52} + \tfrac{4}{52} - \tfrac{1}{52} = \tfrac{16}{52}$$

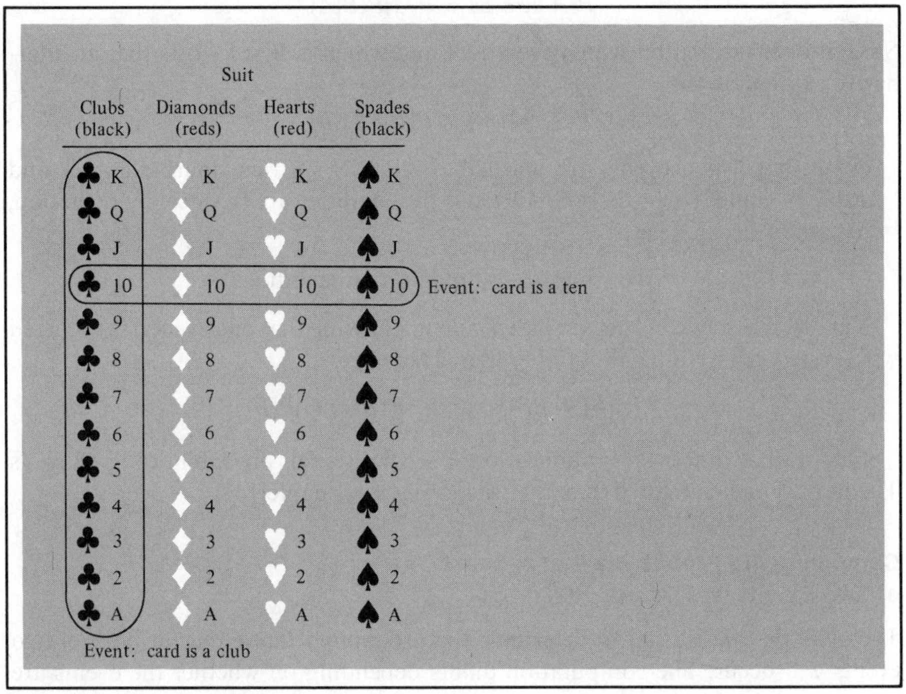

FIGURE 3.4   The events "club" and "ten" overlap.

Another way of looking at this is to check and see that we have included the probability of both occurring in *two* ways, namely, as the probability of a club and also as the probability of a ten. Therefore, we must subtract the *joint* probability of getting a card that is both a ten and a club. The joint probability is the product of the two *marginal* probabilities* ($\frac{13}{52}$ and $\frac{4}{52}$), or $\frac{13}{52} \times \frac{4}{52}$. This amounts to $\frac{13}{52} + \frac{4}{52} - (\frac{13}{52})(\frac{4}{52}) = \frac{16}{52}$.

We can say, in general, that if two outcomes, say, A and B, are mutually exclusive, the probability that *either A or B* will occur is equal to the sum of the probability of A plus the probability of B: $P(A \text{ or } B) = P(A) + P(B)$. If two outcomes are not mutually exclusive, the probability that *either A or B or both* will occur is equal to the sum of the probability of A plus the probability of B minus the probability that both will occur: $P(A) + P(B) - P(A) \cdot P(B)$.

RULES OF PROBABILITY

$P(A \text{ or } B)$, for mutually exclusive events:

$$P(\text{either } A \text{ or } B \text{ will occur}) = P(A) + P(B)$$

for nonmutually exclusive events:

$$P(\text{either } A \text{ or } B \text{ or both will occur}) = P(A) + P(B) - P(A \text{ and } B)$$

$P(A \text{ and } B)$, for independent events:

$$P(A \text{ and } B) = P(A)P(B)$$

for dependent events:

$$P(A \text{ and } B) = P(B)P(A|B) \quad \text{or} \quad P(A)P(B|A)$$

EXERCISES

1. A pair of balanced dice are tossed.
    a. What is the probability that both faces are six?
    b. What is the probability that both faces are two?
    c. What is the probability that both faces are even?
*2. If a pair of dice are tossed, what is the probability that both faces are the same? (Hint: Use conditional probability.)
3. Answer Exercise 1 for three faces when three dice are tossed.
4. Find the probability of drawing a jack of diamonds from a deck of cards using this information:

$$A = \text{diamond} \qquad P(A \text{ and } B) = P(A)P(B|A)$$
$$B = \text{jack}$$

Now use $P(A \text{ and } B) = P(B)P(A|B)$, keeping $A = \text{diamond}$ and $B = \text{jack}$.

---

* This assumes the events are independent. In general it is necessary to know the value of $P(A \text{ and } B)$.

5. Machine breakdowns are independent of each other. If there are four machines, and their respective probabilities of breakdown are 1%, 2%, 5%, and 10% for any given day, find these probabilities:
   a. All break down on a given day.   b. None break down.

6. There were 200 raffle tickets sold, and you bought 2 of them. The prize is one dozen frozen bananas. The stubs are well mixed in a large bowl and a trained monkey will select 2 winning tickets.
   a. What is the probability that a person who holds 1 ticket will win?
   b. What is the probability that you will win one prize? Two prizes? Three prizes?

7. Of the students in a high school, 30% are freshmen, 35% are sophomores, 20% are juniors, and the rest are seniors. One of the students has won $1,000,000 in a state lottery. Find these probabilities:
   a. The student is a senior.
   b. The student is a freshman or sophomore.
   c. The student is not a freshman.
   d. The state refuses to award the prize because the student is a minor.

8. Suppose that $P(A) = .30$, $P(B) = .80$ and $P(A \text{ and } B) = .15$.
   a. Are A and B mutually exclusive? Explain.
   b. Find $P(B')$.
   c. Find $P(A \text{ or } B)$

9. Suppose that A and B are two mutually exclusive events and that $P(A) = .31$ and $P(B) = .29$.
   a. Are A and B collectively exhaustive? Explain.
   b. Find $P(A \text{ or } B)$.
      Find $P(A \text{ or } B)'$.
   d. Find $P(A \text{ and } B)$

10. A fair coin is to be tossed three times. What is the probability that it will land tails up all three times? What is the probability that this will not happen?

11. If three lots of casings each contain 10% defectives, what is the probability of an inspector not finding any defectives if he inspects one casing from each of the three lots?

12. A coin will be tossed four times, and we are given the following probabilities for the number of heads which occur:

$$P(0) = .0625$$
$$P(1) = .2500$$
$$P(2) = .3750$$
$$P(3) = .2500$$
$$P(4) = .0625$$

Find the probability of the following:
   a. one or two heads
   b. less than three heads
   c. five heads
   d. more than three heads
   e. less than two or more than three heads

13. The paper says there is a 40% chance of rain today. Don figures the odds of

his passing his statistics test are 3 : 5. Assuming these events are independent, find the following:

a. *P*(rain and pass)   b. *P*(no rain and does not pass)

14. One card is to be drawn from each of two decks of 52 playing cards. What is the probability of these events?
    a. both red
    b. both clubs
    c. both face cards (J, Q, K of any suit)
    d. one heart and one diamond
    e. a club and either a heart or a diamond

15. What would your answers to the previous exercise be if the two cards are drawn from the same deck *without* replacing the first card prior to drawing the second?

16. The probabilities of 0, 1, 2, 3, 4, 5, 6, or 7 accidents during a weekday between the hours of 1 A.M. and 6 A.M. are, respectively, .08, .15, .20, .25, .18, .07, .04, and .01. Find the probability than on any weekday morning between those hours, there will be the following:
    a. fewer than 3 accidents
    b. 3 or less accidents
    c. exactly 3 accidents
    d. no accidents
    e. more than 7 accidents

17. A firm that manufactures glassware has a four-step inspection process. The probability that a defective will get past any one inspection station is reported to be approximately 20% by the company. Using this 20% figure, find the probability of a defective getting through all four inspection stations without being detected. What would your answer be if a fifth station is added, with a probability of 50% of catching defectives?

18. The probability is 90% that a machine will turn out an acceptable hex-nut. If successive pieces are independent of each other (often a reasonable assumption if the process is "in control"), find the probability of getting the following:
    a. Two pieces in a row that are unacceptable.
    b. A good piece and then a bad piece, in that order.
    c. A good piece and a bad piece, in any order.
    d. Three bad pieces in a row.

19. Find the probability that Alexander Hamilton and Aaron Burr were born on the same day of the week.

20. If the previous question had been same month instead of same day of week, what simplifying assumption would you consider making? Why?

*21. Several sports fans have kept track of the ability of Jimmy the Roman to select winning teams in football. They found his success rate to be .80. Jimmy has picked the winners in four upcoming games. Find these probabilities:
    a. All four game predictions are correct.
    b. None is correct.
    c. One is wrong.
    d. Three are wrong.

22. An oil exploration firm drills a well if it feels that there is at least a 25% chance of finding oil. It drills four wells, and assigns probabilities of .3, .4, .7, and .8 to the wells.

a. Find the probability that none of the wells yields oil, using company figures.

b. Find the probability that all four produce oil.

c. What is the probability that the .3 and .7 probability wells produce oil but the others do not?

23. Mike has two old junkers. On cold mornings there is a 20% chance that one will not start, and a 30% chance that the other will not start.

a. Find the probability that neither starts.

b. Find the probability that only one starts.

24. A flower shop guarantees that "90% of the seeds contained in this packet will germinate." Assume that each seed has a 90% probability of germinating and that there are five seeds per packet.

a. Find the probability of none germinating.

b. Find the probability of all germinating.

25. Ron is anxiously awaiting grades for two courses he has recently completed. He feels there is a .80 probability of getting an A in English literature, and a .40 probability of an A in philosophy. Find the probabilities of these results:

a. both grades A   b. neither A

c. English A, philosophy not A   d. none of the above

26. A packet of mixed flower seeds contains four seeds for red flowers, three for yellow, two for purple, and one for orange.

a. If one seed is chosen from the mix, what is the probability that it is either red or orange?

b. If two seeds are selected from the packet, what is the probability that both are yellow? Red?

c. If three seeds are chosen, what is the probability that one is orange and two are yellow?

d. If three seeds are chosen, what is the probability that one is orange?

27. Refer to Exercise 26. If each seed has a 60% chance of germinating, what are the probabilities for these outcomes?

a. All but the orange germinate.

b. All the Yellow germinate.

c. None of the yellow germinates.

COUNTING TECHNIQUES

To use the classical (a priori) probability approach, it is necessary to know the total number of possible outcomes in a sample or experiment. Counting techniques are usually employed as a means of determining the total number of outcomes. You have already been exposed to several simple counting techniques. For example, in many of the preceding illustrations, it was convenient to *list* the outcomes. This enabled us to visually inspect the outcomes to see if all possible arrangements were accounted for.

A refinement of the listing technique is to use *decision trees*, which provide a rational basis for developing a list of outcomes. However, when the number of outcomes is large, listing methods become cumbersome, and it is necessary to resort to *mathematical formulas* to determine the total number of possible outcomes. Let us consider each of these approaches.

Suppose a student is taking a 20-question true-false test. Suppose, too, that he is guessing at all the answers. What is the probability that he will answer the test perfectly? To solve this problem it is first necessary to determine the total number of outcomes (patterns) possible. For example, he may decide to answer all questions true or all false, or he may alternate true and false, or randomly mix up true and false.

Rather than attempt to solve this problem directly, it will be more instructive to explore scaled-down versions of it first. So imagine that the test consisted only of a single question. The possibilities would be T or F. If there were two questions, the possibilities would be TT, TF, FT, FF. If there were three questions, the possibilities would be TTT, TTF, TFF, TFT, FTF, FTT, FFT, FFF. Obviously, as the number of questions increases, the number of outcomes increases, but at a more *rapid rate*, as shown below.

Number of questions	1	2	3	4
Number of outcomes	2	4	8	16

In fact, unless the number of items to be considered is fairly small, the number of outcomes can be quite large. In such cases listing can be tedious. More importantly, perhaps, it is easy to overlook some of the possibilities.

Tree diagrams provide a systematic approach to enumeration of outcomes as well as a visual presentation. Tree diagrams can be easily constructed, and they are much more illuminating than simple listings. Figure 3.5 portrays a tree diagram for three true-false questions. Since the student has two possible choices for each question, T or F, the tree has two branches at each question.

By expanding the tree diagram, it is possible to enumerate the outcomes with additional true-false questions. However, it would not be practical to do so because the number of possibilities becomes extremely large. Moreover, all that is really necessary is to determine the *total number of outcomes*; there is nothing to be gained by identifying *each outcome*. Fortunately, there is a simple way to determine the total number of outcomes without having to actually count each individual outcome.

Multiplication Principle

The tree diagram illustrated that each successive question *doubled* the total number of outcomes possible, since each new question provided two more choices. The implication is that when there are a number of sequential decisions to be made

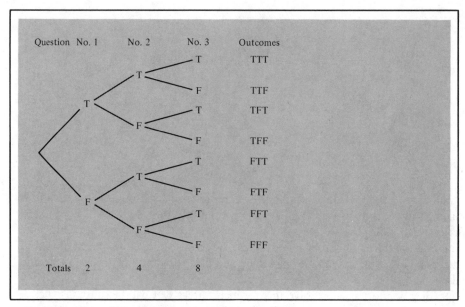

FIGURE 3.5   Using a tree diagram to determine all possible arrangements.

(such as answer true or false for each question), the total number of outcomes possible will be the *product* of the different number of ways that each question (decision) can be made. Thus

Number of questions	Total outcomes
1	$2 = 2$
2	$2 \times 2 = 4$
3	$2 \times 2 \times 2 = 8$
4	$2 \times 2 \times 2 \times 2 = 16$

If this had been a multiple-choice test, say with *four choices* for each question, and there were *three* questions, the total number of outcomes possible would have been $4 \times 4 \times 4 = 64$. If there were four choices for the first question, five for the second, and three for the third, the answer would have been $4 \times 5 \times 3 = 60$.

Let us now apply the multiplication principle to see how many ways of answering the 20-question true-false test there are. With two choices for each of the 20 questions, we would have

$$2 \times 2 \times 2 \times \cdots \times 2 = 2^{20}$$

Although it would be unusual to work out many such problems as this by hand, let us at least examine a simplified approach to the calculations.

$$\underbrace{2 \times 2} \times \underbrace{2 \times 2} \times \underbrace{2 \times 2} \times \underbrace{2 \times 2} \times \underbrace{2 \times 2} \times \underbrace{2 \times 2} \times \underbrace{2 \times 2} \times \underbrace{2 \times 2} \times \underbrace{2 \times 2} \times \underbrace{2 \times 2} = 2^{20}$$

$$\underbrace{4 \times 4} \times \underbrace{4 \times 4} \times \underbrace{4 \times 4} \times \underbrace{4 \times 4} \times \underbrace{4 \times 4} = 4^{10}$$

$$\underbrace{16 \times 16} \times \underbrace{16 \times 16} \times 16 = 16^{5}$$

$$\underbrace{256 \times 256} \times 16 = 1{,}048{,}576$$

In general, if there are *n* sequential decisions, each with *m* choices, the total number of outcomes possible is m^n.

Finally, the probability that the student could guess the correct pattern and thus get all the questions right is

$$\frac{1}{1,048,576}$$

The principle of multiplying the number of choices for each decision is a general rule upon which two additional techniques are based: permutations and combinations. These techniques are useful in situations in which each decision diminishes the number of choices remaining for subsequent decisions.

Permutations and Combinations

When the *order* in which items are arranged is important, the total number of possible outcomes is referred to as a *permutation*. For instance, with answers to a multiple-choice test, there is special significance attached to order. When order has no particular meaning, the total number of possible outcomes is referred to as a *combination*. For example, a committee which consisted of two people, say, Smith and Jones, would be the same as a committee consisting of Jones and Smith. Similarly, both the sum and the product of two numbers are unaffected by which is first and which is second:

$$10 + 5 = 5 + 10 \qquad 10 \times 5 = 5 \times 10$$

Let us first consider permutations. Suppose there are four baseball teams in a playoff. In how many different ways could the final standings turn out? Imagine that we have four slots to fill: winner, second, third, last. If we fill the winner's slot, that might be any one of *four* teams. That would leave three slots remaining, and three teams to choose from. Thus second place would be one of *three* teams. Third place could be one of *two* teams, and *one* team would be last. The total number of outcomes would be

$$\begin{array}{ccccccc} 4 & \times & 3 & \times & 2 & \times & 1 & = 24 \\ \text{(1st)} & & \text{(2d)} & & \text{(3d)} & & \text{(4th)} \end{array}$$

If there had been six teams, then there would have been

$$6 \times 5 \times 4 \times 3 \times 2 \times 1 = 720$$

Whether we select the teams from first to last, in reverse order (last to first), or the any other order, the final result will be the same. For instance, selecting last place first produces $1 \times 2 \times 3 \times 4 = 24$.

When working with permutations, each decision involves one less choice than the previous one. A shorthand way of writing such progressions is to use the symbol "!". For example, $4 \times 3 \times 2 \times 1$ could be written as 4! The exclamation mark means "factorial," and "4!" is read "four factorial." Here are some illustrations of factorials:

$$5! = 5 \times 4 \times 3 \times 2 \times 1 = 120$$

$$12! = 12 \times 11 \times 10 \times 9 \times 8 \times 7 \times \cdots \times 2 \times 1 = 479,001,600$$

Factorials become quite large as the number increases. Fortunately, it is usually not necessary to work out a factorial completely, since factorials often appear in groups when they are used, and canceling is possible. For example,

$$\frac{5!}{7!} = \frac{5 \times 4 \times 3 \times 2 \times 1}{7 \times 6 \times 5 \times 4 \times 3 \times 2 \times 1} = \frac{5!}{7 \times 6 \times 5!} = \frac{1}{7 \times 6} = \frac{1}{42}$$

$$\frac{4!}{2!} = \frac{4 \times 3 \times 2 \times 1}{2 \times 1} = \frac{4 \times 3 \times 2!}{2!} = 4 \times 3 = 12$$

$$\frac{40!}{38!} = \frac{40 \times 39 \times 38!}{38!} = 40 \times 39 = 1560$$

$$\frac{5!}{2!3!} = \frac{5 \times 4 \times 3!}{2 \times 1 \times 3!} = \frac{5 \times 4}{2} = 10$$

Factorials sometimes involve addition and subtraction. When numbers are inside parentheses with the factorial sign outside, it is necessary to complete the addition or subtraction *prior* to finding the factorial:

$$(5 - 3)! = 2! \quad \text{(not } 5! - 3!)$$
$$(9 - 2)! = 7!$$
$$(3 + 1)! = 4!$$
$$\frac{8!}{3!(8-3)!} = \frac{8!}{3!5!} = \frac{8 \times 7 \times 6 \times 5!}{3!5!} = \frac{8 \times 7 \times 6}{3 \times 2}$$

Notice that we canceled out the 5! rather than the 3! The answer would be the same regardless of which one we canceled, but the effort is less when the largest factorials are canceled.

Zero factorial equals 1. That is, $0! = 1$. An intuitive explanation is this: If there were a number of empty chairs to fill, how many different *seating* arrangements are possible if no one arrives to be seated? The answer is one way—with all the seats empty. (If this seems confusing, imagine two people and three seats; then one person and three seats; and finally, no persons.)

If there are seven horses in a race, how many different arrangements of win, place, and show are possible? Intuitively (using the multiplication principle) we can see that there are $7 \times 6 \times 5 = 210$ possible outcomes. Using permutations, we would ask, with seven items (horses, in this case), how many different arrangements of three of the items are possible? In general, the number of permutations of n objects taken x at a time equals $n!/(n - x)!$. More formally, we have

$$_nP_x = \frac{n!}{(n - x)!}$$

Hence the number of ways in which 3 objects can be arranged from a group of 7 objects is

$$_7P_3 = \frac{7!}{(7 - 3)!} = \frac{7 \times 6 \times 5 \times (4!)}{4!} = 210$$

Occasionally we are faced with a situation in which some of the items are identical or *indistinguishable* from each other. For instance, suppose we have three nickels and two dimes. Unless a special effort was made to note the dates on the coins or to otherwise differentiate them, the three nickels would be indistinguishable. So would the two dimes. Because of this, not all the permutations would appear unique. One arrangement would be NNNDD. Switching the two dimes would not change the outward appearance of this arrangement. Hence some of the different arrangements are lost and must be deleted from the total number possible, since the basic concept of a permutation is that each arangement is different.

Now if the coins were (temporarily) identified, say as N_1, N_2, N_3 and D_1, D_2, we could see that there are 2! different arrangements of the dimes and 3! arrangements of the nickels. Moreover, there are 3!(2!) arrangements when nickels and dimes are considered, which must be removed from the total number of permutations in order to find the number of *distinguishable permutations*. This can be accomplished by dividing the total number of permutations, assuming items can be thought of as distinguishable, by the number of patterns which are lost because the items are not really distinguishable. For the case of the three nickels and two dimes, this amounts to

$$\frac{5!}{3!(2!)} = 10$$

In general, the number of distinguishable permutations possible with n items, when there are n_1 indistinguishable items of one kind, n_2 of another kind, and so on, is

$$_nP_{n_1, n_2, \ldots, n_k} = \frac{n!}{n_1!n_2!n_3! \cdots n_k!}$$

where $n = n_1 + n_2 + \cdots + n_k$.

Example 5   How many different eight-letter arrangements can be made using the letters R R R R U U U N?

Solution:
There are 8 letters: 4 R's, 3 U's, and 1 N, which will produce

$$_8P_{4, 3, 1} = \frac{8!}{4!3!1!} = 280$$

When order is not important, the term "combination" is used to denote the different number of groupings possible. The selection of the members of a committee is one example where order is not a factor. Another is selecting two vegetables from a menu that lists five choices. The selection of potatoes and carrots would be equivalent to carrots and potatoes. These equivalent groups must be eliminated from the total number of permutations in order to determine the number of combinations. This is the same situation we saw with indistinguishable permutations, and, in fact, we proceed in exactly the same manner. Thus, in the case of vegetables, each group of two will yield two permutations but only one combination. In other words, the number of permutations is twice the number of combinations. Choosing 2 vegetables from a list of 5, the permutations possible are

$$_5P_2 = \frac{5!}{3!} = 20$$

The number of combinations is half of this, or 10. Using symbols, we write the number of combinations as

$$_5C_2 = \frac{5!}{2!3!} = 10$$

More generally, for groups of size x constructed from a list of n items, the number of combinations possible is

$$_nC_x = \frac{n!}{x!(n-x)!} = \binom{n}{x}$$

Example 6   How many different committees of 3 members can be selected from a group of 10 people?

Solution:

$$_{10}C_3 = \frac{10!}{7!3!} = \frac{10 \times 9 \times 8 \times 7!}{7!(3 \times 2)} = 120$$

Example 7   Suppose we want a committee of 1 woman and 2 men from a group of 4 women and 6 men. How many different arrangements are possible?

Solution:

$$\overset{\text{women}}{(_4C_1)}\ \overset{\text{men}}{(_6C_2)} = \left(\frac{4!}{3!1!}\right)\left(\frac{6!}{4!2!}\right) = 4 \times 15 = 60$$

COUNTING RULES

Multiplication rule: the product of the number of choices for a sequence of decisions.

Permutations: the number of arrangements when order is important.

$$_nP_x = \frac{n!}{(n-x)!}$$

Distinguishable permutations: used when some items appear identical, but order is important.

$$_nP_{n_1, n_2, \ldots, n_k} = \frac{n!}{n_1!n_2! \cdots n_k!}$$

Combinations: used when order is not important.

$$_nC_x = \binom{n}{x} = \frac{n!}{x!(n-x)!}$$

Comparison of Permutations and Combinations

When order is important, the number of possible outcomes is determined by permutations. When order is not important, combinations yield the total number of outcomes possible. Furthermore, the number of combinations possible will always be less than the number of permutations possible.

For instance, suppose we show a person four colors on a paint chart and ask her to select three. The number of sets of three that she could choose would be the number of *combinations*, since order would not be a factor. On the other hand, if we now ask that she pick three and *rank* them according to which she liked best, order would become a factor, and the sets of ranked colors would be *permutations*. Table 3.2 illustrates the comparison of combinations and permutations.

It is interesting to note that when there are *two* groups of indistinguishable items, the number of combinations equals the number of permutations. For instance, in how many ways can a student answer a 10-question true-false test with 5 T's and 5 F's?

$$_{10}P_{5,\,5} = \frac{10!}{5!5!} \qquad _{10}C_5 = \frac{10!}{5!(10-5)!} = \frac{10!}{5!5!}$$

We will use this result in our study of the binomial distribution.

TABLE 3.2   A Comparison of Permutations and Combinations

Choose three colors.
Colors to choose from: red, blue, green, orange

Combinations	Permutations
$_nC_x = \begin{pmatrix} n \\ x \end{pmatrix} = \dfrac{n!}{x!(n-x)!}$	$_nP_x = \dfrac{n!}{(n-x)!}$
	$_4P_3 = \dfrac{4!}{1!} = 24$
$_4C_3 = \begin{pmatrix} n \\ x \end{pmatrix} = \dfrac{4!}{3!(4-3)!}$	
$= 4$	
RBG	RBG, RGB, BGR, BRG, GBR, GRB
RBO	RBO, ROB, BOR, BRO, OBR, ORB
RGO	RGO, ROG, GOR, GRO, OGR, ORG
BGO	BGO, BOG, GOB, GBO, OGB, OBG

EXERCISES

1. Determine each of the following:
   a. 2!   b. 5!   c. 10!   d. 1!   e. 0!
2. Compute the following:

   a. $\begin{pmatrix} 3 \\ 2 \end{pmatrix}$ b. $\begin{pmatrix} 4 \\ 4 \end{pmatrix}$ c. $\begin{pmatrix} 5 \\ 1 \end{pmatrix}$ d. $\begin{pmatrix} 9 \\ 6 \end{pmatrix}$

3. Determine the number of permutations:
   a. $_3P_2$ b. $_4P_4$ c. $_5P_1$ d. $_9P_6$ e. $_1P_0$

4. A new car dealer wants to impress prospective customers with the number of different possible combinations available. One model has three engines, two transmissions, five exterior colors, and two interior colors. How many choices for these options are possible?

5. License plates in one state have three letters followed by four numbers.
   a. How many different plates are possible if all letters and numbers are allowed?
   b. How many different plates are possible if the letter O and the number zero are not used?
   c. How many different plates are possible if the word "sex" is not permitted, but O's and zeros are?
   d. How many different plates are possible if the word "sex" as well as the letter O and number zero are not permitted?

*6. How many distinguishable nine-letter arrangements can be made from the word BLUEBEARD, if nonsense words are permitted?

7. Three wheels, each with the digits 0 through 9, are arranged in a slot machine format, so that each one can be spun individually.
   a. How many different number arrangements are possible?
   b. How many are possible that have the digit 1 in the middle position?

*8. A wine steward inspects bottles of wine and either accepts or rejects each bottle. If 10 bottles are inspected, in how many different ways can each of the following occur? (Hint: The only distinguishing feature is acceptance or rejection.)
   a. 1 is accepted   b. 2 are accepted   c. 3 are accepted

*9. Partners for square dancing are chosen by placing the girls' names in one bowl and the boys' in another and then picking pairs randomly. If there are 10 boys and 10 girls, how many different pairs are possible? If 1 boy and 1 girl are newcomers (still 10 boys and 10 girls total), what is the probability that they will be paired if the pairings are left to chance?

10. A dinner menu features five choices for meat or fish, three salad dressings, two choices on potatoes, and four for vegetables. How many different dinners are possible?

11. If 36 teams are part of a basketball tournament, in how many ways can the teams finish for the first three places?

12. In how many different ways can a supervisor choose a committee of five from the eight people she has working for her?

13. A coin will be tossed seven times. In how many ways can these outcomes happen?
    a. five heads   b. four heads   c. all heads   d. one head

14. Joe's Pizza and Taco Parlor lists these choices on their 12-inch pizzas: sausage, mushrooms, peppers, anchovies, and pepperoni. You can afford only two (all are priced the same). How many different pizzas are there to choose from?

15. Show that for arrangements of two kinds of items, the number of distinguishable permutations equals the number of combinations.

BAYES'S RULE[*]

Bayes's Rule is a method for revising existing (prior) probabilities on the basis of sample information. The following is an intuitive explanation of how revision of probabilities is done and why it is useful to consider this.

Consider the case of the weary manager who hurriedly kisses his wife one rainy morning and then grabs one of the three bags on the kitchen table as he rushes off to work. As he pulls onto the expressway a short time later, it suddenly dawns on him that he may have grabbed the wrong bag. One of the bags contained his lunch: two ham sandwiches. Another contained his daughter's lunch: one ham sandwich and one peanut butter sandwich (which the manager detests with a passion). The third bag contained the garbage. A moment's reflection convinces him that since there were three bags, the probability that he made the correct grab is only $\frac{1}{3}$.

Immediately he reaches over to the bag and fishes out a sandwich. Upon inspection he learns it is ham. Naturally he is somewhat relieved to discover that at least he has not brought along the garbage. At this point the traffic has come to a complete halt. Rather than checking out the other sandwich, the manager decides to pass the time by first determining the probability that he has his own lunch (i.e., the probability that the remaining sandwich is also ham). He remembers that probability is defined as the ratio of the number of favorable outcomes to the total number of outcomes possible. He reasons that if he does, indeed, have his lunch, then there would be two ways of reaching in and getting the ham sandwich. If he has his daughter's lunch, there would be only one way. Thus there are *three ways* in which he could have gotten a ham sandwich, and two of those could be considered favorable. The probability at this point, then, is $\frac{2}{3}$ that he grabbed the correct bag, *given the sample evidence.*

The traffic is beginning to move again, and a faint smile appears on the manager's lips. He confidently puts his hand into the bag and removes the other sandwich. A quick glance tells him that it will be a long day: the sandwich is peanut butter, not ham, demonstrating that probability is a measure of how likely an event is to occur, and not a guarantee that it will occur. Once more, traffic has ground to a standstill. The manager mutters something about investing in a garbage disposal.

With a garbage disposal, presumably there would be only two bags on the table when he rushed through: his and his daughter's. If he were to grab one and then check it on his way to work and find a ham sandwich, what would the probability be of his having taken the correct lunch? The answer it still $\frac{2}{3}$. To see why, remember that the sample evidence (ham sandwich) was the same as before and that in the previous case, once he saw a sandwich, the garbage bag was no longer part of the problem. In other words, with the sample evidence, the garbage disposal is immaterial.

Whether the manager realizes it or not, he has intuitively employed Bayes's Theorem to determine the probability that he had chosen his lunch bag. Undoubtedly, Bayes was himself familiar with the intuitive method of solving problems of this sort. Perhaps he also recognized that a formal approach would be of

---

[*] Optional material. This section can be omitted without loss of continuity.

value in solving similar, but much more complex, problems. He may have reasoned in the following manner: If an event can occur in more than one way, then the probability that it occurred in one particular way would be the ratio of the probability of occurring in that way to the probability of it having occurred at all. In the preceding example the probability of getting a ham sandwich is the probability of selecting the first bag *and* getting ham plus the probability of selecting the second *and* getting ham plus the probability of selecting the third bag *and* getting ham. Thus the posterior (revised) probability that he has the correct bag is

$$P(\text{correct lunch}) = \frac{P(\text{correct bag and ham})}{P(\text{ham})}$$

We can write this in a more detailed fashion:

$$P(\text{correct lunch}|\text{ham sandwich}) = \frac{P(\text{ham sandwich from correct bag})}{P(\text{all ways of getting ham})}$$

$$= \frac{P(\text{c.b.})P(\text{h.s.}|\text{c.b.})}{P(\text{c.b.})P(\text{h.s.}|\text{c.b.}) + P(\text{d.l.})P(\text{h.s.}|\text{d.l.}) + P(\text{g.})P(\text{h.s.}|\text{g.})}$$

c.b. = correct bag

h.s. = ham sandwich

d.l. = daughter's lunch

 g. = garbage

By placing the information in tabular form, the figures become easier to visualize. Thus

	Contents		
	Ham	Peanut butter	Garbage
His bag	2	—	—
Daughter's bag	1	1	—
Garbage bag	—	—	1

By changing these figures to percentages and remembering that the prior (before taking the sample) probability of choosing each bag was $\frac{1}{3}$, the following table evolves.

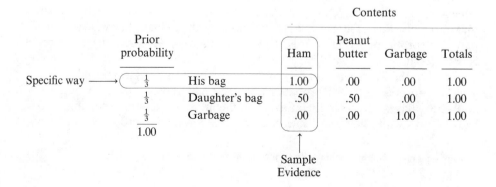

	Prior probability		Ham	Peanut butter	Garbage	Totals
Specific way ⟶	$\frac{1}{3}$	His bag	1.00	.00	.00	1.00
	$\frac{1}{3}$	Daughter's bag	.50	.50	.00	1.00
	$\frac{1}{3}$	Garbage	.00	.00	1.00	1.00
	1.00					

Contents

Sample Evidence

The probability of initially selecting any of the bags is $\frac{1}{3}$. These are the prior probabilities that will be revised using the sample information (that a ham sandwich was pulled out of the bag). The values *within* the table are the probabilities of finding a ham sandwich assuming that a specific bag was initially selected. For example, there would be a 0 probability of finding a ham sandwich if the garbage bag was selected, a 50% chance of ham if the daughter's lunch was selected, and a 100% chance of ham if the manager had selected his own lunch.

Let us now formally compute the probability that the manager has chosen the correct bag given that he finds the ham sandwich.

$$P(\text{correct bag given ham}) = \frac{\frac{1}{3}(1.00)}{\frac{1}{3}(1.00) + \frac{1}{3}(.50) + \frac{1}{3}(.00)} = \frac{2}{3}$$

This same idea is also expressed in Figure 3.6.

> Bayes's Theorem is a technique used to revise initial probability estimates on the basis of sample data.

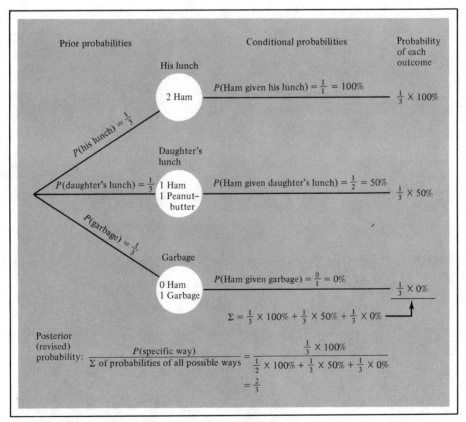

FIGURE 3.6 Computing the probability of correct lunch.

Example 8   Suppose we have four bowls of colored marbles, with 10 marbles in each bowl. The table below summarizes the composition of the bowls.

	Red	White	Blue	Totals
		Marble color		
A	1	6	3	10
B	6	2	2	10
C	8	1	1	10
D	0	6	4	10

One of the bowls has been arbitrarily selected and a single marble drawn from that bowl. If the marble is red, what is the probability that it was drawn from Bowl B?

Solution:

To solve this problem (or any similar problem) we need two things: (1) the prior probability of selecting each bowl and (2) the probability of the event in question (red marble in this instance) occurring, if a particular bowl is selected. The prior probabilities would be $\frac{1}{4}$ for each bowl since there are four bowls and each can be assumed to have an equal chance of being selected. The probability of drawing a red marble from a particular bowl is the ratio of red marbles to total marbles in that bowl. The table below illustrates these probabilities (which were computed using the information from the previous table).

Prior probability	Bowl	Red	White	Blue	Totals
			Color		
$\frac{1}{4}$	A	.10	.60	.30	1.00
$\frac{1}{4}$	B	.60	.20	.20	1.00
$\frac{1}{4}$	C	.80	.10	.10	1.00
$\frac{1}{4}$	D	.00	.60	.40	1.00

The probability that the red marble was drawn from Bowl B is

$$P(\text{Bowl } B|\text{red}) = \frac{\frac{1}{4}(.60)}{\frac{1}{4}(.10) + \frac{1}{4}(.60) + \frac{1}{4}(.80) + \frac{1}{4}(.00)} = \frac{6}{15}$$

As a matter of fact, the probability that the red marble was drawn from any other bowl can be computed in the same manner.

$$P(\text{Bowl } A|\text{red}) = \frac{\frac{1}{4}(.10)}{\frac{1}{4}(.10) + \frac{1}{4}(.60) + \frac{1}{4}(.80) + \frac{1}{4}(.00)} = \frac{1}{15}$$

$$P(\text{Bowl } C|\text{red}) = \frac{\frac{1}{4}(.80)}{\frac{1}{4}(.10) + \frac{1}{4}(.60) + \frac{1}{4}(.80) + \frac{1}{4}(.00)} = \frac{8}{15}$$

$$P(\text{Bowl } D|\text{red}) = \frac{\frac{1}{4}(.00)}{\frac{1}{4}(.10) + \frac{1}{4}(.60) + \frac{1}{4}(.80) + \frac{1}{4}(.00)} = \frac{0}{15}$$

$$\text{Total:} \quad \frac{15}{15}$$

You should notice two things. One is that the sum of the probabilities of the various bowls (ways that red could have occurred) is 1.00 (i.e., $\frac{15}{15}$). The other is that the denominator is the same for all four calculations.

Decision makers frequently use Bayes's Theorem to revise probability estimates in the light of test results. In essence, *the test results are regarded as sample evidence.*

Example 9   A recently completed study indicates that 70% of all college students tend to use fantasies as a mechanism for overcoming frustration caused by solving statistics problems, and that 30% do not turn to fantasies for this reason. An astute assistant professor has developed a test for measuring whether a student fantasizes or not. However, the test is not fully perfected (the professor's six-year grant has not been renewed). Currently the test yields a positive result for 60% of the students who fantasize, and a negative result for 40% of those students. For non-fantasizers the test yields positive for 20% and negative for 80%.

We can summarize this information in tabular form:

Prior probability		Test results	
		Positive	Negative
.70	Fantasizes	.60	.40
.30	Does not indulge	.20	.80
1.00			

Using Bayes's Theorem, we can determine the (posterior) probability that a person fantasizes, given a positive test result:

$$P(\text{fantasizes}|\text{positive}) = \frac{.70(.60)}{.70(.60) + .30(.20)} = \frac{.42}{.42 + .06} = \frac{7}{8} = .88$$

We are now ready to consider a general expression for Bayes's Theorem. If there are a number of states of nature (such as bags on a table or bowls of marbles or have versus do not have) and each has one or more possible sample outcomes or events associated with it (such as ham sandwich or red marble or positive test result), the tabular representation of this would be

		E_1	E_2	$\cdots$	E_j
	S_1	$P(E_1|S_1)$	$P(E_2|S_1)$	$\cdots$	$P(E_j|S_1)$
Possible states	S_2	$P(E_1|S_2)$	$P(E_2|S_2)$	$\cdots$	$P(E_j|S_2)$
of nature	$\vdots$	$\vdots$	$\vdots$		$\vdots$
	S_i	$P(E_1|S_i)$	$P(E_2|S_i)$	$\cdots$	$P(E_j|S_i)$

For example, the probability that a sample outcome, say E_2, occurred as the result of a particular state of nature, say S_1, can be computed in this way:

$$P(S_1|E_2) = \frac{P(S_1)P(E_2|S_1)}{P(S_1)P(E_2|S_1) + P(S_2)P(E_2|S_2) + \cdots + P(S_i)P(E_2|S_i)}$$

The general case would be

$$P(S_i|E_j) = \frac{P(S_i)P(E_j|S_i)}{P(S_1)P(E_j|S_1) + P(S_2)P(E_j|S_2) + \cdots + P(S_i)P(E_j|S_i)}$$

The essence of Bayes's Theorem is the revision of initial (prior) probability estimates given the sample evidence. The revised estimates are called posterior probabilities. The bases for revision are the results of a particular sample plus knowledge of the conditional probabilities (i.e., probabilities for each sample outcome assuming a specific state of nature).

EXERCISES

*1. Police records reveal that 10% of accident victims who are wearing seat belts sustain serious injury, while 50% of those who are not wearing seat belts sustain serious injury. Police estimate that 60% of the people riding in cars use seat belts. Police are called to investigate an accident in which one person is seriously injured. Estimate the probability that he was wearing his seat belt at the time of the crash. The person riding in the other car was not seriously injured. Estimate the probability that he was wearing his seat belt.

2. Your firm recently submitted a bid on a construction project. If your main competitor submits a bid, there is only a .25 chance of the bid being awarded to your firm. If your competitor does not bid, there is a $\frac{2}{3}$ chance of your firm getting the job. There is a .50 chance your competitor will bid.
   a. What is the probability your firm gets the job?
   b. What is the probability that the competitor bid if your firm gets the job?

3. Ed meets a new girl at half of the parties he attends. Three-fourths of the time when he meets a new girl, he has a good time, but the probability of his having a good time when he does not meet a new girl is only 10%. Ed has just told you that he is having a good time. What is the probability that he has met a new girl?

4. Three machines all turn out nonferrous castings. Machine A produces 1% defectives, machine B, 2%, and machine C, 5%. Each machine produces $\frac{1}{3}$ of the output. An inspector examines a single casting, which he determines is non-defective. Estimate the probabilities of its having been produced by each machine.

5. A tree farm estimates that when an experienced serviceman plants trees, 90% survive, but when a novice plants trees, only 50% survive. If a tree previously planted fails to survive, find the probability that the novice planted it, given that novices ordinarily plant $\frac{2}{3}$ of the trees.

SUMMARY

A probability is a number that indicates how likely some future event is. Probabilities are obtained either by conducting a series of trials and noting the relative frequency of occurrence of the event in question (or by treating historical data as a series of identical trials), by realizing that events (or outcomes) are equally likely, or, when these are not possible, by the use of subjective judgment. It is helpful in understanding and utilizing probabilities to envision a sample space of all of the possible outcomes of a sample or experiment.

Rules of probability are designed to aid in the computation of events which are themselves combinations of other events. The addition rule is used when the probability that either or both of two events will occur is desired. There are two variations of the rule, one for events that are mutually exclusive, and one for events that are not. Similarly, the multiplication rule, which is used to determine the probability that two events will both occur, has two variations, one for dependent events and one for independent events.

Counting rules are useful in determining the number of ways something could occur, particularly when the number of ways is large.

REVIEW QUESTIONS

1. Briefly describe the three approaches to the assignment of probabilities.
2. Why is sample size important in the relative frequency approach?
3. What advantage, and what disadvantage, does the subjective approach have over the other two approaches?
4. Explain this statement: There can be a degree of subjectivity in the relative frequency approach.
5. What are odds, and how do they relate to probabilities?
6. Define these terms: mutually exclusive, collectively exhaustive, complement.
7. What is a sample space? What is an event?
8. What are Venn diagrams and how are they useful?
9. What does the expression "independent events" mean?
10. Define what is meant by joint probability. How is joint probability determined when events are independent?
11. The probability that an event will occur plus the probability that the event will not occur always sum to a certain number. What is the number and why must they always sum to it?
12. What is the addition rule of probability for mutually exclusive events? For events which are not mutually exclusive?
13. Contrast permutation and combination.
14. What is the function of counting techniques?
15. What is the connection between counting techniques and classical probability?
16. Explain the multiplication principle.
17. What advantage does the multiplication rule have over a decision tree?
18. What is a factorial?
19. How is Bayes's Theorem used?
20. Define posterior probability.
21. Define prior probability.
22. In the matrix form, which probabilities are the conditional probabilities?
23. In the matrix form, why must the row probabilities always sum to 1.00? Must the column probabilities also sum of 1.00? Why?
24. What does the term "states of nature" mean?

SUPPLEMENTAL EXERCISES

1. Explain why each of the following are erroneous:
   a. $P(A) = -.45$ b. $P(A) = 1.30$
   c. $P(A) = .60$ and $P(A') = .60$ d. $P(A \text{ or } B) = 1.04$
2. The probability that a film will win an award based on acting is .30, the probability of an award for directing is .20, and the probability of an award for both is .05.

a. What is the probability of no awards?

b. What is the probability of at least one award?

*3. Joe has asked a new girl for a date to go to the drive-in on Saturday night. He feels there is a 50 : 50 chance that she will say yes. He feels that there is an 80% chance that he can get his car running by that time. However, the drive-in has a rather unimaginative policy: it closes in the event of rain. The local newspaper reports that the chance of rain is 20% for Saturday night. Find the probability that he gets to the drive-in with both car and girl and no rain. What is the probability of girl and car but rain?

4. As a part of a radio contest, a caller is asked to guess a three-digit number that can range from 000 to 999. Find the probability of guessing the number correctly by using

a. the classical definition approach.

b. the multiplication rule for the three digits.

5. Find the probability of getting the first two digits correct but not the third for the previous problem.

*6. A panel of congressmen is asked to rank seven bills in terms of cost to taxpayers. Assuming ties are not permitted, how many different arrangements are possible?

7. Ed Slammer, using past performance, estimates that his probability of getting par at a certain golf course is about 60% per hole. Find the probability that he pars the first three holes but does not par the next two. Does the assumption of independence seem reasonable? Why?

8. Given that 10% of the students enrolled in a large university have IQs that exceed 145, find these probabilities:

a. If a single student is selected from a list of all students, his IQ will exceed 145.

b. If five students are selected, none will have an IQ that exceeds 145.

9. Henry is late getting to work 25% of the time. He tends to forget his briefcase 20% of the time. Assuming these two misfortunes are independent, find these probabilities:

a. that Henry is late twice in a row

b. that Henry is late and without briefcase

c. that Henry is on time and with briefcase

d. that Henry is on time but without briefcase

*10. In how many ways can five students choose from a list of 11 term projects if:

a. No two can have the same term project?

b. Students are free to choose projects?

11. The public safety commissioner estimates that 5% of the cars parked in the downtown area are left with the keys in the ignition. He feels there is a 10% chance that such a car will be stolen, as opposed to only a .005 chance that a car without keys will be stolen. Given that a car has been stolen, what is the probability the keys were in the ignition?

12. A repair firm has four employees (A, B, C, D). Their respective probabilities for faulty repair are $P(A) = 1\%$, $P(B) = 2\%$, $P(C) = 3\%$, and $P(D) = 3\%$. A and B split 60% of the jobs and C and D split the other 40%. Given that a job is faulty, find these probabilities:

a. A did the job.   b. A or B did the job.

c. C did the job.

4

---

discontinuous probability distributions

Chapter Objectives

After completing this chapter, you should be able to:
1. Explain what a probability distribution is
2. Define a random variable and give examples
3. Tell how a probability distribution can serve as a model
4. State the assumptions that pertain to the binomial distribution
5. State the assumptions related to the Poisson distribution
6. Use the binomial tables and formula to obtain probabilities
7. Use the Poisson tables and formula to obtain probabilities
8. Use the Poisson distribution to approximate binomial probabilities
9. Solve simple problems that involve either binomial or Poisson probabilities

Chapter Outline

Introduction
Random Variables
    Expected value of a random variable
    Sums of random variables
Probability Distributions
Discontinuous Distributions
The Binomial Distribution
    The binomial formula
Binomial Tables
    Individual binomial probabilities
    Cumulative binomial table
    Characteristics of binomial distributions
The Poisson Distribution
    The Poisson formula
    Application involving time
    Application involving area
Poisson Tables
    Individual Poisson probabilities
    The cumulative Poisson table
    The Poisson distribution as an approximation to the binomial
Other Discrete Distributions

INTRODUCTION

WHY DOES a coin that is tossed sometimes land heads up and at other times land heads down? Why does a die that is rolled stop on one face rather than another? We say that these and similar things are determined by chance, but what exactly *is* chance?

Chance can best be thought of as the interaction of a large number of factors—perhaps an extremely large number of factors—that collectively influence the outcome of an experiment or sample. It would not seem unreasonable to suppose, in the case of the die, that the force with which it is rolled, air currents, the angle at which it strikes the table or floor, the "coefficient of bounce" with the surfaces it strikes, how many times it has been shaken, and so on, all play a part. Since it would be virtually impossible to control or regulate all these factors, or to predict how they will interact on any roll to affect the outcome, we cannot precisely specify which outcome will occur on any given roll. Furthermore, the same inability to know in advance which of a set of possible outcomes will occur on any trial is an inherent feature of any process in which chance is a factor, such as would be the case in card shuffling, pulling names from a hat, or *sampling*.

On the other hand, if we are willing to assume that the same factors interact in the same or similar way over many repeated observations, we find that there is *predictability* "over the long run." In other words, certain outcomes may be more likely than others, and this would be apparent given a large number of observations.

RANDOM VARIABLES

When a variable has outcomes or values that tend to vary from observation to observation because of chance-related factors, it is called a *random variable*. As a practical matter it is highly desirable to define a random variable associated with a sample or experiment in such a way that its possible outcomes are *numerical*. For instance, the experiment of tossing a coin once has two possible outcomes, H and T, but these are not numerical. Alternatively, we might consider as our random variable "number of *heads* in one toss," which has the possible *numerical* values 0 and 1. By the same token, our random variable could have been "number of *tails* in one toss." For a coin tossed twice, our random variable could be "number of heads in two tosses" and have the possible outcomes 0, 1, 2. Another random variable could be the number of customers entering a record shop during a 20-minute interval: 0, 1, 2, 3, 4, ... Still another could be the heights of persons in a college classroom, with a continuous range of values which might fall between 4.0 and 7.0 feet.

> A *random variable* is a numerically valued function whose value is governed by chance factors.

Random variables are either discrete or continuous.

> A random variable is considered *discrete* if the values it assumes can be *counted*.

Representative examples of discrete random variables are the number of accidents in a week, the number of defects in shoes, the number of crop failures, the number of earthquakes, the number of forfeited games, and the number of books in a bookcase.

> A random variable is considered *continuous* if it can assume *any* value within a given range.

A continuous variable has infinite possible values. Typical examples are the weights of orange crates, the heights of Douglas fir trees, the length of a telephone conversation, and the time required to complete an essay test.

The distinction between discrete and continuous random variables is important, because different probability models (distributions) are utilized depending on which type of random variable is being considered.

Expected Value of a Random Variable

If a random variable x takes on the values $x_1, x_2, x_3, \ldots, x_n$, with corresponding probabilities $p_1, p_2, p_3, \ldots, p_n$, then the *expected value* of the random variable $E(x)$ is

$$p_1 x_1 + p_2 x_2 + p_3 x_3 + \cdots + p_n x_n$$

Thus*

$$E(x) = \sum_{i=1}^{n} p_i x_i$$

Suppose an appliance store has compiled the following historical sales data on freezers:

---

* Note that this is identical to finding the mean of a frequency distribution using relative frequencies.

x_i Number sold	$P(x)$ Relative frequency
0	.20
1	.30
2	.30
3	.15
4	.05
	1.00

$$E(x) = .20(0) + .30(1) + .30(2) + .15(3) + .05(4) = 1.55$$

Since the firm obviously cannot actually sell 1.55 freezers on any given day (because the number sold is a discrete variable consisting of the *integers* 0, 1, 2, 3, and 4), the obvious question is how to interpret this figure. Quite simply, the expected value is a long-run average.

Similarly, if a balanced die is rolled, what is the expected value of a roll? There are six equally likely outcomes, and the expected value is

$$\tfrac{1}{6}(1) + \tfrac{1}{6}(2) + \tfrac{1}{6}(3) + \tfrac{1}{6}(4) + \tfrac{1}{6}(5) + \tfrac{1}{6}(6) = 3.5$$

Again, 3.5 is an impossible event for any *single* roll, but certainly reasonable in terms of an average computed over many trials.

The *expected value* of an experiment is an average, and can be computed as

$$E(x) = \sum_{i=1}^{n} p_i x_i$$

It is interesting to note that the expected value can be computed even though no sample observations have been made, as was done in the case of rolling a die, and the expected value can be *estimated* from sample data, as was the case with freezer sales.

Example 1 An investor decides he has a .40 probability of making a $25,000 profit and a .60 probability of having a $15,000 loss on an investment. His expected gain is

$$.40(25,000) + .60(-15,000) = \$1,000$$

Note that the $15,000 loss has a minus sign.

Example 2 A contractor makes the following estimates:

Probability	Completion time
.30	10 days
.20	15 days
.50	22 days

The expected number of days for project completion, according to these estimates, is

$$.30(10) + .20(15) + .50(22) = 17 \text{ days}$$

Expected value computations can involve the number of occurrences, such as the number of errors, the number of defectives, the number of accidents, and so on, as well as certain monetary measures, such as profits, gains or losses, returns on investment, and so on.

When monetary decisions are based on expected values, it is assumed that there exists a *linear utility* for dollar amounts. In other words, it is assumed that the value to the decision maker of $2,000 is twice the value of $1,000. Now this is not always the case. If a person needs a dime to make a phone call, nine pennies cannot be considered as 90% of the dime. Similarly, if a small contractor needs $50,000 to remain in business, and must consider two offers—a 10% chance of making $50,000 on a job [expected value = .10(50,000) = $5,000] or a .90 chance of making $30,000 on another job [expected value = .90($30,000) = $27,000]—he would most likely select the more risky job with the lower expected value because he needs the $50,000 to stay in business. We would say that in this case there is a nonlinear utility.

Sums of Random Variables

There are a number of situations in which we will want to consider a random variable which is itself the sum of two or more random variables. In such cases we must be able to determine the mean and the standard deviation for the resulting random variable. Suppose we have two random variables x and y, and we know the mean and standard deviation of each. From this information, we can determine the mean and standard deviation of the sum of these two random variables. If for x we have μ_x and σ_x, and for y we have μ_y and σ_y, then for $x + y$ we have

$$\mu_{x+y} = \mu_x + \mu_y \quad \text{and} \quad \sigma_{x+y} = \sqrt{\sigma_x{}^2 + \sigma_y{}^2}$$

Note that standard deviations are *never* added; only variances can be added. Hence to find the variance of the total, we add the variances. Then we take the square root of the total variance if we want the standard deviation of the total. For example, two pieces of pipe, which come from a distribution with a mean of 10.0 feet and a standard deviation of 3 feet, will be fastened together. We can compute the mean and standard deviation of the two-piece section.

$$\mu_x = \mu_y = 10 \qquad \sigma_x = \sigma_y = 3$$
$$\mu_{x+y} = 10 + 10 = 20 \qquad \sigma_{x+y} = \sqrt{3^2 + 3^2} = 4.24$$

If we had wanted to join four pieces of pipe, the mean and standard deviation of total length would have been

$$\mu = 10 + 10 + 10 + 10 = 40 \qquad \sigma = \sqrt{3^2 + 3^2 + 3^2 + 3^2} = 6.0$$

The *mean* of the sum of two or more random variables is equal to the sum of the means of the random variables.

The *variance* of the sum of two or more mutually independent random variables is the sum of the variances of those random variables.

EXERCISES

1. Classify each of the following random variables as either discrete or continuous:
   a. ages of children in a cafeteria
   b. number of children in a cafeteria
   c. gallons of gasoline sold on Tuesday at a station
   d. number of actors in a play
2. Ten percent of the cars on a used car lot have defective batteries. If there are 82 cars on the lot, what is the expected number of cars with defective batteries on the lot?
3. The number of telephone calls coming into a switchboard and their respective probabilities for a 3-minute interval are as follows:

							Total
Number of calls	0	1	2	3	4	5	
Relative frequency	.60	.20	.10	.04	.03	.03	1.00

   On the average, how many calls might be expected over a 3-minute interval?
4. A firm is working on four independent projects, A, B, C, and D, with expected profits of $4,000, $5,000, $10,000, and $20,000, and with standard deviations of $100, $200, $300, and $400. Find the total expected profit for these four projects and the standard deviation of that total.
5. A random variable x has a mean of 15 and a variance of 2, and a random variable y has a mean of 6 and a variance of 1.
   a. Find μ_{x+y}.   b. Find σ_{x+y}.
6. The National Health Bureau reports that approximately 15% of the adults in the nation will be affected by wild boar flu over the next 12 months. For a city of 250,000 adults, how many can be expected to suffer this affliction?
7. A bakery has developed a record of demand (see the table) for seven-layer devils food cakes. Find the expected number of cakes demanded.

											Total
Number of cakes/day	0	1	2	3	4	5	6	7	8	9	
Relative frequency		.02	.07	.09	.12	.20	.20	.18	.10	.01	.01	1.00

8. A three-step manufacturing operation has an average completion time of 15 minutes for the first step, 25 minutes for the second, and 30 minutes for the third. The respective standard deviations are 3 minutes, 4 minutes, and 5 minutes. Find the mean and variance of the total completion time.
9. A lottery ticket has a .00001 chance of returning $100,000, a .0002 chance of returning $50,000, and a .004 chance of returning $25. What would be a fair price to pay for the ticket?
10. One man is to be chosen from a large group of men. The average weight in the group is 180 pounds and the standard deviation is 20 pounds. A woman will be selected from a group of women that has a mean of 140 pounds and a standard deviation of 15 pounds. Find the mean and variance of the combined weights of one man and one woman.
11. Repeat Exercise 10 for the combined weights of three men.

PROBABILITY DISTRIBUTIONS

A *probability distribution* is a frequency distribution for the outcomes of a sample space (i.e., for the outcomes of a random variable). The frequencies are *relative* frequencies, or *probabilities*. Thus the probabilities indicate the percentage of times over a large number of observations that the various outcomes of a random variable can be expected to occur. Often tables or graphs are used to show how the total probability assigned to a sample space (100%) is *distributed* over the outcomes of that sample space.

> A *probability distribution* is a relative frequency distribution for outcomes in the sample space; it shows the proportion of times the random variable tends to assume various values.

Consider the random variable "number of heads in two tosses of a coin." A list of the points in the sample space and the corresponding values of the random variable are

Result	Value of random variable
TT	0
TH	1
HT	1
HH	2

If the coin is fair, $P(H) = P(T) = \frac{1}{2}$. The probabilities of the various outcomes are

Result	Probability of outcome	Number of heads	$P(x)$
TT	$\frac{1}{2}(\frac{1}{2}) = \frac{1}{4}$	0	.25
1 head $\begin{cases} \text{TH} \\ \text{HT} \end{cases}$	$\left.\begin{array}{l} \frac{1}{2}(\frac{1}{2}) = \frac{1}{4} \\ \frac{1}{2}(\frac{1}{2}) = \frac{1}{4} \end{array}\right\}$	1	.50
HH	$\frac{1}{2}(\frac{1}{2}) = \frac{1}{4}$	2	.25

Thus the probability distribution for the number of heads in two tosses of a fair coin is

Number of heads	$P(x)$
0	.25
1	.50
2	.25
	1.00

Note that the probabilities sum to 1.00, as they must, since the outcomes shown are mutually exclusive and collectively exhaustive. The same distribution can be shown in a *cumulative* form.

Number of heads	$P(x$ or less$)$
0	.25
1	.75
2	1.00

Graphically, these would appear as shown in Figure 4.1.

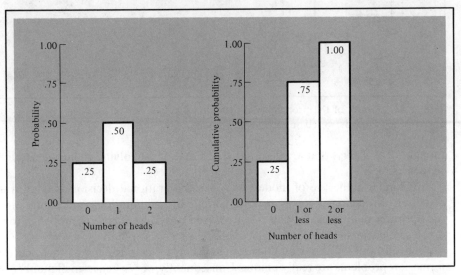

FIGURE 4.1   A probability distribution and a cumulative probability distribution for "number of heads in two tosses of a fair coin."

Suppose a coin is tossed in a situation where $P(H) = .60$ (and thus $P(T) = .40$). We then have a *different* probability distribution for the number of heads in two tosses of the coin.

	Probability		Number of heads	Probability
TT	.40(.40) =	.16	0	.16
TH	.40(.60) =	.24 ⎱	1	.48
HT	.60(.40) =	.24 ⎰		
HH	.60(.60) =	.36	2	.36
		1.00		1.00

Graphically, this distribution would appear as shown in Figure 4.2.

Notice that *given* a probability distribution, it is readily apparent that some outcomes of a random variable are more likely than others. Moreover, the probability of a particular outcome, or group of outcomes, can be found without much effort. As a practical matter, it is usually unnecessary to go to the trouble of computing individual probabilities to obtain a probability distribution. Tables and formulas are readily available for this. Consequently, the real issue is not "how are the values *derived?*" but "how are the distributions *used* to solve problems?"

Now aside from the fact that probability distributions provide a simple approach to the determination of certain probabilities, the distribution types can be

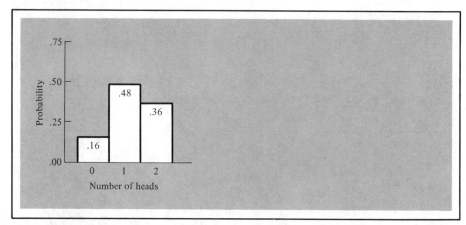

FIGURE 4.2   Graph of the probability distribution for "number of heads in two tosses of a coin" when P(heads) = .60 on each toss.

thought of as *models* that are descriptive of situations involving chance-generated outcomes.

In Chapter 1 the use of models as a basis for rational decision making was discussed. Modeling involves making simplifying assumptions and eliminating unimportant details, and it can often be used to reduce complex problems to a manageable size.

One offshoot of this simplification in using models is that in their purest forms, few problems are really unique. Consequently, very often a small number of basic models can be utilized to obtain solutions for a wide range of problems which appear on the surface to be quite unrelated. This is especially true in statistical work. A few basic models can be used to solve most problems. For example, coin flipping, defectives in a shipment of manufactured goods, and guessing on tests are often handled by the same type of probability distribution. Recognition of this has led to the development of a collection of standardized techniques that can be used to obtain solutions to many "different" problems. This enables a manager or other analyst to bring the power of statistics to bear upon a particular problem without having to start from scratch each time.

There are a variety of probability distribution types in statistics. Each of these has its own set of assumptions that define the conditions under which the distribution type can be validly employed. The key in using probability distributions is to match the assumptions of a distribution type with the characteristics of the real situation. Once correspondence has been achieved, the analysis becomes a relatively simple matter, because probability distributions can be used to handle a class of problems, and all problems within each class are essentially handled in the same manner.

In this chapter a few basic—but very important—types of probability distributions are presented. As you go through the chapter, try to concentrate on the following questions:

1. What basic assumptions or restrictions does each of the probability distributions require? This knowledge is vital for successful matching of a random variable with the real situation.
2. How can probability distributions be used to obtain solutions to problems?

The validity of using a particular distribution for a problem will depend on how closely the problem situation approximates the set of conditions assumed by the probability distribution. Usually, the better the match, the better the answer.

> The essence of statistical analysis is to match the assumptions of some probability distribution with the specifics of a particular problem.

The following discussion of probability distributions is organized into two parts: discontinuous distributions are considered in this chapter and continuous distributions are considered in the next chapter.

DISCONTINUOUS DISTRIBUTIONS

Discontinuous probability distributions involve random variables for count data, such as the number of occurrences per sample or the number of occurrences per unit over an interval of time, area, or distance. In the following pages you will learn about two very important discontinuous distributions, the binomial and the Poisson.

THE BINOMIAL DISTRIBUTION

The term "binomial" is used to designate situations in which the outcomes of a random variable can be grouped into two classes or categories. Hence the data are *nominal*. The categories must be mutually exclusive, so that it is clear to which class any particular observation belongs, and the classes must be collectively exhaustive, so that no other outcome is possible.

There are many examples of random variables that can be classified as binomial variables: answers on a true-false test, yes-no responses to a questionnaire, manufactured products classified as defective or satisfactory, kindergarten students who do or do not have vaccinations, and pass-fail grading systems. Moreover, variables with *multiple* outcomes can often be treated as binomial when only one of the outcomes is of interest. Hence answers to a multiple-choice test can be either correct or incorrect; there may be five colors of beads in a bowl, but if our concern is only with drawing a green bead, the result can be viewed as green-not green; or there may be five applicants for a single job opening, and the final outcome can be viewed in terms of hired or not hired. Likewise, mail can be local or out of town, and telephone calls can be local or long-distance. Even outcomes of a continuous variable can be reduced to two mutually exclusive classes. For instance, automobile speeds can be (and often are) treated as either being within the legal speed limit or exceeding that limit. Similarly, we can say a runner finished a mile in less than 4 minutes or he did not, a person is taller than 6 feet or is not, and so on.

It is fairly standard to refer to the two categories of a binomial distribution as "success" and "failure," although for computational purposes, which category is called success and which failure does not matter, since the two are complements. For instance, if you are involved in a game of chance with a friend, success for you means failure for the friend.

The observations of a binomial experiment are often referred to as "trials." For instance, a problem may require determining the probability of five successes in seven trials (observations).

Note that because success and failure are *mutually exclusive* and *collectively exhaustive*, P(success) + P(failure) = 1.00. Consequently, if we know, for example, that P(success) = .60, we also know that P(failure) = .40.

The binomial distribution is useful in determining the probability of some number of successes in a given number of observations. For instance, suppose it is known that 80% of the registered voters in an urban precinct are over 30 years old. Someone might want to know the probability, in a sample of 10 registered voters, of finding 7 or more voters over 30 years old. We would say, then, that success = registered voter and that P(success) = .80.

Now to utilize the binomial distribution, it is necessary to satisfy certain assumptions. These assumptions are as follows:

---

1. There are n identical observations or trials.
2. Each trial has two possible outcomes, one called "success" and the other "failure."
3. The probabilities of success p and of failure $1 - p$ remain the same for all trials.
4. The outcomes of trials are independent of each other.

There are two approaches to obtaining probabilities for a random variable that is binomially distributed. One approach is to utilize the binomial formula, and the other approach is to refer to a table of binomial probabilities.

The Binomial Formula

To compute a binomial probability, it is necessary to specify n, the number of trials, x, the number of successes, and p, the probability of success on each trial. Suppose that $p = .80$ [and hence, P(failure) = .20], and that we want to determine the probability of getting three successes (and one failure) in four observations. Now there are four ways of getting exactly three successes out of four observations. Each of the ways is shown below, along with its respective probability.

Arrangement	Probability
SSSF	$(.8)(.8)(.8)(.2) = .1024$
SSFS	$(.8)(.8)(.2)(.8) = .1024$
SFSS	$(.8)(.2)(.8)(.8) = .1024$
FSSS	$(.2)(.8)(.8)(.8) = .1024$
	$.4096$

The probability of three successes and one failure is the sum of all the different ways of getting three successes in four observations. In this case the sum is .4096. Notice that each situation has the same probability of occurring because the *same* numbers are multiplied together: only their *order* is different. This will *always* be true.

This observation leads us to the following guidelines. Probabilities for binomial outcomes can be determined mathematically by taking two things into consideration: the *number* of ways the situation can occur and the *probability of one* of those ways. Note, too, that the number of ways is actually the number of distinguishable permutations,

$$\binom{n}{x}$$

Furthermore, there is a table in the Appendix (Table E) of selected values of binomial coefficients—that is,

$$\binom{n}{x}$$

—so that it is usually unnecessary to have to compute these values.

Perhaps the simplest approach for determining the probability of one of the situations is to consider the case in which all the successes come first and all the failures come last. For three successes and one failure, this is SSSF, and the probability for this way is $(.8)(.8)(.8)(.2)$, or $(.8)^3(.2)^1$. Thus $P(x = 3) = 4(.8)^3(.2)^1 = .4096$.

Putting these two ideas together—number of ways and probability of one of the ways—we get the following:

$$P(x) = \binom{n}{x} P(\text{success})^x P(\text{failure})^{n-x}$$

where

$$\binom{n}{x} = \text{number of ways of having } x \text{ successes and } n - x \text{ failures in } n \text{ trials}$$

Note that if we want x successes in n observations, then we also expect $n - x$ failures, because $x + n - x = n$, the total number of observations. (You should always check to make sure that the exponents add to n when using this approach.

Here are a few examples of how to set up the formula for calculations.

n	x	p	$\binom{n}{x} p^x (1 - p)^{n-x}$
5	3	.30	$\binom{5}{3}(.30)^3(.70)^2$
8	6	.11	$\binom{8}{6}(.11)^6(.89)^2$
9	5	.44	$\binom{9}{5}(.44)^5(.56)^4$
10	4	.85	$\binom{10}{4}(.85)^4(.15)^6$

The formula can also be used to obtain *cumulative* probabilities by computing and then *summing* individual probabilities. Here are some examples.

n	p	x	Includes	Calculations	$P(x)$
3	.4	1	1	$\binom{3}{1}(.4)^1(.6)^2$	.4320
5	.2	0	0	$\binom{5}{0}(.2)^0(.8)^5$	.3277
5	.2	1 or less	0, 1	$\binom{5}{0}(.2)^0(.8)^5 + \binom{5}{1}(.2)^1(.8)^4$	.7373
10	.5	8 or more	8, 9, 10	$\binom{10}{8}(.5)^8(.5)^2 + \binom{10}{9}(.5)^9(.5)^1 + \binom{10}{10}(.5)^{10}(.5)^0$	.0547
10	.7	6	6	$\binom{10}{6}(.7)^6(.3)^4$	.2001

EXERCISES

Use the binomial formula to answer these questions.

1. A firm that manufactures billiard tables suspects that 2% of its output is defective in some way. If this suspicion is correct, find the probability that in a sample of nine tables:
   a. There is at least one defective.
   b. There are no defective tables.

2. Of the students at a community college, 41% smoke cigarettes. Six students are selected to be interviewed for their views on smoking.
   a. Find the probability that none of those selected smoke.
   b. Find the probability that all those selected smoke.
   c. Find the probability that at least half of the six smoke.

3. Twelve percent of those holding reservations on a daily commuter flight consistently fail to take the flight. The plane carries 15 passengers.
   a. Find the probability that all 15 persons who hold reservations take the flight.
   b. If 16 reservations are booked, find the probability of:
      (1) one person being bumped
      (2) none being bumped
      (3) more than one being bumped

4. A new car dealer has found that 80% of the cars sold are returned to the service department to correct manufacturing defects during the first 25 days after purchase. Of the 11 cars sold during a 5-day period, what is the probability that:
   a. All return within 25 days for service?
   b. Only one does not return?

5. Assume that 8% of the hot dogs sold at a baseball stadium are ordered without mustard. If seven persons order hot dogs, find the probability that:
   a. all want mustard   ·b. only one does not want mustard

BINOMIAL TABLES

Probability tables offer a very practical approach for statistical analysis; they provide probabilities with very little effort. There are two kinds of binomial tables. One type provides probabilities for single or *individual* outcomes of a random variable, and the other gives probabilities for a *set* of outcomes. While the two tables contain essentially the same information, some problems lend themselves more to one type of table than the other, so we will consider both types.

Individual Binomial Probabilities

When interest lies in determining the probability of a single value in a binomial distribution, such as the probability of obtaining *exactly* four successes in six observations, then a table of individual binomial probabilities can be very useful. As with the formula, three pieces of information are required: n, the number of observations, p, the probability of success, and x, a specified number of successes.

A portion of a binomial table is shown in Table 4.1. In the table selected values of p are shown across the top of the table, and these vary in increments of .05. Down the left side of the table are sample sizes n. Note that for each n the possible number of successes x are listed (0 through n). A more extensive table of binomial probabilities is provided in the Appendix.

Let us use Table 4.1 to find a probability. Suppose we want to find the probability of 5 successes ($x = 5$) in 8 observations ($n = 8$) when the probability of success is .30. The table is used as follows:

1. Read across the top of the table until you find the p you are looking for.
2. Locate the value of n down the side of the table. Find the desired number of successes x in the list of outcomes for that subset.
3. The probability of x successes is found at the intersection of the row found in part 2 and the column found in part 1.

Thus the probability of exactly 5 successes in 8 observations, when the probability of success on each observation is .30, is .0467. This value is circled in Table 4.1.

The following table illustrates probabilities that have been found in Table A in the Appendix. You may find it helpful to use that table to verify the numbers shown.

n	Probability of success p	x	$P(x)$
5	.20	0	.3277
8	.60	3	.1239
11	.30	5	.1321

Cumulative Binomial Table

Many problems in statistics require the combined probability of a group of outcomes instead of a single outcome. Usually the outcomes of interest are those more than, or less than, some specified number. For example, interest might center on the probability of getting 5 *or less* heads in 10 tosses of a fair coin. Although such questions can be answered using a table of individual binomial

TABLE 4.1 Portion of a Table of Individual Binomial Probabilities

n	x	.05	.10	.15	.20	.25	.30	.35	.40	.45	.50	.55	.60	.65	.70	.75	.80	.85	.90	.95
8	0	.6634	.4305	.2725	.1678	.1001	.0576	.0319	.0168	.0084	.0039	.0017	.0007	.0002	.0001	.0000	.0000	.0000	.0000	.0000
	1	.2793	.3826	.3847	.3355	.2670	.1977	.1373	.0896	.0548	.0312	.0164	.0079	.0033	.0012	.0004	.0001	.0000	.0000	.0000
	2	.0515	.1488	.2376	.2936	.3115	.2965	.2587	.2090	.1569	.1094	.0703	.0413	.0217	.0100	.0038	.0011	.0002	.0000	.0000
	3	.0054	.0331	.0839	.1468	.2076	.2541	.2786	.2787	.2568	.2188	.1719	.1239	.0808	.0467	.0231	.0092	.0026	.0004	.0000
	4	.0004	.0046	.0185	.0459	.0865	.1361	.1875	.2322	.2627	.2734	.2627	.2322	.1875	.1361	.0865	.0459	.0185	.0046	.0004
	5	.0000	.0004	.0026	.0092	.0231	(.0467)	.0808	.1239	.1719	.2188	.2568	.2787	.2786	.2541	.2076	.1468	.0839	.0331	.0515
	6	.0000	.0000	.0002	.0011	.0038	.0100	.0217	.0413	.0703	.1094	.1569	.2090	.2587	.2965	.3115	.2936	.2376	.1488	.2793
	7	.0000	.0000	.0000	.0001	.0004	.0012	.0033	.0079	.0164	.0312	.0548	.0896	.1373	.1977	.2670	.3355	.3847	.3826	.2793
	8	.0000	.0000	.0000	.0000	.0000	.0001	.0002	.0007	.0017	.0039	.0084	.0168	.0319	.0576	.1001	.1678	.2725	.4305	.6634
9	0	.6302	.3874	.2316	.1342	.0751	.0404	.0207	.0101	.0046	.0020	.0008	.0003	.0001	.0000	.0000	.0000	.0000	.0000	.0000
	1	.2985	.3874	.3679	.3020	.2253	.1556	.1004	.0605	.0339	.0176	.0083	.0035	.0013	.0004	.0001	.0000	.0000	.0000	.0000
	2	.0629	.1722	.2597	.3020	.3003	.2668	.2162	.1612	.1110	.0703	.0407	.0212	.0098	.0039	.0012	.0003	.0000	.0000	.0000
	3	.0077	.0446	.1069	.1762	.2336	.2668	.2716	.2508	.2119	.1641	.1160	.0743	.0424	.0210	.0087	.0028	.0006	.0001	.0000
	4	.0006	.0074	.0283	.0661	.1168	.1715	.2194	.2508	.2600	.2461	.2128	.1672	.1181	.0735	.0389	.0165	.0050	.0008	.0000
	5	.0000	.0008	.0050	.0165	.0389	.0735	.1181	.1672	.2128	.2461	.2600	.2508	.2194	.1715	.1168	.0661	.0283	.0074	.0006
	6	.0000	.0001	.0006	.0028	.0087	.0210	.0424	.0743	.1160	.1641	.2119	.2508	.2716	.2668	.2336	.1762	.1069	.0446	.0077
	7	.0000	.0000	.0000	.0003	.0012	.0039	.0098	.0212	.0407	.0703	.1110	.1612	.2162	.2668	.3003	.3020	.2597	.1722	.0629
	8	.0000	.0000	.0000	.0000	.0001	.0004	.0013	.0035	.0083	.0176	.0339	.0605	.1004	.1556	.2253	.3020	.3679	.3874	.2985
	9	.0000	.0000	.0000	.0000	.0000	.0000	.0001	.0003	.0008	.0020	.0046	.0101	.0207	.0404	.0751	.1342	.2316	.3874	.6302

probabilities, that approach would require looking up the probabilities in the table and then adding them: $P(0) + P(1) + P(2) + P(3) + P(4) + P(5)$. A more efficient alternative is to use a table of cumulative probabilities, because in a cumulative table the individual values are already summed (accumulated), which saves time and decreases the chance of computational errors.

The format of a cumulative binomial table is nearly identical to the table of individual binomial probabilities. Selected values of p, the probability of success, are listed across the top of the table and the possible number of occurrences (successes) for various sample sizes are shown down the side of the table. The probabilities shown in the body of the table are for x *or less* successes, instead of for the probability of *exactly* x successes as in the individual binomial probability table. A portion of a cumulative table is shown in Table 4.2. The circled value, .9360, is the probability that there will be 2 or less successes (i.e., 0 or 1 or 2) in 3 observations when the probability of success is .40.

A cumulative table can be used in a number of different ways. It can be used to find directly the probability that x will be equal to or less than some specified number of successes. And it can be used indirectly to find both the probability that x will be *greater* than some number of successes and the probability of *exactly* x successes. This is due to the fact that the outcomes are mutually exclusive and collectively exhaustive; their probabilities in any given instance will sum to 1.00. Hence if we find $P(X \le 6) = .72$, then $P(X > 6) = 1.00 - .72 = .28$.

A little trick that can save you a lot of grief is to list the possible outcomes for a given situation and then underline the outcomes for which you desire probabilities. For example, suppose you want to find the probability of 3 or less successes in 7 observations. First, list the possible successes:

$$0 \quad 1 \quad 2 \quad 3 \quad 4 \quad 5 \quad 6 \quad 7$$

Next, underline those of interest:

$$\underline{0 \quad 1 \quad 2 \quad 3} \quad 4 \quad 5 \quad 6 \quad 7$$
(3 or less)

Since the table shows the probability of x *or less* successes, you can look up the probability of 3 or less directly [given n and P(success)]. That is,

$$\underline{0 \quad 1 \quad 2 \quad 3} \quad 4 \quad 5 \quad 6 \quad 7$$

the table shows the probability of any of these number of successes

To find the probability of *more than* 3 (i.e., 4, 5, 6, or 7), find the probability of 3 or less and subtract this from 1.00:

$$100\%$$
$$\underbrace{0 \quad 1 \quad 2 \quad 3} \quad \underbrace{4 \quad 5 \quad 6 \quad 7}$$
$$\text{table value} \quad 1 - \text{table value}$$

A cumulative table can also be used to find individual probabilities. For example, to find the probability of exactly 4 successes, subtract $P(3 \text{ or less})$ from $P(4 \text{ or less})$:

$$P(x \le 4) - P(x \le 3) = P(x = 4)$$

TABLE 4.2 Portion of a Cumulative Binomial Table

n	x	.05	.10	.15	.20	.25	.30	.35	.40	.45	.50	.55	.60	.65
1	0	.9500	.9000	.8500	.8000	.7500	.7000	.6500	.6000	.5500	.5000	.4500	.4000	.3500
	1	1.0000	1.0000	1.0000	1.0000	1.0000	1.0000	1.0000	1.0000	1.0000	1.0000	1.0000	1.0000	1.0000
2	0	.9025	.8100	.7225	.6400	.5625	.4900	.4225	.3600	.3025	.2500	.2025	.1600	.1225
	1	.9975	.9900	.9775	.9600	.9375	.9100	.8775	.8400	.7975	.7500	.6975	.6400	.5775
	2	1.0000	1.0000	1.0000	1.0000	1.0000	1.0000	1.0000	1.0000	1.0000	1.0000	1.0000	1.0000	1.0000
3	0	.8574	.7290	.6141	.5120	.4219	.3430	.2746	.2160	.1664	.1250	.0911	.0640	.0429
	1	.9928	.9720	.9393	.8960	.8438	.7840	.7183	.6430	.5748	.5000	.4253	.3520	.2818
	2	.9999	.9990	.9966	.9920	.9844	.9730	.9571	(.9360)	.9089	.8750	.8336	.7840	.7254
	3	1.0000	1.0000	1.0000	1.0000	1.0000	1.0000	1.0000	1.0000	1.0000	1.0000	1.0000	1.0000	1.0000
4	0	.8145	.6561	.5220	.4096	.3164	.2401	.1785	.1296	.0915	.0625	.0410	.0256	.0150
	1	.9860	.9477	.8905	.8192	.7383	.6517	.5630	.4752	.3910	.3125	.2415	.1792	.1265
	2	.9995	.9963	.9880	.9728	.9492	.9163	.8735	.8208	.7585	.6875	.6090	.5248	.4370
	3	1.0000	.9999	.9995	.9984	.9961	.9919	.9850	.9744	.9590	.9375	.9085	.8704	.8215
	4	1.0000	1.0000	1.0000	1.0000	1.0000	1.0000	1.0000	1.0000	1.0000	1.0000	1.0000	1.0000	1.0000
5	0	.7738	.5905	.4437	.3277	.2373	.1681	.1160	.0778	.0503	.0313	.0185	.0102	.0053
	1	.9774	.9185	.8352	.7373	.6328	.5282	.4284	.3370	.2562	.1875	.1312	.0870	.0540
	2	.9988	.9914	.9734	.9421	.8965	.8369	.7648	.6826	.5931	.5000	.4069	.3174	.2352
	3	1.0000	.9995	.9978	.9933	.9844	.9692	.9460	.9130	.8688	.8125	.7438	.6630	.5716
	4	1.0000	1.0000	.9999	.9997	.9990	.9976	.9947	.9898	.9815	.9688	.9497	.9222	.8840
	5	1.0000	1.0000	1.0000	1.0000	1.0000	1.0000	1.0000	1.0000	1.0000	1.0000	1.0000	1.0000	1.0000

$n = 3 \rightarrow 3$

$x = 2 \rightarrow$

114

Consider this example. If $P(\text{success}) = .50$ and $n = 4$, use the cumulative table to find $P(x = 3)$:

$$P(x \le 3) \text{ includes: } 0 \quad 1 \quad 2 \quad 3 \qquad \text{and equals } .9375$$
$$P(x \le 2) \text{ includes: } 0 \quad 1 \quad 2 \qquad\qquad \text{and equals } \underline{.6875}$$
$$P(x = 3) \text{ includes: } \qquad\qquad\qquad 3 \qquad \text{and equals } .2500$$

Table 4.3 illustrates the various uses of a cumulative table as well as how the desired probabilities can be derived. Study it carefully and you should be able to answer most of the problems you will encounter with little difficulty.

TABLE 4.3   Using a Cumulative Binomial Table

A. Listing desired outcomes

		Outcomes											Read in cumulative table
$n = 10$		0	1	2	3	4	5	6	7	8	9	10	
$P(X \le 6)$	6 or less	0	1	2	3	4	5	6					directly: $P(6)$
$P(X < 6)$	less than 6	0	1	2	3	4	5						directly: $P(5)$
$P(X \ge 6)$	6 or more							6	7	8	9	10	$1 - P(5)$
$P(X > 6)$	more than 6								7	8	9	10	$1 - P(6)$
$P(X = 6)$	6							6					$P(6) - P(5)$

B. Probabilities for above, using $p = .30$ and $n = 10$. Probabilities are from Appendix Table B.

$P(X \le 6)$		.9894
$P(X < 6)$		.9527
$P(X \ge 6)$	$1 - .9527$	.0473
$P(X > 6)$	$1 - .9894$	.0106
$P(X = 6)$	$.9894 - .9527$	.0367

Although tables offer the simplest and most practical method for obtaining probabilities, there are situations in which desired probabilities cannot be found in tables such as the ones we have been working with. For example, suppose $P(\text{success}) = .12$. The table does not include this value. To be sure, larger and more extensive tables are available, and many libraries have them in their reference sections. But it is not always practical to make a trip to the library. For these and other reasons, it is useful to use the binomial formula to obtain desired probabilities.

Characteristics of Binomial Distributions

Every probability distribution type has certain characteristics that differentiate it from other probability distribution types. Very often an awareness of these distinctions provides a better understanding of when to use a distribution type, a better understanding of how some distributions can be used to approximate probabilities for other distribution types, and, in general, a better appreciation of the concepts of statistical analysis.

Since the data are in the form of *counts*, the number of successes must always be an integer value (0, 1, 2, 3, . . .). However, it is sometimes useful to express the number of successes as a percentage of the number of observations. For instance, 2 successes in 10 observations would be .20 or 20%. Also, an alternative method of graphing a binomial distribution is to use a bar graph instead of a histogram.

The bar graph is especially useful for portraying the distribution when working with a percentage of successes instead of a number of successes. See Figure 4.3.

The *mean* of a binomial distribution is the long-run average, or the *expected value*, of a binomial random variable. The standard deviation of a binomial distribution indicates the extent to which sample values will tend to vary from the mean of the distribution. In the case of the binomial, both the mean and the standard deviation can be expressed in terms of the *number* or the *percentage* of successes. The formulas are given below.

	Mean	Standard deviation
Number of successes	np	$\sqrt{np(1-p)}$
Percentage of successes	p	$\sqrt{p(1-p)/n}$

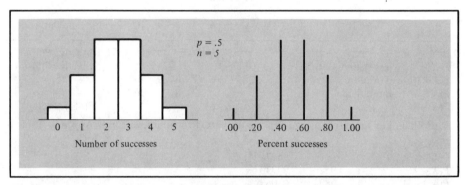

FIGURE 4.3 A histogram is generally used when the random variable is *number* of successes; a bar graph is used for *percentage* of successes.

Example 3 Suppose the probability of success is .10 and the number of observations is 100. Find the mean and standard deviation of the probability distribution both for the number and the percentage of successes.

Solution:

	Mean	Standard deviation
Number of successes	$100(.10) = 10$	$\sqrt{100(.10)(90)} = 3$
Percentage of successes	$.10$	$\sqrt{.10(.90)/100} = .03$

The mean of 10 for the number of successes is interpreted as the long-run average number of successes in samples of 100 observations. Similarly, the long-run percentage of successes in samples of 100 is .10. The two standard deviations reflect the variability that individual samples will exhibit. Note that 3% of 100 is 3; the two alternative forms are equivalent.

The binomial distribution has two parameters: p, the probability of success, and n, the number of observations. Each combination of p and n refers to a unique distribution or sample space. Note how the shaded values in the binomial table have been used to construct the distributions in Figure 4.4.

Individual Terms of the Binomial Distribution

									p								
n	x	.05	.10	.15	.20	.25	.30	.35	.40	.45	.50	.55	.60	.65	.70	.75	.80
1	0	.9500	.9000	.8500	.8000	.7500	.7000	.6500	.6000	.5500	.5000	.4500	.4000	.3500	.3000	.2500	.2000
	1	.0500	.1000	.1500	.2000	.2500	.3000	.3500	.4000	.4500	.5000	.5500	.6000	.6500	.7000	.7500	.8000
2	0	.9025	.8100	.7225	.6400	.5625	.4900	.4225	.3600	.3025	.2500	.2025	.1600	.1225	.0900	.0625	.0400
	1	.0950	.1800	.2550	.3200	.3750	.4200	.4550	.4800	.4950	.5000	.4950	.4800	.4550	.4200	.3750	.3200
	2	.0025	.0100	.0225	.0400	.0625	.0900	.1225	.1600	.2025	.2500	.3025	.3600	.4225	.4900	.5625	.6400
3	0	.8574	.7290	.6141	.5120	.4219	.3430	.2746	.2160	.1664	.1250	.0911	.0640	.0429	.0270	.0156	.0080
	1	.1354	.2430	.3251	.3840	.4219	.4410	.4436	.4320	.4084	.3750	.3341	.2880	.2389	.1890	.1406	.0960
	2	.0071	.0270	.0574	.0960	.1406	.1890	.2389	.2880	.3341	.3750	.4084	.4320	.4436	.4410	.4219	.3840
	3	.0001	.0010	.0034	.0080	.0156	.0270	.0429	.0640	.0911	.1250	.1664	.2160	.2746	.3430	.4219	.5120
4	0	.8145	.6561	.5220	.4096	.3164	.2401	.1785	.1296	.0915	.0625	.0410	.0256	.0150	.0081	.0039	.0016
	1	.1715	.2916	.3685	.4096	.4219	.4116	.3845	.3456	.2995	.2500	.2005	.1536	.1115	.0756	.0469	.0256
	2	.0135	.0486	.0975	.1536	.2109	.2646	.3105	.3456	.3675	.3750	.3675	.3456	.3105	.2646	.2109	.1536
	3	.0005	.0036	.0115	.0256	.0469	.0756	.1115	.1536	.2005	.2500	.2995	.3456	.3845	.4116	.4219	.4096
	4	.0000	.0001	.0005	.0016	.0039	.0081	.0150	.0256	.0410	.0625	.0915	.1296	.1785	.2401	.3164	.4096
5	0	.7738	.5905	.4437	.3277	.2373	.1681	.1160	.0778	.0503	.0313	.0185	.0102	.0053	.0024	.0010	.0003
	1	.2036	.3281	.3915	.4096	.3955	.3602	.3124	.2592	.2059	.1563	.1128	.0768	.0488	.0284	.0146	.0064
	2	.0214	.0729	.1382	.2048	.2637	.3087	.3364	.3456	.3369	.3125	.2757	.2304	.1811	.1323	.0879	.0512
	3	.0012	.0031	.0244	.0512	.0879	.1323	.1811	.2304	.2757	.3125	.3369	.3456	.3364	.3087	.2637	.2048
	4	.0000	.0004	.0022	.0064	.0146	.0283	.0488	.0768	.1128	.1562	.2059	.2592	.3124	.3601	.3955	.4096
	5	.0000	.0000	.0001	.0003	.0010	.0024	.0053	.0102	.0185	.0312	.0503	.0778	.1160	.1681	.2373	.3277

For any given sample size n, a binomial probability distribution will be symmetrical for $p = .50$, but it will be skewed to the right if p is greater than $.50$ and skewed to the left if p is less than $.50$, as illustrated in Figure 4.4. This tendency to be skewed when p is not $.50$ diminishes as n increases.

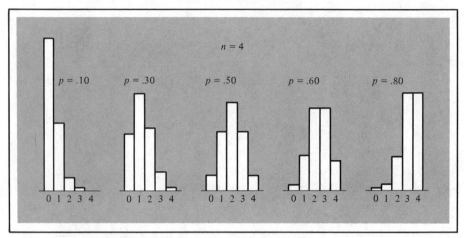

FIGURE 4.4   A binomial distribution will be symmetrical for $p = .5$, skewed to the right for $p < .5$, and skewed to the left for $p > .5$.

EXERCISES

1. Use a binomial table (either individual or cumulative) to determine the probability of x successes:

	Number of observations	P(success)	x
a.	5	.2	0
b.	5	.3	1
c.	5	.5	1 or less
d.	10	.1	2 or less
e.	10	.1	2 or more
f.	10	.9	8 or less
g.	10	.7	2 or 3
h.	12	.7	3 or less

2. Records of a small utility company indicate that 40% of the bills it sends out are paid after the due date. If 14 bills are sent out, find the probability that:
   a. none are late
   b. at most 2 are late
   c. at least half are late

3. An oil exploration firm finds that about 5% of the test wells it drills yield a deposit of natural gas. If it drills six wells, find the probability that at least one will yield gas.

*4. A multiple choice test has 4 choices per question and 14 questions. If a passing grade depends on getting 9 or more answers correct, what is the probability that a student who guesses on all questions will pass the test?

5. A real estate firm has noted that 1 out of 10 prospective homeowners will make an offer on a house if they return for a second visit. In 10 such cases, find the probability that none will make an offer.

6. A recent survey indicates that only 15% of the physicians in a rural area smoke. Two out of eight doctors selected from a list supplied by the county medical board are found to smoke. Assuming the survey was correct, what was the probability of getting this result?

7. Medical research suggests that 20% of the general population suffer adverse side effects from a new drug. If a doctor prescribes the drug for four patients, what is the probability that:
   a. None will have side effects?
   b. All will have them?
   c. At least one will have side effects?

8. A recent government survey suggested that 80% of the families living in a suburban community who earned more than $15,000 gross income owned two cars. Assuming this is true, if a sample of 10 families in this category is taken, find the probability that exactly 80% of the sample own two cars.

*9. A television with 10 circuit boards has one defective board. Eight of the boards are costly to replace. Find the probability that the defective board is not one of those.

10. Traffic records show that 25% of the vehicles stopped on an interstate highway fail to pass a safety check. If 16 vehicles are stopped, find the probability of:
    a. 2 or more failing
    b. 4 or more
    c. 9 or more

11. A local sportswriter picks the winner of 6 out of 10 baseball games correctly. If a person is simply guessing, what is the probability that he could equal or better that record?

12. A balanced coin is flipped three times and called correctly each time. What is the probability of duplicating this feat?

13. Of the students in a junior college, 75% change majors at least once during their first year, according to the college registrar. If 11 students are selected from the freshman class, find the probability that:
    a. all have changed majors at least once
    b. at least 9 have changed
    c. more than half have changed

14. A large bowl contains 10,000 colored marbles:

white	5,000
green	3,000
red	1,500
black	500
	10,000

    a. If 20 marbles are selected, find $P(2 \text{ green})$.
    b. If 19 are selected, what is the probability that at least 3 are green?
    c. If 19 are selected, what is the probability that at least 3 are white?

15. Shipments of 500 bushings each are passed if a random sample of 10 has less than two defectives. If a shipment actually has 5% defectives, what is the probability that it will pass?

16. In Exercise 15 what percentage of lots with 10% defectives would produce samples of 10 pieces in which there were no defectives?

17. A serviceman knows from previous experience that 90% of the spare parts he takes out on a job will be usable. If a job requires five usable parts, what is the minimum number of parts he must take if he desires that the probability of returning for additional parts to be under .12?

18. Compute the mean and standard deviation for the *number* of successes for these cases:
    a. $n = 25, p = .5$ b. $n = 50, p = .2$ c. $n = 80, p = .4$

19. Repeat Exercise 18 for the *percentage* of successes.

20. At times it is impossible for the percentage of successes in the sample to equal the mean percentage. For instance, when $n = 4$ and $p = .3$, the percentage can never be .30.
    a. List the possible sample percentages for this case.
    b. How is the mean of .3 interpreted?

21. Draw two sets of graphs, one for the number of successes and one for the percentage of successes, for these situations:
    a. $n = 5, p = .10$ b. $n = 10, p = .70$

THE POISSON DISTRIBUTION

The Poisson distribution is often useful in describing the probabilities for the number of occurrences over a continuous field or interval (usually time or space). Examples of random variables that can be modeled by the Poisson distribution are defects per square centimeter, accidents per day, customers per hour, telephone calls per minute, mosquitos per square mile, cows per acre, and so on. Note that the unit of measurement (e.g., time, area) is continuous but that the random variable, the number of occurrences, is discrete. Moreover, note that failures are not countable. The number of accidents that did *not* occur cannot be counted. Neither can the number of calls that did not come in or the number of defects that did not occur in a square centimeter. See Figure 4.5.

Use of the Poisson distribution assumes the following:

1. The probability of an occurrence is the same throughout the field of observation.
2. The probability of more than one occurrence at any single point is approximately 0.
3. The number of occurrences in any interval is independent of the number of occurrences in other intervals.

The lower limit for the number of occurrences in all these situations is 0, and the upper limit, at least theoretically, is infinity, even though for most of the examples above, it would be difficult to imagine an unlimited number of occur-

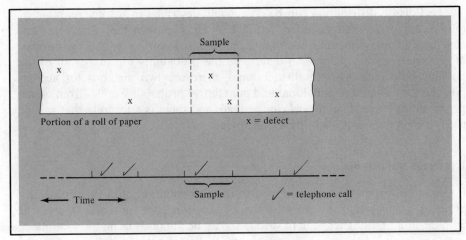

FIGURE 4.5   The Poisson distribution is used for number of occurrences over a continuous field, such as area or time.

rences. So the Poisson distribution, which extends from 0 occurrences per unit to an infinite number of occurrences per unit, may not represent *exactly* any of the random processes mentioned above. Nevertheless, as a *model* the Poisson distribution can often be used to closely approximate such processes.

A typical frequency distribution of observations is illustrated in Figure 4.6. Notice that most of the probability is concentrated near the origin and that the probability of observing large values of the random variable are quite small. Any disparity between what should theoretically be able to occur and what is likely to happen is, therefore, slight. Consequently, when it is said that a random variable is Poisson distributed, what is often meant is that the frequency distribution of occurrences for that variable can be reasonably approximated using a Poisson distribution.

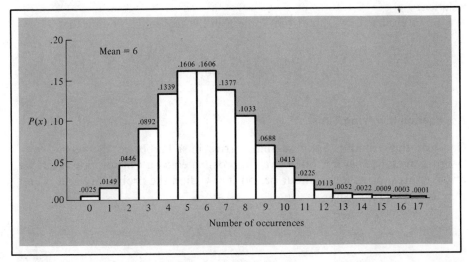

FIGURE 4.6   Histogram of a typical Poisson distribution.

The Poisson distribution can be completely described by a single parameter, the process mean, as suggested in Figure 4.6.* Thus knowing that a random variable has outcomes that are Poisson distributed, and knowing the average number of occurrences per unit, we can determine the probability for any or all of the possible outcomes. As with the binomial, there are two methods for accomplishing this. There are individual and cumulative probability tables from which probabilities for *selected* means can be read, and there is a formula that can be used to compute the probability for *any* mean.

The Poisson Formula

If a random variable is described by a Poisson distribution, then the probability of realizing (observing) any given number of occurrences per unit of measurement (minute, hour, centimeter, square yard, etc.) can be obtained using the formula

$$P(x) = \frac{e^{-\lambda t}(\lambda t)^x}{x!}$$

where x is the number of occurrences; e is the base of natural logarithms (Table F in the Appendix has values for $e^{-\mu}$); λ is the mean rate per unit; and t is the number of units. The quantity λt represents the mean number of occurrences over the interval t. Thus, $\mu = \lambda t$. The formula can be written in a simpler form by substituting the mean μ for λt:

$$P(x) = \frac{e^{-\mu}(\mu)^x}{x!}$$

Example 4   A mechanical process produces shag carpeting that has an average of two defects per yard. Find the probability that a square yard will have exactly one defect, assuming the process can be well approximated by a Poisson distribution.

Solution:
We are given that $\mu = 2$, and from Table F in the Appendix, we find that $e^{-2} = .135$. Thus

$$P(x = 1) = \frac{e^{-2}(2)^1}{1!} = \frac{.135(2)}{1} = .270$$

Application Involving Time

Consider this example. Suppose ships arrive in a harbor at the rate of $\lambda = 2$ ships/hour, and that this rate is well-approximated by a Poisson process. If we observe this process for a $\frac{1}{2}$-hour period $(t = \frac{1}{2})$, find the probability that (a) no ship arrives and (b) 3 ships arrive.

First we find μ.

$$\mu = \lambda t = 2(\tfrac{1}{2}) = 1$$

* The variance of a Poisson distribution equals the mean: mean $= \mu$ and variance $= \mu$.

From Table F we find $e^{-1} = .368$.

(a)
$$P(x = 0) = \frac{e^{-1}(1)^0}{0!} = \frac{e^{-1}(1)}{1} = .368$$

(b)
$$P(x = 3) = \frac{e^{-1}(1)^3}{3!} = \frac{.368}{3 \cdot 2 \cdot 1} = .061$$

Application Involving Area

Suppose that imperfections in yarn can be approximated by a Poisson process with a mean of .2 imperfections/meter ($\lambda = .2$). If lengths of 6 meters ($t = 6$) are inspected, find the probability of less than 2 (i.e., 0 or 1) imperfections.

Again we first determine μ.

$$\mu = \lambda t = .2(6) = 1.2$$

From Table F we find $e^{-1.2} = .301$. Then

$$P(x \leq 1) = P(0) + P(1) = \frac{e^{-1.2}(1.2)^0}{0!} + \frac{e^{-1.2}(1.2)^1}{1!}$$

$$= .301 + .301(1.2) = .6622$$

EXERCISES

*1. Emergency calls come into a police switchboard at the rate of 4/hour during the hours from 1 to 6 A.M. on a nonholiday weekend and can be approximated by the Poisson distribution.
   a. For a 30-minute period, how many emergency calls can be expected?
   b. For a 30-minute period, what is the probability of no calls?
   c. For a 30-minute period, what is the probability of at least 2 calls?
2. The average number of CB radios sold per day by a firm is approximately Poisson, with a mean of 1.5. Find the probability that the firm will sell at least four radios over a:
   a. two-day period   b. three-day period   c. four-day period
3. Defects in a roll of color film average .1 defects/roll, and the distribution of defects is Poisson. Find the probability that any particular roll of color film contains 1 or more defects.
4. Customers arrive at a display room at the rate of 6.5 customers/hour (Poisson). Find the probability that in any given hour:
   a. no customers arrive   b. at least 5 arrive
   c. more than 1 arrive   d. exactly 6.5 arrive

POISSON TABLES

Poisson probability tables provide a convenient method for obtaining probabilities with minimal time and effort. For this reason they should be used whenever possible instead of the formula approach.

Individual Poisson Probabilities

The Poisson tables are actually very similar to the binomial tables, although on the surface they appear quite different. Because the Poisson distribution is a function only of the process mean, the tables are designed to yield probabilities based on the process mean. A portion of the Poisson table from the Appendix is shown in Table 4.4. The selected values of μ, the process mean, (average number of occurrences per unit), are listed across the top of the table, and possible outcomes are listed down the side. The body of the table shows the probability of *exactly x* occurrences per unit.

For example, suppose we have a Poisson process with an average of 3 occurrences per hour, and we want to know the probability of getting exactly 1 occurrence in any given hour. The answer can be found at the intersection of $\mu = 3$ and $x = 1$, as shown in Table 4.4.

TABLE 4.4   Portion of a Poisson Table

x	2.1	2.2	2.3	2.4	2.5	2.6	2.7	2.8	2.9	$\mu \downarrow$ 3.0
0	.1225	.1108	.1003	.0907	.0821	.0743	.0672	.0608	.0550	.0498
→ 1	.2572	.2438	.2306	.2177	.2052	.1931	.1815	.1703	.1596	.1494
2	.2700	.2681	.2652	.2613	.2565	.2510	.2450	.2384	.2314	.2240
3	.1890	.1966	.2033	.2090	.2138	.2176	.2205	.2225	.2237	.2240
4	.0992	.1082	.1169	.1254	.1336	.1414	.1488	.1557	.1622	.1680
5	.0417	.0476	.0538	.0602	.0668	.0735	.0804	.0872	.0940	.1008
6	.0146	.0174	.0206	.0241	.0278	.0319	.0362	.0407	.0455	.0504
7	.0044	.0055	.0068	.0083	.0099	.0118	.0139	.0163	.0188	.0216
8	.0011	.0015	.0019	.0025	.0031	.0038	.0047	.0057	.0068	.0081
9	.0003	.0004	.0005	.0007	.0009	.0011	.0014	.0018	.0022	.0027
10	.0001	.0001	.0001	.0002	.0002	.0003	.0004	.0005	.0006	.0008
11	.0000	.0000	.0000	.0000	.0000	.0001	.0001	.0001	.0002	.0002
12	.0000	.0000	.0000	.0000	.0000	.0000	.0000	.0000	.0000	.0001

Here are some examples of Poisson probabilities obtained from the table of individual probabilities.

μ	x	$P(x)$
2.1	0	.1225
2.4	1	.2177
3.0	2	.2240
2.2	2	.2681
3.0	5	.1008
2.8	10	.0005

Notice in the table that for each mean, the sum of the probabilities of the various possible outcomes equals 1.00.

The Cumulative Poisson Table

The cumulative Poisson table provides sums of probabilities, just as did the cumulative binomial table. The table shows probabilities for x or less occurrences, given the process mean. A portion of a cumulative Poisson table is shown in Table 4.5. And again, listing all the possible outcomes and underlining those outcomes for which you want the probability will simplify working with the cumulative table.

TABLE 4.5   Portion of a Cumulative Poisson Table

	μ									
	3.0	3.1	3.2	3.3	3.4	3.5	3.6	3.7	3.8	3.9
0	.0498	.0450	.0408	.0369	.0334	.0302	.0273	.0247	.0224	.0202
1	.1991	.1847	.1712	.1586	.1468	.1359	.1257	.1162	.1074	.0992
2	.4232	.4012	.3799	.3594	.3397	.3208	.3027	.2854	.2689	.2531
3	.6472	.6248	.6025	.5803	.5584	.5366	.5152	.4942	.4735	.4532
4	.8153	.7982	.7806	.7626	.7442	.7254	.7064	.6872	.6678	.6484
5	.9161	.9057	.8946	.8829	.8705	.8576	.8441	.8301	.8156	.8006
6	.9665	.9612	.9554	.9490	.9421	.9347	.9267	.9182	.9091	.8995
7	.9881	.9858	.9832	.9802	.9769	.9733	.9692	.9648	.9599	.9546
8	.9962	.9953	.9943	.9931	.9917	.9901	.9883	.9863	.9840	.9815
9	.9989	.9986	.9982	.9978	.9973	.9967	.9960	.9952	.9942	.9931
10	.9997	.9996	.9995	.9994	.9992	.9990	.9987	.9984	.9981	.9977
11	.9999	.9999	.9999	.9998	.9998	.9997	.9996	.9995	.9994	.9993
12	1.0000	1.0000	1.0000	1.0000	.9999	.9999	.9999	.9999	.9998	.9998
13	1.0000	1.0000	1.0000	1.0000	1.0000	1.0000	1.0000	1.0000	1.0000	.9999
14	1.0000	1.0000	1.0000	1.0000	1.0000	1.0000	1.0000	1.0000	1.0000	1.0000

Some probabilities that were obtained from the cumulative Poisson table in the Appendix are shown in Table 4.6.

TABLE 4.6   Using the Cumulative Poisson Table

μ	Desired probability for	Includes outcomes	Calculations	$P(x)$
.8	$x \leq 1$	0, 1	read directly	.809
1.2	$x < 3$	0, 1, 2	read $P(x \leq 2)$	.879
1.5	$x = 0$	0	read directly	.223
2.0	$x > 3$	4, 5, 6, …	$1 - P(x \leq 3)$	.143
2.6	$1 < x \leq 4$	2, 3, 4	$P(x \leq 4) - P(x \leq 1)$	.610
3.8	$1 \leq x \leq 4$	1, 2, 3, 4	$P(x \leq 4) - P(x = 0)$	.646
5.6	$1 \leq x \leq 4$	1, 2, 3, 4	$P(x \leq 4) - P(x = 0)$	.338
6.0	$x \geq 5$	5, 6, 7, …	$1 - P(x \leq 4)$	.715

For values of μ that are not in the table, we can find a more extensive table, or interpolate (for approximate values) in the table, or resort to a mathematical formula for Poisson probabilities.

The Poisson Distribution as
an Approximation to the Binomial

Under certain circumstances the Poisson distribution can be used to approximate binomial probabilities. The approximation is most appropriate when the number of observations n is large and the probability of success p is near 0 or near 1.00. It is desirable to have an alternative approach for obtaining binomial probabilities for these reasons:

1. The binomial distribution adequately describes many situations of interest.
2. Most tables are limited to $n \le 20$.
3. The binomial formula can require substantial effort to obtain an exact solution.

The advantages in the approximation are that accuracy suffers very little and that the effort involved is often considerably less. To use the approximation it is necessary to determine only the mean, or expected value, of the binomial distribution. This is then used as the process mean for the Poisson distribution. That is, the process average μ equals the binomial average np.

Example 5 Find the probability of 4 defectives in a sample of 300 taken from a large lot if there are 2% defective in the lot.

Solution:
Since the values $n = 300$ and $p = .02$ are beyond the range of values found in our binomial table, the alternatives would be either to search for a more extensive table, resort to using the binomial probability formula,

$$P(x = 4) = \binom{300}{4}(.02)^4(.98)^{296}$$

(which would turn out to be a monumental task), or use the Poisson approximation, with $\mu = np$. Thus

$$\mu = np = 300(.02) = 6$$

From the Poisson formula,

$$P(x = 4) = \frac{\mu^x \cdot e^{-\mu}}{x!} = \frac{6^4 e^{-6}}{4!} = .135$$

The same result can be obtained by using a Poisson table: when $\mu = 6$, from the table $P(x = 4)$ is .135.

Some of the essential features of the Poisson and binomial distributions are compared in Table 4.7.

TABLE 4.7   A Comparison of the Binomial and Poisson Distributions

	Binomial	Poisson
Possible outcomes	integers 0 to n	integers 0 to $+\infty$
Observations	count of either successes or failures	count successes only
Parameters	n and p	μ

EXERCISES

1. Use a Poisson table to determine each of these probabilities:

Mean	Probability of
1	1
1.5	0
2	1 or less
3	1 or less
3	more than 3
3	3
4	3
4.2	more than 5

2. Rework the Poisson formula exercises listed below using a cumulative Poisson table.
   a. Exercise 1 (page 123)   b. Exercise 3 (page 123)
   c. Exercise 2a (page 123)   d. Exercise 2c (page 123)
3. Trucks arrive at a depot at a mean rate of 2.8 trucks/hour. Find the probability of having 3 or more trucks arriving in a:
   a. 30-minute period   b. 1-hour period   c. 2-hour period
4. Telephone calls come into a switchboard at the rate of 4.6 calls per minute. Find the probability of each of these occurrences during a one-minute interval:
   a. exactly 2 calls
   b. at least 2 calls
   c. no calls
   d. anywhere from 2 to 6 calls
5. Accidents in a large firm are approximately Poisson distributed, with a mean of 3 accidents/month. Find the probability that in any given month there will be:
   a. no accidents   b. 1 accident   c. 3 or 4 accidents
6. If 3% of the people living in a large city are government employees, determine the probability of finding no government employees in a random sample of 50 people in that city. What is the probability of finding 3 or less in the sample?
7. Two percent of the letters mailed at a certain location have incorrect postage. In 400 such letters:
   a. How many with incorrect postage would you expect?
   b. What is the probability of finding 5 or less with incorrect postage?
   c. What is the probability of finding more than 5 with incorrect postage?
   d. What is the probability of finding 5 or more with incorrect postage?
8. The probability of selling an insurance policy to persons who answer a special advertisement is estimated to be .01. On this basis, if 1000 people answer the ad, what is the probability that:
   a. None will buy a policy?
   b. At least 1 will buy a policy?
   c. More than 10 will buy policies?
9. How would your answers differ in Exercise 7 if the percentage of letters with incorrect postage were .4%?

OTHER DISCRETE DISTRIBUTIONS

There are two other distributions worth mentioning at this time, both of which are variations of the binomial distribution.

The *multinomial* distribution is used in situations where there are *more than two* mutually exclusive outcomes. As with the binomial, we have the requirements of independent trials with constant probability. An example of a multinomial variable is rolling a die, which has six possible outcomes. In contrast to previous examples, which treated this by classifying the six outcomes into *two* classes, the multinomial approach would yield from three to six classes, depending on how the outcomes are categorized. For example, we could have these three classes: 1 and 2, 3 and 4, 5 and 6. Another example is drawing beads from a bowl with many different colors of beads. Each color type can be treated as a category, or certain colors can be grouped (thus red and green can be lumped into the same category).

The multinomial probability that, in n observations, outcome E_1 occurs x_1 times, E_2 occurs x_2 times, . . . , and E_k occurs x_k times is expressed by the formula

$$\frac{n!}{n_1!\, n_2! \cdots n_k!}\, (P_1{}^{n_1} P_2{}^{n_2} \cdots P_k{}^{n_k})$$

where

$$n = \sum_{i=1}^{k} n_i$$

and P_i is the probability of event E_i on each observation.

Example 6   A manager learns that 80% of the output of a certain machine is acceptable, 15% needs some reworking, and 5% must be scrapped. In a sample of $n = 10$, what is the probability of obtaining 8 good parts, 2 that must be reworked, and none that must be scrapped?

$$\frac{10!}{8!\, 2!\, 0!}\, (.80)^8 (.15)^2 (.05)^0 = .17$$

The *hypergeometric* distribution pertains to situations with two or more outcomes in which the probability of success *changes* from trial to trial. For example, suppose that there are 10 names written 1 each on 10 pieces of paper and placed in a hat. Your name is on 1 piece of paper. The papers are mixed and 1 name is drawn. The probability it will be yours is $\frac{1}{10}$. When the name is read off, it turns out not to be yours. Then a second name is drawn from the remaining 9 names. The probability that this one will be your name is now $\frac{1}{9}$, whereas previously it was $\frac{1}{10}$. Hence the probability of this outcome on the second draw is *conditional* (dependent) on the results of the first draw. For instance, if that first name had been yours, then the probability that the second name would be yours would drop to 0 assuming that names are not replaced in the hat between draws.

In general, hypergeometric probabilities can be obtained from the formula

$$P(x|N, r, n) = \frac{\dbinom{N - r}{n - x}\dbinom{r}{x}}{\dbinom{N}{n}}$$

where N is the population size, n is the sample size, r is the number of successes in the population, and x is the number of successes in the sample.

Example 7 Two fuses in a box of 10 fuses are defective. If a random sample of 4 fuses is examined, what is the probability of having (a) no defectives; (b) 1 defective; (c) 1 or less defective?

Solution:
We have $N = 10$, $r = 2$, and $n = 4$.

(a)
$$P(x = 0) = \frac{\binom{10-2}{4-0}\binom{2}{0}}{\binom{10}{4}} = \frac{\binom{8}{4}\binom{2}{0}}{\binom{10}{4}} = .333$$

(b)
$$P(x = 1) = \frac{\binom{10-2}{4-1}\binom{2}{1}}{\binom{10}{4}} = \frac{\binom{8}{3}\binom{2}{1}}{\binom{10}{4}} = .533$$

(c)
$$P(x \leq 1) = P(0) + P(1) = .333 + .533 = .866$$

Table 4.8 lists the probability models we have discussed and the situations in which those models are most useful.

TABLE 4.8 Applications of Discrete Probability Distributions

Distribution		Examples	Assumptions
binomial	two outcomes	coin tossing true-false test defective-nondefective	independent observation constant probability
Poisson	occurrences only	accidents/year defects/yard calls/minute	independent observation constant probability
hypergeometric	two or more outcomes	sampling without replacement	dependent observations
multinomial	more than two outcomes	multiple-choice test	independent observation constant probability

EXERCISES

*1. A recent nationwide survey suggested that at 9 P.M. Sunday evening, 40% of the viewing audience were tuned to Network A, 30% to Network B, and 30% to Network C.
   a. In a random sample of 10 viewers, how many would you expect to be tuned to each network?
   b. What is the probability that all are tuned to A?
   c. What is the probability that 4 are tuned to A, 3 to B, and 3 to C?

2. Three vendors supply replacement parts. Vendor A supplies 50% of the parts, B supplies 40%, and C supplies 10%. Five parts are randomly selected from the supply room and inspected for defects.

    a. What is the probability all five have been supplied by Vendor *A*?

    b. What is the probability of two from *A*, two from *B*, and one from *C*?

3. Thirty percent of the students at a university are freshmen, 30% sophomores, 20% juniors, and 20% seniors. A random sample of eight students is taken from a list of all students. Find the probability of these sample results:

    a. two students from each class

    b. three freshmen, three sophomores, two juniors, and no seniors

*4. A series of eight electrical parts are connected in such a way that if one part fails, the system will not operate. Two parts have failed.

    a. What is the probability that the first part that is inspected will be one that failed?

    b. What is the probability of finding both parts that failed if four parts are inspected?

    c. How many parts must be inspected to achieve a 70% probability of finding both bad parts?

5. Seven students have not yet made their class presentations. The instructor must select two students for today's class. However, one student has asked to be excused from consideration due to extenuating circumstances. The instructor has agreed to this but can't remember which student is excused. What is the probability that the excused student will *not* be chosen, assuming random selection among the seven?

REVIEW QUESTIONS

1. Explain what a probability distribution is and indicate how it is useful in obtaining probabilities.
2. State the assumptions that pertain to the binomial distribution.
3. State the assumptions that pertain to the Poisson distribution.
4. What are the parameters of the binomial distribution?
5. What are the parameters of the Poisson distribution?
6. Contrast the term "success" as it relates to the binomial distribution with the term as it relates to the Poisson distribution.
7. Compare and contrast individual and cumulative probability tables.
8. Under what conditions should a formula be used instead of a probability table?
9. Explain how probability distributions serve as models.

SUPPLEMENTAL EXERCISES

1. Ten percent of the tomato plants purchased from local nurseries generally die before bearing fruit.

    a. If you buy 10 plants, what is the probability that no more than 1 die before bearing fruit?

    b. What is the least number of plants that must be purchased if you want to be at least 95% sure that 10 or more will not die before bearing fruit?

2. The probability of any single lottery ticket winning a prize is 1/1000. A man intends to buy 50 tickets.

    a. What is the probability that none will be winning tickets?

    b. What is the probability that at least one will be a winning ticket?

3. Defects in rolls of wallpaper are known to be approximated by a Poisson distribution, with a mean of 2 defects/10-meter roll. You buy half of a roll. Find these probabilities:

    a. 0 defects   b. 1 defect   c. more than 1 defect

4. Suppose 5% of a company's purchasing invoices contain errors in material specifications or in catalog numbers, and a sample of 15 invoices is examined carefully.

    a. How many invoices with such errors would you expect to find?

    b. What is the probability of finding 1 or less with errors?

5. According to insurance company estimates, the probability of a house fire is 1 % per year. The firm insures 400 homes.

    a. If many of the policyholders live in adjacent houses, why might this invalidate use of the binomial or Poisson distribution?

    b. Suppose the policyholders are widely scattered. What is the probability of 0 fires? At least 1 fire?

*6. Answer part b of Exercise 5 if the probability of fire is .1% per year.

7. The average number of prints that do not develop properly on a 12-exposure film is 1.

    a. Find the probability of 0 failures.

    b. Find the probability of 2 or more failures.

    c. Find the probability of 3 or more failures.

8. Suppose the failure rate in Exercise 7 is 1 out of 20. Recompute your answers.

*9. Thread Mills produces bolts of cloth that average 2.2 defects per square yard. Find these probabilities:

    a. A square yard will have no more than 4 defects.

    b. A square yard will have no defects.

    c. A square yard will have at least 2 defects.

    d. There will be exactly 1 defect in 2 square yards.

    e. There will be no defects in 2 square yards.

    f. Two square yards will each have 2 defects.

10. Assume that the percentage of persons in a large eastern city who own municipal bonds of that city is 2%.

    a. Find the probability that in a sample of 10 residents of this city, none own municipal city bonds.

    b. Find the probability that in a sample of 100, more than 2% own bonds.

11. Due to the destructive nature of testing explosion-proof conduit, a fairly small sample of parts is inspected. If 1 part is defective in a lot of 20, what is the probability that it will be found if a sample of 4 parts is taken?

12. Suppose that 20% of the adults living in a large city were born in that city, that 25% of the adults were born in the state but not in the city, that 40% were born in the United States but outside the state, and that the rest were born outside the United States. A sample of four adults is taken. Find these probabilities:

    a. None were born in the city.

    b. Each of the four segments is represented in the sample.

    c. None was born in either the city or the state.

13. Cost estimates for three parts of a remodeling project and their standard deviations are $\mu_a = \$3000$ and $\sigma_a = \$400$, $\mu_b = \$6000$ and $\sigma_b = \$1000$, $\mu_c = \$8000$ and $\sigma_c = \$800$. Find the expected cost for these three parts and the standard deviation of that cost.

14. The probability of a house fire in a certain area is .002. The average damage caused by such a fire is \$20,000. How much should a homeowner be willing to pay for fire insurance?

5

continuous probability distributions

Chapter Objectives

After completing this chapter, you should be able to:
1. Explain the basic differences between continuous and discrete probability distributions
2. Explain why continuous probabilities are related to *areas*
3. Describe the main characteristics of a normal distribution
4. Convert any normal distribution to a standard normal distribution
5. Use the table of normal distribution areas to obtain probabilities
6. Find the area under a normal curve between any two points
7. Use the normal distribution to approximate binomial probabilities
8. Solve problems involving the uniform or exponential distribution

Chapter Outline

Introduction
The Uniform Distribution
Normal Distributions
    Characteristics of normal distributions
    The normal distribution as a model
    The standard normal distribution
    The standard normal table
    The normal distribution as an approximation to the binomial
The Exponential Distribution
Summary

INTRODUCTION

WHEN A discrete random variable has a large number of possible outcomes, or when the random variable under consideration is continuous, discrete probability distributions such as the Poisson and the binomial cannot be used to obtain relevant probabilities. A discrete variable with many possible outcomes would require a very extensive table or a monumental effort in using a formula to obtain probabilities. A continuous variable, because outcomes include noninteger as well as integer values, cannot be adequately handled by a discrete distribution.

The spinner shown in Figure 5.1 illustrates the concept of a continuous variable. Once it is spun, the spinner or pointer could reasonably come to rest at any point along the circle. It certainly does not have to come to rest precisely at one of the integer values shown. Even allowing for the limitations involved in measuring along the circle, there are still an extremely large number of possible stopping points.

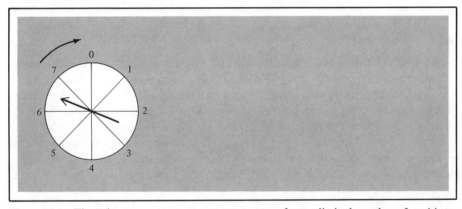

FIGURE 5.1 The spinner can come to rest at any one of an unlimited number of positions.

For instance, imagine that the circle is divided into 8000 equal parts instead of 8. If we assume that each position is as likely a stopping point as any other, we are led to the following conclusion: Since there are so many possible outcomes, the probability that the pointer will stop at *any* particular value is so small, for all practical purposes, it must be regarded as approximately equal to zero.* In fact, modern technology would permit us to identify at least 1 million different positions,

---

* The implication is that it is virtually impossible to predict the precise stopping point of the spinner in advance.

135

so the probability of having the pointer end up at one position would be 1/1,000,000, or .000001.

Because of this peculiarity, it is really meaningless to talk in terms of the probability of some *specific* outcome, as we often did in our discussion of discontinuous probability distributions. Therefore, analysis of continuous variables tends to focus on the probability that a random variable will assume a value *within some range or interval*. Thus while the probability that the pointer will stop at either 3 or 4 is approximately zero, the probability that it will stop *between* those two values is not zero. Since the circle is divided into eight equal areas, it might seem reasonable to assign a probability of $\frac{1}{8}$ to the outcome "stop between 3 and 4," as illustrated in Figure 5.2. Furthermore, since $P(x = 3)$ and $P(x = 4)$ are both approximately equal to zero, it is not necessary to make a distinction between $3 < x < 4$ and $3 \leq x \leq 4$, as it was for discrete probabilities.

FIGURE 5.2   The probability that the point of the spinner will come to rest between two points is equal to the percentage of area between the two points.

Similarly, we would assign a probability of 25% to the event "the pointer comes to rest between the points 4 and 6 ($\frac{1}{4}$ of the circle)." And there is no reason to limit the ranges to integer values, other than for convenience. For instance, the probability of observing a value between 3.217 and 4.217 (note: $4.217 - 3.217 = 1$) would also be $\frac{1}{8}$, and the probability of observing a value between 3.5 and 4 [i.e., $4 - 3.5 = .5$] is $\frac{1}{16}$ [i.e., $\frac{.5}{8}$]. Thus the probability of the pointer coming to a stop between any two points is equal to the percentage of the circle *area* encompassed by those two points. (See Figure 5.3). Moreover, a circle twice as large as this

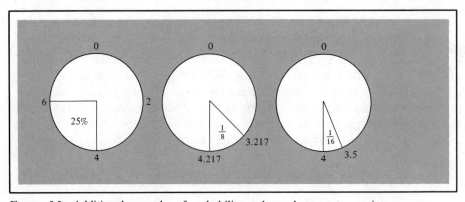

FIGURE 5.3   Additional examples of probability and area between two points.

would yield the same probabilities if its perimeter were numbered in the same way (see Figure 5.4). Hence with a continuous random variable, probability is determined by the percentage of area between two values.

In the following pages three continuous probability distributions are discussed: the uniform, the normal, and the exponential distributions.

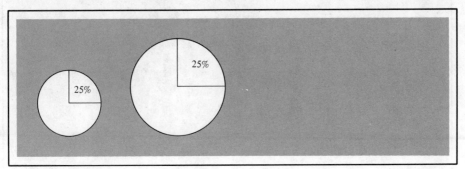

FIGURE 5.4   The *size* of the circle is immaterial.

THE UNIFORM DISTRIBUTION

When a random variable can assume any value on a continuous scale between two points, and do this in such a way that no value is more likely than another, then the probabilities associated with the random variable can be described by the uniform distribution. The preceding example of the spinner fits this category: all points along the edge of the circle are equally likely. Graphically, the uniform distribution is portrayed as a rectangle bounded by points a and b, which represent the range of possible outcomes. See Figure 5.5(a). The height of the rectangle is treated as being equal to $1/b-a$, and the area of the rectangle is to be considered 100%. Consequently, the *area* under the rectangle between any two points c and d is equal to the percentage of the total range included between c and d:

$$P(c \leq x \leq d) = \frac{d - c}{b - a}$$

See Figure 5.5(b).

For instance, suppose a salesperson calls into the home office every afternoon between 3:00 and 4:00, and office records show that no one time is any more likely for the call than any other in that time interval. Because time is measured on a continuous scale, the probability of a call between any two points in time is equal to the ratio of that time to the 1-hour interval. Hence the probability of the call occurring between 3:00 and 3:15 is $\frac{15}{60} = .25$. The probability that the call occurs at exactly 3:15 is treated as being approximately equal to zero, since calls can occur on the minute as well as any of the (infinite) points between, such as 3:15 and .00333 seconds. Now when we say that the probability of a call at exactly 3:15 is zero, this does not mean that a call cannot occur at that time, but only that with an infinite range of possibilities, it would be impossible to select one exact time at which to *predict* that the call will occur. See Figure 5.5(c).

In certain applications it is necessary to utilize the mean and variance of a probability distribution. The mean of a uniform distribution with end points a

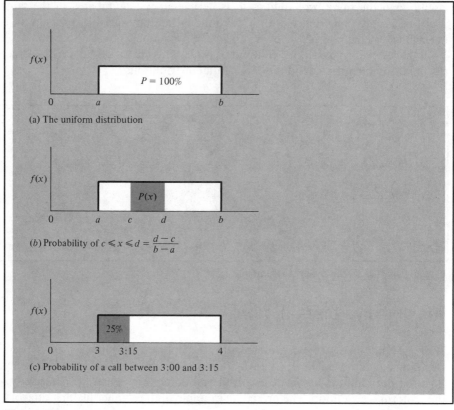

FIGURE 5.5

and b is

$$\mu = \frac{a + b}{2}$$

and the variance is

$$\sigma^2 = \frac{(b - a)^2}{12}$$

EXERCISES

1. Bulk sales of gasoline at a depot have a mean of 40,000 gallons per day and a minimum of 30,000 gallons per day. Assume a uniform distribution is appropriate.
   a. Find the maximum daily sales.
   b. What percentage of the days will sales exceed 34,000 gallons?
2. A small firm cuts and sells logs for fireplaces. Lengths of logs vary uniformly between 2 feet and 3 feet.
   a. What is the average length of a log?
   b. What is the probability that any given log will be:
      (1) longer than 2.6 feet?   (2) more than 3 feet long?
      (3) shorter than average?   (4) exactly 2 feet long?
      (5) between 2 feet and 3 feet?

3. Suppose the daily high temperature in January in a rural area has tended in the past to vary uniformly between 0°C and 6°C.
   a. What percentage of days can be expected to have a high in excess of 3.5°C?
   b. If the weather forecaster wants to minimize prediction error, what temperature should she predict?
   c. What is the probability that on any given January day the temperature will not exceed 1°C?

*4. The amount of ice cream sold on Tuesdays at a soda fountain is known to be uniformly distributed and ranges between 20 and 50 gallons.
   a. What is the probability of selling 40 or more gallons on Tuesday?
   b. What is the probability of selling 40 or more gallons on Monday?
   c. If the store realizes a profit of $.30/gallon, what is the expected profit for Tuesday's sales of ice cream?
   d. What is the probability that Tuesday's profit on ice cream will be below $7.50?

NORMAL DISTRIBUTIONS

Normal distributions occupy a prominent position in both theoretical and applied statistics for a number of reasons. One reason is that they often closely match the observed frequency distributions of many natural and physical measurements. Another reason is that they can be used to approximate binomial probabilities when *n* is large. However, the most important reason for the prominence of the normal distribution is that distributions of both sample means and proportions of large samples tend to be normally distributed, which has important implications in sampling.

Normal distributions were first "discovered" in the eighteenth century. Astronomers and other scientists observed, with some amazement, that repeated measurements of the same quantity (like distance to the moon or mass of an object) tended to vary, and when large numbers of these measurements were collected into a frequency distribution, one shape, similar to that shown in Figure 5.6, kept reappearing. Because the shape was associated with errors of measurement, it soon

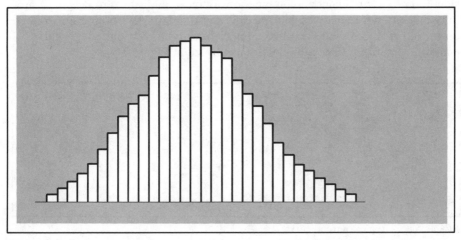

FIGURE 5.6   Frequency distributions of observations often had the same shape.

became known as the "normal distribution of error," or simply the "normal distribution." It was subsequently discovered that the distribution could be closely approximated with a mathematical continuous distribution, like the one shown in Figure 5.7. The distribution is sometimes referred to as a Gaussian distribution in recognition of the contributions of Karl Gauss (1777–1855) to the mathematical theory of the normal distribution.

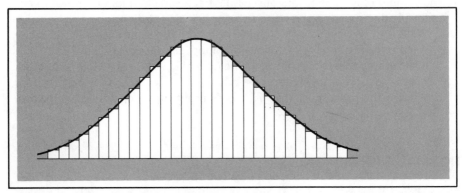

Figure 5.7   A continuous curve that approximates the observed frequency distribution.

Characteristics of Normal Distributions

Normal curves have some rather special characteristics in terms of their shape, how they are specified, and how they are used to obtain probabilities.

The graph of a normal distribution, as we have seen, looks very much like a bell: It is smooth, unimodal, and symmetrical around its mean. Less obvious is the fact that the curve extends forever in either direction from the mean. It comes closer and closer to the horizontal axis as the distance from the mean increases, but it never actually touches the axis. Theoretically, the possible values range from $-\infty$ to $+\infty$. See Figure 5.8.

Another important characteristic is that a normal distribution can be completely specified by two parameters: its mean and its standard deviation. In other words, there is a unique normal distribution for each combination of a mean and a standard deviation. Different combinations of mean and standard deviation produce different normal curves. Since means and standard deviations are measured on a *continuous* scale, the possible number of normal distributions or curves is endless. A few of those possibilities are illustrated in Figure 5.9.

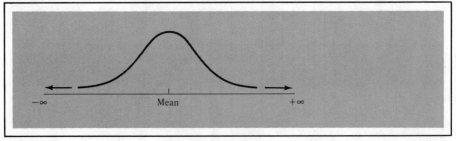

Figure 5.8   A typical normal curve.

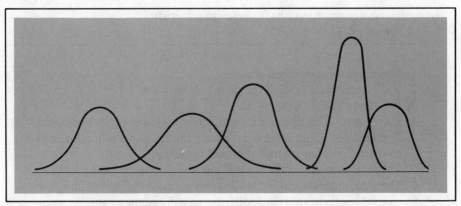

FIGURE 5.9   The combinations of mean and standard deviation are endless.

The total area under any normal curve represents 100% of the probability associated with that variable. Moreover, since the curve is symmetrical around its mean, the probability of observing a value less than the mean is 50%, as is the probability of observing a value greater than the mean. The probability of exactly (predicting) any value is 0 since the scale of measurement is continuous. Hence the probability of observing a value exactly equal to the mean is also 0.

The probability that a random variable which is normally distributed will assume a value between any two points is equal to the area under the normal curve between those two points, as illustrated in Figure 5.10.

> The probability that a random variable will have a value between any two points is equal to the area under the normal curve between those two points.

One important consequence of the fact that a normal curve can be completely specified by its mean and standard deviation is that the area under the curve between any point and the mean is a function only of the number of standard deviations that point is from the mean. *This is the key that enables us to compute probabilities for the normal curve.*

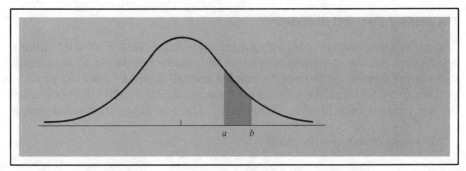

FIGURE 5.10 $P(a < x < b)$ = area under the curve between a and b.

In summary, normal curves have these characteristics:

---

1. The normal curve is bell-shaped.
2. It is symmetrical around the distribution mean.
3. It extends from $-\infty$ to $+\infty$.
4. Each normal distribution is completely specified by its mean and standard deviation; there is a different normal distribution for each combination of mean and standard deviation.
5. The total area under the normal curve is considered to be 100%.
6. The area under the curve between two points is the probability that a variable which is normally distributed will assume a value between those two points.
7. Since there are an unlimited number of values in the range from $-\infty$ to $+\infty$, the probability that a normally distributed random variable will *exactly* equal any given value is approximately zero. Therefore, probabilities are always given for a *range of values.*
8. The area under the curve between the mean and any other point is a function of the number of standard deviations that point is from the mean.

The Normal Distribution as a Model

It is essential to recognize that a normal distribution is a theoretical distribution. For physical measurements that have been grouped into a frequency distribution, it is an ideal distribution, since no set of actual data would conform exactly to it. For instance, real data would not vary between $-\infty$ and $+\infty$. And limitations of measuring instruments will effectively eliminate many other potential values. Nonetheless, such deficiencies are outweighed by the ease of using the normal distribution to obtain probabilities and by the fact that the normal distribution still provides reasonably good approximations to real data. Thus when a random (physical) variable is said to be normally distributed, this should be interpreted as implying that a frequency distribution of its possible outcomes can be approximated reasonably well using a normal probability distribution. Hence the normal curve is a *model.*

The Standard Normal Distribution

The normal distribution is actually an infinitely large "family" of distributions, one for each possible combination of mean and standard deviation. Consequently, it would be fruitless to attempt to develop enough tables to meet the needs of possible users. Likewise, the formula for the normal distribution is not well suited for this purpose because of its complexity.* There is, however, a rather simple

---

* The formula for the normal distribution is

$$f(x) = \frac{1}{\sqrt{2\pi}\sigma} e^{-[(1/2)[(x-\mu)/\sigma]^2]}$$

alternative which avoids these problems. It is conceptually similar to finding "spinner" probabilities. We saw that for the spinner problem the *size* of the circle was unimportant; it was the *shape* that counted. As long as the total area of the circle was taken as 100%, a circle of any size would yield identical probabilities. And so it is with normal distributions: taking the area under the curve as 100% standardizes the curve.

If a variable is normally distributed, then about 68% of its values will fall within one standard deviation of the mean; 95.5% will fall within two standard deviations of the mean; and about 99.7% will fall within three standard deviations of the mean. This idea is illustrated in Figure 5.11. Furthermore, this is true regardless of whatever mean and standard deviation a particular normal distribution has; it is true for *all* normal distributions.

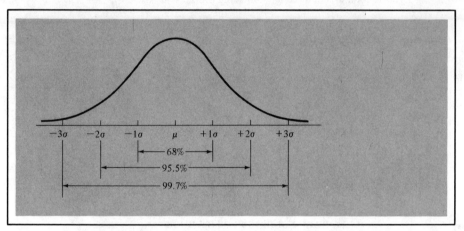

FIGURE 5.11   Area under a normal curve within 1, 2, and 3 standard deviations of the mean.

In a moment we will learn how these and other percentages can be determined. But for now let us just reflect upon the significance of this fact. The implication is that the problem of dealing with an infinite family of normal distributions can be completely avoided if we are willing to work in terms of *relative* values instead of actual values. This amounts to using the mean as a reference point and the standard deviation as a measure of deviation from that reference point. This new scale is commonly known as a *z scale*.

Consider a normal distribution with a mean of 100.0 and a standard deviation of 10.0, as portrayed in Figure 5.12. We can convert this actual scale to a relative, or standardized, scale, by substituting "number of standard deviations from distribution mean" values for actual values.

Although only a few selected values are shown in Figure 5.12, the same concept can be applied to any distribution value. Hence the value 90 is -10 below the mean, or $-\frac{10}{10} = -1$ standard deviation; 120 is $+20$ above the mean, or $\frac{20}{10} = 2$ standard deviations; and so on. The value 95 would be $-.5$ standard deviations ($\frac{5}{10}$ standard deviations below the mean) and 107 would be $+.7$ standard deviations ($\frac{7}{10}$ standard deviations above the mean).

We can summarize this procedure in the following manner: Convert the actual difference between the mean and some other distribution value to a relative

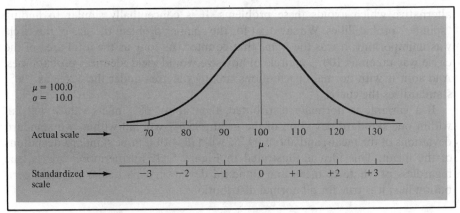

FIGURE 5.12   A comparison of actual and standardized scales.

difference by expressing that difference in terms of the number of standard deviations from the mean. Algebraically, this can be written as shown in the box.

$$z = \frac{x - \mu}{\sigma}$$

where

z = the number of standard deviations from the mean

x = some value of interest

μ = the mean of a normal distribution

σ = the standard deviation

Note that z has a minus sign for values of x that are less than the mean and a plus sign for values greater than the mean.

Here are some examples of the conversion of the actual difference between the mean and another value to the relative distance in terms of the number of standard deviations.

μ Mean	σ Standard deviation	x Value of interest	$x - \mu$ Difference	$(x - \mu)/\sigma = z$ Relative difference
40	1	42	2	+2
25	2	23	−2	−1
30	2.5	37.5	7.5	+3
18	3	13.5	−4.5	−1.5
22	4	22	0	0

It is also necessary to be able to work in reverse, going from z-values to actual values. For instance, we might want to know what actual value would be the equivalent of $z = +2$. Assuming we know the mean and standard deviation and that we are considering a *normal* distribution, the conversion takes the form

$$\text{actual value} = \mu + z\sigma$$

Here are some examples of this.

μ Mean	σ Standard deviation	z	$\mu + z\sigma$ Calculation	Actual value
20	1	+3	20 + 3(1)	23
50	3	−1	50 − 1(3)	47
60	2	−2	60 − 2(2)	56
72	5	+.3	72 + .3(5)	73.5

There is a great advantage in being able to think and work with relative values. It means that instead of having to cope with an unlimited family of normal distributions, a single distribution can be used for all problems. We can convert any value from any normal distribution into a z-value, or z score, which will tell us how many standard deviations that value is from the distribution mean. This permits us to determine various probabilities based on the normal curve by using a *single standardized table*, which is designed solely for this purpose.

The Standard Normal Table

Areas under the curve for any normal distribution can be found by using a standard normal table by changing the scale from actual units to standard units. The distribution mean serves as a reference point and the standard deviation as the yardstick that measures relative distance from the mean. The standard normal table is designed so that it can be read in units of z, the number of standard deviations from the mean. The table shows the area under the curve (i.e., the probability that a value will fall in that range) between the mean and selected values of z. The shaded portion of Figure 5.13 corresponds to the area under the curve that can be read directly from the table. Note that the mean of the distribution is 0, since the mean is 0 standard deviations from itself.

Since the normal distribution is symmetrical around its mean, the left half of the curve is a mirror image of the right half. And because of this symmetry, it is customary to provide only one-half of the distribution in a table. In other words, for each segment on the left side, there is a corresponding segment on the right. It is

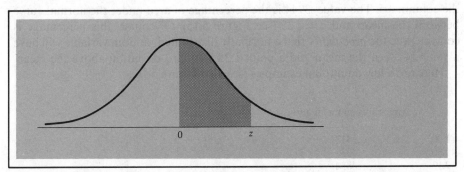

FIGURE 5.13   Area under a normal curve shown in a normal table.

common to provide a table of the *right half* of the distribution. Then if a portion of the left half is needed, those values are treated as positive deviations instead of negative deviations. For example, the area under the curve between the mean and +1 standard deviation is exactly equal to the area under the curve between the mean and −1 standard deviation, as illustrated in Figure 5.14.

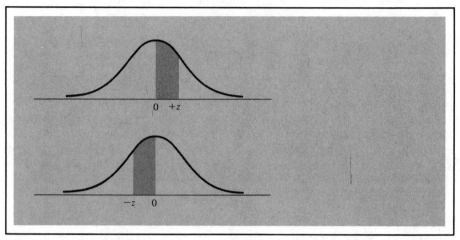

FIGURE 5.14   The area under the curve between the mean and +z equals the area under the curve between the mean and −z.

We can now turn our attention to the table itself. Table 5.1 will be used for discussion purposes here; Table G in the Appendix is identical to Table 5.1. The table is indexed in terms of z-values to two decimals (nearest hundredth), such as 2.78, 1.04, and 2.45. One peculiarity of a typical normal table is that the values of z are shown in two parts, which is always a little confusing for beginners but is not of any consequence once you become familiar with it. Values of the integer and first decimal (like 1.3, 2.5, .7) are listed down the *left side* of the table, while the last digit appears across the *top*. Let us find some areas under the curve between the mean and z to demonstrate the use of the table.

Suppose we want the area between the mean and z when z = 1.25. We must first locate 1.2 on the left side of the table and then locate .05 (5 is the last digit) across the top. The area under the curve can be read at the intersection of the row z = 1.2 and the column .05. The value .3944 is the percentage of area under the normal curve between the mean and z = 1.25 (see Figure 5.15). Of course, this percentage is equivalent to the *probability* that a normally distributed random variable will have a value between the mean and a point 1.25 standard deviation above the mean.

Here are a few additional examples (see also Figure 5.16).

z	Area between mean and z
+1.00	.3413
+1.50	.4332
+2.13	.4834
+2.77	.4972

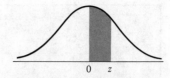

TABLE 5.1   Areas for Standard Normal Probability Distribution

z	.00	.01	.02	.03	.04	.05	.06	.07	.08	.09
.0	.0000	.0040	.0080	.0120	.0160	.0199	.0239	.0279	.0319	.0359
.1	.0398	.0438	.0478	.0517	.0557	.0596	.0636	.0675	.0714	.0753
.2	.0793	.0832	.0871	.0910	.0948	.0987	.1026	.1064	.1103	.1141
.3	.1179	.1217	.1255	.1293	.1331	.1368	.1406	.1443	.1480	.1517
.4	.1554	.1591	.1628	.1664	.1700	.1736	.1772	.1808	.1844	.1879
.5	.1915	.1950	.1985	.2019	.2054	.2088	.2123	.2157	.2190	.2224
.6	.2257	.2291	.2324	.2357	.2389	.2422	.2454	.2486	.2518	.2549
.7	.2580	.2612	.2642	.2673	.2704	.2734	.2764	.2794	.2823	.2852
.8	.2881	.2910	.2939	.2967	.2995	.3023	.3051	.3078	.3106	.3133
.9	.3159	.3186	.3212	.3238	.3264	.3289	.3315	.3340	.3365	.3389
1.0	.3413	.3438	.3461	.3485	.3508	.3531	.3554	.3577	.3599	.3621
1.1	.3643	.3665	.3686	.3708	.3729	.3749	.3770	.3790	.3810	.3830
1.2	.3849	.3869	.3888	.3907	.3925	.3944	.3962	.3980	.3997	.4015
1.3	.4032	.4049	.4066	.4082	.4099	.4115	.4131	.4147	.4162	.4177
1.4	.4192	.4207	.4222	.4236	.4251	.4265	.4279	.4292	.4306	.4319
1.5	.4332	.4345	.4357	.4370	.4382	.4394	.4406	.4418	.4429	.4441
1.6	.4452	.4463	.4474	.4484	.4495	.4505	.4515	.4525	.4535	.4545
1.7	.4554	.4564	.4573	.4582	.4591	.4599	.4608	.4616	.4625	.4633
1.8	.4641	.4649	.4656	.4664	.4671	.4678	.4686	.4693	.4699	.4706
1.9	.4713	.4719	.4726	.4732	.4738	.4744	.4750	.4756	.4761	.4767
2.0	.4772	.4778	.4783	.4788	.4793	.4798	.4803	.4808	.4812	.4817
2.1	.4821	.4826	.4830	.4834	.4838	.4842	.4846	.4850	.4854	.4857
2.2	.4861	.4864	.4868	.4871	.4875	.4878	.4881	.4884	.4887	.4890
2.3	.4893	.4896	.4898	.4901	.4904	.4906	.4909	.4911	.4913	.4916
2.4	.4918	.4920	.4922	.4925	.4927	.4929	.4931	.4932	.4934	.4936
2.5	.4938	.4940	.4941	.4943	.4945	.4946	.4948	.4949	.4951	.4952
2.6	.4953	.4955	.4956	.4957	.4959	.4960	.4961	.4962	.4963	.4964
2.7	.4965	.4966	.4967	.4968	.4969	.4970	.4971	.4972	.4973	.4974
2.8	.4974	.4975	.4976	.4977	.4977	.4978	.4979	.4979	.4980	.4981
2.9	.4981	.4982	.4982	.4983	.4984	.4984	.4985	.4985	.4986	.4986
3.0	.4986	.4987	.4987	.4988	.4988	.4989	.4989	.4989	.4990	.4990
4.0	.49997									

Since the left portion of the curve is essentially the same as the right, if each of the z-values in the previous table had a minus sign in front of it, the areas under the curve would still be the same.

The normal table can also be used to find the area under the curve *beyond* a given value of z. The key here is that one-half of the area is 50%, and so the area beyond z is 50% − table value. For instance, if the table value is 30%, the area beyond z is 50% − 30% = 20%. The area beyond $z = +1$ would be .5000 − .3413 = .1587, since the area *between* the mean and $z = +1$ is .3413. This concept is illustrated in Figure 5.17.

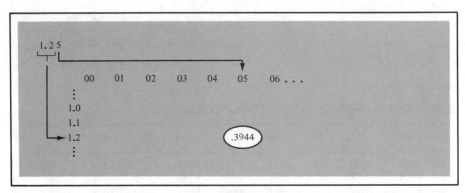

FIGURE 5.15   The area under a normal curve between the mean and $z = 1.25$.

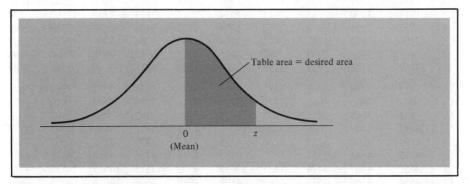

FIGURE 5.16   A normal table gives the area under the standard normal curve between the mean and some value of z.

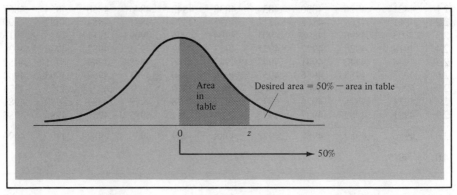

FIGURE 5.17   The area beyond z can be found by subtracting the area between the mean and z from .5000.

Here are some examples.

z	$P(0 < x < z)$	$P(x > z) = .5000 - P(0 < x < z)$
1.65	.4505	.0495
1.96	.4750	.0250
2.33	.4901	.0099

We are not limited to situations bounded by the mean. When an interval or its complement is not bounded by the distribution mean, finding the area under the curve is a two-step process. For example, suppose we want to find the area under the curve between $z = -1$ standard deviation and $z = +1$ standard deviation. Since the mean is always used as the point of reference, we must find the area between the mean and each boundary. We just determined that the area between the mean and $z = +1$ is .3413. Likewise, the area between the mean and $z = -1$ is .3413. Combining the two values will give us the total area: $.3413 + .3413 = .6826$. This is illustrated in Figure 5.18.

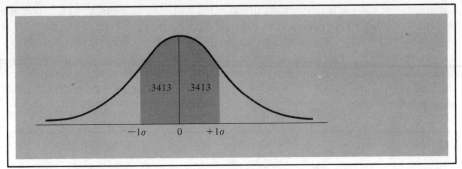

FIGURE 5.18   Finding the area under the curve between two z-values is a two-part problem.

Similarly, if the two boundaries of an interval are both on the same side of the mean, and we want to find the area under the curve between those two boundaries, we again must find the area between each one and the mean. But in this case, we then want to find the *difference* between the two areas. For instance, if we want to find the area between $z = 1$ and $z = 2$ (see Figure 5.19), we must find the area between $z = 1$ and the mean (.3413) and then subtract it from the value for the area between $z = 2$ and the mean (.4772): $.4772 - .3413 = .1359$ is the area between $z = 1$ and $z = 2$.

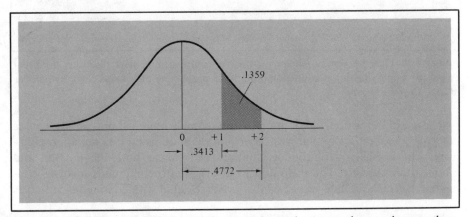

FIGURE 5.19   When two z-values have the same sign and we want the area *between* them, the answer is found by first finding the area between each one and the mean and then finding the difference between the two values.

The Normal Distribution as
an Approximation to the Binomial

Many real life situations are aptly described by the binomial distribution. The trouble is that binomial tables rarely extend beyond $n = 20$, simply because there are so many outcomes that the resulting tables are too large to print. More extensive tables exist, but they are usually not readily available. Formulas can be used provided computer assistance is available; otherwise the computations are too demanding.

In some instances the normal distribution can be used to obtain fairly good approximations to binomial probabilities, and we have just seen that the normal distribution is not particularly difficult to work with. We saw earlier in Chapter 4 that under certain circumstances the Poisson distribution could be used to approximate binomial probabilities when n is large and the probability of success is close to 0 or close to 100%. The normal approximation works best when the probability of success is close to .50, and the approximation improves [and the need to have P(success) close to .50 diminishes] as n gets larger.* Figure 5.20 portrays this concept.

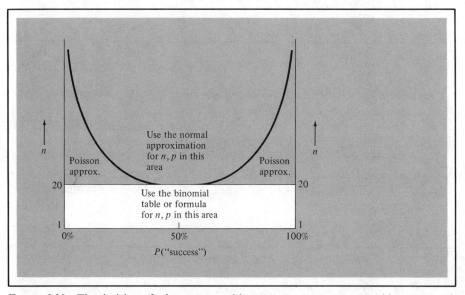

Figure 5.20   The decision of when to use a binomial distribution versus either a normal or Poisson approximation is a function of both the probability of "success" and the number of trials or observations.

The use of the normal distribution to approximate binomial probabilities poses one conceptual difficulty that was not a consideration using Poisson approximations. The normal distribution is continuous, whereas both the Poisson and binomial are discrete. The transition from discrete to continuous involves contending with the noninteger values that are associated with continuous variables

---

* One generally accepted rule of thumb is that $n \cdot p$ or $n(1 - p)$, whichever is smaller, be greater than or equal to 5 in order to use the normal approximation.

but not with discrete variables. For example, the value 3.4523 might be consistent with a continuous variable but probably not with a discrete variable, since discrete variables commonly involve integers only. Discrete probability distributions have lumps of probability at the integers but nothing between integers. Continuous distributions, though, are smooth rather than "lumpy" because all (intervals) values have probabilities associated with them.

The problem is resolved by assigning intervals of the continuous distribution to represent integer values common to discrete variables. In essence, noninteger values of a continuous variable are *rounded* to the nearest integer, and probabilities associated with the noninteger values are then treated as integer probabilities. For example, continuous values in the range from 2.5 to 3.5 would relate to the discrete or integer value 3, continuous values in the range from 6.5 to 7.5 would relate to the discrete value 7, and so on. Thus to find the binomial probability of exactly 7 successes, we would use a normal approximation based on the probability (area under the normal curve) between 6.5 and 7.5.

Let us consider a few examples.

Example 1   Suppose $n = 20$ and $p = .40$. We can easily use a binomial table to find various values. For instance, $P(x = 3)$ is .0124 using Table B in the Appendix. Now let us try using the normal approximation.

Solution:
Remember that the normal distribution is expressed by its mean and standard deviation, so we must first determine the mean and standard deviation of this binomial distribution. The mean is np, or in this case, $20(.40) = 8$, and the standard deviation of the distribution is

$$\sigma_{np} = \sqrt{np(1 - p)} = \sqrt{20(.4)(.6)} = 2.2$$

"Exactly 3" must be interpreted as the range from 2.5 to 3.5 in the normal distribution, as shown in Figure 5.21.

We have a two-part problem, as mentioned previously, because of the way the normal table is constructed. The probability of a value between 2.5 and the mean must be determined, as well as the probability of a value between 3.5 and the mean. The difference between those two probabilities is the probability of a value between 2.5 and 3.5.

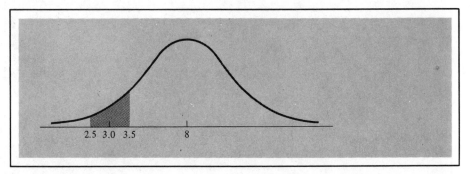

FIGURE 5.21   The normal approximation to the probability of exactly 3.

$$z_1 = \frac{2.5 - 8}{2.2} = \frac{-5.5}{2.2} = -2.50 \qquad P_1 = .4938$$

$$z_2 = \frac{3.5 - 8}{2.2} = \frac{-4.5}{2.2} = -2.05 \qquad P_2 = .4798$$

$$P(x = 3) = P_1 - P_2 = .0140$$

Note that the approximation of .0140 is quite close to the true value of .0124; the error is .0016, which is fairly small.

The normal approximation can also be used to find the probability of a *range* of outcomes.

Example 2 Using the same values of n and p from Example 1, we have $n = 20$ and $p = .40$.
 a. Find the probability of $x \geq 10$.
 b. Find the probability of $x = 9, 10,$ or 11.
(Note: The mean is 8 and the standard deviation is 2.2, as determined in Example 1.)

Solution:
 a. $x \geq 10$ really implies (for a continuous approximation) that $x > 9.5$. The probability of a value in this range is found by determining the probability of observing a value between the mean and 9.5, and then subtracting that probability from 50%, as illustrated in Figure 5.22(a).

$$P(\mu \leq x \leq 9.5): z = \frac{9.5 - 8}{2.2} = \frac{1.5}{2.2} = .68$$

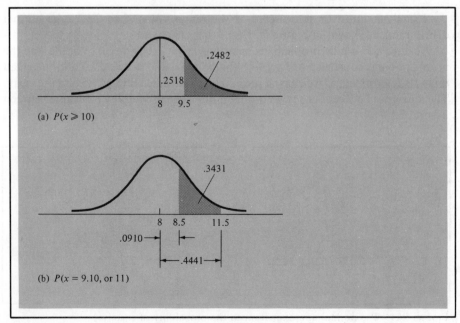

(a) $P(x \geqslant 10)$

(b) $P(x = 9. 10,$ or $11)$

FIGURE 5.22 $P(x \geq 10) = .2482$. (b) $P(x = 9, 10,$ or $11) = .3431$.

We find from the normal table that $z = .68$ translates into a probability of .2518. Therefore,

$$P(x > 9.5) = .5000 - .2518 = .2482$$

b. $x = 9$, 10, or 11 translates into the continuous range of from 8.5 to 11.5.

$$z_1 = \frac{11.5 - 8}{2.2} = \frac{3.5}{2.2} = 1.59 \qquad P_1 = .4441$$

$$z_2 = \frac{8.5 - 8}{2.2} = \frac{.5}{2.2} = .23 \qquad P_2 = .0910$$

$$P(8.5 \leq x \leq 11.5) = P_1 - P_2 = .3531$$

This is illustrated in Figure 5.22(b).

EXERCISES

1. Draw a normal curve and shade in the desired area, and then determine the required information.
    a. Find the area to the right of $z = 1.0$.
    b. Find the area to the left of $z = 1.0$.
    c. Find the area to the right of $z = -.34$.
    d. Find the area between $z = 0$ and $z = 1.5$.
    e. Find the area between $z = 0$ and $z = -2.88$.
    f. Find the area between $z = -.56$ and $z = -.20$.
    g. Find the area between $z = -.49$ and $z = +.49$.
    h. Find the area between $z = +2.5$ and $z = +2.8$.
2. Draw a normal curve and shade in the desired area, and then find the area
    a. to the left of $z = -.2$
    b. to the right of $z = -.2$
    c. between $z = -.2$ and $z = 0$
    d. between $z = -.2$ and $z = +.4$
3. Find the values of z that will produce these areas:
    a. the area to the left of z is .0505
    b. the area to the left of z is .0228
    c. the area to the right of z is .0228
    d. the area between 0 and z is .4772
    e. the area between $+z$ and $-z$ is .0240
    f. the area less than $-z$ or more than $+z$ is .9760
4. Find the values of z that correspond to these probabilities:
    a. the area to the right of z is .0505
    b. the area to the right of z is .5000
    c. the area to the left of z is .0107
    d. the area to the left of z is .3520
    e. the area to the left of z is .8051
    f. the area between $+z$ and $-z$ is .9544
    g. the area between $+z$ and $-z$ is .6826
*5. Given that a population with a mean of 25 and a standard deviation of 2.0 is normally distributed, find z-values for the following population values:
     a. 23.0   b. 23.5   c. 24.0   d. 25.2   e. 25.5

6. A normally distributed population has a mean of 40 and a standard deviation of 3. Find actual values for these z-values:

   a. $+.10$ b. $+2.00$ c. $+.75$

   d. -2.53 e. -3.00 f. -3.20

7. A normal distribution has a mean of 50 and a standard deviation of 5. What percentage of the population of values lie in these intervals:

   a. From 40 to 50?   b. From 49 to 50?   c. From 40 to 45?

   d. From 56 to 60?   e. From 40 to 65?   f. From 45 to 55?

8. After curing for 28 days, ordinary Portland cement has an average compressive strength of 4000 psi. Suppose this compressive strength is normally distributed, with a standard deviation of 120 psi. Find these probabilities for 28-day compressive strength:

   a. less than 3900   c. more than 3850

   b. less than 3850   d. more than 3880

9. Suppose the mean income in a large community can be reasonably approximated by a normal distribution with a mean of $15,000 and a standard deviation of $3,000.

   a. What percentage of the population have incomes exceeding $18,600?

   b. In a random sample of 50 wage earners, about how many persons can be expected to have incomes of less than $10,500?

10. A supplier of wrought iron claims that his product has a tensile strength that is approximately normal, with a mean of 50,000 psi and a variance of 8,100 psi. Assuming his claim is true, what percentage of sample measurements would you expect to be:

    a. Greater than 50,000 psi?

    b. Less than 49,550 psi?

    c. More than $\pm 1,350$ psi from 50,000 psi?

11. A cost estimator for government projects has found that his ability to estimate cost is normally distributed around the true cost, with a standard deviation of $10,000. If this is the case, what percentage of the time should his estimates be:

    a. Within $15,000 of the true cost?

    b. Within $20,000 of the true cost?

    c. Within $27,000 of the true cost?

12. A process for producing pipe makes pieces with a mean diameter of 2.00 inches and a standard deviation of .01 inch. Pipe with diameters that vary by more than .03 from the mean are considered defective. Assume normality.

    a. What percentage of the pipes will be defective?

    b. What is the probability of finding two pieces in a row that are both defective?

    c. What is the probability of finding two pieces in a row that are not defective?

*13. Weights of fish caught by a trawler are approximately normal, with a mean of 4.5 lb and a standard deviation of .5 lb.

    a. What percentage of the fish weight less than 4 lb?

    b. What percentage of the fish weigh within a pound of the average weight?

    c. If two fish are chosen, what is the probability that one will weigh more than the mean and one less?

    d. What is the probability that two fish will both weigh less than the mean?

*14. A fair coin is tossed 64 times. Find the probabilities for these outcomes:

    a. The number of heads equals the number of tails.

b. The number of heads is greater than 34.

c. The number of heads is less than 32.

d. The number of heads is between 30 and 36 but does not include 30 or 36.

e. The number of heads is between, or includes, 30 and 36.

15. It has been said that approximately 30% of the adults living in New York City own shares of stock of private corporations. Assuming this is true, determine these probabilities for a random sample of New Yorkers:

a. Fewer than 20 in a sample of 40 own stock.

b. Twelve or less in a sample of 50 own stock.

c. Twelve or less in a sample of 70 own stock.

16. The amount of beer in a 12-oz can manufactured by Super Suds Beverages, Inc., is known to be well approximated by a normal distribution with a mean of 12 oz and a standard deviation of .25 oz.

a. What percentage of cans should have less than 11.60 oz?

b. What percentage of cans will not vary by more than .30 oz from the mean?

c. Find the probability of getting four cans that all have less than 12 oz if a random sample of four cans is selected.

THE EXPONENTIAL DISTRIBUTION

The exponential distribution involves probabilities for the length of time or distance between occurrences over a continuous range. For example, the exponential distribution is used to model the time between failures of electrical equipment, the time between customer arrivals at a supermarket, the time between calls for service, and so on. There is a close relationship between the exponential and Poisson distributions. In fact, if a Poisson process has a mean of λ occurrences over an interval, the space (or time, etc.) *between* occurrences over that interval will be $1/\lambda$. For example, if calls for service average 6 calls/hour, then the average time *between* calls for service will be $\frac{1}{6}$ hour, or 10 minutes.

Exponential probabilities are expressed in terms of the time or distance until an event or occurrence takes place. See Figure 5.23. For instance, we might wish

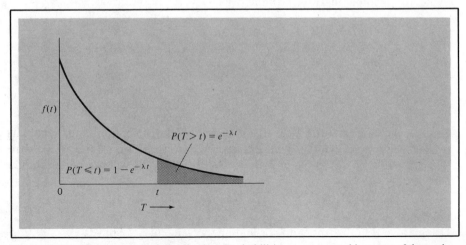

FIGURE 5.23 The exponential distribution. Probabilities are expressed in terms of the probability of an occurrence before, or after, some specified point t.

to determine the probability of no calls over a 2-hour ($t = 2$) period if the average rate (λ) is 1.5 calls/hour. We can use the formula given in the box.

$$P(T > t) = e^{-\lambda t}$$

Using this formula, we can compute the probability that the space (or time) before the first occurrence will be greater than a given space (or time) t.

The probability of an occurrence at or before t is given by this formula:

$$P(T \leq t) = 1 - e^{-\lambda t}$$

Example 3   Suppose that the time it takes to receive your order after placing it in a large restaurant averages 10 minutes. Suppose, too, that this service time is exponentially distributed.
   a. Find the probability that your waiting time is more than 10 minutes.
   b. Find the probability that your waiting time is 10 minutes or less.
   c. Find the probability that your waiting time is 3 minutes or less.

Solution:
From the statement of the problem, we have that $\lambda = \frac{1}{10} = .1$ per minute.

   a.
$$P(T > 10) = e^{-\lambda t} = e^{-.1(10)} = e^{-1} = .368$$

(Note: e^{-1} is found in Table F of the Appendix.)

   b.
$$P(T \leq 10) = 1 - e^{-\lambda t} = 1 - e^{-1} = 1 - .368 = .632$$

   c.
$$P(T \leq 3) = 1 - e^{-\lambda t} = 1 - e^{-.1(3)} = 1 - e^{-.3} = 1 - .741 = .259$$

Example 4   One important use of the exponential distribution is for reliability problems. Suppose that a machine fails on the average of once every two years ($1/\lambda = 2$, so $\lambda = .5$). Find the probability that the machine will not fail during the next year.

Solution:
Using Table F in the Appendix for finding the value of e, we have

$$P(T > 1) = e^{-\lambda t} = e^{-.5(1)} = e^{-.5} = .607$$

EXERCISES

*1. Defects in nylon rope are Poisson distributed, with a mean of 1 defect/meter (this is λ). Find the probability of having an interval between occurrences of at least 3 meters.

2. Service time at a tool crib is well approximated by an exponential distribution, with a mean of 4 minutes. What is the probability that service time will be:
   a. More than 4 minutes?
   b. Less than 4 minutes?
   c. Exactly 4 minutes?

3. Emergency calls during early morning hours on Monday are known to follow an exponential pattern, with a mean time between calls of 1 hour.
   a. Find the probability of a 2-hour period without a call.
   b. Find the probability of a 3-hour period without a call.

4. A communications satellite has a single power source. Find the probability that the satellite will operate for at least 20,000 hours before a power failure if the mean time between failures $(1/\lambda)$ is:
   a. 10,000   b. 20,000   c. 40,000

SUMMARY

Continuous probability distributions are used both to describe continuous random variables and to approximate discrete random variables in certain instances. This chapter considered three continuous distributions: the uniform, the normal, and the exponential distributions. By far the most important of these is the normal distribution, because it is used extensively for inference purposes.

Probabilities of continuous distributions are given in terms of the area under a curve between two points. The probability of any single value is approximately zero due to the (infinitely) large number of potential values a continuous random variable might assume.

The uniform distribution applies when a continuous random variable can assume any value over an interval and all values are equally likely. The exponential distribution is useful in finding probabilities of time or space between occurrences when the rate of occurrence is Poisson distributed.

The normal distribution is a bell-shaped distribution that (theoretically) extends from $-\infty$ to $+\infty$. The distribution is actually a series of distributions, with each combination of a mean and a standard deviation describing a unique distribution. By expressing values of a normally distributed random variable in terms of the number of standard deviations a given value is from the mean, and working with the resulting z scores, the process of obtaining various probabilities is greatly simplified.

One important use of the normal distribution is to approximate binomial probabilities. The approximation works best for P(success) near .5 and n larger than 20.

REVIEW QUESTIONS

1. Why is there a need for continuous probability distributions?
2. What three concepts were illustrated by the spinner example?

3. What three continuous distributions were discussed in this chapter?
4. List five characteristics of normal curves.
5. What is a z score and how is it computed?
6. What is the primary reason for utilizing z scores when working with normal distributions?
7. What is the connection between probability and area for continuous distributions?
8. Why does the normal table only show areas for the right half of the normal curve?
9. What reference point must always be used when working with the z scores to determine probabilities?
10. In what kinds of situations is the exponential distribution useful?
11. How is the exponential distribution related to the Poisson?

SUPPLEMENTAL EXERCISES

1. A small coffee shop sells between 5 and 15 kiloliters of coffee over a seven-day period. The actual amount sold varies uniformly over this range.
   a. What is the average amount of coffee sold in seven days?
   b. What is the probability of selling more than 12 kiloliters in seven days?
   c. If profit is $20/kiloliter, what is the expected profit over the seven-day period?
   d. What is the probability that the profit during the period will be less than $140?
2. The amount of soft drink dispensed into a drinking cup varies uniformly between 4 and 5 ounces.
   a. Find the probability of getting a cup with less than 4.3 ounces.
   b. How much soft drink does the average cup receive?
   c. Find the standard deviation for this distribution.
3. In the standard normal distribution, find the percentage of the values that will exceed z if z equals:
   a. -1.645 b. $+1.645$ c. $+2.33$ d. $+2.0$ e. $+1.96$
4. By keeping careful records an educational testing service has found that the completion time for a standardized mathematics test is approximately normal, with a mean of 80 minutes and a standard deviation of 20 minutes.
   a. What percentage of those taking the test will finish before 80 minutes?
   b. What percentage will not be finished if the maximum time allowed is 2 hours?
   c. If 100 persons take the test, how many would you expect to finish in the first hour?
5. Suppose 5% of a certain model of hand calculators fail within 60 days and must be returned to the dealer for repair. A firm buys 190 calculators.
   a. Roughly how many would you expect to fail in 60 days?
   b. Find the probability of more than 6 failing.
   c. What is the probability that none will fail?
   d. Find the probability of 10 or more failing.
6. Fifty percent of the residents in a township that are of voting age are not registered to vote.

  a. If a random sample of 100 persons of voting age who live in the town is taken, about how many voters would you expect in the sample?

  b. What is the probability that at least 60% of those chosen are, in fact, not registered?

7. The mean trouble-free life of automatic dishwashers is 1.5 years, with a standard deviation of .3 years. What percentage of the dishwashers sold will need repair before the 1-year warranty period expires if dishwasher breakdowns are normally distributed?

8. The number of persons eating lunch at a suburban cafeteria is approximately normal, with a mean of 250 and a standard deviation of 20 per day.

  a. On any given day, what is the probability of having at least 200 customers?

  b. Find the probability that between 225 and 275 customers eat at the cafeteria.

    If the average revenue per customer is $4.00, what is the expected daily lunch revenue?

  d. What is the probability that the revenue will exceed $1100?

9. Large ring gears are to be flame-cut from 3-inch steel plate. Past records indicate that the resulting gears have diameters that are normally distributed with a standard deviation of .0025 inches. What percentage of the gears produced would you expect to be:

  a. Within .005 inches of the nominal setting (mean)?

  b. More than .0075 from the nominal setting?

10. Life of light bulbs is known to be approximately exponential, with a mean life of 1000 hours. Find the percentage of these bulbs that you would expect to fail within:

  a. 500 hours   b. 1000 hours   c. 1500 hours   d. 2000

11. In Exercise 10, after how many hours will 50% of the bulbs have failed?

12. Customers arrive at a barber shop during weekday mornings at the (Poisson) rate of 3 persons/hour. Use the exponential distribution to find the probability that no customers arrive during a 45-minute period.

6
sampling

Chapter Objectives

After completing this chapter, you should be able to:
1. List the situations in which sampling is preferable to taking a census and vice versa
2. Relate the terms "sample" and "population"
3. Explain what is meant by the phrase "simple random sampling"
4. Describe the various methods for obtaining random samples
5. Describe the important characteristics of random number tables
6. Explain the differences between probability sampling and judgment sampling
7. Discuss the variations of simple random sampling and give examples of how each is used

Chapter Outline

Introduction
Samples and Populations
    Sampling from a finite population
    Sample versus census
Random Sampling
    Obtaining a random sample
    Random number tables
Other Sampling Designs
    Probability versus nonprobability sampling
    Judgment sampling
    Probability sampling
Summary

INTRODUCTION

STATISTICAL INFERENCE involves making certain judgments about something after examining only a portion, or *sample*, of it. Thus you are offered a free sample of a new food product at a supermarket; you burn your tongue if you try to sample a piece of freshly baked pie before it has a chance to cool; a cook tastes the soup to see if it needs a little more seasoning. Similarly, when you glance through a new book or magazine, try on new clothes, go out on a first date, or watch a TV program for a few minutes before deciding whether to turn to another channel, you are, in effect, sampling.

Statistical sampling is similar to each of the above examples, although its methods are more formal and precise and typically include a probability statement. Probability and sampling are closely related, and together they form the foundation of inference theory.

In this chapter the basic concepts that underlie sampling are examined. The reasons for sampling and alternative sampling plans are explored. Particular attention is devoted to simple *ramdom sampling* because of its importance in statistical analysis. While *no* sampling plan can guarantee that a sample will be *exactly* like the population from which it has been drawn, a random sample enables one to estimate the amount of possible error (i.e., to say "how close" the sample is in terms of being representative). Nonrandom samples do not have this feature.

You don't have to drink *all* of the punch
to know how it tastes!

SAMPLES AND POPULATIONS

A *census* involves an examination of all of the items in a given group of items, while *sampling* involves an examination of a small portion of the items. The purpose of sampling is to make generalizations about an entire group of items without having to resort to an examination of every single item.

The part of the group of items examined is referred to as the *sample*, and the entire group from which a sample is selected is referred to as the *population* or *universe*. The items that comprise a population can be individuals, corporations, manufactured products, inventories, schools, cities, test scores, prices, or anything else that can be *measured*, *counted*, or *ranked*.

The terms "population" and "sample" are relative to a specific set of circumstances. That is, in one instance the individuals in a classroom might be regarded as a population and a sample of students might be drawn from those students in the classroom. For another problem those same students might be considered as a sample of all students in a college of engineering, or as a sample of the population of students at that particular university. Since the purpose of sampling is to make generalizations about the underlying population, it is axiomatic that the *target population* be established so that meaningful generalizations can be made.

Populations that are limited in size are referred to as *finite* populations, while those that are of unlimited size are referred to as *infinite* populations. Students in a given classroom, the produce in a supermarket, the books in a library, and the automobiles in California are all examples of finite populations. Infinite populations, on the other hand, typically are some sort of *process* that generates items, such as coin flipping, where the number of items (heads and tails) that could be obtained is unlimited. Other examples of infinite population processes are the future output of a machine, draws from a bowl of chips when each chip is replaced before another is drawn, and births of insects (or any other species). From a practical standpoint the important consideration is whether removing one or a small number of items from the population will have any discernible influence on relative probabilities.

Sampling from a Finite Population

The question of whether to return a sampled item to a population before drawing the next observation arises when sampling from a finite population, because the probability of including population items in a sample will depend on whether we are sampling *with replacement* or *without replacement*.

If the size of a sample is small in relation to the size of the population, not returning the sampled items to the population will have a negligible effect on the probabilities of the remaining items, and sampling without replacement will not cause any serious difficulties. On the other hand, relatively large samples tend to distort the probabilities of remaining items when sampling without replacement. Instead of actually replacing items, some sample statistics (e.g., standard deviations) are adjusted to compensate for this.

Although it may not be obvious, selecting an entire sample at once is equivalent to sampling without replacement. When sampling with replacement it would be possible to draw the same item more than once, but by taking the whole sample at once, it would be impossible for that to happen.

There are a number of reasons why sampling without replacement is done in actual practice:

1. As we already mentioned, the effects are often negligible, and it may be more convenient to do so.
2. If destructive testing is involved, it would be impossible to return sampled items to the population.
3. In industrial sampling it can be difficult to convince inspectors not trained in statistics to return sampled items to the population, particularly if the items are defective.
4. When a sampled item is returned to the population, there is a chance that it will be included in a later draw. Thus some items get sampled more than once. If the sampling procedure involves expensive testing or interviewing, it is desirable to avoid examining any item more than once.

If it happens that sampling without replacement is necessary or desirable, but the sample size is relatively large in comparison to the population size, the calculation of relevant probabilities is based on the *hypergeometric* distribution. The calculations can be rather complex, so we merely mention its existence here. More advanced textbooks concern themselves with the hypergeometric distribution.

Sample Versus Census

A sample usually involves the examination of a portion of the items in a population, whereas a census involves an examination of all of the items in a population. Although our focus in inductive statistics will be upon samples, it is nonetheless instructive to consider the alternative to sampling.

On the surface it may seem that a complete or total inspection of all of the items in a population would be more desirable than inspection of a sample of those items. In practice, the opposite is often true: sampling is more desirable than taking a census. Let us explore this last statement in terms of situations in which sampling is advantageous.

1. The population can be *infinite*, in which case it would be impossible to take a census. Since infinite populations are processes that never end, it would obviously not be possible to examine each item in the population.

2. A sample can be more *timely* than a census. If information about a population is needed quickly, a study of an entire population, particularly if there are many items or if the items are widely dispersed, may be too time-consuming to be useful. In the time it would take to examine each case in a trainload of fresh strawberries, the fruit might deteriorate to the point where it was no longer deemed marketable. Moreover, if a population tends to change over time, a complete census may actually combine several populations. A survey of persons in a large community to discover the percentage of individuals who have contracted a certain communicable disease may take so long that by the time the results are in and the appropriate medical action is undertaken, the disease may have spread to such an extent that different action is necessary. In fact, those taking the survey may be a contributing factor in spreading the disease. Thus the study may indicate that enough vaccine is on hand locally to handle the disease, but by that time the disease may have spread out of control and require massive doses of the vaccine.

3. *Destructive testing* may be involved. That is, in the process of examining items, they are destroyed. Items such as flashbulbs, ammunition, and safety devices

often must be destroyed as part of the testing process. Thus a census might provide an accurate picture of a population that no longer existed.

4. *Cost* can be prohibitive in taking a census, particularly when the examination cost per item is high and there are many items in the population. The cost of taking a census of the U.S. population is enormous, and a census is only undertaken once every ten years. As another example, consider trying to obtain a census of the weight of each fish in one of the Great Lakes, or a count of the number of fish in the lake. The population is so large and mobile and the problems of measurement (such as being careful to count each fish only once and being careful not to injure the fish) are so difficult as to clearly exclude taking a census.

5. *Accuracy* may suffer when a census is taken of a large population. Sampling involves fewer observations and thus fewer data collectors. With many data collectors there is less coordination and control possible than there is with a smaller number of collectors, and the chance for errors increases. Thus sampling can usually provide more uniformity in data collection methods and greater comparability among the data than a census can.

6. Finally, the *kind of information* may depend on whether a sample or a census is used. Very often data collection expenditures are subject to budget constraints. Also, a time frame often exists. If a census is used, time and cost considerations might mean that the census has to be limited to one or a few characteristics being measured per item. A sample using the same time and money could produce an in-depth study of a smaller number of items. Note that if all items in a population were identical, then a sample of only one item would provide all the information about the entire population, and little would be gained by the alternative of taking a census. Although this situation would be an extreme one, there are, in fact, many instances in which the items of a population are very similar. In those instances a complete census would contribute very little more than what a relatively small sample would.

There *are* certain situations in which it is more advantageous to inspect all of the items in a population (i.e., o take a census). Among those situations are these:

1. The *population may be so small* that the cost and time to do a census may be only slightly more than for a sample. If the population consisted of a classroom of 20 students, it would undoubtedly make sense to do a census.

2. If the *sample size is large relative to the size of the population*, the additional effort required for a census may be small. For example, if there is much variability among the population items, a fairly large sample may be needed to obtain a representative sample. If it happens that the population is not much larger than the sample size, a census can eliminate sampling variability.

3. If *complete accuracy* is required, a census is the only method of achieving that goal. Because of sampling variability, we can never be exactly sure of what the true population parameters are. A census can give us this information, although errors in data collection and other sorts of biases can obviously affect the accuracy of a census. A bank would not take a random sample of its tellers to learn how much cash was available in all the tellers' drawers; it would count the amount (take a census) in all the drawers. That does not prevent counting errors and arithmetic mistakes in summing up the amounts, but it does avoid problems of deciding if some teller is representative of all the tellers.

4. Occasionally *complete information is already available*, so there is no need to sample.

RANDOM SAMPLING

There are a variety of methods for taking a sample. Perhaps the most important of these, and the one we shall focus on, is random sampling. In fact, most of the statistical tests we will consider are based on random sampling. It is sometimes referred to as "simple random sampling" to differentiate it from other sampling designs that incorporate elements of random sampling.*

Generally speaking, random sampling requires that each "element" in a population have the same opportunity of being included in the sample. This can be interpreted in the following ways:

For *discrete populations* a random sample is one in which each *item* in the population has the same chance of being included in the sample.

For *continuous populations* a random sample is one in which the probability of including any range of values in the sample is equal to the percentage of the population which lies in that range.

A random sample from a discrete population, then, would be a sample in which the probability of drawing any one of the N items in the population in a single draw is $1/N$. It also implies that *groups* of items have the same chance of being included in the sample as other groups *of the same size*. For instance, the probability of including any two items should be equal for all possible groups of two items. An extension of this is that the probability of including an item which is a member of a subgroup of the population in a random sample is proportional to the size of the subgroup. Large subgroups will have a greater probability of having one or more items in a sample than small subgroups, while subgroups of equal size will have equal probabilities. Hence random sampling has the tendency to yield *representative* samples.

Note that when a random sample is selected, it is the *process* of selection that is random and not the items in the sample. Moreover, the process is not hit-or-miss; random must not be associated with haphazard, for the latter might not necessarily satisfy the equally likely situation.

Obtaining a Random Sample

If the target population is *infinite*, such as all future output of a machine, we can regard it as a probabilistic process. Merely recording the items *in the order that they occur*, we can obtain a sample that is representative of the process (i.e., a *random* sample). As long as the process under consideration is stable during the period in which our observations are taken (so that the probability of each possible outcome remains constant), we can treat the process and the resulting sample as being random. This is exactly how we regarded successive tosses of a fair coin and rolls of balanced dice.

---

* Hereafter the term "random sampling" will refer to simple random sampling unless noted otherwise.

Some examples of processes that are generally treated as being random are the arrival times of cars at a tollbooth, telephone calls into a large switchboard, customers at supermarket checkout counters; service times at tollbooths, switchboards, and checkout counters; and the output of any mechanical process.

If the target population is *finite*, there are essentially two ways of selecting a simple random sample. One method involves compiling a list, or "frame," of each of the items in the population and then applying a random method to the list to select the items that are to be sampled. The second approach is used when the items in the population are not clearly identifiable, which makes listing impossible. For instance, in food processing, waste disposal, and pollution control, there is usually not a concept of items that can be sampled. An alternative here would be to sample *locations* instead of items, such as "4 inches over and 7 inches down." This can be accomplished by envisioning the population as being composed of cubes, and then sampling the cubes. Another possibility would be to employ some kind of mixing process, similar to the mixing of chips in a bowl. Clearly, there is the danger that the mixing process will not be complete, so a sample may not be representative after all. Thus it is important to give careful attention to how items are selected and if items are equally likely.

The likelihood of obtaining a truly random sample is much greater when the individual items can be listed. Some examples of things that can be listed are the employees of a firm, the stocks traded on the New York stock exchange, registered motor vehicles in Wisconsin, students taking a certain college course, periodicals available in a library, members of a trade association, 6-A.M. temperature readings at various spots around the country, advertisers in the *Wall Street Journal*, movie theaters in a community, and so on. Note that a list of the items in a population would usually not be considered a census of the population because only a means of item identification is listed. Characteristics of interest must still be obtained through sampling. Thus a list of periodicals does not tell us what is contained in those periodicals; a list of movie theaters does not indicate the box office receipts for the third week in June; a list of students enrolled in some course does not reveal which students had summer jobs; and a list of stocks does not state the net assets of the various firms. *The sole purpose of the list is to be able to select population items for further study.*

The selection process involves assigning consecutive numbers to the listed items and then randomly designating the numbers of the items that will be included in the sample. Conceptually, we could use cards, dice, or numbered chips to generate random numbers corresponding to the numbers on our list. For example, if our population consisted of 46 items, chips numbered 1 through 46 could be placed in a bowl, thoroughly mixed, and then chosen one at a time until the number of chips selected equaled the desired sample size. The numbers on the chips would tell us which population items to include in our sample.

In practice, such random devices are rarely employed, for a variety of reasons. One reason is that each device leaves something to be desired; the methods are not perfectly random. Cards, for instance, may stick together so that shuffling cannot guarantee that each card has an equal chance of being drawn. The edges of dice may become worn, thereby imparting a slight bias to the outcome of rolls of the dice. And there is always the danger that a bowl of chips will not be thoroughly mixed. Moreover, if a large sample is to be selected, or if the need to select random samples from lists arises frequently, procedures involving cards, dice, or numbered chips tend to be both tedious and time-consuming. Because of these problems, and because random sampling is vital to statistical inference, specially designed tables called *random number tables* have been developed for use in conjunction with some forms of random sampling.

Random Number Tables

Random number tables contain the ten digits 0, 1, 2, . . . , 7, 8, 9. These digits can be read singly or in groups, and can be read in any order, such as down columns, up columns, across rows, diagonally, and so on, and can be considered random. The tables are characterized by two things that make them particularly well suited to random sampling. One characteristic is that the digits are so arranged that the probability of any one appearing at a given point in a sequence is equal to the probability of any other ones's occurring. The other characteristic is that combinations of digits have the same probability of occurring as other combinations of an equal number of digits. Note that these two conditions satisfy the requirements for random sampling stated previously. The first condition means that in a sequence of numbers, the probability of any single digit appearing at any point in the sequence is $\frac{1}{10}$. The second condition means that all two-digit combinations are equally likely, all three-digit combinations are equally likely, and so on.

Random number tables could conceptually be constructed by numbering ten chips with the digits 0 through 9 and drawing them from a well-mixed bowl one at a time, recording the result, replacing the chip, drawing again, and so on, until a large number of digits were recorded. Actually, there are more efficient methods for generating random numbers, many of which utilize computers or other electronic devices. Tables developed by these methods are thoroughly tested to insure that they are, in fact, random. However, our concern is not with *constructing* these tables but with *using* the tables.

To illustrate the use of a random number table, let us suppose that a large department store wishes to select a random sample of 15 customers from a list of 830 customers with charge accounts. The purpose of the sample may be to estimate frequency of purchases, to ascertain why people open charge accounts, to determine the average amount purchased, or to uncover complaints about the system.

Hmm, now let me see. . .

The customers may be listed alphabetically or by the date that they opened their accounts. It does not really matter. The numbers 000 to 829 would be assigned consecutively to the list from top to bottom. Since the item identification is a three-digit number, it will be necessary to read three-digit numbers from a random number table so that we can achieve correspondence between the random numbers and the listed numbers. *Any* three-digit sequence read from a random number table will do. Let us use Table 6.1 and read the *first three digits* in the *last column* of the table, *going down* the column. Those digits are 473, 828, 920, 923, 380,

TABLE 6.1   Random Numbers

3690	2492	7171	7720	6509	7549	2330	5733	4730
0813	6790	6858	1489	2669	3743	1901	4971	8280
6477	5289	4092	4223	6454	7632	7577	2816	9202
0772	2160	7236	0812	4195	5589	0830	8261	9232
5692	9870	3583	8997	1533	6466	8830	7271	3809
2080	3828	7880	0586	8482	7811	6807	3309	2729
1039	3382	7600	1077	4455	8806	1822	1669	7501
7227	0104	4141	1521	9104	5563	1392	8238	4882
8506	6348	4612	8252	1062	1757	0964	2983	2244
5086	0303	7423	3298	3979	2831	2257	1508	7642
0092	1629	0377	3590	2209	4839	6332	1490	3092
0935	5565	2315	8030	7651	5189	0075	9353	1921
2605	3973	8204	4143	2677	0034	8601	3340	8383
7277	9889	0390	5579	4620	5650	0210	2082	4664
5484	3900	3485	0741	9069	5920	4326	7704	6525
6905	7127	5933	1137	7583	6450	5658	7678	3444
8387	5323	3753	1859	6043	0294	5110	6340	9137
4094	4957	0163	9717	4118	4276	9465	8820	4127
4951	3781	5101	1815	7068	6379	7252	1086	8919
9047	0199	5068	7447	1664	9278	1708	3625	2864
7274	9512	0074	6677	8676	0222	3335	1976	1645
9192	4011	0255	5458	6942	8043	6201	1587	0972
0554	1690	6333	1931	9433	2661	8690	2313	6999
9231	5627	1815	7171	8036	1832	2031	6298	6073
3995	9677	7765	3194	3222	4191	2734	4469	8617
2402	6250	9362	7373	4757	1716	1942	0417	5921
5295	7385	5474	2123	7035	9983	5192	1840	6176
5177	1191	2106	3351	5057	0967	4538	1246	3374
7315	3365	7203	1231	0546	6612	1038	1425	2709
5775	7517	8974	3961	2183	5295	3096	8536	9442
5500	2276	6307	2346	1285	7000	5306	0414	3383
3251	8902	8843	2112	8567	8131	8116	5270	5994
4675	1435	2192	0874	2897	0262	5092	5541	4014
3543	6130	4247	4859	2660	7852	9096	0578	0097
3521	8772	6612	0721	3899	2999	1263	7017	8057
5573	9396	3464	1702	9204	3389	5678	2589	0288
7478	7569	7551	3380	2152	5411	2647	7242	2800
3339	2854	9691	9562	3252	9848	6030	8472	2266
5505	8474	3167	8552	5409	1556	4247	4652	2953
6381	2086	5457	7703	2758	2963	8167	6712	9820

Source: Donald B. Owen, *Handbook of Statistical Tables*, Reading, Mass: Addison-Wesley, 1962. (Courtesy of U.S. Energy Research and Development Adm.)

272, ... When we come to a number such as 920, we simply discard it because our population only goes to 829. We would also ignore any previously selected numbers that appeared more than once. The process is continued until we have read 15 numbers. These correspond to 15 items from our population. Once we have the 15 numbers, we can refer to our list and select those 15 for further study.

In sum, to use a random number table:

1. Obtain a list of the items in the population.
2. Consecutively number the items on the list, beginning with zero (0,00,000, etc.).
3. Read numbers from a random number table such that the number of digits in each one equals the number of digits of the last numbered item on your list. Thus if the last number was 18, 56, or 72, a two-digit number would be read.
4. Omit any numbers that do not correspond to numbers on the list or that repeat previously selected numbers from the table. Continue until the desired number of observations have been obtained.
5. Use those random numbers to identify the items from the list to include in the sample.

If an accurate list of the items in the population is available, then it is relatively simple to select a random sample by employing a random number table. In fact, the list need not necessarily be of the items themselves. Locations of the items can serve as a feasible alternative. Thus location on a grid or map, sections of a city or county, and office files can be used at times instead of the actual items themselves.

There are, however, certain situations in which the use of lists can be misleading, particularly if the list is incomplete or outdated. When some of the items in the population are not on the list, all items in the population do not have an equal chance of being included in the sample (the excluded items have a zero probability of being included in the sample). This, of course, violates one requirement of random sampling.

In some cases a list may not be available, and it would be too costly or time-consuming to compile a complete list. For example, no single list is available for every person in the United States, or for pipe smokers in New York City, or for shoppers in Atlanta. It would be ridiculous to attempt to develop a complete list in such cases. In instances such as these, it is usually wise to utilize other types of sampling designs. Various alternatives to simple random sampling are considered in the section that follows.

EXERCISES

*1. A numbered list contains 7000 names and addresses. These are numbered consecutively, beginning with the number 1. Briefly describe how you would use a random number table to obtain a sample of 25 names.
   a. How many digits per name must be read?
   b. How would you decide where to start in the table?
   c. What effect, if any, would there be on your approach if the names were evenly numbered (2, 4, . . .) only?

2. A league manager wants to randomly pair 20 teams to begin a playoff. Describe how he might use a random number table to determine the pairings for the initial games. Could he also use the table for subsequent pairings? How?

3. A consumer group wants to determine public sentiment on product labeling.
   In one section of the city, there are 40 blocks, with 10 houses per block.
   a. Design a two-stage approach to random sampling by first selecting 10
      blocks, and then 1 house on each of the 10 blocks. (Total is 10 houses.)
   b. Suppose a one-stage plan was used (i.e., 10 houses were selected directly).
      (1) What problems might there be in selecting houses?
      (2) How would use of the random number table change?
4. Five percent of the output of an automatic screw machine is unacceptable and
   must be reworked.
   a. How could a random number table be used to simulate observations from
      this process?
   b. Use Table 6.1 and simulate 15 observations from this process. Begin at the
      bottom of the first column and read upward, using the first 2 digits.
5. Employees of a firm have identification badges numbered consecutively from
   101 to 873. A safety committee of 10 people will be randomly selected. Use the
   random number table to select the badge numbers. Begin with the second
   column and read down.

OTHER SAMPLING DESIGNS

There are a number of sampling plans, other than simple random sampling, that
are useful in gathering sample information. Some of these other plans are mentioned here to illustrate some of the extensions of simple random sampling and to
provide some additional perspective to random sampling. A word of caution:
much careful planning and knowledge is needed to correctly use these sampling
techniques, particularly in determining which items of the population to sample
and in deciding how to interpret the sample results.

Probability Versus Nonprobability Sampling

Probability sampling plans are designed in such a way that the probability of all
possible sample combinations is known. Because of this the amount of sampling
variability in random sampling can be determined. Under these conditions sampling is objective, and an estimate of sampling error can be readily obtained.
Random sampling is an example of probability sampling. Nonprobability sampling refers to subjective, or judgment, sampling, where the sampling variability
cannot be accurately established. Consequently, no estimate of sampling error
(i.e., sampling variability) is possible. The point is that whenever it is feasible,
probability sampling should be used. There are, nevertheless, some instances in
which nonprobability sampling provides a crude but useful alternative to probability sampling.

Judgment Sampling

If the sample size is quite small, say one to five items, random sampling can yield
results that are not at all representative, whereas a person familiar with the population might be able to specify which items are most representative of the population.
For example, a restaurant chain may wish to try out a new serving technique,

perhaps using heated serving trays. Cost considerations may mean that only two restaurants will be used in the study. The restaurants may differ considerably in terms of size, location, clientele, and profitability. Rather than leave the selection of which two locations to use as a test, it may be wiser to rely upon management's knowledge of conditions to select the two locations.

On occasion sample items are conveniently grouped. Medical research must work with patients available, or perhaps convicts who volunteer for the study. Neither group could be considered as a random sample of the general public, and it would be hazardous to attempt to draw conclusions about the general public based on such a study. However, the results might yield insight that could be used in setting up a probability sample to validate the basic results. The dangers inherent in medical research, as well as other kinds of research, often necessitate limiting the initial research to a small group of volunteers, Other similar examples might be patients with a terminal disease, cadavers, animals, and so on.

Finally, judgment sampling may turn out to be quicker and less costly than random sampling because it is not necessary to construct a list of items in the population.

Keep in mind that judgment sampling does not permit an objective assessment of sampling error, so it is desirable to use probability sampling whenever possible.

Probability Sampling

Let us consider three probabilistic sampling plans: systematic, stratified, and cluster sampling.

Systematic sampling is actually very similar to simple random sampling. It requires the use of a list of the items in the population and, therefore, suffers from the same kinds of problems previously mentioned concerning lists in simple random sampling. If the items on the list are in no particular order, systematic sampling can produce a random sample by sampling every kth item on the list, where k is found by dividing the population size by the sample size (i.e., $k = N/n$). Thus if $N = 200$ and $n = 10$, then $k = 200/10 = 20$. This means that one item out of each sequence of 20 will be sampled. A random number table can be consulted to determine where to begin in the first group, and then every kth item after that will be sampled. For example, if the random number table produces 09, then we would select the 9th item, then the 29th item (i.e., $9 + 20$), the 49th item (i.e., $29 + 20$), the 69th, and so on. Care must be taken to assure that the items in the list are not grouped or periodic in their appearance on the list. Thus names selected alphabetically may be grouped because various ethnic names begin with certain letters or letter combinations. Likewise, selecting houses to sample when the list is based on the order of the houses on a street can be risky since an equal number of houses on each block may mean that the corner house or a middle-of-the-block house will be every kth item. A corner house might have a higher property value, higher taxes, more noise, and so on, meaning that its occupants might be higher salaried, more concerned with the tax structure, hard of hearing, and so on, while the middle houses might exhibit quite different characteristics.

Stratified sampling involves dividing the population into subgroups (strata) of similar items and then sampling in each subgroup. The rationale is that by arranging the population items into *homogeneous* subgroups, the variability is smaller than that of the overall population, and this will necessitate a smaller sample size. This concept can easily be seen by considering an extreme case: suppose that the items in each stratum are identical. In that event, a single observation from each subgroup will indicate what each subgroup is like. Thus the more similar the items in each stratum, the smaller the size of the sample needed.

Sampling within each stratum is usually random, but a census is sometimes useful for some of the subgroups. For example, in a study of inventory systems, it is not unusual to discover that 10% of the *items* on hand in a firm's warehouse account for more than 60% of the *value* of the inventory, and that the other 90% of items account for less than 40% of the value of the inventory. Since there are so few items in the high-value class, it might make sense to take a complete census of those items, but to take only a random sample of the other subgroup(s) containing many lower-value items.

Some other examples of the use of stratified sampling might be a study of the amount of time individuals in various income categories spend on leisure activities, or perhaps the percentage of their salaries spent on recreation, or the kinds of vacations and the number of vacations they take. A study of sales volume versus amount of advertising expediture might also lend itself to stratified sampling if many firms are involved in the study.

Cluster sampling involves arranging items in a population into *heterogeneous subgroups* that are representative of the overall population. Ideally, each cluster could be regarded as a minipopulation. In fact, if the cluster arrangement was perfect, with each cluster exactly like every other cluster (and thus like the parent population), it would be necessary to examine only a single cluster in order to know what the population was like. This rarely occurs in practice, however, because clusters are usually groups of items that are in close physical contact, such as households, city blocks, counties, and so on. More often than not, such subgroups are nearly homogeneous and are selected more for administrative ease and cost savings than for their heterogeneous characteristics. It is usually impractical or impossible to arrange the items into heterogeneous subgroups. Consequently, a larger number of clusters must be sampled to offset this limitation.

Cluster sampling has two very distinct advantages over random sampling. One is that if the items in the population are widely dispersed, a random sample may involve considerable travel and expense to conduct properly, whereas the items within each cluster are close together. For example, suppose the population of interest was automobile owners in Texas. Undoubtedly, a simple random sample would include owners in widely separated locations throughout the state. Coordination and standardization of data collection would be difficult. Clusters of counties or towns, on the other hand, contain car owners in a concentrated area and data collection would be less costly and coordination a good deal easier. Moreover, by randomly selecting clusters from the entire state, a sample that was probably representative of the population could be obtained. Sampling within each cluster might involve random sampling, stratified sampling, or further clustering, since the number of owners even at the county or town levels might be too large to attempt a census.

A second advantage of cluster sampling is that a list of the items in the population is not necessary. A list of the clusters will suffice. Thus a list of all homeowners in the United States could not be readily obtained, but a list of states, counties, and even towns could be. Or the clusters might be city blocks. While lists of homes in a city might not be available, city blocks can often be identified and selected from maps. Then the chosen blocks can be visited and homes for sampling can be identified.

Very often a sampling design will incorporate several of these sampling plans. For example, the items in the population may be people living in a certain state. The state could be divided into counties (clusters) and a random selection of counties for further study could be made. The counties chosen could be divided into metropolitan and rural areas (stratified). The metropolitan areas might be further stratified by commercial and residential zones, or inner-city and suburban areas. The various strata might be randomly sampled, divided into clusters, or further stratified and then sampled or have a census taken. Obviously, the process can become rather complicated.

A comparison of probability sampling plans is presented in Table 6.2.

TABLE 6.2   Comparison of Probability Sampling
Designs

Type	Characterized by
random	list of items
systematic	random list of items
stratified	homogeneous subgroups
cluster	items physically close to each other

SUMMARY

The purpose of sampling is to be able to make inferences about a population after inspecting only a portion of the population. Such factors as cost, time, destructive testing, and infinite populations make sampling preferable to taking a complete survey (census) of a population. It is hoped that a sample will be representative of the population from which it has been drawn. The potential for achieving this goal is good when sampling is random. For discrete populations the term "random" means that each item in the population has the same chance of being included in a sample; for continuous populations it means that the probability of including any value in a given range of values is equal to the proportion of the population with values in that range. Random samples can be obtained by (a) a mixing process, such as shuffling cards, (b) using output of some mechanical *process*, or (c) using a random number table to select items from a list.

Under certain conditions variations of simple random sampling such as systematic (periodic) sampling, stratified (homogeneous subgroups) sampling, and cluster (convenient subgroups) sampling can be more efficient. The primary advantage of random sampling is that the degree of sampling variability can be determined, and this is essential for statistical inference. Nonprobability sampling lacks this feature, although it is sometimes used for other reasons.

REVIEW QUESTIONS

1. Under what circumstances is a sample preferable to a complete census?
2. When is a census preferable to a sample?

3. Define "random sample."
4. Describe the various methods for obtaining a random sample. How would you know which method to use in a particular situation?
5. What is a random number table? How is it used in connection with random sampling?
6. Explain briefly the major features of each of these:
   a. cluster sampling
   b. statified sampling
   c. systematic sampling
7. What is judgment sampling and under what sort of circumstances should it be used?
8. What is probability sampling, and when should it be used?

SUPPLEMENTAL EXERCISES

1. Explain the meaning of "random sample" when a population is:
   a. continuous   b. discrete
2. Explain why each of the following could *not* be considered a random sample:
   a. To ascertain the feeling of the community on a school bond issue, each school child is given a short questionnaire to be filled out by his or her parents.
   b. To measure public sentiment regarding the latest presidential proclamation, a newspaper reporter interviews 25 people on a downtown street corner at midday.
   c. Ten names are randomly selected from the list of members of the House of Representatives in an attempt to predict how various states feel about increasing the public debt ceiling for the third time in a week.
3. A fair coin is tossed 15 times and lands heads 6 times. Answer these questions:
   a. What is the sample proportion?
   b. What is the sample size?
   c. What is the population proportion?
   d. What is the population?
   e. What is the population size?
   f. What was the expected number of heads prior to tossing?
4. A coin is tossed 30 times and lands heads 15 times. It is not known if the coin is fair. Answer these questions:
   a. What is the sample proportion?
   b. What is the population proportion?
   c. Can you say anything at all about the expected number of heads?

7
sampling distributions

Chapter Objectives

After completing this chapter, you should be able to:
1. Explain what is meant by the term "sampling distribution"
2. Describe how population parameters influence sample statistics
3. Tell how sample size influences the dispersion of a sampling distribution
4. Explain why random sampling is important, and explain what its connection with a sampling distribution is
5. Explain what the Central Limit Theorem is and why it is important
6. Contrast deductive and inductive reasoning
7. State what relationship exists between (a) the mean of a population and the mean of a sampling distribution and (b) the standard deviation of a population and the standard deviation of a sampling distribution
8. Tell how formulas for the standard deviations of sampling distributions are modified when sampling from a finite population

Chapter Outline

Introduction
Effect of Population Parameters on a Sampling Distribution
Effect of Sample Size on a Sampling Distribution
Distributions of Sample Means
    The Central Limit Theorem
Distributions of Sample Proportions
Sampling Distribution of Number of Occurrences
Sampling from a Finite Population
Summary

INTRODUCTION

THE PURPOSE of sampling is to get an indication of the value of one or more of the parameters of a population, such as the population mean, the standard deviation, or the proportion of items in the population that possess a certain characteristic. The sample statistics that correspond to these population parameters are used to approximate the unknown values of population parameters. Thus the sample mean is used to estimate the population mean; the sample standard deviation is used to estimate the population standard deviation; and the sample proportion is used to estimate the proportion in the population.

One of the realities of random sampling is that when repeated samples are taken from the same population, there is a tendency for sample statistics to vary from each other and from the true value of the population parameter, simply because of chance factors related to sampling. This tendency is known as *sampling variability*. (For this reason, one can usually be quite sure that a given sample statistic does *not* equal the corresponding population parameter.) Obviously, then, any attempt to draw inferences about a population must take sampling variability into account.

Generally speaking, it might appear that it would be difficult to deal in a rational manner with sampling variability. In the case of *random* sampling, however, it can be shown mathematically that the variability can be described by probability distributions such as the normal and binomial distributions. When probability distributions are used in this way, they are referred to as *sampling distributions*. Since these distributions can be used only when samples are random, it is essential to use only random samples for statistical inference.

The question that must be answered for each sample is this: *How close* is the sample statistic to the actual value of the population parameter? The answer to the question will depend on three factors. One factor is the statistic being considered. Different probability distributions are used to describe the sampling variability associated with different sample statistics. Another factor is the size of the sample. There is less variability among statistics of large samples than there is among statistics of small samples. And the third factor is the variability that exists in the population being sampled. Populations with much variability will produce sample statistics with more variability than populations having little variation among population values.

To understand how sample statistics can be used to make inferences about population parameters, we begin by studying populations with *known* parameters and observe the sample statistics they tend to produce (deductive reasoning). Having done that, we will be in a position to learn how the characteristics of a single sample can be used to make inferences about the parameter(s) of a population (inductive reasoning).

178

> A *sampling distribution* is a probability distribution that indicates the extent to which a sample statistic will tend to vary due to chance variation in random sampling.

The concept of a sampling distribution is often difficult to grasp initially. For that reason let us examine a simple sampling distribution. Suppose a farmer has some pigs that he is considering selling. To keep the example simple, let us limit the population to 5 pigs. For our purposes we assume that we know the weights of the pigs, although the farmer does not. The weights are shown in Table 7.1.

TABLE 7.1   Population of Five Pigs

Pig	Weight (lb)
A	200
B	203
C	206
D	209
E	212
	1030

Let us imagine that any pig that weighs less than 205 pounds is underweight and cannot be sold for a reasonable profit. Hence 2 of the pigs, or $\frac{2}{5}$ of the population, fall into this category. Now the farmer wants to estimate the proportion of his pigs that are underweight. Because it is such a hassle to catch and weigh the pigs, he decides to sample 2 pigs and use the sample proportion to estimate the proportion in the population. The questions we want to answer are these: What sample proportions are possible, and how likely is each one? In other words, we want the sampling distribution for this situation.

Since a sampling distribution should indicate the possible outcomes, we begin by identifying these. Presumably, the farmer would sample without replacement,

TABLE 7.2   Sample Combinations of Two Pigs

Sample size	Number of samples possible	Sample combination	Sample weights	Proportion below 205
2	$\binom{5}{2} = 10$	A, B	200, 203	$\frac{2}{2}$
		A, C	200, 206	$\frac{1}{2}$
		A, D	200, 209	$\frac{1}{2}$
		A, E	200, 212	$\frac{1}{2}$
		B, C	203, 206	$\frac{1}{2}$
		B, D	203, 209	$\frac{1}{2}$
		B, E	203, 212	$\frac{1}{2}$
		C, D	206, 209	$\frac{0}{2}$
		C, E	206, 212	$\frac{0}{2}$
		D, E	209, 212	$\frac{0}{2}$

since he would not want to weigh the same pig twice. Table 7.2 illustrates the possible sample outcomes. The same results are also portrayed in Figure 7.1.

The sampling distribution shows that the possible sample proportions are $\frac{0}{2}$, $\frac{1}{2}$, and $\frac{2}{2}$. It also shows *how probable* each sample proportion is under the assumption that each pig has the same chance of being included in the sample (i.e., *random* sampling). For instance, there is a .60 probability that the sample proportion will be $\frac{1}{2}$, which is close to the actual proportion (since samples of 2 are used, it would be impossible to have a *sample* proportion of $\frac{2}{5}$). If we chose to consider the distribution for samples of 3 observations for the same population, the sampling distribution for the proportion of underweight pigs would look like the one shown in Figure 7.2. Note that the possible sample outcomes are different for samples of 3 than they were for samples of 2.

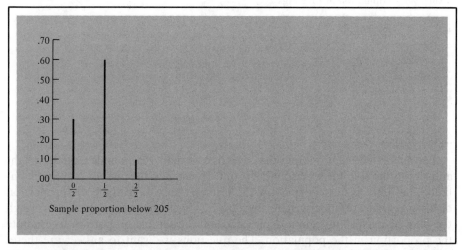

FIGURE 7.1   Distribution of sample proportions of underweight pigs for samples of 2 from a population of 5, with a population proportion of $\frac{2}{5}$.

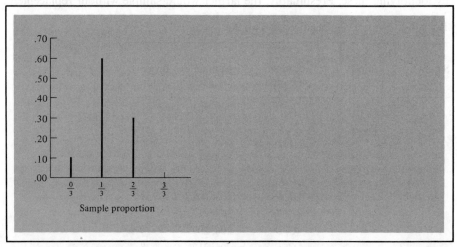

FIGURE 7.2   Sampling distribution for proportion of underweight pigs, with $n = 3$, $p = \frac{2}{5}$.

Although this empirical approach to sampling distributions is impractical because it requires listing all possible outcomes, it does provide a way of considering on a small scale what a sampling distribution is. In practice, sampling distributions are derived mathematically and made available to users in the form of tables and charts. Two of the most widely used sampling distributions are the binomial distribution and the normal distribution, with which you are already familiar. We now need to explore further some of the ways that a population can influence a sampling distribution.

EFFECT OF POPULATION PARAMETERS ON A SAMPLING DISTRIBUTION

It was previously stated that random sampling tends to yield sample statistics that are representative of population parameters. That is, in spite of the fact that random samples tend to exhibit sampling variability, we can say that sample statistics should *approximate* population parameters rather well. This characteristic of being representative results in sample statistics that tend to cluster around actual population values.

We can explore this claim in a number of ways. Perhaps the simplest is to focus our attention on a sampling distribution for the number of occurrences. Suppose we are charged with sampling large containers of jelly beans in order to estimate the percentage that are licorice. We can get some idea of how the percentage in the population (large container) can influence the sample percentage by considering various population proportions (parameters) and examining the related sampling distributions. For instance, suppose we intend to take samples of 10 observations and count the number of licorice jelly beans in the sample. This situation can be adequately described by a binomial distribution with $n = 10$, treating jelly beans as licorice and not licorice. We must assume that the population is so large that the probability of obtaining a licorice jelly bean remains nearly constant from observation to observation, but this does not seem unreasonable.

A table of individual binomial probabilities can be used to obtain the probabilities of the various outcomes (0, 1, 2, . . . , 10 licorice) possible. Converting these outcomes to percentages makes the illustration of how the population proportion influences the sample proportion even clearer. Figure 7.3 shows a succession of sampling (probability) distributions, each with a different percentage of licorice in the population. For instance, the first distribution shows the probability of each sample proportion (0, .1, .2, . . . , 1.0) for a population with 5% licorice, the second shows those probabilities for a population with 10% licorice, and so on. Notice that in each case the distribution of sample proportions seems to reflect the population proportion. That is, the outcomes with the highest probabilities are those closest to the proportion in the population. The implication is that when sampling is random, there is a high probability that the sample statistic will approximate the population parameter. Thus populations with small percentages of some item will tend to generate samples with small percentages of the item; populations with moderate percentages will produce samples that usually have moderate percentages of the item; and populations with large percentages will typically have samples with large percentages. Note, though, that there is some degree of variation; sample statistics do not necessarily equal the population parameter.

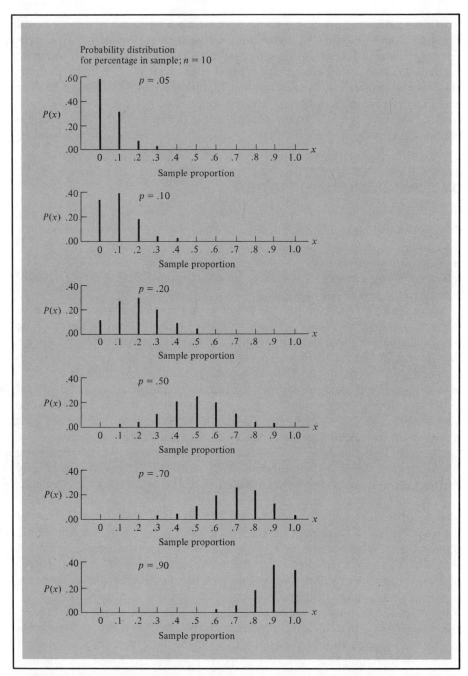

FIGURE 7.3   The distribution of sample proportions is influenced by the population proportion; sample proportions with the highest probabilities are those closest to *p*.

EFFECT OF SAMPLE SIZE ON A SAMPLING DISTRIBUTION

The binomial distribution also provides a convenient method for illustrating the *basic relationship between sample size and variability* in the sampling distribution.

This can be readily observed by selecting a single proportion (probability of success) and comparing outcome probabilities for various sample sizes. Again, the probabilities come from a table of individual binomial probabilities converted to percentage of successes. The series of graphs in Figure 7.4 illustrate the distribution of sample proportions for samples of $n = 2, 4, 8, 16, 32$ for the situation where the proportion of licorice jelly beans in the population is 50%.

There are three very important points illustrated in Figure 7.4. One is that as the sample size increases, the distribution of sample outcomes approaches the

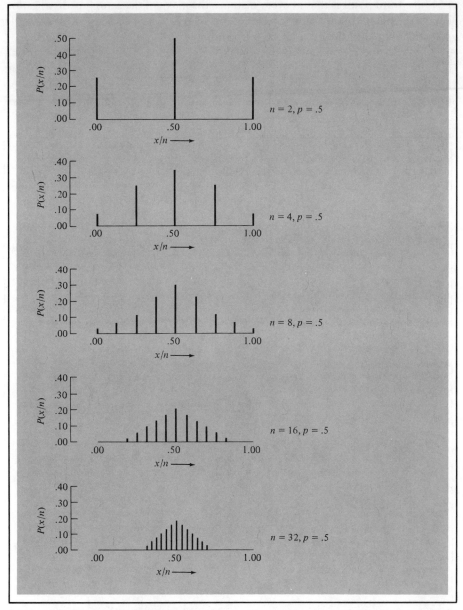

FIGURE 7.4 A series of graphs illustrate that as the sample size increases, (1) the sampling distribution of proportions approaches normality and (2) sampling variability decreases. Note that the mean of the sampling distribution always equals the population proportion.

shape of the normal distribution. The rate at which a sampling distribution approaches normality will depend on how symmetrical the population is: the more symmetrical, the more rapid the approach to normality (and thus the smaller the sample size necessary to "assume" normality).

A second point illustrated in Figure 7.4 is that as the sample size increases, there is less and less variability among sample proportions. The implication of this is that large samples have a stronger tendency to produce sample statistics that are relatively close in value to the population parameter. Thus the potential error will decrease as the sample size increases.

Still a third point is that in every instance the mean of the sampling distribution equals the population parameter. Hence the average or expected value of a sample statistic is equal to the population proportion.

Although the binomial distribution provides a convenient way of illustrating certain properties of sampling distributions, the results are more general than applications involving proportions. For example, the normal distribution is often appropriate for describing distributions of sample means. Figure 7.5(a) demon-

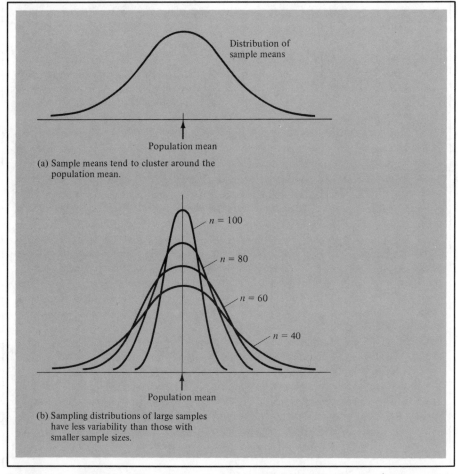

FIGURE 7.5 (a) Sample means tend to cluster around the population mean. (b) Sampling distributions have less variability as the sample size increases.

strates the same tendency for sample means to cluster around the population mean. We know, for instance, that about 68% of the values in a normal distribution lie within one standard deviation of the mean. And unlike the binomial distribution, the sampling distribution is always symmetrical around its mean. Figure 7.5(b) illustrates that increasing the sample size decreases the variability inherent in the sampling distribution.

DISTRIBUTIONS OF SAMPLE MEANS

A sampling distribution of means is a probability distribution that indicates how likely various sample means are. The distribution is a function of the mean and standard deviation of the population and the sample size. For each combination of population mean, population standard deviation, and sample size, there will be a unique sampling distribution of sample means.

Earlier in the chapter we considered a population of five pigs and a farmer who wanted to estimate the proportion of underweight pigs. He might very well focus on the average weight of the pigs, in which case the distribution of sample means would be appropriate. The data from Table 7.1 are repeated in Table 7.3, along with the population parameters.

TABLE 7.3   Population of Five Pigs

Pig	Weight (lb)	Parameters
A	200	mean = $\frac{1030}{5}$ = 206
B	203	standard deviation = 4.24
C	206	
D	209	
E	212	
	1030	

If the farmer wishes to estimate the average weight of his pigs, he might consider taking samples of two, three, or possibly four. And again, it would be possible to list each possible sample mean and construct a frequency distribution. In addition, we could compute the mean and standard deviation of each sampling distribution. As previously noted, mathematical procedures are preferable to this empirical approach. Nonetheless, the results of the empirical method reveal some interesting properties of sampling distributions. The results are shown in Table 7.4.

TABLE 7.4   Summary of Parameters of Sampling
Distributions of Means and the Population
of Five Pigs

	Mean	Standard deviation
Population	206	4.24
Sampling distributions		
$n = 2$	206	2.60
$n = 3$	206	1.73
$n = 4$	206	1.06

Table 7.4 illustrates several things. One is that the mean of the sampling distribution seems to always equal the population mean. And the fact that the mean of a sampling distribution is exactly equal to the population mean in each case is not a coincidence. It results from the fact that a sampling distribution is comprised of "all possible samples" and therefore includes every population item. In essence, computing the mean of a sampling distribution is merely an indirect method of computing the mean of the population. This can be seen with a simple example.

Suppose there are three items in a population: x_1, x_2, and x_3. The population mean is $(x_1 + x_2 + x_3)/3$. If all samples of two items were taken, the combinations would be x_1 and x_2, x_1 and x_3, and x_2 and x_3. The sample means would be

$$\frac{x_1 + x_2}{2} \qquad \frac{x_1 + x_3}{2} \qquad \frac{x_2 + x_3}{2}$$

The mean of the three sample means (and the mean of the sampling distribution) would be

$$\frac{[(x_1 + x_2)/2] + [(x_1 + x_3)/2] + [(x_2 + x_3)/2]}{3} = \frac{\frac{1}{2}(x_1 + x_2 + x_1 + x_3 + x_2 + x_3)}{3}$$

$$= \frac{\frac{1}{2}(2x_1 + 2x_2 + 2x_3)}{3}$$

$$= \frac{x_1 + x_2 + x_3}{3}$$

which is the population mean.

Another feature illustrated in Table 7.4 is that the standard deviation of the sampling distribution appears to be decreasing as the size of samples increases. The same characteristic was noted earlier. The implications are that the average or expected value of the sample mean will equal the population mean and that larger samples tend to be more reliable than smaller samples.

Let us now consider the formulas that are actually used for computations involving sampling distributions of means. The mean of a sampling distribution is always equal to the mean of the population.* Thus

$$\mu_{\bar{x}} = \mu_x$$

where

$$\mu_{\bar{x}} = \text{the mean of sampling distribution}$$

$$\mu_x = \text{the population mean}$$

When the population is very large or infinite, the standard deviation of the sampling distribution of means is

$$\sigma_{\bar{x}} = \frac{\sigma_x}{\sqrt{n}}$$

* Because of this, the symbol μ_x will be used to designate both the population mean and the mean of the sampling distribution after this chapter.

where

$\sigma_{\bar{x}}$ = the standard deviation of the sampling distribution

σ_x = the population standard deviation

n = the sample size

The formula for the standard deviation says, in effect, that the amount of dispersion in the sampling distribution depends on two things:

1. The dispersion in the population.
2. The square root of the sample size.

For instance, for any given population increasing the size of samples taken from that population will result in less variability among possible sample means. And if the same sample size is used with different populations, the populations with the largest amount of dispersion (σ_x) will tend to generate the largest amount of variability among means of samples drawn from those populations.

The Central Limit Theorem

The ability to use samples to draw inferences about population parameters depends on knowledge of the sampling distribution. We have just seen how the mean and standard deviation are determined, but we still need one additional piece of information: the *shape* of the sampling distribution. Earlier it was implied that there is a tendency for the distributions of means and proportions to be normal. In the case of sample means, it can be shown mathematically that if a *population* is normally distributed, the distribution of sample means drawn from that population will also be normally distributed, for *any* sample size. Furthermore, even if the population is nonnormal, the distribution of sample means will be approximately normal if the sample size is large. This is fortunate, indeed, since it tells us that *it is not necessary to know what the population distribution is in order to be able to draw inferences about the population from sample data.* The only restriction is that the sample size be large. A rule of thumb that is used very often is that samples must include 30 or more observations.

These results are known as the *Central Limit Theorem*, and they are perhaps the single most important concept of statistical inference.

The Central Limit Theorem

1. If the population being sampled is normally distributed, the distribution of sample means will be normally distributed for all sample sizes.
2. If the underlying population is nonnormal, the distribution of sample means will be approximately normal for large sample sizes.

Strictly speaking, the Central Limit Theorem applies only to sample means. Nonetheless, you may recall that *except* for very small or very large values of *p*, the normal distribution provides a reasonable approximation to binomial probabilities for large sample sizes. Hence the normal distribution can be utilized for means *and* proportions for large sample sizes.

The Central Limit Theorem is depicted graphically in Figure 7.6.

Let us see how this information can be applied to obtain probabilities of various sample statistics for samples drawn from known populations.

Example 1   A very large population has a mean of 20.0 and a standard deviation of 1.4. A sample of 49 observations will be taken. Answer these questions:

    a. What is the mean of the sampling distribution?
    b. What is the standard deviation of the sampling distribution?
    c. What percentage of possible sample means will differ from the population mean by more than .2?

Solution:
Since $n > 30$, we can assume the sampling distribution is normal.

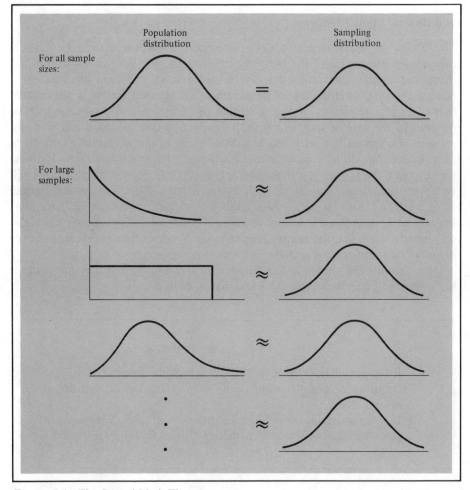

FIGURE 7.6   The Central Limit Theorem.

a. The mean of the sampling distribution always equals the mean of the population. Hence $\mu_{\bar{x}} = 20.0$.

b. The standard deviation of the sampling distribution is

$$\sigma_{\bar{x}} = \frac{\sigma_x}{\sqrt{n}} = \frac{1.4}{\sqrt{49}} = \frac{1.4}{7} = .2$$

c. The percentage of sample means that will differ by more than .2 from the population mean (see Figure 7.7) is

$$\frac{20.2 - 20}{.2} = +1\sigma_{\bar{x}} \qquad \text{proportion: .1587}$$

$$\frac{19.8 - 20}{.2} = -1\sigma_{\bar{x}} \qquad \text{proportion: .1587}$$
$$\text{total: .3174}$$

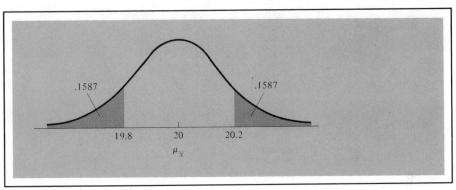

FIGURE 7.7 The shaded portions equal the probability of a sample mean less than 19.8 or greater than 20.2.

Example 2 A manufacturer of car batteries claims that its premium line batteries have an expected (average) life of 50 months. It is known that the standard deviation of battery life is 4 months for premium batteries made by this company. What percentage of samples of 36 observations will have an average mean life within 1 month of 50 months, assuming 50 is the true average life of the batteries? What is the answer if a sample of 64 observations is taken?

Solution:
We know that since $n > 30$ observations, the distribution of sample means will be approximately normal, with a mean equal to the population mean and a standard deviation equal to the population standard deviation divided by the square root of the sample size. Figure 7.8 depicts the unknown probability.

The solution involves determining the number of standard deviations that 49 months and 51 months are from the mean and then referring to a table of areas under the normal curve to obtain the necessary probabilities.

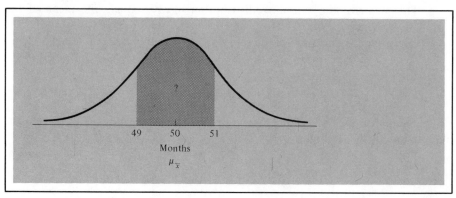

FIGURE 7.8   The problem requires determining the shaded area of the sampling distribution.

First determine the standard deviation of the sampling distribution:

$$\sigma_{\bar{x}} = \frac{\sigma_x}{\sqrt{n}}$$

$$\text{for } n = 36: \sigma_{\bar{x}} = \frac{4}{\sqrt{36}} = \frac{4}{6} = .67$$

$$\text{for } n = 64: \sigma_{\bar{x}} = \frac{4}{\sqrt{64}} = \frac{4}{8} = .50$$

Next find the relative difference from the expected value:

$$z = \frac{\text{statistic} - \text{parameter}}{\sigma_{\bar{x}}}$$

$$\text{for } n = 36: \frac{49 - 50}{.67} = \frac{-1}{.67} = -1.5\sigma_{\bar{x}} \qquad \frac{51 - 50}{.67} = \frac{1}{.67} = 1.5\sigma_{\bar{x}}$$

$$\text{for } n = 64: \frac{49 - 50}{.50} = \frac{-1}{.50} = -2\sigma_{\bar{x}} \qquad \frac{51 - 50}{.50} = \frac{1}{.50} = 2\sigma_{\bar{x}}$$

Now find the areas using Table G in the Appendix:

$$\text{for } n = 36: z = 1.5 \qquad \text{area} = .4332$$
$$P(49 < \bar{x} < 51) = .4332 + .4332 = .8664$$
$$\text{for } n = 64: z = 2.0 \qquad \text{area} = .4773$$
$$P(49 < \bar{x} < 51) = .4773 + .4773 = .9546$$

Observe that even though the range of 49 to 51 remained the same, the answers for samples of 36 and 64 are different. The probability of getting a sample mean in the given range is *larger* for samples of 64 observations than for samples of 36, due to the fact that the standard deviation of the sampling distribution *decreases* as n increases.

Example 3   Using the information contained in Example 2, what would the probability be of getting a sample mean of less than 49.8 months with a sample of 100 observations?

Solution:
Figure 7.9 portrays the unknown area under the normal curve.

$$\sigma_{\bar{x}} = \frac{\sigma_x}{\sqrt{n}} = \frac{4}{10} = .4$$

$$\frac{49.8 - 50}{.4} = -.5\sigma_{\bar{x}}$$

The area beyond $-.5\sigma_{\bar{x}}$ is .3085.

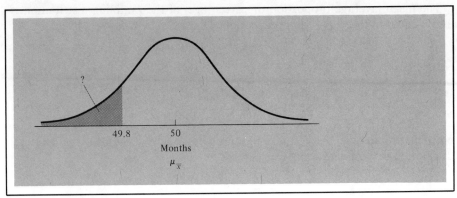

49.8   50

Months

$\mu_{\bar{x}}$

FIGURE 7.9   The shaded portion represents $P(\bar{x} \leq 49.8)$.

EXERCISES

1. If a sample is drawn from a normal distribution, what is the probability that the sample mean will have a value in each of these ranges?
   a. $\mu_x \pm 1.96\sigma_{\bar{x}}$ b. $\mu_x \pm 2.00\sigma_{\bar{x}}$ c. $\mu_x \pm 2.33\sigma_{\bar{x}}$

2. The mean of a sampling distribution of means is 50.0 and its standard deviation is 10.0. Assume the sampling distribution is normal.
   a. What percentage of sample means will be between 45.0 and 55.0?
   b. What percentage of sample means will be between 42.5 and 57.5?
   c. What percentage of sample means will be less than the population mean?
   d. What percentage of sample means will be equal to the population mean?

3. Determine the mean of the distribution of sample means given each of these *population* means:
   a. 5.01   b. 18.41   c. 199.5   d. .008

4. Compute the standard deviation of the sampling distribution of means for each of the following:
   a. $\sigma_x = 5, n = 16$ b. $\sigma_x = 1, n = 36$ c. $\sigma_x = 2, n = 40$
   d. $\sigma_x = 6.2, n = 100$ e. $\sigma_x = 3.2, n = 44$

5. Samples of 36 observations are to be taken from a machine that stamps out commemorative coins. The average thickness of the coins is .20 cm, with a standard deviation of .01 cm.
   a. Is it essential to know that the population is normal in order to state the percentage of sample means that will fall within certain ranges? Explain.
   b. What percentage of sample means will fall in the interval .20 ± .004 cm?
   c. What is the probability of obtaining a sample mean that deviates by more than .005 cm from the process mean?

DISTRIBUTIONS OF SAMPLE PROPORTIONS

A distribution of sample proportions indicates how likely a particular set of sample proportions is, given the sample size and the population proportion. When the sample size is 20 or less, the probabilities of the various possible outcomes can be read directly from a table of *binomial* probabilities simply by converting the number of successes to percentages. For example, 3 occurrences in 10 observations would be 30%, and 5 occurrences in 20 observations would be 25%. For larger sample sizes the normal approximation to the binomial yields fairly decent values.

The mean (average proportion or percentage) of the sampling distribution is always equal to the population proportion. That is,

$$\bar{p} = p$$

where

p = the proportion in the population

$\bar{p}$ = the mean of the sampling distribution of proportions

When the population is very large or infinite, the standard deviation of the sampling distribution is computed using the formula

$$\sigma_p = \sqrt{\frac{p(1-p)}{n}}$$

Example 4   A retailer purchases drinking glasses directly from the factory in large shipments. The glasses are individually wrapped. From time to time the retailer inspects shipments to determine the proportion of broken or chipped glasses. If a large shipment contains 10% chipped or broken glasses, what is the probability that the retailer will obtain a random sample of 100 glasses that has 17% or more defective?

Solution:
The sampling distribution will be centered around 10%, which is the population percentage defective. Figure 7.10 illustrates the unknown percentage. The first step is to compute the standard deviation of the population:

$$\sigma_p = \sqrt{\frac{p(1-p)}{n}} = \sqrt{\frac{(.10)(.90)}{100}} = \frac{.3}{10} = .03$$

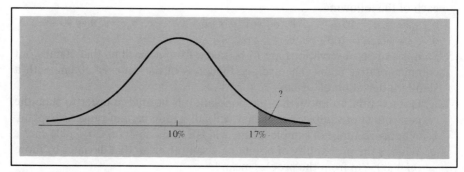

FIGURE 7.10 $P(x/n \geq 17\%)$.

This can now be used to determine the relative variation:

$$\frac{17\% - 10\%}{3\%} = \frac{+7\%}{3\%} = 2.33\sigma_p = z$$

The area beyond $2.33\sigma_p$ is .0099 (from Table G, with $z = 2.33$).

Theoretically, we ought to use a correction for continuity, since we are using the normal distribution to approximate binomial probabilities. From a practical standpoint, the additional effort is usually uncalled for. This is particularly true for large sample sizes with values of z of 2 or more.

SAMPLING DISTRIBUTION OF NUMBER OF OCCURRENCES

The sampling distributions of proportions and number of occurrences are essentially the same. Both pertain to count data rather than measurements, both involve using binomial tables for desired probabilities when the sample size is less than 20, and both can be approximated with the normal distribution for larger sample sizes. The only difference between the two is that the sampling distribution for proportions has values stated as percentages, while the sampling distribution for number of occurrences has values stated as counts. A comparison of the formulas for the mean and standard deviation of each type of sampling distribution is shown in Table 7.5.

TABLE 7.5   Comparison of Formulas for the Sampling Distribution of Proportions and the Sampling Distribution of Number of Occurrences

Sampling distribution	Mean	Standard deviation
proportions	p	$\sigma_p = \sqrt{\dfrac{p(1 - p)}{n}}$
number of occurrences	np	$\sigma_{np} = \sqrt{np(1 - p)}$

Example 5   Suppose that a recently conducted survey revealed that 60% of the adult male population consists of nonsmokers. If a random sample of 600 male adults is taken, find and interpret the mean and standard deviation of the sampling distribution.

Solution:
We have that $n = 600$, $p = .60$, so that $1 - p = .40$.

$$\text{mean} = np = 600(.60) = 360$$
$$\text{standard deviation} = \sqrt{np(1 - p)} = \sqrt{600(.60)(.40)}$$
$$= \sqrt{144} = 12$$

The mean of the sampling distribution, 360, is the number of nonsmokers that we would expect to have in a random sample of 600 male adults, assuming that .60 of the male adults are nonsmokers. Knowing that sampling variability always exists, we would be surprised if there were *exactly* 360 nonsmokers in our sample.

In fact, the standard deviation of the sampling distribution, 12, tells us how much dispersion to expect. For example, 95.5% (2 standard deviations) of such samples ought to fall in the range of ± 24 around 360, or from 336 to 384 nonsmokers.

EXERCISES

1. Find the mean of the distribution of sample proportions when the proportion in the population being sampled is:
   a. 30%   b. 43%   c. 50%   d. 72.3%
2. Find the standard deviation of the sampling distribution of proportions for $n = 100$ and a population proportion of:
   a. 10%   b. 20%   c. 40%   d. 50%
   e. 60%   f. 80%   g. 90%
3. Explain why the normal distribution is used for samples of 20 or more observations when the binomial distribution is theoretically correct when working with proportions. When is the binomial preferable to the normal?
4. Assuming a fairly large sample size, determine the percentage of sample proportions you would expect to fall in these ranges:
   a. $p \pm 1\sigma_p$ b. $p \pm 1.96\sigma_p$ c. $p \pm 2\sigma_p$ d. $p \pm 2.33\sigma_p$
5. Find z if the percentage of sample proportions that is expected to fall in the range $p \pm z\sigma_p$ is:
   a. 90%   b. 95%   c. 99%   d. 99.7%
6. If samples of $n = 100$ observations are to be drawn from a very large population in which the population proportion is 20%, what percentage of the sample proportions might be expected in these ranges?
   a. 16% to 24%   b. greater than 24%   c. 12% to 28%
   d. less than 12% or more than 28%

SAMPLING FROM A FINITE POPULATION

Most sampling is done without replacement, for psychological reasons as well as cost and convenience reasons. As long as the sample size is small *relative* to the size of the population being sampled, sampling without replacement yields essentially the same variability among samples as sampling with replacement does. However, if the sample size is an appreciable percentage of the population (say more than 5%), the results of sampling without replacement are somewhat different than the results obtained with replacement. This is because the probabilities of drawing population items change from draw to draw without replacement. Under such circumstances the hypergeometric distribution is appropriate for determining sample probabilities.

The formulas for the standard deviation of sample means and the standard deviation of sample proportions must be modified to reflect the changing probabilities *if the sample size is more than 5% of the population*. Fortunately, the hypergeometric modification reduces to a simple form:

$$\sqrt{\frac{N - n}{N - 1}}$$

where

$$N = \text{the population size}$$
$$n = \text{the sample size}$$

This formula is referred to as a *finite correction factor*, or sometimes as a *finite population multiplier* since it is multiplied times the usual standard deviation formulas for sampling distributions.

The standard deviation of sample means becomes

$$\sigma_{\bar{x}} = \frac{\sigma_x}{\sqrt{n}} \sqrt{\frac{N-n}{N-1}}$$

The standard deviation of sample proportions is

$$\sigma_p = \sqrt{\frac{p(1-p)}{n}} \sqrt{\frac{N-n}{N-1}}$$

The standard deviation of number of occurrences is

$$\sigma_{np} = \sqrt{np(1-p)} \sqrt{\frac{N-n}{N-1}}$$

Example 6   A machine for coating chocolate-covered cherries is set to give an average thickness of chocolate of 3 mm. The process is normally distributed, with a standard deviation of 1 mm. If the process functions as expected (i.e., mean of 3 mm and standard deviation of 1 mm), what would the probability be of drawing a sample of 25 chocolate-covered cherries from a batch of 169 and finding a sample average of more than 3.4?

Solution:
Figure 7.11 illustrates the unknown probability of getting a sample mean greater than 3.4 mm.

Since the population is finite and the sample size is greater than 5% ($n/N = 25/169 = .15$), the finite correction factor is appropriate. The solution involves finding how far away from the mean 3.4 mm is (in terms of standard deviations

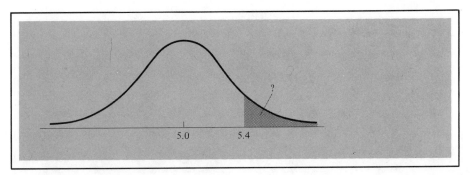

FIGURE 7.11 $P(\bar{x} \geq 5.4)$.

from the mean) and using that value to obtain the probability from the normal curve area table.

$$\sigma_{\bar{x}} = \frac{\sigma_x}{\sqrt{n}} \sqrt{\frac{N - n}{N - 1}} = \frac{1}{\sqrt{25}} \sqrt{\frac{169 - 25}{168}}$$

$$= \tfrac{1}{5}(.92) = .185$$

$$\frac{\bar{x} - \mu}{\sigma_{\bar{x}}} = \frac{3.4 - 3.0}{.185} = \frac{.4}{.185} \approx 2.2\sigma_{\bar{x}}$$

The area under the normal curve beyond $\mu + 2.2\sigma_{\bar{x}}$ is .0139. Thus $P(x > 3.4)$ is 1.39%.

Example 7   A process that fills bottles of cola averages an output in which 10% of the bottles are underfilled. If a sample of 225 bottles are to be selected randomly from a run of 625 bottles filled by this process, what is the probability that the sample proportion of underfilled bottles will be in the range from 9% to 11%?

Solution:
Figure 7.12 illustrates the problem.

   Because the size of the sample is large relative to the size of the population (n/N is 225/625, or 36%), the finite population multiplier is needed. By determining the number of standard deviations from the process average that 9% and 11% are, the desired probability can be determined.

$$\sigma_p = \sqrt{\frac{p(1 - p)}{n}} \sqrt{\frac{N - n}{N - 1}} = \sqrt{\frac{(.10)(.90)}{225}} \sqrt{\frac{625 - 225}{625 - 1}}$$

$$\approx \frac{.3}{15} \cdot \frac{20}{25} = .016$$

$$z_1 = \frac{.09 - .10}{.016} = -.625$$

$$z_2 = \frac{.11 - .10}{.016} = .625$$

The area under the curve in the range z_1 to z_2 is $2(.2340) = .4680$.

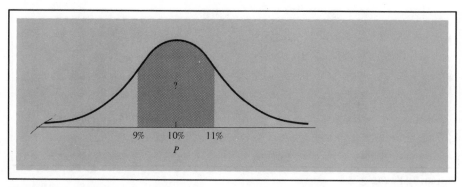

FIGURE 7.12 $P(9\% \le x/n \le 11\%)$.

SUMMARY

Sampling distributions are probability distributions for sample statistics. Hence they indicate how likely various possible values of a sample statistic are. This chapter has considered distributions of sample means, proportions, and number of occurrences. There are other important distributions, which will be considered later.

The importance of sampling distributions to statistical inference cannot be over-emphasized. The purpose of sampling is to be able to learn something about a population without having to examine a large portion of the population. Sampling distributions provide the basis for accomplishing this. When sampling is random, sampling distributions possess certain fundamental characteristics that result in representative samples. One characteristic is that the mean of a sampling distribution (and hence the expected mean of a sample) equals the mean of the population. Another characteristic is that sample values that have the greatest probability of occurrence are those closest to the true population value. And a third feature is that the larger the sample size, the less dispersion there will be among possible sample values.

Sampling distributions are often familiar probability distributions, such as the binomial, hypergeometric, or Poisson, but by far the most important distribution is the normal. This is due to the Central Limit Theorem, which states that large samples tend to yield a sampling distribution that is approximately normal even though the population being sampled is not normal, while any size sample from a normal population will have a sampling distribution that is normal.

Sampling without replacement requires a modification of the usual formulas for computing the standard deviation of a sampling distribution if the sample represents more than 5% of the population. Table 7.6 presents a summary of the formulas discussed in this chapter.

TABLE 7.6   Summary of Sampling Distribution Formulas

		Standard deviation	
Sampling distribution	Mean	Infinite population	Finite population
means	$\mu_{\bar{x}}$	$\sigma_{\bar{x}} = \dfrac{\sigma_x}{\sqrt{n}}$	$\sigma_{\bar{x}} = \dfrac{\sigma_x}{\sqrt{n}} \sqrt{\dfrac{N-n}{N-1}}$
proportions	$\bar{p}$	$\sigma_p = \sqrt{\dfrac{p(1-p)}{n}}$	$\sigma_p = \sqrt{\dfrac{p(1-p)}{n}} \sqrt{\dfrac{N-n}{N-1}}$
number of occurrences	np	$\sigma_{np} = \sqrt{np(1-p)}$	$\sigma_{np} = \sqrt{np(1-p)} \sqrt{\dfrac{N-n}{N-1}}$

REVIEW QUESTIONS

1. Define the term "sampling distribution."
2. What is the connection between random sampling and sampling distributions?
3. What effect does each of the following have on the variability (dispersion) of a sampling distribution of means?
   a. sample size   b. population mean

4. Contrast the effect of increasing the sample size on sampling distributions of proportions with sampling distributions of number of occurrences.
5. What effect does the population mean have on sample means?
6. What is the essence of the Central Limit Theorem?
7. Why is the Central Limit Theorem important?
8. Why do repeated samples taken from the same population tend to vary from each other?
9. What effect does sampling from a finite population have on the variability of a sampling distribution?
10. Contrast inductive and deductive reasoning. Which type of reasoning was used in this chapter? Which type will be used in future chapters?
11. State the relationship that exists between:
   a. The mean of a population and the mean of a sampling distribution of means.
   b. The standard deviation of a population and the standard deviation of a sampling distribution of means.
12. In view of the Central Limit Theorem, when is it necessary to know, or to assume, that a population of measurements is normally distributed?

SUPPLEMENTAL EXERCISES

*1. Approximately 10% of the family-owned stores in a certain region offer trading stamps to their customers. Find the probability that a random sample of 100 stores would indicate that the percentage that give stamps is:
   a. 16% or more
   b. 6% to 16%
   c. more than 18%
2. The purchasing department of a large company routinely rejects shipments of parts if a random sample of 100 from a lot of 10,000 parts has 10 or more defectives. Find the probability that a lot will be rejected if it has a percentage defective of:
   a. 3%   b. 4%   c. 5%   d. 18%   e. 20%
3. If the mean operating life of a flashlight battery is 24 hours and is normally distributed, with a standard deviation of 3 hours, what is the probability that a random sample of 100 flashlight batteries will have a mean that deviates by more than 30 minutes from the average?
4. How would your answer to Exercise 3 differ if the mean of the population was unknown? What, then, is the implication of not knowing the population mean in terms of the extent to which sample means will tend to deviate from the true mean?
*5. It has been established that customer invoices have a standard deviation of $45. If a sample of 225 invoices is taken, what is the probability that the sample mean will deviate from the mean of all 20,000 invoices by $7.50 or more?
*6. How would your answer to Exercise 5 differ if the population consisted of 2000 invoices?
7. A random sample of 400 factory workers at a large plant is taken by a government agency to get an indication of those who might favor unionizing. Find the probability of getting a sample proportion that differs by more than 3% from the actual proportion if the actual proportion of employees who favor unionizing is:
   a. 10%   b. 20%   c. 50%   d. 80%   e. 90%

8

estimation

Chapter Objectives

After completing this chapter, you should be able to:
1. Discuss the meaning of the term "estimation"
2. Describe and compare point and interval estimates
3. Tell why it is desirable to include a probability statement with an interval estimate
4. Explain how sampling distributions are used in estimation
5. Construct confidence intervals for population means and proportions using sample data
6. Use charts to construct intervals for proportions
7. Indicate how sample size, sample dispersion, and confidence level affect the possible error in an estimate

Chapter Outline

Introduction
Point and Interval Estimates
The Rationale of Estimation
Estimating the Mean of a Population
  Population standard deviation known
  Estimation error
  Sample size determination
  Estimating means when σ_x is unknown: the t distribution
  Sampling from small populations: the finite correction factor
  One-sided confidence intervals
Estimating the Proportion in a Population
  Confidence intervals: the formula approach
  Error
  Sample size determination
  Sampling from finite populations
  Confidence intervals: the graphical method
Summary

INTRODUCTION

ESTIMATION IS the process of using sample data to estimate the values of unknown population parameters. Essentially any population characteristic can be estimated from a *random* sample. Among the most common are the mean and standard deviation of a population and the population proportion.

There are countless uses of estimation. Politicians, for example, often attempt to estimate the proportion of their constituents who adhere to various social or economic viewpoints. Manufacturing firms must constantly estimate the percentage of defectives in a lot of parts or pieces. Product performance characteristics must be designed with considerations such as average strain, or weight, or lifetime requirements. Department stores must predict demand for various sale items. Valuation of inventories, cost estimation of project costs, evaluating new energy sources, predicting job performance, and figuring reasonable guesses for job completion times all involve estimation.

"C' mon in, its not very deep."

Estimation is the process of using sample data to estimate the values of unknown population parameters.

POINT AND INTERVAL ESTIMATES

Sample statistics are used as estimators of population parameters. Thus a sample mean is used as an estimate of a population mean; a sample standard deviation is used as an estimate of the population standard deviation; and the proportion of items in a sample with a given characteristic is used to estimate the proportion in a population with that same characteristic. Such estimates are called *point estimates*, because they provide a single-valued estimate of a parameter. However, we now know that random samples have a tendency to produce samples in which the sample mean, for instance, does not equal the population mean, although the two values are generally quite close. Because of sampling variability, it is usually desirable to include an "interval estimate" to accompany the point estimate. It provides a range, or interval, of possible values for the population parameter. Table 8.1 gives some examples of each type of estimate.

Point estimate: A single-valued estimate of a population parameter.

Interval estimate: An estimate that includes a range of possible values in which a population parameter is thought to be.

TABLE 8.1   Examples of Estimates

Population parameter	Type of estimate	
	Point	Interval
Mean	1. The average American consumes 40 lb of beef annually. 2. A typical six-cylinder car averages 15 mi/gal.	1. The mean consumption of beef in this country is between 30 lb and 50 lb per person annually. 2. A typical six-cylinder car averages between 12 mi/gal and 18 mi/gal.
Proportion	1. Twenty-two percent of the residents oppose higher speed limits. 2. The proportion of college students who smoke is 43%.	1. Between 18% and 26% of the residents oppose higher speed limits. 2. The proportion of college students who smoke is between 37% and 49%.
Standard deviation	1. The standard deviation of radial tire mileage is 2000 mi. 2. The standard deviation of temperature in an unheated swimming pool is usually about 5°F.	1. The standard deviation of radial tire mileage is between 1500 mi and 2500 mi. 2. The standard deviation of temperature in an unheated swimming pool usually ranges from 2°F to 8°F.

THE RATIONALE OF ESTIMATION

The ability to estimate population parameters by using sample data is tied directly to knowledge about the sampling distribution of the statistic being used as the *estimator*. You can think of the sample statistic as one observation from that sampling distribution. For instance, suppose we have taken a random sample from a population of graduate students and found that the average age is 24.2 years. We know that this is one of the values from the sampling distribution, but the question is, *which* one? That is, how close *is* 24.2 to the mean of the population?

In formulating our answer to this question, we must take into account the characteristics of the sampling distribution. For example, we learned in Chapter 7 that the distribution of sample means is normal or approximately normal in many instances. Suppose for the moment that this is the case here. Then we know that roughly 68% of the sample statistics will fall within 1 standard deviation of the mean of the sampling distribution (which is equal to the mean of the population) and that about 95% of the sample means will fall within 1.96 standard deviations of the mean. By the same token, we know that 32% of the possible sample means will fall *beyond* 1 standard deviation (i.e., $1.00 - .68$), and that about 5% of the sample means will be more than 1.96 standard deviations from the mean.

Consequently, if we were to make the statement that the mean of a sample is within 1.96 standard deviations of the true mean, we can expect to be right in this assertion 95% of the time and wrong 5% of the time. Thus to say that 24.2 lies within 1.96 standard deviations of the mean carries a *risk* of error of 5%. To be sure, the sample mean may lie much closer to the mean than 1.96—or much further from the actual mean. Since we will never know for certain, we must content ourselves with this *probabilistic assessment* of the interval in which the true value may lie. This is called a *confidence interval*, and our "confidence" is $1 - P(\text{error})$. Hence a 95% confidence interval would carry with it a 5% risk of error; 5% of the intervals so designated would not include the population mean. Similarly, if we say a sample mean lies within 2.33 standard deviations of the mean, the risk that it does not is about 2%, which gives us a 98% confidence interval. Notice that the risk decreases as the value of z increases; an interval with 2.33 has less risk than one with limits of 1.96.* On the other hand, to achieve the decreased risk, it is necessary to settle for a wider range of possible values for the mean of the population.

Now regardless of the confidence level we select, we still cannot say whether a particular sample mean is *less than*, or *greater than*, the unknown value of the population mean. For example, the sample mean might have come from the upper tail of the sampling distribution (i.e., the sample mean might be much greater than the real mean). Or the sample mean might have come from the lower tail of the sampling distribution. Obviously, we have no way of knowing whether a particular sample statistic is too high, too low, or almost equal to the real value. Consequently, we establish a bracket, or interval, of possible values, in which we think the true value of the parameter may lie, keeping in mind the maximum amount of error we are willing to accept. This concept is illustrated in Figure 8.1.

---

* At this point it is natural to entertain thoughts of a 100% confidence interval. However, since a normal distribution ranges between $-\infty$ and $+\infty$ it would be virtually impossible to specify limits that would include all possible sample values.

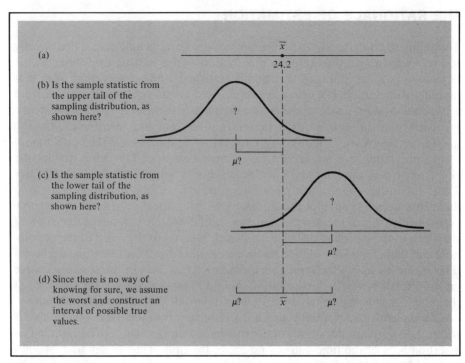

FIGURE 8.1   The concept of an interval estimate.

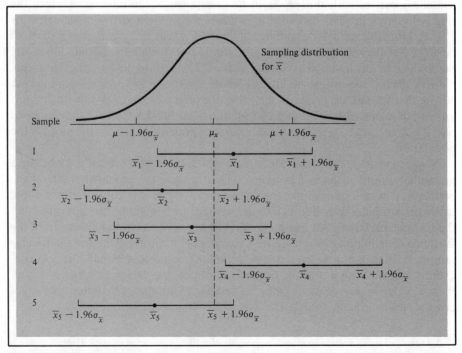

FIGURE 8.2   Interval estimates based on the means of repeated samples will not all contain the true value. 95% confidence intervals ($z = 1.96$) are shown for purposes of illustration.

Our confidence interval has the form $\bar{x} \pm z\sigma_{\bar{x}}$; a 95% interval for the mean with $\bar{x} = 24.2$ would be $24.2 \pm 1.96\ \sigma_{\bar{x}}$. The value of our sample mean is twofold. One significance is that it serves as the midpoint of our confidence interval. In addition, it serves as a point estimate of the real mean. Remember that the sample mean has an expected value that is equal to the population mean. Hence, *on the average*, the sample value will "equal" the population parameter.

Figure 8.2 illustrates that a 95% confidence interval will include the population mean for all but 5% of the sample means. Note, though, that usually only *one* sample needs to be taken; the five samples are shown merely for illustrative purposes.

> A *confidence interval* gives an interval of values, centered on the sample statistic, in which the population parameter is thought to lie, with a known risk of error.

Up to this point we have managed to say in a general sort of way how close our sample mean of 24.2 years is to the mean age of graduate students (in terms of standard deviations), but we have not said anything in terms of how close in *years* our estimate is

ESTIMATING THE MEAN OF A POPULATION

The question of how close a particular sample mean might be to the mean of the sampling distribution, in *actual units*, depends on the variability in the sampling distribution (i.e., the standard deviation of the sampling distribution). Recall that as sample size increases, the standard deviation of the sampling distribution decreases. Hence large samples will tend to yield sample means that are closer to the mean than do small samples. In addition, the variability in the overall population is a factor; the larger the variability in the population, the larger the variability in the sampling distribution.

The method used to estimate the mean of a population depends on whether the standard deviation of the population is known or whether it must be estimated from the sample data. Let us consider first the case in which the population standard deviation is known.

Population Standard Deviation Known

When the standard deviation of the population is known, the point and interval estimates of the population mean are as follows:

$$\text{point estimate of } \mu: \quad \bar{x}$$
$$\text{interval estimate of } \mu: \bar{x} \pm z\sigma_{\bar{x}}$$

where $\sigma_{\bar{x}} = \sigma_x/\sqrt{n}$.

Figure 8.3 illustrates how the confidence interval is constructed with the sample mean as the midpoint.

The interval estimate of the population mean is based on the assumption that the sampling distribution of sample means is normal. For large sample sizes this

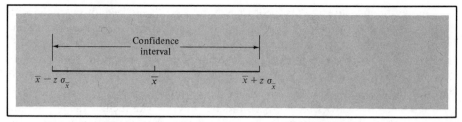

FIGURE 8.3   The confidence interval is centered around the sample mean.

presents no particular difficulty, since the Central Limit Theorem applies. However, *for samples of* 30 *observations or less, it is important to know that the population being sampled is normally distributed*, or at least approximately normal. Otherwise these techniques cannot be utilized.

We can now construct some confidence intervals for the average age of graduate students, using our sample mean of 24.2. To do this we must know the sample size and the population standard deviation. Suppose $n = 36$ and $\sigma_x = 3.0$. Table 8.2 illustrates calculations for 90%, 95%, and 99% confidence intervals.

TABLE 8.2   Confidence Intervals for μ_x When σ_x Is Known

Sample size $= 36$, $\sigma_x = 3$, $\bar{x} = 24.2$

Desired confidence	z	Formula	Calculation	e	Interval
90%	1.65	$\bar{x} \pm 1.65\,\dfrac{\sigma_x}{\sqrt{n}}$	$24.2 \pm 1.65\,\dfrac{3}{\sqrt{36}}$	$24.2 \pm .825$	23.375 to 25.025
95%	1.96	$\bar{x} \pm 1.96\,\dfrac{\sigma_x}{\sqrt{n}}$	$24.2 \pm 1.96\,\dfrac{3}{\sqrt{36}}$	$24.2 \pm .980$	23.220 to 25.180
99%	2.58	$\bar{x} \pm 2.58\,\dfrac{\sigma_x}{\sqrt{n}}$	$24.2 \pm 2.58\,\dfrac{3}{\sqrt{36}}$	24.2 ± 1.290	23.110 to 25.690

Note that since $n > 30$, the question of whether or not the population is normal is immaterial.

Estimation Error

The error in an interval estimate refers to the deviation (difference) between the sample mean and the actual population mean. Since the confidence interval is centered around the sample mean, the *maximum probable error* is one-half the interval width. Hence the interval

$$\bar{x} \pm z\,\frac{\sigma_x}{\sqrt{n}}$$

might be written as

$$\bar{x} \pm \text{error}$$

with the error e being

$$e = z\,\frac{\sigma_x}{\sqrt{n}}$$

Figure 8.4 portrays the confidence interval in terms of error.

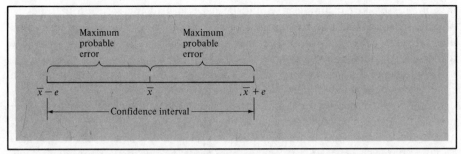

FIGURE 8.4   Error = $\frac{1}{2}$ the width of the confidence interval.

The formula for error reveals that there are actually three determinants of the size or amount of error: (1) the desired confidence, represented by the value of z; (2) the dispersion in the population, σ_x; and (3) the sample size, n. Factors in the numerator have a direct effect on the error since increases in those variables will cause e to increase. That is, the larger the confidence coefficient or the population dispersion, the larger the potential error. The sample size, being in the denominator, has an inverse effect on the error. Larger sample sizes mean less potential for error. The net effect will depend on the values of all three variables. However, it can be instructive to consider briefly the individual effects of each variable (see Figure 8.5).

Figure 8.5(a) shows that increasing the degree of confidence results in a widening of the interval. Figure 8.5(b) indicates that an increase in sample size will cause the interval to decrease. Note, though, that since the factor in the denominator is the square root of n and not n alone, the size of the interval is less sensitive to changes

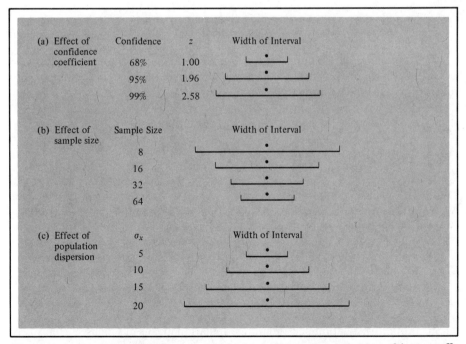

FIGURE 8.5   Factors that influence the width of a confidence interval: (a) confidence coefficient. (b) sample size. (c) population dispersion.

in sample size. For example, it would be necessary to increase n four times to obtain a reduction of one-half in the size of the interval ($1/\sqrt{4} = \frac{1}{2}$). Figure 8.5(c) illustrates how dispersion in a population can affect the interval: the more the dispersion, the larger the interval.

If you refer to the column labeled "e" in Table 8.2, you will see that the maximum error increases as the confidence level increases.

As the formula is presented above, the amount of error associated with a given population dispersion, the sample size, and the level of confidence can be determined. Sometimes, though, we may want to *specify* a *tolerable* error and perhaps find the sample size necessary to achieve that error for a particular confidence level and a known population standard deviation. Or we may want to determine a confidence level, given the other three variables. Interestingly enough, the same basic equation can be used to solve for any unknown variable by simple algebraic manipulation. In the following section special attention is given to one of these variables, the sample size.

Sample Size Determination

One of the most frequently asked questions in statistics is, "What size sample should be taken?" The error formula can be manipulated so that the value of n can be solved for. Thus

$$e = z\, \frac{\sigma_x}{\sqrt{n}}$$

$$\sqrt{n} = z\, \frac{\sigma_x}{e}$$

$$n = \left(z\, \frac{\sigma_x}{e}\right)^2$$

Hence the necessary sample size will depend on (1) the degree of confidence desired, (2) the amount of dispersion among the individual values in the population, and (3) some specified amount of tolerable error.

Example 1 What size sample would be necessary to produce a 90% confidence interval for the true population mean with an error of 1.0 either way if the population standard deviation is 10.0?

Solution:
We know that $\sigma_x = 10.0$ and $e = 1.0$, and we want a 90% confidence interval, which implies a z-value of 1.65. Thus we have

$$n = \left[z\, \frac{\sigma_x}{e}\right]^2 = \left[1.65\, \frac{10.0}{1.0}\right]^2 = 16.5^2 = 272.25 \to 273$$

Note that in solving for n we always round the answer up to the next integer value.

So far our investigation of estimating population means has focused exclusively on situations in which the population standard deviation is known. In practice, it is more common to encounter situations in which the dispersion of the population being sampled is unknown. One very important consequence of not having the population standard deviation is that the normal distribution is no longer the theoretically correct sampling distribution. The following section deals with these matters.

Estimating Means When σ_x is Unknown: The *t* Distribution

When the value of the population standard deviation is not known (which is usually the case), the sample standard deviation is used as an estimate of s_x and replaces σ_x in equations for confidence intervals and errors. This presents no major difficulties, inasmuch as the sample standard deviation provides a reasonably good approximation to the true value in most situations. Furthermore, we know from the Central Limit Theorem that when the sample size is greater than 30, the sampling distribution of means will be approximately normal. However, for samples of 30 or less observations, the normal approximation is inadequate. Instead, computations of confidence intervals must be based on the *t distribution*,* which is the theoretically correct distribution whenever s_x is used.

The shape of the *t* distribution is quite similar to the shape of the normal distribution. Figure 8.6 provides a general comparison of the normal and *t* distributions. The main difference between the two is that the *t* distribution has more area (probability) in the tails. This means that for a given confidence level, the *t*-value will be somewhat larger than the corresponding *z*-value would be.

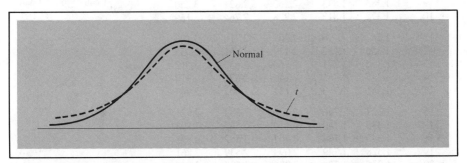

FIGURE 8.6 General comparison of the normal distribution and a *t* distribution. Note that the *t* distribution has more area in the tails.

Now the interesting (and complicating) thing about the *t* distribution is that it is not a standardized distribution in the same sense that the normal distribution is; there is a slightly different *t* distribution for each sample size. Thus while the normal distribution is essentially independent of sample size, the *t* distribution is not. For small sample sizes (say 30 or less observations), the *t* distribution is fairly sensitive to sample size, although for larger sample sizes this sensitivity diminishes. In fact, for large sample sizes it is quite feasible to use *z*-values to approximate *t*-values,

---

* The originator of the *t* distribution was W. S. Gossett, an employee of an Irish brewery in the early 1900s. His firm frowned on employees publishing under their own names, so Gossett assumed the pen name Student in his writings about the mathematical properties of the *t* distribution. Consequently, it acquired the name "Student's *t* distribution."

TABLE 8.3   Values of t for Selected Probabilities

Example.
   Number of degrees of freedom $= 6$.
   The area above $t = 1.440$ *or* below $t = -1.440$ represents 10% of the area under the curve.
   The combined area above $t = 1.440$ *and* below $t = -1.440$ represents 20% of the area under the curve.

		Probabilities (or areas under t distribution curve)			
Area in one tail	.10	.05	.025	.01	.005
Area in two tails	.20	.10	.05	.02	.01

Degrees of freedom			Values of t		
1	3.078	6.314	12.706	31.821	63.657
2	1.886	2.920	4.303	6.965	9.925
3	1.638	2.353	3.182	4.541	5.841
4	1.533	2.132	2.776	3.747	4.604
5	1.476	2.015	2.571	3.365	4.032
6	(1.440)	1.943	2.447	3.143	3.707
7	1.415	1.895	2.365	2.998	3.499
8	1.397	1.860	2.306	2.896	3.355
9	1.383	1.833	2.262	2.821	3.250
10	1.372	1.812	2.228	2.764	3.169
11	1.363	1.796	2.201	2.718	3.106
12	1.356	1.782	2.179	2.681	3.055
13	1.350	1.771	2.160	2.650	3.012
14	1.345	1.761	2.145	2.624	2.977
15	1.341	1.753	2.131	2.602	2.947
16	1.337	1.746	2.120	2.583	2.921
17	1.333	1.740	2.110	2.567	2.898
18	1.330	1.734	2.101	2.552	2.878
19	1.328	1.729	2.093	2.539	2.861
20	1.325	1.725	2.086	2.528	2.845
21	1.323	1.721	2.080	2.518	2.831
22	1.321	1.717	2.074	2.508	2.819
23	1.319	1.714	2.069	2.500	2.807
24	1.318	1.711	2.064	2.492	2.797
25	1.316	1.708	2.060	2.485	2.787
26	1.315	1.706	2.056	2.479	2.779
27	1.314	1.703	2.052	2.473	2.771
28	1.313	1.701	2.048	2.467	2.763
29	1.311	1.699	2.045	2.462	2.756
30	1.310	1.697	2.042	2.457	2.750
40	1.303	1.684	2.021	2.423	2.704
60	1.296	1.671	2.000	2.390	2.660
120	1.289	1.658	1.980	2.358	2.617
∞	1.282	1.645	1.960	2.326	2.576

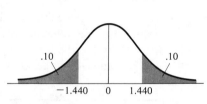

Source: From Ronald A. Fisher: *Statistical Methods for Research Workers*, 14th ed., copyright ©
1970 University of Adelaide.

even though *the t distribution is theoretically correct whenever the population standand deviation is unknown, regardless of the sample size being used.*

There is a table of *t*-values (see Table H in the Appendix) just as there is a table for *z*-values. And the two sets of values are used in much the same way. But because there is a different *t* distribution for each sample size, it would be impractical to attempt to provide complete tables of the distributions. Instead, only the most commonly used values are included in tables.

To use a *t* table you must know two things: the desired confidence level and the *degrees of freedom*. Degrees of freedom are related to the way the sample standard deviation is computed:

$$s_x = \sqrt{\frac{\sum (x - \bar{x})^2}{n - 1}}$$

where

$$s_x = \text{the sample standard deviation}$$
$$n - 1 = \text{the degrees of freedom}$$

Thus the degrees of freedom equal $n - 1$, or one less than sample size.

An intuitive explanation of the degrees of freedom is as follows: Imagine a classroom with 20 empty seats, which will soon be filled by 20 students. As the students begin to arrive, each one selects a seat from those remaining. Naturally the first student has a choice of 20 seats, the second has a choice of 19 seats, and so on down the line until the last student arrives. At that point there is no choice (degree of freedom) and that student simply sits in the remaining seat. Thus 20 students had 19, or $n - 1$, degrees of freedom.

Consider a second example. Suppose we want three numbers whose sum is 10. The first number can be anything (even negative), and so can the second number. But the third number is constrained by the fact that all three must add to 10. Once the first two values are determined, the third value is essentially determined; there is no degree of freedom for that third value. For example, the first number might be $+3$, and the second might be -1, for a total of $+2$. For the three numbers to sum to 10, the third must be 8. There were three numbers, but there were degrees of freedom for only two. (Later on you will learn about situations in which the degrees of freedom are equal to something other than the quantity $n - 1$, so it would be wrong to assume that $n - 1$ will always be the magic number.)

As it turns out, there is the requirement that the sum of the deviations around the sample mean be zero, which means that the last value is forced to make up the difference between the sum to that point and the total sum, which is zero. Hence the degrees of freedom equal $n - 1$.

For purposes of discussion, a *t* table is provided here in Table 8.3; there is also a *t* table (Table H) in the Appendix. Notice that the table is arranged somewhat differently than the normal table is. Areas (percentages or probabilities) are shown across the top of the table rather than in the body of the table; *t*-values are given in the body; and the degrees of freedom are listed down the side of the table.

To use the table you must specify the area in the tails of the distribution (risk) and the degrees of freedom.

Table 8.4 gives some examples of *t*-values for certain sample sizes and risks.

Table 8.4 *t*-values for 95% Confidence
        (.025 in each tail)

Sample size n	Degrees of freedom n − 1	t-value
8	7	2.365
13	12	2.179
23	22	2.074
28	27	2.052

The confidence interval for a sample mean when s_x is used is very similar to the interval with σ_x. The interval is

$$\bar{x} \pm t \frac{s_x}{\sqrt{n}}$$

One last point. The t distribution is theoretically appropriate only when sampling from a normal distribution. As a practical matter, as n increases beyond 30 observations, the need to assume normality diminishes.

> The t distribution assumes that the population being sampled is normally distributed. This assumption is particularly important for $n \leq 30$.

Table 8.5 illustrates confidence intervals employing t.

Table 8.5 Confidence Intervals Using *t*-values

Sample mean	20.0
Sample standard deviation	1.5
Sample size	25 (degrees of freedom are $n - 1 = 24$)

Desired confidence	t	Formula	Calculation	Interval
90%	1.711	$\bar{x} \pm t \dfrac{s_x}{\sqrt{n}}$	$20.0 \pm 1.711 \dfrac{1.5}{\sqrt{25}}$	$20.0 \pm .5133$
95%	2.064	$\bar{x} \pm t \dfrac{s_x}{\sqrt{n}}$	$20.0 \pm 2.064 \dfrac{1.5}{\sqrt{25}}$	$20.0 \pm .6192$
99%	2.797	$\bar{x} \pm t \dfrac{s_x}{\sqrt{n}}$	$20.0 \pm 2.797 \dfrac{1.5}{\sqrt{25}}$	$20.0 \pm .8391$

Note that for samples of 30 or less, both t and z require that the population being sampled be normal, or at least approximately normal. For larger sample sizes this restriction is not necessary. Given a normal population, we have said that z is used when σ_x is known and that t is used if only s_x is known. For cases in which $n > 30$, we can approximate the value of t with z.

Sampling from Small Populations:
The Finite Correction Factor

When the population is finite and the sample size constitutes more than about 5% of the population, the finite correction factor must be used to modify the standard deviations of the formulas:

	Confidence Interval	*Error*
σ_x known:	$\bar{x} \pm z \dfrac{\sigma_x}{\sqrt{n}} \sqrt{\dfrac{N-n}{N-1}}$	$z \dfrac{\sigma_x}{\sqrt{n}} \sqrt{\dfrac{N-n}{N-1}}$
σ_x unknown:	$\bar{x} \pm t \dfrac{s_x}{\sqrt{n}} \sqrt{\dfrac{N-n}{N-1}}$	$t \dfrac{s_x}{\sqrt{n}} \sqrt{\dfrac{N-n}{N-1}}$

Example 2 Determine a 95% confidence interval for these two situations:

a. $\bar{x} = 15.0$ b. $\bar{x} = 15.0$

  $\sigma_x = 2.0$ $s_x = 2.0$

  $n = 100$ $n = 16$

  $N = 1000$ $N = 200$

Solution:
  a.

$$\frac{n}{N} = \frac{100}{1000} = 10\%$$

Therefore, the finite correction factor must be utilized. The formula for the confidence interval is

$$\bar{x} \pm z \frac{\sigma_x}{\sqrt{n}} \sqrt{\frac{N-n}{N-1}}$$

Substituting the problem data yields

$$15.0 \pm 1.96 \frac{2.0}{\sqrt{100}} \sqrt{\frac{1000-100}{999}} = 15.0 \pm 1.96(.2)\sqrt{.901}$$

$$= 15.0 \pm .372$$

  b.

$$\frac{n}{N} = \frac{16}{200} = 8\%$$

With σ_x unknown *and* $n \le 30$, the t distribution is appropriate (assuming the population being sampled is normal), and the formula for the confidence interval is

$$\bar{x} \pm t \frac{s_x}{\sqrt{n}} \sqrt{\frac{N-n}{N-1}}$$

The problem data yield (15 degrees of freedom)

$$15.0 \pm 2.131 \frac{2}{\sqrt{16}} \sqrt{\frac{200 - 16}{200 - 1}} = 15.0 \pm 2.131(.5)\sqrt{.925}$$

$$= 15.0 \pm 1.025$$

Formulas for determining the sample size necessary to achieve an interval with a specified maximum error and confidence level must also be modified when sampling from a finite population. There are two formulas, one when the standard deviation of the population is known and another when it is not known:

$$\sigma_x \text{ known: } n = \frac{z^2 \sigma_x^2 N}{z^2 \sigma_x^2 + e^2(N - 1)}$$

$$\sigma_x \text{ unknown: } n = \frac{t^2 s_x^2 N}{t^2 s_x^2 + e^2(N - 1)}$$

Failure to use these formulas when appropriate can result in a computed sample size that exceeds the size of the population.

One-sided Confidence Intervals

Sometimes the purpose of sampling is to determine if a population parameter is *less than* some minimum standard, with no interest in an upper limit. For example, a resort may desire information on the average expenditure per guest and be particularly concerned if that average is too low to realize a profit. Similarly, other situations exist in which a maximum limit is important but not a minimum. Thus an airline must be concerned with overbooking a flight, although underloaded flights must fly regardless of the number of passengers.

In cases such as these, the risk is concentrated in a *single* tail, instead of being split equally in two tails. The formulas for one-sided confidence intervals for means are given in the box.

	σ_x KNOWN	σ_x UNKNOWN
upper limit only:	$\bar{x} + z\sigma_{\bar{x}}$	$\bar{x} + ts_x$
lower limit only:	$\bar{x} - z\sigma_{\bar{x}}$	$\bar{x} - ts_{\bar{x}}$

Example 3   A random sample of 100 observations has a mean of 30.0 and a standard deviation of 5.

  a. Find a value for which you are 95% confident that the population mean does not exceed.
  b. What is the probability (risk) that $\mu > 31.0$?

Solution:

a. Using $\bar{x} + ts_{\bar{x}}$, we find

$$30.0 + 1.65 \frac{5}{\sqrt{100}} = 30.825$$

b.

$$t = \frac{31 - 30}{5/\sqrt{100}} = 2.0$$

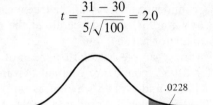

.0228

0 $t = 2$

Using $z \approx t$, from Table G in the Appendix we find that the area beyond $z = 2.0$ is .0228.

EXERCISES

For these exercises assume sampling from a normal population.

1. Determine 95% confidence intervals for each of the following:

	Sample mean	σ	Sample size
a.	16.0	2.0	16
b.	37.5	3.0	36
c.	2.1	.5	25
d.	.6	.1	100

2. Construct 99% confidence intervals for the population mean for each of the cases given in Exercise 1. Are the intervals wider or narrower? Why?

3. Repeat Exercise 1, assuming the standard deviations shown are sample standard deviations instead of population standard deviations.

4. Are the intervals in Exercise 3 wider or narrower than those found in Exercise 1? Why?

*5. In an effort to improve appointment scheduling, a physician has agreed to estimate the average time he spends with each patient. A random sample of 49 patients selected over a three-week period provided a mean of 30 minutes and a standard deviation of 7 minutes.

a. Construct a 95% confidence interval for the true mean time the physician spends with each patient.

b. What is the maximum probable error associated with your estimate in part a?

c. What is the probability the true average exceeds 33 minutes?

6. The state highway patrol recently conducted a secret survey of highway speeds during the early morning hours (2 A.M. to 4 A.M.) on a section of the freeway. During the time of the study, 100 cars passed through a radar net at an average speed of 70 mph, with a standard deviation of 15 mph.

    a. Estimate the true mean (point estimate) of the population.

    b. Describe the population.

    c. Construct a 98% confidence interval for the population mean.

    d. What is the maximum error associated with the interval found in part c?

7. A random sample of 40 noncommercial checking accounts at a branch bank showed an average daily balance of $140 and a standard deviation of $30.

    a. Construct a 95% confidence interval for the true mean.

    b. Construct a 99% confidence interval for the true mean.

    c. What can you say with 95% confidence about the maximum size of the error in your estimate for part a?

8. Rework Exercise 7 using a sample size of 15, a mean of $140, and a standard deviation of $30 for a 95% confidence interval. Assume you are sampling from a normal population and explain why this assumption is necessary.

*9. A firm employs 200 salespeople. In a random sample of 25 expense accounts for a week in December, auditors found an average expense of $220, with a standard deviation of $20.

    a. What is a point estimate for the average amount?

    b. What is a point estimate for the *total* for all 200 salespeople?

    c. Construct a 99% confidence interval for the average amount.

10. One hundred students at a junior college have been asked to keep a record of their expenses for food and beverages for a one-week period. There are 500 students at the school. The result was an average expenditure of $40, with a standard deviation of $10.

    a. Construct a 95% confidence interval for the true mean.

    b. How important is a random sample in this instance?

11. Determine the required number of observations to estimate the mean repair time for emergency plumbing calls if the maximum error is to be .6 hours for a confidence level of 95% and repair time is known to have a standard deviation of 1 hour. Is it necessary to assume that the population is normal?

12. How would your answer to Exercise 11 change if the maximum error could only be .3 hours?

13. How large a sample would be necessary in order to estimate the average time a salesperson in a furniture store spends with each customer within 2 minutes to obtain a 99% confidence level? Assume $\sigma_x = 12$ minutes.

14. Determine values for Exercise 1 that you are 98% confident the true mean *exceeds.*

15. For Exercise 10, determine a value that you are 99% confident the true mean does not exceed.

ESTIMATING THE PROPORTION IN A POPULATION

What percentage of parts in a large shipment are defective? What proportion of beads in a bowl are red? What percentage of the voters favor approval of a bond issue? What is the probability that a schoolchild in this county will not have the required measles vaccination? These and similar questions can be answered by using sample data to *estimate* the population parameter. As before, the estimates are usually in terms of a point estimate and an interval estimate.

    The estimation of population proportions is very similar to the estimation of population means. For instance, large-sample confidence intervals are based on a sampling distribution that is approximately normal, and the sample statistic (in this instance, the sample proportion) is used as a point estimate of the true parameter (population proportion). There is one notable exception. The t distribution is not used at all, and so the issue of t versus z is completely avoided. And there is a new wrinkle: the construction of both 95% and 99% confidence intervals is greatly simplified by the use of special charts. Nevertheless, it will be necessary to consider the formula approach for construction of confidence intervals (an approach similar to that for confidence intervals of means) as well as the use of charts, because the formula approach is used whenever intervals other than 95% or 99% are required.

Confidence Intervals: The Formula Approach*

The expected value of a sample proportion (i.e., the mean of a sampling distribution of sample proportions) always equals the true population proportion. Therefore, the sample proportion is used as the point estimate of the true proportion:

$$\text{point estimate of } p: \hat{p} = \frac{x}{n}$$

The interval estimate of the population parameter (for large sample sizes) is symmetrical around the sample proportion, just as the interval for a population mean was symmetrical around the sample mean. The main difference between estimating means and estimating proportions is in the standard deviations of the sampling distributions. The standard deviation of a proportion is based on the binomial distribution. The estimate of σ_p is given in the box.

$$\sigma_{x/n} = \sqrt{\frac{(x/n)[1 - (x/n)]}{n}}$$

where

$x =$ the number of items in the sample

$z =$ the standard normal deviation

$n =$ the sample size

$$\text{interval estimate of } p: \frac{x}{n} \pm z \sqrt{\frac{(x/n)[1 - (x/n)]}{n}}$$

Example 4 Determine a 98% confidence for the true proportion in the population if $x = 50$ and $n = 200$.

* This approach is limited to large samples (say $n > 40$). For small samples the graphical approach is appropriate (for 95% and 99% confidence intervals).

Solution:

A 98% confidence interval implies $z = 2.33$.

$$\text{estimate} = \frac{x}{n} \pm z \sqrt{\frac{(x/n)[1 - (x/n)]}{n}}$$

$$= .25 \pm 2.33 \sqrt{\frac{(.25)(.75)}{200}}$$

$$= .25 \pm .07 \quad \text{or} \quad .18 \text{ to } .32$$

Error

Again, the amount of error in an estimate is simply one-half the width of the confidence interval. Hence the equation

$$\frac{x}{n} \pm z \sqrt{\frac{(x/n)[1 - (x/n)]}{n}}$$

can be thought of as

$$\frac{x}{n} \pm e$$

where e is

$$z \sqrt{\frac{(x/n)[1 - (x/n)]}{n}}$$

The two factors, z and n, have exactly the same effect that they did for errors in estimates of population means. That is, the larger z is (i.e., the larger the confidence), the greater the possible error will be, while the larger the sample size, the smaller the error will be.

The effect of the sample proportion, however, might not be so obvious, simply because x/n and $1 - (x/n)$ are complements of each other. Thus as one increases, the other decreases. The overall effect of the sample proportion on the width of a confidence interval is shown in Figure 8.7. Note that the interval is widest when $p = .50$, and that it decreases as p gets larger or smaller because of the effect on the product of p times $(1 - p)$. In fact, under conditions of complete uncertainty, p can initially be assumed to be .50, and this will reveal the largest amount of error possible. On the other hand, if some information is available on the size of the sample proportion, say from a small pilot sample, then it may be possible to scale down the size of the interval or to reduce the necessary sample size.

Example 5 A sample of 200 observations has produced 20 defectives in a shipment of batteries. Using a confidence of 99%, find the estimation error.

Solution:

The sample proportion is $\frac{20}{200} = .10$. A 99% confidence requires $z = 2.58$.

$$e = z \sqrt{\frac{(x/n)[1 - (x/n)]}{n}} = 2.58 \sqrt{\frac{(.10)(.90)}{200}} = .055$$

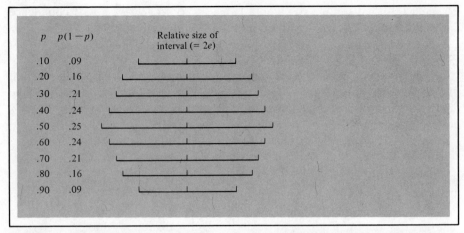

FIGURE 8.7   The confidence interval for a proportion is widest when $x/n = .50$.

Table 8.6 lists some examples of confidence intervals for proportions.

TABLE 8.6   Examples of Confidence Intervals for Proportions

n	x	Desired confidence	z	x/n	Error	Confidence interval
40	8	90%	1.65	$\frac{8}{40} = .20$	$1.65\sqrt{\dfrac{.20(.80)}{40}} = .104$	.096 to .304
80	20	95%	1.96	$\frac{20}{80} = .25$	$1.96\sqrt{\dfrac{.25(.75)}{80}} = .095$	.155 to .345
100	30	98%	2.33	$\frac{30}{100} = .30$	$2.33\sqrt{\dfrac{.30(.70)}{100}} = .107$	.193 to .417

Sample Size Determination

One of the most frequent uses of the error formula is to determine the sample size necessary to achieve a required degree of precision in estimating proportions. The formula for error,

$$e = z\sqrt{\frac{(x/n)[1 - (x/n)]}{n}}$$

can be used to develop a formula for the sample size. Squaring both sides gives

$$e^2 = z^2 \left\{ \frac{(x/n)[1 - (x/n)]}{n} \right\}$$

We can solve for n by interchanging n and e^2:

$$n = z^2 \left\{ \frac{(x/n)[1 - (x/n)]}{e^2} \right\}$$

Example 6   What sample size would be necessary to achieve a 95% confidence interval for the population proportion if the tolerable error is .08?

Solution:
Since the problem statement contains no information about the possible size of the population proportion, computations must be based on the widest possible interval, which occurs when the sample value equals .5. Since we want a 95% interval, we use $z = 1.96$. Thus

$$n = z^2 \left[\frac{p(1-p)}{e^2} \right]$$

becomes

$$n = 1.96^2 \left[\frac{(.5)(.5)}{.08^2} \right] = 3.84 \left[\frac{.25}{.0064} \right] = 149.9 \quad \text{or} \quad 150$$

Example 7   Determine the sample size necessary to estimate the true population percentage within 4%, using a 90% confidence interval. It is reasonable to suspect that the true value is .30 *or less.*

Solution:
Thirty percent would produce the largest interval, so $p = .30$ is used. A 90% confidence interval implies $z = 1.65$. So

$$n = z^2 \left[\frac{p(1-p)}{e^2} \right]$$

becomes

$$n = 1.65^2 \left[\frac{(.3)(.7)}{.04^2} \right] = 2.72 \left[\frac{.21}{.0016} \right] = 357.3 \quad \text{or} \quad 358$$

(the number is rounded *up* in order to obtain *at least* the desired precision.)

Sampling from Finite Populations

When the sample size is more than 5% of the population, the formula for an interval estimate of the population proportion must be modified. As you can see, the change is identical to the one for sample means:

$$\text{interval estimate:} \frac{x}{n} \pm z \sqrt{\frac{(x/n)[1 - (x/n)]}{n}} \cdot \sqrt{\frac{N-n}{N-1}}$$

Example 8   Find a 95% confidence interval for the population percentage defective given this information:

$$N = 2000 \qquad n = 400 \qquad \frac{x}{n} = .10$$

Solution:
Since $n/N = 400/2000 = 20\%$, the finite correction factor is called for.

$$10\% \pm 1.96 \sqrt{\frac{(.10)(.90)}{400}} \sqrt{\frac{2000 - 400}{2000 - 1}} = 10\% \pm 1.96 \sqrt{\frac{.09}{400}} \sqrt{\frac{1600}{1999}}$$

$$= 10\% \pm 1.96 \left(\frac{.3}{20}\right)(.9)$$

$$= 10\% \pm 2.65\% \quad \text{or} \quad 7.35\% \text{ to } 12.65\%$$

The sample size formula for finite populations is

$$n = \frac{z^2(x/n)[1 - (x/n)](N)}{(N - 1)e^2 + z^2(x/n)[1 - (x/n)]}$$

Confidence Intervals: The Graphical Method

For 95% and 99% confidence intervals, charts have been prepared which can be used to quickly obtain confidence intervals for proportions. See Appendix Table K. Formulas typically provide greater *precision* than graphical devices, in terms of the number of decimal places that can be obtained, and can be used for any sample size. However, the charts are superior in that the formula always yields symmetrical confidence intervals when, in fact, the binomial distribution is symmetrical only for $p = .50$. In addition, the ease with which intervals can be determined and the fact that the charts can handle small sample sizes as well as large makes the graphical approach extremely attractive.

A magnified portion of a typical chart is shown in Figure 8.8. The curved lines represent sample sizes, and there are two lines for each sample size. One is used to find the lower end of the confidence interval and the other is used to find the upper end. Possible sample values are listed across the top and bottom of the chart; sample proportions in the range from 0% to 50% are along the bottom

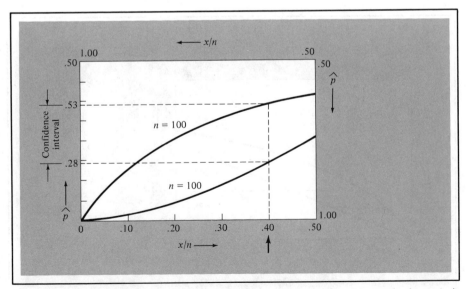

FIGURE 8.8 Using the chart to obtain endpoints of the confidence interval when x/n is found along the bottom scale.

and values in the range from 50% to 100% are across the top. To use the chart, enter at the point along the top or bottom that corresponds to the sample proportion of interest. Next, trace *a vertical* line and note where it intersects the two lines for the sample size used. Finally, trace two horizontal lines from the intersections to the left or right side of the graph (left if $x/n \leq .5$ and right if $x/n \geq .5$) to obtain the endpoints of the confidence interval. Note that actual values are obtained using Table K; Figures 8.8 and 8.9 merely illustrate *how* values are read from the chart.

Suppose we have found a sample proportion, $x/n = .40$, using a sample size of 100, and we now wish to construct a 95% confidence interval for the actual proportion in the population. The first step is to locate the sample proportion along the scale (top or bottom) for sample proportions. In this case we find .40 along the bottom. Next, follow a vertical line through that value of .40 up to the two points where it intersects with the sample size, in this case, with $n = 100$. Now read horizontally over to the left side for the interval endpoints.

Figure 8.8 illustrates that a sample proportion of .40 based on a sample of 100 observations has a confidence interval that ranges from .28 to .53. Thus we can say that the true proportion in the population lies somewhere between these two values, with a confidence of 95%.

For values of x/n larger than 50%, the graph is entered from the top, a vertical line is extended downward from that point to the two intersections, and the endpoints of the confidence interval are read from the right side of the chart. For instance, suppose we use a sample of $n = 200$ and get $x/n = .90$. Figure 8.9 illustrates that the confidence interval will be from 85% to about 94%.

Note that with the formula approach, confidence intervals will always be symmetrical. However, the sampling distribution is actually symmetrical only when $p = .5$, although it is approximately symmetrical over a wider range for large sample sizes. The chart approach is sensitive to this skewness and thus is superior to the formula approach in that respect.

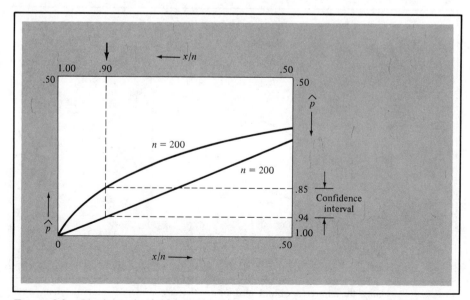

FIGURE 8.9   Obtaining the confidence interval when x/n is found along the upper scale.

EXERCISES

1. Construct a 95% confidence interval for the population proportion for each of these sample proportions. The sample size is 100 in all cases.
   a. .10   b. .20   c. .50   d. .80   e. .90

2. Based on your answers in Exercise 1, how does the value of the sample proportion influence the width of the confidence interval?

3. Construct 99% confidence intervals for each of the sample proportions of Exercise 1. Are 99% intervals wider or narrower than 95% intervals? Why?

4. Use the large-sample approximation formula to construct these confidence intervals:
   a. $x/n = .20$, $n = 50$, 95% confidence interval
   b. $x/n = .10$, $n = 100$, 92% confidence interval

5. Why would Table 8.5 not be appropriate for Exercise 4a? Why would Table K not be appropriate for Exercise 4b?

6. Find 95% confidence intervals for the population proportion by using first Appendix Table K and then the large-sample approximation formula for these cases:
   a. $x/n = 50\%$: $n = 400$, $n = 100$, $n = 25$, $n = 16$
   b. $x/n = 10\%$: $n = 400$, $n = 100$, $n = 25$, $n = 16$

7. Based on your answers to Exercise 6, what general rules can you devise regarding the accuracy of the formula for:
   a. x/n close to .5 versus x/n not close to .5?
   b. n large versus n small?

8. In a recent survey of 200 persons living in a large western city, 40 approved reinstatement of the death penalty for those convicted of using pot.
   a. Construct a 99% confidence interval for the actual proportion of persons living in this city that would agree with the death penalty for users of pot.
   b. What can you say about the size of the maximum error for this confidence interval?

9. A random sample of 100 midmorning shoppers at a supermarket revealed that all but 10 included milk as one of their purchases.
   a. What should the point estimate be of the percentage of midmorning shoppers that purchase milk?
   b. Construct a 90% confidence interval for the true proportion who buy milk.
   c. What can you say regarding the possible error associated with the confidence interval in part b?

10. A marketing research group discovered that 25% of the 200 shoppers it recently interviewed at a large suburban shopping center resided more than 15 miles from that point. Assume that a random sample was taken.
    a. Construct a 95% confidence interval for the actual percentage of shoppers who live more than 15 miles from the shopping center.
    b. What is the maximum probable error associated with the interval in part a?
    c. What does the term "random sample" mean in this case?
    d. Why is it important to obtain a random sample?

11. A random sample of 40 men working on a large building project indicated that 6 men were not wearing hard hats.
    a. Construct a 98% confidence interval for the true portion of men not wearing hard hats on the project.

b. If there are 1000 men working on the building, convert your confidence interval from percentage figures to number of men.

c. What can you say about the maximum size of the error associated with the interval in part a? In part b?

12. Five out of 20 randomly selected secretaries working for a large law firm indicate that they are unhappy with the kind of work they are called upon to do. There are 50 secretaries employed by the firm.

a. Construct a 90% confidence interval for the proportion of unhappy secretaries.

b. Convert the interval in part a to *number* of secretaries.

13. Twenty-five percent of the 48 people randomly selected from a long line of people waiting to enter a movie theater indicated that they felt the main feature contained too much violence.

a. How long would the line have to be before the finite correction factor could be ignored?

b. Construct a 98% confidence interval for the true proportion if there are 100 people standing in line.

c. Construct a 98% confidence interval if there are 500 people in line.

*14. A public library wants to estimate the percentage of books in its collection that have publication dates of 1970 or earlier. How large a random sample must it take to be 90% sure of coming within 5% of the actual proportion in the sample?

15. A manufacturer of flashcubes wants to estimate the probability that a flashcube will flash. Since destructive testing is involved, he wants to keep the sample size as small as possible. Find the number of observations that must be taken to estimate the probability within .04 and with 95% confidence of that if:

a. He has no idea of the percent defective.

b. He believes the percent defective is no more than 6%.

SUMMARY

Estimation involves estimating the value of some population parameter on the basis of sample data. The estimates can be single-valued (point estimate) or can specify a range of values in which the population parameter is thought to be (interval estimate). Confidence intervals are interval estimates that include a probability statement indicating the percentage of intervals that can be expected to contain the actual parameter within their limits. The width of a confidence interval depends on four things: the dispersion of population values, the level of confidence indicated, the tolerable error, and the sample size.

Sampling distributions provide the basis for estimation. Point estimates utilize the fact that the expected sample value equals the population parameter. Interval estimates of means depend on the Central Limit Theorem and the fact that dispersion in a sampling distribution is a function of sample size. Similarly, interval estimates of proportions make use of the tendency of large samples to produce a normal sampling distribution as well as the fact that dispersion is a function of sample size. When the sample size is greater than 5% of the population, formulas for interval estimates of both means and proportions are modified with finite correction factors.

Table 8.7 summarizes the formulas for estimation.

TABLE 8.7   Summary of Formulas

	Population	
	Infinite	Finite
A. Estimating means		
Point estimate	$\bar{x}$	$\bar{x}$
Interval estimate		
σ_x known	$\bar{x} \pm z \dfrac{\sigma_x}{\sqrt{n}}$	$\bar{x} \pm z \dfrac{\sigma_x}{\sqrt{n}} \sqrt{\dfrac{N-n}{N-1}}$
σ_x unknown	$x \pm t \dfrac{s_x}{\sqrt{n}}$	$\bar{x} \pm t \dfrac{s_x}{\sqrt{n}} \sqrt{\dfrac{N-n}{N-1}}$
Sample size		
σ_x known	$n = \dfrac{z^2 \sigma_x^2}{e^2}$	$n = \dfrac{z^2 \sigma_x^2 N}{z^2 \sigma_x^2 + e^2(N-1)}$
σ_x unknown	$n = \dfrac{z^2 s_x^2}{e^2}$	$n = \dfrac{t^2 s_x^2 N}{t^2 s_x^2 + e^2(N-1)}$
Error		
σ_x known	$e = z \dfrac{\sigma_x}{\sqrt{n}}$	$e = z \dfrac{\sigma_x}{\sqrt{n}} \sqrt{\dfrac{N-n}{N-1}}$
σ_x unknown	$e = t \dfrac{s_x}{\sqrt{n}}$	$e = t \dfrac{s_x}{\sqrt{n}} \sqrt{\dfrac{N-n}{N-1}}$
B. Estimating proportions		
Point estimate	$\dfrac{x}{n}$	$\dfrac{x}{n}$
Interval estimate	$\dfrac{x}{n} \pm z \sqrt{\dfrac{(x/n)[1-(x/n)]}{n}}$	$\dfrac{x}{n} \pm z \sqrt{\dfrac{(x/n)[1-(x/n)]}{n}} \sqrt{\dfrac{N-n}{N-1}}$
Sample size	$n = z^2 \left\{ \dfrac{(x/n)[1-(x/n)]}{e^2} \right\}$	$n = \dfrac{z^2(x/n)[1-(x/n)](N)}{(N-1)e^2 + z^2(x/n)[1-(x/n)]}$
Error	$e = z \sqrt{\dfrac{(x/n)[1-(x/n)]}{n}}$	$e = z \sqrt{\dfrac{(x/n)[1-(x/n)]}{n}} \sqrt{\dfrac{N-n}{N-1}}$

REVIEW QUESTIONS

1. Contrast a point estimate with an interval estimate.
2. For a given situation, what effect does increasing the sample size have on the maximum error when estimating a population mean?
3. What is the relationship between maximum error and width of a confidence interval?
4. How are standard error of estimate and standard deviation of a sampling distribution of means related?
5. What effect does increasing the level of confidence have on the width of the resulting confidence interval in a given situation?
6. Under what conditions is it necessary to know that a population distribution is approximately normal?

7. Under what conditions is the t distribution appropriate? When can the normal z-value be used as an approximation to the t-value?
8. Why is an interval estimate of proportions widest when the sample proportion equals 50%?
9. What is the purpose of the finite correction factor? When should it be used?
10. In a confidence interval for the population mean, how does the size of the population (or sample) standard deviation influence the width of the interval?
11. How does a one-sided confidence interval for a population mean differ from a two-sided interval?

SUPPLEMENTAL EXERCISES

*1. Reaction time to a drug taken intravenously averaged 2.1 minutes and had a standard deviation of .1 minute for a group of 28 subjects.
   a. Construct a 90% confidence interval for the mean time for the population of all such people.
   b. Is it necessary to assume the reaction times for the population are normal? Explain.
2. A firm is converting machines it leases to updated versions. Forty machines have been converted so far. The average conversion time was 24 hours and the standard deviation 3 hours.
   a. Determine a 98% confidence interval for the average conversion time.
   b. What is the maximum probable error associated with the interval in part a?
   c. Determine a 98% one-sided confidence interval for the upper limit on the true mean conversion time.
3. Six out of 48 randomly selected time-sharing terminals give incorrect character responses. A firm has 800 of these.
   a. Estimate the percentage of terminals which do this.
   b. Construct a 95% confidence interval for the proportion of the firm's terminals that have this kind of defect.
   c. Is it necessary to assume a normal population? Explain.
4. A random sample of 50 bicycles from a stock of 400 reveal 7 bicycles with flat tires.
   a. Estimate the number of bicycles with flat tires.
   b. Construct a 99% confidence interval for the proportion of bicycles with flat tires.
   c. If it takes an average of 15 minutes per tire to repair each one, how long would you expect it to take to repair the flat tires?
5. Forty out of 52 respondents to a questionnaire indicate they have had difficulties in getting a new car dealer to rectify deficiencies in their new cars.
   a. Construct a 98% confidence interval for the actual proportion in the population that might be expected to give a similar response to this question.
   b. Determine a 95% confidence interval for the proportion.
   c. What is the maximum probable error associated with the interval in part a? In part b?
6. Brite Manufacturing wants to estimate the average life of its 60-watt light bulbs within 25 hours. Light bulb life is known to have a standard deviation of 100 hours and the firm wishes to have a 95.5% confidence interval for the

estimate. How large a sample is necessary? How would your answer differ if the population consists of 300 bulbs?

*7. A restaurant manager wants to determine the average time customers take to finish their salad course. He feels reasonably certain that the standard deviation is 4 minutes, based upon a previous *sample*, and wants to estimate the mean within 1 minute using a 90% confidence interval. What sample size is required?

8. How would you answer Exercise 7 if the manager subjectively estimated that the standard deviation of the time for the salad course was between 3 and 5 minutes?

9. An inspection of 100 randomly selected ball bearings from a lot of 10,000 yields 5 that are unacceptable.

a. Estimate the number of unacceptable ball bearings in the lot.

b. Construct a 95% confidence interval for the number of unacceptable ball bearings in the lot.

c. What is the maximum probable error associated with the interval in part b?

10. How large a sample must the transportation department of a large eastern city contemplate if it wishes to estimate the percentage of parking meters that are faulty if the goal is to be 95% confident of not being off by more than 10%?

11. Repeat Exercise 10 for the situation where the percentage faulty lies between 10% and 20%, based on past experience.

9

significance testing

Chapter Objectives

After completing this chapter, you should be able to:
1. Explain what significance testing is, and explain how significance testing differs from estimation
2. Define such terms as null hypothesis, alternative hypothesis, level of significance, Type I error, Type II error, and critical values
3. Describe how significance testing uses sampling distributions
4. Explain the meaning of the phrase "partition the sampling distribution"

Chapter Outline

Introduction
Chance Variation or Real Variation?
One-sided Tests and Two-sided Tests
Type I and Type II Errors
Summary

INTRODUCTION

THE PURPOSE of this chapter is to *introduce the logic* of significance testing without getting heavily involved in the details of specific tests. The reason for this is that the concepts are pretty much the same for all significance testing. Chapters 10 through 13 and parts of Chapter 14 delve into those details. However, it is easy to become so engrossed with specific details of various tests that the overall theme of significance testing is not clear.

Significance testing and estimation are two main branches of statistical inference. Whereas the goal in estimation is to estimate the value of some population parameter, the goal in significance testing is to decide if a claim about a population parameter is true. For instance, we might wish to determine if claims such as these are true:

1. The average completion time for this test is 80 minutes.
2. Three percent of the output is defective.
3. The coin is fair (i.e., $P(H) = P(T) = .50$).

Occasionally we may be called upon to evaluate a claim that does not actually specify the value of the parameter in question:

4. The percentage unemployed in two neighboring cities is equal.
5. The average miles per gallon rate is the same for three brands of gasoline.

The *purpose of significance testing* is to evaluate claims about the values of population parameters.

We know from our study of estimation that sample statistics such as means and proportions can serve as point estimates of corresponding population parameters. We also learned that because of sampling variability associated with random sampling, sample statistics tend to *approximate* rather than *equal* population parameters. The analysis of a claim concerning the value of a population parameter using sample data must take this into consideration.

Hence the central issue in significance testing is whether the difference between a claimed value of a population parameter and the value of a sample statistic might reasonably be due to sampling variability or whether the discrepancy is too great to be accounted for in this manner.

The basic approach to significance testing can perhaps be best appreciated by working through a simple problem. Consider this situation: A sample of 142 parts from a large shipment is inspected and 8% are found to be defective. The supplier from whom the parts have been purchased has guaranteed that no more than 6% of the parts in any shipment will be defective. The question to be answered by significance testing is whether the vendor's claim is true.

The first step in significance testing is to formulate two hypotheses about the claim. Hypotheses are potential explanations (theories) that attempt to account for observed facts in situations where some unknowns exist. The unknown is this particular instance is the true percentage defective in the shipment. The known fact is that a random sample produced 8% defective. One hypothesis might be that the actual percent defective in the lot is greater than the claimed 6%. Another hypothesis would be that the claim is true. Now if the claim is true, what could account for the fact that a sample produced 8% defective? One possibility is that sampling variability was responsible.

At this point let us more formally define the two kinds of hypotheses we need to formulate. The one that suggests the claim is true is called the *null hypothesis* and is designated by the symbol H_0; the one that suggests the claim is false is called the *alternative hypothesis* and is designated by the symbol H_1.

The *null hypothesis* H_0 is a statement that says that the population parameter is as specified (i.e., that the claim is true).

The *alternative hypothesis* H_1 is a statement that offers an alternative to the claim (e.g., the parameter is greater than the claimed value).

In our previous example our null hypothesis is that the true percent defective is 6%, which we would write in this fashion:

$$H_0: p = 6\%$$

Our alternative is that the percent defective p is greater than 6%, which would be written as

$$H_1: p > 6\%$$

If the decision after analysis is to accept H_0, the implication is that the discrepancy between the observed percent defective in the sample and the claimed percent defective in the population is most likely due to chance variation in sampling. Conversely, a decision to reject H_0 would imply that the variation between the observed value and the claimed value is too great to be due to chance alone.

CHANCE VARIATION OR REAL VARIATION?

The "test" is whether some observed sample statistic could reasonably have come from a population with the claimed parameter. Hence we want to take into account the sampling variability that might arise given such a population as that claimed.

The second step in significance testing is to identify the appropriate sampling distribution, since it will fully describe chance variation. In this instance, where we are dealing with sample proportions and a large sample size ($n = 142$), the appropriate sampling distribution is a normal distribution with a mean of p and a standard deviation of

$$\sigma_p = \sqrt{\frac{p(1-p)}{n}}$$

where

$$p = \text{the population proportion}$$
$$n = \text{the sample size}$$

Thus *if* the claim is true, our sample proportion of 8% has come from a sampling distribution with a mean of 6% and a standard deviation of

$$\sigma_p = \sqrt{\frac{.06(.94)}{142}} = .02$$

Now we can see that our discrepancy of 2% lies one standard deviation above the expected value, assuming .06 is the true proportion in the population:

$$z = \frac{.08 - .06}{.02} = +1.0$$

Furthermore, the probability of obtaining a *greater* discrepancy than 8% with a sample of 142 observations taken from a population with a proportion of 6% is about 16%, as shown in Figure 9.1. This would seem to suggest that chance alone *could* account for the discrepancy. Needless to say, we *cannot* definitely state that the population being sampled does have 6% defective, but in view of the sampling distribution of such a population and the sample statistic observed, the claim does seem reasonable.

On the other hand, if we had gotten a sample proportion of, say, 19%, then

$$z = \frac{.19 - .06}{.02} = +6.5$$

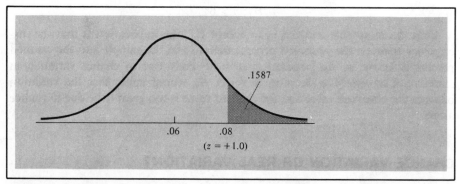

.1587

.06   .08

($z = +1.0$)

FIGURE 9.1   The probability of a sample proportion greater than 8%, given a population proportion of 6%, is .1587.

and it would seem highly unlikely that such a sample statistic could have come from a population with the claimed parameter of 6%. In that case we would be more inclined to reject H_0. Figure 9.2 illustrates a comparison of the two possibilities.

Not all situations will be so obvious, however, that we can "eyeball" them in this manner. Therefore, we will need a more rigorous approach to the problem. The question is, where do we draw the line between what might reasonably be regarded as "chance variation" and what might be regarded as "significant variation"?

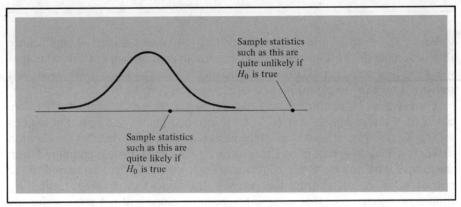

FIGURE 9.2   Sample statistics near the midpoint of the sampling distribution tend to support the claim; those far from the midpoint suggest the claim is false.

In attempting to answer this question, consider the following: Approximately 5% of the sample statistics in a normal distribution will produce a z greater than $+1.65$ (see Figure 9.3). Thus, although the *expected* sample value is 6%, 5% of the possible sample statistics will have values that exceed $p + 1.65\sigma_p$. Hence if we agree to $z = +1.65$ as the dividing line, there is a 5% risk of rejecting H_0 when it is actually true. Another possibility might be to use $z = +2.33$ as our "critical value" since there would only be about a 1% chance of observing a sample statistic more extreme than that when H_0 is true. Of course, the theoretical sampling distribution extends to plus infinity, so we must draw the line somewhere. Moreover, we have agreed that certain values would appear so unlikely that we would

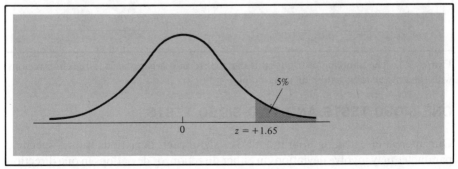

FIGURE 9.3   Approximately 5% of the sample statistics will yield a value of z that exceeds when the null hypothesis is true.

reject them out-of-hand. Commonly selected critical values in significance tests are those that provide risks of 5%, 2.5%, or 1% for rejecting H_0 when true. The probability of rejecting a null hypothesis that is true is called the *level of significance* of a test. It is designated by the symbol α (Greek alpha).

The *level of significance* of a test is the probability that a null hypothesis that is true will be rejected.

Hence the third step in a significance test is to select a level of significance that is acceptable. This, in turn, will indicate a corresponding critical value that will serve as a standard of comparison against which to judge an observed "test statistic" (e.g., the sample proportion of 8% has a z_{test} of $+1.0$).

The essence of a significance test, then, is to partition a sampling distribution, based on the assumption that H_0 is true, into acceptance and rejection regions for H_0. A critical value is selected on the basis of a specified probability the decision maker is willing to accept of rejecting a true H_0. A test statistic is computed from the sample data and the expected (claimed) value which is then compared to the critical value. A test statistic that exceeds the critical value suggests that H_0 should be rejected (i.e., that sampling variability alone will not account for the observed sample statistic), while a test statistic less than the critical value suggests that H_0 should be accepted. The overall concept is illustrated in Figure 9.4.

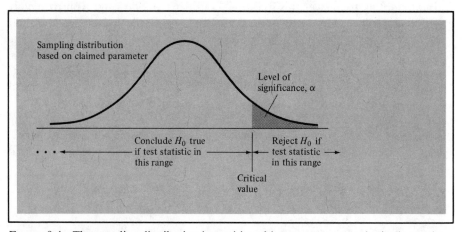

FIGURE 9.4 The sampling distribution is partitioned into acceptance and rejection regions, with the critical value as the dividing point.

ONE-SIDED TESTS AND TWO-SIDED TESTS

Our interest in detecting nonrandom (i.e., significant) deviations from a specified parameter may involve deviations in either direction, or deviations in one direction only. Thus in coin tossing, a coin could be considered unfair if either too many or too few heads appeared. The alternative hypothesis would simply be that the coin is unfair, and deviations in both directions would be investigated. But if we

"Would you call that significant?"

were, say, betting on heads, then our concern would only be with obtaining too few heads. Then the alternative hypothesis would be that too few heads would appear (i.e., that the probability of heads is less than .50), and in our evaluation we would be concerned only with that type of nonrandom deviation from the expected number of heads.

In essence, the alternative hypothesis is used to indicate which aspect of non-random variation is of interest. There are three possible cases: (1) concentrate on *both directions*; (2) concentrate on deviations *below* the expected value; or (3) concentrate on deviations *above* the expected value. Symbolically, for the coin-tossing example, these three cases could be written in the following ways:

$$H_0: p = .50$$

Case 1. $H_1: p \neq .50$ (both directions: too many or too few).
Case 2. $H_1: p < .50$ (deviation below: too few heads).
Case 3. $H_1: p > .50$ (deviation above: too many heads).

Notice that the null hypothesis is written in the same way regardless of what the alternative hypothesis is.* The distinction between these cases is illustrated in Figure 9.5. Note that for a two-tail test, the area in each tail is $\alpha/2$. In the first case either a value too far above or too far below the expected value would cause rejection of the null hypothesis. In the second case, however, only a value too far below the expected value would result in rejecting the null hypothesis. In the third case just the opposite is true, since only values much above the expected value would cause rejection.

* Actually, from the standpoint of completeness, for a one-tail test, the null hypothesis should apply to a range of values. For instance, if H_1 is $p < .5$, then H_0 should be $p \geq .5$, and for $H_1: p > .5$, H_0 should be $p \leq .5$. However, the basis for the sampling distribution used for testing cannot be a range of values; it must be a *single* value. For that reason the format used in this book will be to specify a single value for H_0.

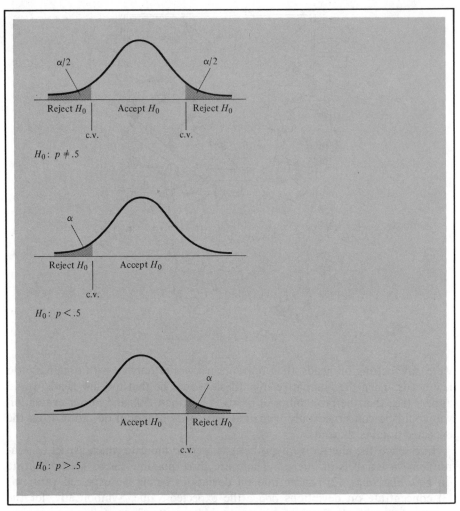

FIGURE 9.5 A comparison of partitioning a sampling distribution in one-sided and two-sided significance tests. Note in one-sided tests, the $>$ or $<$ points toward the tail used.

In practice, the two-sided test is used whenever divergence in *either* direction is critical, as it would be in clothing manufacturing, where shirts that are either too large or too small will not correspond with a stated size. Another example is the case where mating parts must fit together, such as a nut and bolt combination. Too much variation will result in a fit that is either so loose that the parts will not stay together or so tight that the parts cannot be put together at all.

The left-tail test is useful when testing to see if a *minimum* standard has been met. Some examples are a minimum content of butterfat in whole milk, the net weight of packaged products, the tensile strength of seat belts, and the product life as specified in a warranty. A right-tail test is useful when *maximum* standards must not be exceeded. Some examples are the amount of butterfat allowed in skimmed milk, the radiation emitted by nuclear power stations, the number of defectives in a shipment of manufactured goods, and the amount of air pollution flowing from a smokestack.

TYPE I AND II ERRORS

There are two kinds of errors inherent in the significance-testing process. We have already observed that there will be some risk of believing that H_0 is false when it is really true. The probability of committing this error equals the level of significance of a test, α. It is also known as a *Type I error*. A second kind of error that could occur is to accept H_0 when it is not true. This is called a *Type II error* and is designated by the symbol β (Greek beta).

There is the hope, naturally, that H_0 will be accepted when true and rejected when false. Hence there are four possibilities that could result in any test. These are compared in Table 9.1. It is important to recognize that once a decision has been made, either it will be correct or *one* type of error will be made, and the decision (accept or reject) will indicate which type of error is possible. Note, too, that when H_0 is true, there can be no Type II error, and that when H_0 is false, there cannot be a Type I error.

> A *Type I error* is committed by rejecting H_0 when H_0 is true. The probability of a Type I error equals the level of significance of a hypothesis test.

> A *Type II error* is committed by accepting H_0 when it is not true.

TABLE 9.1   Type I and Type II Errors

		If H_0 is	
		True	False
And we take this action	Accept H_0	Correct Decision	Type II Error β
	Reject H_0	Type I Error α	Correct Decision

It was mentioned earlier that the probability of erroneously rejecting H_0 could be reduced by choosing critical values that are extreme (i.e., that leave little area in the tail(s) of a distribution). However, there is an inverse relationship between Type I and II errors: decreasing the probability of a Type I error in this manner will increase the probability of a Type II error.* Ideally, a balance between the

---

* Determining the probability of a Type II error is less straightforward than determining the probability of a Type I error. This matter will be taken up at the end of the next chapter.

cost of committing a Type I versus a Type II error should be minimized, although in practice it is common to select traditional levels of Type I errors and to ignore Type II errors.

SUMMARY

This chapter has introduced the general concept of a significance test without becoming deeply involved with the details of testing. Subsequent chapters will introduce a variety of such tests. However, for the most part, the underlying concepts will essentially be the same as those presented in this chapter.

Significance tests are used to evaluate claims about population parameters. The general procedure is as follows:

1. Formulate the null and alternative hypotheses.
2. Choose the appropriate sampling distribution.
3. Select a level of significance (and thus critical values).
4. Compute a test statistic and compare it to the critical value(s).
5. Reject the null hypothesis if the test statistic exceeds the critical value(s); otherwise, accept.

Central to the entire process is a sampling distribution based on the premise that the claim is true. It indicates the extent to which sample outcomes might vary simply because of chance variation in sampling. The sampling distribution is partitioned into a region that suggests H_0 should be accepted and one (one-tail test) or two (two-tail test) regions where H_0 should be rejected. The probability of making a Type I error is called the level of significance of a test and equals the area of the rejection region. A Type II error occurs if H_0 is accepted when false.

This chapter used a test that required a sampling distribution that was normal. Later chapters will illustrate tests that employ other distributions. The choice of the sampling distribution depends upon such things as the type of data being analyzed (measurements, ranks, or categories), sample size, and whether certain assumptions about the underlying population can be made (e.g., Is the population normal?). The following chapters are organized mainly along the lines of the type of data being analyzed. For example, the next chapter deals with tests of means, and these use measurement data.

REVIEW QUESTIONS

1. Briefly define each of the following:
   - a. hypothesis
   - b. level of significance
   - c. Type I error
   - d. critical value
2. What is the purpose of significance testing?
3. In what ways does significance testing differ from estimation? In what ways are estimation and significance testing similar?
4. Contrast each of the following terms:
   - a. Type I error and Type II error
   - b. null hypothesis and alternative hypothesis
   - c. one-tail test and two-tail test

d. .05 level and .01 level

e. left-tail test and right-tail test

5. Explain the relationship between each of the following pairs:
   a. random sampling and sampling distribution
   b. sampling distribution and significance testing
   c. probability of a Type I error and area in a tail
   d. critical value and area in a tail

6. Explain the meaning of the phrase "partition the sampling distribution."

7. What does it mean when we say that we reject the null hypothesis?

8. Does it mean that H_0 is correct if we accept it? Why?

SUPPLEMENTAL EXERCISES

1. Determine which of these tests are two-tail and which are one-tail. For the one-tail tests, state whether it is a left- or right-tail test.

   a. $H_1: \mu \neq 4.10$ b. $H_1: \mu < 4.10$ c. $H_1: \mu > 81$

   d. $H_1: \mu > .66$ e. $H_1: \mu \neq 1.90$ f. $H_1: \mu < 3$

2. A supplier of metal casings has agreed to send a manufacturing firm shipments that contain no more than 2% defectives. The company takes random samples from the lots as they come in to check lot quality.
   a. State H_0 and H_1.
   b. The supplier does not want to ship lots that have a high risk of being returned because of too many defectives, and he also does not want to send lots with a much smaller percent defective than what was agreed upon, so he, too, is checking the lots as they leave his plant. State H_0 and H_1.

3. Suppose you are given this information:

$$H_0: p = 35\% \qquad H_1: p \neq 35\%$$

   a. Explain why the probability of making a Type II error is 0 if the population proportion is 35%.
   b. Explain why the probability of committing a Type I error is 0 if the population proportion is anything other than 35%.

10

---

significance tests of means

Chapter Objectives

After completing this chapter, you should be able to:
1. State the general purpose of significance tests for means
2. List three different kinds of claims that can be made concerning means
3. Outline the testing procedure for a significance test
4. Use sample data to test claims (i.e., be able to solve typical problems)

Chapter Outline

INTRODUCTION

THE PURPOSE of significance tests of means is to evaluate claims about population means. The various tests require *quantitative data* (i.e., continuous or discrete data).

There are basically three types of claims that are made concerning population means, and each type requires a different evaluation procedure. A claim might involve the mean of a *single* population; evaluation involves a *one-sample* test. Or a claim might be that the means of *two* populations are equal, which requires a *two-sample* test. Finally, a claim might be that the means of *more than two* populations are all equal, and evaluation requires a *k-sample* test. The first two tests are treated in this chapter and the *k*-sample tests are covered in the following chapter.

In the preceding chapter the basic process of significance testing was discussed at length. Briefly, significance tests require the following steps:

1. Set up the null and alternative hypotheses.
2. Identify an appropriate sampling distribution. Most tests of means involve either the normal distribution or the *t* distribution.
3. Partition the sampling distribution into acceptance (probably chance variation) and rejection (probably not chance) regions (see Figure 10.1).
4. Compute a test statistic.
5. Compare the sample statistic to the critical value. Reject H_0 if it is greater than the critical value.

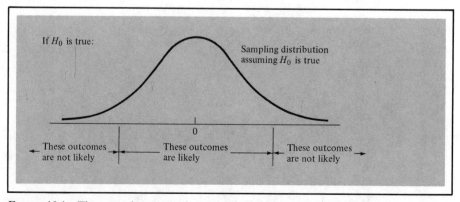

FIGURE 10.1   The general concept of a two-tail significance test.

ONE-SAMPLE TEST OF MEANS

A one-sample test is utilized to test a claim about a single population mean. A sample of n observations is taken and the sample mean is computed. Then the deviation between the claimed value and this sample mean is compared to the variability of the sampling distribution based on the claim. Large deviations suggest the claim is false; small deviations support the claim.

For instance, suppose it is desired to evaluate a manufacturer's claim that its radial tires have an average tread life of 40,000 miles. The null hypothesis becomes

$$H_0: \mu = 40{,}000 \text{ miles}$$

For purposes of illustration let us consider the three possible alternative hypotheses, although ordinarily only one of these would be considered. The three are

$$H_1: \mu \neq 40{,}000 \qquad H_1: \mu > 40{,}000 \qquad H_1: \mu < 40{,}000$$

Our evaluation of any of these must take into account the degree to which some sample statistic might vary, or deviate, from the claimed parameter because of chance variation in sampling. This will be described by a sampling distribution with a mean equal to the value of the claimed parameter. The sampling distribution will be normally distributed for samples drawn from a normal population with a known standard deviation, and it will have a t distribution when the population standard deviation is estimated from the sample standard deviation s_x. When the sample size is greater than 30, the need to assume that you are sampling from a normal population can be relaxed.

Conceptually, the critical values can be stated in values which relate specifically to a given problem. For example, in this case the critical values might be 39,000 miles and 41,000 miles. However, it is far easier to work with standardized test statistics, and standardized critical values, since almost all probability tables are stated in terms of standardized values, as suggested in the previous chapter.

Now it is rather important to establish a level of significance (which, in turn, will lead to a critical value) *prior* to sampling. Otherwise there is the possibility that the person evaluating the sample data will select a level of significance that leads to a decision that corresponds to his or her preconceived notion of how the test "ought" to turn out.

Once the level of significance is chosen, the sample data can be gathered and the test statistic computed.

$$\text{test statistic} = \frac{\text{sample mean} - \text{claimed mean}}{\text{standard deviation of sampling distribution}}$$

If the population standard deviation is known, the test statistic is*

$$z_{\text{test}} = \frac{\bar{x} - \mu_0}{\sigma_x / \sqrt{n}}$$

* μ_0 = claimed mean.

If σ_x is unknown, the test statistic is

$$t_{test} = \frac{\bar{x} - \mu_0}{s_x/\sqrt{n}}$$

σ_x Known

When the population standard deviation is known, the appropriate sampling distribution is the normal distribution. If the population being sampled is normal, the sampling distribution will be normal for *all* sample sizes. If the population is nonnormal, or if its shape is unknown, a one-sample test can be used only for sample sizes of more than 30 observations. Thus *small samples from nonnormal populations cannot be handled with this approach.*

Let us now consider in somewhat greater detail the example of the tire manufacturer who claimed his tires had a tread life of at least 40,000 miles. Suppose the test results were these: a sample of $n = 49$, with a sample mean = 38,000 miles. It is known that the population of tire mileage has a standard deviation of 3,500 miles. We can proceed as follows:

1. State the null and alternative hypotheses:

$$H_0: \mu = 40,000 \text{ miles}$$

Suppose the testing is being done by a consumer group. Naturally this group would want to check to see that consumers were not getting tires that have a shorter tread life, so the alternative hypothesis would be

$$H_1: \mu < 40,000 \text{ miles}$$

2. Choose a level of significance and partition the appropriate sampling distribution. Suppose the group decides to accept a risk of .05 of rejecting H_0 if it is true. Thus $\alpha = .05$. Since σ_x is known and the sample size is large, the normal distribution is used. The value of z that leaves .05 in the tail is -1.65.

3. Compute the test statistic:

$$z_{test} = \frac{\bar{x} - \mu_0}{\sigma_x/\sqrt{n}} = \frac{38,000 - 40,000}{3,500/\sqrt{49}} = \frac{-2,000}{500} = -4.0$$

4. Compare the test statistic to the critical value. Since -4.0 exceeds -1.65, H_0 is rejected. This is illustrated in Figure 10.2. Thus we conclude that the average tread life is less than 40,000 miles. (Thus, we will not test for $\mu > 40,000$.)

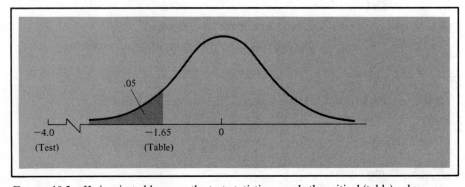

FIGURE 10.2 H_0 is rejected because the test statistic exceeds the critical (table) value.

Note that this *does not* guarantee that the claim is false. We may be committing a Type I error. Hence whenever H_0 is rejected, this means that the sample evidence *suggests* H_0 is not true; there is no way to be *absolutely sure* whether the claim is true or not, short of taking a complete census.

Since we have decided that the true mean is not 40,000 miles, a logical question is this: What *is* the true average tread life? One approach to answering this question is to use the sample data to estimate the mean. Using a $(1 - \alpha)$ confidence level (i.e., 95%), we have

$$\bar{x} \pm 1.96 \frac{\sigma_x}{\sqrt{n}} = 38,000 \pm 1.96(500) = 38,000 \pm 980$$

Now suppose it is the manufacturer who is conducting the test. He might utilize a two-tail test because he wants to guard against giving too little tread life, which would result in false advertising (among other things), and he does not want to build in too much quality, since he also markets a 45,000-mile radial tire for a higher price. Thus we have these facts:

$$\bar{x} = 38,000 \text{ miles}$$
$$n = 49$$
$$\sigma_x = 3,500 \text{ miles}$$

The analysis proceeds as follows:

1. State H_0 and H_1:

$$H_0: \mu = 40,000$$
$$H_1: \mu \neq 40,000$$

2. Choose α and partition the sampling distribution. Using $\alpha = .05$, the critical values of z are ± 1.96.
3. Compute the test statistic. Since we are using the same data, the value of the test statistic remains the same:

$$z_{\text{test}} = \frac{38,000 - 40,000}{3,500/\sqrt{49}} = -4.0$$

4. Since this exceeds the lower critical value, the manufacturer will reject H_0 and conclude that the average life is less than 40,000.

The test is illustrated in Figure 10.3.

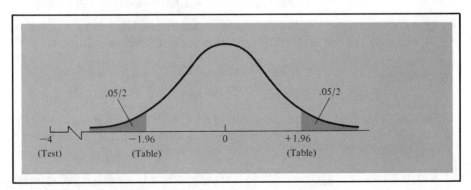

FIGURE 10.3 H_0 is rejected.

σ$_x$ Unknown

When the population standard deviation is unknown, it must be estimated from the sample data using the sample standard deviation. When that happens (in *most* real situations σ_x is unknown), the t distribution is the appropriate sampling distribution. As a practical matter, though, the use of the t distribution is only required when the sample size is 30 or less, since for larger samples the values of t and z are approximately the same, and the normal distribution can be used in place of t.*

Suppose we again consider the example of the 40,000-mile radial tire. This time, however, we will consider the population standard deviation to be unknown. Also, we want to compare the analysis for the large-sample and for the small-sample cases.

As before, let us take as our null hypothesis H_0 that the true mean of the population is 40,000. Furthermore, let us again test the three alternative hypotheses:

1. $H_1: \mu < 40,000$.
2. $H_1: \mu > 40,000$.
3. $H_1: \mu \neq 40,000$.

Example 1 Large sample. Suppose a sample of 36 observations is taken, and the resulting sample mean is 41,200 and the sample standard deviation is 3,000. Let us also use $\alpha = .05$. Now since n is greater than 30, the value of z from a normal table can be used to approximate the value of t. Hence the critical value is $+1.65$ or -1.65 for a one-tail test and ± 1.96 for a two-tail test. For any test, the test statistic is

$$t_{\text{test}} = \frac{\bar{x} - \mu_0}{s_x/\sqrt{n}} = \frac{41,200 - 40,000}{3,000/\sqrt{36}} = +2.4$$

The three possible alternative hypotheses are tested in Figure 10.4. Note that the purpose of the three tests is to illustrate the various tests; in practice, only *one* alternative would be used.

Example 2 Small sample. When the sample size is 30 or less, the t-value is found in a t table. Note that with small sample sizes, the population being sampled must be normally distributed or else this technique cannot be used. Suppose a sample of $n = 25$ resulted in

$$\bar{x} = 41,100 \text{ miles} \qquad s_x = 2,750 \text{ miles}$$

Using $\alpha = .05$ and $25 - 1 = 24$ degrees of freedom, the critical t-value is $+1.71$ or -1.71 for a one-tail test and ± 2.07 for a two-tail test. The test statistic is

$$t_{\text{test}} = \frac{\bar{x} - \mu_0}{s_x/\sqrt{n}} = \frac{41,100 - 40,000}{2,750/\sqrt{25}} = +2.0$$

The three possible tests and the resulting conclusions are illustrated in Figure 10.5. Again, only one such alternative hypothesis would ordinarily be considered.

---

* However, the test statistic is always referred to as t when s_x is used, regardless of the sample size.

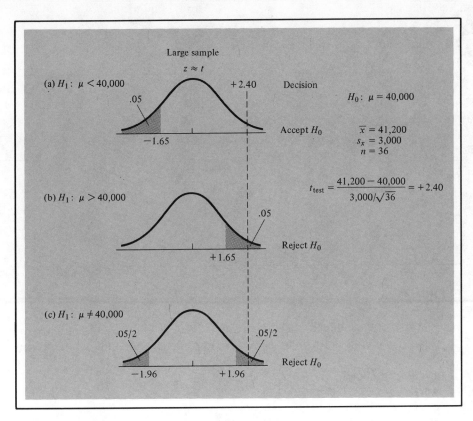

FIGURE 10.4   A comparison of the three alternatives in terms of evaluating the sample data for a large sample.

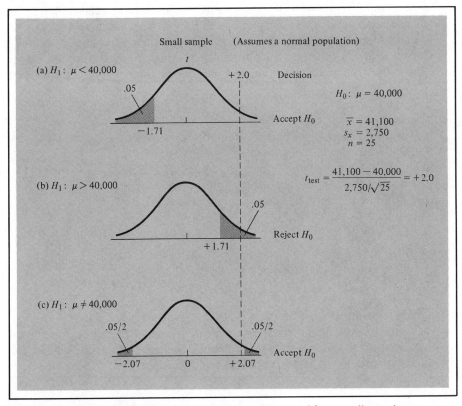

FIGURE 10.5   Three alternative hypothesis tests are illustrated for a small sample.

Test statistic for a one-sample test of means
a. σ_x known:

$$z = \frac{\text{sample mean} - \text{claimed mean}}{\sigma_x/\sqrt{n}}$$

b. σ_x unknown:

$$t = \frac{\text{sample mean} - \text{claimed mean}}{s_x/\sqrt{n}}$$

EXERCISES

1. For each of the following, decide whether a one-tail or a two-tail test is appropriate and then sketch a normal curve illustrating each test. Indicate the area in the tail(s).
   a. $H_0: \mu = 10$, $H_1: \mu \neq 10$, $\alpha = .02$
   b. $H_0: \mu = .037$, $H_1: \mu > .037$, $\alpha = .05$
   c. $H_0: \mu = 3.2$, $H_1: \mu < 3.2$, $\alpha = .01$
   d. $H_0: \mu = 17.45$, $H_1: \mu > 17.45$, $\alpha = .05$
   e. $H_0: \mu_1 = \mu_2$, $H_1: \mu_1 \neq \mu_2$, $\alpha = .02$

2. State the null and alternative hypothesis for each of the following situations:
   a. A product testing organization doubts a manufacturer's claim that flashlight batteries have an average life of 25 hours under continuous operation.
   b. Galvanized pipe must have a mean of 2 inches to be acceptable.
   c. New instructional techniques are not implemented unless it can be shown that the average learning rate will improve in comparison to the current technique being used.
   d. A food processor wants to avoid overfilling 12-oz jars of black raspberry preserves.
   e. The food processor in part d wants to avoid underfilling as well as overfilling 12-oz jars of black raspberry preserves.

3. Referring to the four claims in parts a through d in Exercise 1, test each at the specified level given the additional information below. Develop a $(1 - \alpha)$ confidence interval for any case where H_0 is rejected.

	a.	b.	c.	d.
Sample mean	12.2	.040	3.3	19.05
s_x	1.8	.01	.2	3.5
Sample size	13	81	25	50

4. An employment service advertises that job applicants it has placed in the last six months have salaries that average $9000 a year. A random sample from that group by a government agency found an average salary of $8000 and a standard deviation of $1000 on the basis of 50 people.
   a. What sampling distribution is the *theoretically* correct one to use? Why?

b. What sampling distribution can be used to obtain a reasonable approximation?

c. Test the employment service's claim against the alternative that the average salary is less than $9000, using the .05 level of significance.

*5. The DeBug Company sells bug repellent strips which it claims are effective for at least 400 hours. An analysis of nine randomly selected strips showed an average of 380 hours.

a. Test the company's claim against the alternative that the strips remain effective for less than 400 hours, at the .01 level, if the sample standard deviation is 60 hours.

b. Repeat part a using the knowledge that the population standard deviation is known to be 90 hours.

c. In which of the above parts is it necessary to know that the population is approximately normal? Why?

6. Nine people have followed a special diet plan for two months. At that time their individual weight losses were 1.2, 2.0, 1.0, .8, 1.1, .2, .5, .4, and .1 pounds. Test the null hypothesis of a true average weight loss of 0 pounds against the alternative of a weight loss greater than 0, using $\alpha = .01$. Assume the population is normal.

*7. A process for making steel wire turns out wire with a mean tensile strength of 200 psi. The process standard deviation is 20 psi. The quality control engineer wants to design a test that will indicate whether or not there has been a shift in the process average, using a sample size of 25 and a level of significance of $\alpha = .05$. Assume the population of wire strengths is approximately normal.

a. State H_0 and H_1 for this test.

b. For what range of wire strengths will the process be considered out of control (i.e., be concluded that the process mean has shifted from 200 psi)?

8. An automobile company claims its family–size cars can withstand a head on crash at a speed of 10 mph when equipped with a shock absorbent bumper with repair costs of $100 or less. A sample of six such cars by an independent research bureau had an average repair cost of $150 per car. The sample standard deviation was $30. Assume the distribution of repair costs is approximately normal.

a. Is there sufficient evidence at this point to reject the firm's claim at the .01 level?

b. Is it necessary to know the population is approximately normal? Why?

9. An insurance company will begin an extensive advertising campaign to sell life insurance if it thinks that the average amount carried per family is less than $10,000. A random sample of 50 families in the area has an average of $9,600 and a standard deviation of $1,000.

a. On the basis of the sample evidence, should the claim be accepted or rejected at the .05 level?

b. Might the conclusion reached using the sample evidence be in error? What type of error might it be? Why?

10. Suppose we are given the following information:

$$H_0: \text{mean} = 75 \qquad \alpha = .05$$
$$H_1: \text{mean} > 75 \qquad n = 64$$
$$\sigma_x = 8.0$$

    a. *Prior* to taking a sample, what is P(Type I error)?
    b. If the sample mean is 76.0, what is the probability of a Type I error?
    c. If the sample mean is 77.5, what is the probability of a Type I error?

11. In an effort to speed up the time it takes a pain killer to enter the blood stream, a drug research analyst has added another ingredient to the standard formula. The original formula had a mean time of 43 minutes. In 36 observations of the new mixture, a mean time of 42 minutes was obtained, with a standard deviation of 6 minutes. Assume the distribution of times is approximately normal.
    a. State H_0 and H_1.
    b. What can you conclude about the effectiveness of the new ingredient at the .05 level?
    c. What would your answer be regarding effectiveness of the new ingredient if the .01 level is used?
    d. Is it necessary to assume the population is normal? Why?

12. Sampling from a finite population requires that the estimate of the standard error of the sampling distribution be modified by the correction factor $\sqrt{(N - n)/(N - 1)}$ if the sample size exceeds 5% of the population. A firm's credit manager believes the average credit balance of 400 customers does not exceed \$75. Evaluate this at the .05 level for these cases:
    a. $n = 30$, $s_x = 5$, $\bar{x} = \$77$ b. $n = 50$, $s_x = 5.2$, $\bar{x} = \$76$

TWO-SAMPLE TESTS OF MEANS

Two-sample tests are used to decide if the means of two populations are equal. Two independent samples, one from each of the two populations, are required.* Consider, for instance, a research firm experimenting with two different paint mixtures to see if it can alter the drying time of house paint. Each mixture is tested a number of times, and the mean drying times of the two samples are then compared. One seems to be superior because its average (sample) drying time is 30 minutes less than the other mixture.

But are the true mean drying times of the two paints really different, or is this sample difference nothing more than the chance variation you would expect even if the two formulas have identical mean drying times? Again, *chance* differences must be distinguished from *real* differences.

Two-sample tests are frequently used to compare two methods of instruction, two brands, two cities, two school districts, and other similar things.

The null hypothesis can be that the two populations have equal means:

$$H_0: \mu_1 = \mu_2$$

The alternatives can be one of the following:

$$H_1: \mu_1 \neq \mu_2 \qquad H_1: \mu_1 > \mu_2 \qquad H_1: \mu_1 < \mu_2$$

(Note: $\mu_1 > \mu_2$ is equivalent to $\mu_2 < \mu_1$.)

---

* One note of caution: These two-sample tests require that the samples be independent (i.e., from different groups). This means that before-after data, such as that which might come from a diet study examining average weight before a diet and then after the diet of the same group, cannot be evaluated in this manner. A suitable test for such cases is discussed in Chapter 13.

The test focuses on the relative difference between the means of two samples, one from each population. This difference is divided by the standard deviation of a sampling distribution. The standard deviation is computed by first assuming H_0 is true. In that case the two samples can be regarded as having come from the *same* population, and by pooling (combining) variances of the two populations (or samples, if the population variances are unknown), the variance of the overall population can be determined. When σ_1 and σ_2 are known, the test statistic is as given in the box.

$$z_{\text{test}} = \frac{\bar{X}_1 - \bar{X}_2}{\sqrt{\dfrac{\sigma_1^2}{n_1} + \dfrac{\sigma_2^2}{n_2}}}$$

The actual value of z when H_0 is true can be assumed to be normally distributed with a mean of 0 and a standard deviation of 1.0 (i.e., the standardized normal distribution) for cases in which the *sum* $n_1 + n_2$ is greater than 30. For smaller sample sizes z will be normally distributed only if the two populations being sampled are normally distributed.

When the population standard deviations are unknown, the test statistic is as shown in the box.

$$t_{\text{test}} = \frac{\bar{X}_1 - \bar{X}_2}{\sqrt{\dfrac{s_1^2}{n_1} + \dfrac{s_2^2}{n_2}}}$$

The value of t, assuming H_0 is true, can be well approximated by z if $n_1 + n_2$ exceeds 30.

When the two sample sizes are not equal and their sum is less than 30, the formula for the test statistic becomes:

$$t_{\text{test}} \approx \frac{\bar{X}_1 - \bar{X}_2}{\sqrt{\left[\dfrac{(n_1 - 1)s_1^2 + (n_2 - 1)s_2^2}{n_1 + n_2 - 2}\right]\left(\dfrac{1}{n_1} + \dfrac{1}{n_2}\right)}}$$

The value of t when H_0 is true has a t distribution with $n_1 + n_2 - 2$ degrees of freedom, if it can be assumed that both populations are approximately normal.

The following examples illustrate two sample tests of means for (a) large versus small samples and (b) situations with known versus unknown standard deviations.

Example 3 σ_x is known. Use $\alpha = .05$.

$$H_0: \mu_1 = \mu_2 \qquad H_1: \mu_1 > \mu_2$$
$$\bar{x} = 20 \qquad \bar{x}_2 = 18$$
$$\sigma_1 = \sigma_2 = 3$$
$$n_1 = n_2 = 36$$

Compute the test statistic:

$$z_{\text{test}} = \frac{\bar{x}_1 - \bar{x}_2}{\sqrt{\dfrac{\sigma_1^2}{n_1} + \dfrac{\sigma_2^2}{n_2}}} = \frac{20 - 18}{\sqrt{\dfrac{9}{36} + \dfrac{9}{36}}} = \frac{2}{\sqrt{\dfrac{18}{36}}} = \frac{2}{\sqrt{.5}} = \frac{2}{.7} = 2.9$$

Since the test statistic is greater than 1.65, reject H_0 and conclude that the mean of population 1 is greater than the mean of population 2. See Figure 10.6.

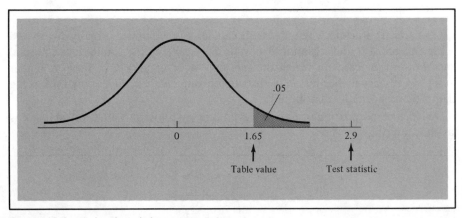

FIGURE 10.6 H_0 is rejected since $z_{\text{test}} > z_{\text{table}}$.

Example 4 σ_x is unknown. Test the hypothesis

$$H_0: \mu_1 = \mu_2$$

when the alternative is

$$H_1: \mu_1 \neq \mu_2$$

Use $\alpha = .05$ and

$$s_{x_1} = 1.1 \qquad s_{x_2} = 1.2$$
$$\bar{x}_1 = 5.4 \qquad \bar{x}_2 = 5.0$$

a. Use $n_1 = n_2 = 36$.
b. Use $n_1 = 15$, $n_2 = 3$ (we must be able to assume a normal population).

Solution:
a. The test statistic is

$$t_{\text{test}} = \frac{\bar{x}_1 - \bar{x}_2}{\sqrt{\dfrac{s_{x_1}^2}{n_1} + \dfrac{s_{x_2}^2}{n_2}}} = \frac{5.4 - 5.0}{\sqrt{\dfrac{1.21}{36} + \dfrac{1.44}{36}}} = \frac{.4}{\sqrt{.2 + .24}} = \frac{.4}{.663} = .6$$

Since $n_1 + n_2 > 30$, $z \approx t$.

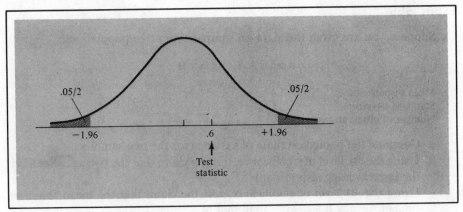

FIGURE 10.7 H_0 is accepted since t_{test} is within the acceptance range.

Since the test statistic is in the acceptance range, the null hypothesis cannot be rejected (see Figure 10.7). We conclude that the difference between the two sample means is probably the result of chance variation due to random sampling.

   b. The test statistic is

$$t_{test} = \frac{\bar{x}_1 - \bar{x}_2}{\sqrt{\left[\dfrac{(n_1 - 1)s_1{}^2 + (n_2 - 1)s_2{}^2}{n_1 + n_2 - 2}\right]\left(\dfrac{1}{n_1} + \dfrac{1}{n_2}\right)}}$$

$$= \frac{5.4 - 5.0}{\sqrt{\left[\dfrac{(14)1.1^2 + (2)1.2^2}{15 + 3 - 2}\right]\left(\dfrac{1}{15} + \dfrac{1}{3}\right)}} = \frac{.4}{.704} = .568$$

With the sum of n_1 and n_2 less than 30, we must use a t table and $n_1 + n_2 - 2$ degrees of freedom to find the critical value. From Table H we find

$$t_{.025,\ 16d.f.} = 2.12$$

Since the test statistic falls in the acceptance region, we cannot conclude that the two populations from which the samples have been drawn have different means. See Figure 10.8.

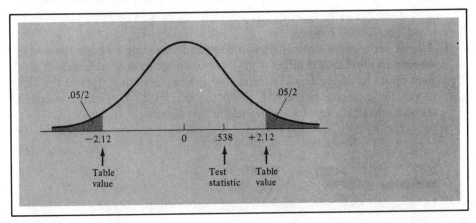

FIGURE 10.8 H_0 is accepted.

EXERCISES

*1. Suppose you are given this data on samples from two populations:

	Agency A	Agency B
Mean response time	4 hr	5 hr
Standard deviation	1 hr	1.2 hr
Number of observations	30	24

a. Compute the pooled estimate of variance for the two samples.

b. Using the .01 level of significance, test the claim that the two agencies have the same average response rate.

c. Using the .01 level of significance, test the claim that the mean response time of Agency B is greater than that of Agency A.

d. Is the assumption of sampling from two normal populations required here? Explain your answer briefly.

2. Two independent wage surveys in two widely separated metropolitan areas revealed the following information about the average wages of heavy equipment operators:

Area

	A	B
$\bar{x}$	$6.50/hr	$7.00/hr
s_x	$1.50/hr	$1.00/hr
n	25	25

Can you conclude that the average wages are different at the .05 level of significance?

3. In a comparison of teaching methods, 12 preschool children in the control group assembled a puzzle in an average time of 3.2 minutes ($s_x = 30$ seconds). The 10 children in the test group, after watching a film related to puzzle solving, completed similar tasks in an average of 2.8 minutes, with $s_x = 30$.

a. Should this be set up as a one-tail test or as a two-tail test? Why?

b. What can you conclude about the effectiveness of the film, using the .05 level?

c. Is it necessary to assume the population of time is normal? Why or why not?

d. Is it necessary to assume that the children have been randomly assigned to the groups? Explain.

4. A large department store chain is interested in deciding whether the average amount of purchases is larger at its downtown location or at a certain shopping center location. Test the claim that the two are equal against the alternative the two are not equal, using the .01 level. A random sample of transactions at the two locations yielded this data:

	Downtown	Shopping center
$\bar{x}$	$45.00	$43.50
Sample size	100	100

(Assume the population standard deviations are both $10.00)

5. Using the .05 level of significance, determine if the mean tensile strengths in two shipments of nylon cord are equal, given these sample observations:

Shipment L	Shipment N
30 psi	32 psi
28	33
27	31
28	30
32	29

CALCULATING THE PROBABILITY OF A TYPE II ERROR*

A Type II error is committed by accepting the null hypothesis when it is false. For purposes of calculating the probability of this occurring, it is helpful to think about the probability as the amount that the sampling distribution, based on the actual population mean, overlaps the acceptance region. This is illustrated in Figure 10.9.

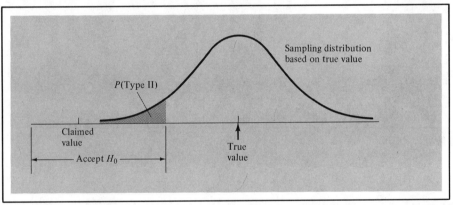

FIGURE 10.9   The probability of a Type II error is the amount that the sampling distribution, based on the true parameter of the population, overlaps the acceptance region for the null hypothesis.

The procedure for determining the probability of a Type II error is as follows (see Figure 10.10):

1. Establish the acceptance region for H_0 using (1) the claimed (assumed) population mean and (2) the specifics of the problem (e.g., standard deviation, sample size, and so on) [Figure 10.10(a)].
2. Add a sampling distribution based on the actual population mean [Figure 10.10(b)].
3. Using the true value as a reference point, determine the area [shown as a Q in Figure 10.10(c)] between it and the decision rule.
4. Add to, or subtract from, 50% to obtain P(Type II), depending on whether the true value is within or outside of the acceptance region. In Figure 10.10

* This section is optional and may be omitted without loss of continuity.

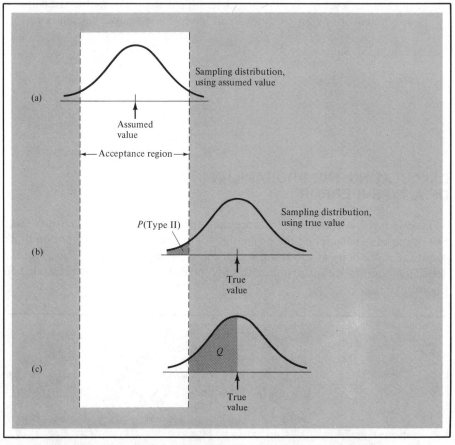

FIGURE 10.10   Steps for calculating the probability of a Type II error.

the true value is outside the region, so the Q area is subtracted from 50%. The Q area would have to be added to 50% if the true value had been inside.

Example 5   Given the following information, compute the probability of making a Type II error if the actual mean of a population is 14.88.

assumed mean	14.00
population standard deviation	2.00
sample size	36
level of significance two-tail test	10%

Solution:

Since σ_x is known, the normal distribution is appropriate. z for a 10%, two-tail test is ± 1.65.

The decision rules are

$$14.00 \pm z\frac{\sigma_x}{\sqrt{n}} = 14.00 \pm 1.65\frac{2}{\sqrt{36}} = 14.00 \pm 1.65\left(\frac{1}{3}\right)$$

$$= 14.00 \pm .55 \quad \text{or} \quad 13.45 \text{ to } 14.55$$

See Figure 10.11.

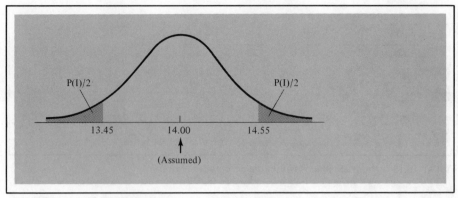

FIGURE 10.11   Decision rule.

If the true mean is 14.88, the probability of a Type II error would look some-thing like the diagram in Figure 10.12.

To determine the area in the tail (which is the probability of a Type II error), it is necessary to find how far the decision rule (14.55) is from the true value:

$$z = \frac{14.55 - 14.88}{2/\sqrt{36}} = \frac{-.33}{.33} = -1.0$$

The area under the normal curve between the mean and 1.0 standard deviation is .3413. Therefore, the area beyond 1.0 standard deviation is .5000 − .3413 = .1587, which is the probability of a Type II error.

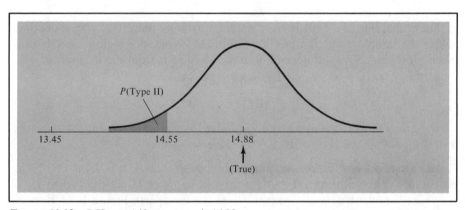

FIGURE 10.12 P(II error) if true mean is 14.88.

Example 6   Using the same information from Example 5, find the probability of making a Type II error if the true value is 14.33 instead of 14.88.

Solution:

The acceptance region would be the same as before, but now the true value is within the acceptance region (note that H_0 is still false because the true value is not equal to the claimed value). See Figure 10.13.

Adding the sampling distribution using the actual mean of 14.33 yields the graph shown in Figure 10.14.

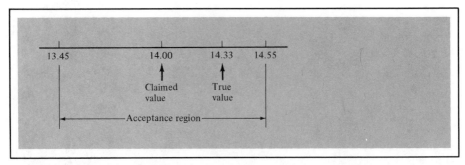

FIGURE 10.13   The true value is within the acceptance region.

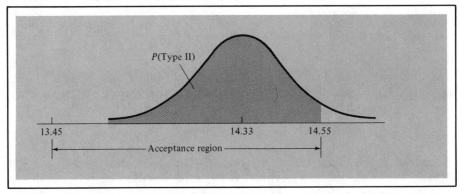

FIGURE 10.14   With an actual mean of 14.33, $P(\text{II})$ is large.

The probability of a Type II error is obviously more than 50%, since more than half of the sampling distribution lies within the acceptance region. Exactly how much more than 50% will depend on how far 14.55 is from the true mean:

$$z = \frac{14.55 - 14.33}{2/\sqrt{36}} = \frac{.22}{.33} = \frac{2}{3}$$

The area between the mean and $\frac{2}{3}$ standard deviations is about .2486, so the probability of a Type II error is $.5000 + .2486 = .7486$.

The size of a Type II error depends on how false H_0 is. If it is slightly false, the probability of committing a Type II error will be much larger than when H_0 is very false (i.e., the true and assumed values are far apart). Figure 10.15 demonstrates this. Note that in order to compute the probability of committing a Type II error, it is necessary to have a particular true value in mind, since each different true value will produce a different $P(\text{Type II error})$.

Notice in Figure 10.15 that in one instance the probability of a Type II error is zero. The reason is the true mean and the assumed mean are the same, so the null hypothesis is true. When that happens, the only kind of error possible is a Type I error.

EXERCISES

1. a. Define a Type I error.
   b. Define a Type II error.

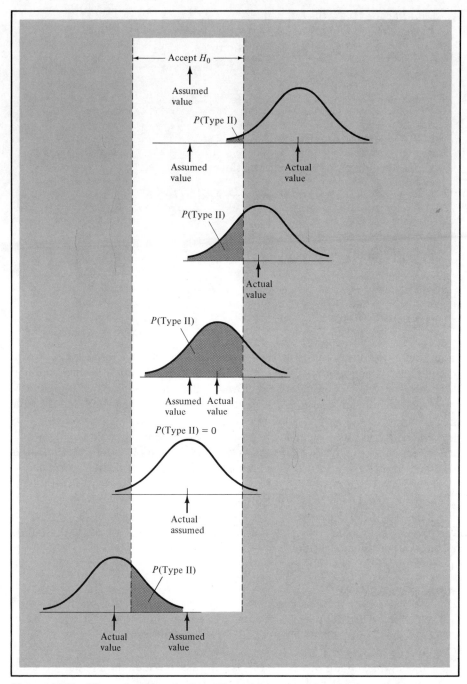

FIGURE 10.15 The probability of a Type II error depends on how far the true (actual) mean is from the assumed mean.

2. Suppose you are given this information:

$$H_0: \mu = 20 \qquad H_1: \mu \neq 20$$
$$n = 100 \qquad \sigma_x = 10$$
$$\alpha = .05$$

Find P(Type II) for the following:

a. $\mu = 19$ b. $\mu = 19.5$ c. $\mu = 20$ d. $\mu = 22$

3. Suppose you are given this information:

$$H_0: \mu = 5 \qquad H_1: \mu > 5$$
$$n = 25 \qquad \sigma_x = 1$$
$$\alpha = .04$$

Find P(Type II) if μ is as follows:

a. 5.2   b. 5.0   c. 5.4   d. 6.0

4. Suppose you are given this information:

$$H_0: \mu = 25 \qquad H_1: \mu < 25$$
$$n = 36 \qquad s_x = 3$$
$$\alpha = .01$$

Find P(Type II) if μ is as follows:

a. 24.5   b. 24   c. 23.5

SUMMARY

The general purpose of tests of means is to evaluate claims about the means of populations. A one-sample test is employed if the claim is about a single population mean; a two-sample test is employed if the claim is that two populations have the same mean; and a k-sample test is used when the claim relates to the means of more than two populations. Claims are evaluated by (1) assuming they are true and then (2) constructing a sampling distribution using that claim, which can be (3) used to judge a particular sample result. Sample means that result in small deviations from the expected (claimed) value are considered to be due to chance variation in sampling; large differences are taken as evidence that the claim is untrue. The standard deviation of the sampling distribution is used as the measure of deviation from the expected value and the level of significance (probability of a Type I error) is used to determine critical values that separate chance and nonchance results.

REVIEW QUESTIONS

1. What is the general purpose of a test of means?
2. List three kinds of claims that can be made about means.
3. Outline the testing procedure for significance tests.
4. Under what conditions is it necessary to assume that the population being sampled has a distribution that is approximately normal?
5. When should the t distribution be used?

SUPPLEMENTAL EXERCISES

Assume samples are drawn from normal populations for each of the following problems.

1. An industrial process produces pieces of fencing that have a mean of 40 cm when the process is in control. The process has a *known* standard deviation of 2.2 cm, which remains constant whether the process is in control or not. Assuming a level of significance of .05, find the minimum and maximum sample averages which would indicate the process is in control for samples of:
   a. 14   b. 22

*2. Determine if the mean number of complaints per day is equal for these two offices:

										Totals
A	18	14	10	13	9	13	8	7	16	108
B	14	15	11	14	20	21	12	10	18	135

3. In a study that compared average time-in-grade for a random sample of 50 men and 50 women at a large industrial complex, these sample statistics emerged:

Men	Women
$\bar{x} = 3.2$ years	$\bar{x} = 3.7$ years
$s_x = .8$ years	$s_x = .9$ years

   Can you conclude at the .01 level that men have a shorter time-in-grade than women employees?

4. In the past a certain group of machines has had an average length of time between repairs of 200 operating hours. Personnel in this department have recently completed a training program which stressed preventive maintenance of equipment. The following 15 breakdowns had a mean of 210 hours between each with a standard deviation of 11 hours. Does this provide sufficient evidence to conclude that the mean time between breakdowns has increased (.025)?

5. A pharmaceutical firm maintains that the average time for a drug to take effect is 24 minutes. In a sample of 19 trials, the average time was 25 minutes, with a standard deviation of 2 minutes. Test the claim against the alternative that the average time is greater than 24 minutes (.01).

6. A company is seeking to purchase a quantity of hand calculators that have a minimum average life of 1.5 years or more. Suppose you are given that such calculators have an operating life with a standard deviation of .3 years. Use the .05 (one-tail) level.
   a. Find the probability that the company will accept $H_0 = 1.5$ based on a sample of 25 calculators (i.e., make a Type II error) if the actual minimum life is:
      (1) 1.3 years   (2) 1.4 years   (3) 1.44 years
   b. Should the claim be accepted if the sample of 25 has a mean of 1.6? Why?

7. In which of the above problems was it necessary to be able to assume the population being sampled was normal?

8. Criticize each of the following statements.
   a. Type I errors are more important than Type II errors.
   b. It is impossible to control both Type I and Type II errors at the same time

because to decrease one type of error means to increase the other type of error.

c. If H_0 is rejected, the probability of a Type I error is equal to the level of significance of the test.

d. A Type I error is made by falsely accepting H_0.

e. A small level of significance is always best because it provides a small probability of committing a Type I error.

11

analysis of variance

Chapter Objectives

After completing this chapter, you should be able to:
1. State what the purpose of analysis of variance is
2. Describe both the similarities and differences between analysis of variance and other tests of means
3. List the assumptions that are necessary when analysis of variance is used
4. Describe the important characteristics of the F distribution
5. Use analysis of variance to analyze a set of sample data and interpret the results
6. Construct an ANOVA table for analysis of variance calculations

Chapter Outline

Introduction
Assumptions
Review of the Procedure for Computing a Sample Variance
The Rationale of Analysis of Variance
The F Ratio
    Characteristics of the F distribution
    Determining the degrees of freedom
    Using the F table
    Calculating the F ratio from sample data
The Analysis of Variance (ANOVA) Table
Comment

INTRODUCTION

ANALYSIS OF variance is a technique that can be used to decide if the means of two or more populations are equal. The test is based on a single sample taken from each population. For example, suppose that the data in Table 11.1 were recorded in a test conducted to determine if the gasoline mileage is the same for four major brands of gasoline. Notice that no two *sample* means are equal. Analysis of variance can be used to determine if the differences among the sample means are indicative of genuine differences among the gasoline mileage yielded by the four brands (populations), or whether the differences between the sample means are more suggestive of sampling variability.

TABLE 11.1   Gasoline Mileage Data

| Observation | Brand | | | |
	1	2	3	4
1	15.1	14.9	15.4	15.6
2	15.0	15.2	15.2	15.5
3	14.9	14.9	16.1	15.8
4	15.7	14.8	15.3	15.3
5	15.4	14.9	15.2	15.7
6	15.1	15.3	15.2	15.7
Sample means	15.2	15.0	15.4	15.6
Sample variances	.088	.040	.124	.032

Accordingly, the null and alternative hypotheses can be stated as follows:

H_0: The population means are all equal.

H_1: The population means are not all equal.

Analysis of variance is used to decide if the means of two or more populations are equal.

If our statistical test (analysis of variance) causes us to accept the null hypothesis, we would conclude that the observed differences among the sample means are due to chance variation in sampling (and thus that the population means of the

265

four brands are equal). If we reject the null hypothesis, we would conclude that the differences among the sample means are too great to be due to chance alone (and thus that the population means are not all equal).

The data for analysis of variance are obtained by taking a sample from each population and computing the sample mean and variance for each sample, as portrayed in Figure 11.1.

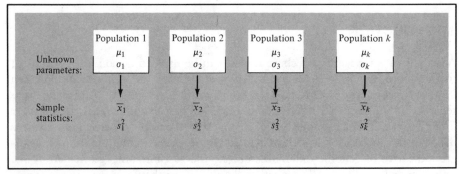

FIGURE 11.1   A sample is taken from each population and the sample mean and variance are computed.

ASSUMPTIONS

There are three basic assumptions that must be satisfied before analysis of variance can be used.

1. The samples must be independent random samples.
2. The samples must be drawn from normal populations.
3. The populations must have equal variances (i.e., $\sigma_1{}^2 = \sigma_2{}^2 = \cdots = \sigma_k{}^2$).

REVIEW OF THE PROCEDURE FOR COMPUTING A SAMPLE VARIANCE

Analysis of variance, as its name implies, involves computing variances. Consequently, a brief review of how this is done should be helpful. The variance of a sample is the average of the squared deviations from the group mean. Symbolically, this is

$$\text{variance} = \frac{\sum(x_i - \bar{x})^2}{n - 1}$$

Note that we must use $n - 1$ because we are working with sample data. Hence to find the sample variance, the procedure is as follows:

1. Compute the sample mean.
2. Subtract the mean from each sample value.
3. Square each of the differences.
4. Sum the squared differences.
5. Divide by $n - 1$.

Example 1 Find the variance of this data: 5, 10, 10, 15, 20, 20, 25.

Solution:
1. Find the mean:

$$\frac{5 + 10 + 10 + 15 + 20 + 20 + 25}{7} = 15$$

2. Subtract the mean from each value:

$$5 - 15 = -10 \qquad 20 - 15 = 5$$
$$10 - 15 = -5 \qquad 20 - 15 = 5$$
$$10 - 15 = -5 \qquad 25 - 15 = 10$$
$$15 - 15 = 0$$

3. Square the differences:

$$100, 25, 25, 0, 25, 25, 100$$

4. Sum the squared differences:

$$\Sigma = 300$$

5. Divide by $n - 1$ to find the variance:

$$\frac{300}{n - 1} = \frac{300}{6} = 50$$

THE RATIONALE OF ANALYSIS OF VARIANCE

Strangely enough, an examination of *variances* can reveal whether or not the population *means* are all equal. Analysis of variance uses two somewhat different approaches for estimating the (equal) population variances. If the two estimates are approximately equal, this tends to confirm H_0; if one of the two estimates is much larger than the other, this tends to confirm H_1. Let us see how the two estimates are made and why they should be approximately the same when H_0 is true.

If the null hypothesis is true, then the samples have all been drawn from populations with equal means. And since it is assumed that all populations are normal and have equal variances, when H_0 is true this is conceptually identical to a situation in which all samples have actually been drawn from a *single* population. This is depicted in Figure 11.2(a). If H_0 is false, then the samples will have come from populations that do not all have the same mean. One such example is shown in Figure 11.2(b). Note, however, that even in that case, we must still assume the populations are normal with equal variances.

One way to estimate the (equal) population variance is to take the average of the sample variances. Of course, any *one* of the sample variances could be used, but the average of all of them will generally provide the best estimate because of the larger number of observations it represents. Since each sample variance reflects only the variation *within* that particular sample, the estimate of variance

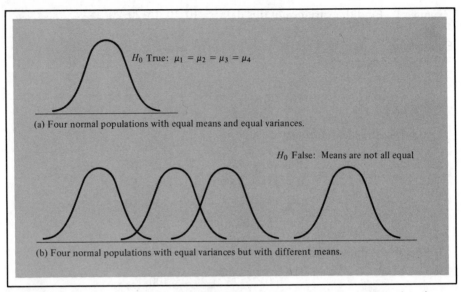

(a) Four normal populations with equal means and equal variances.

(b) Four normal populations with equal variances but with different means.

FIGURE 11.2 (a) Shows four normal populations with equal means and equal variances. (b) Shows four normal populations with equal variances but with different means.

based on the average of sample variances is referred to as the *within estimate of variance*. The within estimate S_w^2 is computed in this way:

Within Estimate of Variance

$$S_w^2 = \frac{s_1^2 + s_2^2 + s_3^2 + s_4^2 + \cdots + s_k^2}{k}$$

where

s_1^2 = variance of sample 1

s_2^2 = variance of sample 2

$\vdots$

s_k^2 = variance of sample k

k = number of samples

For the gasoline mileage data, the average (within) variance is (using the sample variances from Table 11.1)

$$S_w^2 = \frac{.088 + .040 + .124 + .032}{4} = \frac{.284}{4} = .071$$

Since it is assumed that the population variances are equal regardless of whether or not the means are equal, the within estimate of variance is *unaffected* by the truth or falsity of H_0. Therefore, it can not be used, by itself, to judge if the population means might be equal. Nevertheless, it does serve as a standard of comparison against which a second estimate, called the *between estimate of variance*, can be judged. This second estimate, by the way, *is* sensitive to differences between (or among) population means.

> The within estimate of variance serves as a standard against which the between estimate of variance can be compared.

The between sample estimate of variance determines an estimate of the equal population variances in an indirect sort of way—through a sampling distribution of means. Recall that if H_0 is true, this is equivalent to taking all the samples from the *same* normal population. Moreover, we know from the Central Limit Theorem that the sampling distribution of means taken from a normal population will be normally distributed [see Figure 11.3(a)] and that the sampling distribution's standard deviation (square root of its variance) is directly related to the size of the population standard deviation (square root of the population variance). That is,

$$\text{standard deviation of sampling distribution of means} = \frac{\text{population standard deviation}}{\sqrt{\text{sample size}}}$$

or,

$$\sigma_{\bar{x}} = \frac{\sigma_x}{\sqrt{n}}$$

Squaring both sides of this equation yields the relationship in terms of variances:

$$\sigma_{\bar{x}}^2 = \frac{\sigma_x^2}{n}$$

Now if we knew the variance of the sampling distribution, merely multiplying it by sample size would tell us *exactly* the value of σ_x^2. That is,

$$n\sigma_{\bar{x}}^2 = \sigma_x^2$$

Unfortunately, we do not know $\sigma_{\bar{x}}^2$. Nevertheless, it is possible to estimate it. We have frequently used the variance or standard deviation of a sample to estimate the variance or standard deviation of the distribution from which the sample was taken. Hence we now have a set of sample *means* that presumably (if H_0 is true) have all come from the same *sampling* distribution. Finding the variance of the sample means, then, will enable us to estimate the population variance:

$$s_{\bar{x}}^2 = \frac{s_x^2}{n} \quad \text{and} \quad ns_{\bar{x}}^2 = s_x^2$$

Now suppose H_0 is not true. We then have a situation such as that depicted in Figure 11.3(b). One or more of the populations will have a sampling distribution separate from the rest. When the variance of the means is computed, it will reflect this disparity and make it appear as if the sampling distribution of means has a

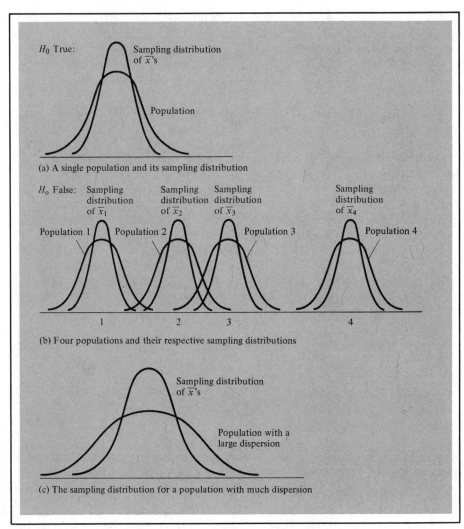

FIGURE 11.3 (a) A single population and its sampling distribution. (b) Four populations and their respective sampling distributions. (c) The sampling distribution for a population with much dispersion.

somewhat larger variance. This, in turn, will cause our estimate of the population variance to be larger, as if the samples had been drawn from a population with wider dispersion, say like that portrayed in Figure 11.3(c).

Thus, the between estimate of variance focuses on the variance between or among sample means and relates this to an estimate of the population variance in terms of a sampling distribution of means. For the gasoline mileage data, the between estimate of variance S_b^2 can be computed in this way:

1. Find $\bar{\bar{x}}$, the mean of the sample means:

$$\bar{\bar{x}} = \frac{\sum\limits_{j=1}^{k} \bar{x}_j}{k}$$

Thus,

$$\bar{\bar{x}} = \frac{15.2 + 15.0 + 15.4 + 15.6}{4} = 15.3$$

2. Find the squared deviations, add them, and divide by $k - 1$:

$$\sum_{j=1}^{k} \frac{(\bar{x}_j - \bar{\bar{x}})^2}{k - 1} = s_{\bar{x}}^2$$

$$= \frac{(15.2 - 15.3)^2 + (15.0 - 15.3)^2 + (15.4 - 15.3)^2 + (15.6 - 15.3)^2}{4 - 1}$$

$$= .067$$

Since each sample consisted of 6 observations, $n = 6$, and our estimate of the population variance is

$$S_b^2 = ns_{\bar{x}}^2 = 6(.067) = .402$$

We now have two estimates of the population variance:

$$S_w^2 = .071 \quad \text{and} \quad S_b^2 = .402$$

Recall that S_w^2 is our standard of comparison, since it is unaffected by H_0's being true or false, while S_b^2 is affected, being approximately equal to S_w^2 when H_0 is true but larger than S_w^2 when H_0 is not true. Now it is apparent at this point that S_b^2 is indeed larger than S_w^2. However, we still do not know for sure that it is *significantly* larger; chance variation due to sampling may be entirely responsible for this. Once more we must refer to a test statistic, and the sampling distribution for that test statistic, to resolve the question.

THE *F* RATIO

In contrast to other tests of means, which rely on the difference between two values, analysis of variance uses the *ratio* of the two estimates, dividing the between estimate by the within estimate:

$$F \text{ ratio} = \frac{S_b^2}{S_w^2} = \frac{ns_{\bar{x}}^2}{(s_1^2 + s_2^2 + \cdots + s_k^2)/k}$$

The resulting value of the test statistic must be compared with a table value of F, which will indicate the maximum value of the test statistic that would occur if H_0 is true, at a chosen level of significance. Before proceeding with this calculation, it will be helpful to consider the F distribution.

Characteristics of the *F* Distribution

1. There is a different F distribution for each combination of sample size and number of samples. So there is one F distribution that applies when five samples

of six observations each are taken, and there is a different F distribution for five samples of seven observations each. As a matter of fact, the number of different sampling distributions is so large that extensive tabulation of distributions would be impractical. Therefore, as with the t distribution, only the most commonly used values are tabulated. In the case of the F distribution, critical values for the .05 and .01 level are usually provided for certain combinations of sample sizes and number of samples.

2. The distribution is continuous over the range from 0 to $+\infty$. The smallest ratio is 0. The ratio cannot be negative since both terms of the F ratio are squared values. On the other hand, large differences between sample means accompanied by small sample variances can result in extremely large values of the F ratio.

3. The shape of each theoretical F sampling distribution depends on the number of degrees of freedom associated with it. Both the numerator and the denominator have related degrees of freedom. Figure 11.4 illustrates some of the different shapes that the F distribution can assume, for various degrees of freedom.

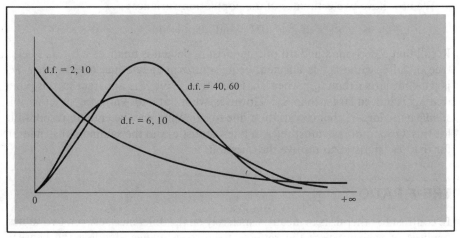

FIGURE 11.4   Some of the different shapes of the F distribution for selected degrees of freedom for numerator and denominator.

Determining the Degrees of Freedom

The degrees of freedom for both the numerator and the denominator of the F ratio are based on the computations necessary to derive each estimate of population variance. The between estimate of variance (numerator) involves dividing the sum of the squared differences by the number of means (samples) minus one, or $k - 1$. Thus $k - 1$ *is the number of degrees of freedom for the numerator.*

Similarly, in computing each sample variance, the sum of the squared differences between the sample mean and each sample value is divided by the number of sample observations minus one, or $n - 1$. The average of the sample variances is then found by dividing the sum of the sample variances by the number of samples, or k. *The denominator degrees of freedom is thus* $k(n - 1)$.

The logic of the degrees of freedom becomes more apparent upon a closer examination of the formulas for computing the between and the within estimates of variance. For the between estimate, we have

$$S_b^2 = ns_{\bar{x}}^2 = n\left[\frac{\sum(\bar{x}_j - \bar{\bar{x}})^2}{\underbrace{k-1}_{\uparrow}}\right]$$
$$\text{d.f.}$$

For the within estimate, we have

$$S_w^2 = \frac{s_1^2 + s_2^2 + \cdots + s_k^2}{k}$$

$$= \frac{\dfrac{\sum(x_i - \bar{x}_1)^2}{n-1} + \dfrac{\sum(x_i - \bar{x}_2)^2}{n-1} + \cdots + \dfrac{\sum(x_i - \bar{x}_k)^2}{n-1}}{k}$$

$$= \left(\frac{1}{n-1}\right)\left[\frac{\sum(x_i - \bar{x}_1)^2 + \sum(x_i - \bar{x}_2)^2 + \cdots + \sum(x_i - \bar{x}_k)^2}{k}\right]$$

$$= \frac{1}{\underbrace{k(n-1)}_{\uparrow}}\left[\sum(x_i - \bar{x}_1)^2 + \sum(x_i - \bar{x}_2)^2 + \cdots + \sum(x_i - \bar{x}_k)^2\right]$$
$$\text{d.f.}$$

In summary, the numerator and denominator degrees of freedom are as follows:

---

numerator: one less than number of samples, or $k - 1$

denominator: number of samples $\times$ (sample size $- 1$), or $k(n - 1)$

Using the *F* Table

The values shown in an *F* table are critical values: the dividing lines that separate random variation from nonrandom variation. In conducting an analysis of variance test, the two sample estimates of variance are used to compute an *F* ratio. The resulting number is then compared to a value of *F* found in the table. If the computed value is *larger* than the table value, the null hypothesis is rejected. If the computed value is *smaller* than the table value, the null hypothesis cannot be rejected. See Figure 11.5.

Table 11.2 illustrates the structure of an *F* table for the .05 level of significance. (*F* tables for both the .01 and .05 levels are included in Table J in the Appendix.) To find an *F*-value in the table, it is necessary to determine the degrees of freedom. The table value is found by locating the numerator degrees of freedom (listed across the top of the table) and the denominator degrees of freedom (listed down the side of the table) corresponding to a given situation. The critical value of *F* is found at the intersection of the row and column that correspond to the denominator and numerator degrees of freedom.

Using the .05 level of significance, with 3 and 20 degrees of freedom, the table value of *F* is 3.10. Notice that there is a *different* value for numerator degrees of freedom of 20 and denominator degrees of freedom of 3, so it is important when

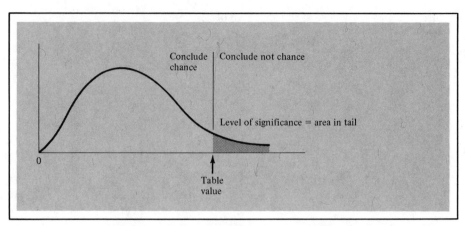

FIGURE 11.5   Illustration of a significance test using the F distribution. If computed F falls to the left of the table value of F, accept H_0; if it falls to the right, reject H_0.

TABLE 11.2   Portion of an F Table

Degrees of freedom in the numerator are recorded at the top of the table, and the degrees of freedom in the denominator are indicated at the sides. The first listed or smaller value is the value on the F scale to the right of which lies 0.05 of the area under the curve. The second listed or larger value is the value on the F scale to the right of which lies 0.01 of the area under the curve.

	Degrees of freedom (numerator)										
	1	2	3	4	5	6	8	10	12	16	20
1	161	200	216	225	230	234	239	242	244	246	248
	4,052	4,999	5,403	5,625	5,764	5,859	5,981	6,056	6,106	6,169	6,208
2	18.51	19.00	19.16	19.25	19.30	19.33	19.37	19.39	19.41	19.43	19.44
	98.49	99.00	99.17	99.25	99.30	99.33	99.36	99.40	99.42	99.44	99.45
3	10.13	9.55	9.28	9.12	9.01	8.94	8.84	8.78	8.74	8.69	8.66
	34.12	30.82	29.46	28.71	28.24	27.91	27.49	27.23	27.05	26.83	26.69
4	7.71	6.94	6.59	6.39	6.26	6.16	6.04	5.96	5.91	5.84	5.80
	21.20	18.00	16.69	15.98	15.52	15.21	14.80	14.54	14.37	14.15	14.02
5	6.61	5.79	5.41	5.19	5.05	4.95	4.82	4.74	4.68	4.60	4.56
	16.26	13.27	12.06	11.39	10.97	10.67	10.27	10.05	9.89	9.68	9.55
6	5.99	5.14	4.76	4.53	4.39	4.28	4.15	4.06	4.00	3.92	3.87
	13.74	10.92	9.78	9.15	8.75	8.47	8.10	7.87	7.72	7.52	7.39
7	5.59	4.74	4.35	4.12	3.97	3.87	3.73	3.63	3.57	3.49	3.44
	12.25	9.55	8.45	7.85	7.46	7.19	6.84	6.62	6.47	6.27	6.15
8	5.32	4.46	4.07	3.84	3.69	3.58	3.44	3.34	3.28	3.20	3.15
	11.26	8.65	7.59	7.01	6.63	6.37	6.03	5.82	5.67	5.48	5.36
9	5.12	4.26	3.86	3.63	3.48	3.37	3.23	3.13	3.07	2.98	2.93
	10.56	8.02	6.99	6.42	6.06	5.80	5.47	5.26	5.11	4.92	4.80
10	4.96	4.10	3.71	3.48	3.33	3.22	3.07	2.97	2.91	2.82	2.77
	10.04	7.56	6.55	5.99	5.64	5.39	5.06	4.85	4.71	4.52	4.41
11	4.84	3.98	3.59	3.36	3.20	3.09	2.95	2.86	2.79	2.70	2.65
	9.65	7.20	6.22	5.67	5.32	5.07	4.74	4.54	4.40	4.21	4.10
12	4.75	3.88	3.49	3.26	3.11	3.00	2.85	2.76	2.69	2.60	2.54
	9.33	6.93	5.95	5.41	5.06	4.82	4.50	4.30	4.16	3.98	3.86

TABLE 11.2 (*Continued*)

				Degrees of freedom (numerator)							
	1	2	3	4	5	6	8	10	12	16	20
13	4.67	3.80	3.41	3.18	3.02	2.92	2.77	2.67	2.60	2.51	2.46
	9.07	6.70	5.74	5.20	4.86	4.62	4.30	4.10	3.96	3.78	3.67
14	4.60	3.74	3.34	3.11	2.96	2.85	2.70	2.60	2.53	2.44	2.39
	8.86	6.51	5.56	5.03	4.69	4.46	4.14	3.94	3.80	3.62	3.51
15	4.54	3.68	3.29	3.06	2.90	2.79	2.64	2.55	2.48	2.39	2.33
	8.68	6.36	5.42	4.89	4.56	4.32	4.00	3.80	3.67	3.48	3.36
16	4.49	3.63	3.24	3.01	2.85	2.74	2.59	2.49	2.42	2.33	2.28
	8.53	6.23	5.29	4.77	4.44	4.20	3.89	3.69	3.55	3.37	3.25
17	4.45	3.59	3.20	2.96	2.81	2.70	2.55	2.45	2.38	2.29	2.23
	8.40	6.11	5.18	4.67	4.34	4.10	3.79	3.59	3.45	3.27	3.16
18	4.41	3.55	3.16	2.93	2.77	2.66	2.51	2.41	2.34	2.25	2.19
	8.28	6.01	5.09	4.58	4.25	4.01	3.71	3.51	3.37	3.19	3.07
19	4.38	3.52	3.13	2.90	2.74	2.63	2.48	2.38	2.31	2.21	2.15
	8.18	5.93	5.01	4.50	4.17	3.94	3.63	3.43	3.30	3.12	3.00
20	4.35	3.49	③.10	2.87	2.71	2.60	2.45	2.35	2.28	2.18	2.12
	8.10	5.85	4.94	4.43	4.10	3.87	3.56	3.37	3.23	3.05	2.94
25	4.24	3.38	2.99	2.76	2.60	2.49	2.34	2.24	2.16	2.06	2.00
	7.77	5.57	4.68	4.18	3.86	3.63	3.32	3.13	2.99	2.81	2.70
30	4.17	3.32	2.92	2.69	2.53	2.42	2.27	2.16	2.09	1.99	1.93
	7.56	5.39	4.51	4.02	3.70	3.47	3.17	2.98	2.84	2.66	2.55
40	4.08	3.23	2.84	2.61	2.45	2.34	2.18	2.07	2.00	1.90	1.84
	7.31	5.18	4.31	3.83	3.51	3.29	2.99	2.80	2.66	2.49	2.37

Source: Reprinted by permission from *Statistical Methods* by George W. Snedecor and William G. Cochran, 6th ed., copyright © 1967 by Iowa State University Press, Ames, Iowa 50010.

using the table to remember that the numerator degrees of freedom are shown across the top and the denominator degrees of freedom are shown down the side of the table.

Example 2 For each of the following sets of conditions, find the table *F*-values for the .01 and .05 levels of significance.

No. of samples, *k*	4	3	6	4	2
Sample size, *n*	11	4	6	6	11

Solution:

No. of samples, k	Numerator degrees of freedom $k - 1$	Sample size n	Denominator degrees of freedom $k(n - 1)$	Table value .05	.01
4	3	11	4(10) = 40	2.84	4.31
3	2	4	3(3) = 9	4.26	8.02
6	5	6	6(5) = 30	2.53	3.70
4	3	6	4(5) = 20	3.10	4.94
2	1	11	2(10) = 20	4.35	8.10

As another example consider the gasoline data. There are four samples ($k = 4$) of six observations each ($n = 6$), so the degrees of freedom are

$$\text{numerator: } k - 1 = 3$$
$$\text{denominator: } k(n - 1) = 4(5) = 20$$

If we decide to test at the .05 level, the table value is 3.10.

Calculating the *F* Ratio from Sample Data

The F ratio is the ratio of the variance estimate based on sample means to the variance estimate based on sample variances. That is, the test statistic is as given in the box.

$$F_{\text{test}} = \frac{\text{between estimate of variance}}{\text{within estimate of variance}}$$

$$= \frac{(\text{sample size}) \times (\text{variance of sample means})}{\text{average of sample variances}}$$

$$= \frac{n \cdot s_{\bar{x}}^2}{(\sum s_k^2)/k}$$

For the gasoline data we have a test statistic of

$$F_{\text{test}} = \frac{S_b^2}{S_w^2} = \frac{.402}{.071} = 5.70$$

Since this value is greater than the table value, H_0 is rejected. Consequently, we conclude that the samples have probably not come from populations with equal means. Thus we conclude that the average miles-per-gallon rate is not the same for all brands. The comparison of the test value of F and the table value is shown in Figure 11.6.

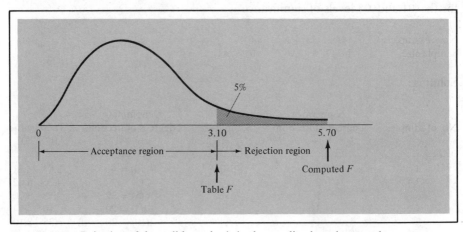

FIGURE 11.6   Rejection of the null hypothesis in the gasoline brands example.

To calculate, *F*, follow this procedure:

WITHIN (DENOMINATOR) ESTIMATE

1. Compute the variance of *each* sample, using the formula

$$\text{variance} = s^2 = \frac{\sum(x_i - \bar{x})^2}{n - 1}$$

2. Find the average sample variance, using the formula

$$S_w^2 = \frac{\sum s^2}{k} = \frac{s_1^2 + s_2^2 + s_3^2 + \cdots + s_k^2}{k}$$

where

$$k = \text{number of samples}$$
$$S_w^2 = \text{within estimate of variance}$$

BETWEEN (NUMERATOR) ESTIMATE

3. Compute the variance of the sample means. To do this first add the sample means and divide by the number of samples to obtain $\bar{\bar{x}}$, the overall mean. Then use the formula

$$\text{variance of means} = s_{\bar{x}}^2 = \frac{\sum(\bar{x} - \bar{\bar{x}})^2}{k - 1}$$

4. Multiply the variance of sample means by *n*:

$$n \cdot s_{\bar{x}}^2$$

5. *F* ratio:

$$\frac{\text{result of step 4}}{\text{result of step 2}} \quad \text{or} \quad \frac{n s_{\bar{x}}^2}{(\sum s^2)/k}$$

If the sample means and variances are not given, they must be computed from the sample data before proceeding. The following example illustrates this.

Example 3   The average hourly wages of auto mechanics in four metropolitan areas were the object of a recent study conducted by a consumers group. The purpose was to determine if any real differences existed between the four locations. The data are shown below. The level of significance used is .05.

Locality (samples)

Observations	A	B	C	D
1	6	12	11	9
2	9	11	8	7
3	9	10	12	10
4	6	8	9	10
5	5	9	10	9
Totals	35	50	50	45

Solution:

First we compute the between means estimate of the variance. To do this we calculate the sample means:

$$\bar{x}_k = \frac{\sum x_i}{n}$$

$$\bar{x}_A = \frac{35}{5} = 7 \qquad \bar{x}_C = \frac{50}{5} = 10$$

$$\bar{x}_B = \frac{50}{5} = 10 \qquad \bar{x}_D = \frac{45}{5} = 9$$

Now we calculate the mean of the sample means:

$$\bar{\bar{x}} = \frac{\sum \bar{x}}{k} = \frac{7 + 10 + 10 + 9}{4} = 9$$

Next we calculate the sum of squares, $\sum (\bar{x}_j - \bar{\bar{x}})^2$:

j	Mean	$\bar{\bar{x}}$	$(\bar{x}_j - \bar{\bar{x}})$	$(\bar{x}_j - \bar{\bar{x}})^2$
1	7	9	-2	4
2	10	9	1	1
3	10	9	1	1
4	9	9	0	0
			$\sum = 0$	$\sum = 6$

Now we calculate the between estimate:

$$S_b{}^2 = \frac{n \sum (\bar{x}_j - \bar{\bar{x}})^2}{k - 1} = \frac{5(6)}{4 - 1} = 10$$

Our next step is to compute the within estimate of variance. To do this we compute the sum of squares for each sample:

A

Observation	x_i	$\bar{x}_A$	$(x_i - \bar{x}_A)$	$(x_i - \bar{x}_A)^2$
1	6	7	-1	1
2	9	7	2	4
3	9	7	2	4
4	6	7	-1	1
5	5	7	-2	4
			$\sum = 0$	$\sum = 14$

B

Observation	x_i	$\bar{x}_B$	$(x_i - \bar{x}_B)$	$(x_i - \bar{x}_B)^2$
1	12	10	2	4
2	11	10	1	1
3	10	10	0	0
4	8	10	-2	4
5	9	10	-1	1
			$\sum = 0$	$\sum = 10$

C

Observation	x_i	$\bar{x}_C$	$(x_i - \bar{x}_C)$	$(x_i - \bar{x}_C)^2$
1	11	10	1	1
2	8	10	-2	4
3	12	10	2	4
4	9	10	-1	1
5	10	10	0	0
			$\sum = 0$	$\sum = 10$

D

Observation	x_i	$\bar{x}_D$	$(x_i - \bar{x}_D)$	$(x_i - \bar{x}_D)^2$
1	9	9	0	0
2	7	9	-2	4
3	10	9	1	1
4	10	9	1	1
5	9	9	0	0
			$\sum = 0$	$\sum = 6$

Now we compute the sample variances:

$$s_k{}^2 = \frac{\sum(x_i - \bar{x}_j)^2}{n - 1}$$

$$s_A{}^2 = \frac{14}{4} \qquad s_B{}^2 = \frac{10}{4} \qquad s_C{}^2 = \frac{10}{4} \qquad s_D{}^2 = \frac{6}{4}$$

Now we compute the within estimate:

$$S_w{}^2 = \frac{\sum s_j{}^2}{k} = \frac{\frac{14}{4} + \frac{10}{4} + \frac{10}{4} + \frac{6}{4}}{4}$$

$$= \frac{1}{4}\left(\frac{40}{4}\right) = \frac{40}{16} = 2.5$$

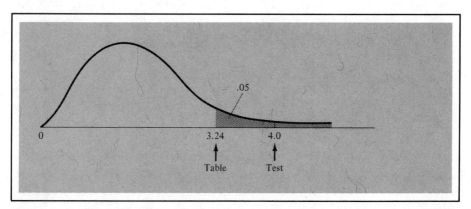

FIGURE 11.7   The null hypothesis is rejected.

Finally, we compute the F ratio:

$$\frac{S_b^2}{S_w^2} = \frac{10.0}{2.5} = 4.0$$

The table value of $F_{.05}$ is 3.24 (d.f.: numerator = 3, denominator = 16). Since the computed F ratio is greater than the table value of F at the chosen level of significance, it can be concluded that the differences between the localities are probably due to more than just chance variation.

Figure 11.7 illustrates the comparison of the two F values.

THE ANALYSIS OF VARIANCE (ANOVA) TABLE

It is customary and often convenient to display the component parts of analysis of variance calculations in tabular form. This not only provides insight into the source of variation, it also provides a mechanism for checking calculations.

Table 11.3 illustrates the symbolic notation of data, and Table 11.4 illustrates an ANOVA table, showing the appropriate formulas. Of course, these are the same formulas used in the preceding examples. The only difference is that now the

TABLE 11.3 Symbolic Representation of Data for Analysis of Variance

	Sample				
	1	2	3	$\cdots$	k
Observations	x_1	x_1	x_1	$\cdots$	x_1
	x_2	x_2	x_2	$\cdots$	x_2
	x_3	x_3	x_3	$\cdots$	x_3
	$\vdots$	$\vdots$	$\vdots$		$\vdots$
	x_n	x_n	x_n	$\cdots$	x_n
Sample means	$\bar{x}_1$	$\bar{x}_2$	$\bar{x}_3$	$\cdots$	$\bar{x}_k$

TABLE 11.4 Symbolic Representation of Analysis of Variance Table

Source of variation	Sum of squares	Degrees of freedom	Variance	F ratio
between means	$n \sum_{j=1}^{k} (\bar{x}_j - \bar{\bar{x}})^2 \div$	$k - 1$	$= S_b^2$	
within samples	$\sum_{j=1}^{k} \left[\sum_{i=1}^{n} (x_i - \bar{x}_j)^2 \right] \div$	$k(n - 1)$	$= S_w^2$	$\frac{S_b^2}{S_w^2} = F$
total	$\sum_{j=1}^{k} \left[\sum_{i=1}^{n} (x_i - \bar{\bar{x}})^2 \right]$	$nk - 1$		

k = number of samples
n = number of observations in each sample
nk = total number of observations

Note: i refers to rows and j refers to columns.

sums of the squared differences are separated from their respective degrees of freedom.

Example 4 Ten random samples of six observations each have been taken from 10 different populations. The results of the computations of the sums of squares and the appropriate degrees of freedom are shown in Table 11.5.

TABLE 11.5   Analysis of Variance

Source of variation	Sum of squares	d.f.	Estimated variance	Calculated F
between means	630	9	70	$\frac{70}{70} = 1.0$
within samples	3500	50	70	
total	4130	59	70	

This table illustrates three important points:

1. There are actually *three* different ways to estimate the true population variance if the null hypothesis is true.
2. The calculations were deliberately designed to show what happens when the estimates of population variance are *exactly* the same (although such an occurrence in practice would be quite rare).
3. The total degrees of freedom can serve as a quick check on the values of the within and between degrees of freedom. Theoretically, the total sum of squares could also serve as a check on the within and between sum of squares, but as a practical matter, the calculations are laborious, so the total is avoided unless the calculations are done by computer.

COMMENT

When the assumptions that underlie analysis of variance are met*, this technique for testing the equality of sample means is extremely powerful. In fact, as long as the distributions from which the samples are taken are not highly skewed, the requirement for normality need not be strictly adhered to. Likewise, if the population variances are approximately the same, the assumption of equal variances will be reasonably satisfied.

Note, however, that analysis of variance does not test the assumption of equality among population variances. Therefore, when sample variances seem to differ considerably, a different test for their equality should be made.[†] If such testing indicates that extreme differences among the population variances are probable, then the F test should not be used. Instead, an alternative method, such as the Kruskal-Wallis test, which does not involve strict assumptions, should be used (See Chapter 13).

---

* The assumptions are *independent samples* drawn from *normal populations* with *equal variances*.

[†] One rule of thumb is that the largest sample variance should be no more than ten times the smallest sample variance.

The discussion and each of the examples in this chapter involved k independent *samples of equal size*. There are situations in which it becomes necessary for one reason or another to take samples of unequal sizes. Consequently, the formulas presented in this chapter must be modified somewhat to accomplish the calculations. Accordingly, the formula for the between estimate of variance becomes:

$$S_b{}^2 = \frac{n_1(\bar{x}_1 - \bar{\bar{x}})^2 + n_2(\bar{x}_2 - \bar{\bar{x}})^2 + \cdots + n_k(\bar{x}_k - \bar{\bar{x}})^2}{k - 1}$$

where

$$n_1 = \text{number of observations in sample 1}$$
$$n_2 = \text{number of observations in sample 2}$$
$$n_k = \text{number of observations in sample } k$$

$$\bar{x}_1 = \text{mean of sample 1}$$
$$\bar{x}_2 = \text{mean of sample 2}$$
$$\bar{x}_k = \text{mean of sample } k$$

$$k = \text{number of samples}$$
$$\bar{\bar{x}} = \text{mean of sample means}$$

For the within estimate of variance, each sample *sum of squares* is adjusted (weighted) by its sample size:

$$S_w{}^2 = \frac{n_1 \sum\limits_{i=1}^{n_1} (x_i - \bar{x}_1)^2 + n_2 \sum\limits_{i=1}^{n_2} (x_i - \bar{x}_2)^2 + \cdots + n_k \sum\limits_{i=1}^{n_k} (x_i - \bar{x}_k)^2}{n_1 + n_2 + \cdots + n_k - k}$$

REVIEW QUESTIONS

1. What is the purpose of analysis of variance?
2. State the null and alternative hypotheses that are used for analysis of variance.
3. List the three basic assumptions of analysis of variance.
4. What do the terms "between estimate of variance" and "within estimate of variance" refer to?
5. Given the standard deviation for each sample, describe how you would determine the within estimate of variance.
6. Given the sample means, describe how you would find the between estimate of variance.
7. What is the F ratio?
8. Briefly describe the characteristics of the F distribution.
9. In what ways is the F distribution similar to the t distribution? In what ways are they different?
10. What does the term "sum of squares" mean?
11. How is a k-sample test of means different from one-and two-sample tests of means?

EXERCISES

1. Determine numerator and denominator degrees of freedom for each of these cases:

	Number of samples	Sample size
a.	5	6
b.	7	4
c.	8	10
d.	4	12

2. Obtain the table F-value for both the .01 and .05 levels for each of the following:
   a. 8 samples, each with 6 observations
   b. 4 samples, each with 7 observations
   c. 5 samples, each with 7 observations
   d. 3 samples, each with 10 observations
   e. 4 samples, each with 12 observations
3. Determine whether to accept or reject the null hypothesis on the basis of these test statistics. Test at both the .01 and .05 levels using your answers from Exercise 2.

	Test statistic	k	n
a.	4.22	8	6
b.	2.10	4	7
c.	3.89	5	7
d.	21.40	3	10
e.	2.01	4	12

4. Find the variance of each of these sets of sample data:
   a. 10, 20, 15, 10, 20
   b. 1, 8, 5, 6, 3, 7
   c. 65, 70, 50, 55, 75, 45
   d. 2, -1, .5, -2, -1.5, 2
5. Use analysis of variance to test the effectiveness of four diet plans. Twenty-four persons were randomly assigned to the plans, with 6 to each plan. The average weight loss and variance for each group are shown in the table. Test this at the .05 level.

Plan	Mean weight loss (lb)	Variance
1 high protein, rigorous exercise	3.0	1.8
2 liquids only	2.5	1.9
3 no grapefruit or cottage cheese	2.6	2.0
4 canned dogfood	5.9	2.3

6. A newspaper reporter is attempting to determine if there are any real differences in average times to repair and return a television set among five repair shops. His data consists of nine sets per shop. What can you conclude about the average repair time?

Shop	Mean repair time (days)	Standard deviation
Dusty's TV	37	3
Speedy's Radio	40	4
AAAA TV Repair	33	3
Zeke Wolfe	20	6
New Location TV	45	5

7. A consumer organization interested in a comparison of selling prices of new cars has taken a random sample of selling price in five metropolitan locations. At each location the selling prices of 10 comparably equipped cars were recorded. Use the .01 level of significance to decide if the mean selling prices differ among the five locations.

Location	Mean price (dollars)	Variance
A	42.5	6
B	44.0	5
C	48.0	7
D	46.0	4
E	44.5	8

8. The Tru-Green Tree Nursery wants to evaluate three strains of hybrid locust trees to determine if they all yield about the same annual growth. What can you conclude about the average annual growths of the three strains?

Strain

1	2	3
14.4	10.8	11.1
14.8	12.2	9.5
12.7	11.2	10.8
12.2	12.8	12.7
10.9	13.0	10.9

*9. The data below show the tread life observed on tires of four ice cream trucks according to tire position. Assuming that the trucks and drivers are comparable, would you say that the mean tread life is independent of position on vehicle in this instance (use the .01 level)? Arrange your calculations into an ANOVA table similar to Table 11.5. How important is the assumption of comparable drivers and trucks?

Tire position

	Right front	Left front	Right rear	Left rear
	17	25	22	26
	19	27	21	24
Tread life (mo)	20	18	19	30
	24	22	26	28

SUPPLEMENTAL EXERCISES

1. Suppose that the critical value of F for analysis of variance is 1.99 at the .05 level. See Figure 11.8.
   a. How would you interpret a test statistic larger than 1.99?
   b. How would you interpret a test statistic smaller than 1.99?
2. Verify the figures given for sample variances for the gasoline brand example at the beginning of this chapter.

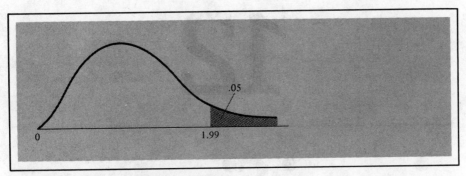

FIGURE 11.8   A hypothetical F distribution.

3. Three sections of Statistics I are given the same final exam. There are 20 students in each section. Viewing the test scores as a *random sample* of the scores that might have resulted (e.g., if the test had been given on another day, at a different time during the day, if different questions had been asked, etc.), can you say that the classes are comparable? Use a .01 level.

	Mean score	Variance
8 o'clock	76	48
9 o'clock	80	40
11 o'clock	87	47

4. Two pit crews at a stock car track are being considered to work in the big race on Sunday. Each crew is given five trials for changing the four tires on a car. Are the crews equivalent, or is one superior? If one is superior, which one is it? Test by using 0.5, and construct an ANOVA table showing your results.

Crew	Times (min)				
red devils	.8	1.0	.8	.7	.7
turnips	.8	.6	.6	.5	.5

5. Rework the data in Exercise 3 and construct an ANOVA table.

12

significance tests for proportions

Chapter Objectives

After completing this chapter, you should be able to:
1. Explain the purpose of tests of proportions
2. Explain the purposes of one-sample, two-sample, and k-sample tests of proportions
3. Solve typical problems using the techniques in this chapter
4. Briefly discuss the chi-square distribution and compare and contrast it with previously learned distributions
5. Use the chi-square table to find probabilities

Chapter Outline

Introduction
One-Sample Test of Proportions
Two-Sample Test of Proportions
k-Sample Test of Proportions
    The Chi-square sampling distribution
    Analysis of an r by k table
χ^2 Goodness-of-fit test
    Degrees of freedom
    Evaluation of test statistic
    Using sample data to develop expected frequencies
Summary

INTRODUCTION

TESTS OF proportions are appropriate when the data being analyzed consist of counts or frequencies of items in two or more classes. The purpose of such tests is to evaluate claims about a population proportion (or percentage). The tests are based on the premise that a sample proportion (i.e., x occurrences in n observations, or x/n) will equal the true population proportion if allowances are made for sampling variability. The tests generally focus on the difference between an expected number of occurrences, assuming a claim is true, and the number actually observed. The difference is compared to the variability prescribed by a sampling distribution based on the assumption that H_0 is really true.

In many respects, tests of proportions closely resemble tests of means, except that for tests of proportions the sample data are in terms of counts rather than measurements. For example, tests of both means and proportions can be used to evaluate claims about (1) a single population parameter (one-sample test), (2) the equality of parameters of two populations (two-sample test), and (3) the equality of parameters of more than two populations (k-sample test). Furthermore, for large sample sizes the appropriate sampling distribution for one- and two-sample proportion tests is approximately normal, just as it is for one- and two-sample tests of means.

The presentation of significance tests for sample proportions is divided into two parts. The first part deals with one- and two-sample tests. The second part deals with tests of more than two proportions and uses a sampling distribution that has not yet been discussed.

ONE-SAMPLE TEST OF PROPORTIONS

When the purpose of sampling is to judge the validity of a claim about a population proportion, a one-sample test is appropriate. The testing methodology depends on whether the number of sample observations is large or small. With samples of more than 20 observations, the normal distribution is acceptable; with smaller sample sizes, the binomial distribution should be used. The large-sample case is considered first, and then the small-sample case is discussed.

As previously noted, large-sample tests of means and proportions are quite similar. Thus test statistics for both tests measure the deviation of a sample statistic from a claimed value. And both tests rely on the standard normal distribution for critical values. Perhaps the only real distinction between the two tests is in the way the standard deviation of the sampling distribution is obtained.

You may recall that the mean and standard deviation of a sampling distribution of means are unrelated, but that the same does not hold true for the mean (p) and standard deviation ($\sigma_p = \sqrt{p(1 - p)/n}$) of a sampling distribution of proportions. However, unlike the approach used in estimation, where the *sample* proportion was inserted into the formula, the value of p used to compute the standard deviation is based on the value stated in H_0.

For example, the null hypothesis may be

$$H_0: p_0 = .20$$

Then the value .20 would be used, along with the sample size n, to compute σ_{p0}. Thus suppose $n = 100$. Then

$$\sigma_{p0} = \sqrt{\frac{(.2)(1 - .2)}{100}} = .04$$

The symbol p_0 is used to denote the value specified in H_0. The test involves computation of the test statistic z:

$$z = \frac{\text{sample proportion} - \text{claimed proportion}}{\text{standard deviation of proportion}} = \frac{(x/n) - p_0}{\sqrt{p_0(1 - p_0)/n}}$$

This value is then compared to the value of z obtained from a normal table at a selected level of significance.

As with a one-sample means test, tests of proportions can be one- or two-tailed. The type of test reflects H_1. For instance, there are three possibilities for H_1:

$$H_1: p > p_0 \qquad H_1: p < p_0 \qquad H_1: p \neq p_0$$

The first alternative dictates a right-tail test, the second a left-tail test, and the third, a two-tail test. The three examples that follow demonstrate these tests.

Example 1 A manufacturer claims a shipment of finishing nails contains less than 1% defective. A random sample of 200 nails contains 4 (i.e., 2%) defectives. Test this claim at the .01 level.

Solution:
The null hypothesis is

$$H_0: p_0 = 1\%$$

The alternative hypothesis might reasonably be

$$H_1: p_0 > 1\%$$

since we want to guard against accepting a shipment with more than 1% but would not worry if the shipment turned out to be better than claimed. Hence we will use a one-tail test, with the dividing line between accepting H_0 and rejecting H_0 in the right tail.

The standard deviation of the sampling distribution, if H_0 is really true, is

$$\sigma_{p_0} = \sqrt{\frac{p_0(1 - p_0)}{n}} = \sqrt{\frac{.01(.99)}{200}} = .007$$

The test statistic can now be computed:

$$z = \frac{.02 - .01}{.007} \approx +1.43$$

The table value, using the .01 level and the normal table, is $z = +2.33$. Consequently, we accept H_0, as illustrated in Figure 12.1.

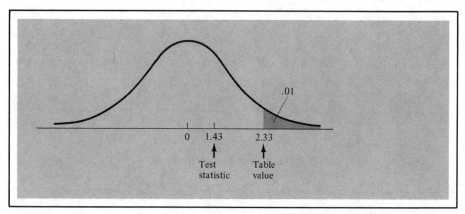

FIGURE 12.1   Evaluation of the test statistic results in accepting H_0.

Example 2   A survey claims that 9 out of 10 doctors (i.e., 90%) recommend aspirin for their patients who have children. Test this claim, at the .05 level of significance, against the alternative that the actual proportion of doctors who do this is less than 90%, if a random sample of 100 doctors results in 80 who indicate that they recommend aspirin.

Solution:

$$H_0: p_0 = 90\%$$
$$H_1: p_0 < 90\%$$

The standard deviation of the sampling distribution, assuming H_0 is true, is

$$\sigma_{p_0} = \sqrt{\frac{.90(.10)}{100}} = .03$$

The test statistic is

$$z = \frac{.80 - .90}{.03} = \frac{-.10}{.03} = -3.33$$

The normal curve table value (.05 level) is $z = -1.65$. Therefore, we reject H_0 and conclude that *less than* 90% of the doctors recommend aspirin. See Figure 12.2.

Example 3   A newspaper states that approximately 25% of the adults in its circulation area are illiterate according to government standards. Test this claim

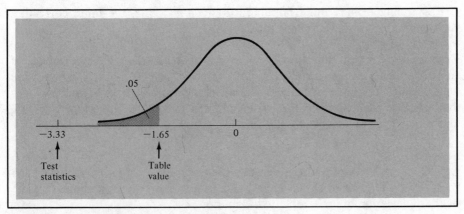

FIGURE 12.2   The null hypothesis is rejected.

against the alternative that the true percentage is not 25%, and use a 5% probability of a Type I error. A sample of 740 persons indicates that 20% would be judged illiterate using the same standards.

Solution:

$$H_0: p_0 = 25\%$$
$$H_1: p_0 \neq 25\%$$

The standard deviation of the sampling distribution is

$$\sigma_{p_0} = \sqrt{\frac{p_0(1 - p_0)}{n}} = \sqrt{\frac{.25(.75)}{740}} \approx .016$$

The test statistic is

$$z = \frac{.20 - .25}{.016} = \frac{-.05}{.016} = -3.1$$

The normal table value for .05 and a two-tail test is ± 1.96. Consequently, we reject H_0 and we conclude that the actual percentage is less than 25%, as shown in Figure 12.3.

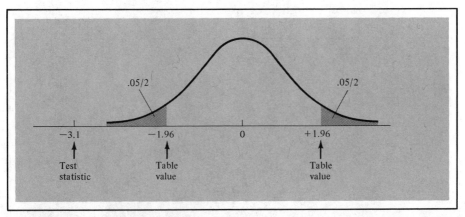

FIGURE 12.3   The null hypothesis is rejected.

If sampling from a finite population (and $n/N > 5\%$), the finite correction factor $\sqrt{(N - n)/(N - 1)}$ must be used.

Example 4 A major candy producer asserts that less than 3% of the bags of chocolate melties are underfilled. A random check reveals 4 out of 50 bags are underfilled. The sample was taken from a shipment of 400 bags of melties. Does the sample evidence refute the manufacturer's claim (i.e., are more than 3% underfilled)?

Solution:
A right-tail test is called for because we want to guard against *too many* underfilled bags. Since the level of significance is not given, suppose we assume .05. The standard deviation of the sampling distribution is

$$\sigma_p = \sqrt{\frac{p_0(1 - p_0)}{n}} \sqrt{\frac{N - n}{N - 1}} = \sqrt{\frac{.03(.97)}{50}} \sqrt{\frac{350}{399}}$$

$$= \sqrt{.00058} \sqrt{.877} \approx .023$$

The test statistic is

$$z = \frac{(x/n) - p_0}{\sigma_p} = \frac{\frac{4}{50} - .03}{.023} = \frac{.08 - .03}{.023} = 2.17$$

H_0 is rejected, as shown in Figure 12.4.

When the number of observations is 20 or less, the cumulative binomial table can be used to evaluate sample data. Consider this example. A tavern owner wants to learn if his regular customers can distinguish between draft and bottled beer. So he selects 11 customers and provides each with two unlabeled mugs, one of which contains draft beer and the other bottled beer. He asks each person to select the one he or she prefers. He feels that there will be a preference for draft beer. If there is no preference, we would expect that about half will select draft and half bottled. If his hunch is correct, few will select bottled beer. Our hypotheses would then be

H_0: no preference (i.e., about half will select each), or $np = 11(\frac{1}{2})$

H_1: few will select bottled, or $np < 11(\frac{1}{2})$

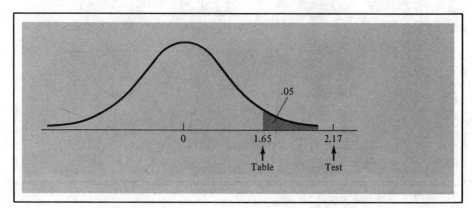

FIGURE 12.4 H_0 is rejected.

Suppose that 4 clients pick bottled beer and the rest pick the draft. The owner wants to test at the .05 level. Does the evidence support H_0 or H_1?

Unlike previously discussed tests, we will not utilize a critical value. Instead we will work with tail probabilities. The reason for this deviation stems from the fact that discrete distributions tend to be "lumpy." We would have to select a critical value such as 1, 2, or 3, and these values will usually not provide the desired level of significance. For example, note from the portion of the cumulative binomial table shown here (with $n = 11$ and $p = .50$) that $P(x \leq 2) = .0327$. Consequently, a critical value of "2 or less choosing bottled beer" would result in a smaller $P(\text{Type I error})$ than specified. On the other hand, a critical value of 3 would leave .1133 in the tail, which is too great. Yet there is nothing between these to choose from. Hence to select a critical value based on the possible outcomes would usually mean having to settle for a level of significance other than what might ordinarily be chosen. In addition, each test would necessitate going through this procedure.

x	$P(x$ or less$)$
0	.0005
1	.0059
2	.0327
3	.1133
4	.2744
5	.5000
⋮	⋮

As an alternative, we can simply note that if we reject in this case, with 4 choosing bottled beer, the probability of rejecting a true H_0 (from the table) is .2744, which exceeds $\alpha = .05$. Therefore, we should accept H_0. However, if only 1 client had selected bottled beer, the cumulative probability would have been small enough $[P(x \leq 1) = .0059]$ that we would have rejected H_0. Hence we can formulate these general rules:

A tail probability less than or equal to α results in rejecting H_0.

A tail probability greater than α results in accepting H_0.

Note that if a two-tail test is being used, the value of α in the above rules should be replaced with $\alpha/2$. In addition, we must be sure to include as part of the tail area the probability of the sample result. In other words, if 4 defectives are found in a sample, the tail area is $P(x \leq 4)$ and not $P(x < 4)$.

EXERCISES

1. For each of the following, sketch the appropriate (large-sample) sampling distribution and indicate on the sketch whether the test is one-tailed or two-tailed and show the area in the tail(s):
   a. $H_0: p = 35\%$, $H_1: p > 35\%$, $\alpha = .05$
   b. $H_0: p = 1\%$, $H_1: p < 1\%$, $\alpha = .05$

c. $H_0: p = 22.5\%$, $H_1: p < 22.5\%$, $\alpha = .01$

d. $H_0: p = 30\%$, $H_1: p \neq 30\%$, $\alpha = .05$

2. A supplier claims that only 2% of the parts he supplies will fail under ordinary operating conditions. A test of 200 randomly selected parts from a shipment of 5000 had 10 failures.

   a. State H_0 and H_1.

   b. Would you be willing to accept the supplier's claim at the .05 level?

3. A supposedly fair coin is flipped 144 times and lands heads 90 times. Do you feel the coin is fair? Explain.

4. A senator maintains that 20% or less of the voters in her state favor a certain bill currently under study by a subcommittee. A random survey of 100 voters show that 11 favor the bill.

   a. Assuming the senator's claim is true, how many supporters would be expected in a sample of 100?

   b. State H_1.

   c. Test at the .01 level.

5. The government claims that 15% or less of the families in a certain area are below poverty levels of income. A random sample of 60 families produces 12 such families. Test the claim against $p > 15\%$.

6. A newspaper article suggests that 40% of the voters in the age group from 18 to 21 years did not vote in the last general election. Suppose a random sample of eight voters in this age group is interviewed, and it turns out that two did not vote. Test $H_0 = .4$ against each of these alternatives at the .01 level:

   a. $H_1: p \neq .4$ b. $H_1: p > .4$ c. $H_1: p < .4$

7. If a new drug has no effect on patients who use it, some will say it was helpful, some will say they feel worse, and some will say they do not feel any different. If it is effective, more should indicate feeling better; if it has a bad effect, more should indicate they feel worse. Suppose out of 20 who try the drug, 11 say they feel better, 3 feel worse, and 6 indicate no change. Ignore the 6 no changes (i.e., use $n = 14$). Test $H_0: p = .5$ against these alternatives using the .05 level:

   a. Drug has a positive effect.   b. Drug has a negative effect.

TWO-SAMPLE TEST OF PROPORTIONS

The purpose of a two-sample test is to decide if the two *independent samples have been drawn* from two populations that both have the same proportion of items with a certain characteristic. The test focuses on the relative difference (difference divided by the standard deviation of the sampling distribution) between the two sample proportions. Small differences imply only chance variation due to sampling (accept H_0), while large differences imply just the opposite (reject H_0). The test statistic (relative difference) is compared to a table value of the normal distribution in order to decide whether to accept or reject H_0. Again, this test closely resembles a two-sample means test.

The null hypothesis in a two-sample test is

$$H_0: p_1 = p_2$$

The possible alternative hypotheses are

$$H_1: p_1 \neq p_2 \qquad H_1: p_1 > p_2 \qquad H_1: p_1 < p_2$$

As usual, the approach is to initially assume that H_0 is true and then use a sampling distribution based on that assumption to conduct the test. However, unlike a one-sample test, there is no stated population parameter in H_0. Therefore, obtaining a value of p to use must be handled somewhat differently. Note that if p_1 does in fact equal p_2, then the two samples, which have been drawn from two populations, can be thought of as two samples from the *same* population. Then each sample proportion might be treated as an estimate of the same population proportion. Furthermore, it would seem reasonable (due to the larger sample size) that combining the two samples would provide an even better estimate of the true value of the population proportion. The combined (pooled) estimate of p can be computed in this manner:

$$p = \frac{x_1 + x_2}{n_1 + n_2}$$

where

$x_1 = $ the number of successes in sample 1

$x_2 = $ the number of successes in sample 2

$n_1 = $ the number of observations in sample 1

$n_2 = $ the number of observations in sample 2

This value of p is used to compute the standard deviation of the proportion, which is similar to previous formulas, except that now it must be "weighted" by the two sample sizes:

$$\sigma_p = \sqrt{p(1-p)[(1/n_1) + (1/n_2)]}$$

Example 5   Consider this situation. Voters in two cities are asked whether they are for or against passage of a bill to clothe farm animals that is currently before the state legislature. To determine if the voters in the two cities differ in terms of the percentage who favor passage of the bill, a sample of 100 voters is taken in each city. Thirty in one city favor passage while twenty in the other favor passage.

First, we must establish the null and alternative hypotheses:

$$H_0: p_1 = p_2$$
$$H_1: p_1 \neq p_2$$
$$\alpha = .01$$

(A two-tail test is called for because the problem does not specify that the percentage in one city is thought to be larger—or higher—than the percentage in the other.)

The test statistic z is

$$z = \frac{(x_1/n_1) - (x_2/n_2)}{\sqrt{p(1-p)[(1/n_1) + (1/n_2)]}} \qquad \text{where} \qquad p = \frac{x_1 + x_2}{n_1 + n_2}$$

Then we have

$$p = \frac{30 + 20}{100 + 100} = .25$$

$$z = \frac{.30 - .20}{\sqrt{.25(.75)[1/100) + (1/100)]}} = \frac{.10}{\sqrt{.00375}} = \frac{.10}{.06} = 1.63$$

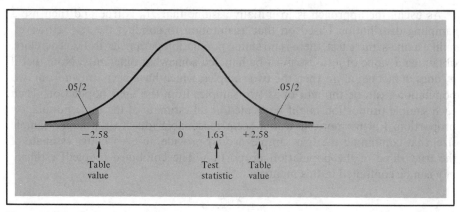

FIGURE 12.5 H_0 is accepted.

Because the test statistic z has a value within the acceptance region, we cannot conclude that the two cities differ in terms of the percentage who favor passage of the bill. See Figure 12.5.

Example 6   Suppose in the preceding example that it had been (H_1) hypothesized that p_1 was greater than p_2. The test would have been set up in the following manner:

$$H_0: p_1 = p_2$$
$$H_1: p_1 > p_2$$
$$\alpha = .05$$

Using the same sample values, z would still equal 1.63. Hence we would accept H_0 at the .05 level, and we *cannot* conclude that the first city has a greater percentage of voters who favor the bill. See Figure 12.6.

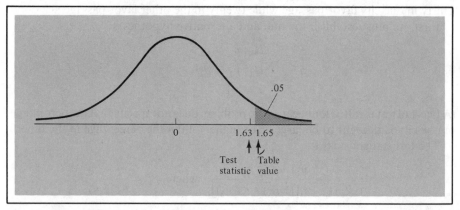

FIGURE 12.6   Accept H_0.

Example 7   Suppose in Example 6 that the alternative had been that $p_1 < p_2$. Graphically, the test would be set up as shown in Figure 12.7.

Since the test statistic z is positive, we would again accept H_0.

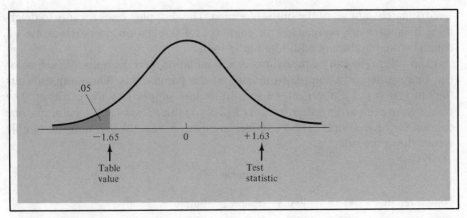

FIGURE 12.7   Accept H_0.

EXERCISES

1. A manufacturer wants to know if a special coating applied to the surface of automobile license plates will improve resistance to rust. Twenty thousand treated plates are distributed, along with 20,000 untreated plates. A random sample of treated plates one year later indicates 360 out of 400 are in excellent condition. A random sample of 225 untreated plates shows 195 plates in excellent condition. Can you conclude from this that either type of plate is superior to the other?

2. A random sample of 200 registered voters in each of two districts resulted in 45 of 200 urban voters supporting property reassessments while 55 suburban voters out of 200 favored reassessment. Would you say the proportion of voters who favor reassessment is the same in these districts?

3. Two potential methods for capping bottles are being tested. In a run of 1000, Machine A generates 30 rejects, while Machine B only has 20 rejects. Can you conclude (.05) that the two machines are different?

k-SAMPLE TEST OF PROPORTIONS

The purpose of a *k*-sample test is to evaluate the claim that k independent samples have all come from populations that contain the same proportion of some item. Accordingly, the null and alternative hypotheses are

H_0: The population proportions are all equal.

H_1: The population proportions are not all equal.

Consider, for instance, this situation. A shopping center purchased and planted 720 tulip bulbs for landscaping in four colors:

white	200
red	160
yellow	240
purple	120
	720

Unfortunately, not all of the bulbs bloomed. The shopping center wants to determine if failures are *independent* of color (i.e., if population proportions are all equal) before purchasing additional tulip bulbs.

Each color type can be thought of as a population, and the bulbs of each color can be regarded as a sample from each of the populations. The sample results (bloom versus not bloom) can be seen from data supplied by the gardener. The results have been arranged into a 2 by k ($2 \times k$) table: 2 rows and k columns, one column for each sample. The k samples are listed across the top, and the sample results down the side:

			Sample		
Sample results	White	Red	Yellow	Purple	Totals
bloomed	176	136	222	114	648
failed to bloom	24	24	18	6	72
total planted	200	160	240	120	720

If the null hypothesis is, in fact, true, then the variations among the samples are only due to chance. Assume initially that this is the case (i.e., that H_0 is true). Then the four samples can be regarded as four samples from the same population. By combining the sample results, we can obtain an estimate of the true population proportion of bulbs that tend to bloom. Accordingly, we find

$$p = \frac{176 + 136 + 222 + 114}{200 + 160 + 240 + 120} = 90\%$$

This estimate of the population percentage can now be employed to find the expected number of "successes" in each category under the assumption that the null hypothesis is true. These expected numbers will then serve as a basis against which the observed (sample) results can be judged. If the differences are small between the two, the conclusion that they may be due to chance would seem reasonable. Large differences, however, would seem to suggest that survival rates are different for different colored bulbs.

The expected number of successes in each category can be found by multiplying the total number of bulbs planted by the estimated percentage in the population:

$$p \times \text{number planted} = \text{expected number}$$

Thus

$$\begin{array}{lll} \text{white:} & 90\% \times 200 = 180 \\ \text{red:} & 90\% \times 160 = 144 \\ \text{yellow:} & 90\% \times 240 = 216 \\ \text{purple:} & 90\% \times 120 = 108 \end{array}$$

The expected number of failures of each color could also be determined in the same manner (i.e., by first finding the percentage of the total that failed and then multiplying that percentage by the number of each flower color). However, because we know the expected number of successes for each color as well as the total number of each color planted, simple subtraction will tell us the expected number of failures:

Color	Number planted	−	Expected blooms	=	Expected failures
white:	200		180		20
red:	160		144		16
yellow:	240		216		24
purple:	120		108		12

It is often convenient to include both the expected and the observed frequencies in a single table for purposes of analysis. The expected frequencies are often shown in parentheses.

	White	Red	Yellow	Purple
Bloomed	(180) 176	(144) 136	(216) 222	(108) 114
Failed	(20) 24	(16) 24	(24) 18	(12) 6

It is important that the *expected* frequency for each square or "cell" be at least 5 in order for the technique demonstrated here to be valid. If this condition is not met, one or more rows (or columns) should be grouped to achieve the minimum expected frequency. In this example the lowest expected frequency is 12, so we need not concern ourselves with this problem. However, if, say, the last two columns had low expected frequencies in some cells, we could consider the category "yellow and purple" as a single column and combine both the observed and the expected frequencies.

The amount of dissimilarity between the two sets of frequencies can be measured by computing this test statistic:

$$\chi^2 = \Sigma \left[\frac{(\text{observed frequency} - \text{expected frequency})^2}{\text{expected frequency}} \right]$$

Procedurally, this amounts to (1) subtracting the expected frequency from the observed frequency for each cell; (2) squaring each of these differences; (3) "standardizing" the squared differences by dividing each one by the expected frequency of that cell; and finally (4) adding all the terms to obtain the total value. The total is called the *chi-square test statistic* (χ^2). Hence the χ^2 test statistic for this problem would be computed in this way:

$$\chi^2 = \frac{(176 - 180)^2}{180} + \frac{(136 - 144)^2}{144} + \frac{(222 - 216)^2}{216} + \frac{(114 - 108)^2}{108}$$

$$+ \frac{(24 - 20)^2}{20} + \frac{(24 - 16)^2}{16} + \frac{(18 - 24)^2}{24} + \frac{(6 - 12)^2}{12}$$

$$= .09 + .44 + .17 + .33 + .80 + 4.00 + 1.50 + 3.00$$

$$= 10.33$$

This test statistic must now be compared to a critical (table) value of the chi-square sampling distribution so as to decide whether to accept or to reject H_0.

The Chi-square Sampling Distribution

Like the t distribution and the F distribution, the chi-square distribution has a shape dependent on the number of degrees of freedom associated with a particular problem. Several of these curves are illustrated in Figure 12.8. Because of this tendency, the critical value (that value which leaves a certain percentage of area in the tail) will be a function of the degrees of freedom. Thus to obtain a critical value from a chi-square table, you must choose a level of significance, and determine the degrees of freedom for the problem being analyzed.

The degrees of freedom are a function of the number of cells in a $2 \times k$ table. That is, degrees of freedom reflect the size of the table. You may remember that in computing the expected frequencies for both the rows and the columns, the expected value of the last cell could simply be obtained by subtracting the sum of the other expected frequencies in that row or column from the row or column total. The expected frequencies are thus constrained by the requirement that they add to the total, and we utilized this knowledge to obtain the final frequencies. To compensate for this, each column is said to lose one degree of freedom. Thus the column degrees of freedom are the number of rows (categories) minus 1, or $r - 1$. Similarly, since the row totals were also known, any one expected value in each row could be obtained using the difference between the row total and the sum of the other frequencies in the row. Thus each row has degrees of freedom

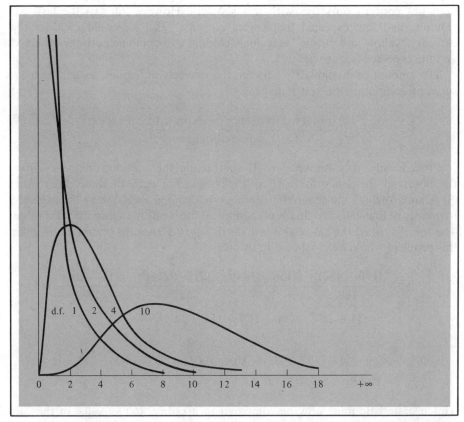

FIGURE 12.8 The shape of the chi-square distribution depends on its degrees of freedom.

equal to the number of columns (samples) minus 1, or $k - 1$. The net effect is that the number of degrees of freedom for the table is the product of (number of rows $- 1$) $\times$ (number of columns $- 1$), or $(r - 1)(k - 1)$. Hence with 2 rows and 4 columns, the degrees of freedom equal $(2 - 1)(4 - 1) = 3$.

Appendix Table I gives critical values of chi-square for various degrees of freedom for selected levels of significance.

The test requires comparing the computed value of chi-square with one obtained from a table of critical values of chi-square, using the appropriate degrees of freedom. If the test statistic is smaller than the table value, the null hypothesis is accepted; if not, H_0 is rejected. This is illustrated in Figure 12.9. (Note that a chi-square value can never be less than zero, since it is computed using squared deviations.)

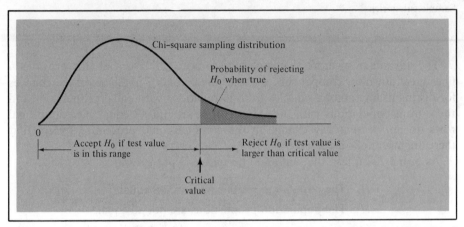

FIGURE 12.9   A value of a chi-square test statistic that is less than or equal to the critical value is regarded as evidence of chance variation; H_0 is accepted.

Comparing our calculated value of χ^2 with one obtained from the table of critical values (see Table I in the Appendix), using, say, the .01 level, reveals that the variation among sample proportions may be due to chance, since the test statistic (10.33) falls within the acceptance region. Hence we cannot conclude that the population proportions are not all equal. The test is illustrated in Figure 12.10.

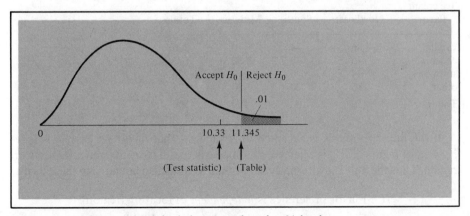

FIGURE 12.10   The null hypothesis is accepted at the .01 level.

Analysis of an *r* by *k* Table

Analysis of an *r* by *k* (i.e., $r \times k$) table is an extension of the analysis of a $2 \times k$ table. Each table still has *k* columns (samples), but now there are more than two rows. The implication is that sample results are classified into *more than two* categories. Thus the populations are treated as *multinomial*. The format of the table is shown here:

	Samples				
	1	2	3	$\cdots$	*k*
	1				
	2				
Sample categories	3				
	$\vdots$				
	r				

The advantage of more than two classes per sample is that this provides a finer breakdown for comparison; the finer the breakdown, the better the chances for distinguishing among samples from populations with equal proportions and those from populations with proportions that are not all equal. The additional rows do not present any change in the computational procedure, except that there are more cells involved.

As in the $2 \times k$ test, the null and alternative hypotheses are

H_0: The population proportions are all equal.

H_1: The population proportions are not all equal.

Consider this example. In a recent study to determine if flavor preferences vary in various parts of the country, the following data were collected. Determine if the three regions are comparable, using the .05 level of significance.

Observed Frequencies

Ice cream flavor	Location			
	Northeast	South	Midwest	Totals
vanilla	86	44	70	200
chocolate	45	30	50	125
strawberry	34	6	10	50
other	85	20	20	125
Totals	250	100	150	500

If the null hypothesis is accepted, this suggests that flavor preference is *independent* of region; if H_0 is rejected, this suggests that flavor preference *depends* on region. Thus the null and alternative hypotheses could also be stated in these terms:

H_0: Flavor preference is *independent* of location (region).

H_1: Flavor preference is *dependent* (related to) location.

The null hypothesis can be interpreted in the following manner: The percentages of each population in category 1 are all equal; the percentages of each population in category 2 are all equal; the percentages of each population in category 3 are all equal; and so on. That is,

population

	1		2		3		k
						$\cdots$	

category

$$
\begin{array}{c|cccc}
1 & p_{1,1} & = & p_{1,2} & = & p_{1,3} & = & p_{1,k} \\
2 & p_{2,1} & = & p_{2,2} & = & p_{2,3} & = & p_{2,k} \\
\vdots & \vdots & & \vdots & & \vdots & & \vdots \\
r & p_{r,1} & = & p_{r,2} & = & p_{r,3} & = & p_{r,k}
\end{array}
$$

The test procedure again involves finding the expected cell frequencies under the assumption that H_0 is true and then computing a test statistic that reflects the squared deviations between each pair of observed and expected cell frequencies. Either the row or the column percentages can be used to obtain the expected frequencies. The results will be the same in either case; the choice of which to use often depends on which frequencies (row totals or column totals) are easiest to work with.

The row percentages are found by computing the ratio of row total to total number of observations:

$$
p_{\text{row}} = \frac{\text{row total}}{\text{total number of observations}}
$$

Similarly, each column percentage could be computed as

$$
p_{\text{col}} = \frac{\text{column total}}{\text{total number of observations}}
$$

The the individual cell expected frequencies are found by computing

$$
p_{\text{row}} \times \text{column total} \quad or \quad p_{\text{col}} \times \text{row total}
$$

The sum of the cell deviations will depend somewhat on the size of the table, which is reflected by the degrees of freedom:

---

degrees of freedom $= (r - 1)(k - 1)$

where

$r =$ the number of rows

$k =$ the number of columns

The computations for the ice cream flavor data proceed as follows: First we determine the row percentages:

$$
\text{row 1 (vanilla):} \quad \frac{200}{500} = .40 = p_1
$$

$$\text{row 2 (chocolate): } \frac{125}{500} = .25 = p_2$$

$$\text{row 3 (strawberry): } \frac{50}{500} = .10 = p_3$$

$$\text{row 4 (other): } \frac{125}{500} = .25 = p_4$$

Now we use the row percentages to obtain expected frequencies for each cell:

Expected number of responses

Flavors	Northeast	South	Midwest
vanilla	250 × .40 = 100	100 × .40 = 40	150 × .40 = 60
chocolate	250 × .25 = 62.5	100 × .25 = 25	150 × .25 = 37.5
strawberry	250 × .10 = 25	100 × .10 = 10	150 × .10 = 15
other	250 × .25 = 62.5	100 × .25 = 25	150 × .25 = 37.5
Total	250.0	100	150.0

Now compute the test statistic,

$$\chi^2 = \sum \left[\frac{(o - e)^2}{e} \right]$$

$$\frac{(86 - 100)^2}{100} + \frac{(44 - 40)^2}{40} + \frac{(70 - 60)^2}{60} = \frac{196}{100} + \frac{16}{40} + \frac{100}{60} = 1.96 + .40 + 1.67$$

$$\frac{(45 - 62.5)^2}{62.5} + \frac{(30 - 25)^2}{25} + \frac{(50 - 37.5)^2}{37.5} = \frac{306.25}{62.5} + \frac{25}{25} + \frac{156.25}{37.5} = 4.90 + 1.00 + 4.17$$

$$\frac{(34 - 25)^2}{25} + \frac{(6 - 10)^2}{10} + \frac{(10 - 15)^2}{15} = \frac{81}{25} + \frac{16}{10} + \frac{25}{15} = 3.24 + 1.60 + 1.67$$

$$\frac{(85 - 62.5)^2}{62.5} + \frac{(20 - 25)^2}{25} + \frac{(20 - 37.5)^2}{37.5} = \frac{506.25}{62.5} + \frac{25}{25} + \frac{306.25}{37.5} = 8.10 + 1.00 + 8.17$$

$$= 37.88$$

Next we determine the table value. The degrees of freedom are $(r - 1)(k - 1) = (4 - 1)(3 - 1) = 6$. The table value is 12.592 (see Table I in the Appendix). Finally, we compare the test statistic and the table value (see Figure 12.11). Since the test statistic lies in the rejection region, the study seems to indicate that the regions are not comparable in terms of flavor preference. In other words, flavor preference seems to *depend* on region.

EXERCISES

1. Each of the following represents the size of an $r \times k$ table:

$$3 \times 4 \quad 4 \times 3 \quad 5 \times 5 \quad 2 \times 5 \quad 3 \times 6 \quad 4 \times 6$$

   a. Determine the number of degrees of freedom for each one.

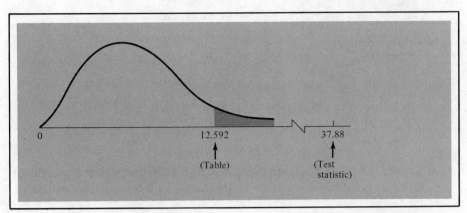

FIGURE 12.11   Comparison of the test statistic to the table value indicates a rejection of H_0.

b. Use the chi-square table to obtain critical values at the .01 and .05 levels for each one.

2. Develop the expected frequencies for this $r \times k$ table:

				Row totals
				200
				200
				200
Column totals 90	120	150	240	600

3. In a study to determine whether four building contractors are comparable in terms of types of complaints registered by new homeowners, a random sample of 100 homes built by each is taken and the owner's major complaint is noted. Do the results suggest (.05) that the builders are comparable?

Major complaint	Builder			
	A	*B*	*C*	*D*
structure	12	10	33	5
heat, plumbing, electric	28	5	17	30
landscaping	40	60	20	40
other	20	25	30	25
	100	100	100	100

4. Five auto service centers were included in a study of repair billings. The data below represent a portion of that investigation which focused on labor charges as a percentage of total bill. Would you say that the five centers are comparable in this respect? Use the .05 level.

Labor (as percentage of total bill)	Service center					
	A	B	C	D	E	
0 to 15	10	5	8	9	13	45
15.1 to 25	10	8	14	10	18	60
25.1 to 35	18	13	4	20	50	105
35.1 to 50	22	4	34	11	19	90
Number of cars	60	30	60	50	100	300

5. A random sample of 50 season ticket holders and 50 purchasers of individual tickets were questioned on seating arrangements for football games, with these results:

	Season	Individual
Approve	35	25
Do not approve	15	25

a. Test these results at the .05 level, using an $r \times k$ analysis. What can you conclude?

b. Test these results using a two-sample z test, using .05. What can you conclude?

c. Square the test and table z-values and compare them with the chi-square test and table values.

6. Four samples of 30 students are asked to comment on their school's policy on cars on campus. Testing at the .01 level, what can you conclude?

	Freshmen	Sophomores	Juniors	Seniors
Approve	5	4	20	27
Disapprove	25	26	10	3

χ^2 GOODNESS-OF-FIT TEST*

Goodness-of-fit tests are used to evaluate claims about the distribution of values in a population. These tests can serve a variety of needs. For example, many statistical procedures are valid only with certain population types (e.g., small-sample tests of means require normal populations). Consequently, it is advantageous to have a way of judging whether a population has the required distribution. Thus if a reasonable doubt exists regarding the population, it may be prudent to run a check on the distribution before proceeding.

A second use of a goodness-of-fit test is to determine if three or more categories in a population are equally likely (a multinomial distribution). Still another use is for situations in which the approach to a problem may differ depending on the type of distribution one is dealing with. For instance, the approach to waiting-line problems (such as waiting lines at supermarket checkouts, stop signs, or

---

* This section may be omitted.

gas stations) depends on the distribution of customer arrivals as well as the distribution of waiting times. If it can be shown that those are of a certain form, standard mathematical equations can be applied to the problem. If not, alternative methods, usually more demanding (e.g., simulation or complex mathematical operations), may be required.

The χ^2 goodness-of-fit test is a variation of the χ^2 test discussed in the preceding section. The computation of the test statistic and its evaluation are very similar in both cases, although there are a few exceptions. The main exceptions involve how H_0 and H_1 are phrased, how expected frequencies are computed, and how the degrees of freedom are determined.

Since goodness-of-fit tests concern distributions, the null and alternative hypotheses must necessarily specify a distribution type. Moreover, the test for a distribution can simply focus on a certain type (e.g., normal), or it can focus on a type plus parameters (e.g., normal with a mean of 5.2 and a standard deviation of 2.4). Thus a typical null hypothesis might be

H_0: The population distribution is Poisson.

This gives only the type of distribution and says nothing about the parameters of the distribution. Or H_0 can be more explicit, such as this:

H_0: The population is Poisson, with a mean of 3.2.

The importance of this distinction is that when the distribution parameters are stated, there is sufficient information to be able to go directly to a probability table (in this instance a Poisson table) and obtain relative expected frequencies. However, a hypothesis in the first form requires additional information about the population mean. And since the mean is not stated, sample data will have to be used to estimate the population mean. Thus the completeness or lack of completeness of H_0 will have a bearing on whether sample statistics must be computed first or whether you can proceed directly to a probability table to obtain expected frequencies. Furthermore, the number of degrees of freedom will also relate to the completeness of H_0: each sample statistic used to obtain expected frequencies results in the loss of one degree of freedom. Thus if you must compute a sample mean, one degree of freedom is lost; if you must compute both a mean and a standard deviation, two degrees of freedom are lost.

A goodness-of-fit test is actually a one-sample test, but one in which the population has been divided into k proportions. Thus it differs from the one-sample test of proportions covered earlier, which dealt with only two categories (success and failure) in the population.

Consider, for example, testing a die to decide if it is balanced. That is, we want to test

H_0: The die is balanced.

H_1: The die is not balanced.

Although the null hypothesis does not explicitly state population parameters, we know from the nature of the problem that if the die is balanced, we would expect the frequency of occurrence of each of the six possible outcomes (categories) to be equally likely. That is, we can determine the expected frequencies directly, without having to use the sample data:

Category	Expected frequency
⚀	$\frac{1}{6} \times n$
⚁	$\frac{1}{6} \times n$
⚂	$\frac{1}{6} \times n$
⚃	$\frac{1}{6} \times n$
⚄	$\frac{1}{6} \times n$
⚅	$\frac{1}{6} \times n$

Consequently, if we were to roll the die, say, 180 times, we would *expect* $\frac{1}{6}$ of the outcomes to fall into each of the categories. Hence for each category the expected frequency would be $\frac{1}{6}(180) = 30$.

Now suppose that the die is rolled 180 times, with these results:

Category	Observed frequency
1	20
2	35
3	25
4	35
5	32
6	33

Notice that the values vary somewhat from the expected value of 30 in each category. Of course, even a balanced die could not be expected to produce exactly 30 of each face, because of chance variation. However, we can use a goodness-of-fit test to determine if the differences are due only to chance variation in sampling or if they suggest that the die is not balanced (i.e., that the categories are not equally likely).

The first step in our problem is to compute the chi-square test statistic, which is

$$\chi^2 = \sum \left[\frac{(o - e)^2}{e} \right]$$

where

$$o = \text{observed frequency for each category}$$

$$e = \text{expected frequency for each category}$$

Using the information above, we can compute the test statistic.

Face	Observed (sample data)	Expected ($\frac{1}{6} \times 180$)	Difference $(o - e)$	$(o - e)^2$	$(o - e)^2/e$
1	20	30	-10	100	3.33
2	35	30	5	25	.83
3	25	30	-5	25	.83
4	35	30	5	25	.83
5	32	30	2	4	.13
6	33	30	3	9	.30
	180	180	0		6.25

Thus $\chi^2 = 6.25$.

Degrees of Freedom

To obtain a table chi-square value for comparison, it is first necessary to determine the degrees of freedom. This, in turn, depends on the number of *restrictions* involved in calculating the test statistic. As a general rule, the degrees of freedom for a goodness-of-fit test equal the number of categories k minus the number of constraints in the sample data. There is always at least one constraint: the expected frequencies must add to the total. Additional constraints occur if sample statistics (mean, standard deviation, etc.) are used to develop the expected frequencies. One degree of freedom is lost for each sample statistic used in this way. Hence the degrees of freedom for a goodness-of-fit test are

$$(k - 1) - c$$

where

> k = number of categories or classes
>
> c = number of sample statistics used in developing expected frequencies

In the case of the die there was a single restriction: the total of the frequencies had to sum to 180. The degrees of freedom, then, are $k - 1$ (where k = number of categories), or $6 - 1 = 5$.

Sometimes categories must be grouped in order to obtain a minimum level for expected frequencies. While there is some disagreement among statisticians, one rule of thumb to use is that no *expected* frequency should be less than 1.0 and that only one or two should be that low. A more conservative rule is to require expected frequencies of at least 5. However, the minimum of 1.0 will be used here. The implication is that when expected frequencies are less than the required minimum, they must be combined.

Evaluation of Test Statistic

With 5 degrees of freedom, the table value at the .05 level is 11.07. Since the test statistic for the die problem (6.25) is less than this, we conclude that the differences between observed and expected frequencies might reasonably be due to chance. Thus the claim of a balanced die is accepted. See Figure 12.12.

Example 8   A machine which fills and caps bottles of beer is said to produce bottles with a mean of 1 liter and a standard deviation of .2 liters. Moreover, it is

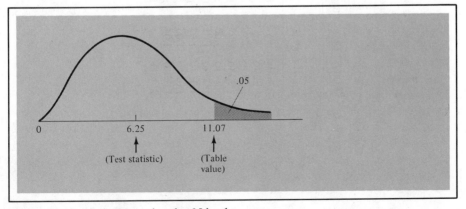

FIGURE 12.12 H_0 is accepted at the .05 level.

Table 12.1 Categories and Data for Example 8

Class	Normal curve	Observed	Expected (normal table × n)		$(o - e)$	$(o - e)^2$	$(o - e)^2/e$
less than .96	less than $\mu - 2\sigma$	4	.0228 × 100 =	2.28	+1.72	2.958	1.30
.96 to <.97	$\mu - 2\sigma$ to $< \mu - 1.5\sigma$	6	.0442 × 100 =	4.42	+1.58	2.496	.56
.97 to <.98	$\mu - 1.5\sigma$ to $< \mu - 1\sigma$	4	.0919 × 100 =	9.19	−5.19	26.936	2.93
.98 to <.99	$\mu - 1\sigma$ to $< \mu - .5\sigma$	16	.1498 × 100 =	14.98	+1.02	1.040	.69
.99 to <1.00	$\mu - .5\sigma$ to < 0	20	.1915 × 100 =	19.15	+.85	.722	.04
1.00 to <1.01	0 to $< \mu + .5\sigma$	18	.1915 × 100 =	19.15	−1.15	1.322	.07
1.01 to <1.02	$\mu + .5\sigma$ to $< \mu + 1\sigma$	16	.1498 × 100 =	14.98	+1.02	1.040	.69
1.02 to <1.03	$\mu + 1\sigma$ to $< \mu + 1.5\sigma$	10	.0919 × 100 =	9.19	+.81	.656	.07
1.03 to <1.04	$\mu + 1.5\sigma$ to $< \mu + 2\sigma$	4	.0442 × 100 =	4.42	−.42	.176	.04
≥1.04	$\geq \mu + 2\sigma$	2	.0228 × 100 =	2.28	−.28	.078	.03
		100		100.00	.00		$\overline{\chi^2 = 6.42}$

claimed the distribution of the amount of beer per bottle is normally distributed. One hundred bottles have been examined and the amount of beer per bottle recorded. Test the claim, using the .025 level of significance.

Solution:
The hypothesis being tested is

H_0: The distribution is normal, with a mean of 1 liter and a standard
deviation of .2 liters.

The alternative hypothesis is

H_1: The distribution is not normal with a mean of 1 liter and a standard
deviation of .2 liters.

The main difference between a goodness-of-fit test that concerns a continuous distribution and one that concerns a discrete distribution is that there are no natural categories in the continuous case. Consequently, we must decide how many categories to use. The main considerations are these: (1) the greater the number of categories, the greater the opportunity for detecting differences between the observed and expected frequencies; and (2) the expected frequencies should not drop below 1.0, and the majority of cell frequencies should be greater than 5. As a rule of thumb, we might attempt to use between 5 and 15 categories. Since there are 100 observations here, we might try about 10 categories.

One possibility for choosing categories (there are many) would be to consider categories such as those shown in Table 12.1. The expected frequencies are derived from a normal table, and the observed frequencies are taken from the sample data. That is, the observed values are measurements converted into a frequency distribution that conforms to the categories shown. Note that the class sizes are unequal. The extreme classes have been grouped together.

The analysis of the data reveals that the variations observed are well within those which might reasonably be attributed to chance variation in sampling. Hence the claim of a normal distribution with a mean of 1 liter and a standard deviation of .2 liters is accepted (see Figure 12.13).

If H_0 had been rejected, this might have been due to any of these factors: (1) the mean was not 1; (2) the standard deviation was not .2; (3) the distribution was not normal; (4) some combination of these three factors; or (5) a Type I error was made. Further analysis would be undertaken to decide which reason was most probable.

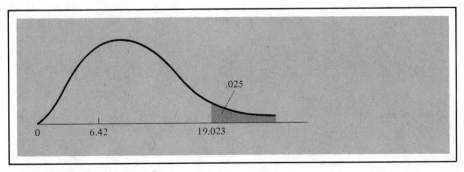

FIGURE 12.13 H_0 is accepted.

Using Sample Data to Develop Expected Frequencies

If expected frequencies cannot be determined without the aid of sample data, additional degrees of freedom are lost at the rate of one degree of freedom for each sample statistic so used. Consider this example, in which one sample statistic, the mean, is used: A traffic engineer wants to test a claim that accidents on a certain two-mile stretch of highway are Poisson distributed. A study of accident data yields these figures:

Number of accidents	Number of weeks
0	86
1	114
2	70
3	60
4	32
5	16
6	9
7	4
8	5
9	4
10 or more	0
	400

The null and alternative hypotheses are

H_0: Accidents are Poisson distributed.

H_1: Accidents are not Poisson distributed.

Since the mean of the hypothesized distribution is not stated (a Poisson distribution is completely specified by its mean), the relative frequencies cannot be obtained directly. The population mean must be estimated from the sample data. Doing this will result in the loss of an additional degree of freedom.

The mean of the frequency distribution can be found using the formula for grouped data:

$$\bar{x} = \frac{\sum xf}{n}$$

where

$$n = \sum f.$$

f frequency	x number	$x \cdot f$
0	86	0
1	114	114
2	70	140
3	60	180
4	32	128
5	16	80
6	9	54
7	4	28
8	5	40
9	4	36
	400	800

$$\text{mean} = \frac{800}{400} = 2.0$$

This sample mean can now be used in conjunction with a table of individual Poisson probabilities to obtain the expected frequencies. The probabilities for each outcome, 0, 1, 2, 3, and so on, are read directly from the table and each is then multiplied by the total frequency. For example, in the Poisson table, $P(0) = .1353$. Multiplying this by 400 gives an expected frequency for 0 of 54.12. The remaining values are obtained in a similar fashion. Table 12.2 shows the calculations for this example. The expected frequencies are given in the third column. The fourth through sixth illustrate the additional calculations necessary to obtain the chi-square test statistic.

One requirement of the chi-square test is that the *expected* frequencies in each category must be 1 or more. Since the last two expected frequencies in Table 12.2 are less than 1, some of the categories will have to be combined. Combining the last two yields an expected value of .44: $.36 + .08 = .44$. Even this is too small, which means that at least one more category must be included. Moving up the column, we see that the next expected frequency is 1.36, which is enough to satisfy the requirement of an expected frequency of 1.0 or more. We are now left with 8 classes, and the last class has an expected frequency of 1.80: $1.36 + .36 + .08 = 1.80$. We must perform a similar pooling for the last three observed frequencies in order to have corresponding observed and expected frequencies. Thus the observed frequency for the last class becomes $4 + 5 + 4 = 13$.

From Table 12.2 we see that the test statistic is 108.66. The degrees of freedom are determined by $(k - 1) - c$. After combining cells, there were 8 categories, so $k = 8$. In addition, there were two restrictions: the total had to equal 400 and the mean was estimated from the sample. So $c = 1$. Thus the degrees of freedom are $(8 - 1) - 1 = 6$.

TABLE 12.2   Data and Calculations for the Highway Accidents Example

Observed frequencies (number of accidents)	Number of weeks	Expected frequencies (Poisson $P \times 400$)	$(o - e)$	$(o - e)^2$	$(o - e)^2/e$
0	86	$.1353 \times 400 = 54.12$	31.88	1016.36	18.78
1	114	$.2707 \times 400 = 108.28$	5.72	32.72	.30
2	70	$.2707 \times 400 = 108.28$	-38.28	1465.36	13.53
3	60	$.1804 \times 400 = 72.16$	-12.16	147.87	2.05
4	32	$.0902 \times 400 = 36.08$	-4.08	16.65	.46
5	16	$.0361 \times 400 = 14.44$	1.56	2.43	.17
6	9	$.0120 \times 400 = 4.80$	4.20	17.64	3.68
7	4 ⎫	$.0034 \times 400 = 1.36$ ⎫			
8	5 ⎬13	$.0009 \times 400 = .36$ ⎬1.80	11.20	125.44	69.69
9	4 ⎭	$.0002 \times 400 = .08$ ⎭			
	400	400.00*	0		108.66

* Total is approximate due to rounding.

Comparing our test statistic with table values at 6 degrees of freedom reveals that the null hypothesis should be rejected, since the test statistic is larger than even the value at .01, as shown in Figure 12.14.

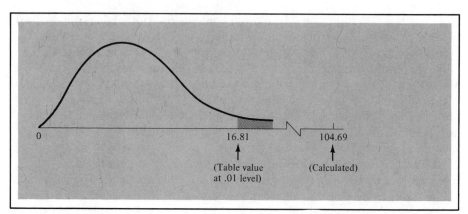

Figure 12.14 H_0 is rejected.

EXERCISES

1. Use a chi-square goodness-of-fit test at the .05 level to determine which of the following sample frequencies are close enough to the expected frequencies so that the null hypothesis can be accepted.

a. Class	Observed frequency	Expected frequency	b. Class	Observed frequency	Expected frequency
0	18	20	0	32	32.7
1	20	25	1	38	41.0
2	20	20	2	22	20.5
3	20	16	3	4	5.1
4	14	12	4	2	.6
5	14	10	5	2	.0
6	6	9		100	100.0
7	9	6			
8	3	4			
9	0	2			
10	1	1			
	125	125			

c. Class	Observed frequency	Expected frequency
1–1.9	27	25
2–2.9	30	25
3–3.9	21	25
4–4.9	22	25
	100	100

2. Over the course of one year, a metal and die firm has experienced 50 lost-time accidents. One aspect of an investigation conducted by the safety engineer concerns the day of the week on which an accident occurred. Does it seem from the data below that the day of week might be a factor? Test the null hypothesis that the days are equally likely.

Day	Number of accidents
Monday	15
Tuesday	6
Wednesday	4
Thursday	9
Friday	16
	50

3. A student has devised a scheme for obtaining random digits. He has generated 1000 digits using his method and wants to determine if the digits are equally likely. Test his data, using a .025 level of significance.

											Total
Digit	0	1	2	3	4	5	6	7	8	9	
Frequency	90	94	95	103	106	99	104	102	104	103	1000

4. The manufacture of iron pipe requires a continuous welded seam. Defects along the seam of 2-inch pipe in the past have been well approximated by a Poisson distribution, with a mean of 3 defects/meter. A new welder is now in use. Determine if the process has changed.

												Total
Number of defects	0	1	2	3	4	5	6	7	8	9	10 or more	
Frequency	5	14	16	20	18	17	3	2	4	0	1	100

5. Determine if the following data might have come from a Poisson process. Estimate the mean from the sample data.

								Total
Births/day	0	1	2	3	4	5	6 or more	
Number of days	3	11	4	2	2	1	2	25

6. Determine if the grades of a large section of introductory psychology can be approximated by a normal distribution with a mean of 50.5 and a standard deviation of 10. Use .05.

< 25.5	14
26 to 30.5	18
31 to 35.5	22
36 to 40.5	20
41 to 45.5	40
46 to 50.5	30
51 to 55.5	22
56 to 60.5	20
61 to 65.5	2
66 to 70.5	6
71 to 75.5	—
76 to 80.5	4
≥ 81	2
	200

SUMMARY

Tests of proportions involve the analysis of count data. The purpose of such tests is to evaluate claims about population proportions. A one-sample test is used to evaluate a specified population proportion, while a two-sample test evaluates the claim that two populations have the same proportion of some item. Test procedures for one- and two-sample tests are very similar to one- and two-sample means tests.

Tests of k-samples involve the use of the chi-square sampling distribution, which is similar in many respects to the t distribution. k-sample tests can be used to test the equality of k population proportions.

Goodness-of-fit tests are one-sample tests that are used to test claims about the shape of a population distribution.

REVIEW QUESTIONS

1. What is the general purpose of a test of proportions?
2. What sampling distribution is appropriate for one- and two-sample tests of proportions when the sample size is small? What sampling distribution provides an approximation that can be used with large samples?
3. Is it necessary to assume that the population in a test of proportions is approximately normal? Explain.
4. State H_0 and H_1 for a typical $r \times k$ table.
5. What advantage is there to having a set of data organized into an $r \times k$ table rather than a $2 \times k$ table? Why, then, is it sometimes necessary to use a $2 \times k$ table?
6. What is the minimum expected frequency required for a chi-square $r \times k$ table? For a chi-square goodness-of-fit test?
7. In what ways is the chi-square distribution like the t distribution? In what ways is it different?
8. Why is a chi-square test usually a one-tail test?
9. What two chi-square tests were described in this chapter?
10. What is the purpose of a goodness-of-fit test?

SUPPLEMENTAL EXERCISES

1. A telephone switchboard was designed under the premise that calls would come in at the rate of 2.2 calls/minute and that the distributions of calls/minute could be approximated by the Poisson distribution. Careful records are kept on the frequency of calls over a period of 1000 minutes, with these results:

Calls/minute	Number of minutes
0	20
1	130
2	150
3	220
4	185
5	140
6	100
7	55
8 or more	0
	1000

Use the χ^2 test at the .01 level to test the claim of Poisson with a mean of 2.2 calls/minute.

*2. Cross-tabulation of data from a questionnaire resulted in the following table:

Attitude Toward U.S. Defense Policies

	Republican	Democrat	Independent
Approve	35	80	50
Disapprove	45	60	80
No opinion	20	60	70
	100	200	200

Does the table show that attitude toward defense policy is independent of political affiliation? Use $\alpha = .01$.

3. Decide if training time can reasonably be approximated by a normal distribution with a mean of 7 and a standard deviation of 2 days, for $\alpha = .05$, given this sample data:

Time	Frequency
2.01–3	1
3.01–4	3
4.01–5	4
5.01–6	10
6.01–7	15
7.01–8	9
8.01–9	4
9.01–10	1
10.01–11	2
11.01–12	1
	50

*4. Arrivals of trucks at a large depot are thought to be Poisson distributed with a mean of 2.4 arrivals/hour. Observations are made over a 50-hour period with these results:

								Total
Number of trucks:	0	1	2	3	4	5	6	
Number of hours:	5	10	15	10	5	2	3	50

a. State H_0 and H_1.
b. What can you conclude about the claim?

*5. A random sample of 16 housewives showed that 11 preferred Brand A and 5 preferred Brand B. Does this data truly reflect a preference for Brand A? Test at the .02 level.

6. A CPA firm is supposed to audit at least 10% of a firm's accounts. A random check of 200 accounts showed that 12 had been audited. Test the claim of 10% against the alternative of less than 10%, using $\alpha = .01$.

7. A national survey indicated that approximately 25% of the charge accounts at large department stores incurred a penalty for late payments. If a local store finds 40 late payments in a random sample of 200 accounts, can the

firm necessarily assume its customers are better than the national average? Test $H_1: p < 25\%$, using the .05 level of significance.

8. A random sample of 40 units from each of three vendors is completely inspected and the number of defectives recorded. On the basis of these results, are you willing to conclude that the percentage defective is approximately equal for the three?

	Vendor		
	A	B	C
Number defective	6	7	3
Number not defective	38	33	37

9. Fourteen automobile owners were given a new pair of windshield wiper blades and asked to report whether the blade for the driver's or passenger's side wore out first. Eleven reported that the passenger's side wore out first. Is this sufficient evidence to conclude that the driver's side blade tends to last longer (use .04)?

10. The marketing department of a toothpaste company wants to determine if the flavor of a new adult toothpaste it will market might influence sales. Fifty adults are given each of the new flavors and then asked their opinion after using the product for one month. Is there a flavor preference?

	Flavor		
	Chocolate	Coffee	Champagne
Liked	20	26	41
Did not like	30	24	9

11. Two vendors supply the same part. A random check of two recent shipments showed Vendor A's shipment had 9 defectives in 200 pieces and Vendor B's shipment had 13 defectives in 200 pieces. Each shipment had 10,000 pieces. Test the alternative that Vendor A's quality is better than Vendor B's.

13

significance tests for ranks and signs

Chapter Objectives

After completing this chapter, you should be able to:
1. Indicate the circumstances under which tests using ranks and signs are useful
2. Contrast the use of such tests with those using means or proportions in terms of advantages and disadvantages over other tests
3. Explain how related samples differ from independent samples
4. Briefly describe the use of each test (i.e., its purpose)
5. Use each of the techniques to solve problems

Chapter Outline

Introduction
Two-Sample Tests: Related Samples
    The sign test
    The ranked sign test
Two Independent Samples
    The Mann-Whitney Test
A *k*-Sample Test Using Ranks
    Kruskal-Wallis one-way analysis of variance
One-Sample Tests
    Analysis of runs
    Sampling distribution of number of runs
    Runs of two kinds of observations: nominal data
    Runs above and below the median
    Runs up and down
    Which test to use?
    Comments
Summary

INTRODUCTION

ALL OF the previously discussed tests have stipulated certain requirements, such as that populations must have equal variances, or that the population be normally distributed, and so on. We will now consider a group of tests called *nonparametric* or *distribution-free* tests, which do not require such assumptions.

Aside from the fact that restrictive assumptions are eliminated, the nonparametric tests are generally easy to use, can be used for small sample sizes, and are intuitively appealing. Thus these tests can be used when the assumptions of some other technique are not met, or when it is not possible to verify that assumptions are met (because of small sample size). Moreover, the tests usually involve qualitative data. Hence, whereas a *t* test or other test of means requires measurement data, these tests do not have that requirement.

Now you rarely get something for nothing; so when you utilize one of the techniques to be discussed here in place of a test with stronger assumptions, you generally end up with a weaker test (i.e., the weaker assumptions result in a more general but less powerful test). The tests tend at times to waste or lose information. In addition, there is a greater probability of accepting H_0 when it is false.

It is important to note that even though these tests make no assumption about the underlying distribution of the *population* being sampled, they do rely on certain sampling distributions, such as the normal and the chi-square, just as previous techniques did.

In the following pages you will be exposed to a variety of tests. There are several kinds of *runs tests*, which are one-sample tests used to detect nonrandom patterns in sequential data. There are two kinds of *two-sample tests*, one for *independent* samples and one for *related* samples. And there is a *k-sample test* for *independent* samples. Table 13.1 outlines the tests that are covered in this chapter. All the tests make the assumption that the variable under consideration is continuous.

TABLE 13.1   Tests Covered in Chapter 13

One-sample	Two-samples	*k*-samples
runs	sign test	Kruskal-Wallis
	ranked sign	
	Mann-Whitney	

TWO-SAMPLE TESTS: RELATED SAMPLES

The purpose of tests involving related samples is to measure the effect of some "treatment" on a variable of interest. The treatment may be a new drug for chemotherapy, a diet plan, a speed-reading course, or some similar thing that we want to evaluate for effectiveness. The evaluation process involves forming two groups: a test group that receives the treatment and a control group that does not receive the treatment, or that receives an alternate treatment. The control group acts as a standard of comparison against which to judge the success of the treatment. To correctly interpret the results of such a comparison, it is necessary to match the two groups as much as possible in terms of important factors. For instance, IQ may be a factor in speed-reading, so in a test concerning speed-reading we would not want one group to have higher IQs than the other. Or, as another example, some individuals may have an easier time dieting than others. Ideally, in evaluating a diet plan, the two groups would be equivalent in this respect.

The need for matching the two groups can cause significant problems. One difficulty often encountered is the ability to successfully identify important factors. Another is measuring those variables, once they have been identified. Still another is assembling the two groups so that they have matching characteristics. One method of avoiding these difficulties is to use each subject as his own control. In this manner all the variables (at least theoretically) are matched, except for the variable under study. Thus initial measurements are made, the subjects are exposed to some treatment, and then a second set of measurements is made on the same subjects. For example, a subject may have his weight taken before starting on a diet plan and then again after completing the plan. Comparison of the two sets of measurements yields information about the effect of the treatment on the subjects.

Two such before-after tests are discussed in the following sections. The first of these, the sign test, involves replacing the data with plus or minus signs, while the second utilizes ranks.

The Sign Test

The sign test is used to test matched pairs to determine if the values in one sample are less than, equal to, or greater than the values in the other sample. The test can be used as long as the two values in each pair can be ranked. The sign test does require that each variable be continuous.

The sign test is so named because it uses plus and minus signs instead of numerical data. If numerical data exist, the values are converted to signs before proceeding. Hence as long as it can be established that the treatment resulted in an improvement $(+)$, a worsening $(-)$, or no measurable change (0), this test can be used. The test data consist of pluses and minuses, with zeros ignored. The null hypothesis is that there is no difference between the two groups, and the alternative hypothesis is that there has been a change. Ordinarily a one-tail test would be used, since the goal is to determine if some treatment is effective.

Consider the following situation: Forty-six people enroll in a creative writing course. At the first session a test that measures writing ability is administered.

After seven sessions, a second test is given. The hypotheses would be

H_0: The course had no effect on writing skills.

H_1: The course caused an improvement in writing skills.

Note that H_1 indicates *direction*, so a one-tail test is appropriate.

Suppose that comparison of the two sets of scores reveals that 30 students showed improvement (30 +'s), 10 were better on the first test (10 −'s), and 6 showed no change (6 0s). Thus we have

$$\left. \begin{array}{l} 30 \ +\text{'s} \\ 10 \ -\text{'s} \end{array} \right\} n = 40$$

6 0s (ignore 0s)

Practically speaking, writing performance is undoubtedly influenced by many interacting factors (e.g., time of test, environment, mood, recent experiences, etc.). Presumably, writing skills would vary from one point in time to another, even without being exposed to a writing course. The question, then, is whether the tests indicate more than chance variation in the changes noted. Chance is suggested when the number of +'s and −'s are approximately equal, while an effective course would be reflected by many +'s and few −'s. The problem, then, is conceptually identical to flipping a coin a certain number of times and deciding if the coin is fair on the basis of the number of heads and tails observed. And for large samples, this situation can be effectively modeled using the normal approximation to the binomial with $p = .5$.

There is, though, one thing that you must be aware of, and that is that H_1 will typically specify a *direction*, which can be translated into a large number of +'s (or −'s) or a small number of +'s (or −'s). Now the question of whether to test the +'s or −'s is really a moot question since the distribution is symmetrical and the number of +'s and −'s sum to n. In other words, the same answer will result regardless of which is used. However, it is important to decide whether a left-tail or a right-tail test will be used. Here, for example, if we decide to focus on +'s, observing many more +'s than −'s (right-tail) would support H_1. But if we focus on −'s, observing few −'s (left-tail) would support H_1. This is illustrated in Figure 13.1.

Suppose we agree here to focus on the number of +'s. We must compare the observed number of +'s to the expected number and compute a value of z. Using the formulas for number of occurrences, we have

expected number of +'s: $np = 40(.50) = 20$

standard deviation of number of +'s: $\sqrt{np(1 - p)} = \sqrt{40(.50)(.50)} = 3.16$

Next we determine z, using

$$z = \frac{\text{observed} - \text{expected}}{\text{standard deviation}} = \frac{30 - 20}{3.16} = 3.16$$

Since this exceeds $z_{\text{table}} = +1.65$ (using the .05 level and a one-tail test), H_0 is rejected, as illustrated in Figure 13.2.

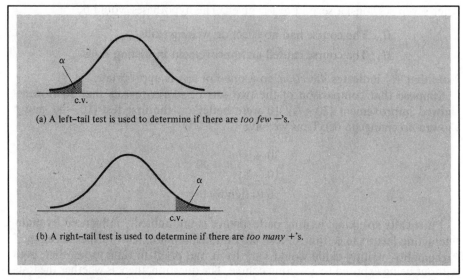

(a) A left–tail test is used to determine if there are *too few* −'s.

(b) A right–tail test is used to determine if there are *too many* +'s.

FIGURE 13.1 A left tail test is used to decide if there are *too few* −'s (or *too few* +'s); a right tail test is used to decide if there are *too many* +'s (or *too many* −'s).

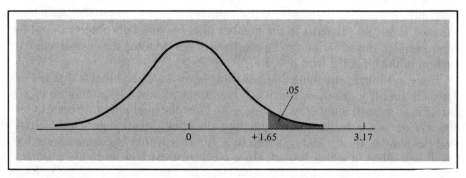

FIGURE 13.2 The number of *t*'s is too great to accept H_0 at the .05 level.

Note that because $p = 1 - p = \frac{1}{2}$ always, the formula for the standard deviation can be written as $\sigma = \sqrt{n(\frac{1}{2})(\frac{1}{2})}$, or $\frac{1}{2}\sqrt{n}$, and that the expected number equals $\frac{1}{2}n$. Thus we have the following result:

$$z = \frac{x - \frac{1}{2}n}{\frac{1}{2}\sqrt{n}}$$

You may wonder why the correction for continuity was not used, especially since we have used the normal approximation to the binomial. The answer is that the additional effort involved is unnecessary unless we have a borderline case. If that does happen, then we will have to rework that portion of the problem. Otherwise, we will be able to avoid getting involved with the correction factor.

When *n* is 20 or less, binomial tables can be used to determine if the probability of observing a result as extreme or more extreme than that in the sample is less than the selected value of alpha.* For example, suppose that in another writing course these results were recorded:

$$\left.\begin{array}{r} 12 +\text{'s} \\ 3 -\text{'s} \end{array}\right\} n = 15$$

$$2 \text{ 0s}$$

If we again focus on +'s, we find from the cumulative binomial table that the probability of 12 or more +'s in $n = 15$ observations with $p = .5$ is .0176. Since this is less than $\alpha = .05$, H_0 is rejected.

The Ranked Sign Test

When data for matched pairs are not measurements, there is little alternative except to use the sign test to evaluate the effect of some treatment. However, when measurements *are* available, using the sign test may lead to an incorrect decision. The reason is that the sign test is quite wasteful of information because it disregards the *magnitude* of change; it measures only the *direction* of change. Consequently, a situation may arise in which the number of plus and minus changes are about equal, but the magnitudes of one type of change are small while the magnitudes of the other are quite large. The sign test might easily suggest that H_0 should be accepted when rejection may seem more reasonable.

Hence when it is possible to determine both the magnitude and direction of change for matched pairs, it is usually more advantageous to use the ranked sign test because the ranked sign test is less wasteful of information. The only assumption of the test is that the underlying variable be continuous. The test focuses on ranked differences.

Before   After

After what?

FIGURE 13.3   Nonparametric statistics can be widely applied.

* The technique for small-sample binomial tests was considered in more detail in Chapter 12.

For example, a chemist claims he has discovered a gasoline additive, B-21, which will, in his words, "revolutionize automobile mileage performance." To test his claim, 18 cars are tested both with and without the additive. Suppose the test results are as shown below.

Mileage/gallon

Car	Without additive	With additive
1	10.4	10.9
2	16.3	16.2
3	15.1	15.8
4	9.2	10.0
5	10.3	10.2
6	8.4	7.9
7	9.7	9.6
8	8.6	9.9
9	11.0	11.9
10	13.2	13.0
11	18.1	18.1
12	7.5	8.1
13	9.5	9.8
14	10.9	10.9
15	8.7	10.3
16	15.1	16.2
17	13.4	13.0
18	12.3	13.8

The hypotheses are

H_0: The additive has no effect.

H_1: The additive has a positive influence.

The test involves computing mileage differences for each pair and then ranking those differences, without regard to whether they are plus or minus differences. If we agree to assign a + to mileage increases and a − to a decrease, we would expect low, medium, and high ranks to be evenly distributed among + and − differences if H_0 is true. Ranking is always from low to high (i.e., give rank of 1 to smallest value). Large ranks (real improvements) associated more often with increases (+'s) would tend to support H_1. Zero changes are again ignored. The test procedure is outlined in the discussion that follows.

First we find the difference for each pair. Then we rank the differences *without regard for sign*, ignoring any 0s. Ties are given the average of the ranks they would receive if they had been slightly different in value. For example, there are three .1s. Since these are the lowest values, they all receive the rank of $(1 + 2 + 3)/3 = 2$. Likewise, there are two values of .5. Had their values been slightly different, they would have been assigned ranks of 7 and 8, but since they are tied, we give each one the average value of 7.5. Note that the ranks 7 and 8 are not used.

Next each rank is given the sign of the difference it is associated with.

Now we determine the sum of the ranks with the fewer signs. There are 6 minus signs and 10 plus signs, so we find the sum of the minus ranks. (Actually either total can be used and the results will be the same, but it is often easier to find the total when fewer numbers are to be added.) The sum T of the negative ranks is 23.5. The steps of the procedure are shown in the accompanying table here.

Mileage/gallon

Car	Without	With	Increases	Rank	Decreases	Rank
1	10.4	10.9	+.5	7.5		
2	16.3	16.2			−.1	2
3	15.1	15.8	+.7	10		
4	9.2	10.0	+.8	11		
5	10.3	10.2			−.1	2
6	8.4	7.9			−.5	7.5
7	9.7	9.6			−.1	2
8	8.6	9.9	+1.3	14		
9	11.0	11.9	+.9	12		
10	13.2	13.0			−.2	4
11	18.1	18.1	0	(ignore)		
12	7.5	8.1	+.6	9		
13	9.5	9.8	+.3	5		
14	10.9	10.9	0	(ignore)		
15	8.7	10.3	+1.6	16		
16	15.1	16.2	+1.1	13		
17	13.4	13.0			−.4	6
18	12.3	13.8	+1.5	15		

$$T = \overline{23.5}$$

If the null hypothesis is true, we would expect the ranks to be equally divided among the + and − values and the two sums to be approximately equal. What we must determine, then, is if the sum of ranks selected differs too much from the expected sum to be due to chance.

The total sum of ranks, when N objects are consecutively assigned ranks, beginning with 1 and ending with N, is

$$\text{sum of ranks} = \frac{N(N + 1)}{2}$$

For example, for the ranks 1, 2, 3, 4, we would have

$$\text{sum of ranks} = 1 + 2 + 3 + 4 = \frac{4(5)}{2} = 10$$

If H_0 is true, the sum U_t of either the −'s or +'s ought to be one-half of the total.

The expected sum of the ranks (+'s or −'s) is

$$U_t = \frac{1}{2}\left[\frac{N(N + 1)}{2}\right] = \frac{N(N + 1)}{4}$$

In this instance, with two zeros, $N = 18 - 2 = 16$, and U_t is

$$U_t = \frac{16(16 + 1)}{4} = 68$$

Assuming H_0 to be true, the difference between U_t and the observed outcome for samples of eight or more is approximately normal, with a standard deviation σ_t as given in the box.

$$\sigma_t = \sqrt{\frac{N(N + 1)(2N + 1)}{24}}$$

In this instance, we find that

$$\sigma_t = \sqrt{\frac{16(16 + 1)(32 + 1)}{24}} = 19.34$$

If H_0 is true, the test statistic z will be approximately normal, with a mean of 0 and a standard deviation of 1.0.

$$z = \frac{\text{observed} - \text{expected}}{\text{standard deviation}} = \frac{T - U_t}{\sigma_t}$$

In our example z is

$$z = \frac{T - U_t}{\sigma_t} = \frac{23.5 - 68}{19.34} = -2.30$$

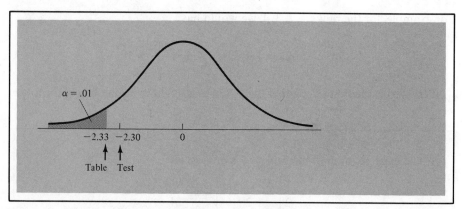

FIGURE 13.4   The null hypothesis is just barely accepted.

Under ordinary circumstances the test would be one-sided. If we had been using a level of significance of .01, for example, we would just barely accept H_0, since the critical z for .01 (one-tail) is -2.33 and our test statistic is -2.30. The test is illustrated in Figure 13.4. As with any one-sided test, care must be used in making sure that the results are in a direction that could lead to rejection of H_0.

EXERCISES

1. In an effort to decrease transportation costs, Central Taxi provided instruction in driving for economy for each of its twenty-four cab drivers. Test the results using a .05 level of significance and the sign test.

	Miles/gallon				Miles/gallon	
Driver	Before	After		Driver	Before	After
1	15.2	15.2		13	15.4	15.8
2	14.3	14.7		14	15.8	15.8
3	13.8	15.0		15	13.2	13.1
4	17.1	17.0		16	13.1	14.4
5	16.4	16.9		17	15.0	16.5
6	15.1	15.7		18	16.4	16.5
7	15.1	16.2		19	13.9	14.0
8	16.2	16.4		20	14.8	15.5
9	16.7	16.4		21	14.4	16.2
10	14.2	15.0		22	15.5	16.1
11	17.2	17.4		23	14.5	14.2
12	16.8	16.0		24	16.0	16.2

2. Verify in the two examples (p. 323 and p. 325) that using the number of $-$'s instead of the number of $+$'s will yield the same answers.

*3. An advertising agency wished to determine the effectiveness of a campaign it was conducting to get voters to approve construction of sidewalks in a suburban area. Two hundred residents were randomly selected and queried on the matter prior to the campaign and then again three weeks after the start of the campaign, with these results:

	After	
Before	for	against
for	20	30
against	90	60

   a. Determine the number of $+$'s, $-$'s, and 0s.
   b. What should the alternative hypothesis be?
   c. What can you conclude using a sign test?
   d. Suppose that out of the 200, only 23 had changed their opinions. Would it still be reasonable to analyze the data in the same way? Why?

4. Following are the results of a two-week crash diet program. Can you conclude that the program is effective? Use a .05 level and the sign test.

Subject	Prediet weight	Postdiet weight
1	132.1	134.3
2	129.0	125.2
3	130.4	127.5
4	127.8	128.9
5	149.0	146.5
6	141.5	140.9
7	137.8	132.3
8	128.7	130.8
9	122.7	125.3
10	151.9	147.0
11	188.1	186.1
12	135.3	130.0
13	142.0	141.5
14	144.4	145.4
15	126.0	123.0
16	98.1	98.1

5. Analyze the B-21 gasoline additive test results using the sum of the positive ranks and compare your result with that shown for the sum of negative ranks.
6. Rework Exercise 1 by using the ranked sign test. Compare your conclusions with those you reached with the sign test.
*7. Rework Exercise 4 using the ranked sign test, and compare the results to those of the sign test. What can you conclude? Why?
8. The ranked sign test cannot be used to analyze the data in Exercise 3. Explain why.
9. Evaluate the success of this five-week diet program using the ranked sign test.

Subject	Prediet weight	Postdiet weight
1	202	204
2	189	177
3	149	154
4	186	169
5	149	140
6	200	200
7	220	214
8	190	189
9	164	167
10	161	150
11	162	155
12	171	172
13	193	183
14	163	158
15	187	184
16	178	192
17	218	210
18	181	166
19	140	143
20	168	164

TWO INDEPENDENT SAMPLES

The Mann-Whitney Test

The Mann-Whitney test is used to test whether two independent samples have come from populations with equal means. The test can be used as an alternative to the two-sample test of means covered earlier, which required that both populations have the same variance. The Mann-Whitney test makes no such requirement. In fact, the only assumption is that the level of measurement be on a continuous scale, and even this assumption is not absolutely rigid. In spite of the weaker assumptions, the Mann-Whitney test is nearly as strong as a two-sample test of means.

The test is based on a sum of ranks. The data are ranked as if the observations are all part of a single sample. If H_0 is true, the low, medium, and high ranks ought to be fairly evenly distributed among the two samples. If H_1 is true, one sample will tend to have more low ranks (and thus a lower sum of ranks), and the other will tend to have a higher sum of ranks. One way of analyzing this tendency is to focus on the sum of ranks of one of the samples and compare it to the expected sum of ranks assuming the means are equal. Either set of ranks may be tested. However, it is crucial to recognize that if one set of ranks is *higher* than expected, the other set must be *lower* than expected. For instance, suppose one sample has a sum of ranks that is 10.5 less than expected. Then the other sample must have a sum that is 10.5 higher than expected. This factor is especially important for a one-tail test, because you must interpret H_1 in terms of the rank sum of the group being tested.

For example, suppose we have

$$H_1: \mu_a > \mu_b$$

Then the sum of the ranks of Group A ought to be *greater* than the sum of the ranks of Group B if H_1 is correct (i.e., greater than the expected sum under H_0). This is equivalent to saying that the sum of ranks for Group B should be *less than* Group A's (i.e., less than the sum under H_0).

The procedure explained here applies when each sample has 10 or more observations.* Again, the total sum of ranks (both columns combined) will be $N(N + 1)/2$. If the two samples are of equal size, the expected sum of either column under H_0 is

$$\frac{1}{2}\left[\frac{N(N + 1)}{2}\right] = \frac{N(N + 1)}{4}$$

If the sample sizes are unequal, the sum of ranks should be split in proportion to the sample sizes. The following formulas are generally used.

---

* For smaller sample sizes, consult Siegel (see the references) for the procedure and tables.

The expected sum of ranks for each column is

$$E(R_1) = \frac{n_1}{N}\left[\frac{N(N+1)}{2}\right] \qquad E(R_2) = \frac{n_2}{N}\left[\frac{N(N+1)}{2}\right]$$

where

n_1 = sample size of Group 1

n_2 = sample size of Group 2

$E(R_1)$ = expected sum of ranks of Group 1

$E(R_2)$ = expected sum of ranks of Group 2

N = total number of observations = $n_1 + n_2$

The sampling distribution is approximately normal and has a standard deviation as given in the box.

$$\sigma_u = \sqrt{\frac{n_1 n_2(n_1 + n_2 + 1)}{12}}$$

The test statistic z is

$$z = \frac{R - E(R)}{\sigma_u}$$

where R is the sum of the ranks being tested.

Example 1 Compare the mean typing speeds of two groups of business school students. Group 2 learned typing by using a traditional approach, while Group 1 learned by typing blindfolded. Test the claim that the blindfolded students did worse, using $\alpha = .05$.

Group 1 (words/min)	Group 2 (words/min)
36.0	38.2
32.5	40.1
41.3	29.8
40.1	30.3
50.8	32.8
39.2	40.4
41.2	37.2
29.7	34.1
32.5	36.2
37.8	41.5
46.6	35.5
	42.5
	44.9

Solution:

If the claim (H_1) is true, the second group should show a higher rank total (and thus the first group a lower total), which would indicate a higher mean for Group 2.

Before ranking, we array both groups from lowest to highest. Then we rank as if all are a single set; give ties the average rank.

Now we sum the ranks for each group.

Group 1 (ranks)	Group 2 (ranks)
29.7 (1)	29.8 (2)
32.5 (4.5)	30.3 (3)
32.5 (4.5)	32.8(6)
36.0 (9)	34.1 (7)
37.8 (12)	35.5 (8)
39.2 (14)	36.2 (10)
40.1 (15.5)	37.2 (11)
41.2 (18)	38.2 (13)
41.3 (19)	40.1 (15.5)
46.6 (23)	40.4 (17)
50.8 (24)	41.5 (20)
	42.5 (21)
	44.9 (22)
$\sum R_1 = 144.5$	$\sum R_2 = 155.5$
$n_1 = 11$	$n_2 = 13$

Next we compute the expected sum of ranks for one of the groups (either one) and compare it with the observed sum of ranks for that group. Suppose we focus on Group 1.

$$E(R_1) = \frac{n_1}{N}\left[\frac{N(N+1)}{2}\right] = \frac{11}{24}\left[\frac{24(25)}{2}\right] = 137.5$$

Now we compute the standard deviation of the sampling distribution:

$$\sigma_u = \sqrt{\frac{n_1 n_2(n_1 + n_2 + 1)}{12}} = \sqrt{\frac{11(13)(11 + 13 + 1)}{12}} = \sqrt{297.9} = 17.26$$

Finally we compute z (see Figure 13.5):

$$z = \frac{R_1 - E(R_1)}{\sigma_u} = \frac{144.5 - 137.5}{17.26} = \frac{7}{17.26} = +.406$$

If we had decided to focus on Group 2, the expected sum of ranks would then be

$$E(R_2) = \frac{n_2}{N}\left[\frac{N(N+1)}{2}\right] = \frac{13}{24}\left[\frac{24(25)}{2}\right] = 162.5$$

The standard deviation is unaffected by this. Hence (see Figure 13.6)

$$\sigma_u = 17.26$$

$$z = \frac{R_2 - E(R_2)}{\sigma_u} = \frac{155.5 - 162.5}{17.26} = -\frac{7}{17.26} = -.406$$

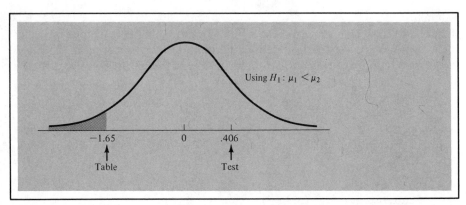

FIGURE 13.5   We cannot conclude that the two methods are different with respect to average typing speed.

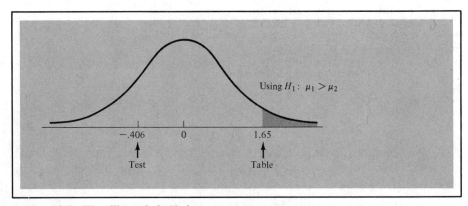

FIGURE 13.6   We still conclude H_0 is true.

EXERCISES

*1. Use the Mann-Whitney tests to determine if the mean of Group A is larger than the mean of Group B. Use $\alpha = .01$.

A	5.2	5.9	6.3	6.8	7.0	8.1	8.2	8.9	9.5	10.0
B	4.5	5.0	5.1	5.6	5.9	6.3	6.8	7.2	7.8	8.1

2. Determine if the average amount of sale is different for these two stores:

Store 30	Store 25
$10.50	$22.25
18.71	17.65
9.16	15.62
8.75	9.10
2.00	10.80
11.53	6.78
4.56	8.75
3.88	12.34
9.16	8.99
12.34	9.90
10.75	
16.41	

3. Twelve tires randomly selected from each of two tire manufacturers are subjected to life testing. Would you say that the average tire life differs for the populations from which the tires have been chosen? Test at the .05 level.

Manufacturer 1	Manufacturer 2
35,500	33,400
25,400	29,650
24,605	25,500
25,670	27,900
30,645	24,570
27,850	23,800
24,570	27,890
31,800	30,100
27,760	28,865
28,875	27,700
21,900	24,450
26,560	32,300

4. What would be the effect on the outcome of Exercise 2 if each value is doubled? Explain.

A *k*-SAMPLE TEST USING RANKS

Kruskal-Wallis One-Way Analysis of Variance

Classical analysis of variance (*F* test) requires some fairly strong assumptions concerning the sample data. For example, it is necessary to assume that samples have been drawn from *normal populations* with *equal variances*. The researcher may not be willing to make these assumptions and there may be too few observations to test for normality. To proceed under such circumstances can invalidate the results.

An alternative approach for testing whether three or more independent samples have been drawn from populations with equal means is to use the Kruskal-Wallis test. It is a one-way analysis of variance test that employs ranks rather than actual measurements, and its assumptions concerning the data are relatively weak. For instance, while both the *F* test and the Kruskal-Wallis (K-W) test require independent random samples, the only additional requirement for the K-W test is that the underlying variable be continuously distributed.

The procedure for the test is to convert each observation to a rank. This is accomplished by treating all observations as if they belong to a single sample. The lowest value receives a rank of 1, the next lowest a rank of 2, and so on, until all observations have been ranked. Ties are assigned the average values that they would have received if the values were slightly different. For example, if there are two values tied for the lowest, instead of having ranks 1 and 2, they would each have a rank of 1.5.

The sum of ranks in each sample, the sample sizes, and the total number of observations are used to compute the statistic *H*, where

$$H = \frac{12}{N(N + 1)} \sum_{j=1}^{k} \frac{(R_j)^2}{n_j} - 3(N + 1)$$

and

$$N = \text{total number of observations}$$
$$k = \text{the number of samples}$$
$$n_j = \text{the number of observations in the } j\text{th sample}$$
$$R_j = \text{the sum of ranks in the } j\text{th sample}$$

If the null hypothesis of equal means is true, the ranks should be well scattered among the samples. The squared sum of ranks divided by their respective sample sizes should be approximately equal. The test statistic H will have a chi-square distribution with $k - 1$ degrees of freedom. Hence the computed value of H can be compared to a table value of chi-square and the null hypothesis rejected if the computed value is greater than the table value at the desired level of significance.

If the number of ties is large, it will affect the value of H. Consequently, it may be necessary to adjust the value of H by dividing it by the quantity

$$1 - \frac{\sum(t^3 - t)}{N^3 - N}$$

where t is the number of ties in a group of ties.

As an example of a situation where the K-W test could be applied, consider the following example: To examine the merits of three different instructional techniques, each of 16 students was randomly assigned to one of three sections, each of which used a different one of the three techniques. After a two-hour session, each student was asked to solve the same problem. Their times (in minutes) were as shown below.

Lecture	Programmed materials	Video tapes
15	10	11
12	21	19
18	16	17
20	13	22
10	14	24
	9	

The procedure is as follows: First we assign a rank to each value. It is usually easier to do this if the values are first arrayed within each sample:

Lecture	Rank	Programmed	Rank	Video	Rank
10	2.5	9	1	11	4
12	5	10	2.5	17	10
15	8	13	6	19	12
18	11	14	7	22	15
20	13	16	9	24	16
	39.5	21	14		57
			39.5		

Now the sum of ranks for each column is determined (see the table). Thus $R_1 = 39.5$, $R_2 = 39.5$, and $R_3 = 57$.

The test statistic *H* is

$$H = \frac{12}{16(16 + 1)} \left[\frac{39.5^2}{5} + \frac{39.5^2}{6} + \frac{57^2}{5} \right] - 3(16 + 1) = 2.90$$

If H_0 is true, then *H* will have a chi-square distribution with $k - 1 = 2$ degrees of freedom. Comparing the calculated value with the table values reveals that we should accept H_0, since *H* is smaller than even the value at the .10 level. There were only two ties, so no adjustment is called for. See Figure 13.7.

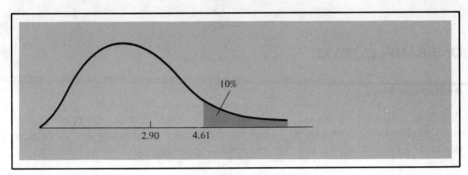

FIGURE 13.7 The null hypothesis is accepted.

EXERCISES

1. Four different paint mixtures have been tested to determine if any differences in mean drying time exist, with these results:

Mixture A	14.3	18.7	15.0	17.2	18.1	17.6	15.8
Mixture B	10.8	12.4	11.6	16.1	13.4	13.8	
Mixture C	14.5	14.8	15.3	14.0	16.3	10.8	
Mixture D	16.0	17.2	17.7	13.3	16.8		

   Test, using the .025 level of significance.

*2. Each of 16 overweight persons was assigned randomly to one of three diet plans. The weight losses were as given below.

Plan 1	1.3	5.1	2.8	0.5	3.0
Plan 2	4.5	3.2	3.4	2.8	3.2
Plan 3	10.0	4.9	1.0	2.2	0.0

   Use the .01 level to test these results.

3. Five brands of fluorescent light bulbs were compared to determine if operating lives were different. Test, using the .05 level.

Brand A	1010	905	989	859	910	1035	875	888
Brand B	690	850	824	856	915	734	799	700
Brand C	1203	978	918	816	992	1021	666	873
Brand D	752	709	717	921	761	991	809	981
Brand E	591	723	672	924	881	1038	604	704

4. In a study of accident prevention and predictability, reaction times of various categories of drivers were obtained. Does there seem to be any significant difference among them?

Cab drivers	Bus drivers	Power company truck drivers
3.5	4.6	3.7
3.4	4.0	3.0
2.0	2.9	2.1
3.2	3.2	2.9
2.6	3.8	1.9
	4.5	3.6

ONE-SAMPLE TESTS

Analysis of Runs

A crucial assumption in statistical inference is that sample observations are random. It would seem logical, therefore, that methods for testing whether randomness is present would be developed. One of these methods involves the analysis of runs.

For our purposes a run is defined as an unbroken sequence of observations that possess a like characteristic. Suppose the characteristic of interest was color and a sequence such as green, green, green, red, red, green occurred. For convenience, we can replace each color with a symbol (say the first letter of the color). Thus the series becomes GGGRRG. There are three runs. They are counted as GGG RR G (length is unimportant).

Runs focus attention on the sequence or *order of occurrence* of observations. The observations might be in a temporal (time-ordered) sequence or a spatial (position-ordered) sequence. Examples of time sequences include records of daily temperature highs, the order of output from some industrial process, and daily volume on the New York stock exchange. Some position-ordered sequences are final standings in some competitive event, place in line, position on a shelf or in a file cabinet, and so on. The data can be nominal categories, like true-false, male-female, and so on, or measurements, like height, weight, IQ, and so on. Regardless of the nature of the actual data, observations can be transformed into a series of symbols in which the number of runs can be counted.

A *run* is an unbroken sequence of observations that possess a common characteristic.

A test for runs is used to detect nonrandom patterns in data when the order of observation is known. A sequence can be nonrandom in a variety of ways. Here are a few examples of identifiable patterns:

ABABABABABABABABABAB

Notice that there is a regular back and forth movement. This would be suggestive of cycling.

<u>AAAAAAAAAAAA BBBBBBBBBB</u>

There is a trend from A to B in the data.

<u>AAAA</u> <u>BBBBB</u> <u>AAAAAA</u> <u>BBBB</u> <u>AAA</u>

Here there are clusters of like elements.

Figure 13.8 illustrates some graphs of nonrandom patterns.

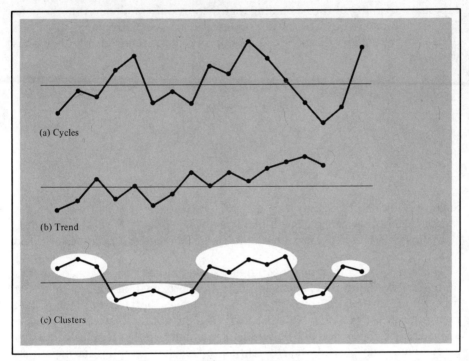

(a) Cycles

(b) Trend

(c) Clusters

FIGURE 13.8   Examples of some nonrandom patterns.

Of course, these are extreme cases, and the patterns are rather easy to spot. In practice, patterns may be more difficult to identify. Consequently, a somewhat more rigorous approach than mere visual inspection is desirable.

Sampling Distribution of Number of Runs

The number of runs in a series of n observations will tend to vary from sample to sample, just as other sample statistics do. Thus a set of such data is regarded as a sample, even though it may not be feasible to select another sample.

To be able to say that a series of observations exhibits the characteristics of a random process, it is first necessary to have an idea of what a process that is random would produce. This can then serve as a standard against which to judge some actual situation. The sampling distribution provides a definition of randomness by indicating the expected (average) number of runs and by revealing how much variability between the number of runs expected and the number actually observed is reasonable for a random series.

When the series in question involves a large number of observations (say 30 or more)* the sampling distribution of the number of runs is well approximated by a *normal* distribution.

The null hypothesis in a runs test is that the difference between the expected number of runs and the number actually observed is the result of chance variation in sampling (i.e., the sequence of observations is random). The alternative hypothesis is that the difference between the observed and expected number of runs is too great to be due to chance alone. The difference is tested by comparing it to the expected variability of runs assuming that there is only randomness in the data. That is, the difference between the observed and expected number of runs is divided by the standard deviation of the appropriate sampling distribution. Thus we have

$$z = \frac{\text{observed number of runs} - \text{expected number of runs}}{\text{standard deviation of runs}}$$

or

$$z = \frac{r - R}{\sigma_R}$$

Small absolute values of z (say less than 1.96 for $\alpha = .05$) imply that the sequence is random, while large values suggest that it is not random.

Ordinarily a two-tail test is used, although occasionally a one-tail test is called for.

Theoretically, a correction for continuity should be used, because a continuous (normal) distribution is being employed as an approximation with discrete data (number of runs). To correct for continuity, reduce the absolute value of the numerator in the preceding equation by $\frac{1}{2}$. In practice, the correction is usually applied only if H_0 is rejected by a very narrow margin. In that case the correction for continuity may offset the narrow margin and result in accepting the hypothesis of randomness.

Runs of Two Kinds of Observations: Nominal Data

When the data under investigation consist of items assigned to one of two mutually exclusive categories, such as true-false, yes-no, good-bad, and so on, we say that the data are dichotomized (two categories). For example, we may have a sequence like TFTTFTTFFF and we would like to know if the sequence is random. To make a decision it is necessary to count the number of runs in the data and then compare this to the number of runs expected.

The sampling distribution for the number of runs with two types of observations is approximately normal for large sample sizes (either type of observation greater than 20). We will concern ourselves with large samples only. The expected number

* The exact number will vary, depending on the type of data.

of runs is

$$R = \frac{2n_1 n_2}{N} + 1$$

where

R = the expected number of runs

n_1 = the number of one kind of observation

n_2 = the number of the other kind of observation

N = total number of observations

Note that n_1 and n_2 are counts of elements of each type, not runs of each type. Also, $n_1 + n_2 = N$.

The standard deviation of the sampling distribution of the number of runs is

$$\sigma_R = \sqrt{\frac{2n_1 n_2 (2n_1 n_2 - n_1 - n_2)}{(n_1 + n_2)^2 (n_1 + n_2 - 1)}}$$

Fortunately, it is possible to reduce this rather formidable equation to a much simpler form:

$$\sigma_R = \sqrt{\frac{(R - 1)(R - 2)}{N - 1}}$$

Example 2 Forty students are lined up outside the Central High gym awaiting the start of the Valley High-Central High basketball game. Would you say that the sequence is random?

Solution:

Letting V stand for a Valley High student and C for a Central High student, the sequence is

<u>CCCCC</u> <u>VV</u> <u>CC</u> <u>VV</u> <u>CCCC</u> <u>VVV</u> <u>CCCCCC</u> <u>VVVVV</u> <u>C</u> <u>VVV</u> <u>CCCCCC</u> <u>V</u>

The runs are underlined. If we arbitrarily let n_1 = the number of C's and n_2 = the number of V's, we find that $n_1 = 24$ and $n_2 = 16$. There are 12 runs ($r = 12$). The expected number of runs is

$$R = \frac{2n_1 n_2}{N} + 1 = \frac{2(24)(16)}{40} + 1 = 19.2 + 1 = 20.2$$

The standard deviation is

$$\sigma_R = \sqrt{\frac{(R - 1)(R - 2)}{N - 1}} = \sqrt{\frac{(19.2)(18.2)}{39}} = 2.99$$

Using the standard deviation as the measure of relative difference between the actual number of runs counted and the number expected, we find that

$$z = \frac{r - R}{\sigma_R} = \frac{12 - 20.2}{2.99} = \frac{-8.2}{2.99} \approx -2.7$$

As shown in Figure 13.9, the difference is beyond what might be considered chance, so we conclude that the sequence is not random. In fact, the probability of getting a difference larger than -8.2 (i.e., $12 - 20.2$) with a random process would be .0035 (the area in the tail of the standardized normal distribution beyond $z = -2.7$ standard deviations).

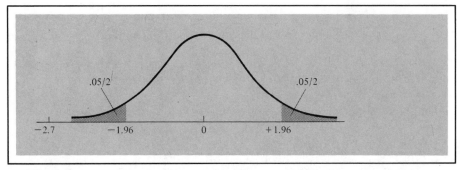

FIGURE 13.9   Our test reveals there are too few runs; H_0 is rejected.

Runs Above and Below the Median

When the data being investigated are numerical instead of symbolic, a common method of testing a sequence for randomness focuses on any patterns that might form with respect to the sample median. That is, each observation is designated as being above (A) or below (B) the sample median. Values that fall on the median are ignored. Then the number of runs of A's and B's are counted.

The process of converting each value to either an A or a B reduces the data to two kinds of observations, and the previous formulas could be applied to this data just as they were in the preceding case. However, since the number of A's will equal the number of B's (by definition one-half of the observations fall above the median and one-half below the median), the previous formulas can be reduced to a simpler form:

$$R = \frac{N}{2} + 1 \qquad \sigma_R \approx \sqrt{\frac{N-1}{4}}$$

where N is the total number of observations.

For large sample sizes (say $N \geq 40$), the sampling distribution of the number of runs above and below the median is well approximated by the normal distribution. For smaller sample sizes, tables are readily available.*

Example 3   The county board of health in a large midwestern city records the amount of sulfur dioxide in the atmosphere as one meaure of the amount of air pollution. Using the following data, which were recorded on 44 successive days in this city, what can be concluded about the randomness of the sequence? It has been determined from historical data that the median is .050.

* Refer, for example, to the texts by Bradley, Duncan, or Siegel in the references.

Day	SO$_2$		Day	SO$_2$	
1	.057	A|	23	.051	A|
2	.040	B|	24	.063	A
3	.059	A|	25	.060	A
4	.063	A	26	.049	B|
5	.061	A	27	.040	B
6	.040	B	28	.044	B|
7	.009	B	29	.058	A|
8	.003	B	30	.032	B|
9	.031	B	31	.018	B
10	.067	A|	32	.017	B
11	.071	A	33	.017	B
12	.083	A	34	.030	B
13	.081	A	35	.053	A|
14	.093	A	36	.054	A
15	.065	A	37	.085	A
16	.023	B|	38	.081	A
17	.029	B	39	.041	B|
18	.018	B	40	.037	B
19	.001	B	41	.063	A|
20	.010	B|	42	.073	A
21	.055	A|	43	.055	A|
22	.056	A|	44	.048	B|

Solution:

The data show that there are 14 runs. If the sequence is random, we would expect

$$R = \frac{N}{2} + 1 = \frac{44}{2} + 1 = 23 \text{ runs}$$

and the standard deviation of the related sampling distribution would be

$$\sigma_R = \sqrt{\frac{N-1}{4}} = \sqrt{\frac{43}{4}} = \sqrt{10.75} \approx 3.28$$

The real question, then, is whether a process which is truly random could yield as few as 14 runs when 23 runs are expected. Using the standard deviation as a measure of the difference between the two, we find that

$$z = \frac{r - R}{\sigma_R} = \frac{14 - 23}{3.28} = \frac{-9.0}{3.28} \approx -2.74$$

If we test, say, at the .01 level, H_0 would be rejected, and we would conclude that the sequence is not random. This is illustrated in Figure 13.10.

There are undoubtedly many possible explanations for this result. Among them are that pollution may remain in an area for days when the air is still, while at other times, wind and rain may keep pollution levels down. Moreover, polluting agents, such as automobiles, factories, and so on, may follow definite patterns related to weekdays versus weekends, vacations and holidays, and so on.

When working with data that has already been graphed (and the actual figures are not available), if the data are plotted around the median, the number of runs can be counted as the number of times the line connecting the data points crosses the median plus 1. If the central line is the mean instead of the median, as long as the distribution is symmetrical (e.g., uniform or normal) the mean and median will be

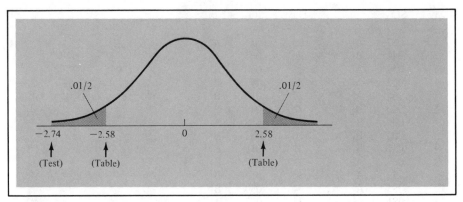

FIGURE 13.10 H_0 is rejected.

the same, so the median test can still be used. Otherwise, the more general formula for two kinds of observations must be used.

Runs Up and Down

Another kind of runs test uses runs up and down as a measure of randomness. Each value in a sequence is measured relative to the previous value. Each numerical value is replaced either with a U for up or D for down, relative to the previous value. For example, the sequence

$$28 \quad 29 \quad 31 \quad 25 \quad 24$$
$$\underline{U} \quad \underline{U} \quad \underline{D} \quad \underline{D}$$

would yield two runs: first a run of 2 up, and then a run of 2 down. The first value is not assigned a symbol, since it does not follow another value.

Again, the sampling distribution of the number of runs up and down is normally distributed for large sample sizes ($N \geq 40$), and tables are available for smaller sample sizes.* The formulas for the mean and standard deviation of the sampling distribution are not the same, though. The reason is that the two previous tests involved elements with *constant* probability. For instance, the probability of getting a value on either side of the median is always $\frac{1}{2}$ and is independent of the previous observation's value. Such is not the case with runs up and down. If the sequence is really random, the probability of a high value being followed by an even higher value would be much less than $\frac{1}{2}$, and the probability of its being followed by a smaller value would be much more than $\frac{1}{2}$. The formulas take this matter of "positional" probability into account.

The expected number of runs up and down is

$$R = \frac{2N - 1}{3}$$

where N is the total number of observations. The standard deviation of the number of runs up and down is

$$\sigma_R = \sqrt{\frac{16N - 29}{90}}$$

* See for example, Bradley or Duncan, listed in the references.

Example 4   The following sequence of numbers was developed by a random number "generator." Use a test of runs up and down to test for nonrandom patterns.

76 88 01 35 34 49 17 89 19 41 14 99 13 23 79 40 15 19 01 66
   U D U D U D U D U D U D U U D D U D U

33 31 15 16 54 03 11 93 78 87 50 23 46 14 27 12 38 12 20 15
D D D U U D U U D U D D U D U D U D U D

Solution:

There are 40 two-digit numbers. If the sequence is random, we would expect the number of runs up and down to be

$$R = \frac{2N - 1}{3} = \frac{2(40) - 1}{3} = \frac{79}{3} \approx 26$$

with a standard deviation of

$$\sigma_R = \sqrt{\frac{16N - 29}{90}} = \sqrt{\frac{16(40) - 29}{90}} = \sqrt{\frac{611}{90}} \approx \sqrt{6.79} \approx 2.61$$

The observed number of runs, r, is 32, so the difference between the number expected and the number observed is 6. The relative difference is

$$z = \frac{r - R}{\sigma_R} = \frac{32 - 26}{2.61} = \frac{6.0}{2.61} = +2.30$$

If we are testing at the .05 level, we would reject H_0, but we would accept H_0 at the .01 level, as illustrated in Figure 13.11.

Which Test to Use?

An interesting situation arises when data are subjected to both a runs up and down test and a runs above and below the median test if one test indicates a nonrandom pattern of variability while the other test does not. This often results in the question, "Which test will I believe?" Moreover, there is the temptation to collect additional data to resolve the issue. And occasionally, the issue is completely avoided by using only one of the tests.

Each of these "solutions" ignores the real issue. The fact of the matter is that each type of runs test is sensitive to different kinds of nonrandom patterns. In

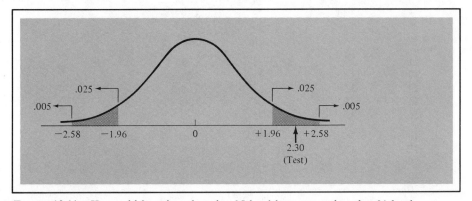

FIGURE 13.11 H_0 would be rejected at the .05 level but accepted at the .01 level.

other words, a sequence of observations can be nonrandom in a variety of ways. Some of these ways are more apt to be discovered using a runs up and down approach while others are more likely to be found by examining runs above and below the median. Consequently, if both tests are applied and one indicates the sequence is not random, there is not really a conflict, the sequence is nonrandom in some way.

Comments

This section has focused on the number of runs with large samples. Consideration of small-sample tests and appropriate tables is taken up in Bradley, Siegel, and Duncan, listed in the references. A very useful kind of runs test involves the *length* of the longest run instead of the *number* of runs. Bradley and Duncan both include good discussions of those tests. The underlying concept in those tests is that long runs are another indicator of nonrandomness in a sequence of observations.

For problems with more than two kinds of observations, Wallis and Roberts (see the references) provide the necessary formulas and simple examples.

Although runs tests are not among the strongest of the nonparametrics tests, they do have a number of rather important advantages:

1. They are easy to apply and interpret.
2. With large amounts of data, the risk of accepting a false H_0 diminishes.
3. The necessary assumptions are relatively weak.

EXERCISES

*1. The quality control department has monitored a grinding process over the last several weeks, recording sample means in the order they were taken, obtaining the following data:

Observation	Mean	Observation	Mean
1	3.21	21	3.83
2	3.49	22	3.47
3	3.91	23	3.92
4	3.77	24	4.13
5	3.67	25	4.20
6	3.88	26	3.86
7	3.51	27	3.42
8	3.40	28	3.59
9	3.89	29	3.99
10	3.43	30	3.81
11	3.22	31	3.78
12	3.35	32	4.06
13	3.60	33	3.65
14	4.02	34	3.72
15	3.61	35	3.38
16	3.90	36	4.01
17	4.23	37	3.69
18	3.91	38	3.95
19	3.41	39	4.03
20	3.67		

a. Plot the data on a graph.
b. Analyze the data using a median runs test.
c. Analyze the data using an up and down test.
d. Are the means random?

2. Traffic citations for the month of May in a small community were written for this number of motorists:

Day	1	2	3	4	5	6	7	8	9	10	11	12	13	14	15
Number	34	37	44	59	20	28	24	25	35	48	52	22	27	30	22

Day	16	17	18	19	20	21	22	23	24	25	26	27	28	29	30	31
Number	32	49	53	23	29	30	18	34	46	51	21	30	29	60	40	50

a. Analyze the data using a runs up and down test at the .01 level.
b. Analyze the data with a median test, using the .01 level.

3. Test each of the graphs in Figure 13.12 to determine if nonrandom patterns are present. Use $\alpha = .05$. There are 40 observations in each graph.

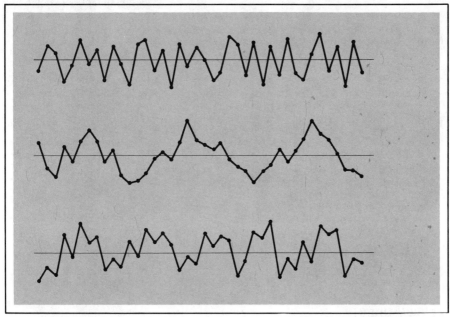

FIGURE 13.12 Data for Exercise 3.

4. An automatic screw machine's output is monitored for defective (D) pieces. Determine if the sequence is random in terms of where in the series defectives occur. Nondefectives are denoted by G. Use the .01 level.

GGGGGGG D GGGGG DD GGGGGG D GGGGG D G D GGGGGGGGGGGG

SUMMARY

The tests covered in this chapter are useful alternatives to some of the tests considered in previous chapters, tests which make certain assumptions about the populations being sampled or about population parameters. The nonparametric tests are somewhat less efficient and less discriminating than the previous tests, but the only assumption they require is that the variables being analyzed be continuous. The tests are also useful when the variable(s) being analyzed cannot be measured on a quantitative scale.

Table 13.2 presents a summary of the tests discussed in this chapter.

TABLE 13.2   Nonparametric Formulas

Test	Test statistic	Comment
sign	$z = \dfrac{x - \frac{1}{2}n}{\frac{1}{2}\sqrt{n}}$	n = no. of +'s and −'s
ranked sign	$z = \dfrac{T - [N(N+1)/4]}{\sqrt{N(N+1)(2N+1)/24}}$	N = no. of changes T = sum of ranks of either +'s or −'s
Mann-Whitney	$z = \dfrac{R_1 - (n_1/N)[N(N+1)/2]}{\sqrt{n_1 n_2 (n_1 + n_2 + 1)/12}}$	$N = n_1 + n_2$ R_1 = sum of ranks of sample 1
Kruskal-Wallis	$\chi^2 = \dfrac{12}{N(N+1)}$ $\times \left[\dfrac{(\sum R_1)^2}{n_1} + \cdots + \dfrac{(\sum R_k)^2}{n_k} \right]$ $- 3(N+1)$	$N = n_1 + n_2 + \cdots + n_k$
runs		
nominal data	$z = \dfrac{r - [(2n_1 n_2/N) + 1]}{\sqrt{(R-1)(R-2)/(N-1)}}$	$N = n_1 + n_2$ r = observed no. of runs $R = (2n_1 n_2/N) + 1$
median	$z = \dfrac{r - [(N/2) + 1]}{\sqrt{(N-1)/4}}$	N = total no. of observations r = observed no. of runs
up and down	$z = \dfrac{r - [(2N-1)/3]}{\sqrt{(16N - 29)/90}}$	N = total no. of observations r = observed no. of runs

REVIEW QUESTIONS

1. In what ways do the tests covered in this chapter differ from previous tests?
2. What is the one assumption that most nonparametric tests require?
3. How do tests for related samples differ from tests for independent samples?
4. Why can't there be a one-sample related samples test?
5. Briefly state the purpose of each of these tests:
   a. runs test
   b. Kruskal-Wallis
   c. Mann-Whitney
   d. sign test
   e. ranked sign
6. Contrast the sign test with the ranked sign test. Which is the better test?

SUPPLEMENTAL EXERCISES

1. Nineteen main courses served by three restaurants (*A, B, C*) have been ranked for taste and visual appeal by members of a gourmet club. Would you say the three are comparable (.01)?

Restaurant	A	B	B	C	A	B	A	A	A	B	C	B	A	C	B	B	C	C	B
Rank	1	2	3	4	5	6	7	8	9	10	11	12	13	14	15	16	17	18	19

2. Twenty-eight salespeople were rated on their sales presentation and then asked to view a training film on selling. Each was rated a second time. Decide if the film had a positive impact on the ratings (.05).

	Rating after film	
Rating before film	Acceptable	Not acceptable
acceptable	5	4
not acceptable	13	6

3. Solve Exercise 9, Chapter 11, page 284, using the Kruskal-Wallis test (.01).
4. Twenty-four students took a midterm and a final exam. Use the data below to determine if there was any change in grades for the two tests at the .01 level (treat as a large sample).
   a. Use a sign test.   b. Use a ranked sign test.
   c. In view of the results of the two tests, what conclusion can you make?

Improvements	Decreases
+1 +2 +3 +4 +6 +8	−2 −3 −5 −6 −7 −8 −9 −10 −11 −12 −13 −14 −15

(5 showed no change)

5. Analyze the data in Exercise 2, Chapter 10, page 261, using the appropriate nonparametric test (.01 level).
6. Use the Mann-Whitney test to determine if a new training procedure results in a decrease in average repair time (.05).

Regular	15.0	15.1	15.3	15.5	15.6	15.6	16.0	16.2
New	15.1	15.2	15.7	15.8	15.9			

7. The table below shows annual snowfall for Syracuse, New York, for winters beginning with 1902–03 and ending with the 1975–76 season. Snowfall for the 1975–1976 season is only given through February, and you may want to take that into account.
   a. Analyze the data by using both runs up and down and runs above and below the median. (Hint: Use 90 inches as the median.)
   b. Plot the data and visually compare it with the results of the runs tests.

Season	Total	Season	Total
1902–03	79.6	1942–43	76.5
1903–04	112.6	1943–44	66.5
1904–05	54.4	1944–45	128.7
1905–06	59.4	1945–46	67.8
1906–07	91.6	1946–47	110.6
1907–08	93.2	1947–48	75.8
1908–09	93.2	1948–49	76.6
1909–10	87.5	1949–50	104.2
1910–11	98.9	1950–51	92.8
1911–12	72.1	1951–52	100.5
1912–13	57.7	1952–53	77.5
1913–14	57.7	1953–54	85.9
1914–15	66.2	1954–55	101.4
1915–16	102.0	1955–56	146.8
1916–17	90.7	1956–57	76.1
1917–18	101.4	1957–58	141.1
1918–19	64.4	1958–59	137.2
1919–20	101.3	1959–60	134.8
1920–21	43.7	1960–61	130.5
1921–22	77.6	1961–62	77.3
1922–23	90.3	1962–63	116.5
1923–24	53.9	1963–64	83.3
1924–25	91.7	1964–65	97.3
1925–26	97.5	1965–66	118.8
1926–27	82.7	1966–67	83.0
1927–28	87.1	1967–68	81.2
1928–29	76.6	1968–69	127.9
1929–30	43.6	1969–70	125.5
1930–31	45.3	1970–71	157.2
1931–32	81.8	1971–72	133.7
1932–33	37.6	1972–73	81.2
1933–34	73.2	1973–74	123.2
1934–35	59.5	1974–75	105.5
1935–36	87.0	1975–76	103.0*
1936–37	79.8		
1937–38	60.7		
1938–39	102.5		
1939–40	112.7		
1940–41	93.7		
1941–42	84.7		

* Through February. (Courtesy: U.S. Weather Bureau)

REFERENCES

1. Bradley, James V., *Distribution-Free Statistical Tests*, Englewood Cliffs, N.J.: Prentice-Hall, Inc., 1968.

2. Duncan, Acheson J., *Quality Control and Industrial Statistics*, Homewood, Ill.: Richard D. Irwin, Inc., 1965, 3d ed.
3. Siegel, Sidney, *Nonparametric Statistics for the Behavioral Sciences*, New York: McGraw-Hill, 1956.
4. Wallis, W. Allen, and Harry V. Roberts, *Statistics: A New Approach*, New York: The Free Press, 1956.
5. Wonnacott, Thomas H., and Ronald J. Wonnacott, *Introductory Statistics*, New York: John Wiley & Sons, 1972; 2d ed.

14

regression and correlation

Chapter Objectives

After completing this chapter, you should be able to:
1. State the purpose of a regression analysis
2. State the purpose of correlation analysis
3. List the assumptions that underlie each of the three correlation techniques
4. List the assumptions that underlie the use of regression analysis
5. Contrast linear regression with curvilinear regression, and contrast simple regression with multiple regression analysis
6. Explain the advantages and weaknesses of multiple correlation and regression analysis in contrast to simple correlation and regression
7. Compute regression lines and correlation coefficients for problems similar to those presented in this chapter
8. Interpret correlation coefficients and regression equations
9. Develop confidence intervals for and test the significance of regression and correlation coefficients
10. Intuitively explain what correlation analysis does

Chapter Outline

Introduction
Linear Regression
    The linear equation
    Deciding on a type of relationship
Determining the Mathematical Equation
The Least Squares Method
Inferences in Regression Analysis
    The standard error of estimate
    Inferences about the slope of a regression line
    The coefficient of determination, r^2
    Analysis of variance for simple regression
    Prediction intervals in regression analysis
Multiple Linear Regression Analysis
Correlation Analysis
Continuous Data: Pearson's r
    Characteristics of r
    Product-moment correlation: conceptual approach
    Interpreting r
    A practical approach for computing r

INTRODUCTION

REGRESSION AND correlation are two closely related techniques that involve a form of estimation. The difference between these techniques and the kind of estimation discussed previously is that the previous techniques were utilized to estimate a *single population parameter,* whereas the techniques presented in this chapter are concerned with estimating a *relationship* that may exist in the population.

More specifically, *correlation and regression analysis* involve analyzing sample data to learn if and *how two or more variables relate to each other in a population.* Our concern will be mainly with two-variable situations. *Correlation* analysis yields a number that *summarizes* the *degree of relationship* between two variables; *regression* analysis results in a *mathematical equation* that *describes* the relationship. The equation can be used to estimate or *predict* future values of one variable when values of the other variable are known or assumed. *Correlation* analysis is often helpful in exploratory work when a researcher or analyst is trying to determine which variables are potentially important and the interest lies basically in the *strength of the relationship.* Very often in education and psychology, the major emphasis is on determining the strength of relationship. In other disciplines, such as business administration, economics, medical research, and agriculture, attention is focused more upon the *nature* of the relationship (i.e., the predictive equation), and *regression* analysis is the main tool.

Correlation measures the strength of a relationship between variables; *regression* yields an equation that describes the relationship in mathematical terms.

The data necessary for regression and correlation analysis come from observations of *matched variables.* For a two-variable problem, this means that each observation provides two values, one for each variable. For example, a study involving physical characteristics might focus on the age and height of each individual in the study. The two variables of interest, each person's age and height, would be matched. For a three-variable problem, each observation provides three values. For instance, in addition to each person's age and height, we might also want to include the person's weight in the analysis.

We will begin our discussion of the investigation of relationships in a population by considering regression analysis. The matter of correlation analysis will be taken up later in the chapter.

LINEAR REGRESSION

Simple linear regression involves the attempt to develop a straight-line or linear mathematical equation that describes the relationship between two variables.

There are a number of ways in which regression equations are used. One use is for situations in which the two variables measure approximately the same thing but one variable is relatively expensive, or otherwise unattractive to work with, while the other variable is not. For example, strength of a metal and hardness may be related, so that if we know the hardness of the metal, we can pretty much estimate its strength. If the test for strength destroys the metal, while the test for hardness does not, someone interested in estimating strength might obviously prefer to rely on hardness test results to estimate strength. The purpose of a regression equation would be to *estimate* values of one variable based on known values of the other.

Another way regression equations are used is to explain values of the one variable in terms of the other variable. That is, we may suspect a cause and effect relationship between two variables. For instance, an economist may attempt to explain changes in demand for used automobiles in terms of the level of unemployment. A farmer might suspect that the amount of fertilizer he used influenced crop yield. A car's speed would presumably by a factor in braking distance. It should be noted, however, that the logic of a causal relationship must come from theories outside of the realm of statistics. Regression analysis merely indicates what, if any, mathematical relationship there might be. In other words, neither regression or correlation can show that one variable tends to "cause" certain values of another variable.

Still a third use of a regression equation is to predict *future* values of a variable. For instance, screening tests are often administered to potential employees or students in an effort to predict potential for success in school or on a job. Presumably there is a mathematical relationship between test score and future potential.

Although such relationships might assume a wide variety of forms, the discussion here will be limited to linear equations. Linear, or straight-line, equations are important because they closely approximate many real world relationships and because they are relatively easy to work with and interpret. Other forms of regression analysis, such as multiple (more than two variables) and curvilinear (other than straight-line relationships) regression, involve extensions of the same concepts used in simple linear regression.

The Linear Equation

Two important features of a linear equation are (1) the slope of the line and (2) the height, or location, of the line at some point. A linear equation has the form

$$y = a + bx$$

where a and b are values determined from sample data; a indicates the height of the line at $x = 0$ and b indicates its slope. The variable y is the variable to be predicted and x is the predictor variable.

Figure 14.1 illustrates the relationship between the graph of a straight line and its equation. The line, with equation $y = a + bx$, intersects the y-axis at the point $y = a$. This point is called the y intercept. The slope of the line, b, indicates the amount of change in y per one unit change in x, or $\Delta y / \Delta x$.

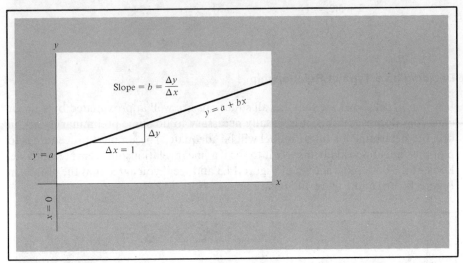

FIGURE 14.1   The equation $y = a + bx$ is a straight line with slope b and y intercept a.

Consider the linear equation $y = 5 + 3x$, which is shown in Figure 14.2. The line intersects the y-axis at the point where $y = 5$. The slope of the line is 3, which indicates that for every 1-unit change in x, there will be a corresponding three-unit change in y. The equation can be used to determine values of y for various values of x, as shown in the table that follows. This latter approach (i.e., substituting values of x in the mathematical equation and solving for y) is usually preferable to reading values from the graph because it permits a much higher degree

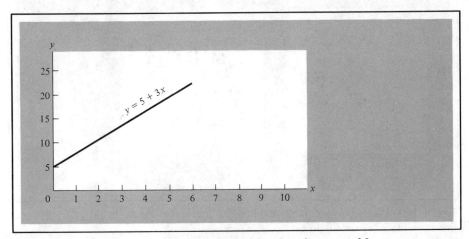

FIGURE 14.2   The line $y = 5 + 3x$ has a slope of 3 and a y intercept of 5.

of precision than is possible using an ordinary graph. These graphs are important, though, because they create a mental image of the relationship. Also, in the initial part of data analysis, they can be useful in deciding if a linear relationship is appropriate.

| | $y = 5 + 3x$ |
Value of x	Computed value of y
2	$5 + 3(2) = 11$
3.1	$5 + 3(3.1) = 14.3$
7.2	$5 + 3(7.2) = 26.6$

Deciding on a Type of Relationship

It is important to realize that not all situations are well approximated by a linear equation. Because of this, it is usually necessary to do some preliminary work in order to determine if a linear model will be adequate. The simplest procedure is to plot the data and visually inspect it to see if a linear relationship seems reasonable. Look at the data plots shown in Figure 14.3 and see if you agree that the graphs in Figure 14.3(b) and Figure 14.3(c) are linear.

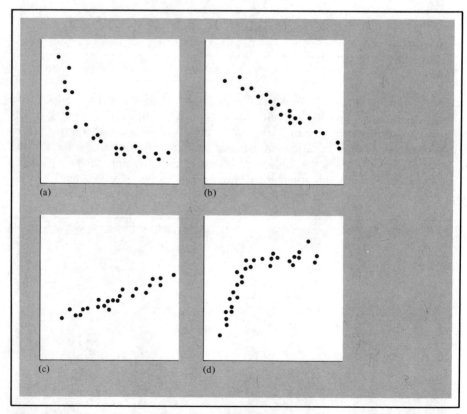

FIGURE 14.3   Not all two-variable relationships are linear. Points in (b) and (c) appear linear; points in (a) and (d) do not.

When data cannot be approximated with a linear model, the alternatives are either to search for a suitable *nonlinear* model* or to transform the data into a linear form. For example, converting one or both scales to logarithms sometimes yields a linear model. This would probably produce a straight line for the data shown in Figure 14.3(a).

EXERCISES

1. What is the equation of a straight line with these characteristics?
   a. slope of 10.2 and y-intercept of 5.0
   b. slope of 55 and y-intercept of 0
   c. slope of 27 and y-intercept of -2
   d. slope of -13 and y-intercept of 200
   e. slope of zero and y-intercept of 2.4
2. Estimate the values of a and b in the linear equation $y_c = a + bx$ from the graphs shown in Figure 14.4.

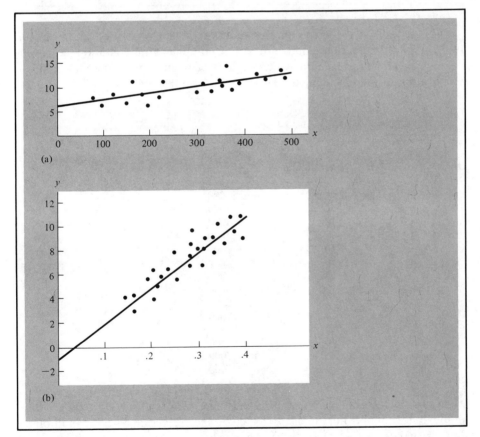

FIGURE 14.4

* These will be mentioned briefly. More detailed explanations can be found in more advanced books.

DETERMINING THE MATHEMATICAL EQUATION

Let us now turn our attention to the mechanics of obtaining the equation of a straight line that best describes a set of observations. As an example, suppose we want to determine if there is a relationship between the mileage of a used car and its selling price. That is, we want to learn if price depends on a car's mileage. In regression terms, mileage would be designated as the *independent*, or "explaining," variable, and selling price the *dependent*, or "explained," variable. It is traditional to use the symbol x to represent values of the independent variable and the symbol y for values of the dependent variable.

> In regression, the y-values are predicted from given or known values of x. The variable y is called the *dependent* variable and the variable x is called the *independent* variable.

Suppose we have gathered data from area car dealers on mileage and prices of 1975 cars of a certain brand and with certain equipment (air conditioning, power steering, etc.). The *sample* data, which might have come from a random sample of area dealers, would look something like the data shown in Table 14.1.

TABLE 14.1   Hypothetical Sample Data: Car Mileage and Selling Price

i Observation	x_i Mileage (in thousands)	y_i Selling price
1	40	$1000
2	30	1500
3	30	1200
4	25	1800
5	50	800
6	60	1000
7	65	500
8	10	3000
9	15	2500
10	20	2000
11	55	800
12	40	1500
13	35	2000
14	30	2000

To simplify the example, the mileage and price figures have been rounded. And although it would be more realistic to include such things as general condition of the car (e.g., rust, dents, etc.), color, and dealer location, for purposes of illustrating the technique for finding a suitable equation, only mileage is included here.

The data of Table 14.1 is plotted in Figure 14.5 for the purpose of deciding if a straight line can adequately describe the data. Now, while it is apparent that it would be impossible to find a straight line that would go through each and every

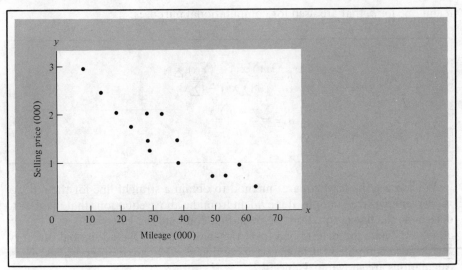

FIGURE 14.5   The data seem to show a linear relationship between mileage and selling price.

point, it does appear that a linear relationship would be reasonably consistent with the sample data.

THE LEAST SQUARES METHOD

The most widely used method for fitting a straight line to a set of points is known as the *least squares* technique. The resulting line has two important characteristics: (1) the sum of the *vertical* deviations of the points from the line is zero, and (2) the sum of the squared vertical deviations is minimized (i.e., no other line would have a smaller sum of squared deviations). Symbolically, the value that is minimized is

$$\sum (y_i - y_c)^2$$

where

y_i = an observed value of y

y_c = the computed value of y using the least squares equation with the matching value of x for y_i

The values of a and b for the line $y_c = a + bx$, which minimizes the sum of the squared deviations, are the solutions to the so-called "*normal equations*":

$$\sum y = na + b(\sum x)$$
$$\sum xy = a(\sum x) + b(\sum x^2)$$

where n is the number of paired observations. Thus obtaining the various quantities such as $\sum x, \sum xy$, and so on, we could solve these two simultaneous equations for a and b. However, the equation can be solved algebraically for a and b, and this provides a much simpler format to work with. The result is two formulas, one for *a* and one for *b*, that are used for computational purposes:

$$b = \frac{n(\sum xy) - (\sum x)(\sum y)}{n(\sum x^2) - (\sum x)^2}$$

$$a = \frac{\sum y - b \sum x}{n}$$

We can use the least squares method to obtain a straight line for the mileage versus selling price example. It is evident from the above equations that in order to determine the linear equation, we must first compute the values of $\sum x$, $\sum y$, $\sum x^2$, and $\sum xy$. These are determined from the sample data. One additional quantity, $\sum y^2$, is also computed for later use. Note that $n = 14$ paired observations. These calculations are shown in Table 14.2.

TABLE 14.2 Calculations for the Data of Table 14.1

Observation	Mileage (in thousands) x	Selling price y	xy	x^2	y^2
1	40	$1,000	40,000	1600	1,000,000
2	30	1,500	45,000	900	2,250,000
3	30	1,200	36,000	900	1,440,000
4	25	1,800	45,000	625	3,240,000
5	50	800	40,000	2500	640,000
6	60	1,000	60,000	3600	1,000,000
7	65	500	32,500	4225	250,000
8	10	3,000	30,000	100	9,000,000
9	15	2,500	37,500	225	6,250,000
10	20	2,000	40,000	400	4,000,000
11	55	800	44,000	3025	640,000
12	40	1,500	60,000	1600	2,250,000
13	35	2,000	70,000	1225	4,000,000
14	30	2,000	60,000	900	4,000,000
	$\sum x = 505$	$\sum y = 21,600$	$\sum xy = 640,000$	$\sum x^2 = 21,825$	$\sum y^2 = 39,960,000$

From Table 14.2, we have

$$b = \frac{14(640,000) - (505)(21,600)}{14(21,825) - (505)^2} = \frac{8,960,000 - 10,908,000}{305,550 - 255,025}$$

$$= \frac{-1,948,000}{50,525} = -38.56$$

$$a = \frac{\sum y - b(\sum x)}{n} = \frac{21,600 - (-38.56)(505)}{14} = \frac{40,979.4}{14} = 2,934$$

The resulting regression equation, $y_c = a + bx$, is then

$$y_c = 2,934 - 38.56x$$

The equation can be interpreted in the following manner. The expected selling price of a 1975 car is $2,934 minus $38.56 for each thousand miles the car has been driven. For example, for a car with 20,000 miles, the equation suggests a selling price of $2,934 − 38.56(20) = $2,163.

It is important to recognize certain facts concerning a regression equation. One is that it pertains to an *average* relationship; so a car with some given mileage will not necessarily bring the *exact* selling price indicated by the equation. Another important point is that it would by very risky to attempt to use this equation for prices and mileage outside of the range of data. In other words, although we were reasonably satisfied that the relationship was linear from a quick plot of the data, higher- or lower-mileage cars need not necessarily exhibit the same relationship between price and mileage. Figure 14.6 illustrates what can happen.

The regression line has the interesting property of always passing through the point $\bar{x}, \bar{y}$. This information is helpful in dealing with certain kinds of problems.

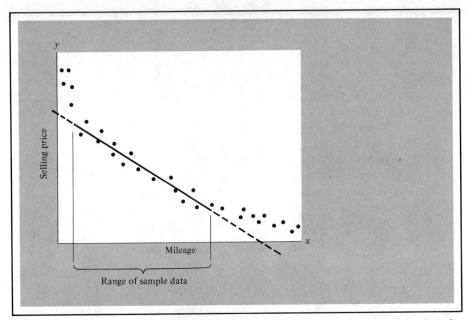

FIGURE 14.6   The danger in extrapolating beyond the range of sampled data is that the same relationship may not exist.

EXERCISES

1. Suppose that a supermarket chain financed a study of annual expenditures on groceries for families of four. The investigation was limited to families with incomes after taxes in a range of $8,000 to $20,000. The following equation was derived:

$$y_c = -200 + .10x$$

   where

$$y_c = \text{estimated annual expenditures on groceries}$$
$$x = \text{annual income after taxes}$$

Assume the equation provides a reasonably good fit and that the data were obtained through random sampling methods.

a. Estimate expenditures for a family of four with an annual income of $15,000.

b. One of the vice-presidents of the firm is disturbed by the fact that the equation apparently suggests that a family with an income of $2,000 would not spend anything on groceries. How would you answer her?

c. Explain briefly why the above equation *could not* be used for each of these:

(1) Extimating grocery expenditures for families of five.

(2) Estimating grocery expenditures for families with net incomes of $20,000 to $35,000.

d. Plot the equation on a sheet of graph paper and label each axis.

2. An engineering consulting team has established the following relationship for city mileage for six-cylinder American cars in the weight range of 1500 lb to 3000 lb (150-lb driver):

$$y_c = 30 - .002x$$

where

$$y = \text{estimated miles per gallon}$$
$$x = \text{car weight}$$

a. Plot this relationship on a graph and label the axes.

b. Estimate gas mileage for a car that weighs:

(1) 2000 lb   (2) 1500 lb   (3) 2500 lb

(Use your graph and check the answers using the equation.)

3. Use the summary values given in the following to determine the regression equations:

a. $\sum x = 200$, $\sum y = 300$, $\sum xy = 6200$, $\sum x^2 = 3600$, $n = 20$

b. $\sum x = 7.2$, $\sum y = 37$, $\sum xy = 3100$, $\sum x^2 = 620$, $n = 36$

c. $\sum x = 700$, $\sum y = -250$, $\sum xy = -1,400$, $\sum x^2 = 21,000$, $n = 30$

d. $\sum x = 33$, $\sum y = 207$, $\sum xy = 525$, $\sum x^2 = 750$, $n = 40$

4. For each set of data, plot the data on a graph and, if a linear equation seems appropriate, determine the coefficients a and b from the data.

a.

Size of order x	Total cost y
25	$2000
20	3500
40	1000
45	800
22	3000
63	1300
70	1500
60	1100
55	950
50	900
30	1600

b.

Sales (in thousands) x	Revenue (in thousands) y
201	17
225	20
305	21
380	23
560	25
600	24
685	27
735	27
510	22
725	30
450	21
370	19
150	15

5. Determine an equation that describes the relationship between accident frequency and level of preventive (educational) effort for these data:

Man-hours per month for education	Accidents per million man-hours
200	7.0
500	6.4
450	5.2
800	4.0
900	3.1
150	8.0
300	6.5
600	4.4

6. A company with 15 suburban department stores has compiled data on square footage of sales area versus monthly revenues. Plot the data, and if a linear model seems appropriate, determine the regression equation.

Store	Monthly revenue (in thousands)	Square feet (in thousands)
A	45	55
B	115	200
C	120	180
D	95	110
E	75	90
F	170	260
G	110	140
H	140	215
I	130	200
J	75	85
K	80	90
L	105	180
M	200	300
N	95	130
O	60	80

7. Rework Exercise 5 using accidents per month as the x variable and level of education as the y variable. Compare the resulting equation to the one obtained in Exercise 5.

8. Use the data below for the following:
   a. Compute the coefficients of the regression equation.
   b. Double each value of x and recompute the coefficients.
   c. Double both the original x's and y's and recompute the coefficients.
   d. Use the original x's but add 2 to each original y and recompute the regression equation.

								Totals
x	1	2	3	4	5	6	7	28
y	2	4	5	6	7	7	9	40

9. Determine a predictive equation for amount of term insurance as a function of annual income for these data:

Annual income (in thousands)	Insurance
20	10
25	12
26	15
18	10
16	15
17	20
32	30
13	5
38	40
40	50
42	40

INFERENCES IN REGRESSION ANALYSIS

The sample data used to compute a regression line can be thought of as a relatively small number of possible observations from an infinite population of paired values. In this sense the computed regression line can be regarded as an *estimate* of the real, but unknown, relationship that exists between the two variables in the population. Hence the regression coefficients a and b serve as point estimates of two corresponding population parameters, A and B, and the equation

$$y_c = a + bx$$

is an estimate of the population relationship $y = A + Bx + e$, where e represents scatter in the population. The concept of a population of paired values is portrayed in Figure 14.7. Note that even in the population the values do not fall on a single straight line but tend to exhibit some degree of scatter or dispersion. In fact, if there were no dispersion in the population, all the sample observations would fall on a single straight line, and there would be no need to develop inferences about the true values in the population. Unfortunately, few real life examples of populations with no scatter exist.

A reasonable question at this point might be, "Why is there scatter?" The answer lies in the fact that there is not a perfect relationship between the two variables in the population. There are other variables that influence values of the dependent variable, perhaps a surprisingly large number of other variables, which are not included in the regression analysis. In the case of selling price, factors in

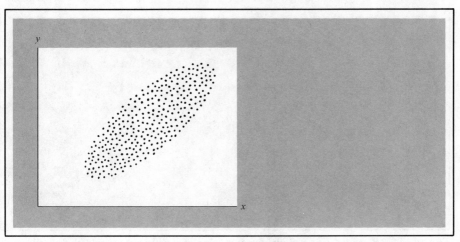

FIGURE 14.7   Population of possible values, with relationship $y = A + B + e$.

addition to mileage that might influence selling price are general condition of the car, location of the dealer with respect to other dealers and in relationship to a buyer's residence or place of work, the dealer's reputation for service, advertising, skill of the salesperson, time of day, weather, how desperately the buyer wants the car, and so on. You might wonder why these other variables are not included in the study. The answer is that the influence of each is probably slight, and the cost of including such factors often outweighs the benefit that might be derived by including them. Moreover, one or two variables usually account for most of the variation in the dependent variable, so there is little to be gained by trying to completely explain how selling price is determined. What is more, the number of potential explaining variables is so great that it would undoubtedly be impossible— or highly improbable—to achieve a perfect description anyway. One consequence of this is that there will always be some scatter present. And this scatter means that sample statistics will tend to differ from actual population parameters. Thus there are many different regression equations which could conceivably be obtained, as suggested in Figure 14.8.

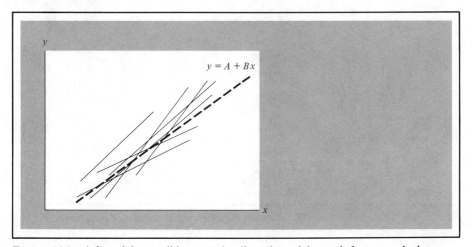

FIGURE 14.8   A few of the possible regression lines that might result from sample data.

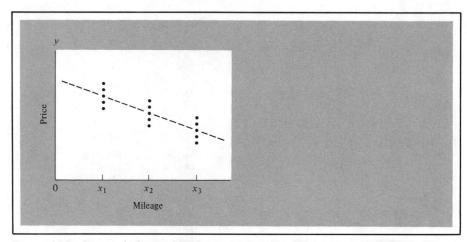

FIGURE 14.9   Repeated observations for any value of x will tend to yield slightly different values of y. Three possible x's are shown.

The scatter in the population means that for any given value of x, there will be many possible values of y. Thus if a number of cars with identical mileage are sold, prices for that mileage will vary, as illustrated in Figure 14.9.

Regression analysis assumes that for each possible value of x there is a distribution of potential y's that is *normally* distributed. This is called a *conditional* (i.e., given x) distribution. The conditional distribution amounts to a thin vertical slice of the population taken at a given value of x. The mean of each conditional distribution is equal to the average value of y in the population for that particular x: $y = A + Bx$ is estimated by $y_c = a + bx$. See Figure 14.10. It is further assumed

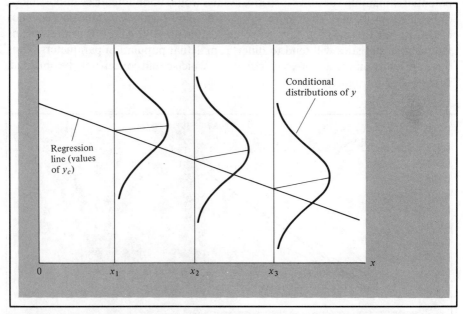

FIGURE 14.10   Regression analysis assumes that for each possible value of x, there is a conditional distribution of possible y's that is normal. Three possible x's are shown.

that all conditional distributions have the same standard deviation and that y is a random variable (i.e., x's may be preselected but not y's). Thus the assumptions for regression analysis are as follows:

1. There are measurement data for both x and y.
2. The dependent variable is a random variable.
3. For each value of x, there is a conditional distribution of y's which is normally distributed.
4. The standard deviations of all the conditional distributions are equal.

The Standard Error of Estimate

The question that naturally arises in regression analysis is, "How accurate are the various regression estimates?" The primary determinant of accuracy is the amount of scatter in the population: the greater the scatter, the less the accuracy of the estimates. The amount of scatter in the population can be estimated from the scatter of sample observations around the computed regression line, using the formula

$$s_e = \sqrt{\frac{\sum (y_i - y_c)^2}{n - 2}}$$

where

$y_i =$ each y-value

$y_c =$ corresponding regression line value from regression equation

$n =$ number of observations

This is simply a computation of standard deviation, with y_c replacing the sample mean and with $n - 2$ in the denominator instead of $n - 1$. The reason for $n - 2$ is that two degrees of freedom are lost in computing the two constants a and b in the regression equation. The use of y_c instead of $\bar{y}$ stems from the fact that we want to use the regression line as our center, or reference point, rather than the sample mean in order to measure the *scatter around the line*.

The above formula is not ordinarily used for actual computations because a shortcut formula (obtained by substituting the regression equation for y_c and completing the square) is easier to work with. It is

$$s_e = \sqrt{\frac{\sum y^2 - a \sum y - b \sum xy}{n - 2}}$$

The computation of the standard error is predicated on the assumption that there is uniform scatter* of the points around the regression line, which is another way of saying the conditional distributions of y-values are assumed to have equal standard deviations.

* The technical name for this is "homoscedasticity."

The standard error of estimate for the mileage versus selling price data would be computed in the following way:*

$$s_e = \sqrt{\frac{\sum y^2 - a \sum y - b \sum xy}{n - 2}}$$

$$= \sqrt{\frac{39,960,000 - 2,934(21,600) - (-38.56)(640,000)}{14 - 2}}$$

$$= \sqrt{\frac{39,960,000 - 63,374,400 + 24,678,400}{12}} = \sqrt{105,333} = 324.55$$

This is the standard deviation of the distribution of points around the regression line. In the following pages you will learn how this information can be used to construct confidence intervals and to measure the goodness of fit of the line.

Inferences About the Slope of a Regression Line

Even when there is little or no relationship between two variables in a population, it is still possible to obtain sample values that make it appear that the variables are related. For example, Figure 14.11(a) depicts a *population* in which x and y are unrelated, as evidenced by the scatter of the points on the graph. Figure 14.11(b) shows some possible *sample* observations from the same population. Notice that there does seem to be a relationship, since we can easily imagine a straight line which would fit the points. What has happened is that chance factors in sampling have produced a "relationship" where none exists.

It is important, then, to test the results of such computations in order to decide if the results are significant (i.e., if the true parameters are nonzero). Hence we want to distinguish between those occasions in which two variables are related and those in which the variables are not related. If there is no relationship, we would expect a slope of zero. Thus we want to test the null hypothesis

$$H_0: B = 0$$

against the alternative

$$H_1: B \neq 0$$

The significance of the regression coefficient can be tested by comparing it to its standard deviation s_b. That is,*

$$t = \frac{\text{sample value} - \text{expected value}}{\text{standard deviation}} = \frac{b - 0}{s_b} = \frac{b}{s_b}$$

If this ratio is relatively small, this would tend to imply that the true value may actually be 0, while if the ratio is relatively large, the opposite would be implied. Figure 14.12 illustrates this concept. The sampling distribution of the relative

---

* Using figures obtained previously in the chapter. The exact answer will vary with the extent of rounding used.

** It is also possible to test the hypothesis that $b = B$; that is, the hypothesis that the slope is a certain specified value. The formula for t thus becomes

$$t = \frac{b - B}{s_b}$$

and the alternative could be either one- or two-sided.

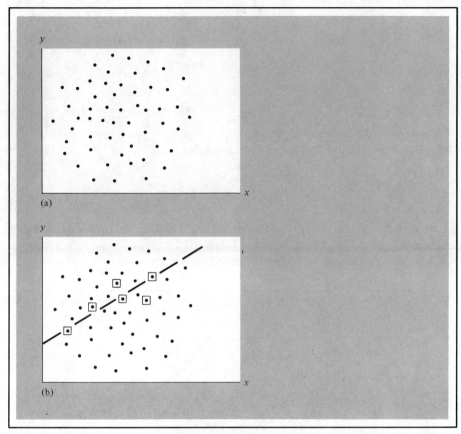

FIGURE 14.11 (a) A population with no relationship between two variables. (b) Hypothetical sample observations from the population make it appear that there is a relationship.

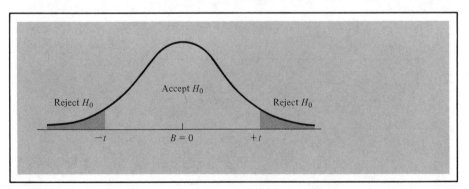

FIGURE 14.12 The slope is considered nonzero if t_{test} exceeds $\pm t_{\text{table}}$

difference is a t distribution with $n - 2$ degrees of freedom. Thus the critical value obtained from a t table is used to determine whether the relative size of b is large or small.

The standard deviation of the sampling distribution for the slope is calculated using the formula

$$s_b = s_e \sqrt{\frac{1}{\sum x^2 - [(\sum x)^2 / n]}}$$

For the mileage example, using the previously determined values

$$s_e = 324.55 \qquad \sum x^2 = 21{,}825 \qquad (\sum x)^2 = 255{,}025$$

we find

$$s_b = 324.55 \sqrt{\frac{1}{21{,}825 - (255{,}025/14)}} = 324.55 \sqrt{\frac{1}{3608.9}} = 5.40$$

Using $b = -38.56$ and $n = 14$, the test statistic is

$$t_{\text{test}} = \frac{b - 0}{s_b} = \frac{-38.56}{5.4} = -7.14$$

As illustrated in Figure 14.13, this is significant at the .01 level (with 12 degrees of freedom, $t_{.005} = 3.055$). Hence there is some relationship; the slope is not zero. Some additional examples of significance testing are provided in Table 14.3.

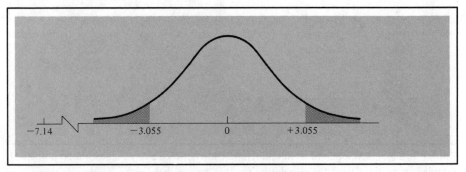

FIGURE 14.13   Conclude the slope is nonzero.

TABLE 14.3   Examples of Significance Tests for the Slope of a Line

	Given		Compute	From t table	Decision
b	s_b	$n-2$	b/s_b	$t_{.025}$	Conclude
2.0	1.0	10	2.0	2.23	Accept H_0
.5	.1	18	5.0	2.10	Reject H_0
−9.0	1.5	25	−6.0	2.06	Reject H_0
−.6	.4	30	−1.5	2.04	Accept H_0
4.0	1.0	100	4.0	≈1.96	Reject H_0

Note: $H_0: B = 0$ and $H_1: B \neq 0$.

It may be more informative to establish a confidence interval for the true value B rather than to merely test the significance of b. That is, the significance test may indicate that the true value is probably not zero. The natural question, then, is, "What *is* the true value?" This leads us back to the confidence interval for B. The confidence interval is $b \pm ts_b$, or, alternatively,

$$b - ts_b \leq B \leq b + ts_b$$

Actually, the confidence interval can serve a dual purpose. To be sure, it indicates the probable range in which the true value may lie, but it also can be used to test the significance of a sample slope. For example, if a confidence interval for B includes zero, this would be equivalent to a significance test in which $H_0: B = 0$ could not be rejected. If H_0 specifies some value other than zero, and this value is included in the confidence interval, then that claim could not be rejected. The main reason for even considering the significance test for slope is that such a test is typical of regression analysis on a computer.

Table 14.4 shows some examples with 95% confidence intervals which use the data from Table 14.3. Notice that for intervals that overlap $B = 0$, our previous significance test indicated we would accept H_0.

TABLE 14.4   95% Confidence Intervals for the Slope of a Regression Line

b	s_b	$n - 2$	$t_{.025}$	Interval	Comment
2.0	1.0	10	2.23	$-.23 \leq B \leq 4.23$	B may be 0 since 0 is in the interval
.5	.1	18	2.10	$.29 \leq B \leq .71$	
-9.0	1.5	25	2.06	$-12.09 \leq B \leq -5.91$	
$-.6$	.4	30	2.04	$-1.42 \leq B \leq +.22$	B may be 0
4.0	1.0	100	≈ 1.96	$2.04 \leq B \leq 5.96$	

For the mileage data, a 95% confidence interval for the slope of the regression line is

$$b \pm ts_b = -38.56 \pm 2.179(5.4)$$

or

$$-26.79 \text{ to } -50.33$$

The Coefficient of Determination, r^2

One useful measure associated with the regression line is the degree to which predictions based on the regression equation are superior to predictions based on $\bar{y}$. That is, if predictions based on the line are no better than using the average value of y, there is no value in having a regression equation. A significance test for B will indicate whether or not the slope is nonzero, but it is difficult to translate that into a measure which reflects the extent to which values of y are related to values of x. On the other hand, the coefficient of determination, r^2, is directly concerned with this. For example, consider the dispersion of points in Figure 14.14(a) around $\bar{y}$ as opposed to the (vertical) dispersion of points around the regression line as depicted in Figure 14.14(b). If the dispersion (error) associated with the line is much smaller than the dispersion (error) associated with $\bar{y}$, predictions based on the line will be better than those based on $\bar{y}$. The variation of points around $\bar{y}$ is called the *total* variation, and it is computed as the sum of the squared deviations:

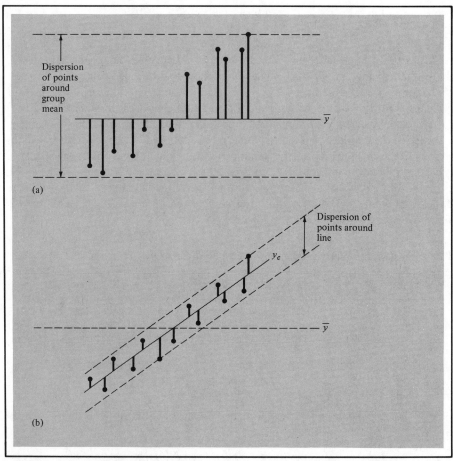

FIGURE 14.14 A comparison of a scatter of y's around the regression line against a scatter of y's around $\bar{y}$ indicates the extent to which predictions based on the line are superior to those based on $\bar{y}$.

$$\text{total variation} = \sum(y_i - \bar{y})^2$$

The vertical deviations of y_i's around the regression line are called the "unexplained" variation, because they cannot be explained by the value of x alone (i.e., there is *still* dispersion even after the line is taken into account). The unexplained variation is computed as the sum of the squared deviations around the line:

$$\text{unexplained variation} = \sum(y_i - y_c)^2$$

The amount of deviation explained by the regression line is the difference between the total variation and the unexplained variation:

$$\text{explained variation} = \text{total variation} - \text{unexplained variation}$$

The percentage of explained variation, r^2, is the ratio of the explained variation to the total variation:

$$r^2 = \frac{\text{explained variation}}{\text{total variation}} = \frac{\text{total variation} - \text{unexplained variation}}{\text{total variation}}$$

From a computational standpoint, the use of variances instead of sums of squares is a useful alternative. It is important to note that in correlation and regression equations, the computation of the variance of y values, s_y, has $n - 2$ in the denominator, rather than the usual $n - 1$.

$$s_y^2 = \frac{n(\sum y^2) - (\sum y)^2/n}{n - 2}$$

Using variances, the formula for computing r^2 is:

$$r^2 = \frac{s_y^2 - s_e^2}{s_y^2} = 1 - \frac{s_e^2}{s_y^2} = 1 - \frac{[\sum(y_i - y_c)^2]/(n - 2)}{[\sum(y_i - \bar{y})^2]/(n - 2)}$$

For the mileage versus selling price example, we can compute s_y^2:

$$s_y^2 = \frac{39{,}960{,}000 - 21{,}600^2/14}{14 - 2} = 552{,}857.1$$

$$r^2 = 1 - \frac{s_e^2}{s_y^2} = 1 - \frac{(324.55)^2}{552{,}857.1} = .81$$

The value of r^2 can range from 0 to 1.00. When the unexplained variation is a large percentage of the total variation (i.e., the explained variation is a small percentage of the total), r^2 will be small. Conversely, when scatter is small around the regression line relative to the total variation of the y-values around their mean, this means that the explained variation accounts for a large percentage of the total variation, and r^2 will be much closer to 1.00.

Hence the fact that $r^2 = .81$ in our example indicates that approximately 81% of the *variation* in selling price of 1975 automobiles is related to variation in mileage. In other words, 19% of the variation is unexplained by mileage. This means that predictions based on the regression equation will match fairly well the actual prices. Thus the fact that r^2 is not near 0 suggests that the equation represents quite an improvement over using the mean $\bar{y}$ as a predictor. The problem here does not seem to be one of using a linear equation when perhaps a curvilinear equation would do better, because we checked that initially by plotting the data before proceeding with the computations. Instead, it would seem more reasonable to suppose that other variables that were not included in the study may be important. When more than two variables are analyzed using regression techniques, the term "multiple regression analysis" is used. This topic is briefly discussed later in this chapter.

Analysis of Variance for Simple Regression*

The significance of the regression line can be tested using analysis of variance techniques. You may recall that the F test is valid if it can be assumed that k *independent* samples have been drawn from normal populations with equal variances (homoscedasticity). Hence we assume the observations have come from normal populations with equal variances, and we test for *independence* among the k (which is equal to 2) variables.

Recall the form of the F test:

$$F = \frac{\text{between estimate of variance}}{\text{within estimate of variance}}$$

In terms of regression analysis, this is

$$F = \frac{\sum(y_c - \bar{y})^2/1}{\sum(y_i - y_c)^2/(n-2)}$$

or

$$F = \frac{\text{between sum of squares (SSR)}/1}{\text{within sum of squares (SSE)}/(n-2)}$$

Note that the total sum of squares, SST, is equal to SSR + SSE. Ordinarily, the quantities SST and SSE are easily obtained, and SSR is found by subtraction SSR = SST − SSE. Thus for the mileage versus selling price example, we have

$$\text{SSR} = 6,634,286.9 - 1,263,992 = 5,370,295$$

and F is

$$F = \frac{5,370,295/1}{1,263,992/12} = 50.98$$

The computations are summarized in Table 14.5, and the results portrayed in Figure 14.15. Since the table value of F (.05 level, with numerator d.f. = 1 and

---

* This section may be omitted without loss of continuity.

TABLE 14.5   Summary of Analysis of Variance Computations for the Mileage Versus Selling Price Example

Source of variation	Sum of squares	Degrees of freedom	Mean square
regression line (between)	$\text{SSR} = \sum(y_c - \bar{y})^2$ $= 5{,}370{,}295$	1	$\sum(y_c - \bar{y})^2/1 = 5{,}370{,}295$
error (within)	$\text{SSE} = \sum(y_i - y_c)^2$ $= 1{,}263{,}992$	$n - 2 = 12$	$\sum(y_i - y_c)^2/(n - 2) = s_e^2$ $= 105{,}333$
total	$\text{SST} = \sum(y_i - \bar{y})^2$ $= 6{,}634{,}286.9$	$n - 1 = 13$	$s_y^2 = 510{,}330$

$$F = \frac{\text{mean square (between)}}{\text{mean square (within)}} = \frac{5{,}370{,}295}{105{,}333} = 50.98$$

denominator d.f. = 12) is much less than the computed value, the null hypothesis of no relationship is rejected, as shown in Figure 14.15.

It is worthwhile to note that the test value of F is exactly equal to the square of the value of t we found when testing the slope of the line for significance [i.e., $t = -7.14$, $t^2 = (-7.14)^2 = 50.98$]. This is no mere coincidence. The F test with numerator degrees of freedom equal to 1 is equivalent to a t test.

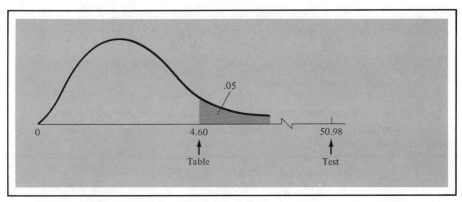

FIGURE 14.15 H_0 is rejected; there is a relationship.

Prediction Intervals in Regression Analysis

The predicted value of y obtained from the regression equation for a specified value of x can be viewed in two ways. It can refer to the average or *mean* value of y for a given value of x, or it can refer to an individual value of y that might be expected. The value in either case would be the same, but the confidence interval for that prediction will depend on which viewpoint is being used. For instance, the local trade organization of automobile dealers may want to estimate the *average* selling price for a car with 18,000 miles; a dealer may want to estimate the price he can expect for an *individual* car.

The confidence intervals for these predictions are based on the standard deviations of their respective quantities. For the average value of y, the standard deviation of y_c is

$$s_{y_c} = s_e \sqrt{\frac{1}{n} + \frac{(x_g - \bar{x})^2}{\sum x^2 - [(\sum x)^2/n]}}$$

where x_g is a given value of x. And for the individual values of y, a single term, 1, is added to the expression under the square root sign:

$$s_{y_i} = s_e \sqrt{1 + \frac{1}{n} + \frac{(x_g - \bar{x})^2}{\sum x^2 - [(\sum x)^2/n]}}$$

The implication of these last two equations is that the confidence interval for individual y-values for a given value of x is slightly larger than the interval for the average value of y. The individual values are analogous to a *population* of values, while the average values are analogous to a *sampling distribution of means* from that population. The latter would always tend to have a smaller standard deviation than the population standard deviation.

Since it is apparent from the standard deviation formulas that the width of the confidence intervals for y_c and y_i are different for different values of x_g, it will be necessary to choose some value of x_g for purposes of illustration. Suppose we want confidence intervals for $x = 20$ (i.e., 20,000) miles. Thus $x_g = 20$. Remember, too, that $\bar{x} = 505/14 = 36.07$. The standard errors are

$$s_{y_c} = 324.55 \sqrt{\frac{1}{14} + \frac{(x_g - \bar{x})^2}{3608.9}} = 324.55 \sqrt{.071 + \frac{258.25}{3608.9}}$$

$$= 324.55 \sqrt{.071 + .072} = 324.55 \sqrt{.143} = 324.55(.378) = 122.68$$

$$s_{y_i} = 324.55(1.069) = 346.98$$

In summary, we can compute standard deviations for the average value of y for a given value of x and for the individual of y for that same x. Using $x = 20$, we have:

average y when $x = 20$: $s_{y_c} = 122.68$

individual y when $x = 20$: $s_{y_i} = 346.98$

y_c when $x = 20$: $y_c = 2934 - 38.56(20) = 2163$

$t_{.025}$ with $n - 2 = 12$ d.f.: 2.179

The corresponding 95% confidence intervals are

average y: $y_c \pm ts_{y_c} = 2163 \pm 2.179(122.68)$ or $1896 to $2430

individual y: $y_i \pm ts_{y_i} = 2163 \pm 2.179(346.98)$ or $1407 to $2919

If it were possible to compute confidence intervals for all the possible values of x, the result would be a pair of *confidence bands* around the regression line, as shown in Figure 14.16. Note that the bands (and hence the confidence intervals) are narrowest when $x_g = \bar{x}$, and that they get progressively wider as the distance of x_g from the mean increases.

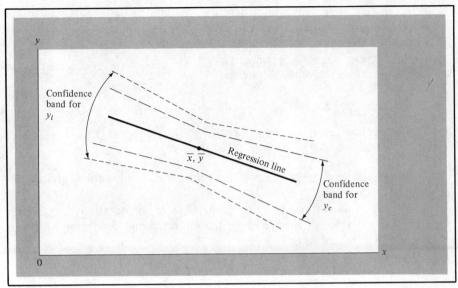

FIGURE 14.16   Confidence bands for both y_i and $\bar{y}$ for a given x increase as the distance from $\bar{x}$ increases.

EXERCISES

1. Determine which slopes for the following data are significant at the .05 level. Use $n - 2$ degrees of freedom.

	a.	b.	c.	d.	e.	f.
b	4	−.15	1.2	.6	−212	.015
s_b	1	.10	.6	.2	38	.001
n	12	20	25	31	50	100

2. Determine 99% confidence intervals for each of these regression coefficients and indicate which slopes are significant:

	a.	b.	c.	d.	e.
b	8.2	.13	5.213	145	−7.1
s_b	4.1	.04	1.50	40	3.0
n	50	30	20	66	9

3. Use the data below for the following:
   a. Compute the regression equation.
   b. Compute s_e and then s_b.
   c. Determine if b is significant using a confidence interval with $\alpha = .05$.

Test scores	A	B	C	D	E	F	G	H	I	J	Totals
1st test	80	95	88	98	94	74	81	86	90	69	855
2nd test	78	90	85	98	90	76	80	78	89	62	826

4. Write the equation that would describe the data in the preceding exercise if the second test score in each case exactly equaled the first.
5. Compute r^2 using the data in Exercise 8, page 366.
6. Explain why r^2 can never be negative.
7. Compute r^2 for each of the following:

	a.	b.	c.	d.	e.
s_e^2	14,400	14,400	2,025	2,025	606
s_y^2	28,800	57,600	2,500	2,200	6,060

8. Determine the degrees of freedom for the between and within variation for each of these cases:
   a. 40 paired observations   b. 23 paired observations
9. Compute the value of F for each of the following and determine which are significant at the .01 level.

	n	$\sum x$	$\sum y$	$\sum xy$	$\sum x^2$	$\sum y^2$
a	25	60	52	200	400	592
b	50	15	20	146	204.5	400
c	100	+20	25	−3.5	5	125

10. Use analysis of variance to analyze the summary statistics in Exercise 7, parts a–e, using the .05 level and $n = 42$. Assume $n − 1$ used to compute s_y^2.
11. Use the following information for the computations:

$$y_c = 13 + 2x \qquad s_e = 3 \qquad n = 10$$
$$\sum x = 40 \qquad \sum x^2 = 600$$

   a. Compute a 95% confidence interval for the average (expected) value of y, if x_g is:
      (1) 1.0   (2) 4.0   (3) 8.0
   b. Compute a 95% confidence interval for an individual value of y when x_g is:
      (1) 1.0   (2) 4.0   (3) 8.0
12. When x_g is set equal to 0, the resulting confidence interval for the average y becomes the interval for the y-intercept a.
   a. Find a 95% confidence interval for a in Exercise 11.
   b. Obtain both a 95% and a 99% confidence interval for a for the example on page 362.

MULTIPLE LINEAR REGRESSION ANALYSIS

Multiple regression involves three or more variables. There is still a single dependent variable, but there are two or more independent (explaining) variables. The theory is an extension of simple linear regression analysis. Again, the analysis is concerned with developing an equation that can be used to predict values of y for given values of the various independent variables. The purpose of additional independent variables is to improve predictive ability over that for simple linear regression. Computational techniques are quite involved, however, and beyond the scope of this text. Therefore, the discussion here will only briefly describe multiple regression analysis.

Least squares techniques are used to obtain the regression equation, although, from a practical standpoint, computerized solutions are highly desirable, owing to the fact that even moderate-sized problems require fairly burdensome computations. The regression equation has the form

$$y_c = a + b_1 x_1 + b_2 x_2 + \cdots + b_k x_k$$

where

$$a = y\text{-intercept}$$
$$b_i = \text{slopes}$$
$$k = \text{number of independent variables}$$

Whereas a two-variable simple regression analysis results in the equation of a *line*, a three-variable problem implies a *plane*, and a k-variable problem implies $a(k + 1)$-dimensional *hyperplane*. The k-variable hyperplane does not lend itself to graphical display, but since the three-variable plane does, and because the *concepts* are identical, the discussion here will focus on three-variable problems.

Figure 14.17 illustrates a regression *plane*.* Data points would be scattered around the plane rather than around a regression line. Again, the less the scatter, the better the fit, and hence the more the accuracy in the predictions.

While in many situations a simple linear regression equation will provide a satisfactory predictive equation, we discovered in the case of trying to estimate selling prices of used cars on the basis of mileage alone that a single independent variable did not accomplish this. If we are reasonably satisfied that the relationship is not curvilinear, the next step would be to search for additional variables

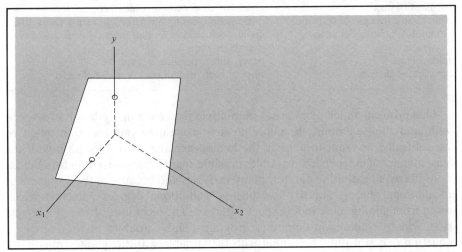

FIGURE 14.17   When a problem involves two independent variables and a dependent variable, the result is a regression plane instead of a regression line.

---

* You can get some idea of how a regression plane might look by using a book to represent the plane. Imagine all the different ways it might be tilted, say, with respect to one corner of a room.

that might have some bearing on prices. General condition of car body is probably an important factor, although it can be difficult to quantify. One way around this problem would be to develop a rating scale in which cars are assigned a two-digit number from 0 to 1 (e.g., .65), with a score of 1 representing a car in mint condition and 0 a pile of rusted metal.

The resulting equation might be

$$y_c = 2900 - 40x_1 + 800x_2$$

where

$$x_1 = \text{mileage}$$
$$x_2 = \text{body rating}$$

We can use this equation to estimate the selling price of a car with 20,000 miles that has a body rating of .80:

$$y_c = 2900 - 40(20) + 800(.80) = \$2540$$

Before actually using the equation, we would want to consider the dispersion around the regression plane, which is measured in a manner similar to that of simple regression.

Some other examples of cases where multiple independent variables might provide better estimates than single independent variables are shown in Table 14.6.

TABLE 14.6   Examples of Situations in Which Multiple Regression Might be Useful

Dependent variable	Possible predictor (independent) variables
crop yield	amount of fertilizer, rainfall, soil type
annual salary	years with company, years of college
hardness of steel	annealing time, carbon content, cooling rate
compressive strength of concrete	composition, curing time, average curing temperature
automobile braking distance	speed, coefficient of friction for road surface and tires, reaction time
sales volume	advertising expenditures, price
demand for chicken	price of beef, price of pork, price of chicken

One problem which often arises in multiple regression analysis is how to cope with, and choose among, the many possible explaining variables that might be used. Ideally, we want to achieve the highest explanatory relationship with the least number of independent variables possible, mainly because of practical limitations of cost in gathering data for many variables and because of the requirement of additional observations to offset the loss of additional degrees of freedom which result from adding more independent variables. The technique of *stepwise* regression, widely available in computer programs, adds variables to the regression equation one at a time, beginning with the variable with the greatest predictive strength. The remaining variables are then entered (added to the equation) one at a time, with the strongest ones first. A revised equation and measure of r^2 are indicated at each step. This permits the analyst to make a trade-off decision between addition of variables to increase predictability and the added cost and effort that might be required to obtain necessary data.

EXERCISES

1. Given the multiple regression equation $y_c = -420 + 50x_1 + 2.5x_2$, find y_c for these cases:
   a. $x_1 = 15$, $x_2 = 3000$
   b. $x_1 = 10$, $x_2 = 2000$
   c. $x_1 = 20$, $x_2 = 1000$
2. Given the multiple regression equation $y_c = .40 + 3x_1 - 2x_2 - x_3$, compute y_c for these cases:
   a. $x_1 = 1$, $x_2 = .5$, $x_3 = 1.4$
   b. $x_1 = .6$, $x_2 = .4$, $x_3 = 2$
   c. $x_1 = 0$, $x_2 = 0$, $x_3 = 0$

CORRELATION ANALYSIS

The objective of a correlational study is to determine the strength of a relationship between paired observations. The term "correlation" literally means "co-relationship," since it indicates the extent to which values of one variable are related to values of another variable. There are many instances in which a possible relationship between two variables may exist. Consider, for example, such questions as these:

1. Are age and physical endurance related?
2. Do persons with high incomes tend to have completed more years of school than those with lower incomes?
3. Can job success be predicted from test scores?
4. Does temperature seem to influence crime rate?
5. Do students with high reading ability tend to perform better in mathematics courses than those with lesser reading abilities?

These and similar problems lend themselves to correlation analysis. The result of such an analysis is a coefficient of correlation, a value which quantifies the degree of correlation. In the following pages, you will learn (1) the important characteristics of correlational coefficients, (2) computational procedures, and (3) how these coefficients can be used to draw inferences about relationships in a population. We will consider three techniques of correlation: one for measurement data, one for ranked data, and one for nominal classifications.

CONTINUOUS DATA: PEARSON'S *r*

The most common form of correlation analysis involves continuous data. The amount of relationship between two continuous variables is summarized by a correlation coefficient which is referred to as "Pearson's *r*" in honor of the great mathematician Karl Pearson who developed the technique. This technique is valid only if certain fairly rigid assumptions can be made. The assumptions are as follows:

1. Both x and y are continuous *random* variables. That is, unlike regression analysis, it is not acceptable to select certain x-values and then measure y; *both x and y must be free to vary* (i.e., taken "as is").
2. The joint frequency distribution (i.e., the distribution of values of x, y pairs) is normal. This is called a *bivariate normal distribution* and is illustrated in Figure 14.18.

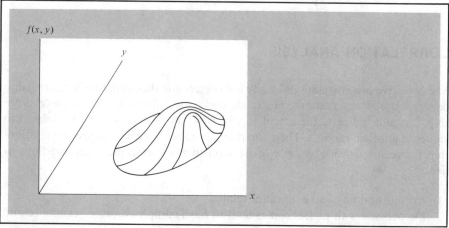

FIGURE 14.18   Correlation analysis assumes that x and y have a joint frequency distribution that is normal.

Characteristics of r

The correlation coefficient has two properties that communicate the nature of a relationship between two variables. One is its sign ($+$ or $-$) and the other is its magnitude. The sign is the same as the sign of the slope of an imaginary straight line which might "fit" the data if it were plotted in a scatter diagram, and the magnitude of r indicates how close the individual points are to the "line." For example, values close to -1.00 or $+1.00$ indicate that the values are fairly close or on the line, while values near 0 suggest more scatter. These concepts are illustrated in Figure 14.19.

More precisely, we can say the following:

1. The value of r can range from -1.00 to $+1.00$. Thus $-1.00 \leq r \leq +1.00$.
2. A *positive* relationship (r is $+$) between two variables means that high values of one variable are paired with high values of the other and that low values of one are paired with low values of the other.
3. A *negative* relationship (r is $-$) means that high values of one variable are paired with low values of the other.
4. A *zero* relationship ($r \approx 0$) means that some high values are paired with low values and others are paired with high values.

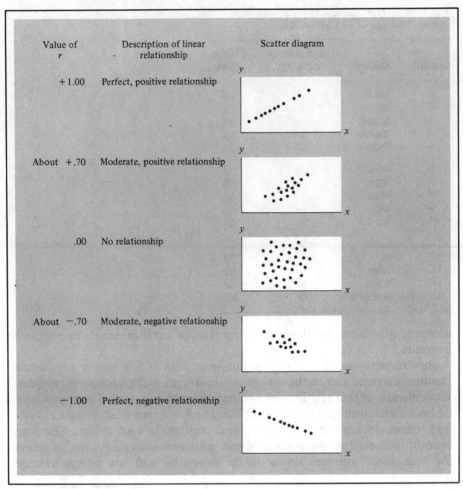

Value of r	Description of linear relationship	Scatter diagram
+1.00	Perfect, positive relationship	
About +.70	Moderate, positive relationship	
.00	No relationship	
About −.70	Moderate, negative relationship	
−1.00	Perfect, negative relationship	

FIGURE 14.19 Various scatter diagrams and corresponding values of the correlation coefficient.

5. The sign of r is always the same as the sign of b, the slope of an imaginary line fit to the data. Note that it is *not* necessary to compute a line.

Product-Moment Correlation: Conceptual Approach

The term "product-moment" is descriptive of the way in which paired values are combined to obtain the correlation coefficient. To demonstrate the concept, consider the following hypothetical example. Suppose we are interested in whether scholastic performance in college is related to scholastic performance in high school. It might seem reasonable to expect that students would tend to achieve approximately the same grades in college that they did in high school. To measure this, imagine that 15 college seniors at a large eastern university have been randomly selected and that both their high school and college averages have been obtained. The data might look like that shown in Table 14.7.

If there is a strong relationship between grade point average in high school and quality point average in college, the university may incorporate this into its

TABLE 14.7   Hypothetical High School and
College Averages of 15 College Seniors

Number	Student	High School GPA (%)	College QPA
1	Jim C.	80	1.0
2	Ed	82	1.0
3	Karen	84	2.1
4	Marcia	85	1.4
5	Peter	87	2.1
6	Beverly	88	1.7
7	Tom	88	2.0
8	Marc	89	3.5
9	Sid	90	3.1
10	Jim L.	91	2.4
11	Linda	91	2.7
12	Al	92	3.0
13	John	94	3.9
14	Susan	96	3.6
15	Ann Marie	98	4.0

screening procedures. Or this information may be useful in establishing remedial programs.

An extremely useful first step in analyzing data of this sort is to construct a scatter diagram, such as the one shown in Figure 14.20, because it provides a visual display of the relationship. Among other things, such a plot can reveal if a linear relationship is conceivable. The graph is constructed using an x-value (high school average) and a y-value (college average) for each student. Our graph seems to indicate that there is a moderate positive relationship since, in general, low high school averages appear to be associated with low college averages,

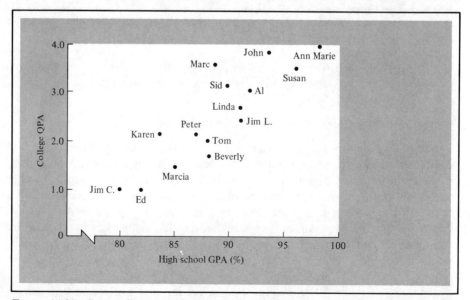

FIGURE 14.20   Scatter diagram of high school and college averages of 15 college seniors.

while high college averages and high high school averages seem to correspond, although there are some exceptions.

It is not surprising to find this kind of relationship between high school and college performance. In fact, you may have felt that the relationship would be even stronger. Let us pause for a moment, then, to reflect on why there is not a *perfect* positive relationship. Among the explanations which seem most plausible are these:

1. Students probably have come from different high schools with different grading policies.
2. Motivation and ability can change over a period of time.
3. College programs differ in difficulty and grading policies.
4. There is undoubtedly some chance variation present.

It is prudent to construct a scatter diagram of the data whenever possible. The visual portrayal is especially helpful in exploring the data. Nevertheless, unless there is a perfect relationship between the two variables, it will be necessary to resort to computational methods to obtain a statistic that *summarizes* the extent of the relationship.

Our goal is to learn whether a student's relative standing in one group of scores is related to his relative standing in the other group of scores. It is possible to measure the relative position of any score in a group of scores in terms of the group mean and group standard deviation. That is, subtracting the group mean and then dividing by the group standard deviation will indicate each value's position relative to the other values in the group. This, in effect, standardizes the

TABLE 14.8   Standardizing the Scores

		x Scores (high school GPAs) $\bar{x} = 89$ $s_x = 5$			y Scores (college QPAs) $\bar{y} = 2.5$ $s_y = 1.0$		
Number	Student	x_i GPA (%)	$(x_i - \bar{x})$	z_x $(x_i - \bar{x})/s_x$	y_i QPA	$(y_i - \bar{y})$	z_y $(y_i - \bar{y})/s_y$
1	Jim C.	80	−9	−1.8	1.0	−1.5	−1.5
2	Ed	82	−7	−1.4	1.0	−1.5	−1.5
3	Karen	84	−5	−1.0	2.1	−.4	−.4
4	Marcia	85	−4	−.8	1.4	−1.1	−1.1
5	Peter	87	−2	−.4	2.1	−.4	−.4
6	Beverly	88	−1	−.2	1.7	−.8	−.8
7	Tom	88	−1	−.2	2.0	−.5	−.5
8	Marc	89	0	0	3.5	+1.0	+1.0
9	Sid	90	+1	+.2	3.1	+.6	+.6
10	Jim L.	91	+2	+.4	2.4	−.1	−.1
11	Linda	91	+2	+.4	2.7	+.2	+.2
12	Al	92	+3	+.6	3.0	+.5	+.5
13	John	94	+5	+1.0	3.9	+1.4	+1.4
14	Susan	96	+7	+1.4	3.6	+1.1	+1.1
15	Ann Marie	98	+9	+1.8	4.0	+1.5	+1.5
			$\overline{0}$			$\overline{0}$	

scores and has the desirable property of making groups of scores comparable even though the group means or standard deviations might be quite different. The standardizing procedure is illustrated for our two sets of scores in Table 14.8.

These standardized scores can now be used to determine a figure that measures the combined standing (i.e., relative position in *both* groups) by finding the product of the two standardized scores for each student. For example, if there is a positive relationship between the two sets of scores, then high scores will be paired with high scores and low scores with low scores. In addition, the products of these pairs will reflect a positive relationship since they will tend to be positive. If there is a negative relationship, lows and highs will be paired, yielding negative products. This can be seen in Figure 14.21.

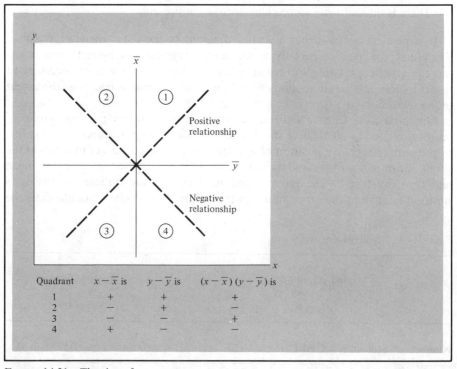

FIGURE 14.21   The sign of r.

The correlation coefficient will be the average of these products. Hence the procedure is as follows:

1. Convert actual scores of each group to standardized scores.
2. Find the product of each pair of standardized scores.
3. Add the products.
4. Determine the average product.

The average is obtained by summing the products and dividing by $n - 1$ rather than n, for the same reason that the standard deviation is found using $n - 1$. Our formula, then, will be

$$r = \frac{\sum z_x z_y}{n - 1}$$

The computations necessary are illustrated in Table 14.9 for the high school and college scores.

TABLE 14.9   Computations for r Using the Standardized Scores

Number	Student	z_y	z_x	$z_x z_y$
1	Jim C.	−1.5	−1.8	+2.70
2	Ed	−1.5	−1.4	+2.10
3	Karen	−.4	−1.0	+.40
4	Marcia	−1.1	−.8	+.88
5	Peter	−.4	−.4	+.16
6	Beverly	−.8	−.2	+.16
7	Tom	−.5	−.2	+.10
8	Marc	+1.0	0	.00
9	Sid	+.6	+.2	+.12
10	Jim L.	−.1	+.4	−.04
11	Linda	+.2	+.4	+.08
12	Al	+.5	+.6	+.30
13	John	+1.4	+1.0	+1.40
14	Susan	+1.1	+1.4	+1.54
15	Ann Marie	+1.5	+1.8	+2.70
				12.60

$$r = \frac{\sum z_x z_y}{n - 1} = \frac{+12.60}{14} = +.90$$

Interpreting r

Our purpose in computing the value of r was to determine if there was any statistical relationship between a student's high school grade point average and his or her college quality point average. We have found that $r = +.90$. The plus sign tells us that there is a positive relationship between the two sets of scores. Since we know that r has an upper limit of $+1.00$, this seems to suggest that the two variables are closely related. However, the value of r can be misleading. In fact, a more meaningful statistic is r^2, the coefficient of determination,* which shows the percentage of variation in one variable that is statistically "explained," or accounted for, by variation in the other variable. For instance, in this case, with $r = +.90$, $r^2 = .81$, meaning that 81% of the variation of the points around the two group means can be explained by the relationship between the two variables. Conversely, $1 - r^2$, or 19% of the variation, cannot be explained by the relationship, and so must be considered to be due to other factors that have not been included in the study. Some possibilities are motivation, grading procedures, and so on.

A Practical Approach for Computing r

The preceding discussion of the correlation coefficient provided an intuitive basis for correlation. However, as a practical matter, the technique of standardizing

---

* This is the same r^2 mentioned in connection with the explained variation of a regression line.

observations is not useful because the necessary computations can be fairly time-consuming, especially subtracting the group means from each observation and then squaring those differences. Fortunately, there is a more suitable version of the formula which simplifies calculations, although on the surface it might appear a bit overwhelming:

$$r = \frac{n(\sum xy) - (\sum x)(\sum y)}{\sqrt{n(\sum x^2) - (\sum x)^2} \cdot \sqrt{n(\sum y^2) - (\sum y)^2}}$$

The necessary calculations using this approach for finding r are illustrated in Table 14.10. Even with this formula the computations are rather long and involved.

TABLE 14.10   Calculations Necessary to Compute r

Number	Student	x_i GPA	y_i QPA	$x_i y_i$	x_i^2	y_i^2
1	Jim C.	80	1.0	80.0	6,400	1.00
2	Ed	82	1.0	82.0	6,724	1.00
3	Karen	84	2.1	176.4	7,056	4.41
4	Marcia	85	1.4	119.0	7,225	1.96
5	Peter	87	2.1	182.7	7,569	4.41
6	Beverly	88	1.7	149.6	7,744	2.89
7	Tom	88	2.0	176.0	7,744	4.00
8	Marc	89	3.5	311.5	7,921	12.25
9	Sid	90	3.1	279.0	8,100	9.61
10	Jim L.	91	2.4	218.4	8,281	5.76
11	Linda	91	2.7	245.7	8,281	7.29
12	Al	92	3.0	276.0	8,464	9.00
13	John	94	3.9	366.6	8,836	15.21
14	Susan	96	3.6	345.6	9,216	12.96
15	Ann Marie	98	4.0	392.0	9,604	16.00
		$\sum x_i = 1,335$	$\sum y_i = 37.5$	$\sum xy = 3,400.5$	$\sum x_i^2 = 119,155$	$\sum y_i^2 = 107.75$

$$r = \frac{15(3,400.5) - 1,335(37.5)}{\sqrt{15(119,155) - (1,335)^2} \cdot \sqrt{15(107.75) - (37.5)^2}} = +.90$$

TABLE 14.11   Three Alternative Methods for Obtaining r

Method	Comment
$r = \sqrt{1 - (s_e^2/s_y^2)}$	Correlation in terms of regression. The sign of r is the same as the sign of b. Correlation is inversely related to the scatter around the line: the less scatter, the higher the correlation. Use $n - 2$ in computing s_y^2.
Standardized values	Correlation measures the relationship between two variables with the mean and standard deviation of each variable "equalized."
$r = \dfrac{n \sum xy - \sum x \sum y}{\sqrt{n(\sum x^2) - (\sum x)^2} \cdot \sqrt{n(\sum y^2) - (\sum y)^2}}$	Most suitable for mechanical computation.

Pocket and desk calculators eliminate much of the burden, but the most realistic approach for computing r is to utilize computer programs when they are available.

There are, in effect, *three* alternative ways of obtaining the value of r for measurement data: standardize each set of scores and find the average cross product, use the formula, or compute the coefficient of determination r^2 and find the square root. For a given set of data, all three methods will yield the same value for r. Nonetheless, each approach adds something to our understanding of the meaning of the term "correlation." The three methods are briefly compared in Table 14.11.

EXERCISES

1. Standardize each set of scores and compute the coefficient of correlation.

a.	x	y	b.	x	y
	34	21		3.9	46
	30	22		4.6	46
	40	25		6.0	52
	34	28		2.8	50
	39	15		3.1	48
	35	24		3.4	40
	42	24		4.2	42
	45	22		4.0	44
	43	17		$\bar{x} = 4$	$\bar{y} = 46$
	$\bar{x} = 38$	$\bar{y} = 22$		$s_x = 1$	$s_x = 4$
	$s_x = 5$	$s_y = 4$			

2. Recompute r for Exercise 1a treating the x's as y's and the y's as x's. Justify your answer in terms of the formula for r.
3. Refer to the data in Exercise 1a.
   a. Double each value of x and recompute the mean and standard deviation of the x's.
   b. Standardize the values of x.
   c. Compare these standardized values to the standardized values you obtained for the x's in Exercise 1a.
   d. What effect does doubling the x's have on r?
   e. Can you explain why?
4. Refer to the data in Exercise 1a.
   a. Add 12 to each value of x and subtract 2 from each value of y.
   b. Compute the mean and standard deviation of each set using the values obtained in part a.
   c. Standardize the values and compare them to the standardized values you obtained in Exercise 1a.
   d. What effect does adding or subtracting a constant for either the x- or the y-values have on r?
   e. Can you explain why?
5. Determine the correlation coefficient for these two sets of test scores:

Student	First exam	Second exam
1	82	92
2	84	91
3	86	90
4	83	92
5	88	87
6	87	86
7	85	89
8	83	90
9	86	92
10	85	90
11	87	91
	$\bar{x} = 85$	$\bar{y} = 90$

6. Given the following sets, compute the value of r:

n	$\sum x$	$\sum y$	$\sum xy$	$\sum x^2$	$\sum y^2$
a. 25	60	52	200	400	592
b. 50	15	20	146	204.5	400
c. 100	−20	25	−3.5	5	12.5

7. Verbal and math scores on college entrance exams for seven freshman students are given below.
   a. Divide each score by 100.
   b. Compute the correlation coefficient.

Student	Verbal score	Math score
1	420	550
2	450	600
3	410	520
4	360	400
5	320	410
6	440	425
7	400	475

8. Determine the correlation coefficient for the data in Exercise 5, page 365.
9. Given the following data on violent crimes and average temperature between the hours of 9 P.M. and 2 A.M. on Saturday evenings in a large eastern community, plot the data and compute the correlation coefficient:

Violent crimes/1000 residents	Average temperature (°F)
5.0	87
2.2	50
4.1	75
5.4	90
2.8	55
3.0	54
3.6	68
4.9	85
4.1	82
4.2	80
2.0	45
2.7	58
3.1	66

10. Determine the correlation coefficient for hours studied by 11 students versus grades they received on a test.

Hours spent studying	Grade
$2\frac{1}{2}$	89
3	95
6	80
4	82
6	85
$4\frac{1}{2}$	90
7	75
10	70
$5\frac{1}{2}$	91
5	93
$8\frac{1}{2}$	74

11. a. Would you be surprised if your computations for a given set of paired observations yielded $r = +.9$ and $b = -.9$? Why or why not?
    b. Given the data below, would you be surprised if both sets had a positive correlation? Explain.
    c. Would you be surprised if both yielded $r = +1.00$? Explain.

Set 1		Set 2	
x	y	x	y
1	0	0	1
5	8	10	4

12. For each of the following situations, state whether correlation analysis or regression analysis would be more appropriate and why:
    a. A team of researchers wants to determine if grades in college are indicative of success in a chosen field.
    b. Estimate the number of miles a set of radial tires can be expected to travel before needing replacement.
    c. Predict how long it will take a person to complete a job based on the number of weeks of training.
    d. Decide if the number of weeks spent in training is an important variable in how long it takes to do a job.
    e. A store manager wants to estimate weekly sales on the basis of Monday and Tuesday sales.

INFERENCES ABOUT THE CORRELATION COEFFICIENT

A Confidence Interval for the Population Correlation

The value of the sample correlation coefficient can be used as an estimate of the true correlation in the population, ρ. Stating r as a single value, though, may give the mistaken impression that this is the actual value. Consequently, it is usually more desirable to include a confidence interval for the true value along with the sample statistic. There are several methods for obtaining a confidence interval for ρ, but perhaps the most straightforward method is to utilize a chart such as that shown in Figure 14.22. Once r has been calculated, the chart can be used to determine the upper and lower values of the interval for the sample size used.

If you examine the chart, you will see that the range of potential (unknown) values of ρ is shown along the vertical scale, possible sample r's are shown along the bottom scale, and a series of curves represent selected sample sizes. Note that there are two curves for each sample size. The chart is used in the following manner. Suppose a sample of 50 observations ($N = 50$) yields an r of $+.80$. Enter the chart at the point on the bottom scale at $r = +.80$ and follow the vertical line up until it intersects the first curve for $N = 50$. Now read horizontally across the chart. You will find the value of $\rho = +.68$. This is the lower limit of the confidence interval. The upper limit is determined in the same way, except that the vertical line through $r = +.80$ is followed up to the intersection with the second curve for $N = 50$. Reading across the chart, we find that the upper limit is about .88. Hence the confidence interval becomes

$$.68 \le \rho \le .88$$

Notice that the interval is not symmetrical. This is because the sampling distribution of ρ is only symmetrical when the true correlation in the population is approximately 0.

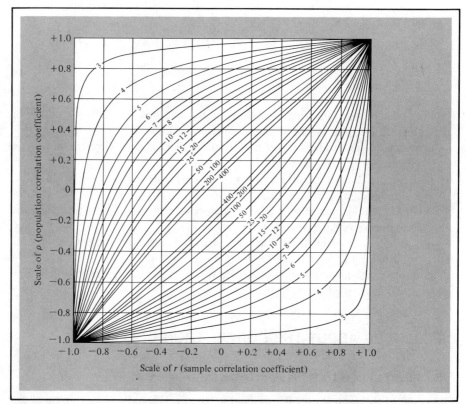

FIGURE 14.22 Confidence bands for the population correlation coefficient (95%).
Source: E. S. Pearson and H. O. Hartley, *Biometrika Tables for Statisticians*, Vol. 1 (1962), p. 140.
    Reprinted by permission of the *Biometrika* Trustees.

A Significance Test of r

It may be necessary to evaluate a claim concerning the value of ρ. The simplest way to do this is to construct a confidence interval for r and note whether or not the claimed value is included in the interval. If it is, accept H_0; if not, reject H_0 and accept the alternative. For example, suppose we have H_0: $\rho = .3$ and H_1: $\rho \neq .3$. If we find a confidence interval of $+.05$ to $+.26$, we would reject H_0 because $+.3$ is not in the interval.

If a confidence interval for ρ includes the value 0, then we say that r is not significant, meaning that ρ may be 0 and that the value of r may be due to nothing more than sampling variability.

Some examples showing how Figure 14.22 is used to determine confidence intervals for the population correlation coefficient are given in Table 14.12.

TABLE 14.12   Examples of Confidence Intervals for the Population Correlation Coefficient

Sample r	Sample size	Confidence interval (from Figure 14.22)	Comment
.60	20	$+.21 \leq \rho \leq +.82$	The small sample size produces a wide confidence interval.
.70	100	$+.58 \leq \rho \leq +.78$	
.50	40	$+.20 \leq \rho \leq +.70$	Interpolation on the graph is necessary to obtain the limits.
$-.20$	50	$-.46 \leq \rho \leq +.08$	Since the interval includes 0, there is the possibility that the true value is 0.

Another approach that can be used to test the significance of a sample r is to use the formula

$$t = \frac{r - 0}{\sqrt{(1 - r^2)/(n - 2)}}$$

This approach obviously requires some computations, which the chart method avoids. Moreover, it is only useful in testing the null hypothesis that $\rho = 0$. On the other hand, other levels of significance can be employed, and the formula can handle virtually any sample size, with no need for interpolation.

Example 1   A sample of 24 observations yields $r = .50$, and we want to know if r is significant at the .01 level. The test statistic is

$$t = \frac{.50 - 0}{\sqrt{(1 - .50^2)/(24 - 2)}} = 5.42$$

The two-tail table value of t, with $n - 2$ (note the $n - 2$ in the formula) degrees of freedom for the .01 level, is 2.819. Thus we can conclude that $r \neq 0$, as illustrated in Figure 14.23.

A Word of Caution

It is necessary to exercise some degree of caution when examining the relationship between two variables on the basis of sample data. Thus, although it turns out

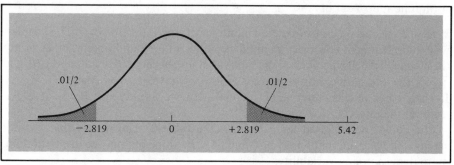

FIGURE 14.23 H_0 is rejected; $\rho \neq 0$.

that r is not significant, this does not necessarily imply that two variables are unrelated. Let us consider this apparent paradox a bit further.

Figure 14.24(a) depicts a situation in which the relationship between the two variables is perfect but *nonlinear*. The preceding formulas, which measure only *linear correlation*, would produce $r = 0$. Still another possibility is shown in Figure 14.24(b). Although there appears to be a strong relationship overall, the sample data (inside the box) suggest otherwise. Unless care is taken to insure *random sampling* by not restricting the range of potential values, this situation may occur. Hence a study whose aim is to predict college performance on the basis of entrance examinations may include only a small portion of the possible scores of all high school students (i.e., only those who continued on to college) and so seem to indicate little or no relationship.

In the first instance, plotting the data helps to prevent dismissing curvilinear relationships. In the second, the dangers of obtaining data taken from a restricted range are more subtle and hence more difficult to handle.

Conversely, when $r \neq 0$, there may still be a problem. For example, the data may not be randomly scattered around the regression line (assuming it has been derived from the data), as illustrated in Figure 14.25. The moral is clear: *plot the data*.

EXERCISES

1. For each sample correlation coefficient, obtain a 95% confidence interval, using Figure 14.22, for the population correlation coefficient and then decide if the sample r is significantly different than zero.

r	a.	b.	c.	d.	e.
r	+.80	+.10	−.30	−.30	−.30
n	15	15	25	50	100

2. Obtain 95% confidence intervals for the true correlation in the population for each of these cases, and then decide which r's are not significant at the .05 level.

	a.	b.	c.	d.	e.	f.
r	+.10	+.10	+.10	+.70	−.70	0.00
n	20	50	200	50	50	25

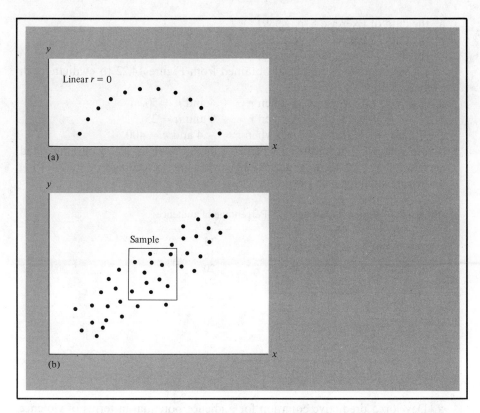

FIGURE 14.24   A nonlinear relationship may produce $r = 0$, while sampling only a limited portion of the population can make it appear there is no relationship between two variables.

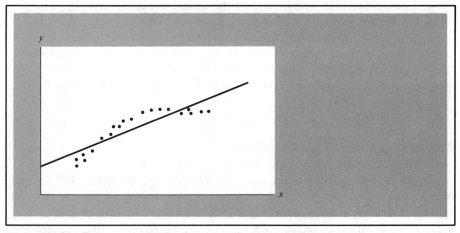

FIGURE 14.25   Data are not randomly scattered around the line.

3. Use the formula

$$t = \frac{r - 0}{\sqrt{(1 - r^2)/(n - 2)}}$$

and the .01 level and decide which of these are significant:

    a. the data of Exercise 5, page 391
    b. the data of Exercise 9, page 392
    c. the data of Exercise 10, page 393

4. Use a 95% confidence interval obtained from Figure 14.22 to evaluate each of these claims:

    a. $H_0: \rho = +.6$, $H_1: \rho \neq .6$, when $r = +.4$ and $n = 50$
    b. $H_0: \rho = +.9$, $H_1: \rho \neq .9$, when $r = +.8$ and $n = 25$
    c. $H_0: \rho = -.5$, $H_1: \rho \neq -.5$, when $r = -.4$ and $n = 400$

*5. A research group developed a violence quotient scale for TV programs, rated each of 10 programs, and gathered data on the percentage of the viewing audience watching each program.

Program	Violence quotient	Percentage of audience
1	10	15
2	20	16
3	30	20
4	40	24
5	40	25
6	50	30
7	55	30
8	65	35
9	70	35
10	70	35
	450	265

    a. Develop a predictive equation for audience potential in terms of violence quotient.
    b. Determine the percentage of explained variation.
    c. Compute or otherwise determine the correlation coefficient.
    d. What assumptions were necessary for part a? Part c?
    e. Is b significant? Is r? (Use .05.)
    f. What is a 95% confidence interval for the percentage of the viewing audience of the new program Gotcha, which has a violence quotient of 60?

6. Use a confidence interval to evaluate this claim: $H_0: \rho = -.45$, $H_1: \rho \neq -.45$, $\alpha = .05$, $n = 200$, $r = -.5$.

RANKED DATA: SPEARMAN'S *r*

Spearman rank correlation is a nonparametric technique for measuring strength of relationship between paired observations of two variables when the data are in ranked form. Preference data is quite common in such areas as food tasting, competitive events (e.g., beauty contests, art shows, athletic contests), and attitudinal studies. The objective in computing a correlation coefficient in such instances is to determine the extent to which two sets of rankings are in agreement or disagreement. The technique can also be extended to scores or other measurements if these are converted to ranks.

    Consider this simple example. Two experts are to judge 12 wines. Each will assign ranks denoting preference from 1 (highest) to 12 (lowest). The data are shown in Table 14.13. If the experts are essentially in agreement, we would expect the ranks they assign to the various wines to be roughly the same. If the experts disagreement, high ranks will be paired with low ranks, and vice versa. One measure of the extent of agreement is the squared differences between the two sets of ranks. If the sum of these is small, this suggests agreement; if the sum is large, this suggests disagreement. The actual computation of correlation involves the formula

$$r_{sp} = 1 - \frac{6 \sum d^2}{n(n^2 - 1)}$$

where n is the number of observations and $\sum d^2$ is the sum of the squared differences between the ranks. The coefficient of rank correlation obtained is called Spearman's r. The necessary computations are shown in Table 14.13. Note that the sum of the differences adds to 0. This serves as a useful check on the calculations, although it is not needed in the formula. Pearson's product-moment formula applied to the *ranked* data would yield exactly the same correlation coefficient that the Spearman formula did.* Nevertheless, it should be evident that the computations here are a great deal easier than those the Pearson's formula would entail, particularly since only two pieces of information, sample size and sum of squared differences, are necessary.

The procedure is as follows:

1. Find the difference in ranks for each pair of observations.
2. As a check, see that the differences add to 0.
3. Square the differences.
4. Sum the squared differences, obtaining $\sum d^2$.
5. Compute r_{sp}.

TABLE 14.13   Example Illustrating Computation of r_{sp}

Wine	Preferences Judge 1	Judge 2	Difference d	(Difference)^2 d^2
1	1	3	+2	4
2	5	4	−1	1
3	2	1	−1	1
4	7	5	−2	4
5	4	2	−2	4
6	8	9	+1	1
7	3	7	+4	16
8	6	6	0	0
9	9	8	−1	1
10	12	10	−2	4
11	11	11	0	0
12	10	12	+2	4
			$\sum d = 0$	$\sum d^2 = 40$

$$r_{sp} = 1 - \frac{6 \sum d^2}{n(n^2 - 1)} = 1 - \frac{6(40)}{12(144 - 1)} = +.86$$

* The reverse does not hold; converting measurement data to ranks and computing r_{sp} will generally result in a different value than the Pearson value for *nonranked* data.

The Spearman rank correlation coefficient can range from -1.00 to $+1.00$, just as Pearson's r can. Thus the $+.86$ calculated in the table implies that the judges were consistent (in agreement) in their rankings. Had the result been $-.86$, the implication would have been that the judges strongly disagreed in their assessments of the wines. So when r_{sp} is close to $+1.00$, this indicates that the two sets of ranks are very similar, while if r_{sp} is close to -1.00, this means that the rankings are quite different. If there is agreement on some items and disagreement on others, r_{sp} is apt to equal approximately 0, which would suggest no relationship between the two judges' rankings.

Since sample data invariably differ somewhat due to chance, there is always the potential for obtaining what appears to be a relationship when, in fact, there is none. Consequently, it is desirable to test the significance of r_{sp}, particularly if the sample size is small or if the value of r_{sp} is small. For situations where n is greater than 10, the null hypothesis of $r_{sp} = 0$ can be tested using the formula

$$t = \frac{r_{sp} - 0}{\sqrt{(1 - r_{sp}^2)/(n - 2)}}$$

with $n - 2$ degrees of freedom. Using the preceding calculations, which yielded $r_{sp} = +.86$, we find

$$t = \frac{+.86}{\sqrt{(1 - .86^2)/(12 - 2)}} = 4.53$$

Since it would be necessary to use the .001 level in order to accept H_0, it seems safe to conclude that the value $+.86$ is significant in this instance.

EXERCISES

1. Test each correlation coefficient at the .05 level for significance, using

$$H_0: p = 0 \qquad H_1: p \neq 0$$

   a. $r_{sp} = +.60, n = 17$ c. $r_{sp} = .91, n = 11$
   b. $r_{sp} = -.45, n = 22$ d. $r_{sp} = .25, n = 32$

2. a. Compute r_{sp} for Exercise 7, page 392. (Do not neglect to rank the data prior to computation.) Do the results agree with the value obtained using Pearson's r? Why?

   b. Which approach, Pearson or Spearman, is the better correlation technique? Explain briefly.

3. Compute the rank correlation coefficient for these data and test for significance at the .01 level:

	1	2	3	4	5	6	7	8	9	10	11	12	13	14
Number 1	3	2	4	1	9	5	6	10	8	11	7	14	12	13
Number 2	1	2	3	5	6	4	7	11	9	10	8	12	13	14

4. Write the ranks 1 through 6, in order, and then pair them with the ranks 1 through 6 in the opposite order. Compute r_{sp}. Compute r_{sp} for the case when both sets of ranks (1 through 6) are in the same order. Now try to rearrange the data so that r_{sp} is approximately zero.

5. Two managers are asked to rank 11 young workers according to management potential. Determine the extent to which the two managers agree or disagree and decide if the relationship is significant or not.

	Rank	
Employee	A	B
Al S.	6	9
Ed. B.	7	10
Ann D.	5	8
Ron Z.	4	7
Biff K.	9	11
Peaches	1	1
Al J.	8	6
Bob T.	2	2
Ned T.	3	4
Joan H.	11	3
Sam P.	10	5

NOMINAL DATA: THE CONTINGENCY COEFFICIENT

When both variables are measured on nominal scales (i.e., categories), the analysis is facilitated by developing a contingency table similar to that used with analysis of k proportions (chi-square test). In fact, the procedure is actually an extension of the analysis of an $r \times k$ table. For example, suppose data on income and education for a large sample of persons are available, and we want to test to determine if these two variables are related in the population. The data might be as shown in the table that follows.

	Income (in thousands)				
Education	Less than 8	8 to 12.9	13 to 18.9	19 or more	Row Totals
high school	55	20	55	10	140
some college	55	50	30	5	140
bachelor degree	60	60	10	10	140
graduate degree	30	70	5	35	140
Column Totals	200	200	100	60	560

Note that there are two important differences between the contingency table here and the previous $r \times k$ tables used in tests for independence. Whereas our concern before involved k *samples*, contingency data involve a *single sample* in which each observation has been classified according to two separate variables. In addition, the variables are arranged from low to high or high to low; there is *direction* in the categories.

If there is a high positive relationship in the data, the values should fall along the diagonal from low income and education to high income and education. If there is a high negative relationship, the data should fall along the other diagonal. If there is little or no relationship, the values should be scattered throughout the table. The first step in the analysis, then, is to compute the chi-square value and compare it to the table value for $(r - 1)(k - 1)$ degrees of freedom. This will indicate if there is anything more than chance scatter.

Calculations for the data above are shown in the table that follows and yield

$$\chi^2 = 138.0$$

which is significant at all levels shown in the chi-square table. Thus we know that there is some relationship between these two variables, but we still do not know how much.

Row percentages		Expected values		
$140/560 = \frac{1}{4}$	$200(\frac{1}{4}) = 50$	$200(\frac{1}{4}) = 50$	$100(\frac{1}{4}) = 25$	$60(\frac{1}{4}) = 15$
$140/560 = \frac{1}{4}$	$200(\frac{1}{4}) = 50$	$200(\frac{1}{4}) = 50$	$100(\frac{1}{4}) = 25$	$60(\frac{1}{4}) = 15$
$140/560 = \frac{1}{4}$	$200(\frac{1}{4}) = 50$	$200(\frac{1}{4}) = 50$	$100(\frac{1}{4}) = 25$	$60(\frac{1}{4}) = 15$
$140/560 = \frac{1}{4}$	$200(\frac{1}{4}) = 50$	$200(\frac{1}{4}) = 50$	$100(\frac{1}{4}) = 25$	$60(\frac{1}{4}) = 15$

$$\chi^2 = \sum \frac{(o - e)^2}{e} = \frac{(55 - 50)^2}{50} + \frac{(20 - 50)^2}{50} + \frac{(55 - 25)^2}{25} + \frac{(10 - 15)^2}{15} = .5 + 18 + 36 + 1.67$$

$$+ \frac{(55 - 50)^2}{50} + \frac{(50 - 50)^2}{50} + \frac{(30 - 25)^2}{25} + \frac{(5 - 15)^2}{15} = .5 + 0 + 1 + 6.67$$

$$+ \frac{(60 - 50)^2}{50} + \frac{(60 - 50)^2}{50} + \frac{(10 - 25)^2}{25} + \frac{(10 - 15)^2}{15} = 2 + 2 + 9 + 1.67$$

$$+ \frac{(30 - 50)^2}{50} + \frac{(70 - 50)^2}{50} + \frac{(5 - 25)^2}{25} + \frac{(35 - 15)^2}{15} = 8 + 8 + 16 + 26.67$$

$$= 137.68 \approx 138$$

One measure of the relationship is to compute the *contingency coefficient C*, where

$$C = \sqrt{\frac{\chi^2}{\chi^2 + N}}$$

An interesting feature of a chi-square table is that the maximum size of χ^2 possible is a function of N, the number of observations, and the size of the table. For *square* tables, this leads to a maximum value of C of

$$C_{max} = \sqrt{\frac{k - 1}{k}}$$

where k is the number of rows or columns. By comparing C to C_{max} an indication of the strength of the association between the two variables can be obtained.

Unlike other measures of correlation, C_{max} does not vary between -1.00 and $+1.00$. Instead, its smallest value is 0, and the largest value is less than 1.00, since the ratio $(k - 1)/k$ must always be less than 1.00.* This somewhat limits the utility of the contingency coefficient, since only tables of the same size (and only square tables) can be compared. Moreover, it is easy to misinterpret the strength

* As the size (number of rows and columns) increases, C_{max} becomes closer and closer to 1.00.

of association. For instance, with a 3 × 3 table, $C = .60$ versus C_{max} of $\sqrt{\frac{2}{3}} \approx .82$ represents a fairly high correlation, while with an 8 × 8 table, the same value of $C = .60$ versus C_{max} of $\sqrt{\frac{7}{8}} \approx .94$ is not nearly so strong.

For the previous data,

$$C = \sqrt{\frac{\chi^2}{\chi^2 + N}} \qquad C_{max} = \sqrt{\frac{k-1}{k}}$$

$$= \sqrt{\frac{138}{138 + 540}} \qquad = \sqrt{\frac{3}{4}}$$

$$\approx .45 \qquad\qquad = .87$$

This is a moderate, but not strong, relationship. The exact interpretation of strength depends in part on the nature of the data and comparable results from other studies, so it is difficult to state definite values for strong, weak, and so on.

Note that the formula does not automatically produce the *sign* of the contingency coefficient. Hence it is not always obvious whether there is a positive or negative relationship. Careful visual examination of the data is necessary to determine this, and you are strongly urged to plot and examine your data as part of your analysis each time you use this technique.

Some of the more important advantages and limitations of this technique are summarized below.

ADVANTAGES

1. No assumptions about the shape of the population are necessary.
2. Only nominal measurement (i.e., categories) is required.

LIMITATIONS

1. The upper limit of C is less than 1.00, even for perfect correlation.
2. The upper limit depends on the size of the table, so contingency coefficients from tables of different size are not comparable.
3. The contingency coefficient is not directly comparable with other measures of correlation, such as Pearson's r and Spearman's r, or even other contingency tables of different sizes.
4. Each cell must have an expected frequency of at least 5.
5. C_{max} can only be computed for square tables.

EXERCISES

1. For each of the following, determine if there is a significant relationship between the two variables, and if there is, decide how strong the relationship is.

	Size of table	χ^2	N	α
a.	4 × 4	150	200	.02
b.	5 × 5	40	200	.05
c.	3 × 3	250	250	.01
d.	6 × 6	130	150	.05
e.	4 × 4	16	100	.05

2. Grades in reading and grades in math for fifth-grade children were collected, with these results. Determine if there is any relationship between the two for this group.

Grade in math

Grade in Reading	A	B	C	D	Totals
A	20	40	30	0	90
B	30	60	20	10	120
C	50	50	80	60	240
D	0	50	70	30	150
Totals	100	200	200	100	600

3. Explain how the chi-square contingency table and the chi-square test of independence table (Chapter 12) differ with regard to number of samples and how the rows and columns are labeled.

4. A firm is considering the possibility of offering its employees a monetary incentive to give up or reduce smoking if there is a direct correlation between smoking and absenteeism. Analyze the data provided by the firm and decide whether or not the incentive should be offered.

Days absent per year	Nonsmoker	Light	Moderate	Heavy	Totals
0–2	10	10	55	65	140
3–4	5	50	30	55	140
5–6	10	70	10	50	140
7 or more	35	70	5	30	140
Totals	60	200	100	200	560

MULTIPLE CORRELATION

When more than one independent (or predictor) variable is used in a correlation analysis, the term "multiple correlation analysis" applies. Although the same basic theory which underlies simple correlation applies to multiple correlation, the computations are more demanding and interpretation of results is somewhat more complex. Furthermore, the inclusion of additional variables increases the necessary data and can add substantial cost to the study. The major reasons for shifting analysis from one to two or more independent variables are that (1) there is a logical relationship and (2) a single independent variable does not yield a sufficiently high correlation coefficient to be deemed satisfactory. For example, the ability to predict college performance might be enhanced if college entrance examination scores were included as a third variable.

A complete discussion of multiple correlation analysis is beyond the scope of this text. The brief discussion here is meant to give added perspective to simple correlation analysis.

Whereas the coefficient of determination r^2 served as the measure of association, or "explained variation," for simple correlation, a coefficient of multiple determination, R^2, serves as the measure of the collective association for all independent variables taken together in multiple correlation. In addition, it can be enlightening to compute *partial correlation coefficients*. These show the correlation between the dependent variable and each of the independent variables when the influence of the others is removed. In other words, the amount of variation explained by each independent variable is isolated.

CORRELATION AND CAUSATION

> Father to young son: "Why do you have that picture of a mouse in your bedroom window?"
> Son: "To keep the dragons away."
> Father: "There aren't any dragons around here."
> Son: "Gee, it really works!"

When two variables are correlated, it is possible to predict values of one from knowledge of the other. This often leads to the mistaken conclusion that one variable has *caused* the other variable. This is particularly true when the "causal" variable precedes the other variable in time. However, merely because there is a mathematical relationship between two variables tells us nothing about cause and effect. Hence there are three possible explanations for obtaining a correlation: there is a cause and effect relationship; both variables are related to a third variable; or the correlation is due to chance.

The "third variable" case is exemplified by leaves falling from trees shortly before snow begins in many northern sections of the country. Does this mean that the falling leaves have somehow triggered the snow, or are both occurrences related to the changing seasons? Studies have shown a remarkable correlation between rises in alcohol consumption and increases in teachers salaries. Are we to believe that teachers are using pay increases to drown their sorrows, or is it that as general levels of income rise (including teachers' incomes), consumption of many products also rises, and one of these is liquor?

There are many interesting examples of spurious, or nonsense, types of relationships. For instance, one study revealed a high correlation between price movements on the New York stock exchange and changes in the heights of women's hemlines. Others have shown correlation between births in England and pig iron production in the United States.

The point is that there is more to establishing relationships than simply pairing anything and everything until a correlation is found. Instead, correlational studies are used as initial exploratory inquiries in order to identify future areas for research. Results that appear promising on the basis of logic or theory must be submitted to further analysis (such as controlled experiments) to determine if a cause and effect relationship exists.

The real danger in using relationships for predictive purposes that have not been validated in terms of cause and effect is that the "relationships" may change or that deliberate changes in the "causal" variable may not lead to expected changes in the "effect" variable.

Table 14.14 summarizes the methods of correlational analysis discussed in this chapter.

TABLE 14.14   Summary of Correlation Analysis

Form of data	measurements	categories	ranks
Technique	Pearson product-moment	contingency	Spearman rank correlation
Method	1. Data	1. $r \times k$ table	1. ranked data
	$x \quad y$		No. 1 No. 2
	1		1
	2		2
	3		3
	$\vdots$		$\vdots$
	n		n
	2. compute r	2. compute χ^2	2. compute r
	3. confidence interval for ρ	3. If χ^2 is significant, then compute C_{table} and compare to C_{max}	3. Confidence interval for ρ
Assumptions	1. x and y are *continuous, random* variables. 2. x and y have a joint frequency distribution that is approximately *normal.*	1. The two variables are *continuous* and *random.*	1. The two variables are *continuous* and *random.* 2. Data can be ranked.

SUMMARY

Regression and correlation are techniques concerned with estimating relationships between two or more variables. Correlation summarizes the strength of the relationship, while regression provides a mathematical equation of the relationship. The equation can be used to *predict* values of one variable given values of the other. This chapter deals primarily with two-variable linear relationships. Linear relationships are important because the necessary calculations are relatively simple, they are easy to interpret, and they approximate many real world relationships.

Linear regression equations have the form $y_c = a + bx$, where y_c is the dependent, or predicted, variable, x is the independent, or predictor, variable, and a and b indicate the height and slope, respectively, of the line. The most widely used technique for determining the regression equation is called the *least squares* technique; the term is used because the resulting line minimizes the sum of the *squared* deviations of points from the line. Obtaining the equation of the line is simplified by the use of two formulas. The line describes the relationship between two variables, and it can be used to predict values of the dependent variable (y) from given values of the independent variable (x) in the sampled range.

Regression analysis involves making inferences about the true relationship that exists in the population. It requires that x and y be continuous variables and that for each x the distribution of possible y-values be normal. Inferences involve both tests of significance and construction of confidence intervals. In addition, a value r^2 can be computed that serves as a measure of how well the line "fits" the set of points.

Multiple regression analysis involves the use of two or more independent variables. Conceptually, multiple regression is simply an extension of simple linear regression. However, the computations are considerably more complex and typically are done with the assistance of a computer program.

Three types of correlation analysis were covered in this chapter: one for measurement data, one for ranked data, and one for nominal data. All three methods dealt with two-variable, linear relationships, and all require that both variables be random. Inferences can involve tests of significance as well as construction of confidence intervals.

TABLE 14.15   Regression and Correlation Formulas

Least squares equation

$$y_c = a + bx$$

$$b = \frac{n\sum xy - \sum x \sum y}{n\sum x^2 - (\sum x)^2} \qquad a = \frac{\sum y - b\sum x}{n}$$

Standard error

of estimate, $s_e = \sqrt{\dfrac{\sum y^2 - a\sum y - b\sum xy}{n - 2}}$

of slope, $s_b = s_e \sqrt{\dfrac{1}{\sum x^2 - [(\sum x)^2/n]}}$

Slope

significance test $(H_0: B = 0)$ $\qquad t_{\text{test}} = \dfrac{b}{s_b}$

confidence interval $b \pm ts_b$

Confidence intervals for predicted values of y, given x_g

individual $y_c \pm t \cdot s_e \sqrt{1 + \dfrac{1}{n} + \dfrac{(x_g - \bar{x})^2}{\sum x^2 - [(\sum x)^2/n]}}$

average $y_c \pm t \cdot s_e \sqrt{\dfrac{1}{n} + \dfrac{(x_g - \bar{x})^2}{\sum x^2 - [(\sum x)^2/n]}}$

Coefficient of determination

$$r^2 = 1 - \frac{s_e^2}{s_y^2}$$

Correlation

Pearson's $r = \dfrac{n\sum xy - \sum x \sum y}{\sqrt{n\sum x^2 - (\sum x)^2} \cdot \sqrt{n\sum y^2 - (\sum y)^2}}$

significance test $(H_0: \rho = 0)$ $\qquad t_{\text{test}} = \dfrac{r}{\sqrt{(1 - r^2)/(n - 2)}}$

confidence interval (chart)

Spearman's $r = 1 - \dfrac{6\sum d^2}{n(n^2 - 1)}$

contingency $C = \sqrt{\dfrac{\chi^2}{\chi^2 + N}}$

REVIEW QUESTIONS

1. What is a regression line?
2. How are regression lines used?
3. Contrast the terms "independent variable" and "dependent variable."
4. What does the standard error of estimate measure?
5. Explain what is meant by the term "conditional distribution."
6. What are two ways the slope can be tested for significance?
7. What does it mean if the slope is not significant?
8. What does r^2 measure?
9. What is the value of computing a confidence interval for the regression line?
10. Why is the confidence band for individual predicted values wider than the band for the predicted mean values?
11. Why are computers generally used for multiple regression problems?
12. Explain briefly the term "stepwise regression." What is the criterion for "stepping"?
13. What advantage does multiple regression have over linear regression? What disadvantages?
14. How would you decide which technique, simple or multiple regression, was most appropriate for a particular situation?
15. Compare the purpose of correlation analysis with the purpose of regression analysis.
16. What assumptions underlie each of these techniques?
    a. regression analysis
    b. correlation analysis
17. Contrast these pairs:
    a. independent and dependent variables
    b. s_y and s_e
    c. positive slope and negative slope
    d. r and b
18. Why is it important to plot a scatter diagram for two-variable correlation or regression techniques?
19. Why is it risky to make estimates of y for values of x, y that are outside the range of the sample data?
20. Contrast these pairs:
    a. linear regression and curvilinear regression
    b. simple regression and multiple regression
    c. confidence interval for a regression line and a confidence interval for an individual value
21. a. Does a high correlation imply causation?
    b. Does a low correlation always mean that there is no relationship between two variables?
22. What advantages would multiple correlation have over simple correlation? What disadvantages?
23. What does r^2 measure in regard to a regression line?
24. What does a minus sign before r imply? Before b?
25. If Pearson product-moment correlation and Spearman rank correlation coefficients are both computed for the same set of data, and one of the coefficients is significant but the other is not, how would you decide which measure was valid? (Note: additional data is not available.)

26. What does it mean when a test shows that r is not significant?
27. In most business applications, which technique, correlation or regression, is more useful? Why?

SUPPLEMENTAL EXERCISES

1. A farm cooperative studying the relationship between yield per acre and application of fertilizer selected 15 acres of land and randomly selected 3 one-acre plots which received the same application of fertilizer, with these results:

Amount of fertilizer (lb/acre)	200	250	300	350	400
Yield (rounded thousand bu/acre)	1, 1.5, 2	2.5, 3, 4	5.5, 6, 6	6.5, 7, 8	9, 10, 11

   a. Plot the data.
   b. Compute the regression equation for this data.
   c. Determine a 95% confidence interval for the real slope.
   d. Compute r^2.

*2. Cross-tabulation of two areas of response on a survey conducted recently by Anonymous Friends, Inc., yielded the following data for 120 households. Determine if there is a positive or negative correlation and how strong the relationship is.

Number of TV sets household

Income per household	0	1	2	3
low	7	11	6	0
moderate	4	4	3	13
above average	3	7	28	10
high	1	3	8	12

3. Compute the correlation coefficient for the income versus life insurance data in Exercise 9, page 366, and determine if it is significant at the .05 level.
4. Develop a predictive equation for the high school GPA and college QPA example, page 386, and predict the QPA for a student in that population who has a GPA of 81.
5. The following data comprise a random sample of sales versus feet of shelf display for paperback books in a supermarket:

Sales (books/day)	Shelf space (feet)
40	7.0
25	4.0
30	4.4
32	5.0
17	3.2
38	6.0
44	8.0
27	4.2
30	4.8
20	3.4
303	50.0

    a. Plot this data.

    b. Compute the values of a and b for a least squares line.

    c. Compute the standard error of estimate.

    d. Compute r.

    e. Is b significant? Is r? (Use .05.)

    f. The manager of the store wants to use the least squares equation to predict sales if shelf space is 20 feet. Comment on this.

6. Use analysis of variance on the data in Exercise 1. What can you conclude about the relationship from your analysis?

7. Use analysis of variance to analyze the data in Exercise 5. What can you conclude about the relationship?

8. Compute the coefficient of rank correlation for the data in Exercise 5 and compare it to the value of r found in Exercise 5d. Are they the same? Are they ordinarily the same? Explain.

*9. Compute r_{sp} for this data and check for significance at the .01 level.

Weight	145	162	136	178	143	153	149	169	181	137	164	201	155
Order of finish in 100-yard dash	1	2	3	4	5	6	7	8	9	10	11	12	13

15

---

index numbers

Chapter Objectives

After completing this chapter, you should be able to:
1. Explain what index numbers are and how they are used
2. Explain what a simple index number is and compute price, quantity, and value index numbers for a given set of data
3. Explain what a composite index number is and compute price and quantity index numbers using the method of averaging relatives and the method of aggregates
4. List and briefly discuss the special problems and considerations related to construction and use of index numbers
5. Tell how, and why, the base of an index number is shifted
6. List and briefly describe four business indexes

Chapter Outline

INTRODUCTION

INDEX NUMBERS are one important way of summarizing change in economic variables over a period of time. These numbers indicate the relative change in price, quantity, or value between some previous point in time (base period) and, usually, the current period. For example, when the family shopper notes that the cost of a loaf of bread is double what it was ten years ago, he or she is actually making use of one kind of index number.

When only a single product or commodity is involved, the index is called a *simple index*, while a comparison that involves a group of items is called a *composite index*. For instance, in addition to the loaf of bread, a shopper might reasonably include prices of such staples as milk, butter, ground meat, lettuce, and dried beans in the comparison. Some of these items may have undergone relatively large price increases, some very little change, and some may have even decreased in price. The purpose of using a composite index would be to summarize the overall price changes for this group of grocery products. By the same token, the family's purchases of these items may have changed over the years. Perhaps consumption of milk and ground meat has increased. This would likely be the case if the family increased in size, and as the children entered the teenage years. Consumption of butter, on the other hand, may have decreased, particularly if mom or dad is weight-conscious. Hence it may be necessary to include quantity changes as well as price changes in order to obtain a more accurate picture of overall change.

Business and industry are also faced with situations that call for some way to deal with such changes. They, too, experience price and quantity changes in raw materials, semifinished goods, replacement parts, supplies, labor, fuel, and sales. Index numbers offer them a way to measure these changes.

> *Index numbers* are used to indicate relative changes in quantities, prices, or value of a commodity over a given time period.

Strictly speaking, index numbers need not refer only to comparisons between different time periods; they can also be used for comparisons within the same time frame. For example, the comparison of dropout rates among a city's schools, or a comparison of crime rates, housing costs, or food costs among various cities,

413

involve *spatial* comparisons. However, the emphasis here will be on comparisons between time periods. It is also worthwhile to note that the use of index numbers to summarize economic change is relevant in any economy, regardless of its political and social structure.

There are three classifications of business and economic index numbers: price, quantity, and value indexes. The following discussion will include the construction of each kind of index, general comments on the problems of developing and using index numbers, and a brief discussion of four important business and economic indexes: the consumer price index, the Dow-Jones index, the wholesale price index, and the index of industrial production.

All index numbers have certain features in common. One is that they are *ratios* of amount in a current time period to amount in a *base period*. The ratios are stated as percentages, usually to either the nearest one percent or tenth of a percent, but without the percent sign (e.g., 123, 145.2). The amount in the base period is usually taken as 100%.

> An *index number* is a *ratio* used to measure relative change between two time periods.

SIMPLE INDEX NUMBERS

A simple index number measures relative change in a *single* item or economic variable between two time periods. It is computed as the ratio of price, quantity, or value in a given period to the corresponding price, quantity, or value in a base period.

Consider, for example, average price and volume for a local new car dealership for a specific model type with standard factory equipment. The data are shown in Table 15.1.

TABLE 15.1   Price and Volume Data for Car Dealers

(1) Year	(2) Average selling price	(3) Number sold	(2) × (3) Revenue (in thousands)
1972	3000	60	180.0
1973	3300	63	207.9
1974	3900	60	234.0
1975	4500	66	297.0
1976	4500	72	324.0
1977	4800	75	336.0
1978	4950	66	326.7

Simple index numbers for price, quantity, and value *relatives* can be computed using these formulas:

$$\text{price relative} = \frac{p_n}{p_0} \times 100$$

$$\text{quantity relative} = \frac{q_n}{q_0} \times 100$$

$$\text{value relative} = \frac{p_n q_n}{p_0 q_0} \times 100$$

where

p_0 = price of an item in the base year

q_0 = quantity of an item in the base year

p_n = price of an item in a given year

q_n = quantity of an item in a given year

Suppose we agree to use 1972 as the base year. This means that we are treating the price of \$3,000 as equal to 100% and that other year's prices will be measured *relative* to that price. Similarly, volume will be measured using the 60 units sold in 1972 as 100%, and revenue measured using \$180,000 as 100%.

The index numbers (relatives) for price, quantity, and value for 1976 cars are

$$\text{price:} \frac{p_{1976}}{p_{1972}} \times 100 = \frac{4500}{3000} \times 100 = 150$$

$$\text{quantity:} \frac{q_{1976}}{q_{1972}} \times 100 = \frac{72}{60} \times 100 = 120$$

$$\text{value:} \frac{(p_{1976})(q_{1976})}{(p_{1972})(q_{1972})} \times 100 = \frac{(4500)(72)}{(3000)(60)} \times 100 = 180$$

These figures can be interpreted in the following way. Automobile prices increased 50% between 1972 and 1976, the quantity sold increased by 20%, and the value (revenue) increased by 80%. The relatives for other years can be computed in a similar manner. They are shown in Table 15.2.

TABLE 15.2   Annual Price Quantity, and Value Indexes for Car Example, Using 1972 Base Figures

	Price		Quantity		Revenue	
Year	Dollars	Index	Units	Index	Dollars	Index
1972	3000	100	60	100	180.0	100
1973	3300	110	63	105	207.9	116
1974	3900	130	60	100	234.0	130
1975	4500	150	66	110	297.0	165
1976	4500	150	72	120	324.0	180
1977	4800	160	75	125	360.0	200
1978	4950	165	66	110	326.7	182

Simple index numbers using a common base period are called *fixed-base relatives*. Another form of index number, called *link relatives*, focuses attention on yearly changes. Each year's price, quantity, or value is measured as a ratio with respect to the previous year. Link relatives can be computed directly, using the raw data, or they can be determined from fixed-base index numbers, if these are available. Link relatives are also expressed as percentages. For instance, for the data shown in Table 15.2, the link relative for quantity for 1976 could be computed in either of two ways. Using the raw data, we find

$$\text{quantity link relative}_{1976} = \frac{q_{1976}}{q_{1975}} \times 100 = \frac{72}{66} \times 100 = 109$$

Alternatively, the indexes for 1975 and 1976 can be used to obtain the same result:

$$\text{quantity link relative}_{1976} = \frac{I_{1976}}{I_{1975}} \times 100 = \frac{120}{110} \times 100 = 109$$

The link relatives for other years can be obtained in a similar fashion (see Exercise 3). They are shown in Table 15.3.

TABLE 15.3   Link Relatives for the Car Example

Year	Price Actual	Price Relative	Volume Actual	Volume Relative	Revenue Actual	Revenue Relative
1972	30,000	—	60	—	180.9	—
1973	33,000	110	63	105	207.9	116
1974	39,000	118	60	95	234.0	113
1975	45,000	115	66	110	297.0	127
1976	45,000	100	72	109	324.0	109
1977	48,000	107	75	104	260.0	111
1978	49,500	103	66	88	326.7	91

The main limitation of simple relatives is that they can handle only *single* items, whereas it is often desirable to be able to summarize changes for an entire *group* of items. Index numbers for groups are called *composite* index numbers, and we now turn our attention to them.

COMPOSITE INDEX NUMBERS

Composite index numbers are used to indicate relative change in the price, quantity, or value of a *group* of items or commodities. For instance, you might wonder whether grocery *prices*, in general, have risen or fallen over a given time period. To be sure, many prices have risen, but some have fallen. What can you say overall? To find out it is necessary to examine some *combination* of items instead of individual items. Similarly, it may be useful to know if quantities of grocery items have changed, and if they have, what the direction of change is. Two methods for obtaining composite index numbers are considered: the weighted aggregates method and the average of price relatives.

The Weighted Aggregates Method

The problem in measuring *price changes* for a group of commodities is that usually there are changes in quantities purchased as well as changes in prices. Therefore, in order to focus on price alone, changes in quantities of the various items must be factored out. In other words, we want to know to what extent changes in value are due to changes in price, without having to consider changes in quantities. One way to accomplish this is to let the current year quantities equal the base year quantities. In this way, the only difference will be the prices in the two years.

Consider the example of a late night shopper who purchases four items: marshmallows, lemons, cupcakes, and the evening paper. The data are given in Table 15.4. Note that both prices and quantities have changed from 1970 to 1978. If we want to learn what the overall change in prices has been, we can imagine that quantities have remained unchanged. The formula for a price index is as follows:

$$\text{price index (base year weights)} = \frac{\sum p_n q_0}{\sum p_0 q_0} \times 100$$

where q_0 denotes the base year weights.

Using the figures from the table, we find

TABLE 15.4   Late Shopper Data

	1970		1978	
	Price$_0$	Quantity$_0$	Price$_0$	Quantity$_0$
marshmallows	.80/lb	2 lb	1.20/lb	1.5 lb
lemons	.10 each	4	.08 each	6
cupcakes	1.00/doz	1 doz	2.00/doz	.5 doz
evening paper	.10	1	.25	1

$$I_{\text{price}} = \frac{\sum(p_{1978}q_{1970})}{\sum(p_{1970}q_{1970})} \times 100$$

$$= \frac{1.20(2.0) + .08(4) + 2.00(1) + .25(1)}{.80(2.0) + .10(4) + 1.00(1) + .10(1)} \times 100 = 160$$

The price index suggests that, overall, prices have increased by 60%.

In similar fashion, we can compute a quantity index by holding prices constant and thus isolate quantity changes.

$$\text{quantity index (base year weights)} = \frac{\sum q_n q_0}{\sum q_0 p_0} \times 100$$

where p_0 denotes the base year weights.

Referring to the figures in Table 15.4, our quantity index, using base year weights (prices), is

$$I_{\text{quantity}} = \frac{\sum(q_{1978} p_{1970})}{\sum(q_{1970} p_{1970})} \times 100$$

$$= \frac{1.5(.80) + 6(.10) + .5(1.00) + 1(.10)}{2(.80) + 4(.10) + 1(1.00) + 1(.10)} \times 100 = 77$$

The index can be interpreted as showing that the overall quantities of these items purchased by this shopper have declined 23% (i.e., $10\% - 77\% = 23\%$).

A value index would have this form:

$$\text{value index} = \frac{\sum p_n q_n}{\sum p_0 q_0} \times 100$$

For the late shopper, the index would be

$$I_{\text{value}} = \frac{1.20(1.5) + .08(6) + 2.00(.5) + .25(1)}{.80(2) + .10(4) + 1.00(1) + .10(1)} \times 100 = 114$$

It is not absolutely necessary to use base year prices or quantities as weights for these indexes. Current year weights, for example, are sometimes used. However, one disadvantage of current year weights is that they must be revised with each new year. Still another approach might be to use weights for some other year between the base and current years.

Weighted Average of Relatives Method

This method is an alternative approach to the weighted aggregates method; it yields exactly the same numbers. There are computational considerations which influence the choice of methods for a given situation. For instance, as a general rule, the weighted aggregate approach often requires less computational effort. However, in working with published data, original prices and quantities are sometimes not available. Instead, relatives are given, so they must be used. The corresponding price and quantity indexes using relatives are as follows:

$$\text{price index (base year weights)} = \frac{\sum[(p_n/p_0)p_0q_0]}{\sum p_0q_0} \times 100$$

$$\text{quantity index (base year weights)} = \frac{\sum[(q_n/q_0)p_0q_0]}{\sum p_0q_0} \times 100$$

The indexes for our late shopper are

$$I_{price} = \frac{\sum[(p_{1978}/p_{1970})p_{1970}q_{1970}]}{\sum p_{1970}q_{1970}} \times 100$$

$$= \frac{(1.20/.80)(.80)(2) + (.08/.10)(.10)(4) + (2.00/1.00)(1.00)(1) + (.25/.10)(.10)(1)}{.80(2) + .10(4) + 1.00(1) + .10(1)} \times 100$$

$$= 160$$

$$I_{quantity} = \frac{\sum[(q_{1978}/q_{1970})p_{1970}q_{1970}]}{p_{1970}q_{1970}} \times 100$$

$$= \frac{(1.5/2)(.80)(2) + (6/4)(.10)(4) + (.5/1)(1.00)(1) + (1/1)(.10)(1)}{.80(2) + .10(4) + 1.00(1) + .10(1)} \times 100$$

$$= 77$$

which are identical to those previously computed with weighted aggregates.

SPECIAL CONSIDERATIONS AND PROBLEMS

Index numbers are crude attempts to capture economic change. There are inherent dangers in using and interpreting such indicators. For example, quality changes and the frequent introduction of new products (calculators, color TV, mini-computers, and so on) distort comparisons over long time periods. Then, too, definitional changes, such as what constitutes a household, or a dependent, or a voter (e.g., lowering the minimum voting age) distort comparisons. And many situations involve so many items that only a small number of "representative" items are included. The choice of which items to include opens the door to possible biases. In addition, the problems are compounded by the mere fact that consumer buying habits and preferences often tend to change over time, so the "typical market basket" of, say, 1977 can differ substantially from what may be "typical" in, say, 1987.

The choice of a base period is important. Ideally, the base should be fairly recent, and have stable prices, in order to obtain meaningful comparisons. One way to improve stability is to use an average of two or three years for the base period.

Finally, the choice of index is important. Are price changes important? Quality changes? Both? Availability of data can figure in, too. If monthly or weekly data are not available, a quarterly or annual index may be the only alternative.

SHIFTING THE BASE OF AN INDEX NUMBER

It is sometimes desirable to shift the base of an index from one period to another. One objective of such a shift might be to make the base period more recent. This provides a more current measure of change. Another objective might be to make two series with different bases comparable.

The procedure for accomplishing the shift is actually quite simple, given a series of index numbers using the old base. It merely requires that each number in the series be divided by the index number of the new base period. Table 15.5 illustrates this procedure. Note that values are stated in percentage form. For instance, 80/80 = 1, which represents 100%.

TABLE 15.5   Shifting the Base of an Index Number

Index of housing costs		
Old index number (1957–59 = 100)		New index number (1973 = 100)
1973	80	80/80 = 100
1974	76	76/80 = 95
1975	84	84/80 = 105
1976	82	82/80 = 101
1977	88	88/80 = 110
1978	90	90/80 = 120

FOUR IMPORTANT BUSINESS AND ECONOMIC INDEXES

Index numbers in business and economics are often looked upon as barometers of financial and economic activity, supposedly indicating periods of inflation, recession, business cycles, and stagnation. Among the most widely used indexes are the consumer price index, the wholesale price index, and Dow-Jones industrial average, and index of industrial production. Each of these, for example, is widely reported by the news media.

The Consumer Price Index

This index is published monthly by the Department of Labor's Bureau of Labor Statistics. This is what is generally referred to by the news media as the cost-of-living index. It actually measures price changes of goods and services purchased by urban wage earners and clerical workers. The index measures price changes of a typical market basket of approximately 400 items, including such things as food, clothing, housing and transportation costs, medical expenses, and the like. The items on the list should not be construed as a random sample. Instead, they are carefully selected as being typical of the purchases of households in the groups mentioned.

It is not unusual to find "escalator" clauses in collective bargaining agreements that tie wage increases to the consumer price index (CPI). Moreover, Social Security payments and some trusts include provisions for change which take the level of the CPI into account.

The consumer price index values are stated both as annual averages and as monthly averages. Table 15.6 lists some annual averages, beginning with 1951. Note that the base year is 1967 (which is equal to 100). The steady upward trend in the index is quite apparent. Table 15.7 gives a monthly summary of the consumer

TABLE 15.6 Consumer Price Index, Annual Averages and Changes, 1951–76 [1967 = 100]

	Consumer prices					
	All items		Commodities		Services	
Year	Index	Percentage change	Index	Percentage change	Index	Percentage change
1951	77.8	7.9	85.9	9.0	61.8	5.3
1952	79.5	2.2	87.0	1.3	64.5	4.4
1953	80.1	.8	86.7	−.3	67.3	4.3
1954	80.5	.5	85.9	−.9	69.5	3.3
1955	80.2	−.4	85.1	−.9	70.9	2.0
1956	81.4	1.5	85.9	.9	72.7	2.5
1957	84.3	3.6	88.6	3.1	75.6	4.0
1958	86.6	2.7	90.6	2.3	78.5	3.8
1959	87.3	.8	90.7	.1	80.8	2.9
1960	88.7	1.6	91.5	.9	83.5	3.3
1961	89.6	1.0	92.0	.5	85.2	2.0
1962	90.6	1.1	92.8	.9	86.8	1.9
1963	91.7	1.2	93.6	.9	88.5	2.0
1964	92.9	1.3	94.6	1.1	90.2	1.9
1965	94.5	1.7	95.7	1.2	92.2	2.2
1966	97.2	2.9	98.2	2.6	95.8	3.9
1967	100.0	2.9	100.0	1.8	100.0	4.4
1968	104.2	4.2	103.7	3.7	105.2	5.2
1969	109.8	5.4	108.4	4.5	112.5	6.9
1970	116.3	5.9	113.5	4.7	121.6	8.1
1971	121.3	4.3	117.4	3.4	128.4	5.6
1972	125.3	3.3	120.9	3.0	133.3	3.8
1973	133.1	6.2	129.9	7.4	139.1	4.4
1974	147.7	11.0	145.5	12.0	152.0	9.3
1975	161.2	9.1	158.4	8.9	166.6	9.5
1976	170.5	5.8	165.2	4.3	180.4	8.3

Source: U.S. Department of Labor, Bureau of Labor Statistics, Monthly Labor Review, Vol. 100, Nos. 1 and 4.

TABLE 15.7 Consumer Price Index, U.S. Average, General Summary and Groups, Subgroups, and Selected Items [1967 = 100 unless otherwise specified]

General summary	Annual average 1975	1975 Nov.	1975 Dec.	1976 Jan.	Feb.	Mar.	Apr.	May	June	July	Aug.	Sept.	Oct.	Nov.	Dec.
All items	161.2	165.6	166.3	166.7	167.1	167.5	168.2	169.2	170.1	171.1	171.9	172.6	173.3	173.8	155
All items (1957–59 = 100)	187.5	192.6	193.4	193.9	194.4	194.8	195.6	196.7	197.9	199.0	200.0	200.8	201.5	202.1	180
Food	175.4	179.8	180.7	180.8	180.0	178.7	179.2	180.0	180.9	182.1	182.4	181.6	181.6	181.1	169
food at home	175.8	180.0	180.9	180.9	179.6	177.7	178.1	178.8	179.7	180.9	181.0	179.9	179.6	178.9	170
food away from home	174.3	179.2	180.0	180.9	181.9	182.8	183.8	184.8	185.6	186.9	187.8	188.7	189.3	190.0	167
Housing	166.8	171.3	172.2	173.2	173.8	174.5	174.9	175.6	176.5	177.5	178.4	179.5	180.1	180.7	159
rent	137.3	139.9	140.6	141.2	142.1	142.7	143.2	143.8	144.4	145.0	145.6	146.2	146.9	147.5	133
homeownership	181.7	186.8	187.8	188.8	188.6	188.7	188.9	189.6	190.7	192.2	193.4	194.4	194.8	194.8	174
Apparel and upkeep	142.3	145.5	145.2	143.3	144.0	145.0	145.7	146.8	146.9	146.5	148.1	150.2	150.9	151.9	141
Transportation	150.6	157.4	157.6	158.1	158.5	159.8	161.3	163.5	165.9	167.6	168.5	169.5	170.9	171.4	143
Health and recreation	153.5	156.5	157.5	158.6	159.7	160.6	161.4	162.1	162.8	163.7	164.4	165.3	166.1	167.3	147
medical care	168.6	173.3	174.7	176.6	178.8	180.6	181.6	182.6	183.7	185.5	186.8	187.9	188.9	191.3	159
Special groups															
all items less food	159.1	163.4	164.1	164.4	164.9	165.3	166.1	167.1	168.1	169.0	169.7	170.4	171.0	171.6	153
all items less shelter	157.1	161.5	162.1	162.6	163.4	164.2	165.0	166.0	167.0	167.9	168.9	170.0	170.8	171.6	151
all items less medical care	160.9	165.2	165.8	166.2	166.5	166.8	167.4	168.4	169.4	170.3	171.1	171.7	172.4	172.7	155
appliances (including radio and TV)	118.4	120.9	120.8	121.3	121.8	122.1	122.7	123.0	123.3	123.5	123.6	124.2	124.4	124.8	115
Commodities	158.4	162.2	162.7	162.4	162.3	162.3	163.1	164.2	165.2	166.0	166.6	167.0	167.4	167.7	153
nondurables	163.2	167.1	167.6	167.3	167.2	166.7	167.2	168.2	169.0	169.7	170.4	170.7	171.0	171.3	158
durables	145.5	149.2	149.3	149.0	149.3	150.4	151.9	153.5	154.7	155.8	156.4	156.9	157.8	158.0	138
Services	166.6	172.0	173.1	174.9	176.1	177.2	177.7	178.4	179.5	180.7	181.8	183.2	184.1	185.1	160
Commodities less food	149.1	152.6	152.8	152.3	152.7	153.3	154.2	155.5	156.5	157.1	158.0	158.9	159.6	160.3	143
nondurables less food	151.7	155.1	155.4	154.7	155.2	155.5	156.0	157.0	157.9	158.1	159.1	160.4	161.0	161.9	147
apparel commodities	141.2	144.4	143.9	141.5	142.2	143.1	143.9	145.1	145.0	144.4	146.2	148.5	149.2	150.1	141
apparel commodities less footwear	140.6	144.1	143.6	140.9	141.4	142.2	142.8	144.2	144.1	143.4	145.2	147.8	148.5	149.4	141
nondurables less food and apparel	157.9	161.5	162.2	162.6	162.9	162.8	163.2	164.2	165.6	166.3	166.8	167.4	168.1	169.0	151
household durables	140.3	142.9	143.0	143.3	144.0	144.8	145.5	145.8	146.1	146.5	146.3	146.7	147.2	147.8	136
housefurnishings	144.4	147.4	147.5	147.4	148.5	149.5	150.1	150.3	150.9	150.9	150.8	151.7	152.2	152.9	140
Services less rent	171.9	177.7	179.0	181.0	182.2	183.4	184.0	184.7	185.8	187.2	188.4	189.8	190.8	191.8	164
household services less rent	184.7	190.7	192.0	193.7	194.4	195.1	195.4	196.1	197.3	198.7	200.1	201.5	202.3	202.6	177
transportation services	152.7	161.7	163.2	167.0	168.9	171.1	171.7	172.3	173.2	174.7	175.5	177.3	178.9	180.2	146
medical care services	179.1	184.2	185.8	188.0	190.4	192.5	193.5	194.6	195.8	197.9	199.4	200.6	201.7	204.5	168
other services	152.1	155.2	155.7	156.6	157.4	158.4	159.1	159.7	160.5	161.2	162.0	163.6	164.3	165.2	147

Source: U.S. Department of Labor, Bureau of Labor Statistics: Monthly Labor Review, Vol. 100, No. 4.

price index for 1974, and provides a finer breakdown of the elements which comprise the index.

There are many uses of this index. One common use is to measure "consumer purchasing power," or the purchasing power of the dollar. This is nothing more than the reciprocal of the CPI. Table 15.8 illustrates how these values are obtained.

TABLE 15.8   Computing the Purchasing
Power of the Dollar Using 1967
as the Base Year

Year	CPI	$(1/\text{CPI}) \times 100 = $ purchasing power
1961	89.6	$1.12
1962	90.6	1.10
1963	91.7	1.09
1964	92.9	1.08
1965	94.5	1.06
1966	97.2	1.03
1967	100.0	1.00
1968	104.2	.96
1969	109.8	.91
1970	116.3	.86
1971	121.3	.82
1972	125.3	.80
1973	133.1	.75
1974	147.7	.68
1975	161.2	.62

The CPI is also used to measure "real" income, which is income adjusted for price changes. Thus dividing take-home pay by the current value of CPI in any year will reveal real income for that year. Comparison between years is also possible. Consider a factory worker who received $10,000 in take-home pay in 1970 and $12,600 in 1974. How did his real income change? Dividing each year's take-home pay by the value of the CPI for that year, we find his real income as shown below.

	Take-home pay	CPI	Real income
1970	$10,000	116.3	$10,000/116.3 = $8,598
1974	$12,600	147.7	$12,600/147.7 = $8,531

In other words, this person was slightly worse off in terms of real income in 1974 than in 1970, in spite of the higher takehome pay, because prices measured by the CPI rose faster than take-home pay.

In 1977 the method of compiling the CPI underwent a major revision in an attempt to modernize the index. The weights assigned to various spending categories such as food, clothing, medical care, and the like were revised to more closely reflect reality. Furthermore, the sample of items priced and the sample of retail stores was updated. Presently, the index represents about 80% of the population, whereas previously it represented only about 40% of the population.*

* Julius Shiskin, "The Consumer Price Index: How Will the 1977 Revision Affect It?" *Statistical Reporter* (December 1975).

The Wholesale Price Index

This index is also published by the Bureau of Labor Statistics. It is intended to measure relative changes in the prices manufacturers pay for raw materials, and it includes all major products and materials used in American industry. Industrial contracts sometimes contain provisions for price changes related to future values of this index. Values of the wholesale price index (WPI) are published monthly and annually. Some recent values are shown in Table 15.9.

TABLE 15.9   Wholesale Price Index, 1951–76 [1967 = 100]

	Wholesale prices					
	All commodities		Farm products, processed foods and feeds		Industrial commodities	
Year	Index	Percentage change	Index	Percentage change	Index	Percentage change
1951	91.1	11.4	106.9	13.8	86.1	10.4
1952	88.6	−2.7	102.7	−3.9	84.1	−2.3
1953	87.4	−1.4	96.0	−6.5	84.8	.8
1954	87.6	.2	95.7	−.3	85.0	.2
1955	87.8	.2	91.2	−4.7	86.9	2.2
1956	90.7	3.3	90.6	−.7	90.8	4.5
1957	93.3	2.9	93.7	3.4	93.3	2.8
1958	94.6	1.4	98.1	4.7	93.6	.3
1959	94.8	.2	93.5	−4.7	95.3	1.8
1960	94.9	.1	93.7	.2	95.3	0
1961	94.5	−.4	93.7	0	94.8	−.5
1962	94.8	.3	94.7	1.1	94.8	0
1963	94.5	−.3	93.8	−1.0	94.7	−.1
1964	94.7	.2	93.2	−.6	95.2	.5
1965	96.6	2.0	97.1	4.2	96.4	1.3
1966	99.8	3.3	103.5	6.6	98.5	2.2
1967	100.0	.2	100.0	−3.4	100.0	1.5
1968	102.5	2.5	102.4	2.4	102.5	2.5
1969	106.5	3.9	108.0	5.5	106.0	3.4
1970	110.4	3.7	111.7	3.4	110.0	3.8
1971	113.9	3.2	113.8	2.0	114.0	3.6
1972	119.1	4.6	122.4	7.6	117.9	3.4
1973	134.7	13.1	159.1	30.0	125.9	6.8
1974	160.1	18.9	177.4	11.5	153.8	22.2
1975	174.9	9.2	184.2	3.8	171.5	11.5
1976	182.9	4.6	183.1	−.6	182.3	6.3

Source: U.S. Department of Labor, Bureau of Labor Statistics: Monthly Labor Review, Vol. 100, Nos. 1 and 4.

The Dow-Jones Industrial Average

This is perhaps the best known of a group of indexes which purport to show changes in stock market prices. The Dow-Jones index includes 30 industrial common stocks. Like the group of items included in the consumer price index, this is also not a random sample of the roughly 1800 stocks listed on the New York stock exchange. Instead, the 30 stocks are supposedly representative of stock prices in general, although there is considerable doubt as to how representative these industrial stocks actually are. Other stock indexes are the Standard and Poor's 500, the New York Stock Exchange Composite Index of All Stocks, and the American Stock Exchange Index.

Index of Industrial Production

This index is published by the Federal Reserve Board on the basis of information compiled from other government agencies. It measures changes in the volume of output of manufacturing, mining, and utility companies, and includes approximately 100 components. These industries account for about 70% to 80% of the total U.S. production of goods and services in the private sector. The index is usually regarded as an indicator of general business conditions.

DEFLATING A TIME SERIES

When annual figures are stated in dollar amounts, those amounts include both quantity and price changes. The price changes, often due to inflation or deflation, can obscure quantity changes. Consider, for example, the data shown in Figure 15.1. Although dollar sales appear to indicate sizable gains for the period shown, sales in units indicate only moderate gains. Evidently price increases account for the major portion of dollar sales gains.

If there is only a single product, the use of units rather than dollar sales avoids this difficulty. However, most problems of interest involve transactions with

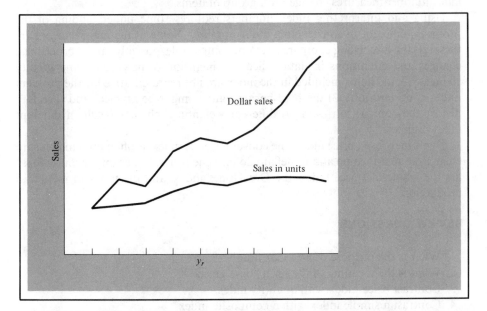

FIGURE 15.1 Dollar changes often obscure quantity changes.

multiple products. For example, department store sales, supermarket sales, and so on, are of this nature. In such cases dollar sales can be converted to quantity figures by factoring out overall price changes, as measured by an index like the CPI. Original dollar amounts are "deflated" (divided) by the value of the CPI for the corresponding period. The net result is a clearer picture of real changes.

$$\text{deflated value:} \frac{\text{original dollar value}}{\text{price index}} \times 100$$

Example 1 The table below shows how deflated values are computed.

Year	Dollar sales (in thousands)	CPI	Deflated values
1970	$880	116.3	$880/116.3 \times 100 = 757$
1971	940	121.3	$940/121.3 \times 100 = 775$
1972	1100	125.3	$1100/125.3 \times 100 = 878$
1973	1450	133.1	$1450/133.1 \times 100 = 1089$
1974	1790	147.7	$1790/147.7 \times 100 = 1212$
1975	1825	161.2	$1825/161.2 \times 100 = 1132$

SUMMARY

Index numbers are ratios that measure the relative change in prices, quantities, or values between two time periods. There are simple and composite index numbers. A simple index number focuses on changes in a single item; a composite index number measures change for a group of items.

Using and interpreting index numbers requires some understanding of the problems inherent in constructing index numbers. Some of the main dangers are these: (1) the data being compared are not comparable, possibly due to procedural changes and definitions in data collection, inclusion of new items, and quality changes; (2) the items included in the index are not representative for the problem under consideration; (3) the base period figures might be atypical and therefore distort the comparison; and (4) different weighting schemes result in different index numbers.

One widely used price index, the consumer price index, is often used to measure changes in real income and to deflate dollar time series. Other important indexes are the wholesale price index, the Dow-Jones index, and the index of industrial production.

REVIEW QUESTIONS

1. What is the purpose of an index number?
2. What is the meaning of the term "base period"?
3. Contrast price index with quantity index.
4. Contrast a simple index with a composite index.
5. How do link relatives differ from fixed-based relatives?

6. Explain how the average of price relatives differs from the weighted aggregate method.
7. List four special problems or considerations generally associated with the construction or use of index numbers.
8. Why is it sometimes desirable to shift the base of an index number?
9. List four commonly used index numbers.
10. Describe some of the ways the consumer price index is used.
11. What happens to the purchasing power of the dollar when the CPI increases? What happens if the CPI decreases?

EXERCISES

1. The owner of a small doughnut shop wants to compare sales and prices in 1976 with those for the year after he took over from the previous owner. Data represent values for the first week in June. Compute a simple price index, a quality index, and a value index for these data, using 1966 as 100%.

	1966	1976
Sales	650 dozen	600 dozen
Price	$.90/doz	$1.40/doz

2. A trucking firm wants to compare prices, quantities, and values using 1970 as a base year. Compute suitable index numbers.

	1970	1978
Tons shipped (in thousands)	300	360
Cost per ton	$50	$70

3. Compute link relatives for the data shown in Table 15.2 and compare your answers to those given in Table 15.3.
4. The night manager of a dairy store has kept accurate records of prices and quantities of his leading products and now wants to make comparisons, using August figures.

	1972		1978	
	price	quantity	price	quantity
Milk				
whole, $\frac{1}{2}$ gal	.49	400,000	.79	450,000
skim, qt	.30	80,000	.40	100,000
chocolate, qt	.35	20,000	.40	22,000
heavy cream, $\frac{1}{2}$ pt	.22	1,000	.29	1,000
Ice cream				
economy, gal	1.09	30,000	1.39	40,000
deluxe, $\frac{1}{2}$ gal	1.49	10,000	1.79	12,000
sherbert, pt	.40	3,000	.40	3,600
Eggs				
small, doz	.39	30,000	.59	20,000
medium, doz	.45	40,000	.65	35,000
large, doz	.49	60,000	.75	80,000
x-large, doz	.53	30,000	.79	40,000

a. Use the weighted aggregate method to obtain price, quantity, and value index numbers for ice cream products, with 1972 weights.

b. Use the weighted aggregate method to obtain a price index and a quantity index for *all* products combined, using 1972 weights.

c. Compute price relatives for *each* of the eleven products, using 1972 = 100%.

*5. The plant manager is reviewing production figures for his injection molding department of the plastics division. The data (first quarter of each year) are given below. Compute both price and quantity indexes for 1974, 1976, and 1978, using the weighted aggregates method with 1972 base weights.

	1972		1974		1976		1978	
	Cost	Quantity	Cost	Quantity	Cost	Quantity	Cost	Quantity
Labor, price/h	4.00	10,400	4.10	10,920	4.80	9360	5.20	10,400
Materials, price/ton	28	12	30	15	36	10	38	14
Overhead, price/ft^2	50	800	55	800	70	800	70	1000

6. Rework Exercise 5 using the average of relatives method.

7. Obtain the latest monthly value of the CPI and last week's closing value of the Dow-Jones industrial index.

8. Name five commonly used indexes *other than* those mentioned in this chapter. (Hint: Check government publications such as *Survey of Current Business*, *Monthly Labor Review*, or *Business Conditions Digest*.)

*9. Shift the base of the CPI values given in Table 15.8 to 1970, and then compute the purchasing power of the dollar for the years 1961 to 1975, using 1970 as the base year.

10. Use the annual values of the WPI industrial commodities to deflate the prices paid by a manufacturer for cleaning supplies. Use 1967 = 100%.

Year	Price per barrel
1968	$4.80
1969	4.85
1970	4.85
1971	5.00
1972	5.00
1973	5.25
1974	5.40
1975	5.70
1976	6.11

16

analysis of
time series

Chapter Objectives

After completing this section, you should be able to:
1. Explain the term "time series"
2. Describe the classical approach to analysis of time series, identifying the four components of a series and explaining how the components are isolated
3. Solve simple problems using these techniques
4. Contrast the additive and multiplicative models
5. Explain the term "exponential smoothing"
6. Tell how exponential smoothing differs from the classical approach to the analysis of time series data.

Chapter Outline

The Classical Model
    Multiplicative and additive models
Trend
    Isolating trend using regression analysis
    Moving averages
Cyclical and Irregular Variations
Seasonal Variations
    Ratio-to-moving-average method
Recomposition
Exponential Smoothing
    Choice of smoothing constant
Comment
Summary

INTRODUCTION

A TIME series is a chronological (time-ordered) set of observations. Examples of time series include such things as records of daily precipitation, weekly sales, quarterly GNP, hourly measurements in a hospital of a patient's temperature and blood pressure, EKG and EEG tests which may be given as part of a routine physical examination, and radar monitoring of the launching of a spaceship.

The purpose of analyzing such data is to determine if any nonrandom patterns are present. Sometimes the desire is to discover nonrandom patterns, which can then be used for predicting the future. For instance, sales forecasting is one area where past data is explored with the hopes of finding something that will be useful for predicting future demand. At other times the desire is to assure that nonrandom patterns are not present. In these cases nonrandom patterns are viewed as a signal that a system or process is "out of control."

For instance, industrial quality control makes extensive use of time series data in monitoring and adjusting manufacturing processes. A machine that is functioning properly will produce pieces with average dimensions that are statistically independent of each other (i.e., there will be no historical relationship among observations.) Instead, values appear to be random observations from some probability distribution, such as the normal distribution. While significance tests of means and proportions are quite useful in evaluating deviations from a norm (critical values of these tests are treated as "control limits"), those tests focus on extreme values. They completely ignore the possibility of nonrandom patterns *within* the control limits. Detecting this sort of nonrandom behavior requires more attention to the *sequence* of observations. The runs tests discussed previously are useful in detecting nonrandom patterns of this nature. If any nonrandom patterns are found in the data, this is regarded as evidence that the machine or process is out of control and corrective measures would be taken to return the process to a state of statistical control.

The emphasis in this section will be on time series in which there is some *historical* relationship among the observations. The purpose of the analysis is to determine what that relationship is so that it can be used in planning or forecasting. Cash register receipts, stock market prices, living expenses, production costs, and many other economic, political, and social variables often exhibit historical patterns. Sometimes these patterns seem to be related to *extrinsic* variables (i.e., they can be explained in terms of other variables). For example, sales of consumer durables such as refrigerators, dishwashers, clothes dryers, and the like are often sensitive to such factors as housing starts and employment levels. Thus the more people there are working, or the greater the number of new houses

431

under construction, the greater the potential for sales of consumer durables. Econometric models, similar to multiple regression models, are often useful in these analyses, although a discussion of such techniques is beyond the scope of this book.

The discussion that follows pertains to *intrinsic* analysis, which focuses on historical data of the variable of interest. It should be noted that intrinsic analysis is widely used in business and industry. The avowed purpose of intrinsic analysis is to *describe* rather than to *explain* historical patterns of the data (i.e., to identify various patterns). Moreover, the underlying assumption of intrinsic analysis is that there is a constant causal system related to time which exerts an influence on the data. In other words, the historical data presumably reflect the influence of all factors—and reflect these uniformly over time. For instance, a study of past sales over a 14-year period may reveal that sales have steadily increased at a rate of about 10% annually. A projection of future sales is made on this basis, assuming that whatever forces have created this pattern will continue in the future.

In the following pages two intrinsic models that are widely used for analysis of time series data are explained. The first is commonly referred to as the *classical model*, and the second is called *exponential smoothing*.

THE CLASSICAL MODEL

The classical, or decomposition, model, regards time series data as being composed of four basic patterns:

1. Trend.
2. Cyclical variations.
3. Seasonal variations.
4. Irregular variations.

The term "trend" refers to a smooth, long-term upward or downward movement in the data. Trends can be related to such things as population changes (perhaps influenced by the growth of retirement communities or decreases in the birth rate), establishment or abolishment of draft regulations, changes in consumer preferences, increasing emphasis on energy conservation, and so on. A linear trend is illustrated in Figure 16.1(a).

A *cyclical* pattern exists when fluctuations exhibit some degree of regularity. A typical pattern is shown in Figure 16.1(b). Economists have found cyclical patterns in the demand for durable goods and agricultural products, business inventories, stock market prices, and prosperity. There is also evidence that sunspots, rainfall, and certain animal populations have cyclical patterns. The cycles tend to vary in terms of regularity, some being fairly regular and others more erratic. There is little agreement even among experts as to the causes or cures for these cycles.

Seasonal variations are relatively short-term cyclical variations (a year or less), which are often related to the changing seasons (weather) or to holidays. For example, there are seasonal patterns in sales of recreational goods that are used primarily in one season, such as skis, sleds, boats, fishing gear, and so on. Greeting cards, textbooks, clothing, automobiles, and garden supplies also exhibit seasonal

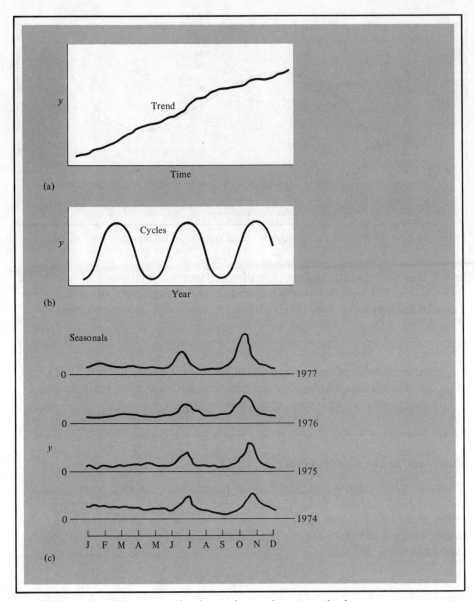

FIGURE 16.1   The components of a time series can be separately shown.

patterns in sales. Figure 16.1(c) portrays a series of seasonal patterns. The pattern tends to stand out due to the way the years are aligned.

Finally, *irregular variations* are composed of such things as "acts of God," strikes, and whatever else is left after the first three factors have been accounted for.

In the classical model the approach is to decompose a time series into each of these basic components of variation, analyze each component separately, and then recombine the series in order to describe the observed variations in the variable of interest. The decomposition process involves the systematic removal of each component from the data, beginning with trend. Figure 16.2 illustrates

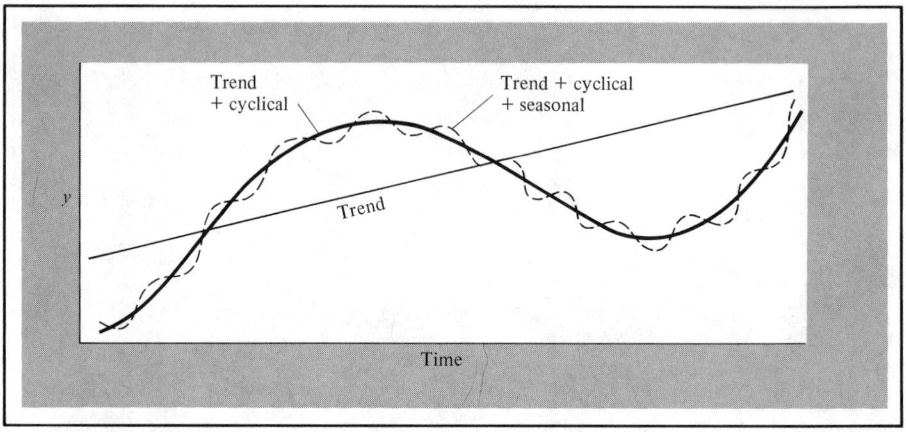

FIGURE 16.2 A time series may be composed of trend, cyclical, and seasonal variations.

how a time series might incorporate all components. Note that each pattern is shown in its ideal form. Furthermore, random and irregular variations have been excluded for simplicity. Real life data rarely produce such smooth patterns.

The *classical approach* to analysis of time series data attempts to sort out trend, cyclical, irregular, and seasonal components of the data in order to analyze each component separately.

Multiplicative and Additive Models

There are two variations of the classical model. One is called "multiplicative" and the other "additive." The first of these treats a time series as if it is the resultant of the *product* of the individual components, while the latter treats a time series as the resultant of the *sum* of the individual components. Thus the *multiplicative* model has the form

$$Y = T \times C \times S \times I$$

where

$$T = \text{trend component}$$
$$C = \text{cyclical component}$$
$$S = \text{seasonal component}$$
$$I = \text{irregular component}$$

and the *additive* model has the form

$$Y = T + C + S + I$$

In both models the trend figure is an actual amount (e.g., 20,000 bushels). In the additive model, C, S, and I are also actual amounts, but in the multiplicative model, *C*, *S*, and *I* are expressed as *percentages* of trend. Although the additive model may appear somewhat easier to work with, the multiplicative model is more widely used, mainly because it more closely portrays actual experience. However, the ultimate criterion for a given situation is *to use the model that best fits the data.*

TREND

Secular trend refers to long-term upward or downward movements in the data. There are two basic purposes for isolating the trend component of a time series. One is to identify the trend and use it, say, in forecasting. The other is to remove trend so that the other components of a time series can be studied. Thus in terms of forecasting, investigation of trend may yield insight into the long-term direction of a time series.

The long-term direction of demand is of vital concern to almost any firm or business. Very often, the strategies adopted by the firm will depend on whether demand is expected to increase, decrease, or remain steady over an extended period. Increasing demand may suggest the need for expansion of present facilities, investment in capital equipment, additional funding, and so on. Conversely, decreasing demand may suggest the need to consider advertising and promotional schemes, a search for new products, budget curtailment, and so on. Furthermore, trends in such variables as population growth, government deficits, taxes, weather, and the like are also sources of concern and merit analysis.

On the other hand, trend movements can often obscure other components of a time series. For instance, seasonal and cyclical patterns can be less apparent when trend is present. Short-range strategies often depend more on seasonal and cyclical factors than on long-range trend. For instance, factories work overtime or temporarily lay off workers according to seasonal variations in demand. Similarly, the cost of borrowed funds may exhibit cyclical patterns, and a firm may be able to plan its budget accordingly.

Two important purposes for isolating the trend component of a time series are (1) to remove it so that other components can be analyzed and (2) to identify it so that trend considerations can be taken into account in planning decisions.

There are two general methods for isolating trend. One is to use regression models similar to those discussed previously. The other is to use a moving average approach to smooth out the nontrend components.

Isolating Trend Using Regression Analysis

The regression models developed in Chapter 14 can be applied to the analysis of time series data by substituting time ($t = 1, 2, 3, \ldots$) for the independent variable

x and by using the corresponding values of the time series observations as the dependent variable Y. The underlying rationale is that the causal system that influences the time series is assumed to be a function (varies systematically) of time.

Trend can be linear or curvilinear. For instance, very often growth of a product or industry follows a curvilinear pattern such as that illustrated in Figure 16.3. However, there are many instances in which a *linear* model is appropriate. In fact, the discussion here will be limited to linear trends because of the broad applicability of linear models in practice and because of the simplicity of such models.

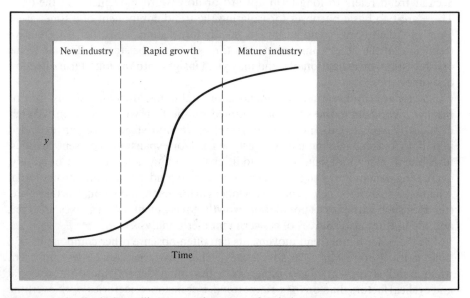

FIGURE 16.3   Typical curvilinear growth pattern of an industry.

Figure 16.4 contains time series data for a 20-year period. Observe from the graph that a linear trend line seems reasonable. Let us see how linear regression techniques can be used to obtain a trend line.

Year	Tons	Year	Tons
1954	10	1964	14
1955	11	1965	10
1956	9	1966	18
1957	11	1967	16
1958	12	1968	20
1959	15	1969	22
1960	13	1970	14
1961	17	1971	21
1962	16	1972	17
1963	13	1973	21

Rewriting the previous linear regression equations, substituting a time scale (t) for the independent variable scale (x), we obtain an equation of the form

$$Y_t = a + bt$$

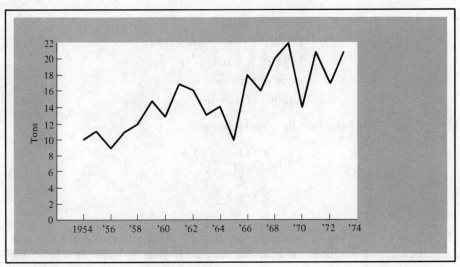

FIGURE 16.4   Time series graph of data.

TABLE 16.1   Calculation of a Linear Trend Equation

Year	Period t	Data Y	tY	t^2
1954	1	10	10	1
1955	2	11	22	4
1956	3	9	27	9
1957	4	11	44	16
1958	5	12	60	25
1959	6	15	90	36
1960	7	13	91	49
1961	8	17	136	64
1962	9	16	144	81
1963	10	13	130	100
1964	11	14	154	121
1965	12	10	120	144
1966	13	18	234	169
1967	14	16	224	196
1968	15	20	300	225
1969	16	22	352	256
1970	17	14	238	289
1971	18	21	378	324
1972	19	17	323	361
1973	20	21	420	400

$$\sum t = 210 \qquad \sum Y = 300 \qquad \sum tY = 3497 \qquad \sum t^2 = 2870$$

$$b = \frac{n \sum tY - \sum t \sum Y}{n \sum t^2 - (\sum t)^2} = \frac{20(3497) - 210(300)}{20(2870) - (210)^2} = .52$$

$$a = \frac{\sum Y - b \sum t}{n} = \frac{300 - .52(210)}{20} = 9.52$$

$$Y = 9.52 + .52t$$

where

$$Y_t = \text{predicted value of time series}$$
$$a = \text{value of } Y_t \text{ when } t = 0$$
$$b = \text{slope of the line}$$
$$t = \text{number of time periods}$$

The corresponding equations for a and b become

$$b = \frac{n \sum tY - \sum t \sum Y}{n \sum t^2 - (\sum t)^2}$$

$$a = \frac{\sum Y - b \sum t}{n}$$

where n is the number of observations. For all practical purposes, then, the computations are identical to those illustrated previously. Table 16.1 provides an example of the necessary calculations and the resulting trend equation.

TABLE 16.2 Values of $\sum t$ and $\sum t^2$

n	$\sum t$	$\sum t^2$
1	1	1
2	3	5
3	6	14
4	10	30
5	15	55
6	21	91
7	28	140
8	36	204
9	45	285
10	55	385
11	66	506
12	78	650
13	91	819
14	105	1015
15	120	1240
16	136	1496
17	153	1785
18	171	2109
19	190	2470
20	210	2870
21	231	3311
22	253	3795
23	276	4324
24	300	4900
25	325	5525
26	351	6201
27	378	6930
28	406	7714
29	435	8555
30	465	9455

Notice that the years are "coded." That is, the actual values, 1954, 1955, 1956, and so on, are replaced by the numbers 1, 2, 3, and so on. This simplifies computations and results in an a-value at $t = 0$. In addition, you will see that the values $\sum t, \sum t^2, \sum tY$, and $\sum Y$ are required in the formulas. Table 16.2 can easily be used to obtain the $\sum t$ and the $\sum t^2$.

Thus the linear component of these data is represented by the equation $Y = 9.52 + .52t$. The line can be plotted by identifying any *two* points. Of course, we already have one point: the value of a. Hence for $t = 0\,(1953)$, $Y = a = 9.52$. Another point might be the value of Y when $t = 10$: $Y = 9.52 + .52(10) = 14.72$. The line is plotted in Figure 16.5.

If the data are annual sales, in thousands of units, and the purpose of the analysis is to predict future sales, values of t can be substituted into the equation to obtain the projected sales in future years. For example, the sales estimate for 1974 $(t = 21)$ would be

$$Y = 9.52 + .52(21) = 20.44 \text{ thousands} \qquad \text{or } 2{,}044{,}000$$

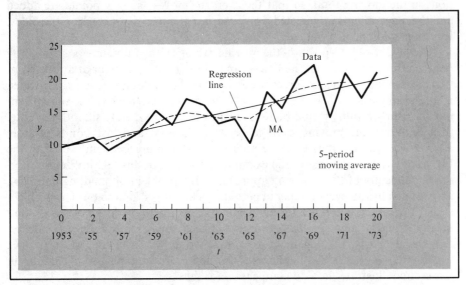

FIGURE 16.5   Original data, the linear trend, and a five-period moving average.

Moving Averages

A second method for trend analysis is the use of a moving average. A moving average is an average of the last k data points, say the last 10, 15, or 22 observations. For example, if the average is composed of the last 12 observations $(k = 12)$, then as each new observation is considered (included in the average), the oldest (12th back in the data) is dropped. A moving average is the arithmetic average of the last k observations:

$$MA = \frac{\sum\limits_{i=t-k}^{t} Y_i}{k}$$

Consider the following series, for which a five-period moving average has been developed.

Y	Moving total (5 periods)	$MT/5$	MA
9			
10			
12			
8			
6	$45 (= 9 + 10 + 12 + 8 + 6)$	$45/5 = 9$	
14	$50 (= 45 + 14 - 9)$	$50/5 = 10$	
20	$60 (= 50 + 20 - 10)$	$60/5 = 12$	
16	$64 (= 60 + 16 - 12)$	$64/5 = 12.8$	
6	$62 (= 64 + 6 - 8)$	$62/5 = 12.4$	

Note that a five-period *moving total* (sum of the last five observations) is first computed, and that the moving average is found by dividing the moving total by the number of periods (values) in that total. Thus there are always k observations in the moving total, so that the average "moves" as new points are added and the oldest points are deleted. Hence to find the next average, drop the oldest value and add one new value.

Usual practice is to position the moving average either at a time point midway between the time points of the newest and oldest observations or at a time point that corresponds to the most recent observation. The latter approach is illustrated in the example above. If the purpose is to predict *the next value*, the current moving average value would be used. If the intent is to merely smooth the data, then centering the moving average between the first and last points is more appropriate. In fact, the centering approach is the more frequently used of the two approaches, and most of the examples presented in this text utilize it.

One difficulty of the centering approach is the problem of handling a moving average that has an even number of periods, such as 4, 6, 8, and so on. The problem is that the centered average for an even number of periods does not correspond to any of the original periods, and certain techniques require correspondence. For instance, a two-period moving average would be centered first at 1.5 (i.e., between data points 1 and 2), then 2.5, and so on. An example presented later in this section illustrates how to compensate for this.

The effect of using a moving average is to smooth out (remove) seasonal, cyclical, irregular, and random variations, and what remains is considered as trend. The problem is that it is almost impossible to completely remove cyclical and irregular variations in this way. Ideally, by selecting a long enough time period for the moving average, cyclical and some irregular variations can be removed. However, the more data included in the average, the less sensitive the average is to recent observations. Sometimes a weighting scheme is used that gives more weight to recent periods than to earlier data points. A later section in this chapter deals with one such technique.

Table 16.3 illustrates a five-period moving average for the same data analyzed in Table 16.1 using linear regression. Note the comparison of the two approaches in Figure 16.5. One advantage of a moving average over a linear trend approach is that it can handle nonlinear trends as well as linear trends. A disadvantage is

TABLE 16.3   Illustration of a Five-Year Moving Average

Year	Period t	Data Y	Five-period moving average includes	Five-period moving average (MA)
1954	1	10		
1955	2	11		
1956	3	9		10.6
1957	4	11		11.6
1958	5	12		12.0
1959	6	15		13.6
1960	7	13		14.6
1961	8	17		14.8
1962	9	16		14.6
1963	10	13		14.0
1964	11	14		14.2
1965	12	10		14.2
1966	13	18		15.6
1967	14	16		17.2
1968	15	20		18.0
1969	16	22		18.6
1970	17	14		18.8
1971	18	21		19.0
1972	19	17		
1973	20	21		

that the first few data points, and the last few, do not have corresponding moving average values, while they do have linear trend values.

CYCLICAL AND IRREGULAR VARIATIONS

Cyclical variations are periodic variations of more than one year in length. Ordinarily such variations cannot be separated from irregular variations, so the two are analyzed together. To isolate cyclical variations, the other variations (trend and seasonal) must be removed from the time series data. Seasonal variations are effectively removed by using annual figures (since seasonal variations are defined as cycles of a year or less in duration, annual figures will not show seasonal fluctuations), or, if monthly figures are being analyzed, by using a 12-month moving average. Next, the trend is extracted from the data, and what is left is considered to be the total of the cyclical and the irregular fluctuations.

The removal of trend requires obtaining a trend line (or curve). This can be done by using a regression equation or a long-term moving average. Removing the trend from the data depends on whether an additive or multiplicative model is being used. In the additive model each observation is subtracted from the corresponding trend value. The result is a series of deviations from trend. Figure 16.6 illustrates the concept. Table 16.4 illustrates the method for eliminating trend in data in the additive model, given a linear regression equation derived from the data.

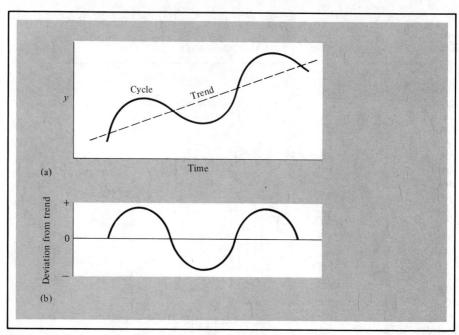

FIGURE 16.6   (a) original data with trend and cyles; (b) data with trend removed, leaving cycles.

TABLE 16.4   Removing Trend in an Additive Model, Using Linear Regression

t	Original data Y	Trend, $Y_t = 10 + 2t$	Data without trend, $Y - Y_t$
1	12	12	0
2	15	14	+1
3	18	16	+2
4	19	18	+1
5	20	20	0
6	21	22	−1
7	22	24	−2
8	25	26	−1
9	28	28	0
10	31	30	+1
11	34	32	+2
12	35	34	+1
13	36	36	0
14	37	38	−1
15	38	40	−2
16	41	42	−1
17	44	44	0
18	47	46	+1
19	50	48	+2
20	51	50	+1

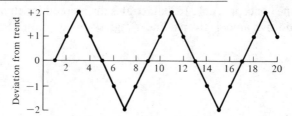

In this simple example random and irregular variations have been excluded from the data. Consequently, the resulting cycles are uniform. Ordinarily, we might expect to use a moving average to smooth some of these variations after eliminating the trend from the data, if a linear trend equation was used. If a moving average was used, the random variations may have been smoothed already.

Table 16.5 illustrates the method for eliminating trend in data when a multiplicative model is used, given a linear regression equation for the data. Note that at each point in time, the original data are divided by the regression value for that time and then multiplied by 100. The result is that each observation is expressed as a percentage of trend. The data with trend removed is shown in the accompanying plot. Once again, the cycles appear to be fairly regular, with a length (peak-to-peak) of about eight periods. If the cycles contain irregularities, a moving average could be used to smooth them in order to obtain a better picture of the cyclical variations.

TABLE 16.5 Removing Trend in a Multiplicative Model, Using Linear Regression

t	Original data Y	Trend, $Y_t = 100 + 10t$	Data without trend, $(Y/Y_t) \cdot 100$
1	110	110	100%
2	124	120	103
3	140	130	108
4	148	140	106
5	150	150	100
6	158	160	99
7	165	170	97
8	170	180	94
9	190	190	100
10	209	200	105
11	230	210	110
12	229	220	104
13	230	230	100
14	230	240	96
15	225	250	90
16	250	260	96
17	270	270	100
18	292	280	104
19	320	290	110
20	310	300	103
21	290	310	94

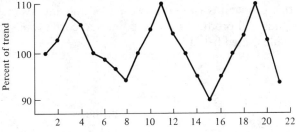

SEASONAL VARIATIONS

Seasonal fluctuations are regularly recurring variations within the period of one year. There are two general purposes in isolating the seasonal component of a time series. One is to remove that pattern in order to study cyclical fluctuations. This was illustrated in the previous section. The second purpose is to identify seasonal factors so that they may be taken into account in making decisions. For example, if a manufacturing firm realizes that there are seasonal fluctuations in the demand for a certain product, it may want to adjust budgets, production schedules, manpower, and inventory with this in mind. Often such adjustments are costly. Alternatively, the firm may search for a complementary product—a product with seasonal variations in demand that are the opposite for this product. Demand for winter snow skis and demand for water skis may exhibit such patterns. Similarly, demand for heating equipment and demand for air-conditioning equipment may have opposite seasonal patterns. At other times advertising and promotional schemes may offset seasonal variations in demand.

To try and cope with seasonal patterns, it is first necessary to identify and determine the extent of these variations. The most commonly used technique for seasonal analysis is the ratio-to-moving-average method.

Ratio-to-Moving-Average Method

This approach produces weekly, monthly, or quarterly indexes which state time series observations in terms of a percentage of annual total (i.e., as seasonal *relatives*). For example, if the month of June has a seasonal index of .80, this indicates that average sales in June are 80% of the monthly average. If a quarter has a seasonal index of 2.00, this says that sales for that quarter are about double the average amount for all quarters.

Here is a step-by-step approach for the method.

1. The first step is to obtain an annual moving average in order to remove the seasonal variations. Hence if data are in quarterly form, a moving average of 4 periods is required; if monthly data are involved, a 12-period moving average is called for. If data are yearly, it will be impossible to determine seasonal indices, since seasonal variations will automatically be excluded.

Now a problem arises in centering the data if an even number of periods is used for the annual moving average, because the center will not correspond to any of the original data points. For instance, with quarterly data the center is *between* the second and third quarters and hence does not correspond to any one quarter. Similarly, with monthly data the center is between the sixth and seventh months. One way around this problem is to find a two-period moving average of the moving averages, and this will produce a center point that corresponds to a data point. This solution is illustrated below.

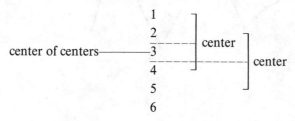

2. The next step is to divide the original data by the corresponding values of the moving average. In effect, this removes trend and cyclical variations from the data, leaving only seasonal, irregular, and random variations. Symbolically, this is

$$\frac{Y}{MA} = \frac{T \times C \times S \times I}{T \times C} = S \times I$$

3. Next, group the relatives of like periods and find the average seasonal ratio for each period. If monthly data are used, for example, group all Januaries and find the January average; group all Februaries and find the February average; and so on. Likewise, if quarterly data are used, average all first quarters, all second quarters, and so on. Very often a "modified mean" is computed. This involves the removal of both the highest and the lowest figures in each group before finding the average.

4. Finally, the resulting figures are "standardized." This is accomplished by adjusting the relatives so that they add to the number of periods. Hence if there were 12 periods, the total of the seasonal relatives should be 12. In this example below there are 4 periods, so the sum of the relatives should be made to equal 4. Coincidentally, due to rounding, the figures already sum to 4. Suppose that the sum turned out to be 5 instead of 4, though. The adjustment would be accomplished by multiplying each seasonal relative by $\frac{4}{5}$. Thus divide the number of periods in the moving average by the sum of the relatives, and multiply each relative by the result.

Example 1 Given quarterly sales data, use the ratio-to-moving-average method to obtain quarter relatives, following the procedure outlined above.

Quarter	Y Data	Four-period Moving Total	Four-period MA	B, MA of Two MA's	Y/B
I	20				
II	18				
III	22		21.00	21.50	1.02
IV	24	84	22.00	22.50	1.07
I	24	88	23.00	23.50	1.02
II	22	92	24.00	24.68	.89
III	26	96	25.25	27.75	.94
IV	29	101	26.25	26.62	1.09
I	28	105	27.00	27.62	1.01
II	25	108	28.25	28.88	.87
III	31	113	29.50	30.00	1.03
IV	34	118	30.50	31.00	1.10
I	32	122	31.50	32.00	1.00
II	29	126	32.50	33.00	.88
III	35	130	33.50	34.00	1.03
IV	38	134	34.50	34.88	1.09
I	36	138	35.25	35.38	1.02
II	32	141	36.50	37.12	.86
III	40	146	37.75	38.25	1.05
IV	43	151	38.75	39.25	1.10
I	40	155	39.75	40.25	.99
II	36	159	40.75	41.38	.87
III	44	163	42.00		
IV	48	168			

Grouping relatives (Y/B) by quarter, we obtain the following results:

	I	II	III	IV
			1.02	1.07
	1.02	.89	.94	1.09
	1.01	.87	1.03	1.10
	1.00	.88	1.03	1.09
	1.02	.86	1.05	1.10
	.99	.87		
Modified totals	3.03	2.62	3.08	3.28
Modified means (seasonal relatives)	1.01	.87	1.03	1.09

RECOMPOSITION

If the purpose of a time series analysis is to focus upon a single component of the series, the preceding techniques are appropriate. Sometimes, however, it is desirable to put the components all together. For example, a company may want to predict sales for June, having established the fact that there are seasonal variations in demand as well as cyclical and trend factors. Therefore, it will be useful to see how the individual components can be combined to achieve a total figure.

TABLE 16.6   Comparison of Multiplicative and Additive Models

Month	Additive $Y = T + S + CI$				Multiplicative $Y = T \times S \times CI$			
	Trend	Seasonal	Cyclical	Y	Trend	Seasonal	Cyclical	Y
Feb.	90	−5	−22	63	90	.90	.70	56.7
Mar.	94	−4	−22	68	94	.92	.70	60.5
Apr.	98	−4	−22	72	98	.92	.70	63.1
May	102	−6	−22	74	102	.86	.70	61.4
June	106	−7	−22	77	106	.82	.70	60.8
July	110	−3	−20	87	110	.94	.80	82.8
Aug.	114	−1	−20	93	114	.95	.80	86.6
Sept.	118	+5	−20	103	118	1.10	.80	103.8
Oct.	122	+5	−20	107	122	1.10	.80	107.4

The recomposition process will differ depending on whether a multiplicative model or an additive model is being used. In the examples that are shown in Table 16.6, both models are illustrated using monthly data. Notice that the trend values are identical for the two approaches, signifying that the trend equation is independent of the model used. Note, though, that the predicted values of Y differ considerably between the two models. Since both cannot obviously be correct, this simply demonstrates that it is important to give careful consideration to the choice of model in each situation.

EXERCISES

1. Using the following linear trend equation, predict return on investment for 1980 and 1984.

$$Y = .15 + .01t$$

where

$$Y = \text{return on investment in year } t$$
$$t = \text{year } (1974 = 0)$$

2. From the graph of sales revenue in Figure 16.7, estimate the values of a and b for the equation for linear trend. Use the equation to project revenues for 1979 and check your answer on the graph by extrapolating the line to 1979. Use 1969 as the base year ($t_{1969} = 0$).

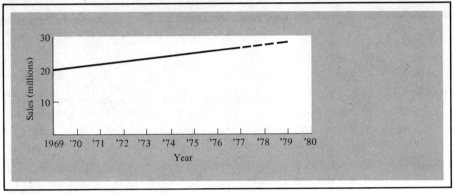

FIGURE 16.7   Annual revenue, 1969–1977.

3. For each of these time series, plot the data on a graph and compute and plot the least squares trend line.

a.

Year	Federal income tax as a percentage of gross pay	Year	Sales (no. of units)
		1960	500
		1961	610
1964	8.5	1962	700
1965	9.2	1963	780
1966	9.5	1964	900
1967	9.6	1965	1,080
1968	9.7	1966	1,160
1969	10.0	1967	1,200
1970	10.2	1968	1,190
1971	10.7	1969	1,210
1972	11.0	1970	1,250
1973	12.0	1971	1,300
1974	12.3	1972	1,340
1975	11.8	1973	1,360
1976	12.5	1974	1,250
1977	13.0	1975	1,370
	150.0	1976	1,400
			18,600

4. Compute a three-year and a seven-year moving average for the data below, and plot them and the original data on the same graph.

Year	Rainfall (nearest inch)	Year	Rainfall
1948	12	1965	18
1949	10	1966	22
1950	13	1967	17
1951	11	1968	23
1952	16	1969	24
1953	15	1970	11
1954	20	1971	18
1955	21	1972	20
1956	18	1973	20
1957	13	1974	14
1958	24	1975	16
1959	20	1976	17
1960	27	1977	13
1961	15	1978	21
1962	16		
1963	12		
1964	18		

5. A monthly record of cloudy days (days that have 40% or less of the possible sunshine) for Sun Mountain for five years is given below. Using a 12-month moving average and the ratio-to-moving-average method, obtain seasonal relatives for each month.

	Jan.	Feb.	Mar.	Apr.	May	June	July	Aug.	Sept.	Oct.	Nov.	Dec.
1972	16	15	13	7	8	7	5	5	3	8	10	14
1973	18	14	16	9	11	10	4	5	4	9	12	16
1974	20	17	17	12	13	9	3	6	3	7	10	16
1975	19	15	15	11	10	7	4	6	2	8	11	14
1976	15	13	13	10	10	7	3	4	2	9	10	11

*6. Obtain seasonal (quarterly) relatives for these plant utilization data. Utilization figures are percentages of total capacity (e.g., the plant operated at 50% utilization during the fourth quarter of 1968).

	Quarter			
Year	I	II	III	IV
1968			16	50
1969	52	60	22	66
1970	56	65	24	74
1971	54	70	26	78
1972	60	72	30	82
1973	62	73	20	75
1974	40	62	22	66
1975	60	64	28	72
1976	70	72		

7. Remove the seasonal variation from these monthly department store sales (Divide monthly sales by the seasonal index):

Month	Sales (in thousands)	SI/100
Jan.	800	.90
Feb.	750	.75
Mar.	710	.40
Apr.	825	.90
May	830	.99
June	800	1.00
July	850	1.01
Aug.	860	1.01
Sept.	900	1.04
Oct.	1000	1.10
Nov.	1300	1.50
Dec.	1200	1.40

8. Given the following data and a linear trend line $Y_c = 50 + 2t$, compute and plot cyclical variations around the trend line, using an additive model.

t	Amount
1	60
2	53
3	45
4	51
5	57
6	56
7	60
8	65
9	70
10	85
11	78
12	82
13	90
14	75
15	74
16	77
17	80
18	85
19	93
20	90
21	108
22	88
23	91
24	87
	1800

*9. The volume of mail to the governor's mansion may be one indicator of public concern over current issues. From the data presented below, plot the data and the least squares trend line, and then compute and plot cyclical relatives.

Year	Volume (thousand pieces)	Year	Volume (thousand pieces)
1958	12	1968	73
1959	15	1969	88
1960	25	1970	104
1961	40	1971	122
1962	50	1972	131
1963	66	1973	140
1964	70	1974	144
1965	69	1975	134
1966	68	1976	136
1967	67	1977	139

10. Rework Exercise 9 using a five-year moving average instead of the least squares linear trend.

*11. Recompose the following time series for an additive model for the years 1964 to 1978 for annual sales.

$$\text{trend}: Y_c = 384 + 24t \quad (t_0 = 1960)$$

Seasonal Deviations:

Jan.	Feb.	Mar.	Apr.	May	June	July	Aug.	Sept.	Oct.	Nov.	Dec.
-18	-22	-14	4	$+37$	$+20$	$+10$	0	0	-7	-14	-6

Cyclical Deviations:

1964	1965	1966	1967	1968	1969	1970	1971	1972	1973	1974	1975	1976	1977	1978
0	-12	-60	-120	-60	-12	0	$+12$	$+60$	$+120$	$+60$	$+12$	0	-12	-60

b. What will the model predict for 1981?

c. Estimate monthly sales for 1981.

12. a. Recompose the following time series, using a multiplicative model for the years 1960 to 1976 for annual sales.

b. Estimate sales for 1982.

$$\text{trend}: Y_c = 250 + 50t \quad (t_0 = 1960)$$

Cyclical Relatives:

1960	1961	1962	1963	1964	1965	1966	1967	1968	1969	1970	1971
1.05	1.10	1.05	1.00	.94	.92	.96	1.00	1.05	1.10	1.05	1.00

1972	1973	1974	1975	1976
.94	.92	.96	1.00	1.05

c. Estimate monthly sales for 1982.

Seasonal Relatives:

Jan.	Feb.	Mar.	Apr.	May	June	July	Aug.	Sept.	Oct.	Nov.	Dec.
.5	.4	.6	1.0	2.2	2.0	1.2	1.0	1.0	.7	.6	.8

EXPONENTIAL SMOOTHING

Exponential smoothing is a technique that utilizes an exponentially weighted moving average equation which smoothes *random* variations in time series data. The purpose of the smoothing is to try and obtain a clearer picture of any nonrandom patterns that might be present in the data. Again, the data presumably are composed of trend, seasonal, and cyclical variations and the random fluctuations.

Exponential smoothing adds one slight variation to our previous work in that there is also a component for "average." There are separate smoothing equations for each of the basic components of variation. All equations are devoted to removing or reducing the influence of random variation, and all follow essentially the same lines. Consequently, since our purpose is to gain an intuitive understanding of the technique, the discussion here will be limited to only one of these equations, that for average.

Generally speaking, when a moving average technique is used, the question of how many periods to include in the moving average must be considered. The greater the number of periods (data) included in an average, the less sensitive the average will be to each new piece of data; while the fewer the number of periods included, the more sensitive the average will be to new data. Ideally, a balance can be struck between high and low sensitivity. The optimum degree of smoothing depends to a large extent on the magnitude of random fluctuations. If these are fairly large, a great deal of smoothing will be required to reduce their impact; if the random fluctuations are minor, there will be less need for smoothing. The exponentially weighted moving average technique is somewhat superior to other moving average techniques because of the ease of adjusting the amount of smoothing.

A second consideration of some importance is the quantity of data required to support the moving average technique. For example, if the moving average includes the last 100 observations, this places considerable burden on storing and maintaining the data, even if computations are computerized. Again, exponential smoothing is superior to other approaches because it eliminates the need for storing data by condensing data into a single figure. This will become evident as we examine the equation used for exponential smoothing.

The equation for exponential smoothing is

$$V_s = V_{s-1} + \alpha(D - V_{s-1})$$

where

$$V_s = \text{new smoothed value}$$
$$V_{s-1} = \text{previous smoothed value}$$
$$D = \text{next data point}$$
$$\alpha = \text{smoothing factor}$$

The smoothed value V_s is equal to the previous value plus a percentage (α) of the difference between that previous value and the next data point. (The smoothing factor α should not be confused with the α used in significance testing; *the two are unrelated*.)

Observe that the effect of the smoothing factor is to take a percentage of the difference between the last average and the next individual piece of data and to add to (or subtract from) the last average to obtain the new average. For example, suppose the last average was 100, the new data point is 150, and α is .10. The new average would be computed as

$$V_s = 100 + .10(150 - 100) = 100 + .10(50)$$
$$= 100 + 5 = 105$$

Had the next data point been 75, the new value would have been

$$V_s = 100 + .10(75 - 100) = 100 + .10(-25)$$
$$= 100 - 2.5 = 97.5$$

Because each previous average has been computed in exactly the same manner, theoretically *all* past data points are embodied in V_{s-1}. This greatly reduces the need to store historical data; the only information required is the old or previous value, the new data point, and the smoothing factor. Furthermore, the weighting arrangement is embodied in α; to change the rate of smoothing, change α. Commonly used values of α range from .01 to .30. When α is small, there are a large number of previous data points included in V_{s-1}; when α is large, there are relatively few data points in V_{s-1}. The table below illustrates the number of data points included in the moving average for selected values of α.

α	Approximate number of periods included in average
.01	230
.05	77
.10	45
.20	22
.30	16
.40	11

Note in the table that as the size of α increases, the number of previous data points included in the smoothing decreases. Although theoretically all past data points are included, as a practical matter, beyond a certain point the weights become so small that they have a negligible effect on the average.

Choice of Smoothing Constant

The degree or amount of smoothing depends on the size of the smoothing constant. The table below provides a comparison of weights for the previous periods for smoothing constants of .05, .10, and .20. Although $\alpha = .05$ carries a lesser weight per period initially, the gap narrows rapidly. After about 10 periods, $\alpha = .05$ carries more weight per period than either .10 or .20.

Period weights

Period	$\alpha = .05$	$\alpha = .10$	$\alpha = .20$
t	.05	.10	.20
$t-1$	.0475	.09	.16
$t-2$	.045125	.081	.128
$t-3$	.0428687	.07296	.1024
$t-4$	.0407252	.06561	.08192
$t-5$	.0386889	.059049	.065536
$t-6$	.0367544	.0531441	.0524288
$\vdots$	$\vdots$	$\vdots$	$\vdots$
	1.0000000	1.0000000	1.0000000

When random variations are *large*, a *small* value of α is necessary to smooth them (i.e., these large variations are given less weight). Conversely, when random variations are *small*, a *large* value of α is desirable; there is less need to smooth the data.

Consider the data in the table below, and compare the effect of using smoothing constants of .1 and .3 on these data, as shown in the graph in Figure 16.8. Notice that the larger smoothing constant (.3) yields values that tend to follow the original data more closely than the values yielded by the smaller constant (.1).

Year	Data	Smoothed values $\alpha = .1$	$\alpha = .3$
1941	37	37.000	37.000
1942	33	36.600	35.800
1943	40	36.940	37.060
1944	50	38.246	40.942
1945	52	39.621	44.259
1946	46	50.259	44.782
1947	44	40.633	44.547
1948	46	41.170	44.983
1949	40	41.053	43.488
1950	47	41.648	44.542
1951	42	41.683	43.779
1952	40	41.515	42.645
1953	40	41.363	41.852
1954	37	40.927	40.392
1955	41	40.934	40.577
1956	40	40.841	40.404
1957	43	41.057	41.183
1958	40	40.951	40.828
1959	30	39.856	37.580
1960	36	39.470	37.106
1961	34	38.923	36.174
1962	41	39.131	37.622
1963	40	39.218	38.335
1964	36	38.896	37.635
1965	46	39.606	40.144
1966	48	40.446	42.501
1967	38	40.201	41.151

Year	Data	Smoothed values $\alpha = .1$	$\alpha = .3$
1968	42	40.381	41.405
1969	52	41.543	44.584
1970	46	41.989	45.009
1971	46	42.390	45.306
1972	47	42.851	45.814
1973	44	42.966	45.270
1974	42	42.869	44.289
1975	46	43.182	44.802
1976	38	42.664	42.762
1977	40	42.398	41.933
1978	35	41.658	39.853

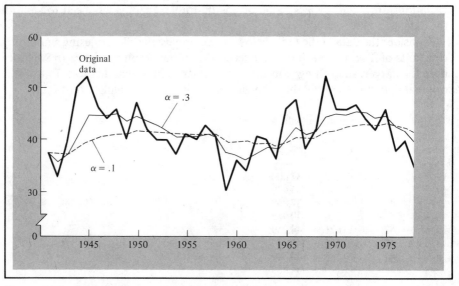

FIGURE 16.8   Smoothed values plotted against original data.

Because of the limited data requirements and the ease with which α can be adjusted, exponential smoothing lends itself well to computerization. Furthermore, it is particularly well suited to handling large numbers of different time series. One application of time series analysis is in analyzing product demand. A firm with hundreds or even thousands of products can easily use exponential smoothing to handle this load. Moreover, some computer programs are constructed in such a way that the computer can automatically adjust the smoothing constant if the moving average departs too much from the original data.

COMMENT

The analysis of time series is as much an art as it is a science, and successful analysis often includes some combination of skill and luck. This is simply another way of saying that there are many complexities involved in time series data, and a certain degree of caution is required in interpreting the results of an analysis. It might be fair to say that there is still much to learn about the analysis of time series data. In fact, efforts to upgrade existing knowledge are continuing. There is currently a wide range of statistical packages available for use on computers with which to attack time series data. However, interpretation is usually left to the user and many require considerable expertise in statistics and perhaps some other disciplines. In addition, a certain amount of care must be taken to ensure that the data points are comparable. This is especially true if the data cover a long time span, because definitions and methods of data collection can change over time in ways that may not be apparent from the data alone.

SUMMARY

Time series data consist of observations taken over a period of time. The purpose in analyzing such data is to determine if historical patterns can be identified, patterns which might be useful in either explaining past occurrences or in predicting future occurrences. This chapter concentrated on two widely used techniques, the classical model, which attempts to decompose a time series into trend, seasonal, and cyclical variation, and exponential smoothing, which seeks to smooth out random variations in the data and to thereby give a clearer picture of real variations in the data.

REVIEW QUESTIONS

1. What is time series data?
2. Why is sequence important in analyzing time series data?
3. Explain briefly what is meant by the term "classical approach to time series analysis" and the purpose of that approach.
4. List and briefly describe the four components of time series.
5. Explain briefly the meaning of these equations:
   a. $Y = T + S + C + I$ b. $Y = TSCI$
6. Explain briefly each of these terms:
   a. ratio-to-moving-average method
   b. modified mean
   c. seasonal relative
7. Suggest two ways that seasonal variations can be removed from time series data.
8. What is meant by the term "exponential smoothing"?
9. What effect does changing the value of the smoothing constant have on the number of data points included in an exponentially weighted moving average?

EXERCISES

1. Use the rainfall data of Exercise 4, page 448. Plot the data.
   a. Smooth the data, using $\alpha = .1$.
   b. Smooth the data, using $\alpha = .3$.

    c. Plot the original data and the smoothed values on the same graph.

    d. Which of these two values for α seems more appropriate in this instance? Why?

*2. Use exponential smoothing, with $\alpha = .1$, to smooth the data for Exercise 9, page 449. Plot the original data and the smoothed values on the same graph. Are you satisfied with the results? Why not? Would a different value of α solve this problem? Explain briefly

17

summary and conclusions

"Great moments in statistics"

AT THIS point you should have a pretty fair understanding of what statistics is all about and how it works. The purposes of this final chapter are to briefly review what you have studied in an effort to help you to put it all together and to suggest some possible future directions for your consideration.

SUMMARY

This book presented statistics in two parts. The first part dealt with descriptive statistics and the second (the predominant part of the book) with inferential statistics.

Descriptive statistics is concerned with the organization and summarizing of statistical data. This involves the calculation and interpretation of numerical summary measures, such as the mean, median, and standard deviation, as well as the construction and use of graphical devices, such as frequency distributions. Probability is used with these techniques as a way of summarizing how likely the occurrence of some event is. These descriptive techniques have two uses—either as an end in themselves, in which case the purpose is to clarify, visualize, or communicate some concept or idea, or else as an initial step in an inferential process.

Inferential statistics focuses on the use of samples as a method of obtaining information about a population without having to actually examine each item in the population. We began our study with a discussion of sampling. This included the reasons for sampling, various techniques for sampling, and alternatives to sampling. A major portion of the discussion was devoted to simple random sampling because of its importance in inference theory. Random sampling is intuitively appealing because it requires that each item in a discrete population have the same opportunity of being included in the sample. In the case of continuous populations, it requires that a range of values have a probability of being included in the sample that is proportional to the percentage of the population that falls within that range.

The mathematical properties of random sampling are highly attractive. Random sampling yields a sampling distribution with a known form. Sampling distributions are probability distributions for sample statistics such as means, proportions, and the like. Whereas sampling is the mechanism by which data are obtained, sampling distributions are the tools of analysis. Initially our discussion of sampling distributions was deductive in nature. The purpose was to discover some of the properties of sampling distributions, as well as the effects population parameters and sample sizes had on certain sampling distributions. We also learned about the Central Limit Theorem, which reveals that distributions of sample means will be approximately normal for large sample sizes. The general knowledge of the characteristics of sampling distributions, plus the specific knowledge provided by a sample, enables us to draw inferences about population parameters.

The study of inference was divided into two parts, estimation and significance testing. *Estimation* involves making an educated guess as to how far some sample statistic is from the unknown population parameter, taking into consideration the sample size, the dispersion in the sample, and the desired level of confidence. Estimates can be single-valued point estimates, or they can be confidence intervals. *Significance testing* is used to evaluate a claim about a population parameter. The result is usually a yes-no type of decision to either accept or reject a claim. Testing takes into consideration the knowledge that, because of sampling variability, sample statistics will almost never equal exactly corresponding population parameters.

In significance testing sampling distributions are important because they describe the extent to which chance can affect sample statistics. The sampling distribution is partitioned into two general areas: (1) a region in which the difference between the claimed and sample values is so small that it might realistically be nothing more than chance variation and (2) a region in which the difference is too great to be considered merely the result of chance variation.

We examined a variety of tests under three general headings: continuous data, count data, and ranks and signs, and it was strongly suggested that the choice of which test to use depended on the type of data that might be available for testing purposes as well as the assumptions upon which each test is based. Matching assumptions with a problem situation is vital if the test results are to be meaningful.

Correlation and regression deal with *estimating* relationships involving paired, or bivariate, data. The ultimate purpose of correlation is to summarize the strength of a relationship, while the purpose of regression is to establish a mathematical equation that describes the relationship. Correlation analysis lends itself to the three-types-of-data approach.

The use of models constitutes an important aspect of statistical analysis. The rationale for using models is that they simplify problems by eliminating unimportant details, and they often serve as "ideals." You have been introduced to a variety of models in this text. For instance, summary measures, such as the mean and the proportion, as well as frequency distributions, probability distributions, and particularly the normal distribution ("is well approximated by a normal distribution"), are models. Random sampling is an ideal that some claim is never actually achieved and hence is a model. And sampling distributions are models which purportedly indicate how chance tends to influence sample statistics.

USING WHAT YOU HAVE LEARNED

At this stage there is still a considerable amount of statistics to be learned, a matter which is covered below. Nonetheless, by studying this book and working through the various exercises, you have achieved a solid foundation that can serve you in a number of ways. First of all, your skills should be useful in other courses that involve applications of statistics or the use of models. Secondly, there will be on-the-job applications of your knowledge of statistics. Your ability to read and understand professional journals should be much improved over what it was previously. Finally, you should get more from your reading of the daily newspapers, and you should be more discriminating as you weigh the claims made in TV commercials and by other forms of advertising.

Naturally, the extent to which you actually achieve each of the above applications will depend on the degree to which you seek applications and the degree to which you choose to incorporate what you have learned. One suggestion in this respect is to glance over from time to time the review questions that follow each chapter to reinforce the important concepts covered in the chapters.

BEYOND THIS BOOK

Your study of statistics need not end here. In fact, I hope this book has whetted your appetite a bit for additional knowledge. The following paragraphs suggest a number of different areas of statistics for your consideration.

Multivariate techniques are an extension of the correlation and regression techniques covered in Chapter 14. They deal with situations that involve three or more variables, and they include curvilinear relationships as well as linear relationships. These techniques, particularly regression analysis, are powerful tools that are widely used throughout business and economics.

Design of experiments is an extension of analysis of variance. It involves setting up, or designing, investigations so as to separate the effects of multiple factors. For example, factors affecting gasoline consumption might be the type of car, the driver, and the brand of gasoline, and it can be extremely illuminating to discover which factor or factors contribute the most to mileage efficiency.

Nonparametric statistics involves significance tests and estimation, using methods that are often quick and that require relatively weak assumptions. These methods often involve data in the form of ranks or signs and are generally wasteful of information. Chapter 13 illustrated a few such methods, but there are many others.

Mathematical statistics focuses on the mathematical basis for statistics and covers such things as the derivation of sampling distributions, probability functions, moments of probability distributions, and so on. It requires some knowledge of calculus.

Although the thrust of this book has been almost entirely toward *classical* statistics, another entire field of statistics is that of *Bayesian* statistics. While classical statistics relies on either a logical approach to probability or the long-run relative frequency approach via sampling, the Bayesian approach utilizes subjective probabilities, which are combined with the results of sample data in making an analysis. Consequently, in using the classical approach, unless the analyst is dealing with a situation involving equally likely outcomes, he or she must await sample data before determining probabilities, whereas in using the Bayesian approach, there is an opportunity to incorporate what might be expert opinion (which is essentially ignored by classical theory). This can offset some of the effects of sampling variability and may lead to superior decisions. Such things as decision trees, payoff tables, and utilities are often part of Bayesian analysis. These techniques are being increasingly utilized in the business world.

appendix

TABLE A Individual Terms of the Binomial Distribution

n	x	.05	.10	.15	.20	.25	.30	.35	.40	.45	.50	.55	.60	.65	.70	.75	.80	.85	.90	.95
1	0	.9500	.9000	.8500	.8000	.7500	.7000	.6500	.6000	.5500	.5000	.4500	.4000	.3500	.3000	.2500	.2000	.1500	.1000	.0500
	1	.0500	.1000	.1500	.2000	.2500	.3000	.3500	.4000	.4500	.5000	.5500	.6000	.6500	.7000	.7500	.8000	.8500	.9000	.9500
2	0	.9025	.8100	.7225	.6400	.5625	.4900	.4225	.3600	.3025	.2500	.2025	.1600	.1225	.0900	.0625	.0400	.0225	.0100	.0025
	1	.0950	.1800	.2550	.3200	.3750	.4200	.4550	.4800	.4950	.5000	.4950	.4800	.4550	.4200	.3750	.3200	.2550	.1800	.0950
	2	.0025	.0100	.0225	.0400	.0625	.0900	.1225	.1600	.2025	.2500	.3025	.3600	.4225	.4900	.5625	.6400	.7225	.8100	.9025
3	0	.8574	.7290	.6141	.5120	.4219	.3430	.2746	.2160	.1664	.1250	.0911	.0640	.0429	.0270	.0156	.0080	.0034	.0010	.0001
	1	.1354	.2430	.3251	.3840	.4219	.4410	.4436	.4320	.4084	.3750	.3341	.2880	.2389	.1890	.1406	.0960	.0574	.0270	.0071
	2	.0071	.0270	.0574	.0960	.1406	.1890	.2389	.2880	.3341	.3750	.4084	.4320	.4436	.4410	.4219	.3840	.3251	.2430	.1354
	3	.0001	.0010	.0034	.0080	.0156	.0270	.0429	.0640	.0911	.1250	.1664	.2160	.2746	.3430	.4219	.5120	.6141	.7290	.8574
4	0	.8145	.6561	.5220	.4096	.3164	.2401	.1785	.1296	.0915	.0625	.0410	.0256	.0150	.0081	.0039	.0016	.0005	.0001	.0000
	1	.1715	.2916	.3685	.4096	.4219	.4116	.3845	.3456	.2995	.2500	.2005	.1536	.1115	.0756	.0469	.0256	.0115	.0036	.0005
	2	.0135	.0486	.0975	.1536	.2109	.2646	.3105	.3456	.3675	.3750	.3675	.3456	.3105	.2646	.2109	.1536	.0975	.0486	.0135
	3	.0005	.0036	.0115	.0256	.0469	.0756	.1115	.1536	.2005	.2500	.2995	.3456	.3845	.4116	.4219	.4096	.3685	.2916	.1715
	4	.0000	.0001	.0005	.0016	.0039	.0081	.0150	.0256	.0410	.0625	.0915	.1296	.1785	.2401	.3164	.4096	.5220	.6561	.8145
5	0	.7738	.5905	.4437	.3277	.2373	.1681	.1160	.0778	.0503	.0313	.0185	.0102	.0053	.0024	.0010	.0003	.0001	.0000	.0000
	1	.2036	.3281	.3915	.4096	.3955	.3602	.3124	.2592	.2059	.1563	.1128	.0768	.0488	.0284	.0146	.0064	.0022	.0004	.0000
	2	.0214	.0729	.1382	.2048	.2637	.3087	.3364	.3456	.3369	.3125	.2757	.2304	.1811	.1323	.0879	.0512	.0244	.0081	.0011
	3	.0011	.0081	.0244	.0512	.0879	.1323	.1811	.2304	.2757	.3125	.3369	.3456	.3364	.3087	.2637	.2048	.1382	.0729	.0214
	4	.0000	.0004	.0022	.0064	.0146	.0283	.0488	.0768	.1128	.1562	.2059	.2592	.3124	.3601	.3955	.4096	.3915	.3281	.2036
	5	.0000	.0000	.0001	.0003	.0010	.0024	.0053	.0102	.0185	.0312	.0503	.0778	.1160	.1681	.2373	.3277	.4437	.5905	.7738
6	0	.7351	.5314	.3771	.2621	.1780	.1176	.0754	.0467	.0277	.0156	.0083	.0041	.0018	.0007	.0002	.0001	.0000	.0000	.0000
	1	.2321	.3543	.3993	.3932	.3560	.3025	.2437	.1866	.1359	.0938	.0609	.0369	.0205	.0102	.0044	.0015	.0004	.0001	.0000
	2	.0305	.0984	.1762	.2458	.2966	.3241	.3280	.3110	.2780	.2344	.1861	.1382	.0951	.0595	.0330	.0154	.0055	.0012	.0001
	3	.0021	.0146	.0415	.0819	.1318	.1852	.2355	.2765	.3032	.3125	.3032	.2765	.2355	.1852	.1318	.0819	.0415	.0146	.0021
	4	.0001	.0012	.0055	.0154	.0330	.0595	.0951	.1382	.1861	.2344	.2780	.3110	.3280	.3241	.2966	.2458	.1762	.0984	.0305
	5	.0000	.0001	.0004	.0015	.0044	.0102	.0205	.0369	.0609	.0937	.1359	.1866	.2437	.3025	.3560	.3932	.3993	.3543	.2321
	6	.0000	.0000	.0000	.0001	.0002	.0007	.0018	.0041	.0083	.0156	.0277	.0467	.0754	.1176	.1780	.2621	.3771	.5314	.7351

Binomial probability table — individual terms $b(x;n,p)=\binom{n}{x}p^x(1-p)^{n-x}$. Columns give p (from $p=.95$ at left to $p=.05$ at right); rows grouped by n and x.

n	x	.95	.90	.85	.80	.75	.70	.65	.60	.55	.50	.45	.40	.35	.30	.25	.20	.15	.10	.05
7	0	.0000	.0000	.0000	.0000	.0001	.0002	.0006	.0016	.0037	.0078	.0152	.0280	.0490	.0824	.1335	.2097	.3206	.4783	.6983
	1	.0000	.0000	.0001	.0004	.0013	.0036	.0084	.0172	.0320	.0547	.0872	.1306	.1848	.2471	.3115	.3670	.3960	.3720	.2573
	2	.0000	.0002	.0012	.0043	.0115	.0250	.0466	.0774	.1172	.1641	.2140	.2613	.2985	.3177	.3115	.2753	.2097	.1240	.0406
	3	.0002	.0026	.0109	.0287	.0577	.0972	.1442	.1935	.2388	.2734	.2918	.2903	.2679	.2269	.1730	.1147	.0617	.0230	.0036
	4	.0036	.0230	.0617	.1147	.1730	.2269	.2679	.2903	.2918	.2734	.2388	.1935	.1442	.0972	.0577	.0287	.0109	.0026	.0002
	5	.0406	.1240	.2097	.2753	.3115	.3177	.2985	.2613	.2140	.1641	.1172	.0774	.0466	.0250	.0115	.0043	.0012	.0002	.0000
	6	.2573	.3720	.3960	.3670	.3115	.2471	.1848	.1306	.0872	.0547	.0320	.0172	.0084	.0036	.0013	.0004	.0001	.0000	.0000
	7	.6983	.4783	.3206	.2097	.1335	.0824	.0490	.0280	.0152	.0078	.0037	.0016	.0006	.0002	.0001	.0000	.0000	.0000	.0000
8	0	.0000	.0000	.0000	.0000	.0000	.0001	.0002	.0007	.0017	.0039	.0084	.0168	.0319	.0576	.1001	.1678	.2725	.4305	.6634
	1	.0000	.0000	.0000	.0001	.0004	.0012	.0033	.0079	.0164	.0313	.0548	.0896	.1373	.1977	.2670	.3355	.3847	.3826	.2793
	2	.0000	.0000	.0002	.0011	.0038	.0100	.0217	.0413	.0703	.1094	.1569	.2090	.2587	.2965	.3115	.2936	.2376	.1488	.0515
	3	.0000	.0004	.0026	.0092	.0231	.0467	.0808	.1239	.1719	.2188	.2568	.2787	.2786	.2541	.2076	.1468	.0839	.0331	.0054
	4	.0004	.0046	.0185	.0459	.0865	.1361	.1875	.2322	.2627	.2734	.2627	.2322	.1875	.1361	.0865	.0459	.0185	.0046	.0004
	5	.0054	.0331	.0839	.1468	.2076	.2541	.2786	.2787	.2568	.2188	.1719	.1239	.0808	.0467	.0231	.0092	.0026	.0004	.0000
	6	.0515	.1488	.2376	.2936	.3115	.2965	.2587	.2090	.1569	.1094	.0703	.0413	.0217	.0100	.0038	.0011	.0002	.0000	.0000
	7	.2793	.3826	.3847	.3355	.2670	.1977	.1373	.0896	.0548	.0313	.0164	.0079	.0033	.0012	.0004	.0001	.0000	.0000	.0000
	8	.6634	.4305	.2725	.1678	.1001	.0576	.0319	.0168	.0084	.0039	.0017	.0007	.0002	.0001	.0000	.0000	.0000	.0000	.0000
9	0	.0000	.0000	.0000	.0000	.0000	.0000	.0001	.0003	.0008	.0020	.0046	.0101	.0207	.0404	.0751	.1342	.2316	.3874	.6302
	1	.0000	.0000	.0000	.0000	.0001	.0004	.0013	.0035	.0083	.0176	.0339	.0605	.1004	.1556	.2253	.3020	.3679	.3874	.2986
	2	.0000	.0000	.0000	.0003	.0012	.0039	.0098	.0212	.0407	.0703	.1110	.1612	.2162	.2668	.3003	.3020	.2597	.1722	.0629
	3	.0000	.0001	.0006	.0028	.0087	.0210	.0424	.0743	.1160	.1641	.2119	.2508	.2716	.2668	.2336	.1762	.1069	.0446	.0077
	4	.0000	.0008	.0050	.0165	.0389	.0735	.1181	.1672	.2128	.2461	.2600	.2508	.2194	.1715	.1168	.0661	.0283	.0074	.0006
	5	.0006	.0074	.0283	.0661	.1168	.1715	.2194	.2508	.2600	.2461	.2128	.1672	.1181	.0735	.0389	.0165	.0050	.0008	.0000
	6	.0077	.0446	.1069	.1762	.2336	.2668	.2716	.2508	.2119	.1641	.1160	.0743	.0424	.0210	.0087	.0028	.0006	.0001	.0000
	7	.0629	.1722	.2597	.3020	.3003	.2668	.2162	.1612	.1110	.0703	.0407	.0212	.0098	.0039	.0012	.0003	.0000	.0000	.0000
	8	.2986	.3874	.3679	.3020	.2253	.1556	.1004	.0605	.0339	.0176	.0083	.0035	.0013	.0004	.0001	.0000	.0000	.0000	.0000
	9	.6302	.3874	.2316	.1342	.0751	.0404	.0207	.0101	.0046	.0020	.0008	.0003	.0001	.0000	.0000	.0000	.0000	.0000	.0000
10	0	.0000	.0000	.0000	.0000	.0000	.0000	.0000	.0001	.0003	.0010	.0025	.0060	.0135	.0282	.0563	.1074	.1969	.3487	.5987
	1	.0000	.0000	.0000	.0000	.0000	.0001	.0005	.0016	.0042	.0098	.0207	.0403	.0725	.1211	.1877	.2684	.3474	.3874	.3151
	2	.0000	.0000	.0000	.0001	.0004	.0014	.0043	.0106	.0229	.0439	.0763	.1209	.1757	.2335	.2816	.3020	.2759	.1937	.0746
	3	.0000	.0000	.0001	.0008	.0031	.0090	.0212	.0425	.0746	.1172	.1665	.2150	.2522	.2668	.2503	.2013	.1298	.0574	.0105
	4	.0000	.0001	.0012	.0055	.0162	.0368	.0689	.1115	.1596	.2051	.2384	.2508	.2377	.2001	.1460	.0881	.0401	.0112	.0010
	5	.0001	.0015	.0085	.0264	.0584	.1029	.1536	.2007	.2340	.2461	.2340	.2007	.1536	.1029	.0584	.0264	.0085	.0015	.0001
	6	.0010	.0112	.0401	.0881	.1460	.2001	.2377	.2508	.2384	.2051	.1596	.1115	.0689	.0368	.0162	.0055	.0012	.0001	.0000
	7	.0105	.0574	.1298	.2013	.2503	.2668	.2522	.2150	.1665	.1172	.0746	.0425	.0212	.0090	.0031	.0008	.0001	.0000	.0000
	8	.0746	.1937	.2759	.3020	.2816	.2335	.1757	.1209	.0763	.0439	.0229	.0106	.0043	.0014	.0004	.0001	.0000	.0000	.0000
	9	.3151	.3874	.3474	.2684	.1877	.1211	.0725	.0403	.0207	.0098	.0042	.0016	.0005	.0001	.0000	.0000	.0000	.0000	.0000
	10	.5987	.3487	.1969	.1074	.0563	.0282	.0135	.0060	.0025	.0010	.0003	.0001	.0000	.0000	.0000	.0000	.0000	.0000	.0000

TABLE A (Continued)

n	x	.05	.10	.15	.20	.25	.30	.35	.40	.45	.50	.55	.60	.65	.70	.75	.80	.85	.90	.95
11	0	.5688	.3138	.1673	.0859	.0422	.0198	.0088	.0036	.0014	.0005	.0002	.0000	.0000	.0000	.0000	.0000	.0000	.0000	.0000
	1	.3293	.3835	.3248	.2362	.1549	.0932	.0518	.0266	.0125	.0054	.0021	.0007	.0002	.0000	.0000	.0000	.0000	.0000	.0000
	2	.0867	.2131	.2866	.2953	.2581	.1998	.1395	.0887	.0513	.0269	.0126	.0052	.0018	.0005	.0001	.0000	.0000	.0000	.0000
	3	.0137	.0710	.1517	.2215	.2581	.2568	.2254	.1774	.1259	.0806	.0462	.0234	.0102	.0037	.0011	.0002	.0000	.0000	.0000
	4	.0014	.0158	.0536	.1107	.1721	.2201	.2428	.2365	.2060	.1611	.1128	.0701	.0379	.0173	.0064	.0017	.0003	.0000	.0000
	5	.0001	.0025	.0132	.0388	.0803	.1321	.1830	.2207	.2360	.2256	.1931	.1471	.0985	.0566	.0268	.0097	.0023	.0003	.0000
	6	.0000	.0003	.0023	.0097	.0268	.0566	.0985	.1471	.1931	.2256	.2360	.2207	.1830	.1321	.0803	.0388	.0132	.0025	.0001
	7	.0000	.0000	.0003	.0017	.0064	.0173	.0379	.0701	.1128	.1611	.2060	.2365	.2428	.2201	.1721	.1107	.0536	.0158	.0014
	8	.0000	.0000	.0000	.0002	.0011	.0037	.0102	.0234	.0462	.0806	.1259	.1774	.2254	.2568	.2581	.2215	.1517	.0710	.0137
	9	.0000	.0000	.0000	.0000	.0001	.0005	.0018	.0052	.0126	.0269	.0513	.0887	.1395	.1998	.2581	.2953	.2866	.2131	.0867
	10	.0000	.0000	.0000	.0000	.0000	.0000	.0002	.0007	.0021	.0054	.0125	.0266	.0518	.0932	.1549	.2362	.3248	.3835	.3293
	11	.0000	.0000	.0000	.0000	.0000	.0000	.0000	.0000	.0001	.0005	.0014	.0036	.0088	.0198	.0422	.0859	.1673	.3138	.5688
12	0	.5404	.2824	.1422	.0687	.0317	.0138	.0057	.0022	.0008	.0002	.0001	.0000	.0000	.0000	.0000	.0000	.0000	.0000	.0000
	1	.3413	.3766	.3012	.2062	.1267	.0712	.0368	.0174	.0075	.0029	.0010	.0003	.0001	.0000	.0000	.0000	.0000	.0000	.0000
	2	.0988	.2301	.2924	.2835	.2323	.1678	.1088	.0639	.0339	.0161	.0068	.0025	.0008	.0002	.0000	.0000	.0000	.0000	.0000
	3	.0173	.0852	.1720	.2362	.2581	.2397	.1954	.1419	.0923	.0537	.0277	.0125	.0048	.0015	.0004	.0001	.0000	.0000	.0000
	4	.0021	.0213	.0683	.1329	.1936	.2311	.2367	.2128	.1700	.1208	.0762	.0420	.0199	.0078	.0024	.0005	.0001	.0000	.0000
	5	.0002	.0038	.0193	.0532	.1032	.1585	.2039	.2270	.2225	.1934	.1489	.1009	.0591	.0291	.0115	.0033	.0006	.0000	.0000
	6	.0000	.0005	.0040	.0155	.0401	.0792	.1281	.1766	.2124	.2256	.2124	.1766	.1281	.0792	.0401	.0155	.0040	.0005	.0000
	7	.0000	.0000	.0006	.0033	.0115	.0291	.0591	.1009	.1489	.1934	.2225	.2270	.2039	.1585	.1032	.0532	.0193	.0038	.0002
	8	.0000	.0000	.0001	.0005	.0024	.0078	.0199	.0420	.0762	.1208	.1700	.2128	.2367	.2311	.1936	.1329	.0683	.0213	.0021
	9	.0000	.0000	.0000	.0001	.0004	.0015	.0048	.0125	.0277	.0537	.0923	.1419	.1954	.2397	.2581	.2362	.1720	.0852	.0173
	10	.0000	.0000	.0000	.0000	.0000	.0002	.0008	.0025	.0068	.0161	.0339	.0639	.1088	.1678	.2323	.2835	.2924	.2301	.0988
	11	.0000	.0000	.0000	.0000	.0000	.0000	.0001	.0003	.0010	.0029	.0075	.0174	.0368	.0712	.1267	.2062	.3012	.3766	.3413
	12	.0000	.0000	.0000	.0000	.0000	.0000	.0000	.0000	.0002	.0002	.0008	.0022	.0057	.0138	.0317	.0687	.1422	.2824	.5404

TABLE B Cumulative Binomial Probabilities

n	x		.05	.10	.15	.20	.25	.30	.35	.40	.45	.50	.55	.60	.65	.70	.75	.80	.85	.90	.95
												p										
1	0		.9500	.9000	.8500	.8000	.7500	.7000	.6500	.6000	.5500	.5000	.4500	.4000	.3500	.3000	.2500	.2000	.1500	.1000	.0500
	1		1.0000	1.0000	1.0000	1.0000	1.0000	1.0000	1.0000	1.0000	1.0000	1.0000	1.0000	1.0000	1.0000	1.0000	1.0000	1.0000	1.0000	1.0000	1.0000
2	0		.9025	.8100	.7225	.6400	.5625	.4900	.4225	.3600	.3025	.2500	.2025	.1600	.1225	.0900	.0625	.0400	.0225	.0100	.0025
	1		.9975	.9900	.9775	.9600	.9375	.9100	.8775	.8400	.7975	.7500	.6975	.6400	.5775	.5100	.4375	.3600	.2775	.1900	.0975
	2		1.0000	1.0000	1.0000	1.0000	1.0000	1.0000	1.0000	1.0000	1.0000	1.0000	1.0000	1.0000	1.0000	1.0000	1.0000	1.0000	1.0000	1.0000	1.0000
3	0		.8574	.7290	.6141	.5120	.4219	.3430	.2746	.2160	.1664	.1250	.0911	.0640	.0429	.0270	.0156	.0080	.0034	.0010	.0001
	1		.9928	.9720	.9393	.8960	.8438	.7840	.7183	.6480	.5748	.5000	.4253	.3520	.2818	.2160	.1563	.1040	.0608	.0280	.0073
	2		.9999	.9990	.9966	.9920	.9844	.9730	.9571	.9360	.9089	.8750	.8336	.7840	.7254	.6570	.5781	.4880	.3859	.2710	.1426
	3		1.0000	1.0000	1.0000	1.0000	1.0000	1.0000	1.0000	1.0000	1.0000	1.0000	1.0000	1.0000	1.0000	1.0000	1.0000	1.0000	1.0000	1.0000	1.0000
4	0		.8145	.6561	.5220	.4096	.3164	.2401	.1785	.1296	.0915	.0625	.0410	.0256	.0150	.0081	.0039	.0016	.0005	.0001	.0000
	1		.9860	.9477	.8905	.8192	.7383	.6517	.5630	.4752	.3910	.3125	.2415	.1792	.1265	.0837	.0508	.0272	.0120	.0037	.0005
	2		.9995	.9963	.9880	.9728	.9492	.9163	.8735	.8208	.7585	.6875	.6090	.5248	.4370	.3483	.2617	.1808	.1095	.0523	.0140
	3		1.0000	.9999	.9995	.9984	.9961	.9919	.9850	.9744	.9590	.9375	.9085	.8704	.8215	.7599	.6836	.5904	.4780	.3439	.1855
	4		1.0000	1.0000	1.0000	1.0000	1.0000	1.0000	1.0000	1.0000	1.0000	1.0000	1.0000	1.0000	1.0000	1.0000	1.0000	1.0000	1.0000	1.0000	1.0000
5	0		.7738	.5905	.4437	.3277	.2373	.1681	.1160	.0778	.0503	.0313	.0185	.0102	.0053	.0024	.0010	.0003	.0001	.0000	.0000
	1		.9974	.9185	.8352	.7373	.6328	.5282	.4284	.3370	.2562	.1875	.1312	.0870	.0540	.0308	.0156	.0067	.0022	.0005	.0000
	2		.9988	.9914	.9734	.9421	.8965	.8369	.7648	.6826	.5931	.5000	.4069	.3174	.2352	.1631	.1035	.0579	.0266	.0086	.0012
	3		1.0000	.9995	.9978	.9933	.9844	.9692	.9460	.9130	.8688	.8125	.7438	.6630	.5716	.4718	.3672	.2627	.1648	.0815	.0226
	4		1.0000	1.0000	.9999	.9997	.9990	.9976	.9947	.9898	.9815	.9688	.9497	.9222	.8840	.8319	.7627	.6723	.5563	.4095	.2262
	5		1.0000	1.0000	1.0000	1.0000	1.0000	1.0000	1.0000	1.0000	1.0000	1.0000	1.0000	1.0000	1.0000	1.0000	1.0000	1.0000	1.0000	1.0000	1.0000
6	0		.7351	.5314	.3771	.2621	.1780	.1176	.0754	.0467	.0277	.0156	.0083	.0041	.0018	.0007	.0002	.0001	.0000	.0000	.0000
	1		.9672	.8857	.7765	.6554	.5339	.4202	.3191	.2333	.1636	.1094	.0692	.0410	.0223	.0109	.0046	.0016	.0004	.0001	.0000
	2		.9978	.9842	.9527	.9011	.8306	.7443	.6471	.5443	.4415	.3438	.2553	.1792	.1174	.0705	.0376	.0170	.0059	.0013	.0001
	3		.9999	.9987	.9941	.9830	.9624	.9295	.8826	.8208	.7447	.6563	.5585	.4557	.3529	.2557	.1694	.0989	.0473	.0159	.0022
	4		1.0000	.9999	.9996	.9984	.9954	.9891	.9777	.9590	.9308	.8906	.8364	.7667	.6809	.5798	.4661	.3446	.2235	.1143	.0328
	5		1.0000	1.0000	1.0000	.9999	.9998	.9993	.9982	.9959	.9917	.9844	.9723	.9533	.9246	.8824	.8220	.7379	.6229	.4686	.2649
	6		1.0000	1.0000	1.0000	1.0000	1.0000	1.0000	1.0000	1.0000	1.0000	1.0000	1.0000	1.0000	1.0000	1.0000	1.0000	1.0000	1.0000	1.0000	1.0000

TABLE B (*Continued*)

n	x																			
		.05	**.10**	**.15**	**.20**	**.25**	**.30**	**.35**	**.40**	**.45**	**.50**	**.55**	**.60**	**.65**	**.70**	**.75**	**.80**	**.85**	**.90**	**.95**
7	0	.6983	.4783	.3206	.2097	.1335	.0824	.0490	.0280	.0152	.0078	.0037	.0016	.0006	.0002	.0001	.0000	.0000	.0000	.0000
	1	.9556	.8503	.7166	.5767	.4449	.3294	.2338	.1586	.1024	.0625	.0357	.0188	.0090	.0038	.0013	.0004	.0001	.0000	.0000
	2	.9962	.9743	.9262	.8520	.7564	.6471	.5323	.4199	.3164	.2266	.1529	.0963	.0556	.0288	.0129	.0047	.0012	.0002	.0000
	3	.9998	.9973	.9879	.9667	.9294	.8740	.8002	.7102	.6083	.5000	.3917	.2898	.1998	.1260	.0706	.0333	.0121	.0027	.0002
	4	1.0000	.9998	.9988	.9953	.9871	.9712	.9444	.9037	.8471	.7734	.6836	.5801	.4677	.3529	.2436	.1480	.0738	.0257	.0038
	5	1.0000	1.0000	.9999	.9996	.9987	.9962	.9910	.9812	.9643	.9375	.8976	.8414	.7662	.6706	.5551	.4233	.2834	.1497	.0444
	6	1.0000	1.0000	1.0000	1.0000	.9999	.9998	.9994	.9984	.9963	.9922	.9848	.9720	.9510	.9176	.8665	.7903	.6794	.5217	.3017
	7	1.0000	1.0000	1.0000	1.0000	1.0000	1.0000	1.0000	1.0000	1.0000	1.0000	1.0000	1.0000	1.0000	1.0000	1.0000	1.0000	1.0000	1.0000	1.0000
8	0	.6634	.4305	.2725	.1678	.1001	.0576	.0319	.0168	.0084	.0039	.0017	.0007	.0002	.0001	.0000	.0000	.0000	.0000	.0000
	1	.9428	.8131	.6572	.5033	.3671	.2553	.1691	.1064	.0632	.0352	.0181	.0085	.0036	.0013	.0004	.0001	.0000	.0000	.0000
	2	.9942	.9619	.8948	.7969	.6785	.5518	.4278	.3154	.2201	.1445	.0885	.0498	.0253	.0113	.0042	.0012	.0002	.0000	.0000
	3	.9996	.9950	.9786	.9437	.8862	.8059	.7064	.5941	.4770	.3633	.2604	.1737	.1061	.0580	.0273	.0104	.0029	.0004	.0000
	4	1.0000	.9996	.9971	.9896	.9727	.9420	.8939	.8263	.7396	.6367	.5230	.4059	.2936	.1941	.1138	.0563	.0214	.0050	.0004
	5	1.0000	1.0000	.9998	.9988	.9958	.9887	.9747	.9502	.9115	.8555	.7799	.6846	.5722	.4482	.3215	.2031	.1052	.0381	.0058
	6	1.0000	1.0000	1.0000	.9999	.9996	.9987	.9964	.9915	.9819	.9648	.9368	.8936	.8309	.7447	.6329	.4967	.3428	.1869	.0572
	7	1.0000	1.0000	1.0000	1.0000	1.0000	.9999	.9998	.9993	.9983	.9961	.9916	.9832	.9681	.9424	.8999	.8322	.7275	.5695	.3366
	8	1.0000	1.0000	1.0000	1.0000	1.0000	1.0000	1.0000	1.0000	1.0000	1.0000	1.0000	1.0000	1.0000	1.0000	1.0000	1.0000	1.0000	1.0000	1.0000
9	0	.6302	.3874	.2316	.1342	.0751	.0404	.0207	.0101	.0046	.0020	.0008	.0003	.0001	.0000	.0000	.0000	.0000	.0000	.0000
	1	.9288	.7748	.5995	.4362	.3003	.1960	.1211	.0705	.0385	.0195	.0091	.0038	.0014	.0004	.0001	.0000	.0000	.0000	.0000
	2	.9916	.9470	.8591	.7382	.6007	.4628	.3373	.2318	.1495	.0898	.0498	.0250	.0112	.0043	.0013	.0003	.0000	.0000	.0000
	3	.9994	.9917	.9661	.9144	.8343	.7297	.6089	.4826	.3614	.2539	.1658	.0994	.0536	.0253	.0100	.0031	.0006	.0001	.0000
	4	1.0000	.9991	.9944	.9804	.9511	.9012	.8283	.7334	.6214	.5000	.3786	.2666	.1717	.0988	.0489	.0196	.0056	.0009	.0000
	5	1.0000	.9999	.9994	.9969	.9900	.9747	.9464	.9006	.8342	.7461	.6386	.5174	.3911	.2703	.1657	.0856	.0339	.0083	.0006
	6	1.0000	1.0000	1.0000	.9997	.9987	.9957	.9888	.9750	.9502	.9102	.8505	.7682	.6627	.5372	.3993	.2618	.1409	.0530	.0084
	7	1.0000	1.0000	1.0000	1.0000	.9999	.9996	.9986	.9962	.9909	.9805	.9615	.9295	.8789	.8040	.6997	.5638	.4005	.2252	.0712
	8	1.0000	1.0000	1.0000	1.0000	1.0000	1.0000	.9999	.9997	.9992	.9980	.9954	.9899	.9793	.9596	.9249	.8658	.7684	.6126	.3698
	9	1.0000	1.0000	1.0000	1.0000	1.0000	1.0000	1.0000	1.0000	1.0000	1.0000	1.0000	1.0000	1.0000	1.0000	1.0000	1.0000	1.0000	1.0000	1.0000
10	0	.5987	.3487	.1969	.1074	.0563	.0282	.0135	.0060	.0025	.0010	.0003	.0001	.0000	.0000	.0000	.0000	.0000	.0000	.0000
	1	.9139	.7361	.5443	.3758	.2440	.1493	.0860	.0464	.0233	.0107	.0045	.0017	.0005	.0001	.0000	.0000	.0000	.0000	.0000
	2	.9885	.9298	.8202	.6778	.5256	.3828	.2616	.1673	.0996	.0547	.0274	.0123	.0048	.0016	.0004	.0001	.0000	.0000	.0000
	3	.9990	.9872	.9500	.8791	.7759	.6496	.5138	.3823	.2660	.1719	.1020	.0548	.0260	.0106	.0035	.0009	.0001	.0000	.0000

This page is a **cumulative binomial distribution table**, giving $P(X \le x)$ for $n = 11, 12, 13$. The table is printed in landscape (rotated). The column headers (probability p) are not printed on this page fragment; the data columns run, left to right, from $p = .95$ down to $p = .05$ in steps of $.05$.

n	x	.95	.90	.85	.80	.75	.70	.65	.60	.55	.50	.45	.40	.35	.30	.25	.20	.15	.10	.05
11	4	.0000	.0000	.0003	.0020	.0076	.0216	.0501	.0994	.1738	.2744	.3972	.5328	.6683	.7897	.8854	.9496	.9841	.9972	.9999
	5	.0000	.0003	.0027	.0117	.0343	.0782	.1487	.2465	.3669	.5000	.6332	.7535	.8513	.9218	.9657	.9883	.9973	.9997	1.0000
	6	.0001	.0028	.0159	.0504	.1146	.2103	.3317	.4672	.6029	.7256	.8263	.9006	.9499	.9784	.9924	.9980	.9997	1.0000	1.0000
	7	.0016	.0185	.0694	.1611	.2867	.4304	.5744	.7037	.8089	.8867	.9390	.9707	.9878	.9957	.9988	.9998	1.0000	1.0000	1.0000
	8	.0152	.0896	.2212	.3826	.5448	.6873	.7999	.8811	.9348	.9673	.9853	.9941	.9980	.9994	.9999	1.0000	1.0000	1.0000	1.0000
	9	.1019	.3026	.5078	.6779	.8029	.8870	.9394	.9698	.9861	.9941	.9979	.9993	.9998	1.0000	1.0000	1.0000	1.0000	1.0000	1.0000
	10	.4312	.6862	.8327	.9141	.9578	.9802	.9912	.9964	.9986	.9995	.9999	1.0000	1.0000	1.0000	1.0000	1.0000	1.0000	1.0000	1.0000
12	0	.0000	.0000	.0000	.0000	.0000	.0000	.0000	.0000	.0001	.0002	.0008	.0022	.0057	.0138	.0317	.0687	.1422	.2824	.5404
	1	.0000	.0000	.0000	.0000	.0000	.0000	.0001	.0003	.0011	.0032	.0083	.0196	.0424	.0850	.1584	.2749	.4435	.6590	.8816
	2	.0000	.0000	.0000	.0000	.0000	.0002	.0008	.0028	.0079	.0193	.0421	.0834	.1513	.2528	.3907	.5583	.7358	.8891	.9804
	3	.0000	.0000	.0000	.0001	.0004	.0017	.0056	.0153	.0356	.0730	.1345	.2253	.3467	.4925	.6488	.7946	.9078	.9744	.9978
	4	.0000	.0000	.0001	.0006	.0028	.0095	.0255	.0573	.1117	.1938	.3044	.4382	.5833	.7237	.8424	.9274	.9761	.9957	.9998
	5	.0000	.0001	.0007	.0039	.0143	.0386	.0846	.1582	.2607	.3872	.5269	.6652	.7873	.8822	.9456	.9806	.9954	.9995	1.0000
	6	.0000	.0005	.0046	.0194	.0544	.1178	.2127	.3348	.4731	.6128	.7393	.8418	.9154	.9614	.9857	.9961	.9993	.9999	1.0000
	7	.0002	.0043	.0239	.0726	.1576	.2763	.4167	.5618	.6956	.8062	.8883	.9427	.9745	.9905	.9972	.9994	.9999	1.0000	1.0000
	8	.0022	.0256	.0922	.2054	.3512	.5075	.6533	.7747	.8655	.9270	.9644	.9847	.9944	.9983	.9996	.9999	1.0000	1.0000	1.0000
	9	.0196	.1109	.2642	.4417	.6093	.7472	.8487	.9166	.9579	.9807	.9921	.9972	.9992	.9998	1.0000	1.0000	1.0000	1.0000	1.0000
	10	.1184	.3410	.5565	.7251	.8416	.9150	.9576	.9804	.9917	.9968	.9989	.9997	.9999	1.0000	1.0000	1.0000	1.0000	1.0000	1.0000
	11	.4596	.7176	.8578	.9313	.9683	.9862	.9943	.9978	.9992	.9998	.9999	1.0000	1.0000	1.0000	1.0000	1.0000	1.0000	1.0000	1.0000
13	0	.0000	.0000	.0000	.0000	.0000	.0000	.0000	.0000	.0000	.0001	.0004	.0013	.0037	.0097	.0238	.0550	.1209	.2542	.5133
	1	.0000	.0000	.0000	.0000	.0000	.0000	.0000	.0001	.0005	.0017	.0049	.0126	.0296	.0637	.1267	.2336	.3983	.6213	.8646
	2	.0000	.0000	.0000	.0000	.0000	.0001	.0003	.0013	.0041	.0112	.0269	.0579	.1132	.2025	.3326	.5017	.6920	.8661	.9755
	3	.0000	.0000	.0000	.0000	.0001	.0007	.0025	.0078	.0203	.0461	.0929	.1686	.2783	.4206	.5843	.7473	.8820	.9658	.9969

TABLE B (Continued)

n	x	.05	.10	.15	.20	.25	.30	.35	.40	.45	.50	.55	.60	.65	.70	.75	.80	.85	.90	.95
											p									
	4	.9997	.9935	.9658	.9009	.7940	.6543	.5005	.3530	.2279	.1334	.0698	.0321	.0126	.0040	.0010	.0002	.0000	.0000	.0000
	5	1.0000	.9991	.9925	.9700	.9198	.8346	.7159	.5744	.4268	.2905	.1788	.0977	.0462	.0182	.0056	.0012	.0002	.0000	.0000
	6	1.0000	.9999	.9987	.9930	.9757	.9376	.8705	.7712	.6437	.5000	.3563	.2288	.1295	.0624	.0243	.0070	.0013	.0001	.0000
	7	1.0000	1.0000	.9998	.9988	.9944	.9818	.9538	.9023	.8212	.7095	.5732	.4256	.2841	.1654	.0802	.0300	.0075	.0009	.0000
	8	1.0000	1.0000	1.0000	.9998	.9990	.9960	.9874	.9679	.9302	.8666	.7721	.6470	.4995	.3457	.2060	.0991	.0342	.0065	.0003
	9	1.0000	1.0000	1.0000	1.0000	.9999	.9993	.9975	.9922	.9797	.9539	.9071	.8314	.7217	.5794	.4157	.2527	.1180	.0342	.0031
	10	1.0000	1.0000	1.0000	1.0000	1.0000	.9999	.9997	.9987	.9959	.9888	.9731	.9421	.8868	.7975	.6674	.4983	.3080	.1339	.0245
	11	1.0000	1.0000	1.0000	1.0000	1.0000	1.0000	1.0000	.9999	.9995	.9983	.9951	.9874	.9704	.9363	.8733	.7664	.6017	.3787	.1354
	12	1.0000	1.0000	1.0000	1.0000	1.0000	1.0000	1.0000	1.0000	1.0000	.9999	.9996	.9987	.9963	.9903	.9762	.9450	.8791	.7458	.4867
	13	1.0000	1.0000	1.0000	1.0000	1.0000	1.0000	1.0000	1.0000	1.0000	1.0000	1.0000	1.0000	1.0000	1.0000	1.0000	1.0000	1.0000	1.0000	1.0000
14	0	.4877	.2288	.1028	.0440	.0178	.0068	.0024	.0008	.0002	.0001	.0000	.0000	.0000	.0000	.0000	.0000	.0000	.0000	.0000
	1	.8470	.5846	.3567	.1979	.1010	.0475	.0205	.0081	.0029	.0009	.0003	.0001	.0000	.0000	.0000	.0000	.0000	.0000	.0000
	2	.9699	.8416	.6479	.4481	.2811	.1608	.0839	.0398	.0170	.0065	.0022	.0006	.0001	.0000	.0000	.0000	.0000	.0000	.0000
	3	.9958	.9559	.8535	.6982	.5213	.3552	.2205	.1243	.0632	.0287	.0114	.0039	.0011	.0002	.0000	.0000	.0000	.0000	.0000
	4	.9996	.9908	.9533	.8702	.7415	.5842	.4227	.2793	.1672	.0898	.0426	.0175	.0060	.0017	.0003	.0000	.0000	.0000	.0000
	5	1.0000	.9985	.9885	.9561	.8883	.7805	.6405	.4859	.3373	.2120	.1189	.0583	.0243	.0083	.0022	.0004	.0000	.0000	.0000
	6	1.0000	.9998	.9978	.9884	.9617	.9067	.8164	.6925	.5461	.3953	.2586	.1501	.0753	.0315	.0103	.0024	.0003	.0000	.0000
	7	1.0000	1.0000	.9997	.9976	.9897	.9685	.9247	.8499	.7414	.6047	.4539	.3075	.1836	.0933	.0383	.0116	.0022	.0002	.0000
	8	1.0000	1.0000	1.0000	.9996	.9978	.9917	.9757	.9417	.8811	.7880	.6627	.5141	.3595	.2195	.1117	.0439	.0115	.0015	.0000
	9	1.0000	1.0000	1.0000	1.0000	.9997	.9983	.9940	.9825	.9574	.9102	.8328	.7207	.5773	.4158	.2585	.1298	.0467	.0092	.0004
	10	1.0000	1.0000	1.0000	1.0000	1.0000	.9998	.9989	.9961	.9886	.9713	.9368	.8757	.7795	.6448	.4787	.3018	.1465	.0441	.0042
	11	1.0000	1.0000	1.0000	1.0000	1.0000	1.0000	.9999	.9994	.9978	.9935	.9830	.9602	.9161	.8392	.7189	.5519	.3521	.1584	.0301
	12	1.0000	1.0000	1.0000	1.0000	1.0000	1.0000	1.0000	.9999	.9997	.9991	.9971	.9919	.9795	.9525	.8990	.8021	.6433	.4154	.1530
	13	1.0000	1.0000	1.0000	1.0000	1.0000	1.0000	1.0000	1.0000	1.0000	.9999	.9998	.9992	.9976	.9932	.9822	.9560	.8972	.7712	.5123
	14	1.0000	1.0000	1.0000	1.0000	1.0000	1.0000	1.0000	1.0000	1.0000	1.0000	1.0000	1.0000	1.0000	1.0000	1.0000	1.0000	1.0000	1.0000	1.0000
15	0	.4633	.2059	.0874	.0352	.0134	.0047	.0016	.0005	.0001	.0000	.0000	.0000	.0000	.0000	.0000	.0000	.0000	.0000	.0000
	1	.8290	.5490	.3186	.1671	.0802	.0353	.0142	.0052	.0017	.0005	.0001	.0000	.0000	.0000	.0000	.0000	.0000	.0000	.0000
	2	.9638	.8159	.6042	.3980	.2361	.1268	.0617	.0271	.0107	.0037	.0011	.0003	.0001	.0000	.0000	.0000	.0000	.0000	.0000
	3	.9945	.9444	.8227	.6482	.4613	.2969	.1727	.0905	.0424	.0176	.0063	.0019	.0005	.0001	.0000	.0000	.0000	.0000	.0000
	4	.9994	.9873	.9383	.8358	.6865	.5155	.3519	.2173	.1204	.0592	.0255	.0093	.0028	.0007	.0001	.0000	.0000	.0000	.0000
	5	.9999	.9978	.9832	.9389	.8516	.7216	.5643	.4032	.2608	.1509	.0769	.0338	.0124	.0037	.0008	.0001	.0000	.0000	.0000

n	x																			
	6	.0000	.0000	.0001	.0008	.0042	.0152	.0422	.0950	.1818	.3036	.4522	.6098	.7548	.8689	.9434	.9819	.9964	.9997	1.0000
	7	.0000	.0000	.0006	.0042	.0173	.0500	.1132	.2131	.3465	.5000	.6535	.7869	.8868	.9500	.9827	.9958	.9994	1.0000	1.0000
	8	.0000	.0003	.0036	.0181	.0566	.1311	.2452	.3902	.5478	.6964	.8182	.9050	.9578	.9848	.9958	.9992	.9999	1.0000	1.0000
	9	.0001	.0022	.0168	.0611	.1484	.2784	.4357	.5968	.7392	.8491	.9231	.9662	.9876	.9963	.9992	.9999	1.0000	1.0000	1.0000
	10	.0006	.0127	.0617	.1642	.3135	.4845	.6481	.7827	.8796	.9408	.9745	.9907	.9972	.9993	.9999	1.0000	1.0000	1.0000	1.0000
	11	.0055	.0556	.1773	.3518	.5387	.7031	.8273	.9095	.9576	.9824	.9937	.9981	.9995	.9999	1.0000	1.0000	1.0000	1.0000	1.0000
	12	.0362	.1841	.3958	.6020	.7639	.8732	.9383	.9729	.9893	.9963	.9989	.9997	.9999	1.0000	1.0000	1.0000	1.0000	1.0000	1.0000
	13	.1710	.4510	.6814	.8329	.9198	.9647	.9858	.9948	.9983	.9995	.9999	1.0000	1.0000	1.0000	1.0000	1.0000	1.0000	1.0000	1.0000
	14	.5367	.7941	.9126	.9648	.9866	.9953	.9984	.9995	.9999	1.0000	1.0000	1.0000	1.0000	1.0000	1.0000	1.0000	1.0000	1.0000	1.0000
	15	1.0000	1.0000	1.0000	1.0000	1.0000	1.0000	1.0000	1.0000	1.0000	1.0000	1.0000	1.0000	1.0000	1.0000	1.0000	1.0000	1.0000	1.0000	1.0000
16	0	.0000	.0000	.0000	.0000	.0000	.0000	.0000	.0000	.0000	.0000	.0001	.0003	.0010	.0033	.0100	.0281	.0743	.1853	.4401
	1	.0000	.0000	.0000	.0000	.0000	.0000	.0000	.0000	.0001	.0003	.0010	.0033	.0098	.0261	.0635	.1407	.2839	.5147	.8108
	2	.0000	.0000	.0000	.0000	.0000	.0000	.0000	.0001	.0006	.0021	.0066	.0183	.0451	.0994	.1971	.3518	.5614	.7892	.9571
	3	.0000	.0000	.0000	.0000	.0000	.0000	.0002	.0009	.0035	.0106	.0281	.0651	.1339	.2459	.4050	.5981	.7899	.9316	.9930
	4	.0000	.0000	.0000	.0000	.0000	.0003	.0013	.0049	.0149	.0384	.0853	.1666	.2892	.4499	.6302	.7982	.9209	.9830	.9991
	5	.0000	.0000	.0000	.0000	.0003	.0016	.0062	.0191	.0486	.1051	.1976	.3288	.4900	.6598	.8103	.9183	.9765	.9967	.9999
	6	.0000	.0000	.0000	.0002	.0016	.0071	.0229	.0583	.1241	.2272	.3660	.5272	.6881	.8247	.9204	.9733	.9944	.9995	1.0000
	7	.0000	.0000	.0002	.0015	.0075	.0257	.0671	.1423	.2559	.4018	.5629	.7161	.8406	.9256	.9729	.9930	.9989	.9999	1.0000
	8	.0000	.0001	.0011	.0070	.0271	.0744	.1594	.2839	.4371	.5982	.7441	.8577	.9329	.9743	.9925	.9985	.9998	1.0000	1.0000
	9	.0000	.0005	.0056	.0267	.0796	.1753	.3119	.4728	.6340	.7728	.8759	.9417	.9771	.9929	.9984	.9998	1.0000	1.0000	1.0000
	10	.0001	.0033	.0235	.0817	.1897	.3402	.5100	.6712	.8024	.8949	.9514	.9809	.9938	.9984	.9997	1.0000	1.0000	1.0000	1.0000
	11	.0009	.0170	.0791	.2018	.3698	.5501	.7108	.8334	.9147	.9616	.9851	.9951	.9987	.9997	1.0000	1.0000	1.0000	1.0000	1.0000
	12	.0070	.0684	.2101	.4019	.5950	.7541	.8661	.9349	.9719	.9894	.9965	.9991	.9998	1.0000	1.0000	1.0000	1.0000	1.0000	1.0000
	13	.0429	.2108	.4386	.6482	.8029	.9006	.9549	.9817	.9934	.9979	.9994	.9999	1.0000	1.0000	1.0000	1.0000	1.0000	1.0000	1.0000
	14	.1892	.4853	.7161	.8593	.9365	.9739	.9902	.9967	.9990	.9997	.9999	1.0000	1.0000	1.0000	1.0000	1.0000	1.0000	1.0000	1.0000
	15	.5599	.8147	.9257	.9719	.9900	.9967	.9990	.9997	.9999	1.0000	1.0000	1.0000	1.0000	1.0000	1.0000	1.0000	1.0000	1.0000	1.0000
	16	1.0000	1.0000	1.0000	1.0000	1.0000	1.0000	1.0000	1.0000	1.0000	1.0000	1.0000	1.0000	1.0000	1.0000	1.0000	1.0000	1.0000	1.0000	1.0000
17	0	.0000	.0000	.0000	.0000	.0000	.0000	.0000	.0000	.0000	.0000	.0001	.0002	.0007	.0023	.0075	.0225	.0631	.1668	.4181
	1	.0000	.0000	.0000	.0000	.0000	.0000	.0000	.0000	.0000	.0001	.0006	.0021	.0067	.0193	.0501	.1182	.2525	.4818	.7922
	2	.0000	.0000	.0000	.0000	.0000	.0000	.0000	.0001	.0003	.0012	.0041	.0123	.0327	.0774	.1637	.3096	.5198	.7618	.9497
	3	.0000	.0000	.0000	.0000	.0000	.0000	.0001	.0005	.0019	.0064	.0184	.0464	.1028	.2019	.3530	.5489	.7556	.9174	.9912
	4	.0000	.0000	.0000	.0000	.0000	.0001	.0006	.0025	.0086	.0245	.0596	.1260	.2348	.3887	.5739	.7582	.9013	.9779	.9988
	5	.0000	.0000	.0000	.0000	.0001	.0007	.0030	.0106	.0301	.0717	.1471	.2639	.4197	.5968	.7653	.8943	.9681	.9953	.9999
	6	.0000	.0000	.0000	.0001	.0006	.0032	.0120	.0348	.0826	.1662	.2902	.4478	.6188	.7752	.8929	.9623	.9917	.9992	1.0000
	7	.0000	.0000	.0001	.0005	.0031	.0127	.0383	.0919	.1834	.3145	.4743	.6405	.7872	.8954	.9598	.9891	.9983	.9999	1.0000
	8	.0000	.0000	.0003	.0026	.0124	.0403	.0994	.1989	.3374	.5000	.6626	.8011	.9006	.9597	.9876	.9974	.9997	1.0000	1.0000
	9	.0000	.0001	.0017	.0109	.0402	.1046	.2128	.3595	.5257	.6855	.8166	.9081	.9617	.9873	.9969	.9995	1.0000	1.0000	1.0000

TABLE B (*Continued*)

n	x										*p*									
		.05	.10	.15	.20	.25	.30	.35	.40	.45	.50	.55	.60	.65	.70	.75	.80	.85	.90	.95
	10	1.0000	1.0000	1.0000	.9999	.9994	.9968	.9880	.9652	.9174	.8338	.7098	.5522	.3812	.2248	.1071	.0377	.0083	.0008	.0000
	11	1.0000	1.0000	1.0000	1.0000	.9999	.9993	.9970	.9894	.9699	.9283	.8529	.7361	.5803	.4032	.2347	.1057	.0319	.0047	.0001
	12	1.0000	1.0000	1.0000	1.0000	1.0000	.9999	.9994	.9975	.9914	.9755	.9404	.8740	.7652	.6113	.4261	.2418	.0987	.0221	.0012
	13	1.0000	1.0000	1.0000	1.0000	1.0000	1.0000	.9999	.9995	.9981	.9936	.9816	.9536	.8972	.7981	.6470	.4511	.2444	.0826	.0088
	14	1.0000	1.0000	1.0000	1.0000	1.0000	1.0000	1.0000	.9999	.9997	.9988	.9959	.9877	.9673	.9226	.8363	.6904	.4802	.2382	.0503
	15	1.0000	1.0000	1.0000	1.0000	1.0000	1.0000	1.0000	1.0000	1.0000	.9999	.9994	.9979	.9933	.9807	.9499	.8818	.7475	.5182	.2078
	16	1.0000	1.0000	1.0000	1.0000	1.0000	1.0000	1.0000	1.0000	1.0000	1.0000	1.0000	.9998	.9993	.9977	.9925	.9775	.9369	.8332	.5819
	17	1.0000	1.0000	1.0000	1.0000	1.0000	1.0000	1.0000	1.0000	1.0000	1.0000	1.0000	1.0000	1.0000	1.0000	1.0000	1.0000	1.0000	1.0000	1.0000
18	0	.3972	.1501	.0536	.0180	.0056	.0016	.0004	.0001	.0000	.0000	.0000	.0000	.0000	.0000	.0000	.0000	.0000	.0000	.0000
	1	.7735	.4503	.2241	.0991	.0395	.0142	.0046	.0013	.0003	.0001	.0000	.0000	.0000	.0000	.0000	.0000	.0000	.0000	.0000
	2	.9419	.7338	.4797	.2713	.1353	.0600	.0236	.0082	.0025	.0007	.0001	.0000	.0000	.0000	.0000	.0000	.0000	.0000	.0000
	3	.9891	.9018	.7202	.5010	.3057	.1646	.0783	.0328	.0120	.0038	.0010	.0002	.0000	.0000	.0000	.0000	.0000	.0000	.0000
	4	.9985	.9718	.8794	.7164	.5187	.3327	.1886	.0942	.0411	.0154	.0049	.0013	.0003	.0000	.0000	.0000	.0000	.0000	.0000
	5	.9998	.9936	.9581	.8671	.7175	.5344	.3550	.2088	.1077	.0481	.0183	.0058	.0014	.0003	.0000	.0000	.0000	.0000	.0000
	6	1.0000	.9988	.9882	.9487	.8610	.7217	.5491	.3743	.2258	.1189	.0537	.0203	.0062	.0014	.0002	.0000	.0000	.0000	.0000
	7	1.0000	.9998	.9973	.9837	.9431	.8593	.7283	.5634	.3915	.2403	.1280	.0576	.0212	.0061	.0012	.0002	.0000	.0000	.0000
	8	1.0000	1.0000	.9995	.9957	.9807	.9404	.8609	.7368	.5778	.4073	.2527	.1347	.0597	.0210	.0054	.0009	.0001	.0000	.0000
	9	1.0000	1.0000	.9999	.9991	.9946	.9790	.9403	.8653	.7473	.5927	.4222	.2632	.1391	.0596	.0193	.0043	.0005	.0000	.0000
	10	1.0000	1.0000	1.0000	.9998	.9988	.9939	.9788	.9424	.8720	.7597	.6085	.4366	.2717	.1407	.0569	.0163	.0027	.0002	.0000
	11	1.0000	1.0000	1.0000	1.0000	.9998	.9986	.9938	.9797	.9463	.8811	.7742	.6257	.4509	.2783	.1390	.0513	.0118	.0012	.0000
	12	1.0000	1.0000	1.0000	1.0000	1.0000	.9997	.9986	.9942	.9817	.9519	.8923	.7912	.6450	.4656	.2825	.1329	.0419	.0064	.0002
	13	1.0000	1.0000	1.0000	1.0000	1.0000	1.0000	.9997	.9987	.9951	.9846	.9589	.9058	.8114	.6673	.4813	.2836	.1206	.0282	.0015
	14	1.0000	1.0000	1.0000	1.0000	1.0000	1.0000	1.0000	.9998	.9990	.9962	.9880	.9672	.9217	.8354	.6943	.4990	.2798	.0982	.0109
	15	1.0000	1.0000	1.0000	1.0000	1.0000	1.0000	1.0000	1.0000	.9999	.9993	.9975	.9918	.9764	.9400	.8647	.7287	.5203	.2662	.0581
	16	1.0000	1.0000	1.0000	1.0000	1.0000	1.0000	1.0000	1.0000	1.0000	.9999	.9997	.9987	.9954	.9858	.9605	.9009	.7759	.5497	.2265
	17	1.0000	1.0000	1.0000	1.0000	1.0000	1.0000	1.0000	1.0000	1.0000	1.0000	.9997	.9999	.9996	.9984	.9944	.9820	.9464	.8499	.6028
	18	1.0000	1.0000	1.0000	1.0000	1.0000	1.0000	1.0000	1.0000	1.0000	1.0000	1.0000	1.0000	1.0000	1.0000	1.0000	1.0000	1.0000	1.0000	1.0000
19	0	.3774	.1351	.0456	.0144	.0042	.0011	.0003	.0001	.0000	.0000	.0000	.0000	.0000	.0000	.0000	.0000	.0000	.0000	.0000
	1	.7547	.4203	.1985	.0829	.0310	.0104	.0031	.0008	.0002	.0000	.0000	.0000	.0000	.0000	.0000	.0000	.0000	.0000	.0000
	2	.9335	.7054	.4413	.2369	.1113	.0462	.0170	.0055	.0015	.0004	.0001	.0000	.0000	.0000	.0000	.0000	.0000	.0000	.0000
	3	.9868	.8850	.6841	.4551	.2631	.1332	.0591	.0230	.0077	.0022	.0005	.0001	.0000	.0000	.0000	.0000	.0000	.0000	.0000

Cumulative binomial probabilities. The table continued at the top of this page is for $n = 19$ (rows $x = 4$ through 19); the lower block is for $n = 20$ (rows $x = 0$ through 20). Columns are values of p.

$n = 19$ (continued)

x	.95	.90	.85	.80	.75	.70	.65	.60	.55	.50	.45	.40	.35	.30	.25	.20	.15	.10	.05
4	.0000	.0000	.0000	.0000	.0000	.0000	.0001	.0006	.0028	.0096	.0280	.0696	.1500	.2822	.4654	.6733	.8556	.9648	.9980
5	.0000	.0000	.0000	.0000	.0000	.0001	.0007	.0031	.0109	.0318	.0777	.1629	.2968	.4739	.6678	.8369	.9463	.9914	.9998
6	.0000	.0000	.0000	.0000	.0001	.0006	.0031	.0116	.0342	.0835	.1727	.3081	.4812	.6655	.8251	.9324	.9837	.9983	1.0000
7	.0000	.0000	.0000	.0000	.0005	.0028	.0114	.0352	.0871	.1796	.3169	.4878	.6656	.8180	.9225	.9767	.9959	.9997	1.0000
8	.0000	.0000	.0000	.0003	.0023	.0105	.0347	.0885	.1841	.3238	.4940	.6675	.8145	.9161	.9713	.9933	.9992	1.0000	1.0000
9	.0000	.0000	.0001	.0016	.0089	.0326	.0875	.1861	.3290	.5000	.6710	.8139	.9125	.9674	.9911	.9984	.9999	1.0000	1.0000
10	.0000	.0000	.0008	.0067	.0287	.0839	.1855	.3325	.5060	.6762	.8159	.9115	.9653	.9895	.9977	.9997	1.0000	1.0000	1.0000
11	.0000	.0003	.0041	.0233	.0775	.1820	.3344	.5122	.6831	.8204	.9129	.9648	.9886	.9972	.9995	1.0000	1.0000	1.0000	1.0000
12	.0000	.0017	.0163	.0676	.1749	.3345	.5188	.6919	.8273	.9165	.9658	.9884	.9969	.9994	.9999	1.0000	1.0000	1.0000	1.0000
13	.0002	.0086	.0537	.1631	.3322	.5261	.7032	.8371	.9223	.9682	.9891	.9969	.9993	.9999	1.0000	1.0000	1.0000	1.0000	1.0000
14	.0020	.0352	.1444	.3267	.5346	.7178	.8500	.9304	.9720	.9904	.9972	.9994	.9999	1.0000	1.0000	1.0000	1.0000	1.0000	1.0000
15	.0132	.1150	.3159	.5449	.7369	.8668	.9409	.9770	.9923	.9978	.9995	.9999	1.0000	1.0000	1.0000	1.0000	1.0000	1.0000	1.0000
16	.0665	.2946	.5587	.7631	.8887	.9538	.9830	.9945	.9985	.9996	.9999	1.0000	1.0000	1.0000	1.0000	1.0000	1.0000	1.0000	1.0000
17	.2453	.5797	.8015	.9171	.9690	.9896	.9969	.9992	.9998	1.0000	1.0000	1.0000	1.0000	1.0000	1.0000	1.0000	1.0000	1.0000	1.0000
18	.6226	.8649	.9544	.9856	.9958	.9989	.9997	.9999	1.0000	1.0000	1.0000	1.0000	1.0000	1.0000	1.0000	1.0000	1.0000	1.0000	1.0000
19	1.0000	1.0000	1.0000	1.0000	1.0000	1.0000	1.0000	1.0000	1.0000	1.0000	1.0000	1.0000	1.0000	1.0000	1.0000	1.0000	1.0000	1.0000	1.0000

$n = 20$

x	.95	.90	.85	.80	.75	.70	.65	.60	.55	.50	.45	.40	.35	.30	.25	.20	.15	.10	.05
0	.0000	.0000	.0000	.0000	.0000	.0000	.0000	.0000	.0000	.0000	.0000	.0000	.0002	.0008	.0032	.0115	.0388	.1216	.3585
1	.0000	.0000	.0000	.0000	.0000	.0000	.0000	.0000	.0000	.0000	.0001	.0005	.0021	.0076	.0243	.0692	.1756	.3917	.7358
2	.0000	.0000	.0000	.0000	.0000	.0000	.0000	.0000	.0000	.0002	.0009	.0036	.0121	.0355	.0913	.2061	.4049	.6769	.9245
3	.0000	.0000	.0000	.0000	.0000	.0000	.0000	.0000	.0003	.0013	.0049	.0160	.0444	.1071	.2252	.4114	.6477	.8670	.9841
4	.0000	.0000	.0000	.0000	.0000	.0000	.0000	.0003	.0015	.0059	.0189	.0510	.1182	.2375	.4148	.6296	.8298	.9568	.9974
5	.0000	.0000	.0000	.0000	.0000	.0000	.0003	.0016	.0064	.0207	.0553	.1256	.2454	.4164	.6172	.8042	.9327	.9887	.9997
6	.0000	.0000	.0000	.0000	.0000	.0003	.0015	.0065	.0214	.0577	.1299	.2500	.4166	.6080	.7858	.9133	.9781	.9976	1.0000
7	.0000	.0000	.0000	.0000	.0002	.0013	.0060	.0210	.0580	.1316	.2520	.4159	.6010	.7723	.8982	.9679	.9941	.9996	1.0000
8	.0000	.0000	.0000	.0001	.0009	.0051	.0196	.0565	.1308	.2517	.4143	.5956	.7624	.8867	.9591	.9900	.9987	.9999	1.0000
9	.0000	.0000	.0000	.0006	.0039	.0171	.0532	.1275	.2493	.4119	.5914	.7553	.8782	.9520	.9861	.9974	.9998	1.0000	1.0000
10	.0000	.0000	.0002	.0026	.0139	.0480	.1218	.2447	.4086	.5881	.7507	.8725	.9468	.9829	.9961	.9994	1.0000	1.0000	1.0000
11	.0000	.0001	.0013	.0100	.0409	.1133	.2376	.4044	.5857	.7483	.8692	.9435	.9804	.9949	.9991	.9999	1.0000	1.0000	1.0000
12	.0000	.0004	.0059	.0321	.1018	.2277	.3990	.5841	.7480	.8684	.9420	.9790	.9940	.9987	.9998	1.0000	1.0000	1.0000	1.0000
13	.0000	.0024	.0219	.0867	.2142	.3920	.5834	.7500	.8701	.9423	.9786	.9935	.9985	.9997	1.0000	1.0000	1.0000	1.0000	1.0000
14	.0003	.0113	.0673	.1958	.3828	.5836	.7546	.8744	.9447	.9793	.9936	.9984	.9997	1.0000	1.0000	1.0000	1.0000	1.0000	1.0000
15	.0026	.0432	.1702	.3704	.5852	.7625	.8818	.9490	.9811	.9941	.9985	.9997	1.0000	1.0000	1.0000	1.0000	1.0000	1.0000	1.0000
16	.0159	.1330	.3523	.5886	.7748	.8929	.9556	.9840	.9951	.9987	.9997	1.0000	1.0000	1.0000	1.0000	1.0000	1.0000	1.0000	1.0000
17	.0755	.3231	.5951	.7939	.9087	.9645	.9879	.9964	.9991	.9998	1.0000	1.0000	1.0000	1.0000	1.0000	1.0000	1.0000	1.0000	1.0000
18	.2642	.6083	.8244	.9308	.9757	.9924	.9979	.9995	.9999	1.0000	1.0000	1.0000	1.0000	1.0000	1.0000	1.0000	1.0000	1.0000	1.0000
19	.6415	.8784	.9612	.9885	.9968	.9992	.9998	1.0000	1.0000	1.0000	1.0000	1.0000	1.0000	1.0000	1.0000	1.0000	1.0000	1.0000	1.0000
20	1.0000	1.0000	1.0000	1.0000	1.0000	1.0000	1.0000	1.0000	1.0000	1.0000	1.0000	1.0000	1.0000	1.0000	1.0000	1.0000	1.0000	1.0000	1.0000

TABLE C   Poisson Probabilities

x	0.005	0.01	0.02	0.03	0.04	μ 0.05	0.06	0.07	0.08	0.09
0	0.9950	0.9900	0.9802	0.9704	0.9608	0.9512	0.9418	0.9324	0.9231	0.9139
1	0.0050	0.0099	0.0192	0.0291	0.0384	0.0476	0.0565	0.0653	0.0738	0.0823
2	0.0000	0.0000	0.0002	0.0004	0.0008	0.0012	0.0017	0.0023	0.0030	0.0037
3	0.0000	0.0000	0.0000	0.0000	0.0000	0.0000	0.0000	0.0001	0.0001	0.0001

x	0.1	0.2	0.3	0.4	0.5	0.6	0.7	0.8	0.9	1.0
0	0.9048	0.8187	0.7408	0.6703	0.6065	0.5488	0.4966	0.4493	0.4066	0.3679
1	0.0905	0.1637	0.2222	0.2681	0.3033	0.3293	0.3476	0.3595	0.3659	0.3679
2	0.0045	0.0164	0.0333	0.0536	0.0758	0.0988	0.1217	0.1438	0.1647	0.1839
3	0.0002	0.0011	0.0033	0.0072	0.0126	0.0198	0.0284	0.0383	0.0494	0.0613
4	0.0000	0.0001	0.0002	0.0007	0.0016	0.0030	0.0050	0.0077	0.0111	0.0153
5	0.0000	0.0000	0.0000	0.0001	0.0002	0.0004	0.0007	0.0012	0.0020	0.0031
6	0.0000	0.0000	0.0000	0.0000	0.0000	0.0000	0.0001	0.0002	0.0003	0.0005
7	0.0000	0.0000	0.0000	0.0000	0.0000	0.0000	0.0000	0.0000	0.0000	0.0001

x	1.1	1.2	1.3	1.4	1.5	1.6	1.7	1.8	1.9	2.0
0	0.3329	0.3012	0.2725	0.2466	0.2231	0.2019	0.1827	0.1653	0.1496	0.1353
1	0.3662	0.3614	0.3543	0.3452	0.3347	0.3230	0.3106	0.2975	0.2842	0.2707
2	0.2014	0.2169	0.2303	0.2417	0.2510	0.2584	0.2640	0.2678	0.2700	0.2707
3	0.0738	0.0867	0.0998	0.1128	0.1255	0.1378	0.1496	0.1607	0.1710	0.1804
4	0.0203	0.0260	0.0324	0.0395	0.0471	0.0551	0.0636	0.0723	0.0812	0.0902
5	0.0045	0.0062	0.0084	0.0111	0.0141	0.0176	0.0216	0.0260	0.0309	0.0361
6	0.0008	0.0012	0.0018	0.0026	0.0035	0.0047	0.0061	0.0078	0.0098	0.0120
7	0.0001	0.0002	0.0003	0.0005	0.0008	0.0011	0.0015	0.0020	0.0027	0.0034
8	0.0000	0.0000	0.0001	0.0001	0.0001	0.0002	0.0003	0.0005	0.0006	0.0009
9	0.0000	0.0000	0.0000	0.0000	0.0000	0.0000	0.0001	0.0001	0.0001	0.0002

x	2.1	2.2	2.3	2.4	2.5	2.6	2.7	2.8	2.9	3.0
0	0.1225	0.1108	0.1003	0.0907	0.0821	0.0743	0.0672	0.0608	0.0550	0.0498
1	0.2572	0.2438	0.2306	0.2177	0.2052	0.1931	0.1815	0.1703	0.1596	0.1494
2	0.2700	0.2681	0.2652	0.2613	0.2565	0.2510	0.2450	0.2384	0.2314	0.2240
3	0.1890	0.1966	0.2033	0.2090	0.2138	0.2176	0.2205	0.2225	0.2237	0.2240
4	0.0992	0.1082	0.1169	0.1254	0.1336	0.1414	0.1488	0.1557	0.1622	0.1680
5	0.0417	0.0476	0.0538	0.0602	0.0668	0.0735	0.0804	0.0872	0.0940	0.1008
6	0.0146	0.0174	0.0206	0.0241	0.0278	0.0319	0.0362	0.0407	0.0455	0.0504
7	0.0044	0.0055	0.0068	0.0083	0.0099	0.0118	0.0139	0.0163	0.0188	0.0216
8	0.0011	0.0015	0.0019	0.0025	0.0031	0.0038	0.0047	0.0057	0.0068	0.0081
9	0.0003	0.0004	0.0005	0.0007	0.0009	0.0011	0.0014	0.0018	0.0022	0.0027
10	0.0001	0.0001	0.0001	0.0002	0.0002	0.0003	0.0004	0.0005	0.0006	0.0008
11	0.0000	0.0000	0.0000	0.0000	0.0000	0.0001	0.0001	0.0001	0.0002	0.0002
12	0.0000	0.0000	0.0000	0.0000	0.0000	0.0000	0.0000	0.0000	0.0000	0.0001

x	3.1	3.2	3.3	3.4	3.5	3.6	3.7	3.8	3.9	4.0
0	0.0450	0.0408	0.0369	0.0334	0.0302	0.0273	0.0247	0.0224	0.0202	0.0183
1	0.1397	0.1304	0.1217	0.1135	0.1057	0.0984	0.0915	0.0850	0.0789	0.0733
2	0.2165	0.2087	0.2008	0.1929	0.1850	0.1771	0.1692	0.1615	0.1539	0.1465
3	0.2237	0.2226	0.2209	0.2186	0.2158	0.2125	0.2087	0.2046	0.2001	0.1954
4	0.1734	0.1781	0.1823	0.1858	0.1888	0.1912	0.1931	0.1944	0.1951	0.1954
5	0.1075	0.1140	0.1203	0.1264	0.1322	0.1377	0.1429	0.1477	0.1522	0.1563
6	0.0555	0.0608	0.0662	0.0716	0.0771	0.0826	0.0881	0.0936	0.0989	0.1042
7	0.0246	0.0278	0.0312	0.0348	0.0385	0.0425	0.0466	0.0508	0.0551	0.0595
8	0.0095	0.0111	0.0129	0.0148	0.0169	0.0191	0.0215	0.0241	0.0269	0.0298
9	0.0033	0.0040	0.0047	0.0056	0.0066	0.0076	0.0089	0.0102	0.0116	0.0132

TABLE C (*Continued*)

10	0.0010	0.0013	0.0016	0.0019	0.0023	0.0028	0.0033	0.0039	0.0045	0.0053
11	0.0003	0.0004	0.0005	0.0006	0.0007	0.0009	0.0011	0.0013	0.0016	0.0019
12	0.0001	0.0001	0.0001	0.0002	0.0002	0.0003	0.0003	0.0004	0.0005	0.0006
13	0.0000	0.0000	0.0000	0.0000	0.0001	0.0001	0.0001	0.0001	0.0002	0.0002
14	0.0000	0.0000	0.0000	0.0000	0.0000	0.0000	0.0000	0.0000	0.0000	0.0001

x	4.1	4.2	4.3	4.4	4.5	4.6	4.7	4.8	4.9	5.0
0	0.0166	0.0150	0.0136	0.0123	0.0111	0.0101	0.0091	0.0082	0.0074	0.0067
1	0.0679	0.0630	0.0583	0.0540	0.0500	0.0462	0.0427	0.0395	0.0365	0.0337
2	0.1393	0.1323	0.1254	0.1188	0.1125	0.1063	0.1005	0.0948	0.0894	0.0842
3	0.1904	0.1852	0.1798	0.1743	0.1687	0.1631	0.1574	0.1517	0.1460	0.1404
4	0.1951	0.1944	0.1933	0.1917	0.1898	0.1875	0.1849	0.1820	0.1789	0.1755
5	0.1600	0.1633	0.1662	0.1687	0.1708	0.1725	0.1738	0.1747	0.1753	0.1755
6	0.1093	0.1143	0.1191	0.1237	0.1281	0.1323	0.1362	0.1398	0.1432	0.1462
7	0.0640	0.0686	0.0732	0.0778	0.0824	0.0869	0.0914	0.0959	0.1002	0.1044
8	0.0328	0.0360	0.0393	0.0428	0.0463	0.0500	0.0537	0.0575	0.0614	0.0653
9	0.0150	0.0168	0.0188	0.0209	0.0232	0.0255	0.0280	0.0307	0.0334	0.0363
10	0.0061	0.0071	0.0081	0.0092	0.0104	0.0118	0.0132	0.0147	0.0164	0.0181
11	0.0023	0.0027	0.0032	0.0037	0.0043	0.0049	0.0056	0.0064	0.0073	0.0082
12	0.0008	0.0009	0.0011	0.0014	0.0016	0.0019	0.0022	0.0026	0.0030	0.0034
13	0.0002	0.0003	0.0004	0.0005	0.0006	0.0007	0.0008	0.0009	0.0011	0.0013
14	0.0001	0.0001	0.0001	0.0001	0.0002	0.0002	0.0003	0.0003	0.0004	0.0005
15	0.0000	0.0000	0.0000	0.0000	0.0001	0.0001	0.0001	0.0001	0.0001	0.0002

x	5.1	5.2	5.3	5.4	5.5	5.6	5.7	5.8	5.9	6.0
0	0.0061	0.0055	0.0050	0.0045	0.0041	0.0037	0.0033	0.0030	0.0027	0.0025
1	0.0311	0.0287	0.0265	0.0244	0.0225	0.0207	0.0191	0.0176	0.0162	0.0149
2	0.0793	0.0746	0.0701	0.0659	0.0618	0.0580	0.0544	0.0509	0.0477	0.0446
3	0.1348	0.1293	0.1239	0.1185	0.1133	0.1082	0.1033	0.0985	0.0938	0.0892
4	0.1719	0.1681	0.1641	0.1600	0.1558	0.1515	0.1472	0.1428	0.1383	0.1339
5	0.1753	0.1748	0.1740	0.1728	0.1714	0.1697	0.1678	0.1656	0.1632	0.1606
6	0.1490	0.1515	0.1537	0.1555	0.1571	0.1584	0.1594	0.1601	0.1605	0.1606
7	0.1086	0.1125	0.1163	0.1200	0.1234	0.1267	0.1298	0.1326	0.1353	0.1377
8	0.0692	0.0731	0.0771	0.0810	0.0849	0.0887	0.0925	0.0962	0.0998	0.1033
9	0.0392	0.0423	0.0454	0.0486	0.0519	0.0552	0.0586	0.0620	0.0654	0.0688
10	0.0200	0.0220	0.0241	0.0262	0.0285	0.0309	0.0334	0.0359	0.0386	0.0413
11	0.0093	0.0104	0.0116	0.0129	0.0143	0.0157	0.0173	0.0190	0.0207	0.0225
12	0.0039	0.0045	0.0051	0.0058	0.0065	0.0073	0.0082	0.0092	0.0102	0.0113
13	0.0015	0.0018	0.0021	0.0024	0.0028	0.0032	0.0036	0.0041	0.0046	0.0052
14	0.0006	0.0007	0.0008	0.0009	0.0011	0.0013	0.0015	0.0017	0.0019	0.0022
15	0.0002	0.0002	0.0003	0.0003	0.0004	0.0005	0.0006	0.0007	0.0008	0.0009
16	0.0001	0.0001	0.0001	0.0001	0.0001	0.0002	0.0002	0.0002	0.0003	0.0003
17	0.0000	0.0000	0.0000	0.0000	0.0000	0.0001	0.0001	0.0001	0.0001	0.0001

x	6.1	6.2	6.3	6.4	6.5	6.6	6.7	6.8	6.9	7.0
0	0.0022	0.0020	0.0018	0.0017	0.0015	0.0014	0.0012	0.0011	0.0010	0.0009
1	0.0137	0.0126	0.0116	0.0106	0.0098	0.0090	0.0082	0.0076	0.0070	0.0064
2	0.0417	0.0390	0.0364	0.0340	0.0318	0.0296	0.0276	0.0258	0.0240	0.0223
3	0.0848	0.0806	0.0765	0.0726	0.0688	0.0652	0.0617	0.0584	0.0552	0.0521
4	0.1294	0.1249	0.1205	0.1162	0.1118	0.1076	0.1034	0.0992	0.0952	0.0912
5	0.1579	0.1549	0.1519	0.1487	0.1454	0.1420	0.1385	0.1349	0.1314	0.1277
6	0.1605	0.1601	0.1595	0.1586	0.1575	0.1562	0.1546	0.1529	0.1511	0.1490
7	0.1399	0.1418	0.1435	0.1450	0.1462	0.1472	0.1480	0.1486	0.1489	0.1490
8	0.1066	0.1099	0.1130	0.1160	0.1188	0.1215	0.1240	0.1263	0.1284	0.1304
9	0.0723	0.0757	0.0791	0.0825	0.0858	0.0891	0.0923	0.0954	0.0985	0.1014

Table C   (*Continued*)

10	0.0441	0.0469	0.0498	0.0528	0.0558	0.0588	0.0618	0.0649	0.0679	0.0710
11	0.0245	0.0265	0.0285	0.0307	0.0330	0.0353	0.0377	0.0401	0.0426	0.0452
12	0.0124	0.0137	0.0150	0.0164	0.0179	0.0194	0.0210	0.0227	0.0245	0.0264
13	0.0058	0.0065	0.0073	0.0081	0.0089	0.0098	0.0108	0.0119	0.0130	0.0142
14	0.0025	0.0029	0.0033	0.0037	0.0041	0.0046	0.0052	0.0058	0.0064	0.0071
15	0.0010	0.0012	0.0014	0.0016	0.0018	0.0020	0.0023	0.0026	0.0029	0.0033
16	0.0004	0.0005	0.0005	0.0006	0.0007	0.0008	0.0010	0.0011	0.0013	0.0014
17	0.0001	0.0002	0.0002	0.0002	0.0003	0.0003	0.0004	0.0004	0.0005	0.0006
18	0.0000	0.0001	0.0001	0.0001	0.0001	0.0001	0.0001	0.0002	0.0002	0.0002
19	0.0000	0.0000	0.0000	0.0000	0.0000	0.0000	0.0000	0.0001	0.0001	0.0001

x	7.1	7.2	7.3	7.4	7.5	7.6	7.7	7.8	7.9	8.0
0	0.0008	0.0007	0.0007	0.0006	0.0006	0.0005	0.0005	0.0004	0.0004	0.0003
1	0.0059	0.0054	0.0049	0.0045	0.0041	0.0038	0.0035	0.0032	0.0029	0.0027
2	0.0208	0.0194	0.0180	0.0167	0.0156	0.0145	0.0134	0.0125	0.0116	0.0107
3	0.0492	0.0464	0.0438	0.0413	0.0389	0.0366	0.0345	0.0324	0.0305	0.0286
4	0.0874	0.0836	0.0799	0.0764	0.0729	0.0696	0.0663	0.0632	0.0602	0.0573
5	0.1241	0.1204	0.1167	0.1130	0.1094	0.1057	0.1021	0.0986	0.0951	0.0916
6	0.1468	0.1445	0.1420	0.1394	0.1367	0.1339	0.1311	0.1282	0.1252	0.1221
7	0.1489	0.1486	0.1481	0.1474	0.1465	0.1454	0.1442	0.1428	0.1413	0.1396
8	0.1321	0.1337	0.1351	0.1363	0.1373	0.1382	0.1388	0.1392	0.1395	0.1396
9	0.1042	0.1070	0.1096	0.1121	0.1144	0.1167	0.1187	0.1207	0.1224	0.1241
10	0.0740	0.0770	0.0800	0.0829	0.0858	0.0887	0.0914	0.0941	0.0967	0.0993
11	0.0478	0.0504	0.0531	0.0558	0.0585	0.0613	0.0640	0.0667	0.0695	0.0722
12	0.0283	0.0303	0.0323	0.0344	0.0366	0.0388	0.0411	0.0434	0.0457	0.0481
13	0.0154	0.0168	0.0181	0.0196	0.0211	0.0227	0.0243	0.0260	0.0278	0.0296
14	0.0078	0.0086	0.0095	0.0104	0.0113	0.0123	0.0134	0.0145	0.0157	0.0169
15	0.0037	0.0041	0.0046	0.0051	0.0057	0.0062	0.0069	0.0075	0.0083	0.0090
16	0.0016	0.0019	0.0021	0.0024	0.0026	0.0030	0.0033	0.0037	0.0041	0.0045
17	0.0007	0.0008	0.0009	0.0010	0.0012	0.0013	0.0015	0.0017	0.0019	0.0021
18	0.0003	0.0003	0.0004	0.0004	0.0005	0.0006	0.0006	0.0007	0.0008	0.0009
19	0.0001	0.0001	0.0001	0.0002	0.0002	0.0002	0.0003	0.0003	0.0003	0.0004
20	0.0000	0.0000	0.0001	0.0001	0.0001	0.0001	0.0001	0.0001	0.0001	0.0002
21	0.0000	0.0000	0.0000	0.0000	0.0000	0.0000	0.0000	0.0000	0.0001	0.0001

x	8.1	8.2	8.3	8.4	8.5	8.6	8.7	8.8	8.9	9.0
0	0.0003	0.0003	0.0002	0.0002	0.0002	0.0002	0.0002	0.0002	0.0001	0.0001
1	0.0025	0.0023	0.0021	0.0019	0.0017	0.0016	0.0014	0.0013	0.0012	0.0011
2	0.0100	0.0092	0.0086	0.0079	0.0074	0.0068	0.0063	0.0058	0.0054	0.0050
3	0.0269	0.0252	0.0237	0.0222	0.0208	0.0195	0.0183	0.0171	0.0160	0.0150
4	0.0544	0.0517	0.0491	0.0466	0.0443	0.0420	0.0398	0.0377	0.0357	0.0337
5	0.0882	0.0849	0.0816	0.0784	0.0752	0.0722	0.0692	0.0663	0.0635	0.0607
6	0.1191	0.1160	0.1128	0.1097	0.1066	0.1034	0.1003	0.0972	0.0941	0.0911
7	0.1378	0.1358	0.1338	0.1317	0.1294	0.1271	0.1247	0.1222	0.1197	0.1171
8	0.1395	0.1392	0.1388	0.1382	0.1375	0.1366	0.1356	0.1344	0.1332	0.1318
9	0.1256	0.1269	0.1280	0.1290	0.1299	0.1306	0.1311	0.1315	0.1317	0.1318
10	0.1017	0.1040	0.1063	0.1084	0.1104	0.1123	0.1140	0.1157	0.1172	0.1186
11	0.0749	0.0776	0.0802	0.0828	0.0853	0.0878	0.0902	0.0925	0.0948	0.0970
12	0.0505	0.0530	0.0555	0.0579	0.0604	0.0629	0.0654	0.0679	0.0703	0.0728
13	0.0315	0.0334	0.0354	0.0374	0.0395	0.0416	0.0438	0.0459	0.0481	0.0504
14	0.0182	0.0196	0.0210	0.0225	0.0240	0.0256	0.0272	0.0289	0.0306	0.0324
15	0.0098	0.0107	0.0116	0.0126	0.0136	0.0147	0.0158	0.0169	0.0182	0.0194
16	0.0050	0.0055	0.0060	0.0066	0.0072	0.0079	0.0086	0.0093	0.0101	0.0109
17	0.0024	0.0026	0.0029	0.0033	0.0036	0.0040	0.0044	0.0048	0.0053	0.0058
18	0.0011	0.0012	0.0014	0.0015	0.0017	0.0019	0.0021	0.0024	0.0026	0.0029
19	0.0005	0.0005	0.0006	0.0007	0.0008	0.0009	0.0010	0.0011	0.0012	0.0014

TABLE C (*Continued*)

20	0.0002	0.0002	0.0002	0.0003	0.0003	0.0004	0.0004	0.0005	0.0005	0.0006
21	0.0001	0.0001	0.0001	0.0001	0.0001	0.0002	0.0002	0.0002	0.0002	0.0003
22	0.0000	0.0000	0.0000	0.0000	0.0001	0.0001	0.0001	0.0001	0.0001	0.0001

x	9.1	9.2	9.3	9.4	9.5	9.6	9.7	9.8	9.9	10.0
0	0.0001	0.0001	0.0001	0.0001	0.0001	0.0001	0.0001	0.0001	0.0001	0.0000
1	0.0010	0.0009	0.0009	0.0008	0.0007	0.0007	0.0006	0.0005	0.0005	0.0005
2	0.0046	0.0043	0.0040	0.0037	0.0034	0.0031	0.0029	0.0027	0.0025	0.0023
3	0.0140	0.0131	0.0123	0.0115	0.0107	0.0100	0.0093	0.0087	0.0081	0.0076
4	0.0319	0.0302	0.0285	0.0269	0.0254	0.0240	0.0226	0.0213	0.0201	0.0189
5	0.0581	0.0555	0.0530	0.0506	0.0483	0.0460	0.0439	0.0418	0.0398	0.0378
6	0.0881	0.0851	0.0822	0.0793	0.0764	0.0736	0.0709	0.0682	0.0656	0.0631
7	0.1145	0.1118	0.1091	0.1064	0.1037	0.1010	0.0982	0.0955	0.0928	0.0901
8	0.1302	0.1286	0.1269	0.1251	0.1232	0.1212	0.1191	0.1170	0.1148	0.1126
9	0.1317	0.1315	0.1311	0.1306	0.1300	0.1293	0.1284	0.1274	0.1263	0.1251
10	0.1198	0.1210	0.1219	0.1228	0.1235	0.1241	0.1245	0.1249	0.1250	0.1251
11	0.0991	0.1012	0.1031	0.1049	0.1067	0.1083	0.1098	0.1112	0.1125	0.1137
12	0.0752	0.0776	0.0799	0.0822	0.0844	0.0866	0.0888	0.0908	0.0928	0.0948
13	0.0526	0.0549	0.0572	0.0594	0.0617	0.0640	0.0662	0.0685	0.0707	0.0729
14	0.0342	0.0361	0.0380	0.0399	0.0419	0.0439	0.0459	0.0479	0.0500	0.0521
15	0.0208	0.0221	0.0235	0.0250	0.0265	0.0281	0.0297	0.0313	0.0330	0.0347
16	0.0118	0.0127	0.0137	0.0147	0.0157	0.0168	0.0180	0.0192	0.0204	0.0217
17	0.0063	0.0069	0.0075	0.0081	0.0088	0.0095	0.0103	0.0111	0.0119	0.0128
18	0.0032	0.0035	0.0039	0.0042	0.0046	0.0051	0.0055	0.0060	0.0065	0.0071
19	0.0015	0.0017	0.0019	0.0021	0.0023	0.0026	0.0028	0.0031	0.0034	0.0037
20	0.0007	0.0008	0.0009	0.0010	0.0011	0.0012	0.0014	0.0015	0.0017	0.0019
21	0.0003	0.0003	0.0004	0.0004	0.0005	0.0006	0.0006	0.0007	0.0008	0.0009
22	0.0001	0.0001	0.0002	0.0002	0.0002	0.0002	0.0003	0.0003	0.0004	0.0004
23	0.0000	0.0001	0.0001	0.0001	0.0001	0.0001	0.0001	0.0001	0.0002	0.0002
24	0.0000	0.0000	0.0000	0.0000	0.0000	0.0000	0.0000	0.0001	0.0001	0.0001

Table D   Cumulative Poisson Probabilities

					μ					
x	.005	.01	.02	.03	.04	.05	.06	.07	.08	.09
0	.9950	.9900	.9802	.9704	.9608	.9512	.9418	.9324	.9231	.9139
1	1.0000	1.0000	.9998	.9996	.9992	.9988	.9983	.9977	.9970	.9962
2	1.0000	1.0000	1.0000	1.0000	1.0000	1.0000	1.0000	.9999	.9999	.9999

					μ					
x	.10	.11	.12	.13	.14	.15	.16	.17	.18	.19
0	.9048	.8958	.8869	.8781	.8694	.8607	.8521	.8437	.8353	.8870
1	.9953	.9944	.9934	.9922	.9911	.9898	.9885	.9871	.9856	.9841
2	.9998	.9998	.9997	.9997	.9996	.9995	.9994	.9993	.9992	.9990
3	1.0000	1.0000	1.0000	1.0000	1.0000	1.0000	1.0000	1.0000	1.0000	1.0000

					μ					
x	.20	.21	.22	.23	.24	.25	.26	.27	.28	.29
0	.8187	.8106	.8025	.7945	.7866	.7788	.7711	.7634	.7558	.7483
1	.9825	.9808	.9791	.9773	.9754	.9735	.9715	.9695	.9674	.9653
2	.9989	.9987	.9985	.9983	.9981	.9978	.9976	.9973	.9970	.9967
3	.9999	.9999	.9999	.9999	.9999	.9999	.9998	.9998	.9998	.9998
4	1.0000	1.0000	1.0000	1.0000	1.0000	1.0000	1.0000	1.0000	1.0000	1.0000

					μ					
x	.30	.32	.34	.36	.38	.40	.42	.44	.46	.48
0	.7408	.7261	.7118	.6977	.6839	.6703	.6570	.6440	.6313	.6188
1	.9631	.9585	.9538	.9488	.9437	.9384	.9330	.9274	.9217	.9158
2	.9964	.9957	.9949	.9940	.9931	.9921	.9910	.9898	.9885	.9871
3	.9997	.9997	.9996	.9995	.9994	.9992	.9991	.9989	.9987	.9985
4	1.0000	1.0000	1.0000	1.0000	1.0000	.9999	.9999	.9999	.9999	.9999

					μ					
x	.50	.55	.60	.65	.70	.75	.80	.85	.90	.95
0	.6065	.5769	.5488	.5220	.4966	.4724	.4493	.4274	.4066	.3867
1	.9098	.8943	.8781	.8614	.8442	.8266	.8088	.7907	.7725	.7541
2	.9856	.9815	.9769	.9717	.9659	.9595	.9526	.9451	.9371	.9287
3	.9982	.9975	.9966	.9956	.9942	.9927	.9909	.9889	.9865	.9839
4	.9998	.9997	.9996	.9994	.9992	.9989	.9986	.9982	.9977	.9971
5	1.0000	1.0000	1.0000	.9999	.9999	.9999	.9998	.9997	.9997	.9995
6	1.0000	1.0000	1.0000	1.0000	1.0000	1.0000	1.0000	1.0000	1.0000	.9999

TABLE D   (*Continued*)

x	1.0	1.1	1.2	1.3	1.4	1.5	1.6	1.7	1.8	1.9
0	.3679	.3329	.3012	.2725	.2466	.2231	.2019	.1827	.1653	.1496
1	.7358	.6990	.6626	.6268	.5918	.5578	.5249	.4932	.4628	.4337
2	.9197	.9004	.8795	.8571	.8335	.8088	.7834	.7572	.7306	.7037
3	.9810	.9743	.9662	.9569	.9463	.9344	.9212	.9068	.8913	.8747
4	.9963	.9946	.9923	.9893	.9857	.9814	.9763	.9704	.9636	.9559
5	.9994	.9990	.9985	.9978	.9968	.9955	.9940	.9920	.9896	.9868
6	.9999	.9999	.9997	.9996	.9994	.9991	.9987	.9981	.9974	.9966
7	1.0000	1.0000	1.0000	.9999	.9999	.9998	.9997	.9996	.9994	.9992
8	1.0000	1.0000	1.0000	1.0000	1.0000	1.0000	1.0000	.9999	.9999	.9998
9	1.0000	1.0000	1.0000	1.0000	1.0000	1.0000	1.0000	1.0000	1.0000	1.0000

μ

x	2.0	2.1	2.2	2.3	2.4	2.5	2.6	2.7	2.8	2.9
0	.1353	.1225	.1108	.1003	.0907	.0821	.0743	.0672	.0608	.0550
1	.4060	.3796	.3546	.3309	.3084	.2873	.2674	.2487	.2311	.2146
2	.6767	.6496	.6227	.5960	.5697	.5438	.5184	.4936	.4695	.4460
3	.8571	.8386	.8194	.7993	.7787	.7576	.7360	.7141	.6919	.6696
4	.9473	.9379	.9275	.9162	.9041	.8912	.8774	.8629	.8477	.8318
5	.9834	.9796	.9751	.9700	.9643	.9580	.9510	.9433	.9349	.9258
6	.9955	.9941	.9925	.9906	.9884	.9858	.9828	.9794	.9756	.9713
7	.9989	.9985	.9980	.9974	.9967	.9958	.9947	.9934	.9919	.9901
8	.9998	.9997	.9995	.9994	.9991	.9989	.9985	.9981	.9976	.9969
9	1.0000	.9999	.9999	.9999	.9998	.9997	.9996	.9995	.9993	.9991
10	1.0000	1.0000	1.0000	1.0000	1.0000	.9999	.9999	.9999	.9998	.9998
11	1.0000	1.0000	1.0000	1.0000	1.0000	1.0000	1.0000	1.0000	1.0000	.9999
12	1.0000	1.0000	1.0000	1.0000	1.0000	1.0000	1.0000	1.0000	1.0000	1.0000

μ

x	3.0	3.1	3.2	3.3	3.4	3.5	3.6	3.7	3.8	3.9
0	.0498	.0450	.0408	.0369	.0334	.0302	.0273	.0247	.0224	.0202
1	.1991	.1847	.1712	.1586	.1468	.1359	.1257	.1162	.1074	.0992
2	.4232	.4012	.3799	.3594	.3397	.3208	.3027	.2854	.2689	.2531
3	.6472	.6248	.6025	.5803	.5584	.5366	.5152	.4942	.4735	.4532
4	.8153	.7982	.7806	.7626	.7442	.7254	.7064	.6872	.6678	.6484
5	.9161	.9057	.8946	.8829	.8705	.8576	.8441	.8301	.8156	.8006
6	.9665	.9612	.9554	.9490	.9421	.9347	.9267	.9182	.9091	.8995
7	.9881	.9858	.9832	.9802	.9769	.9733	.9692	.9648	.9599	.9546
8	.9962	.9953	.9943	.9931	.9917	.9901	.9883	.9863	.9840	.9815
9	.9989	.9986	.9982	.9978	.9973	.9967	.9960	.9952	.9942	.9931
10	.9997	.9996	.9995	.9994	.9992	.9990	.9987	.9984	.9981	.9977
11	.9999	.9999	.9999	.9998	.9998	.9997	.9996	.9995	.9994	.9993
12	1.0000	1.0000	1.0000	1.0000	.9999	.9999	.9999	.9999	.9998	.9998
13	1.0000	1.0000	1.0000	1.0000	1.0000	1.0000	1.0000	1.0000 ˙	1.0000	.9999
14	1.0000	1.0000	1.0000	1.0000	1.0000	1.0000	1.0000	1.0000	1.0000	1.0000

TABLE D   (*Continued*)

| | | | | | μ | | | | | |
x	4.0	4.2	4.4	4.6	4.8	5.0	5.2	5.4	5.6	5.8
0	.0183	.0150	.0123	.0101	.0082	.0067	.0055	.0045	.0037	.0030
1	.0916	.0780	.0663	.0563	.0477	.0404	.0342	.0289	.0244	.0206
2	.2381	.2102	.1851	.1626	.1425	.1247	.1088	.0948	.0824	.0715
3	.4335	.3954	.3594	.3257	.2942	.2650	.2381	.2133	.1906	.1700
4	.6288	.5898	.5512	.5132	.4763	.4405	.4061	.3733	.3421	.3127
5	.7851	.7531	.7199	.6858	.6510	.6160	.5809	.5461	.5119	.4783
6	.8893	.8675	.8436	.8180	.7908	.7622	.7324	.7017	.6703	.6384
7	.9489	.9361	.9214	.9049	.8867	.8666	.8449	.8217	.7970	.7710
8	.9786	.9721	.9642	.9549	.9442	.9319	.9181	.9026	.8857	.8672
9	.9919	.9889	.9851	.9805	.9749	.9682	.9603	.9512	.9409	.9292
10	.9972	.9959	.9943	.9922	.9896	.9863	.9823	.9775	.9718	.9651
11	.9991	.9986	.9980	.9971	.9960	.9945	.9927	.9904	.9875	.9840
12	.9997	.9996	.9993	.9990	.9986	.9980	.9972	.9962	.9949	.9932
13	.9999	.9999	.9998	.9997	.9995	.9993	.9990	.9986	.9980	.9973
14	1.0000	1.0000	.9999	.9999	.9999	.9998	.9997	.9995	.9993	.9990
15	1.0000	1.0000	1.0000	1.0000	1.0000	.9999	.9999	.9998	.9998	.9996
16	1.0000	1.0000	1.0000	1.0000	1.0000	1.0000	1.0000	.9999	.9999	.9999
17	1.0000	1.0000	1.0000	1.0000	1.0000	1.0000	1.0000	1.0000	1.0000	1.0000

| | | | | | μ | | | | | |
x	6.0	6.2	6.4	6.6	6.8	7.0	7.2	7.6	7.6	7.8
0	.0025	.0020	.0017	.0014	.0011	.0009	.0007	.0006	.0005	.0004
2	.0174	.0146	.0123	.0103	.0087	.0073	.0061	.0051	.0043	.0036
2	.0620	.0536	.0463	.0400	.0344	.0296	.0255	.0219	.0188	.0161
3	.1512	.1342	.1189	.1052	.0928	.0818	.0719	.0632	.0554	.0485
4	.2851	.2592	.2351	.2127	.1920	.1730	.1555	.1395	.1249	.1117
5	.4457	.4141	.3837	.3547	.3270	.3007	.2759	.2526	.2307	.2103
6	.6063	.5742	.5423	.5108	.4799	.4497	.4204	.3920	.3646	.3384
7	.7440	.7160	.6873	.6581	.6285	.5987	.5689	.5393	.5100	.4812
8	.8472	.8259	.8033	.7796	.7548	.7291	.7027	.6757	.6482	.6204
9	.9161	.9016	.8858	.8686	.8502	.8305	.8096	.7877	.7649	.7411
10	.9574	.9486	.9386	.9274	.9151	.9015	.8867	.8707	.8535	.8352
11	.9799	.9750	.9693	.9627	.9552	.9466	.9371	.9265	.9148	.9020
12	.9912	.9887	.9857	.9821	.9779	.9730	.9673	.9609	.9536	.9454
13	.9964	.9952	.9937	.9920	.9898	.9872	.9841	.9805	.9762	.9714
14	.9986	.9981	.9974	.9966	.9956	.9943	.9927	.9908	.9886	.9859
15	.9995	.9993	.9990	.9986	.9982	.9976	.9969	.9959	.9948	.9934
16	.9998	.9997	.9996	.9995	.9993	.9990	.9987	.9983	.9978	.9971
17	.9999	.9999	.9999	.9998	.9997	.9996	.9995	.9993	.9991	.9988
18	1.0000	1.0000	1.0000	.9999	.9999	.9999	.9998	.9997	.9996	.9995
19	1.0000	1.0000	1.0000	1.0000	1.0000	1.0000	.9999	.9999	.9999	.9998
20	1.0000	1.0000	1.0000	1.0000	1.0000	1.0000	1.0000	1.0000	1.0000	.9999
21	1.0000	1.0000	1.0000	1.0000	1.0000	1.0000	1.0000	1.0000	1.0000	1.0000

TABLE D   (*Continued*)

					μ					
x	8.0	8.5	9.0	9.5	10.0	10.5	11.0	11.5	12.0	12.5
0	.0003	.0002	.0001	.0001	.0000	.0000	.0000	.0000	.0000	.0000
1	.0030	.0019	.0012	.0008	.0005	.0003	.0002	.0001	.0001	.0001
2	.0138	.0093	.0062	.0042	.0028	.0018	.0012	.0008	.0005	.0003
3	.0424	.0301	.0212	.0149	.0103	.0071	.0049	.0034	.0023	.0016
4	.0996	.0744	.0550	.0403	.0293	.0211	.0151	.0107	.0076	.0053
5	.1912	.1496	.1157	.0885	.0671	.0504	.0375	.0277	.0203	.0148
6	.3134	.2562	.2068	.1649	.1301	.1016	.0786	.0603	.0458	.0346
7	.4530	.3856	.3239	.2687	.2202	.1785	.1432	.1137	.0895	.0698
8	.5925	.5231	.4557	.3918	.3328	.2794	.2320	.1906	.1550	.1249
9	.7166	.6530	.5874	.5218	.4579	.3971	.3405	.2888	.2424	.2014
10	.8159	.7634	.7060	.6453	.5830	.5207	.4599	.4017	.3472	.2971
11	.8881	.8487	.8030	.7520	.6968	.6387	.5793	.5198	.4616	.4058
12	.9362	.9091	.8758	.8364	.7916	.7420	.6887	.6329	.5760	.5190
13	.9658	.9486	.9261	.8981	.8645	.8253	.7813	.7330	.6815	.6278
14	.9827	.9726	.9585	.9400	.9165	.8879	.8540	.8153	.7720	.7250
15	.9918	.9862	.9780	.9665	.9513	.9317	.9074	.8783	.8444	.8060
16	.9963	.9934	.9889	.9823	.9730	.9604	.9441	.9236	.8987	.8693
17	.9984	.9970	.9947	.9911	.9857	.9781	.9678	.9542	.9370	.9158
18	.9993	.9987	.9976	.9957	.9928	.9885	.9823	.9738	.9626	.9481
19	.9997	.9995	.9989	.9980	.9965	.9942	.9907	.9857	.9787	.9694
20	.9999	.9998	.9996	.9991	.9984	.9972	.9953	.9925	.9884	.9827
21	1.0000	.9999	.9998	.9996	.9993	.9987	.9977	.9962	.9939	.9906
22	1.0000	1.0000	.9999	.9999	.9997	.9994	.9990	.9982	.9970	.9951
23	1.0000	1.0000	1.0000	.9999	.9999	.9998	.9995	.9992	.9985	.9975
24	1.0000	1.0000	1.0000	1.0000	1.0000	.9999	.9998	.9996	.9993	.9988
25	1.0000	1.0000	1.0000	1.0000	1.0000	1.0000	.9999	.9998	.9997	.9994
26	1.0000	1.0000	1.0000	1.0000	1.0000	1.0000	1.0000	.9999	.9999	.9997
27	1.0000	1.0000	1.0000	1.0000	1.0000	1.0000	1.0000	1.0000	.9999	.9999

TABLE E   Binomial Coefficients

n	$\binom{n}{0}$	$\binom{n}{1}$	$\binom{n}{2}$	$\binom{n}{3}$	$\binom{n}{4}$	$\binom{n}{5}$	$\binom{n}{6}$	$\binom{n}{7}$	$\binom{n}{8}$	$\binom{n}{9}$	$\binom{n}{10}$
0	1										
1	1	1									
2	1	2	1								
3	1	3	3	1							
4	1	4	6	4	1						
5	1	5	10	10	5	1					
6	1	6	15	20	15	6	1				
7	1	7	21	35	35	21	7	1			
8	1	8	28	56	70	56	28	8	1		
9	1	9	36	84	126	126	84	36	9	1	
10	1	10	45	120	210	252	210	120	45	10	1
11	1	11	55	165	330	462	462	330	165	55	11
12	1	12	66	220	495	792	924	792	495	220	66
13	1	13	78	286	715	1287	1716	1716	1287	715	286
14	1	14	91	364	1001	2002	3003	3432	3003	2002	1001
15	1	15	105	455	1365	3003	5005	6435	6435	5005	3003
16	1	16	120	560	1820	4368	8008	11440	12870	11440	8008
17	1	17	136	680	2380	6188	12376	19448	24310	24310	19448
18	1	18	153	816	3060	8568	18564	31824	43758	48620	43758
19	1	19	171	969	3876	11628	27132	50388	75582	92378	92378
20	1	20	190	1140	4845	15504	38760	77520	125970	167960	184756

TABLE F   Values of $e^{-\mu}$

μ	$e^{-\mu}$	μ	$e^{-\mu}$	μ	$e^{-\mu}$	μ	$e^{-\mu}$
.10	.9048	1.90	.1496	3.60	.0273	5.40	.0045
.20	.8187	2.00	.1353	3.70	.0247	5.50	.0041
.30	.7408			3.80	.0224		
.40	.6703	2.10	.1225	3.90	.0202	5.60	.0037
.50	.6065	2.20	.1108	4.00	.0183	5.70	.0033
		2.30	.1003			5.80	.0030
.60	.5488	2.40	.0907	4.10	.0166	5.90	.0027
.70	.4966	2.50	.0821	4.20	.0150	6.00	.0025
.80	.4493			4.30	.0136		
.90	.4066	2.60	.0743	4.40	.0123	6.10	.0022
1.00	.3679	2.70	.0672	4.50	.0111	6.20	.0020
		2.80	.0608			6.30	.0018
1.10	.3329	2.90	.0550	4.60	.0101	6.40	.0017
1.20	.3012	3.00	.0498	4.70	.0091	6.50	.0015
1.30	.2725			4.80	.0082		
1.40	.2466	3.10	.0450	4.90	.0074	6.60	.0014
1.50	.2231	3.20	.0408	5.00	.0067	6.70	.0012
		3.30	.0369			6.80	.0011
1.60	.2019	3.40	.0334	5.10	.0061	6.90	.0010
1.70	.1827	3.50	.0302	5.20	.0055	7.00	.0009
1.80	.1653			5.30	.0050		

TABLE G   Right Tail Areas Under the Standard Normal Probability Distribution

Each entry in the table indicates the proportion of the total area under the normal curve contained in the segment bounded by a perpendicular raised at the mean and a perpendicular raised at a distance of z standard deviation units.

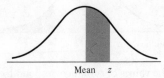

Mean z

To illustrate: 43.57 percent of the area under a normal curve lies between the maximum ordinate and a point 1.52 standard deviation units away.

z	0.00	0.01	0.02	0.03	0.04	0.05	0.06	0.07	0.08	0.09
0.0	0.0000	0.0040	0.0080	0.0120	0.0160	0.0199	0.0239	0.0279	0.0319	0.0359
0.1	0.0398	0.0438	0.0478	0.0517	0.0557	0.0596	0.0636	0.0675	0.0714	0.0753
0.2	0.0793	0.0832	0.0871	0.0910	0.0948	0.0987	0.1026	0.1064	0.1103	0.1141
0.3	0.1179	0.1217	0.1255	0.1293	0.1331	0.1368	0.1406	0.1443	0.1480	0.1517
0.4	0.1554	0.1591	0.1628	0.1664	0.1700	0.1736	0.1772	0.1808	0.1844	0.1879
0.5	0.1915	0.1950	0.1985	0.2019	0.2054	0.2088	0.2123	0.2157	0.2190	0.2224
0.6	0.2257	0.2291	0.2324	0.2357	0.2389	0.2422	0.2454	0.2486	0.2518	0.2549
0.7	0.2580	0.2612	0.2642	0.2673	0.2704	0.2734	0.2764	0.2794	0.2823	0.2852
0.8	0.2881	0.2910	0.2939	0.2967	0.2995	0.3023	0.3051	0.3078	0.3106	0.3133
0.9	0.3159	0.3186	0.3212	0.3238	0.3264	0.3289	0.3315	0.3340	0.3365	0.3389
1.0	0.3413	0.3438	0.3461	0.3485	0.3508	0.3531	0.3554	0.3577	0.3599	0.3621
1.1	0.3643	0.3665	0.3686	0.3708	0.3729	0.3749	0.3770	0.3790	0.3810	0.3830
1.2	0.3849	0.3869	0.3888	0.3907	0.3925	0.3944	0.3962	0.3980	0.3997	0.4015
1.3	0.4032	0.4049	0.4066	0.4082	0.4099	0.4115	0.4131	0.4147	0.4162	0.4177
1.4	0.4192	0.4207	0.4222	0.4236	0.4251	0.4265	0.4279	0.4292	0.4306	0.4319
1.5	0.4332	0.4345	0.4357	0.4370	0.4382	0.4394	0.4406	0.4418	0.4429	0.4441
1.6	0.4452	0.4463	0.4474	0.4484	0.4495	0.4505	0.4515	0.4525	0.4535	0.4545
1.7	0.4554	0.4564	0.4573	0.4582	0.4591	0.4599	0.4608	0.4616	0.4625	0.4633
1.8	0.4641	0.4649	0.4656	0.4664	0.4671	0.4678	0.4686	0.4693	0.4699	0.4706
1.9	0.4713	0.4719	0.4726	0.4732	0.4738	0.4744	0.4750	0.4756	0.4761	0.4767
2.0	0.4772	0.4778	0.4783	0.4788	0.4793	0.4798	0.4803	0.4808	0.4812	0.4817
2.1	0.4821	0.4826	0.4830	0.4834	0.4838	0.4842	0.4846	0.4850	0.4854	0.4857
2.2	0.4861	0.4864	0.4868	0.4871	0.4875	0.4878	0.4881	0.4884	0.4887	0.4890
2.3	0.4893	0.4896	0.4898	0.4901	0.4904	0.4906	0.4909	0.4911	0.4913	0.4916
2.4	0.4918	0.4920	0.4922	0.4925	0.4927	0.4929	0.4931	0.4932	0.4934	0.4936
2.5	0.4938	0.4940	0.4941	0.4943	0.4945	0.4946	0.4948	0.4949	0.4951	0.4952
2.6	0.4953	0.4955	0.4956	0.4957	0.4959	0.4960	0.4961	0.4962	0.4963	0.4964
2.7	0.4965	0.4966	0.4967	0.4968	0.4969	0.4970	0.4971	0.4972	0.4973	0.4974
2.8	0.4974	0.4975	0.4976	0.4977	0.4977	0.4978	0.4979	0.4979	0.4980	0.4981
2.9	0.4981	0.4982	0.4982	0.4983	0.4984	0.4984	0.4985	0.4985	0.4986	0.4986
3.0	0.4986	0.4987	0.4987	0.4988	0.4988	0.4989	0.4989	0.4989	0.4990	0.4990
3.1	0.4990	0.4991	0.4991	0.4991	0.4992	0.4992	0.4992	0.4992	0.4993	0.4993
3.2	0.4993	0.4993	0.4994	0.4994	0.4994	0.4994	0.4994	0.4995	0.4995	0.4995
3.3	0.4995	0.4995	0.4995	0.4996	0.4996	0.4996	0.4996	0.4996	0.4996	0.4997
3.4	0.4997	0.4997	0.4997	0.4997	0.4997	0.4997	0.4997	0.4997	0.4998	0.4998
3.5	0.4998	0.4998	0.4998	0.4998	0.4998	0.4998	0.4998	0.4998	0.4998	0.4998
3.6	0.4998	0.4998	0.4999	0.4999	0.4999	0.4999	0.4999	0.4999	0.4999	0.4999
3.7	0.4999	0.4999	0.4999	0.4999	0.4999	0.4999	0.4999	0.4999	0.4999	0.4999
3.8	0.4999	0.4999	0.4999	0.4999	0.4999	0.4999	0.4999	0.5000	0.5000	0.5000
3.9	0.5000	0.5000	0.5000	0.5000	0.5000	0.5000	0.5000	0.5000	0.5000	0.5000

TABLE H   *t* Distributions

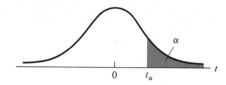

The following table provides the values of t_α that correspond to a given upper-tail area α and a specified number of degrees of freedom.

Degrees of freedom	Upper-tail area α							
	.1	.05	.025	.01	.005	.0025	.001	.0005
1	3.078	6.314	12.706	31.821	63.657	127.32	318.31	636.62
2	1.886	2.920	4.303	6.965	9.925	14.089	22.327	31.598
3	1.638	2.353	3.182	4.541	5.841	7.453	10.214	12.924
4	1.533	2.132	2.776	3.747	4.604	5.598	7.173	8.610
5	1.476	2.015	2.571	3.365	4.032	4.773	5.893	6.869
6	1.440	1.943	2.447	3.143	3.707	4.317	5.208	5.959
7	1.415	1.895	2.365	2.998	3.499	4.029	4.785	5.408
8	1.397	1.860	2.306	2.896	3.355	3.833	4.501	5.041
9	1.383	1.833	2.262	2.821	3.250	3.690	4.297	4.781
10	1.371	1.812	2.228	2.764	3.169	3.581	4.144	4.587
11	1.363	1.796	2.201	2.718	3.106	3.497	4.025	4.437
12	1.356	1.782	2.179	2.681	3.055	3.428	3.930	4.318
13	1.350	1.771	2.160	2.650	3.012	3.372	3.852	4.221
14	1.345	1.761	2.145	2.624	2.977	3.326	3.787	4.140
15	1.341	1.753	2.131	2.602	2.947	3.286	3.733	4.073
16	1.337	1.746	2.120	2.583	2.921	3.252	3.686	4.015
17	1.333	1.740	2.110	2.567	2.898	3.222	3.646	3.965
18	1.330	1.734	2.101	2.552	2.878	3.197	3.610	3.922
19	1.328	1.729	2.093	2.539	2.861	3.174	3.579	3.883
20	1.325	1.725	2.086	2.528	2.845	3.153	3.552	3.850
21	1.323	1.721	2.080	2.518	2.831	3.135	3.527	3.819
22	1.321	1.717	2.074	2.508	2.819	3.119	3.505	3.792
23	1.319	1.714	2.069	2.500	2.807	3.104	3.485	3.767
24	1.318	1.711	2.064	2.492	2.797	3.091	3.467	3.745
25	1.316	1.708	2.060	2.485	2.787	3.078	3.450	3.725
26	1.315	1.706	2.056	2.479	2.779	3.067	3.435	3.707
27	1.314	1.703	2.052	2.473	2.771	3.057	3.421	3.690
28	1.313	1.701	2.048	2.467	2.763	3.047	3.408	3.674
29	1.311	1.699	2.045	2.462	2.756	3.038	3.396	3.659
30	1.310	1.697	2.042	2.457	2.750	3.030	3.385	3.646
40	1.303	1.684	2.021	2.423	2.704	2.971	3.307	3.551
60	1.296	1.671	2.000	2.390	2.660	2.915	3.232	3.460
120	1.289	1.658	1.980	2.358	2.617	2.860	3.160	3.373
∞	1.282	1.645	1.960	2.326	2.576	2.807	3.090	3.291

Source: From Ronald A. Fisher: *Statistical Methods for Research Workers*, 14th ed., copyright © 1970 University of Adelaide.

TABLE I   Chi-square Distributions

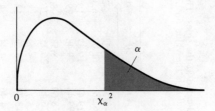

0.10	0.05	0.025	0.01	0.005	P / d.f.
2.71	3.84	5.02	6.63	7.88	1
4.61	5.99	7.38	9.21	10.60	2
6.25	7.81	9.35	11.34	12.84	3
7.78	9.49	11.14	13.28	14.86	4
9.24	11.07	12.83	15.09	16.75	5
10.64	12.59	14.45	16.81	18.55	6
12.02	14.07	16.01	18.48	20.3	7
13.36	15.51	17.53	20.1	22.0	8
14.68	16.92	19.02	21.7	23.6	9
15.99	18.31	20.5	23.2	25.2	10
17.28	19.68	21.9	24.7	26.8	11
18.55	21.0	23.3	26.2	28.3	12
19.81	22.4	24.7	27.7	29.8	13
21.1	23.7	26.1	29.1	31.3	14
22.3	25.0	27.5	30.6	32.8	15
23.5	26.3	28.8	32.0	34.3	16
24.8	27.6	30.2	33.4	35.7	17
26.0	28.9	31.5	34.8	37.2	18
27.2	30.1	32.9	36.2	38.6	19
28.4	31.4	34.2	37.6	40.0	20
29.6	32.7	35.5	38.9	41.4	21
30.8	33.9	36.8	40.3	42.8	22
32.0	35.2	38.1	41.6	44.2	23
33.2	36.4	39.4	43.0	45.6	24
34.4	37.7	40.6	44.3	46.9	25
35.6	38.9	41.9	45.6	48.3	26
36.7	40.1	43.2	47.0	49.6	27
37.9	41.3	44.5	48.3	51.0	28
39.1	42.6	45.7	49.6	52.3	29
40.3	43.8	47.0	50.9	53.7	30
51.8	55.8	59.3	63.7	66.8	40
63.2	67.5	71.4	76.2	79.5	50
74.4	79.1	83.3	88.4	92.0	60
85.5	90.5	95.0	100.4	104.2	70
96.6	101.9	106.6	112.3	116.3	80
107.6	113.1	118.1	124.1	128.3	90
118.5	124.3	129.6	135.8	140.2	100

Source: Abridged from "Table of percentage points of the χ^2 distribution" by Catherine M. Thompson, *Biometrika*, Vol. 32 (1941), pp. 187–191, and reprinted here by permission of the author and editor of *Biometrika*.

TABLE J F Distributions[a]

Degrees of freedom in the numerator are recorded at the top of the table, and the degrees of freedom in the denominator are indicated at the sides. The first listed or smaller value is the value on the F scale to the right of which lies 0.05 of the area under the curve. The second listed or larger value is the value on the F scale to the right of which lies 0.01 of the area under the curve.

degrees of freedom (numerator)

	1	2	3	4	5	6	8	10	12	16	20	30	40	50	100
1	161 / 4,052	200 / 4,999	216 / 5,403	225 / 5,625	230 / 5,764	234 / 5,859	239 / 5,981	242 / 6,056	244 / 6,106	246 / 6,169	248 / 6,208	250 / 6,258	251 / 6,286	252 / 6,302	253 / 6,334
2	18.51 / 98.49	19.00 / 99.00	19.16 / 99.17	19.25 / 99.25	19.30 / 99.30	19.33 / 99.33	19.37 / 99.36	19.39 / 99.40	19.41 / 99.42	19.43 / 99.44	19.44 / 99.45	19.46 / 99.47	19.47 / 99.48	19.47 / 99.48	19.49 / 99.49
3	10.13 / 34.12	9.55 / 30.82	9.28 / 29.46	9.12 / 28.71	9.01 / 28.24	8.94 / 27.91	8.84 / 27.49	8.78 / 27.23	8.74 / 27.05	8.69 / 26.83	8.66 / 26.69	8.62 / 26.50	8.60 / 26.41	8.58 / 26.35	8.56 / 26.23
4	7.71 / 21.20	6.94 / 18.00	6.59 / 16.69	6.39 / 15.98	6.26 / 15.52	6.16 / 15.21	6.04 / 14.80	5.96 / 14.54	5.91 / 14.37	5.84 / 14.15	5.80 / 14.02	5.74 / 13.83	5.71 / 13.74	5.70 / 13.69	5.66 / 13.57
5	6.61 / 16.26	5.79 / 13.27	5.41 / 12.06	5.19 / 11.39	5.05 / 10.97	4.95 / 10.67	4.82 / 10.27	4.74 / 10.05	4.68 / 9.89	4.60 / 9.68	4.56 / 9.55	4.50 / 9.38	4.46 / 9.29	4.44 / 9.24	4.40 / 9.13
6	5.99 / 13.74	5.14 / 10.92	4.76 / 9.78	4.53 / 9.15	4.39 / 8.75	4.28 / 8.47	4.15 / 8.10	4.06 / 7.87	4.00 / 7.72	3.92 / 7.52	3.87 / 7.39	3.81 / 7.23	3.77 / 7.14	3.75 / 7.09	3.71 / 6.99
7	5.59 / 12.25	4.74 / 9.55	4.35 / 8.45	4.12 / 7.85	3.97 / 7.46	3.87 / 7.19	3.73 / 6.84	3.63 / 6.62	3.57 / 6.47	3.49 / 6.27	3.44 / 6.15	3.38 / 5.98	3.34 / 5.90	3.32 / 5.85	3.28 / 5.75
8	5.32 / 11.26	4.46 / 8.65	4.07 / 7.59	3.84 / 7.01	3.69 / 6.63	3.58 / 6.37	3.44 / 6.03	3.34 / 5.82	3.28 / 5.67	3.20 / 5.48	3.15 / 5.36	3.08 / 5.20	3.05 / 5.11	3.03 / 5.06	2.98 / 4.96

degrees of freedom (numerator)

ϕ_d	1	2	3	4	5	6	8	10	12	16	20	30	40	50	100
9	5.12 / 10.56	4.26 / 8.02	3.86 / 6.99	3.63 / 6.42	3.48 / 6.06	3.37 / 5.80	3.23 / 5.47	3.13 / 5.26	3.07 / 5.11	2.98 / 4.92	2.93 / 4.80	2.86 / 4.64	2.82 / 4.56	2.80 / 4.51	2.76 / 4.41
10	4.96 / 10.04	4.10 / 7.56	3.71 / 6.55	3.48 / 5.99	3.33 / 5.64	3.22 / 5.39	3.07 / 5.06	2.97 / 4.85	2.91 / 4.71	2.82 / 4.52	2.77 / 4.41	2.70 / 4.25	2.67 / 4.17	2.64 / 4.12	2.59 / 4.01
11	4.84 / 9.65	3.98 / 7.20	3.59 / 6.22	3.36 / 5.67	3.20 / 5.32	3.09 / 5.07	2.95 / 4.74	2.86 / 4.54	2.79 / 4.40	2.70 / 4.21	2.65 / 4.10	2.57 / 3.94	2.53 / 3.86	2.50 / 3.80	2.45 / 3.70
12	4.75 / 9.33	3.88 / 6.93	3.49 / 5.95	3.26 / 5.41	3.11 / 5.06	3.00 / 4.82	2.85 / 4.50	2.76 / 4.30	2.69 / 4.16	2.60 / 3.98	2.54 / 3.86	2.46 / 3.70	2.42 / 3.61	2.40 / 3.56	2.35 / 3.46
13	4.67 / 9.07	3.80 / 6.70	3.41 / 5.74	3.18 / 5.20	3.02 / 4.86	2.92 / 4.62	2.77 / 4.30	2.67 / 4.10	2.60 / 3.96	2.51 / 3.78	2.46 / 3.67	2.38 / 3.51	2.34 / 3.42	2.32 / 3.37	2.26 / 3.27
14	4.60 / 8.86	3.74 / 6.51	3.34 / 5.56	3.11 / 5.03	2.96 / 4.69	2.85 / 4.46	2.70 / 4.14	2.60 / 3.94	2.53 / 3.80	2.44 / 3.62	2.39 / 3.51	2.31 / 3.34	2.27 / 3.26	2.24 / 3.21	2.19 / 3.11
15	4.54 / 8.68	3.68 / 6.36	3.29 / 5.42	3.06 / 4.89	2.90 / 4.56	2.79 / 4.32	2.64 / 4.00	2.55 / 3.80	2.48 / 3.67	2.39 / 3.48	2.33 / 3.36	2.25 / 3.20	2.21 / 3.12	2.18 / 3.07	2.12 / 2.97
16	4.49 / 8.53	3.63 / 6.23	3.24 / 5.29	3.01 / 4.77	2.85 / 4.44	2.74 / 4.20	2.59 / 3.89	2.49 / 3.69	2.42 / 3.55	2.33 / 3.37	2.28 / 3.25	2.20 / 3.10	2.16 / 3.01	2.13 / 2.96	2.07 / 2.86
17	4.45 / 8.40	3.59 / 6.11	3.20 / 5.18	2.96 / 4.67	2.81 / 4.34	2.70 / 4.10	2.55 / 3.79	2.45 / 3.59	2.38 / 3.45	2.29 / 3.27	2.23 / 3.16	2.15 / 3.00	2.11 / 2.92	2.08 / 2.86	2.02 / 2.76
18	4.41 / 8.28	3.55 / 6.01	3.16 / 5.09	2.93 / 4.58	2.77 / 4.25	2.66 / 4.01	2.51 / 3.71	2.41 / 3.51	2.34 / 3.37	2.25 / 3.19	2.19 / 3.07	2.11 / 2.91	2.07 / 2.83	2.04 / 2.78	1.98 / 2.68
19	4.38 / 8.18	3.52 / 5.93	3.13 / 5.01	2.90 / 4.50	2.74 / 4.17	2.63 / 3.94	2.48 / 3.63	2.38 / 3.43	2.31 / 3.30	2.21 / 3.12	2.15 / 3.00	2.07 / 2.84	2.02 / 2.76	2.00 / 2.70	1.94 / 2.60
20	4.35 / 8.10	3.49 / 5.85	3.10 / 4.94	2.87 / 4.43	2.71 / 4.10	2.60 / 3.87	2.45 / 3.56	2.35 / 3.37	2.28 / 3.23	2.18 / 3.05	2.12 / 2.94	2.04 / 2.77	1.99 / 2.69	1.96 / 2.63	1.90 / 2.53

TABLE J (Continued)

degrees of freedom (numerator)

	1	2	3	4	5	6	8	10	12	16	20	30	40	50	100	ϕ_d
25	4.24 7.77	3.38 5.57	2.99 4.68	2.76 4.18	2.60 3.86	2.49 3.63	2.34 3.32	2.24 3.13	2.16 2.99	2.06 2.81	2.00 2.70	1.92 2.54	1.87 2.45	1.84 2.40	1.77 2.29	25
30	4.17 7.56	3.32 5.39	2.92 4.51	2.69 4.02	2.53 3.70	2.42 3.47	2.27 3.17	2.16 2.98	2.09 2.84	1.99 2.66	1.93 2.55	1.84 2.38	1.79 2.29	1.76 2.24	1.69 2.13	30
40	4.08 7.31	3.23 5.18	2.84 4.31	2.61 3.83	2.45 3.51	2.34 3.29	2.18 2.99	2.07 2.80	2.00 2.66	1.90 2.49	1.84 2.37	1.74 2.20	1.69 2.11	1.66 2.05	1.59 1.94	40
50	4.03 7.17	3.18 5.06	2.79 4.20	2.56 3.72	2.40 3.41	2.29 3.18	2.13 2.88	2.02 2.70	1.95 2.56	1.85 2.39	1.78 2.26	1.69 2.10	1.63 2.00	1.60 1.94	1.52 1.82	50
60	4.00 7.08	3.15 4.98	2.76 4.13	2.52 3.65	2.37 3.34	2.25 3.12	2.10 2.82	1.99 2.63	1.92 2.50	1.81 2.32	1.75 2.20	1.65 2.03	1.59 1.93	1.56 1.87	1.48 1.74	60
80	3.96 6.96	3.11 4.88	2.72 4.04	2.48 3.56	2.33 3.25	2.21 3.04	2.05 2.74	1.95 2.55	1.88 2.41	1.77 2.24	1.70 2.11	1.60 1.94	1.54 1.84	1.51 1.78	1.42 1.65	80
100	3.94 6.90	3.09 4.82	2.70 3.98	2.46 3.51	2.30 3.20	2.19 2.99	2.03 2.69	1.92 2.51	1.85 2.36	1.75 2.19	1.68 2.06	1.57 1.89	1.51 1.79	1.48 1.73	1.39 1.59	100
150	3.91 6.81	3.06 4.75	2.67 3.91	2.43 3.44	2.27 3.14	2.16 2.92	2.00 2.62	1.89 2.44	1.82 2.30	1.71 2.12	1.64 2.00	1.54 1.83	1.47 1.72	1.44 1.66	1.34 1.51	150
200	3.89 6.76	3.04 4.71	2.65 3.88	2.41 3.41	2.26 3.11	2.14 2.90	1.98 2.60	1.87 2.41	1.80 2.28	1.69 2.09	1.62 1.97	1.52 1.79	1.45 1.69	1.42 1.62	1.32 1.48	200
400	3.86 6.70	3.02 4.66	2.62 3.83	2.39 3.36	2.23 3.06	2.12 2.85	1.96 2.55	1.85 2.37	1.78 2.23	1.67 2.04	1.60 1.92	1.49 1.74	1.42 1.64	1.38 1.57	1.28 1.42	400
1000	3.85 6.66	3.00 4.62	2.61 3.80	2.38 3.34	2.22 3.04	2.10 2.82	1.95 2.53	1.84 2.34	1.76 2.20	1.65 2.01	1.58 1.89	1.47 1.71	1.41 1.61	1.36 1.54	1.26 1.38	1000
∞	3.84 6.64	2.99 4.60	2.60 3.78	2.37 3.32	2.21 3.02	2.09 2.80	1.94 2.51	1.83 2.32	1.75 2.18	1.64 1.99	1.57 1.87	1.46 1.69	1.40 1.59	1.35 1.52	1.24 1.36	∞

Source: Reprinted by permission from *Statistical Methods* by George W. Snedecor and William G. Cochran, 6th ed., copyright © 1967 by The Iowa State University Press, Ames, Iowa 50010.

488

TABLE K   .95 Confidence Intervals for Proportions

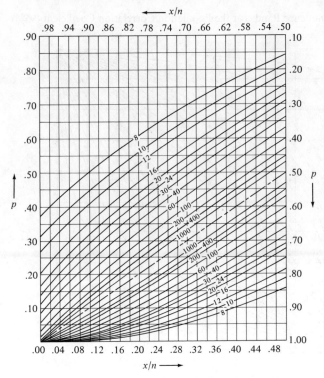

TABLE K   (*Continued*) .99 Confidence Intervals for Proportions

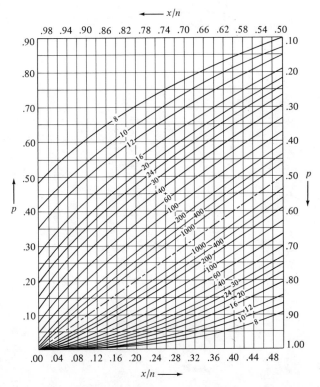

TABLE L   Confidence Bands for the Population Correlation Coefficient (95%).

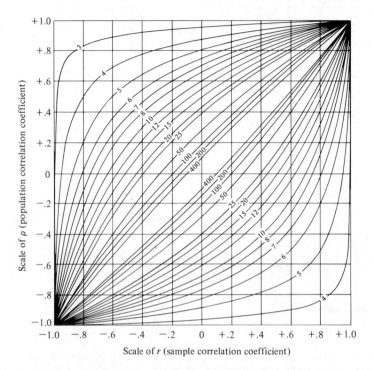

Scale of r (sample correlation coefficient)

Source: From E. S. Pearson and H. O. Hartley, *Biometrika Tables for Statisticians*, Vol. 1 (1962), p. 140. Reprinted by permission of the *Biometrika* Trustees.

TABLE M   Squares, Square Roots, and Reciprocals

n	n^2	$\sqrt{n}$	$\sqrt{10n}$	$1/n$	n	n^2	$\sqrt{n}$	$\sqrt{10n}$	$1/n$
1	1	1.000	3.162	1.00000	51	2601	7.141	22.583	.01961
2	4	1.414	4.472	.50000	52	2704	7.211	22.804	.01923
3	9	1.732	5.477	.33333	53	2809	7.280	23.022	.01887
4	16	2.000	6.325	.25000	54	2916	7.348	23.238	.01852
5	25	2.236	7.071	.20000	55	3025	7.416	23.452	.01818
6	36	2.449	7.746	.16667	56	3136	7.483	23.664	.01786
7	49	2.646	8.367	.14286	57	3249	7.550	23.875	.01754
8	64	2.828	8.944	.12500	58	3364	7.616	24.083	.01724
9	81	3.000	9.487	.11111	59	3481	7.681	24.290	.01695
10	100	3.162	10.000	.10000	60	3600	7.746	24.495	.01667
11	121	3.317	10.488	.09091	61	3721	7.810	24.698	.01639
12	144	3.464	10.954	.08333	62	3844	7.874	24.900	.01613
13	169	3.606	11.402	.07692	63	3969	7.937	25.100	.01587
14	196	3.742	11.832	.07143	64	4096	8.000	25.298	.01562
15	225	3.873	12.247	.06667	65	4225	8.062	25.495	.01538
16	256	4.000	12.649	.06250	66	4356	8.124	25.690	.01515
17	289	4.123	13.038	.05882	67	4489	8.185	25.884	.01493
18	324	4.243	13.416	.05556	68	4624	8.246	26.077	.01471
19	361	4.359	13.784	.05263	69	4761	8.307	26.268	.01449
20	400	4.472	14.142	.05000	70	4900	8.367	26.458	.01429
21	441	4.583	14.491	.04762	71	5041	8.426	26.646	.01408
22	484	4.690	14.832	.04545	72	5184	8.485	26.833	.01389
23	529	4.796	15.166	.04348	73	5329	8.544	27.019	.01370
24	576	4.899	15.492	.04167	74	5476	8.602	27.203	.01351
25	625	5.000	15.811	.04000	75	5625	8.660	27.386	.01333
26	676	5.099	16.125	.03846	76	5776	8.718	27.568	.01316
27	729	5.196	16.432	.03704	77	5929	8.775	27.749	.01299
28	784	5.292	16.733	.03571	78	6084	8.832	27.928	.01282
29	841	5.385	17.029	.03448	79	6241	8.888	28.107	.01266
30	900	5.477	17.321	.03333	80	6400	8.944	28.284	.01250
31	961	5.568	17.607	.03226	81	6561	9.000	28.460	.01235
32	1024	5.657	17.889	.03125	82	6724	9.055	28.636	.01220
33	1089	5.745	18.166	.03030	83	6889	9.110	28.810	.01205
34	1156	5.831	18.439	.02941	84	7056	9.165	28.983	.01190
35	1225	5.916	18.708	.02857	85	7225	9.220	29.155	.01176
36	1296	6.000	18.974	.02778	86	7396	9.274	29.326	.01163
37	1369	6.083	19.235	.02703	87	7569	9.327	29.496	.01149
38	1444	6.164	19.494	.02632	88	7744	9.381	29.665	.01136
39	1521	6.245	19.748	.02564	89	7921	9.434	29.833	.01124
40	1600	6.325	20.000	.02500	90	8100	9.487	30.000	.01111
41	1681	6.403	20.248	.02439	91	8281	9.539	30.166	.01099
42	1764	6.481	20.494	.02381	92	8464	9.592	30.332	.01087
43	1849	6.557	20.736	.02326	93	8649	9.644	30.496	.01075
44	1936	6.633	20.976	.02273	94	8836	9.695	30.659	.01064
45	2025	6.708	21.213	.02222	95	9025	9.747	30.822	.01053
46	2116	6.782	21.448	.02174	96	9216	9.798	30.984	.01042
47	2209	6.856	21.679	.02128	97	9409	9.849	31.145	.01031
48	2304	6.928	21.909	.02083	98	9604	9.899	31.305	.01020
49	2401	7.000	22.136	.02041	99	9801	9.950	31.464	.01010
50	2500	7.071	22.361	.02000	100	10000	10.000	31.623	.01000

answers

page 16
1. continuous: a, b, f; discrete: c, h; nominal: d, e; rank: g, i

page 19
1. a. $x_1 + x_2 + x_3 + x_4 + x_5$
   b. $f_1 x_1^2 + f_2 x_2^2 + f_3 x_3^2 + f_4 x_4^2 + f_5 x_5^2$
   c. $x_1 y_1 + x_2 y_2 + x_3 y_3 + x_4 y_4 + x_5 y_5$
   d. $\frac{1}{8}(x_1 + x_2 + x_3 + x_4 + x_5 + x_6 + x_7 + x_8)$
   e. $|x_1 - \bar{x}| + |x_2 - \bar{x}| + |x_3 - \bar{x}| + |x_4 - \bar{x}|$
   f. $3(4 + 5 + 6 + 7 + 8) = 90$
   g. $(x_1 - \bar{x})^2 + (x_2 - \bar{x})^2 + (x_3 - \bar{x})^2 + (x_4 - \bar{x})^2 + (x_5 - \bar{x})^2 + (x_6 - \bar{x})^2$

2. a. $\sum_{i=1}^{n} x_i$ b. $\left(\sum_{i=1}^{n} x_i\right)^2$ c. $\sum_{i=1}^{7} x_i$ d. $\sum_{i=1}^{4} \left[\frac{(o_i - e_i)^2}{e_i}\right]$

3. a. 96   b. 1352   c. 9216   d. 28.57
   e. 0   f. 200   g. 28.57
4. a. 102   b. 30   c. 478   d. 8098
5. a. 12   b. 29   c. 45   d. 10

page 26
1. a. mean = 5.5, median = 5.5   b. mean = 4, median = 4
   c. mean = .019, median = .020   d. mean = 245.1, median = 232
2. mean = 1.33, median = 1, mode = 1
3. a. $2.30   b. (1) 149.5   (2) 2.30   c. (1) $2.30   (2) $368
4. The mean may be zero if a set contains all zeros, or some positive and some negative numbers. Similarly, the mean can be negative.
5. See answer 4.

page 32
1. a. The standard deviation will be zero only when all values equal the mean in a set. It can never be negative since it is always the positive square root of the variance.
   b. Similarly, the mean absolute deviation can be zero but never negative since it is the positive (absolute) value.

2. mean = 7200, standard deviation = 2284
3. a. mean = 4.89, median = 5   b. mean = 6.20, median = 7
   c. mean = 32.14, median = 30   d. mean = .029, median = .032
   e. mean = 86, median = 86   f. mean = 32.71, median = 32
4. a. $\bar{x}_{new} = \bar{x}_{old} + (10/n)$ b. $\bar{x}_{new} = \bar{x}_{old} + 10$
5. a. $\bar{x} = 87$, $s^2 = 119.5$ b. $\mu = 87$, $\sigma^2 = 109.5$
6. a. 10.93   b. 10.46
7. mean = 2.25; median = 2; 3 modes: 1, 2, 4 (mode is not meaningful)
8. $s^2 = 1.84$, $s = 1.36$
9. $Q_1 = 1$, $Q_2 = 2$, $Q_3 = 3.5$ 10. $\bar{x} = 2.39$, $s = .44$
11. 2.4   12. a. 4580 to 10,640   b. 57 to 100   c. 0 to 4
13. $Q_1 = 2.1$, $Q_2 = 2.4$, $Q_3 = 2.7$ 14. both double
15. a. 23.4 to 27.5   b. .89   c. 1.22   d. 1.5
16. a. 5/25 or .20   b. 7/9 = .78   c. 3/12 or .25, 4/12 or .33, 5/12 or .42
17. a. 15/30 or .5   b. 3/30 or .10   c. 0/4 or 0,   d. 2/22 or .091   e. 0

page 43
1. without loss: x: 0   1   2   3   4   5   6   7   8   9   10   11
                  f: 3   10 15 13 5   3   4   3   2   1   0   1

   with loss: x: 0–1   2–3   4–5   6–7   8–9   10–11
              f: 13   28   8   7   3   1

2.		3.	
10 to <15	.06	22 to <33	3
15 to <20	.12	33 to <44	3
20 to <25	.14	44 to <55	15
25 to <30	.32	55 to <66	14
30 to <35	.18	66 to <77	5
35 to <40	.12	77 to <88	3
40 to <45	.06	88 to <99	2
	1.00		45

4. the frequency distribution (1) has gaps, (2) classes overlap, (3) has too few classes, and (4) does not cover the range of data.

5. a.		b.		c.		d.	
0	3	0–1	13	10 to <15	.06	22 to <33	3
1	13	2–3	41	15 to <20	.18	33 to <44	6
2	28	4–5	49	20 to <25	.32	44 to <55	21
3	41	6–7	56	25 to <30	.64	55 to <66	35
4	46	8–9	59	30 to <35	.82	66 to <77	40
5	49	10–11	60	35 to <40	.94	77 to <88	43
6	53			40 to <45	1.00	88 to <99	45
7	56						
8	58						
9	59						
10	59						
11	60						

page 50
1. mean: 1380/50 = 27.6; median is in 3d class (20 to 30)
2. mean: 1099.5/99 = 11.11; median is first score in 12–13 class

3. $\bar{x} = 5.44$; $s = 4.70$
4. a. $10-<20$ b. $14-15$ and $2-3$ c. 0 to <5
5. a. 361.98 b. 37.59 c. 22.12
6. a. 0 to < 70 years b. 2 to < 27 mo c. 0 to < 30 min
7. a. 21.365 b. 12.09 c. 3.99
8. a. $\bar{x} = 3.25$, $s = 2.36$ b. $\bar{x} = 3.45$, $s = 2.16$ c. with-loss groups
 d. without loss is better; with loss is only an approximation

CHAPTER 3

page 62

1.

Experiment	Sample space
a. giving math test	grades 0–100
b. giving medical exam	no. who pass or fail
c. weighing turkeys	weights ranging from 6 lb to 30 lb

3. a, b, c, f, g   4. b, e, f
5. a. lose b. lose or tie c. diamond, club, or spade
 d. black card e. 1, 4, 5 or 6 f. 10 or more
 g. more than 10 h. not pine paneling

page 69
1. a. $\frac{4}{52}$ b. $\frac{12}{52}$ c. $\frac{26}{52}$ d. $\frac{13}{52}$ e. $\frac{1}{52}$ f. $\frac{4}{52}$
2. $\frac{1}{6}$ each; sum $= 1.00$
3. a. $\frac{1}{6}$ b. $\frac{2}{6}$ c. $\frac{3}{6}$ d. $\frac{3}{6}$
4. a. $\frac{5}{50}$ b. $\frac{20}{50}$ c. $\frac{25}{50}$ d. $\frac{35}{50}$ e. $\frac{20}{50}$ f. $\frac{0}{50}$ g. $\frac{50}{50}$
5. a. $\frac{1}{10}$ b. $\frac{5}{10}$ c. $\frac{4}{10}$ d. $\frac{0}{10}$
6. $.20$ 7. a. 50% b. $.50$ c. $.50$ d. $.20$ e. $.70$
8. $\frac{1}{7}$; $\frac{1}{7}$; equally likely; yes
9. a. $\frac{1}{10}$ b. $\frac{2}{10}$ c. $\frac{3}{10}$ 10. a. $\frac{2}{6}$ b. $\frac{4}{6}$
11. $4 : 48$; $48 : 4$ 12. $12 : 40$ 13. $1 : 3$ 14. $3 : 7$; $7 : 3$
15. a. $\frac{38}{90}$ b. $52 : 38$
16. $\frac{9}{10}$; $9 : 1$ 17. $\frac{10}{40}$; $3 : 1$ 18. $\frac{915}{1500}$
19. $\frac{45}{300}$ 20. $\frac{175}{200}$
21. $\frac{79}{100}$ b. no trends, etc.; probably
22. a. "representative" or typical b. $.12 + .32 = .44$ c. $.80$
23. a. $\frac{6}{10}$ b. $\frac{4}{10}$ c. $\frac{10}{20}$ 24. a. $\frac{4}{10}$ b. $\frac{6}{10}$ c. $\frac{10}{20}$
25. a. no b. Tim (larger samples generally yield more reliable answers)
26. $2 : 3$ 27. $\frac{2}{15}$ 28. $3 : 4$
30. 9 out of 10 times under same circumstances

page 77
1. a. $\frac{1}{36}$ b. $\frac{1}{36}$ c. $\frac{1}{4}$ 2. $\frac{1}{6}$
3. a. $\left(\frac{1}{6}\right)^3$ b. $\left(\frac{1}{6}\right)^3$ c. $\left(\frac{1}{2}\right)^3$
5. a. $.01(.02)(.05)(.10) = .000001$ b. $.99(.98)(.95)(.90) = .83$
6. a. $\frac{2}{200}$ b. (1) $.01990$ (2) $.00005$ (3) zero (impossible)

7. a. .15   b. .65   c. .70

8. a. no, $P(A) + P(B) > 1.00$ b. .20   c. .95

9. a. no, $P(A) + P(B) < 1.00$ b. .60   c. .40   d. 0

10. a. $(\frac{1}{2})^3$ b. $\frac{7}{8}$ 11. $.9^3$

12. a. .6250   b. .6875   c. 0   d. .0625   e. .3750

13. a. .15   b. .375

14. a. $(\frac{26}{52})^2$ b. $(\frac{1}{4})^2$ c. $(\frac{12}{52})^2$ d. $\frac{2}{16}$ e. $\frac{2}{8}$

15. a. $(\frac{26}{52})(\frac{25}{51})$ b. $(\frac{13}{52})(\frac{12}{51})$ c. $(\frac{12}{52})(\frac{11}{51})$ d. $2(\frac{13}{52})(\frac{13}{51})$

    e. $(\frac{13}{52})(\frac{26}{51}) + (\frac{26}{52})(\frac{13}{51})$

16. a. .43   b. .68   c. .25   d. .08   e. .02

17. a. $.20^4$ b. $.20^4(.50)$

18. a. $.10^2$ b. $.90(.10)$ c. $.90(.10) + (.10)(.90)$ d. $.10^3$

19. $\frac{1}{7}$ 20. month = 30 days

21. a. $.80^4$ b. $.20^4$ c. $4(.80)^3(.20)^1$ d. $4(.20)^3(.80)^1$

22. a. $(.7)(.6)(.3)(.2)$ b. $(.3)(.4)(.7)(.8)$ c. $(.3)(.6)(.7)(.2)$

23. a. $(.20)(.30)$ b. $(.20)(.70) + (.80)(.30)$

24. a. $(1 - .90)^5$ b. $.9^5$

25. a. $(.8)(.4) = .32$ b. $.2(.6) = .12$ c. $.8(.6) = .48$ d. $.2(.4) = .08$

26. a. $\frac{5}{10}$ b. (1) $\frac{6}{90}$ (2) $\frac{12}{90}$ c. $\frac{6}{720} + \frac{6}{720} + \frac{6}{720} = \frac{18}{720}$

    d. $\frac{1}{10} + \frac{1}{10} + \frac{1}{10} = \frac{3}{10}$

27. a. $.6^9(.4)^1$ b. $.6^3$ c. $.4^3$

page 87

1. a. 2   b. 120   c. 3,628,800   d. 1   e. 1

2. a. 3   b. 1   c. 5   d. 84

3. a. 6   b. 24   c. 5   d. 60,480   e. 1

4. $3(2)(5)(2)$

5. a. $26^3(10)^4$ b. $25^3(9)^4$ c. $(26^3 - 1)(10)^4$ d. $(25^3 - 1)(9)^4$

6. $9!/(2!2!)$ 7. a. 10^3 b. $10(1)(10)$

8. a. 10   b. $10!/(2!8!)$ c. $10!/(7!3!)$

9. a. $10!$ b. $\frac{1}{10}$ 10. $5(3)(2)(4)$ 11. $36(35)(34)$

12. $\binom{8}{5} = 56$ 13. a. 21   b. 35   c. 1   d. 7

14. 10

page 94

1. a. $(.6)(.1)/[.6(.1) + .4(.5)] = .23$ b. $.6(.9)/[.6(.9) + .4(.5)] = .73$

2. a. .458   b. $\frac{1}{2}(.25)/[\frac{1}{2}(.25) + \frac{1}{2}(\frac{2}{3})] = .273$

3. $.5(.75)/[.5(.75) + .5(.10)] = .882$

4. $P(A)$: $(\frac{1}{3})(.99)/[(\frac{1}{3})(.99) + (\frac{1}{3})(.98) + (\frac{1}{3})(.95)] = .33/.973 = .339$

    $P(B)$: $(\frac{1}{3})(.98)/.973 = .336$

    $P(C)$: $(\frac{1}{3})(.95)/.973 = .325$

5. $(\frac{2}{3})(.5)/[(\frac{2}{3})(.5) + (\frac{1}{3})(.1)] = .909$

CHAPTER 4

page 103

1. continuous: a and c; discrete: b and d   2. 8.2

3. .79

4. $\mu = \$39{,}000$, $\sigma = \$547.7$

5. a. $\mu = 21$ b. $\sigma = 1.73$

6. 37,500   7. 4.36

8. mean: 70; variance: 50

9. $11.10

10. mean: 320 lb; variance: 625 lb^2

11. mean: 540 lb; variance: 1200 lb^2

page 110

1. a. .166   b. .834

2. a. .042   b. .0048   c. .4766

3. a. .1470   b. (1) .1296   (2) .8706   (3) impossible

4. a. .086   b. .236

5. a. .5578   b. .3396

page 118

1. a. .3277   b. .3602   c. .1875   d. .9298   e. .2639   f. .2639

  g. .0104   h. .0017

2. a. .0008   b. .0398   c. .3075   3. .2648   4. .0022

5. .3487   6. .2376

7. a. .4096   b. .0016   c. .5904   8. .3020   9. .20

10. a. .9365   b. .5950   c. .0075   11. .3770   12. .1250

13. a. .0422   b. .4552   c. .9657   14. a. .0279   b. .9538   c. .9996

15. .9139   16. .3487   17. 6

18. a. $\mu = 12.5$, $\sigma = 2.5$ b. $\mu = 10$, $\sigma = 2.83$ c. $\mu = 32$, $\sigma = 4.38$

19. a. $\mu = .5$, $\sigma = .10$ b. $\mu = .20$, $\sigma = .057$ c. $\mu = .40$, $\sigma = .055$

20. a. .00, .25, .50, .75, 1.00   b. as a long-run average

page 123

1. a. $\mu = \frac{2}{30}$ min   b. .1353   c. .5941

2. a. .3528   b. .6577   c. .8488   3. .0952

4. a. .0015   b. .776   c. .989   d. impossible

page 127

1. a. .3679   b. .2231   c. .4060   d. .1991   e. .3528   f. .2240

  g. .1465   h. .2469

3. a. $\mu = 1.4$, .1665   b. $\mu = 2.8$, .5305   c. $\mu = 5.6$, .9176

4. a. .1063   b. .9437   c. .0101   d. .7617

5. a. .0498   b. .1493   c. .3921

6. $\mu = 1.5$, $P(x = 0) = .2231$, $P(x \leq 3) = .9344$

7. a. 8   b. .191   c. .809   d. .900

8. a. ≈ 0 b. $\approx 100\%$ c. .417

9. a. 1.6   b. .9940   c. .0060   d. .0237

page 129

1. a. A: 4; B: 3; C: 3   b. .0001   c. .0784

2. a. .031   b. .12   3. a. .0326   b. .0163

4. a. $\frac{2}{8}$ b. $\frac{12}{56}$ c. 7   5. $\frac{5}{7}$

CHAPTER 5

page 138

1. a. 50,000   b. .80

2. a. 2.5   b. (1) .4/1   (2) 0   (3) 50%   (4) 0   (5) 100%
3. a. .417   b. 3   c. $\frac{1}{6}$
4. a. $\frac{10}{30}$ b. unknown   c. $10.50   d. $\frac{1}{6}$

page 153
1. a. .1587   b. .8413   c. .6331   d. .4332   e. .4980   f. .1330
   g. .3758   h. .0036
2. a. .4207   b. .5793   c. .0793   d. .2347
3. a. -1.64 b. -2.0 c. $+2.0$ d. $+2.0$ e. $\pm.03$ f. $\pm.03$
4. a. $+1.64$ b. $z = 0$ c. -2.3 d. $-.38$ e. $+.86$ f. $+2.0$
   g. $+1.0$
5. a. -1.0 b. $-.75$ c. $-.50$ d. $+.1$ e. $+.25$
6. a. 40.3   b. 46   c. 42.25   d. 32.41   e. 31   f. 30.40
7. a. .4772   b. .0793   c. .1359   d. .0923   e. .9758   f. .6826
8. a. .2033   b. .1056   c. .8944   d. .8413
9. a. .1151   b. 3.34   10. a. 50%   b. .3085   c. .1336
11. a. .8664   b. .9544   c. .9930
12. a. .0028   b. $.0028^2$ c. $(1 - .0028)^2$
13. a. .1587   b. .9544   c. .50   d. .25
14. a. .0956   b. .2676   c. .4522   d. .4586   e. .6010
15. a. .9952   b. .2206   c. .0132
16. a. .0548   b. .7698   c. $.5^4$

page 157
1. .05   2. a. .368   b. .632   c. ≈ 0
3. a. .135   b. .05   4. a. .135   b. .368   c. .607

CHAPTER 6

pages 170–171
1. a. 4
   b. In a way which would not always lead to the same point (e.g., arbitrarily place finger in middle of table and use first digit to locate column and second to locate row)
   c. $N = 14,000$; must read 5 digits/name
2. (1) number teams 00 to 19
   (2) determine pairings: read 2 digits for first team, 2 for second (ignore repeats)
   (3) continue until all are paired
   For playoffs, repeat procedure pairing 10 teams.
3. a. (1) number blocks 00 to 39
      (2) select 10 using random number table
      (3) for each block, read a single digit (0–9), which corresponds to a house on that block (houses are numbered 0 to 9)
   b. (1) It might be more difficult to identify which houses are to be sampled.
      (2) There would be 400 houses, numbered 000 to 399.
4. a. 00 to 04 could represent a defective; 05 to 99 nondefective
   b. 63, 55, 33, 74, 55, 35, 35, 46, 32, 55, 57, 73, 51, 52, 24 (all are acceptable).

5. 249, 679, 528, 216, 987 (unusable), 382, 338, 010 (unusable), 634, 030 (unusable), 162, 556, 397.

page 175
1. (see p. 166)
2. a. The community undoubtedly consists of others besides parents of school-children; and even parents are not fairly represented since some have more children in school than others, increasing chances of being selected.
   b. Many persons would not be apt to be on a downtown street corner at midday (e.g., factory workers, students, etc.).
   c. Membership in the House is based on *population*, so populous states would tend to be overrepresented.
3. a. $\frac{6}{15}$ b. 15   c. $\frac{1}{2}$ d. all possible future tosses   e. ∞
   f. $15(\frac{1}{2}) = 7.5$
4. a. $\frac{15}{30}$ b. unknown
   c. It equals the population percentage, which is unknown.

CHAPTER 7

page 191
1. a. $\approx 95\%$ b. $\approx 95.5\%$ c. $\approx 98\%$
2. a. .3830   b. .5468   c. 50%   d. ≈ 0
3. a. 5.01   b. 18.41   c. 199.5   d. .008
4. a. 1.25   b. $\frac{1}{6}$ c. .316   d. .62   e. .482
5. a. No, the distribution of sample means will be approximately normal because the sample size is greater than 30.
   b. .9836   c. .0028

page 194
1. a. 30%   b. 43%   c. 50%   d. 72.3%
2. a. .03   b. .04   c. .049   d. .05   e. .049   f. .04   g. .03
3. Tables rarely extend beyond $n = 20$, and the normal distribution provides a good approximation to the binomial as long as p is not too close to 0 or 1.0. The binomial is preferable for values of n and p included in the tables.
4. a. $\approx 68\%$ b. $\approx 95\%$ c. $\approx 95.5\%$ d. $\approx 98\%$
5. a. ± 1.65 b. ± 1.96 c. ± 2.58 d. ± 3.0
6. a. $\approx 68\%$ b. .1587   c. $\approx 95.5\%$ d. $\approx .045$

CHAPTER 8

page 215
1. a. $16 \pm .98$ b. $37.5 \pm .98$ c. $2.1 \pm .196$ d. $.6 \pm .0196$
2. a. 16 ± 1.29 b. 37.5 ± 1.29 c. $2.1 \pm .258$ d. $.6 \pm .0258$
3. a. 16 ± 1.065 b. $37.5 \pm .98$ c. $2.1 \pm .2064$ d. $.6 \pm .0196$
4. generally wider, since $t \geq z$
5. a. 30 ± 1.96 b. $e = 1.96$ c. .0014

6. a. $\bar{x} = 70$ b. all cars on that section between 2 and 4 A.M.
   c. 70 ± 3.50 d. $e = 3.50$
7. a. 140 ± 5.88 b. 140 ± 7.74 c. 5.88
8. a. 140 ± 12.38
9. a. \$220   b. 200(220)   c. 220 ± 10.49
10. a. 40 ± 1.755 b. A random sample is always necessary.
11. $n = 11$; since n is less than 30, it is necessary to know the population is normal, or at least approximately normal.
12. $n = 43$; it is not necessary to assume a normal population.
13. $n = 240$
14. (use $z = 2.055$)   a. 14.97   b. 36.47   c. 1.87   d. $+.58$
15. \$42.09

page 223
1. a. 5% to 17.5%   b. 13% to 29%   c. 40% to 60%   d. 71% to 87%
   e. 82.5% to 95%
2. The intervals are widest at $p = .50$
3. Intervals are wider at 99% since $z_{.99} > z_{.95}$
   a. 4% to 20%   b. 11% to 32%   c. 37% to 63%   d. 68% to 89%
   e. 80% to 96%
4. a. $.20 \pm .11$ b. $.10 \pm .05$
5. a. $n = 50$ b. 92% confidence (not on chart)

6.

	50%		10%	
	Formula	Chart	Formula	Chart
400	$.50 \pm .049$	.45 to .55	$.10 \pm .0294$	.07 to .13
100	$.50 \pm .098$	.40 to .60	$.10 \pm .0588$	.05 to .175
25	$.50 \pm .196$	.30 to .70	$.10 \pm .1176$	.02 to .28
16	$.50 \pm .245$	.25 to .75	$.10 \pm .147$	.01 to .35

7. a. formula best when p is near .50   b. formula best for large n
8. a. .13 to .28 (longest "side" is .08)   b. $e \le .07$
9. a. .90   b. $.90 \pm .0495$ c. $e \le .0495$
10. a. (chart) .19 to .32   b. "longest side" $= .32 - .25 = .07$
    c. Each person has the same chance of being selected among all shoppers.
    d. to be able to use a sampling distribution
11. a. $.15 \pm .13$ b. 150 ± 130 c. .13, 130
12. a. $.25 \pm .16$ b. 12.5 ± 8.0
13. a. 960   b. $.25 \pm .07$ c. $.25 \pm .04$
14. 273   15. a. 600   b. 136

CHAPTER 9

page 239
1. a. two tail   b. left tail   c. right tail   d. right tail   e. two tail
   f. left tail
2. a. $H_0: p = 2\%$ defective; $H_1: p > 2\%$
   b. $H_0: p = 2\%$ defective; $H_1: p \ne 2\%$

3. a. To accept would be the correct decision, while to reject would be a Type I error.
    b. To reject would be the correct decision; to accept would be a Type II error.

CHAPTER 10

page 248

1. a. two tail

    b. right tail

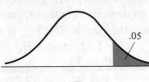

    c. left tail

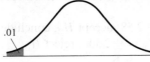

    d. right tail

    e. two tail

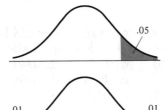

2.

H_0	H_1
a. $\mu = 25$ hr	$\mu < 25$ hr
b. $\mu = 2$ in.	$\mu \neq 2$ in.
c. $\mu_{current} = \mu_{new}$	$\mu_{new} > \mu_{current}$
d. $\mu = 12$ oz	$\mu > 12$ oz
e. $\mu = 12$ oz	$\mu \neq 12$ oz

3. a. $t_{test} = 4.41$; $t_{.01, 12} = 2.68$; reject H_0; μ: 10.86 to 13.54
    b. $t_{test} = +2.7$; $t_{.05} \approx +1.65$; reject H_0; μ: .038 to .042
    c. $t_{test} = 2.5$; $t_{.005, 24} = -2.49$; accept H_0
    d. $t_{test} = 3.23$; $t_{.05} \approx +1.65$; reject H_0; μ: 18.08 to 20.02
4. a. t is used since σ_x is unknown   b. normal, since $n > 30$
    c. $t_{test} = -7.07$; $t_{.05} \approx -1.65$; reject H_0, conclude $\mu < \$9000$
5. a. $t_{test} = -1$; $t_{.01, 8} = -2.90$; accept H_0
    b. $z_{test} = -.67$; $z_{.01} = -2.33$; accept H_0
    c. a and b since $n < 30$ in both
6. $t_{test} = 4.12$; $t_{.01, 8} = 2.9$; reject H_0
7. a. $H_0: \mu = 200$; $H_1: \mu \neq 200$ b. reject if $z > \pm 1.96$; 198.43 to 201.57
8. a. $t_{test} = 4.08$; $t_{.01, 5} = 3.37$; reject H_0 b. $n < 30$, yes

9. a. $t_{test} = -2.83$; $t_{.05} \approx -1.65$; reject H_0 b. Type I if H_0 true
10. a. .05   b. $z = +1.0$, $P(\text{Type I}) = 0$ c. $z = 2.5$, $P(\text{Type I}) = .0062$
11. a. $H_0: \mu = 43$; $H_1: \mu < 43$ b. $t_{test} = -1$; $t_{.05} \approx -1.65$; accept H_0
    c. same   d. no, since $n > 30$
12. a. $t_{test} = +2.28$; $t_{.05, 29} = +1.70$; reject H_0
    b. $t_{test} = +1.45$; $t_{.05} \approx +1.65$; accept H_0

page 254
1. a. .093   b. $t_{test} = -3.28$, $t_{.005} \approx \pm 2.58$; reject H_0, means are not equal.
   c. $t_{test} = 3.28$ vs $t_{.01} = 2.33$; reject H_0, conclude $B > A$ d. no, large n.
2. $t_{test} = -1.37$; $t_{.025} \approx \pm 1.96$; accept H_0, conclude average salaries may be equal
3. a. One tail; we want to demonstrate that training film decreases average time
      required to complete the puzzle. $H_1: \mu_{test} < \mu_{control}$
   b. $t_{test} = -1.87$; $t_{.05, 20} = -1.725$; reject H_0
   c. yes, since $n_1 + n_2$ is less than 30
   d. Yes; otherwise, we will not be able to specify an appropriate sampling
      distribution.
4. $z_{test} = 1.06$; $z_{.005} = \pm 2.58$; accept H_0, conclude that the two may be equal
5. $t_{test} = -1.75$ vs $t_{.025, 8} = \pm 2.306$; reject H_0.

page 258
1. a. A Type I error occurs when H_0 is rejected when true.
   b. A Type II error occurs if H_0 is accepted when false.
2. a. .8300   b. .9210   c. 0   d. .4840
3. a. .7734   b. 0   c. .4013   d. .0006
4. a. .9066   b. .6255   c. .0465

CHAPTER 11

page 282
1.

	a.	b.	c.	d.
Numerator	4	6	7	3
Denominator	25	21	72	44

	Degree of freedom		F_{table}	
	Numerator	Denominator	.01	.05
a.	7	40	≈ 3.12	≈ 2.25
b.	3	24	4.72	3.01
c.	4	30	4.02	2.69
d.	2	27	5.49	3.35
e.	3	44	≈ 4.20	≈ 2.80

3. a. reject at both levels   b. accept H_0 at both levels
   c. accept at .01, reject at .05   d. reject at both levels
   e. accept at both levels

4. a. 25   b. 6.8   c. 140   d. 3.10
5. $F_{test} = 7.82$; $F_{.05, 3, 20} = 3.10$; reject H_0, conclude diets are not equally effective
6. $F_{test} = 42.39$; $F_{.01, 4, 40} = 3.83$; reject H_0, conclude average repair times differ
7. $F_{test} = 7.29$; $F_{.01, 4, 45} \approx 3.8$; reject H_0, conclude some differences exist in average selling prices among five locations
8. $F_{test} = 3.11$; accept at .05 and .01 levels
9. $F_{test} = 3.53$; $F_{.01, 3, 12} = 5.95$; accept H_0. The assumption of comparable trucks and drivers is important because the test does not allow for or measure any factor other than tire position. Additional factors such as driver or truck differences could easily distort the results, if present.

CHAPTER 12

page 293
1. a. right tail   b. left tail   c. left tail   d. two tail
2. a. $H_0: p = 2\%$; $H_1: p > 2\%$
   b. $z_{test} = 3.03$; $z_{table} = +1.65$; reject H_0, conclude percentage defective greater than 2%
3. $z = 3$, $P(z \geq 3) = .0013$; conclude coin not fair
4. a. 20 or less   b. $H_1; p > .20$ c. $z_{test} = -2.25$; agree with senator
5. $z = -1.08$; accept H_0
6. $P(x \leq 2) = .3154$; accept a, b, and c.
7. positive effect; $P(x \geq 11) = .0288$

page 297
1. $z_{test} = +1.28$; accept H_0
2. $z_{test} = 1.155$; accept H_0 at all levels, conclude proportion of voters is the same in two districts
3. $z_{test} = 1.428$; $z_{.025} = \pm 1.96$; accept H_0; conclude machines are not different

page 304

1.

	3×4	4×3	5×5	2×5	3×6	4×6
Degrees of freedom	6	6	16	4	10	15
$\chi^2_{.05}$	12.59	12.59	26.3	9.49	18.31	25.0
$\chi^2_{.01}$	16.81	16.81	32.0	13.28	23.2	30.6

2. each row: 30, 40, 50, 80
3. $\chi^2_{test} = 72.43$; $\chi^2_{.05, 9} = 16.92$; reject H_0, builders are not comparable
4. $\chi^2_{test} = 46.23$; $\chi^2_{.05, 12} = 21.0$; reject H_0, conclude labor charges differ
5. a. $\chi^2_{test} = 4.17$; $\chi^2_{.05} = 3.84$; reject H_0, conclude the proportion of ticket holders approving of seating differ depending on whether season or individual
   b. $z_{test} = 2.041$; $z_{.025} = \pm 1.96$ c. these are the same (for 1 d.f.)
6. $\chi^2_{test} = 51.70$; $\chi^2_{.01, 3} = 11.34$

page 314
1. a. $\chi^2_{test} = 8.88$; $\chi^2_{.05, 10} = 18.3$; accept H_0
   b. $\chi^2_{test} = 1.28$; $\chi^2_{.05, 3} = 7.81$; accept H_0
   c. $\chi^2_{test} = 2.16$; $\chi^2_{.05, 3} = 7.81$; accept H_0

2. $\chi^2_{\text{test}} = 11.4$; $\chi^2_{.05, 4} = 9.49$; reject H_0, conclude days are not equally likely
3. $\chi^2_{\text{test}} = 2.52$; $\chi^2_{.025, 9} = 19.02$; accept H_0, conclude digits equally likely
4. $\chi^2_{\text{test}} = 19.853$; $\chi^2_{.05, 8} = 15.51$; reject H_0; $\chi^2_{.01, 8} = 20.1$; accept (thus accept versus reject depends on level of significance chosen)
5. $\chi^2_{\text{test}} = 5.609$; $\chi^2_{\text{table}, 4}$ (accept at all levels)
6. $\chi^2_{\text{test}} = 272.49$; $\chi^2_{.05, 11} = 19.68$; conclude not normal with mean of 50.5 and standard deviation of 10

CHAPTER 13

page 329

1. $z_{\text{test}} = 1.28$ (no correction for continuity); $z_{.05} = +1.65$; accept H_0, conclude miles/gallon did not improve
3. a. 90 +'s, 30 −'s, 80 no change ($n = 90 + 30 = 120$)
   b. H_1: increase in percentage who approve (i.e., more +'s, few −'s)
   c. $z = +5.48$; $z_{.01} = +2.33$; reject H_0, conclude campaign effective
   d. too many no changes
4. $P(x \geq 10) = .1509 > .05$, conclude chance variation only
5. results are identical
6. $z_{\text{test}} = 2.86$; $z_{.05} = 1.65$; reject H_0, conclude miles/gallon improved
7. $z_{\text{test}} = 1.76$; $z_{.05} = 1.65$; reject H_0, conclude diet effective (previously, sign test indicated diet not effective; however, you should more readily accept results of stronger ranked sign test)
8. Magnitudes of change cannot be determined from data given.
9. $z_{\text{test}} = 2.21$; reject all .05 level, accept at .01

page 334

1. $z_{\text{test}} = +1.96$; $z_{.01} = +2.33$; conclude means are equal
2. $z_{\text{test}} = +.7$; conclude average sales are equal
3. $z_{\text{test}} = .317$; $z_{.025} = \pm 1.96$; conclude average tire lives do not differ
4. no effect since relative positions (ranks) would not change

page 337

1. $H = 10.044$; $\chi^2_{.025, 3} = 9.35$; reject H_0, conclude mean drying times not equal
2. $H = 1.115$; $\chi^2_{.01, 2} = 9.210$; accept H_0, diets equally effective
3. $H = 9.571$; $\chi^2_{.05, 4} = 9.49$; reject H_0, conclude average operating lives differ among brands
4. $H = 4.89$; $\chi^2_{.05, 2} = 5.991$; accept H_0, also accept at .01 level

page 346

1. median: $z = .00$; Up and Down; $z = -1.04$; conclude only random variation
2. Up and Down: $z = -.57$; median: $z = -2.60$; conclude not random

3.

	Up and Down z	Median z	Conclusion
a.	+1.41	+3.21	not random
b.	−3.56	−1.60	not random
c.	+3.70	−1.28	not random

4. $z = -.190$, conclude chance variation

CHAPTER 14

page 359
1. a. $y = 5 + 10.2x$ b. $y = 55x$ c. $y = -2 + 27x$ d. $y = 200 - 13x$
   e. $y = 2.4$
2. a. $y = 6 + (7.5/500)x$ b. $y = -1 + (12/.4)x$

page 363
1. a. $y_c = -200 + .10(15,000) = \$1300$
   b. The equation is relevant only for families of four with incomes in the range $8000 to $20,000. The y-intercept is a convenient point at which the *height of the line* can be specified.
   c. (1) equation based on studies of families of *four*
      (2) These amounts are beyond the range of the estimating equation.
   d.

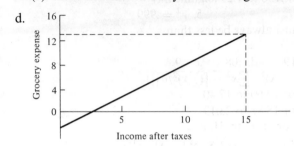

2. a.

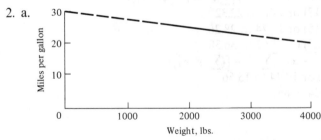

   b. (1) 26 mpg (2) 27 mpg (3) 25 mpg
3. a. $y_c = -5 + 2x$ b. $y_c = .028 + 5x$
   c. $y_c = -30.5 + .95x$ d. $y_c = 4.77 + .49x$
4. a. nonlinear
   b. $y_c = 13.48 + .02x$ ($\sum x = 5896$; $\sum y = 291$; $\sum xy = 141,502$; $\sum x^2 = 3,159,126$)
5. $y_c = 8.44 - .006x$ ($\sum x = 3900$; $\sum y = 44.6$; $\sum xy = 18,720$; $\sum x^2 = 2,415,000$)
6. $y_c = 22.11 + .554x$ ($\sum x = 2315$; $\sum y = 1,615$; $\sum xy = 289,600$; $\sum x^2 = 430,075$)
7. $y_c = 1348 - 154.4x$ ($\sum x = 44.6$; $\sum y = 3,900$; $\sum xy = 18,720$; $\sum x^2 = 268.22$)
8. a. $y_c = 1.57 + 1.036x$ ($\sum x = 28$; $\sum y = 40$; $\sum xy = 189$; $\sum x^2 = 140$)
   b. $y_c = 1.57 + .52x$ ($\sum x = 56$; $\sum y = 40$; $\sum xy = 378$; $\sum x^2 = 560$)
   c. $y_c = 3.14 + 1.036x$ ($\sum x = 56$; $\sum y = 80$; $\sum xy = 756$; $\sum x^2 = 560$)
   d. $y_c = 3.57 + 1.036x$ ($\sum x = 28$; $\sum y = 54$; $\sum xy = 245$; $\sum x^2 = 140$)
9. $y_c = -12.0 + 1.32x$ ($\sum x = 287$; $\sum y = 247$; $\sum xy = 7875$; $\sum x^2 = 8571$)

page 379

1. $t_{test} = (b - 0)/s_b$ (if $n > 32$, use $z \approx t$)

	a.	b.	c.	d.	e.	f.
t_{test}	4	-1.5	2.0	3.0	-5.58	15.0
t_{table}	2.228	2.101	2.069	2.045	1.96	1.96
Decision	significant	accept H_0	accept H_0	significant	significant	significant

2. intervals are $b \pm ts_b$ (not significant if 0 in interval)
   a. $8.2 \pm 2.58(4.1)$ or -2.38 to 18.78 (not significant)
   b. $.13 \pm 2.76(.04)$ or .02 to .24
   c. $5.213 \pm 2.878(1.5)$ or .90 to 9.53
   d. $145 \pm 2.58(40)$ or 41.8 to 248.2
   e. $-7.1 \pm 3.499(3.0)$ or -17.6 to $+3.4$ (not significant)

3. a. $y_c = -4.02 + 1.013x$ b. $s_e = 3.33$; $s_b = .12$
   c. $1.013 \pm 2.77(.12)$ or $+.736$ to 1.29 (significant)

4. $y_c = 1x$ 5. $r^2 = .999$

6. $r^2 = 1 - (s_e^2/s_y^2)$; s_e^2 must always be less than s_y^2

7. $r^2 = 1 - (s_e^2/s_y^2)$.
   a. .5   b. .75   c. .19   d. .08   e. .9

11. a. $y_c \pm t(s_e\sqrt{(1/n) + (x_g - \bar{x})^2/\{\sum x^2 - [(\sum x)^2/n]\}})$
    (1) $15 \pm 2.306(1.04)$ or 12.60 to 17.40
    (2) $21 \pm 2.306(.949)$ or 18.81 to 23.19
    (3) $29 \pm 2.306(1.108)$ or 26.44 to 31.56
    b. $y_c \pm t(s_e\sqrt{1 + (1/n) + (x_g - \bar{x})^2/\{\sum x^2 - [(\sum x)^2/n]\}})$
    (1) $15 \pm 2.306(3.17)$ or 7.68 to 22.32
    (2) $21 \pm 2.306(3.15)$ or 13.74 to 28.26
    (3) $29 \pm 2.306(3.20)$ or 21.62 to 36.38

12. $y_c \pm t(s_e\sqrt{(1/n) + (x_g - \bar{x})^2/\{\sum x^2 - [(\sum x)^2/n]\}})$
    a. $13 \pm 2.306(1.108)$ or 10.44 to 15.56
    b. 2934 ± 464.8; 2934 ± 651.7

page 383

1. a. 7830   b. 5080   c. 3080
2. a. 1   b. 3.4   c. .40

page 391

1. a.

x	z_x	y	z_y	$z_x z_y$
34	$-.8$	21	-2.5	$+.2$
30	-1.6	22	0	0
40	$+.4$	25	$+.75$	$+.3$
34	$-.8$	28	$+1.5$	-1.2
39	$+.2$	15	-1.75	$-.35$
35	$-.6$	24	$+.50$	$-.3$
42	$+.8$	24	$+.50$	$+.4$
45	$+1.4$	22	0	0
43	$+1.0$	17	-1.25	-1.25
				-2.2

$$r = \frac{-2.2}{9 - 1} = -.275$$

b.

x	z_x	y	z_y	$z_x z_y$
3.9	−.1	46	0	0
4.6	+.6	46	0	0
6.0	+.2	52	+1.5	+3
2.8	−1.2	50	+1.0	−1.2
3.1	−.9	48	+.5	−.45
3.4	−.6	40	−1.5	+.9
4.2	+.2	42	−1.0	−.2
4.0	0	44	−.5	0
				+2.05

$$r = \frac{+2.05}{8-1} = +.29$$

2. The value of r is unaffected.
3. a. $\bar{x} = 76$, $s_x = 10$
   c. standardized values are same as in Exercise 25
   d. none
4. b. $\bar{x} = 50$, $s_x = 5$; $\bar{y} = 20$, $s_y = 4$
   c. standardized values are same as in Exercise 25
   d. none
5. $r = -.50$
6. a. +.214   b. +.500   c. +.60   7. $r = +.68$
8. $r = -.95$ 9. $r = +.973$ 10. $r = -.834$
11. a. You should be surprised, because r and b must always have the same sign.
    b. You should not be surprised, since in both cases increases in x are accom-
       panied by increases in y (plot the data).
    c. Both yield $r = +1$ because there is *no scatter* around the line with only two
       points.
12. a. correlation   b. regression   c. regression
    d. correlation   e. regression

page 396
1. (not significant if zero is in the interval)
   a. +.48 to +.92
   b. −.42 to +.57 (not significant)
   c. −.62 to +.10 (not significant)
   d. −.53 to −.03
   e. −.47 to −.11
2. (not significant if zero is in the interval)
   a. −.35 to +.51 (not significant)
   b. −.18 to +.37 (not significant)
   c. −.04 to +.23 (not significant)
   d. +.54 to +.81   e. −.81 to −.54
   f. −.39 to +.39 (not significant)
3. a. $r = -.50$, $n = 11$, $t_{table} = \pm 2.262$, $t_{test} = -1.737$ (not significant)
   b. $r = +.973$, $n = 13$, $t_{table} = \pm 3.106$, $t_{test} = +13.98$ (significant)
   c. $r = -.814$, $n = 11$, $t_{table} = \pm 3.250$, $t_{test} = -4.53$ (significant)
4. a. +.14 to +.61, accept H_0
   b. +.58 to +.90, accept H_0
   c. −.32 to −.48, reject H_0

5. a. $10 + .37x$ b. $.98$ c. $.99$ d. regression assumptions
    e. correlation assumptions   f. $12.22 \pm 2.306(1.13)(1.05)$

6. $-.6 < \rho < -.4$; accept H_0

page 400

1. a. $t_{table} = \pm 2.131$, $t_{test} = +2.90$, reject H_0
   b. $t_{table} = \pm 2.086$, $t_{test} = -2.55$, reject H_0
   c. $t_{table} = \pm 2.262$, $t_{test} = +6.58$, reject H_0
   d. $t_{table} = \pm 2.042$, $t_{test} = +1.41$, accept H_0 (not significant)

2. a. $r_{sp} = +.75$ (Pearson's $r = +.68$); ranking wastes some information.
   b. If data are in ranks, or if the assumptions necessary for Pearson are not satisfied, Spearman is preferable. If assumptions of Pearson are met, it should be used because it is less wasteful of information.

3. $r_{sp} = +.908$, $t_{test} = +7.51$, $t_{table} = \pm 3.055$ (significant)

4. Opposite ranks give $r_{sp} = -1$; same ranks give $r_{sp} = +1$.

5. $r_{sp} = +.391$, $t_{test} = 1.27$, accept at all levels (not significant)

page 403

1.

	χ^2_{table}	Significant	C	C_{max}	Strength
a.	19.679	yes	.655	.866	moderate to strong
b.	26.296	yes	.408	.894	moderate
c.	13.277	yes	.707	.816	strong
d.	37.652	yes	.464	.913	moderate
e.	16.919	no	—	—	—

2. $\chi^2_{test} = 107.75$ (significant at all levels); $C = .39$ versus $C_{max} = .866$; moderate relationship

3. In a contingency table there is a *single* sample with results cross-classified into the cells; with an $r \times k$ table, there are k (or r) samples. The scales of a contingency table have direction; they do not usually have direction in an $r \times k$ table.

4. $\chi^2_{test} = 160$ (significant at all levels); $C = .47$ versus $C_{max} = .866$. The analysis fails to reveal that the correlation is *negative*. This can only be seen by inspection. Consequently, the incentive should not be offered.

CHAPTER 15

page 427

1. price: 156; quantity: 92; value: 144

2. price: 14; quantity: 12; value: 168

3.

Year	Price	Quantity	Revenue
1973	110	105	116
1974	118	95	113*
1975	115	110	127
1976	100	109	109
1977	107	104	111
1978	103	88	91

   * Rounding may give 112.

4. a. price: 157; quantity: 114; value: 178
   b. price: 151; quantity: 115

Milk		Ice cream		Eggs	
whole	161	economy	128	small	151
skim	133	deluxe	120	medium	144
chocolate	114	sherbert	100	large	153
heavy cream	132			extra large	149

5. price: 1974 = 106, 1976 = 130, 1978 = 135;
   quantity: 1974 = 103, 1976 = 94.9, 1978 = 112

6. answers are same as answer 5

9.

Year	Purchasing power	Year	Purchasing power
1961	$1.30	1969	$1.06
1962	1.28	1970	1.00
1963	1.27	1971	.96
1964	1.25	1972	.93
1965	1.23	1973	.87
1966	1.20	1974	.79
1967	1.16	1975	.72
1968	1.12	1976	.68

10.

Year	(Price/barrel) ÷ WPI
1968	$4.68
1969	4.58
1970	4.41
1971	4.39
1972	4.24
1973	4.17
1974	3.51
1975	3.15
1976	3.35

CHAPTER 16

page 447

1. 1980: .21; 1984: .25

2. $y = 20 + .8t$

3. a. $y = 8.25 + .328t$ b. $y = 623.6 + 52.28t$

4.

	3 year	7 year		3 year	7 year
1948			1964	16.00	16.86
1949	11.67		1965	19.33	18.00
1950	11.33		1966	19.00	19.14
1951	13.33	13.86	1967	20.67	19.00
1952	14.00	15.15	1968	21.33	19.00
1953	17.00	16.29	1969	19.67	19.29
1954	18.67	16.29	1970	17.67	19.00
1955	19.67	18.14	1971	16.33	18.29
1956	17.33	18.71	1972	19.33	17.29
1957	18.33	19.00	1973	18.00	16.29
1958	19.00	17.71	1974	16.67	16.86
1959	23.67	19.00	1975	15.67	17.29
1960	20.67	18.14	1976	15.33	
1961	19.33	18.86	1977		
1962	14.33	18.00	1978		
1963	15.33	18.29			

5.
Jan	1.740	July	.383
Feb	1.422	Aug	.538
Mar	1.464	Sep	.296
Apr	1.059	Oct	.805
May	1.062	Nov	1.020
June	.786	Dec	1.424

6.
I	1.031
II	1.221
III	.448
IV	1.300

7.
Jan	888.9	July	841.7
Feb	1000.0	Aug	851.5
Mar	1775.0	Sep	865.4
Apr	916.7	Oct	909.1
May	838.4	Nov	866.7
June	800.0	Dec	857.1

8.

t	$y - y_c$	t	$y - y_c$	t	$y - y_c$
1	+8	9	2	17	−4
2	−1	10	15	18	−1
3	−11	11	6	19	5
4	−7	12	12	20	0
5	−3	13	14	21	16
6	−6	14	−3	22	−6
7	−4	15	−6	23	−5
8	−1	16	−5	24	−11

9. $y_c = 8.53 + 7.25t$

Year	y/y_c	Year	y/y_c
1958	.76	1968	.83
1959	.65	1969	.92
1960	.83	1970	1.01
1961	1.07	1971	1.11
1962	1.12	1972	1.12
1963	1.27	1973	1.12
1964	1.18	1974	1.09
1965	1.19	1975	.96
1966	.92	1976	.93
1967	.83	1977	.91

10.

Year	y/y_{ma}	Year	y/y_{ma}
1960	.88	1968	.91
1961	1.02	1969	.97
1962	1.00	1970	1.00
1963	1.12	1971	1.04
1964	1.08	1972	1.02
1965	1.01	1973	1.04
1966	.98	1974	1.05
1967	.92	1975	.97

11. a.
1964	480	1972	732
1965	492	1973	816
1966	468	1974	780
1967	432	1975	756
1968	516	1976	768
1969	588	1977	780
1970	624	1978	756
1971	660		

b. 852

c. January   53
   February   49
   March   57
   April   75
   May   108
   June   91
   July   81
   August   71
   September   71
   October   64
   November   57
   December   61

12. a.

					c.		
1960	262	1969	770		January	54.0
1961	330	1970	787.5		February	43.2
1962	367.5	1971	800		March	64.8
1963	400	1972	799		April	108.0
1964	423	1973	828		May	237.6
1965	460	1974	912		June	216.0
1966	528	1975	1000		July	129.6
1967	600	1976	1102.5		August	108.0
1968	682.5				September	108.0
					October	75.6
1350					November	64.8
					December	86.4

page 455

1.

	$\alpha = .1$	$\alpha = .3$		$\alpha = .1$	$\alpha = .3$
1948	12.00	12.00	1964	16.45	16.94
1949	11.80	11.40	1965	16.60	17.26
1950	11.92	11.88	1966	17.14	18.68
1951	11.83	11.62	1967	17.13	18.18
1952	12.25	12.93	1968	17.72	19.63
1953	12.53	13.55	1969	18.35	20.94
1954	13.28	15.48	1970	17.62	17.96
1955	14.05	17.14	1971	17.66	17.97
1956	14.74	17.40	1972	17.89	18.58
1957	14.57	16.08	1973	18.10	19.01
1958	15.51	18.46	1974	17.69	17.51
1959	15.96	18.92	1975	17.52	17.06
1960	17.06	21.34	1976	17.47	17.04
1961	16.85	19.44	1977	17.02	15.83
1962	16.76	18.41	1978	17.42	17.38
1963	16.28	16.49			

2. The smoothing does not allow for trend, and hence the smoothed values lag the real data; the values are all low.

index

Printer and Binder: Halliday Lithograr

79 80 81 9 8 7 6 5